THE KING'S GOOD SERVANT

Page from More's *Book of Hours* with the
first words of his "Godly Meditation".

JAMES MONTI

The King's Good Servant but God's First

The Life and Writings
of Saint Thomas More

IGNATIUS PRESS   SAN FRANCISCO

Nihil Obstat: Francis J. McAree, S.T.D.,
            Censor Librorum

Imprimatur: + Patrick Sheridan, D.D., Vicar General,
            Archdiocese of New York.

The *Nihil Obstat* and *Imprimatur* are official declarations that a book or pamphlet is free of doctrinal or moral error. No implication is contained therein that those who have granted the *Nihil Obstat* and *Imprimatur* agree with the contents, opinions, or statements expressed.

To Our Lady of Walsingham
that the land once known as "Our Lady's Dowry"
may one day return to full and joyful communion
with the See of Peter

Contents

PART ONE

THE JOURNEY TO GOD BEGINS

PART TWO

THE BATTLE FOR
THE SOUL OF ENGLAND

Contents

Contents

Acknowledgments

I wish to express my deep gratitude to the entire staff of the Corrigan Memorial Library of Saint Joseph's Seminary in Yonkers, New York, for making available to me their outstanding collection of books and periodicals. I also wish to thank the library staffs of the College of New Rochelle (New Rochelle, New York) and Marymount College (Tarrytown, New York) for permitting me to use their excellent collections of publications regarding the life and times of Saint Thomas More; I likewise wish to thank the staff of the Irvington Public Library for obtaining for me several key interlibrary loans of books essential to the completion of this work.

Sources for Chapter Epigraphs

Introduction, p. 15: In *The Fame of Blessed Thomas More: Being Addresses Delivered in His Honour in Chelsea, July 1929,* ed. R. W. Chambers (London and New York: Sheed and Ward, 1933), 63.

Chapter 2, p. 57: Quoted and translated in E. E. Reynolds, *Margaret Roper: Eldest Daughter of St. Thomas More* (New York: P. J. Kenedy and Sons, 1960), 46–47; for original Latin text, see letter no. 2750 in *Opus Epistolarum Des. Erasmi Roterdami,* vol. 10, *1532–1534,* ed. P. S. Allen, H. M. Allen, and H. W. Garrod (1941; reprint, Oxford: Clarendon Press, 1963), 139.

Chapter 5, p. 117: Letter no. 46, in Elizabeth Rogers, ed., *St. Thomas More: Selected Letters* (New Haven: Yale Univ. Press, 1961), 180.

Chapter 6, p. 148: *The Apology,* ed. J. B. Trapp, vol. 9 of *Complete Works of St. Thomas More* (New Haven: Yale Univ. Press, 1979), chap. 10, p. 49.

Chapter 13, p. 362: Letter no. 214, More to Margaret Roper, May 2 or 3, 1535, in Elizabeth Rogers, ed., *The Correspondence of Sir Thomas More* (Princeton: Princeton Univ. Press, 1947), 552.

Chapter 14, p. 405: More admonishing his wife and children, in William Roper, *The Lyfe of Sir Thomas Moore, Knighte,* ed. Elsie V. Hitchcock, Early English Text Society, original series, no. 197 (London: Early English Text Society, 1935), 26.

Epilogue, p. 453: Quoted in E. E. Reynolds, *Thomas More and Erasmus* (London: Burns and Oates, 1965), 239; for original Latin text, see *Ecclesiastes sive Concionator Evangelicus,* preface, in *Desiderii Erasmi Roterodami: Opera Omnia,* vol. 5 (Lyons: Peter Vander, 1704), cols. 769–70.

Introduction

Blessed Thomas More is more important at this moment than at any moment since his death, even perhaps the great moment of his dying; but he is not quite so important as he will be in about a hundred years time. He may come to be counted the greatest Englishman, or at least the greatest historical character in English history. For he was above all things historic; he represented at once a type, a turning point and an ultimate destiny. If there had not happened to be that particular man at that particular moment, the whole of history would have been different.

— G. K. Chesterton, "A Turning Point in History"

In the vast and sweeping drama of human history we sometimes encounter individuals whose lives especially captivate each succeeding generation—men and women who shaped their own time and have helped to shape our own. Indeed, it is a testimony to the awesome dignity that Almighty God has bestowed on each human soul that just one man can exert such a marked and lasting influence on the course of human events—an influence for good or for evil.

Just such a figure is Saint Thomas More. Over the course of time this popular humanist scholar and Lord Chancellor of England has won the hearts of many with a universal appeal that often seems to transcend religious and ideological boundaries. Unfortunately, this very popularity has tended to obscure the underlying force that molded More's destiny—his faith. Certainly this reality is obvious enough from the circumstances of his death, yet the events of his life have sometimes been interpreted as more a secular quest for freedom of thought and conscience than a journey to God. If More has been misunderstood, it is undoubtedly due in part to the fact that for most of the four and a half centuries that have passed since his death, almost all of the saint's voluminous writings have lain in relative obscurity, with his complete English works available only in a rare folio edition dating from 1557. The extremely wide circulation of only one work, the *Utopia*, removed from the context of More's other writings, has surely led to at least some erroneous perceptions. The publication over the past three decades of a definitive edition of the complete Latin and English works of Saint Thomas More (filling over eleven thousand pages) has made it possible as never before to venture into More's soul and learn the real force behind his convictions—and it is unmistakably More the man of faith who emerges from these pages.

It is hence our purpose here to present a new portrait of Thomas More in the light of his writings—most especially his writings on the Church and on the spiritual life. We will explore More's lifelong, uncompromising commitment to his Catholic faith, a commitment that in his earlier years almost led him to select a life in the cloister. In this context we will discover a fundamental theme of More's apologetical writings: a passionate dedication to the unity of the Church, a unity of faith that he saw as necessitating assent to all her teachings and obedience to her ordained ministers. It was to be this fundamental conviction that would pit the saint in an increasingly intense intellectual struggle over a span of fifteen years with the vanguards of the definitive religious revolution of his age—the Protestant Reformation. Thus we will be able to see More's trial for treason in Westminster Hall and his execution on Tower Hill, not as the product of some sudden impulse of heroism, but rather as the concluding and crowning act of witness in a long-fought battle to preserve England's thousand-year communion with the See of Peter.

It is likewise important to understand that Thomas More not only believed in Catholicism, he *lived* it. Hence we will devote much of this book to exploring the roots and expressions of More's own spirituality—dimensions of the man that have heretofore not received as full a treatment as they justifiably deserve. Key to our understanding will be the recognition of three fundamental traits of the saint's inner life: his consciousness of the mystery of man's mortality, his pervasive devotion to the Passion of Christ, and his deep love for the Holy Eucharist. These elements permeate his spiritual writings, having largely shaped his thoughts, words, and actions. But it is also possible to discern other characteristics of More's spirituality: his intense prayer life, his acts of penance and works of mercy, his devotion to the Heart of Christ and the Blessed Virgin Mary, as well as his love of the Scriptures and the sacred liturgy. These too will receive our attention.

Few periods of human history have been written about so copiously as the first half of the sixteenth century. It is simply impossible to compass every aspect of the central event of this period—the Reformation—within the confines of one book, let alone in a work such as this, which is intended to be primarily the biography of one man. What the author has attempted to do is to give the reader an outline of the major facets of the Reformation relevant to the life of Thomas More, and particularly a sampling of the newest studies in this field, which are in many cases rewriting conventional ideas about what caused the dividing of Western Christendom. Such is especially the case with regard to the state of the "pre-Reformation Church" in England. It should also be noted that the portrayal of Reformation developments presented in this work is shaped with the intent of helping the reader to perceive the event as Thomas More saw it.

It should be declared from the outset that the following book is an unashamedly sympathetic account of Thomas More, yet an account nonetheless based upon the actual facts and demonstrable interpretations of More's life and writings. Over the last twenty years it seems that the saint has been put on trial again, charged with the supposed "treason" of being too ardent a defender of Catholic orthodoxy. More than one biography has appeared of late painting him in a less than favorable light for this very reason. It will be our purpose here to demonstrate that the secret to More's greatness lay precisely in the reasoned ardor of his Catholic convictions.

A few comments on sources should be made. Except where otherwise noted, all quotations from the writings of Saint Thomas More are from the Yale University Press edition of his complete works (sixteen volumes, 1963–).[1] Quotations from two of More's works, *The Four Last Things* and *The Life of John Picus* (not yet available in the Yale edition), are from William Rastell's 1557 edition of More's complete works, as reproduced in volume 1 of *The English Works of Sir Thomas More,* edited in 1931 by W. E. Campbell.[2] As for More's letters, the

---

[1] *The Complete Works of St. Thomas More* (New Haven: Yale Univ. Press, 1963–).

[2] London: Eyre and Spottiswoode; New York: Lincoln MacVeagh, Dial Press, 1931.

majority of these are quoted from Elizabeth Rogers' 1947 edition of the saint's correspondence.[3] While quotes from More's Latin works are taken unaltered from the translations of the Yale scholars (or from the letter translations of E. M. G. Routh[4] and Francis Nichols[5]), those from his English works and letters the author has rendered closer to modern English by very slight modifications in spelling, punctuation, and capitalization, with occasional substitutions of a modern equivalent for an antiquated word. Such alterations, nonetheless, have been kept to a discreet minimum. Finally, except where otherwise noted, all quoted scriptural texts are taken from the Catholic edition of the Revised Standard Version of the Holy Bible © 1965, 1966 by the Division of Christian Education of the National Council of Churches of Christ in the United States of America.

In the pages to follow there will be repeated references to the five major early biographies of Thomas More that, aside from the saint's own writings and the correspondence of his friend Erasmus of Rotterdam, are the only sources for most of the details of his life. Thus it would be helpful to the reader at this juncture to know precisely what these five works are:[6]

William Roper, *The Lyfe of Sir Thomas Moore, Knighte.*[7] This short but invaluable biography was written by More's son-in-law, husband of his daughter Margaret.

Nicholas Harpsfield, *The Life and Death of Sir Thomas More.*[8] Archdeacon Harpsfield composed his biography during the reign of Queen Mary I (1553–1558).

---

[3] *The Correspondence of Sir Thomas More* (Princeton, N.J.: Princeton Univ. Press, 1947).

[4] *Sir Thomas More and His Friends, 1477–1535* (1934; reprint, New York: Russell and Russell, 1963).

[5] *The Epistles of Erasmus: From His Earliest Letters to His Fifty-first Year*, trans. and ed. Francis M. Nichols, 3 vols. (1901–1918; reprint, New York: Russell and Russell, 1962).

[6] The following description of these biographies is based on information provided by R. W. Chambers in his classic work *Thomas More* (1935; reprint, Ann Arbor, Mich.: Ann Arbor Paperbacks, Univ. of Michigan Press, 1973), 24–42.

[7] *The Lyfe of Sir Thomas Moore, Knighte*, ed. Elsie Vaughan Hitchcock, Early English Text Society, original series, no. 197 (London: Early English Text Society, 1935).

[8] *Lives of Saint Thomas More* (Roper biography and Harpsfield biography), ed. E. E. Reynolds, Everyman's Library, no. 19 (London: J. M. Dent and Sons), 1963.

Thomas Stapleton, *The Life and Illustrious Martyrdom of Sir Thomas More.*[9] One of the English Catholic refugees who fled to the Continent following the accession of Queen Elizabeth I to the throne, Stapleton, a priest and theologian, published his biography in 1588 (in Latin).

Ro: Ba:, *The Lyfe of Syr Thomas More, Sometymes Lord Chancellor of England.*[10] The anonymous author of this biography, known only as "Ro: Ba:", has never been identified, but his work dates from about 1599.

Cresacre More, *The Life and Death of Sir Thomas Moore.*[11] This biography was composed by More's great-grandson in the first part of the seventeenth century.

Finally, please note that in all quotations from the Roper, "Ro: Ba:", and Cresacre More biographies, the spelling and punctuation have been modernized by the author.

---

[9] *The Life and Illustrious Martyrdom of Sir Thomas More,* ed. E. E. Reynolds (Bronx, N.Y.: Fordham Univ. Press), 1966.

[10] *The Lyfe of Syr Thomas More, Sometymes Lord Chancellor of England by Ro: Ba:,* ed. E. V. Hitchcock and Msgr. P. E. Hallett, Early English Text Society, original series, no. 222 (London: Early English Text Society, 1950).

[11] *The Life and Death of Sir Thomas Moore (1630),* facsimile of 1st ed. English Recusant Literature, 1558–1640, ed. D. M. Rogers, vol. 66 (Menston, Yorkshire, England: Scolar Press, 1971).

PART ONE

The Journey to God Begins

CHAPTER I

More's Early Years

We can state with reasonable certainty that Thomas More entered this world on February 6, 1478, during the reign of King Edward IV.[1] His father, John More, a citizen of London, recorded his son's birth in the back pages of a book, Geoffrey of Monmouth's *History of the Kings of Britain*, where earlier he had recorded the date of his marriage to Agnes Graunger, April 24, 1474.[2] Thomas was the second of six children to be born to John and Agnes More: three girls (Joan, 1475–1542; Agatha, 1479–?; Elizabeth, 1482–1528) and two other boys (John, 1480–c. 1512; Edward, 1481–?).[3] Their father began his career as a butler at Lincoln's Inn; only much later in his life, probably at the age of sixty-six, was he raised to the office of "Judge of the Common Pleas" and, about six years later, to that of "Judge of the King's Bench".[4]

About the year 1485, when Thomas More would have been in his seventh year, his father enrolled him in the institution reputed to be one of London's finest schools for young students: Saint Anthony's on Threadneedle Street.[5] It was here that the boy would have received his first systematic training in Latin, the language that was to serve as the cornerstone of his lifelong endeavors as an accomplished scholar.[6]

---

[1] R. W. Chambers, *Thomas More* (1935; reprint, Ann Arbor, Mich.: Ann Arbor Paperbacks, Univ. of Michigan, 1973), 48–49; E. E. Reynolds, *The Field Is Won: The Life and Death of Saint Thomas More* (Milwaukee: Bruce Publishing Co., 1968), 383.

[2] Chambers, *More*, 49–50.

[3] Ibid., 52–53; E. E. Reynolds, *Saint Thomas More* (New York: P. J. Kenedy and Sons, 1953), family tree chart.

[4] Chambers, *More*, 52–53.

[5] Reynolds, *Field Is Won*, 21, 25.

[6] Ibid.

Around the age of twelve, Thomas was received as a page into the household of John Morton, the Archbishop of Canterbury (who was later to become a cardinal).[7] So impressed was the Archbishop with the young More that he was wont to say of him, "This child here waiting at the table, whosoever shall live to see it, will prove a marvellous man."[8]

Probably in 1492, the year of Columbus' landmark voyage to the New World, More became a student at Oxford University, sponsored by Archbishop Morton.[9] Oxford, then as now, consisted of several different colleges on the same grounds, and according to More's greatgrandson, Cresacre More, it was at Oxford's Canterbury College that Thomas studied for the duration of his short stay at the university—a period of less than two years, according to Harpsfield.[10] From other evidence it appears that his actual place of residence on the campus was in Oxford's "Hall of Saint Mary the Virgin", although this by no means excludes his affiliation with Canterbury College; the two institutions were in close proximity to each other.[11] The individual facets of More's intellectual and spiritual formation during this period would be of great interest to us, as they undoubtedly would serve to shed light upon his subsequent writings. Unfortunately, we are hampered in this effort by the paucity of testimony in this regard from either More himself or from his biographers. From other sources, however, we may piece together a picture of student life at Oxford in the late fifteenth century. Statutes issued for the university in 1489, only about three years prior to More's arrival, are of particular interest in this regard. On all but special occasions students were required to communicate with one another and the faculty in Latin—violators were fined. Members of the student body were required to attend Mass

---

[7] Chambers, *More*, 58–59, 60.

[8] William Roper, *The Lyfe of Sir Thomas Moore, Knighte*, ed. Elsie V. Hitchcock, Early English Text Society, original series, no. 197 (London: Early English Text Society, 1935), 5.

[9] Thomas Stapleton, *The Life and Illustrious Martyrdom of Sir Thomas More*, ed. E. E. Reynolds (Bronx, N.Y.: Fordham Univ. Press, 1966), chap. 1, p. 4; Reynolds, *Field Is Won*, 23, 25.

[10] Cresacre More, *The Life and Death of Sir Thomas Moore (1630)*, facsimile of 1st ed. English Recusant Literature, 1558–1640, ed. D. M. Rogers, vol. 66 (Menston, Yorkshire, England: Scolar Press, 1971), chap. 1, no. 3, p. 20; Nicholas Harpsfield, *The Life and Death of Sir Thomas More*, in *Lives of Saint Thomas More* (William Roper and Nicholas Harpsfield), ed. E. E. Reynolds, Everyman's Library, no. 19 (London: J. M. Dent and Sons, 1963), 59.

[11] H. Baker, "Thomas More at Oxford", *Moreana* 11 (November 1974): 7–10.

daily, a habit that we know More observed the rest of his life. Medieval university lectures generally began around six in the morning, and at Oxford, according to the 1489 statutes, the day ended with the communal singing of the *Salve Regina* or the antiphon of the Blessed Virgin from the Divine Office.[12] As for the Oxford curriculum, it is difficult to say precisely which courses More would have taken, as we do not know what particular degree he was preparing for; William Roper does tell of his father-in-law learning Greek and deepening his proficiency in Latin at Oxford, while Cresacre More speaks of his great-grandfather studying rhetoric, logic, and philosophy at the university.[13] A statute dating from 1431 specifying the requirements for a licentiate in arts gives us a broad idea of the subjects taught, listing courses in the seven traditional disciplines of grammar, rhetoric, logic, arithmetic, music, geometry, and astronomy, and utilizing the works of Aristotle, Boethius, Cicero, Ovid, and Ptolemy; the study of the three branches of philosophy—natural, moral, and metaphysical—are also prescribed, with Aristotle used in all three cases.[14] In addition to arts degrees, Oxford also granted degrees in theology, medicine, civil law, canon law, and (by the early sixteenth century) even music.[15]

It may possibly be that More's love for the Fathers of the Church, particularly for the writings of Saint Augustine, could have first taken root during his brief sojourn at Oxford. It is particularly likely that his knowledge of the theology of Saint Thomas Aquinas began at Oxford, for the university was a stronghold of medieval scholasticism.[16]

While Oxford may have nurtured the young More's aspirations to seek "the things that are above" (Col 3:1), John More had very different ambitions for his son. Hence it seems likely that Thomas' transfer around 1494 from the halls of the university to a London institution that trained students destined for a career in law, the "New Inn",[17] was prompted by the young man's desire to comply with his father's wishes. Subsequently, by the age of eighteen, he had sufficiently advanced in his legal formation to receive admission into the prestigious

---

[12] Hastings Rashdall, *The Universities of Europe in the Middle Ages,* rev. ed., ed. F. M. Powicke and A. B. Emdem (Oxford: Oxford Univ. Press, 1936), 3:373–74, 401.

[13] Roper, *Lyfe,* 5; Cresacre More, *Life,* 20.

[14] Rashdall, *Universities,* 3:153–156.

[15] Ibid., 156–60.

[16] Reynolds, *Field Is Won,* 24.

[17] Ibid., 25, 27.

Lincoln's Inn on February 12, 1496.[18] Nonetheless, these changes in academic setting and curriculum could not divert Thomas from his love for ecclesiastical studies. It was also at this time that the seeds of More's career as a writer were sown when several epigrams composed by the young scholar were published as part of a student grammar book, *Lac puerorum* (Milk of children), which first appeared sometime between 1497 and 1500.[19] Hence More's debut on the printed page would have occurred when he was only twenty-two or younger, not a minor accomplishment considering that the printing press had been introduced scarcely half a century before.

It was at this juncture that there entered into the life of the young More two significant figures: the humanist scholars John Colet (1466–1519) and Desiderius Erasmus of Rotterdam (1466?–1536). One of the foremost English intellects of his age, the clergyman John Colet had for a time studied in Italy, from which he would have brought back to his native land the Italian humanists' passion for biblical, patristic, and Greek studies.[20] In 1499 we find him lecturing at Oxford University on the Epistles of Saint Paul; six years later he was appointed to the prestigious London office of dean of Saint Paul's Cathedral.[21] It is not possible to date precisely when More first came into contact with Colet, but we do know that by 1504 he had begun to avail himself of Colet's spiritual direction.[22]

It appears certain that More initially met Erasmus in the year 1499, when the famous Dutch scholar visited England for the first time. Included in Erasmus' voluminous correspondence is a letter dating from October 28, 1499, in which he gently berates More for failing to send him a letter.[23] On December 5 of the same year, writing to one of his students of his tremendous satisfaction with his stay in England, Erasmus lists his young English friend as one of many examples of

---

[18] Ibid., 27.

[19] Chambers, *More*, 81; note/commentary, in *Latin Poems,* ed. Clarence H. Miller et al., vol. 3, pt. 2 of *Complete Works of St. Thomas More* (New Haven: Yale Univ. Press, 1984), 65, 417. Hereafter cited as *CW* 3/2.

[20] J. H. Lupton, *A Life of John Colet, D.D.* (London: George Bell and Sons, 1909), 43–48.

[21] John Gleason, *John Colet* (Berkeley, Calif.: Univ. of California Press, 1989), 32; Francis M. Nichols, trans. and ed., *The Epistles of Erasmus: From His Earliest Letters to His Fifty-First Year* (1901–1918; reprint, New York: Russell and Russell, 1962), 1:204–5 (commentary).

[22] Letter no. 3, from More to Colet, October 23, 1504, in Elizabeth Rogers, ed., *The Correspondence of Sir Thomas More* (Princeton, N.J.: Princeton Univ. Press, 1947), 5–9.

[23] Nichols, *Epistles,* 1:200 (commentary), 212–13.

"the harvest of ancient learning in this country": "What has Nature ever created more gentle, more sweet, more happy than the genius of Thomas More?"[24] The earliest incident involving both men of which we have record dates from the second half of 1499 or the beginning of 1500 and centers upon yet another figure who was to loom so large in More's future: Henry VIII. As Erasmus tells the story, More had come to visit him at the country home of one Lord Mountjoy (a student of Erasmus) and had persuaded him to join him on a stroll to the next village (evidently Eltham), where the royal children of the king then reigning, Henry VII, were in residence. Entering a hall where the children were gathered, More went up to the nine-year-old Henry VIII and presented him with a written composition he had prepared for the occasion. Not having anticipated this visit with the royal family, Erasmus found himself deeply embarrassed that he had nothing to offer Henry. He later confessed to being angry with More for having put him in this awkward position; yet nonetheless the two forged a friendship that lasted a lifetime.[25] In a letter written only six years later (May 1, 1506), Erasmus described the personality and intellectual gifts of his English friend in the most effusive terms:

> . . . I do not think, unless the vehemence of my love leads me astray, that Nature ever formed a mind more present, ready, sharpsighted and subtle, or in a word more absolutely furnished with every kind of faculty than his. Add to this a power of expression equal to his intellect, a singular cheerfulness of character and an abundance of wit, but only of the candid sort; and you miss nothing that should be found in a perfect advocate.[26]

The name of Erasmus will appear frequently in the pages to follow; we must however note that More's friendship with this renowned Dutch scholar should not be misunderstood as implying that the two men always thought alike. Indeed, the differences in their respective outlooks are important and were particularly brought to the fore by their divergent reactions to the Reformation. Perhaps these differences serve to account for a comment made by Erasmus in August 1535, when rumors of More's execution a month earlier first began reaching him: "Would that he [More] had never embroiled himself

---

[24] Letter of Erasmus to Robert Fisher, in ibid., 226.

[25] Erasmus, *Catalogue of Lucubrations,* quoted in Nichols, *Epistles,* 1:201–2, plus commentary, 200–201; Chambers, *More,* 70.

[26] Letter to Richard Whitford, in Nichols, *Epistles,* 1:406–7.

in this dangerous business and had left theological questions to the theologians."[27] A mutual understanding of their differences is implicit in the curious absence of any notable manifestations of More's own deep spirituality in his earlier letters to his Dutch clerical friend.[28] Nonetheless, even in his dealings with Erasmus, More's religious motivations are ever present just below the surface and, indeed, come to the surface when in the spring of 1520 he finds it necessary to admonish his friend to put an end to his quarrel with the humanist Edward Lee:

> You need not be warned, or exhorted to such modesty as befits a true Christian, since in all the drudgery this affair has inflicted on you, Christ has been your sole aim. He alone, then, should be now before your eyes.[29]

It is a testimony to the integrity of More's concept of friendship that he was able to appreciate and share in the laudable qualities of his friends without slavishly imitating their imperfections or assimilating their mistaken ideas.

Whatever may be said of the possible role of Oxford in initiating Thomas' fascination with the Church Fathers, we can say with considerably greater confidence that John Colet would certainly have fostered such a devotion in More, for Colet crusaded for a return in theology to the works of Saint Jerome, Saint Augustine, and Saint Ambrose.[30] Similarly we find Erasmus preoccupied with publishing accurate texts of the works of the Church Fathers in order to make their writings more widely available;[31] undoubtedly Erasmus' interest in this matter would have also exerted an influence on More. The saint appears to have made a point of furthering his knowledge of the ecclesiastical disciplines by regularly attending the lectures of

---

[27] Letter to Bartholomew Latomus, August 24, 1535, in E. E. Reynolds, *Thomas More and Erasmus* (London: Burns and Oates, 1965), 238; for original Latin text, see letter no. 3048 in *Opus Epistolarum Des. Erasmi Roterdami*, vol. 11, *1534–1536*, ed. P. S. Allen, H. M. Allen, and H. W. Garrod (1947; reprint, Oxford: Clarendon Press, 1963), 216.

[28] Fr. Germain Marc'hadour, "Thomas More's Spirituality", in *St. Thomas More: Action and Contemplation: Proceedings of the Symposium Held at St. John's University, October 9–10, 1970*, ed. Richard Sylvester (New Haven: Yale Univ. Press, 1972), 147–50.

[29] Letter of More to Erasmus, April 1520, in ibid., 150; for original Latin text, see letter no. 1090 in *Opus Epistolarum Des. Erasmi Roterdami*, vol. 4, *1519–1521*, ed. P. S. Allen and H. M. Allen (Oxford: Clarendon Press, 1922), 234.

[30] Chambers, *More*, 80.

[31] Ibid.

noted scholars in these fields. Thus in a letter dating from the autumn of 1501[32] he speaks of the lectures of the cleric William Grocyn on the *De Ecclesiastica Hierarchia*, a work until then universally attributed to Dionysius the Areopagite, a figure in the early Church briefly mentioned in the Acts of the Apostles as one of the few Greeks who were converted following Saint Paul's discourse to the Athenians (Acts 17:34).[33] Grocyn originally believed this book was truly from the pen of Dionysius, but after further study he concluded that it could not have been written by him and presented this finding in his lectures.[34] Subsequent scholarship has confirmed Grocyn's view on this matter, so that the term "Pseudo-Dionysius the Areopagite" is now routinely used to identify the unknown author of *De Ecclesiastica Hierarchia*. Thomas More humorously describes the audience attending Grocyn's lectures as "a group of students, whose numbers, unfortunately, are greater than their learning, but it also includes a large number of educated people".[35]

It was this same William Grocyn who shortly thereafter invited More, only about twenty-three at the time, to lecture upon Saint Augustine's *City of God* at Grocyn's parish of "Saint Lawrence Jewry" in London. We are told that More's talks focused upon the historical and philosophical aspects of Saint Augustine's book rather than upon its theological dimensions, but unfortunately we have no further details concerning his presentation.[36] Nonetheless, Thomas Stapleton does state that the lectures proved an enormous success for the young scholar, eventually attracting a larger audience than did Grocyn,[37] with "old men and priests not being ashamed to take a lesson in divinity from a young layman, and not at all sorry to have done so", according to Erasmus.[38] As for the oratorical skills that More would have brought to occasions such as this, Erasmus further testifies:

> It would be difficult to find any one more successful in speaking *ex tempore*, the happiest thoughts being attended by the happiest language;

---

[32] Letter no. 2, from More to John Holt, c. November 1501, in Rogers, *Correspondence*, 4.

[33] Chambers, *More*, 82.

[34] Rogers, *Correspondence*, 4 n; Reynolds, *Field Is Won*, 31.

[35] Letter no. 2, to John Holt, in Rogers, *Correspondence*, 4, quoted and translated in Reynolds, *Field Is Won*, 31.

[36] Stapleton, *Life*, chap. 2, pp. 7–8; Reynolds, *Field Is Won*, 31; Chambers, *More*, 82–83.

[37] Stapleton, *Life*, chap. 2, p. 8.

[38] Letter of Erasmus to Ulrich von Hutten, July 23, 1517, in Nichols, *Epistles*, 3:393.

while a mind that catches and anticipates all that passes, and a ready memory, having everything as it were in stock, promptly supply whatever the time, or the occasion, demands. In disputations nothing can be imagined more acute, so that the most eminent theologians often find their match, when he meets them on their own ground.[39]

Already versed in Latin, the young More was at this time studying the other great language of ancient Western civilization—Greek. His tutors in this pursuit were Grocyn[40] and Thomas Linacre, the latter a cleric who was proficient in medicine and whose lectures on Aristotle's scientific treatise *Meteorologica* More had also made a point of attending.[41] Thomas' interest in Greek was yet another manifestation of his preoccupation with the sacred sciences, for Greek was the language of ancient texts of the New Testament and of the Eastern Church Fathers such as Saint John Chrysostom and Saint Cyril of Jerusalem.

More's range of work and studies at this time in his life was most remarkable; yet there were other forces at work in his soul, as we are told by Stapleton:

> . . . [H]e was far more zealous to become a saint than a scholar. For, even as a youth, he wore a hairshirt, and slept on the ground or on bare boards with perhaps a log of wood as his pillow. At the most he took four or five hours' sleep, and he was frequent in watchings and fastings. Although he was practising such austerities, yet he hid them so carefully that no sign of them could be perceived.[42]

It also appears that in 1499, when More was about twenty-one, he suffered what would have been a most painful reminder of the shortness of human life: the death of his own mother. While there are no definitive statements by his early biographers as to precisely when this event took place, there is evidence to suggest that the following sepulchral epitaph (translated from the Latin) is that composed for the tomb of More's mother, Agnes, and her brother-in-law, Abel More.

---

[39] Ibid., 398.

[40] Letter no. 2, to John Holt, in Rogers, *Correspondence*, 4.

[41] More, letter to Martin Dorp, October 21, 1515, in *In Defense of Humanism: Letters to Dorp, Oxford, Lee, and a Monk,* ed. Daniel Kinney, vol. 15 of *Complete Works of St. Thomas More* (New Haven: Yale Univ. Press, 1986), 103. Hereafter identified as *CW* 15. Chambers, *More*, 83–84.

[42] Stapleton, *Life,* chap. 2, p. 8.

The structure and style of the epitaph strongly suggest that Thomas
More himself may have been the author:[43]

> Come hither, wayfarer, and measure with thine eyes
> How small an urn holds two [persons] enclosed.
> What thou art today, this man once was,
> and so was this woman,
> Now each of them is part of this icy soil.
> His name was ABEL, MORE his surname, and at Exeter
> City was he once a doctor of Civil Law.
> AGNES was the other's name,
> and she was the wife of JOHN MORE,
> once the brother of this ABEL here.
> As thou wishest, then,
> the living should do to thee after thy demise,
> So thyself, now, whoever thou art,
> utter this short prayer:
> "May this ABEL in the first place and this AGNES
> be relieved by the Lamb
> Who previously washed the sheep
> in his 'agnine' [lamblike] blood."
> ABEL died 1486, AGNES 1499. May their souls
> (through the mercy of God rest in peace).[44]

While none of More's biographers is able to tell us anything of his reaction to the loss of his mother, we are justified in assuming it elicited
deep emotions in the young man, judging from his reaction to his
father's death some thirty years later.

It was in or around 1501 that a new chapter opened in More's
life, perhaps prompted in part by a deepened introspection following
the recent loss of his mother. The young Thomas had felt the call
to perfection and sought to answer it as best he could; and so he
spent the next four years contemplating what state in life God might
be calling him to. Thus he gave serious consideration to the idea of
entering the priesthood and the religious life. For this reason, from
around the age of twenty-three to about his twenty-seventh year, he

---

[43] Fr. Germain Marc'hadour, "The Death-Year of Thomas More's Mother", *Moreana/
Thomas More Gazette* 16 (1979): 13–16.

[44] Ibid., 14.

spent at least part of each day participating in the spiritual exercises of the Carthusian monks of London's Charterhouse. He did not actually reside within the monastery or become a member of the order by any vows or profession but rather lived in quarters nearby, so that he continued his work in the world while nourishing his soul with Carthusian spirituality.[45] We cannot underestimate the importance of this episode in his life; it served to shape all his remaining years. Once again we are confronted with a relative paucity of information from More's biographers; but by examining the horarium of Carthusian communities (which has changed very little over nine centuries) we may gain some picture of his four years at the Charterhouse. It is immediately obvious from More's selection of the Carthusians that he was quite serious about the question of his vocation. Their rule is among the most demanding of any in the Church, and, unlike all too many other religious communities in early sixteenth-century Europe, the Carthusians had not in any way slackened in the observance of the constitutions of their founder, Saint Bruno. Their life is strictly and totally "contemplative", as distinguished from the "active" life of other orders that exercise their ministry in some fairly visible form in the outside world. The daily exercises of the Carthusians,[46] hidden from the eyes of the world but nonetheless seen by God, would have begun with the sacristan ringing the bell between ten and eleven o'clock at night, signaling the start of Matins, the first "hour" of the Divine Office for the upcoming day. The monks rose in their cells and knelt to recite by themselves Matins and Lauds (the second hour) of the Little Office of the Blessed Virgin Mary, an abbreviated version of the Breviary dating back to the tenth century or earlier and consisting of psalms and canticles selected in honor of our Lady, accompanied by appropriate Marian antiphons and prayers. This was followed by prayers for the restoration of the Holy Land to the Christians, after which the monks were allowed a short interval of time before they were summoned from their cells by a second bell, calling them to the

---

[45] Roper, *Lyfe*, 6; Ro: Ba:, *The Lyfe of Syr Thomas More, Sometymes Lord Chancellor of England by Ro: Ba:,* ed. E. V. Hitchcock and Msgr. P. E. Hallett, Early English Text Society, original series, no. 222 (London: Early English Text Society, 1950), bk. 1, chap. 4, pp. 25–26; Cresacre More, *Life,* chap. 1, no. 5, p. 29.

[46] The following account of Carthusian life is based upon Dom Lawrence Hendriks, *The London Charterhouse: Its Monks and Its Martyrs* (London: Kegan Paul, Trench and Co., 1889), 26–35.

communal recital in the chapel of Matins and Lauds from the official Divine Office. Much of the Office was chanted, thereby adding to the amount of time and stamina required to perform this daily function. It is recorded of London's Charterhouse in the sixteenth century that the chanting there was particularly slow and thus even more demanding.[47] The Breviary of the Carthusians was longer still than the *Roman Breviary* of Pope Saint Pius V; hence the first hours of the Divine Office were not completed until about two o'clock in the morning, at which time the monks returned to their rooms to recite another hour of the Little Office of the Blessed Virgin Mary, that of Prime; after a few other prayers, they were allowed to sleep until around dawn (between five and six in the morning). Upon rising, the monks now attended Mass, which was followed by periods for meditation, spiritual reading, and the recitation of more of the Divine Office, lasting until about ten o'clock. The interval from ten until two-thirty in the afternoon was spent mostly in mental or manual labors performed in solitude, with a little time set aside for a meal (also taken in solitude) and the recitation of a bit more of the Office. At a quarter to three the monks, having assembled in the chapel, recited the hour of Vespers from the Divine Office; this was followed by other spiritual exercises that lasted until six-thirty or seven, at which time they retired for the day so as to be rested for the beginning of the next day's Office that night. Coupled with this grueling daily routine were a number of extraordinary austerities, including the continual wearing of a hair shirt, a perpetual abstinence from meat and animal fat, a Lenten fast extended to last six months, as well as a weekly fast on only bread and water (usually on Fridays) throughout the year.[48]

The members of the Carthusian community who were not destined for Holy Orders, known as "lay brothers", followed a horarium that was a bit less strenuous than that described above; nonetheless, their rule was quite austere as well. In the case of Thomas More, we should keep in mind that his biographers speak of him aspiring specifically to the priesthood, and hence had More chosen priesthood in the Carthusians, he would have had to follow the demanding rule

---

[47] Ibid., 28.

[48] Fr. Herbert Thurston, S.J., *The Life of Saint Hugh of Lincoln* (London: Burns and Oates, 1898), 48; *The Carthusians: Origin, Spirit, Family Life,* 2d ed. (Westminster, Md.: Newman Press, 1952), 53.

of the ordained monks, and not the "easier" rule of the lay brothers. In this light we cannot but admire the depth of More's faith in
considering such a life, which he took the opportunity to see for
himself. Remember also that this was no mere passing fancy or im-
pulsive venture on the part of a naïve young man ignorant of what
would be required of him, for Thomas, far from being repelled by
his first tastes of the Carthusian rule, chose to continue sharing in
the spiritual exercises of the London Charterhouse over a period of
four years. The fortitude of those called to the Carthusian state was to
be amply demonstrated years later as eighteen members of this order,
mostly from the London Charterhouse, were eventually to die for
their fidelity to the papacy.[49]

It was sometime during or shortly after this period of More's life
that he completed a translation of the biography of a recently deceased Italian scholar, Giovanni Pico della Mirandola (1463–1494).
Pico's life as an unmarried layman, devoted to ecclesiastical studies,
who shortly before dying had sought admittance into the Dominican
Order, stirred the interest of More, whose academic pursuits and ascetical practices resembled in certain ways those of Pico. Stapleton
and Cresacre More indicate that the young Thomas turned to the life
of Pico as an example for the lay state only after he had decided not
to become a priest or religious,[50] but the renowned twentieth-century
Morean biographer E. E. Reynolds proposes quite logically that this
translation was more likely a product of the Charterhouse years when
More was still considering a clerical vocation.[51] Nonetheless, the Pico
biography must have continued to serve as something of a blueprint
for More's own spirituality even after he had come to a final decision on the lay state; the ideals it embodies would remain with him
throughout his life.[52]

More's translation bears a dedicatory preface to a young woman
who had decided upon her vocation: Joyeuce Leigh, who had entered the community of Poor Clares of the House of Minoresses in

[49] Dom Bede Camm, O.S.B., *Martyrs under Henry VIII*, vol. 1 of *Lives of the English Martyrs* (London: Burns and Oates, 1904), lx–lxi, 1–16, 37–46, 249–68.

[50] Stapleton, *Life*, chap. 2, p. 9; Cresacre More, *Life*, chap. 1, pp. 31–32.

[51] Reynolds, *Field Is Won*, 43–45.

[52] The judgment that the Pico translation constitutes an "autobiography" of More's ideals is endorsed in Vittorio Gabrieli, "Giovanni Pico and Thomas More", *Moreana* 15 (1967): 46.

Aldgate.[53] The members of the Leigh family had been friends of the Mores over the years; both families had attended the same parish of Saint Stephen's Walbrook.[54] It appears likely that Joyeuce and her brother Edward were playmates of John More's children, and thus we see that the preface is addressed to a young woman Thomas had known since childhood. Interestingly Stapleton mentions that for a while More had considered becoming a Franciscan;[55] it seems possible that Joyeuce's decision to consecrate her life to Christ as a daughter of Saint Francis may have inspired the young More with the idea of entering the same order. In any event this preface and the translation of the *Life of John Picus* accompanying it constitute two of the earliest surviving examples of More's prose:

> It is, and of long time hath been, my well beloved sister, a custom in the beginning of the new year, friends to send between, presents or gifts, as the witnesses of their love and friendship and also signifying that they desire each to other that year a good continuance and prosperous end of that lucky beginning . . . But forasmuch as the love and amity of Christian folk should be rather ghostly friendship than bodily . . . I therefore, mine heartily beloved sister, in good luck of this new year have sent you such a present, as may bear witness of my tender love and zeal to the happy continuance and gracious increase of virtue in your soul; and where as the gifts of other folk declare that they wisheth their friends to be worldly fortunate, mine testifyeth that I desire to have you godly prosperous.[56]

Twice in the above passage More refers to Joyeuce as his "beloved sister"; this and the whole tone of the letter suggest that More deeply admired Joyeuce's dedication of herself to God and that he shared her aspirations as her spiritual brother in Christ. As we will later see, More was never to lose his sense of reverence for the religious life and was to defend it in his subsequent apologetical writings. As to Joyeuce Leigh, we have no further details of her life in the Franciscan community of Aldgate, but it is recorded that her mother later came to live in the convent.[57] It seems that Joyeuce may have died in 1515, when twenty-seven of the nuns of Aldgate perished in an outbreak of

---

[53] Reynolds, *Field Is Won*, 44.
[54] Introduction to letter no. 4, to Joyeuce Leigh, in Rogers, *Correspondence*, 9.
[55] Stapleton, *Life*, chap. 2, p. 8.
[56] Letter no. 4, to Joyeuce Leigh, in Rogers, *Correspondence*, 9–10.
[57] Introduction to letter no. 4, in ibid., 9.

the plague.[58] Perhaps she was fortunate not to have lived long enough to see the dissolution of her convent in 1539 and the desecration of her mother's grave.[59]

An examination of More's translation of the Pico biography reveals a great deal about his state of mind at this time. Although he basically provides the reader with a literal translation of the Italian text authored by Pico's nephew, he does exercise a certain amount of editorial discretion in his omission of some passages and in his glosses upon others.[60] From these little liberties of the translator we can see that he was discerning enough to have recognized Pico's deficiencies and failures as well as his virtues. Thus after presenting the ecclesiastical investigation of Pico in Rome regarding certain statements in the Italian scholar's writings that nearly led to him being condemned for heresy, More, recognizing the pitfalls of excessive ambition in the pursuit of scholarship, observes:

> Lo, this end had Picus of his high mind and proud purpose: that where he thought to have gotten perpetual praise; there had he much work to keep himself upright; that he ran not in[to] perpetual infamy and slander.[61]

The above incident brought about a conversion in Pico, prompting him to turn from a life of intellectual and bodily self-gratification and instead to pursue the way of perfection followed by penitents and ascetics: ". . . [H]e drew back his mind flowing in riot, and turned it to Christ."[62] It is particularly in this phase of Pico's life that we find parallels with the young More, parallels that serve to explain his desire to translate the Pico biography. There is an echo of More's participation in the horarium of the Carthusians in Pico's devoting himself to prayer "[e]very day at certain hours" and his contentment "with mean fare at his table".[63] When in More's translation we are told that

---

[58] Reynolds, *Field Is Won*, 44 n.

[59] Ibid.; Chambers, *More*, 93.

[60] W. Doyle-Davidson, "The Earlier Works of Sir Thomas More", in *Essential Articles for the Study of Thomas More*, ed. R. S. Sylvester and G. P. Marc'hadour (Hamden, Conn.: Archon Books, 1977), 364, 366–67.

[61] *Life of John Picus*, in *The Workes of Sir Thomas More Knight . . . in the English Tongue* (1557), as reproduced in *The English Works of Sir Thomas More*, ed. W. E. Campbell (London: Eyre and Spottiswoode; New York: Lincoln MacVeagh, Dial Press, 1931), 1:4.

[62] Ibid., 4–6 (quote on 4).

[63] Ibid., 6.

Pico "[on] many days (and namely those days, which represent unto us the passion and death that Christ suffered for our sake) beat and scourged his own flesh",[64] we find reflections of More's absorption of Carthusian asceticism, as manifested by the latter's daily use of a hair shirt and frequent use of the discipline (small thongs for penitential self-scourging). Equally significant here is the parenthetical comment linking Pico's penance to the days of the liturgical year associated with our Lord's Passion. Devotion to the Passion is perhaps the single most pervasive aspect of More's spirituality, an aspect to which he was to give particular expression every Friday and on Good Friday, as we shall later see. It is probably no mere coincidence that the title page of the first printed edition of More's *Life of John Picus*, thought to date from before 1510,[65] features a woodcut image of Christ on the Cross, surrounded by the various instruments of the Passion, with a kneeling figure below.[66] Moreover, the death scene in the Pico biography serves as a prefiguration of More's subsequent expressions of love for the image of the crucifix:

> . . . [T]hey offered unto him the crucifix (that in the image of Christ's ineffable passion, suffered for our sake, he might ere he gave up the ghost, receive his full draught of love and compassion in the beholding of that pitiful figure, as a strong defense against all adversity, and a sure portcullis against wicked spirits:) . . .[67]

More's generosity to, and solicitude for, the underprivileged is presaged in Pico's distribution of his "silver vessel[s] and plate, with other precious and costly utensils" among the poor.[68] Then there was Pico's zeal for the sacred sciences—especially his day-and-night study of the Scriptures and his encyclopedic knowledge of the Church Fathers[69] —pursuits that we already know were dear to More. He would also have identified with Pico's indecision over the question of whether to enter the priesthood and religious life.[70] Pico's commitment following his conversion "to seek the glory and profit of Christ's Church",

---

[64] Ibid.
[65] Reynolds, *Field Is Won*, 44.
[66] Marc'hadour, "Spirituality", 128.
[67] *Life of Picus*, 8.
[68] Ibid., 6.
[69] Ibid., 4–5.
[70] Ibid., 8–9.

along with his diligence in "those observances, which the Church commandeth", are attributes shared by More and which will come to the fore in his later apologetical writings.[71] More's passionate defense in these latter works of the doctrine of Purgatory is anticipated in the oration given at Pico's funeral, as reproduced in More's translation:

> . . . [T]hough his soul be not yet in the bosom of our Lord in the heavenly joy, yet is it not on that other side deputed unto perpetual pain; but he is adjudged for a while to the fire of purgatory, there to suffer pain for a season, which I am the gladder to show you in this behalf; to the intent that they, which knew him, and such in especially, as for his manifold benefices are singularly beholden unto him; should now in their prayers, alms, and other suffrages help him.[72]

Following the text of the biography, More gives us a greater insight into what interests him about Pico by providing a selection of the Italian humanist's letters, all of which consist of instructions in Christian spirituality. In these, major themes of More's own spiritual life readily emerge, as in Pico's comments on the value of the Scriptures in nourishing the needs of the soul:

> Thou mayest do nothing more pleasant to God, nothing more profitable to thyself, than if thine hand cease not day nor night to turn and read the volumes of Holy Scripture. There lieth privily in them a certain heavenly strength, quick and effectual, which with a marvelous power transformeth and changeth the reader's mind into the love of God . . .[73]

Describing prayer and almsgiving as the two wings with which we are to rise from earth to heaven, Pico advises that we cannot expect God to hear our prayers if we turn a deaf ear to the cries of the poor.[74] If we desire health and protection from the devil, our enemies, and the vicissitudes of this life, and if we wish to make ourselves pleasing to God, let no day pass, Pico recommends, without at least some prayer to the Almighty, "falling down before him flat to the ground with an humble affection of devout mind".[75]

In an uncanny foreshadowing of later events in More's own life, Pico speaks at length on the suffering of ostracism for Christ, reas-

---

[71] Ibid., 4, 8.
[72] Ibid., 9–10.
[73] Ibid., 13.
[74] Ibid.
[75] Ibid.

suring his nephew that God provides not only the grace to live virtuously but also the grace to endure criticism for His sake. He recalls Christ's promise in the Beatitudes to reward those who are maligned on His account (Mt 5:11–12), as well as the rejoicing of the apostles in having suffered at the hands of the high priest and the Council of Jerusalem for the name of Jesus (Acts 5:41). Pico likewise draws upon our Lord's words at the Last Supper in this regard:

> And if we suffer of the world any thing that is grievous or bitter, let this sweet voice of our Lord be our consolation . . . If the world (saith our Lord) hate you, know ye, that it hated me before you.[76]

Pico adds that when men do praise us for our virtues, we resemble Christ insofar as we possess such virtues, but we fail to resemble Him insofar as we are praised, for He suffered for His goodness death on the Cross.[77]

More also translated Pico's commentary on Psalm 16. The opening words of the psalm, "Preserve me, O God" (v. 1), are for Pico an expression of humility, an acknowledgment that the just man is dependent upon God for his virtues, as Saint Paul indicates in asking, "What have you that you did not receive?" (1 Cor 4:7).[78] As to the psalm's words on taking refuge in God, Pico explains that when we turn to God for assistance in any matter, we should ask with hope and trust, and with the understanding that we only desire Him to give us what is truly for our good.[79] The Psalmist's declaration, "Thou art my Lord" (v. 2), serves as the basis for Pico's reflection on who or what a man really worships as his god in the place of the true God. Misers worship their money, gluttons worship their carnal appetite, and the ambitious worship their own glory. Hence there are few who can truly say only God is their God:

> For only he may truly say it, which is content with God alone; so that if there were offered him all the kingdoms of the world, and all the good that is in earth, and all the good that is in heaven, he would not once offend God to have them all.[80]

---

[76] Ibid., 15.

[77] Ibid.

[78] Ibid., 17.

[79] Ibid., 17–18.

[80] Ibid., 18.

The Psalmist's reference to "the saints in the land" (v. 3) provides Pico with an opportunity to advocate the veneration of the saints, as More himself will zealously do years later in his apologetical writings:

> To his saints that are in the land of him, he hath made marvelous his wills. After God should we specially love them, which are nearest joined unto God, as be the holy angels and blessed saints, that are in their country of heaven.[81]

The last third of More's edition of the *Life of John Picus* is taken up with poems that are in large part the translator's own compositions inspired by the ideas of Pico.[82] The first set of verses, "Twelve Rules" of "Spiritual Battle", treats of the soul's ongoing war with its enemies, the world, the flesh, and the devil. Thus the "Seventh Rule" addresses the temptation of taking pride in one's good actions, proposing humility as the antidote:

> Sometime he [the devil] secretly casteth in thy mind,
> Some laudable deed to stir thee to pride,
> As vainglory maketh many a man blind,
> But let humility be thy sure guide,
> Thy good work to God let it be applied
> Think it not thine, but a gift of his,
> Of whose grace undoubtedly all goodness is.[83]

The Passion of Christ permeates the stanzas of the "Fourth Rule", which stresses that in resisting each particular temptation, we conform ourselves to a corresponding attribute of Christ in His sufferings:

> If thou withdraw thine hands, and forbear,
> The ravin of anything, remember then,
> How his innocent hands nailed were,
> If thou be tempted with pride, think how that when
> He was in form of God, yet of a bond man,
> He took the shape and humbled himself for thee
> To the most odious and vile death of a tree.

---

[81] Ibid.
[82] Doyle-Davidson, "Earlier Works", 364.
[83] *Life of Picus*, 23.

Consider when thou art moved to be wroth,
He who that was God, and of all men the best,
Seeing himself scorned and scourged both,
And as a thief between two thieves threft,
With all rebuke and shame; yet from his breast
Came never sign of wrath or of disdain,
But patiently endured all the pain.[84]

The concluding words of the twelfth and last rule reflect a common-place of More's meditations and a recurring motif in his life: the remembrance of death:

. . . [P]eradventure death within one hour,
Shall us bereave, wealth, riches and honour,
And bring us down full low both small and great,
To vile carrion and wretched worms' meat.[85]

The "Twelve Rules" are followed by reflections on what are termed the "Twelve Weapons of Spiritual Battle", twelve considerations that can be brought to mind when confronting temptation. The soul is advised to recall in the face of such a trial that the pleasure from the proposed sinful act will be short-lived and minimal, only to be followed by sorrows and an even greater loss:

When thou laborest thy pleasure for to buy,
Upon the price look thou thee well advise,
Thou sellest thy soul therefore even by and by,
To thy most utter dispiteous enemies,
O mad merchant, O foolish merchandise,
To buy a trifle, O childish reckoning,
And pay therefore so dear a precious thing.[86]

There is also the need to remember that life is as fleeting as "a dream or shadow on the wall" and that death is ever near, with the danger that the soul in serious sin will die unrepentant, doomed to eternal torments.[87] But in addition to the sad consequences of succumbing to temptation, the soul is also advised to weigh the good that comes

---

[84] Ibid., 21–22.
[85] Ibid., 25.
[86] Ibid., 25–26.
[87] Ibid., 26.

from resisting temptation, for of all the joys one can experience in this life, "Thou shalt no pleasure comparable find / To the inward gladness of a virtuous mind."[88] The examples of the saints and martyrs prove that temptation can with God's assistance be resisted.[89] And we are invited to consider our dignity as rational beings made in the image and likeness of God,[90] as well as to recall the many gifts God has bestowed upon us:

> How mayest thou then to him unloving be,
> That ever hath been so loving unto thee?[91]

Here again the leitmotif of More's spirituality—the remembrance of the Savior's Passion—returns, this time manifesting an additional dimension of his inner life: devotion to the Heart of Christ, evidence of which will appear repeatedly in his subsequent writings:

> When thou in flame of the temptation friest,
> Think on the very lamentable pain,
> Think on the piteous cross of woeful Christ,
> Think on his blood beat out at every vein,
> Think on his precious heart carved in twain,
> Think how for thy redemption all was wrought,
> Let him not lose that he so dear hath bought.[92]

After providing a translation of Pico's "Twelve Properties or Conditions of a Lover", More proceeds to give his own commentary in poetic verse upon these "Twelve Properties", interpreting them in the spiritual sense as depicting the love a soul has for God. Thus Pico's first property, "To love one alone . . .",[93] prompts More to write:

> . . . [T]hou that hast thy love set unto God,
> In thy remembrance this imprint and grave,
> As he in sovereign dignity is odd [singular],
> So will he in love no parting fellows have;

---

[88] Ibid., 26–27.
[89] Ibid., 27.
[90] Ibid., 26.
[91] Ibid., 27.
[92] Ibid.
[93] Ibid.

Love him therefore with all that he thee gave,
For body, soul, wit, cunning, mind and thought
Part will he none, but either all or nought.[94]

Pico's seventh property, "To love all things that pertaineth unto his love",[95] provides More with the opportunity to advocate the reverencing of relics and religious images, thereby demonstrating that his belief in these traditional Catholic devotional practices can be traced back to his early life. It dispels any notion that his impassioned defense of these practices years later in the wake of the Reformation somehow represented a break with the spirituality of his youth:

. . . [E]very relic, image, or picture,
That doth pertain to God's magnificence,
The lover of God should with all busy cure
Have it in love, honour, and reverence . . .[96]

In this context More adds a further idea illustrative of his deep eucharistic piety and reminiscent of Saint Francis of Assisi: that so great is the dignity of priests in their ability to celebrate Mass that they are most precious relics in and of themselves:

And specially give them preeminence,
which daily done his blessed body work,
The quick [living] relics,
the ministers of his Church.[97]

As his edition of Pico draws to a close with a prayer of the latter, More makes the Italian humanist's thoughts distinctively his own by rendering the original into beautiful English verse, as in the following stanza that describes the Passion as a work of divine love:

What but our sin hath showed that mighty love,
which able was thy dreadful majesty,
To draw down into earth from heaven above,
And crucify God, that we poor wretches we,
Should from our filthy sin cleansed be,

---

[94] Ibid., 28.
[95] Ibid., 27.
[96] Ibid., 30.
[97] Ibid.

with blood and water of thine own side,
That streamed from thy blessed wounds wide.[98]

The theme of God's love is carried with commensurate eloquence onward to the end of the prayer, which closes with the vision of heaven and God's unfathomable mercy:

Grant me good Lord, and Creator of all,
The flame to quench of all sinful desire,
And in thy love set all mine heart afire.

That when the journey of this deadly life
My silly ghost [soul] hath finished, and thence
Depart must, without his fleshly wife
Alone into his Lord's high presence
He may thee find, O well of indulgence,
In thy lordship not as a lord, but rather
As a very tender loving Father.[99]

While More was straddling the line between the world and the cloister, he was elected, in 1504, as a burgess of Parliament, thus drawing him for the first time into the thickets of public affairs. All too soon More proved to be a courageous politician, beginning his career in public office by engaging in a head-on confrontation with the reigning monarch over a question of revenue. After King Henry VII's son Prince Arthur died, the monarch sought to obtain from Parliament two grants of financial support, one for the posthumous knighting of Arthur, the other for the marriage of Henry's daughter Margaret to the King of Scotland; in the case of the latter, he requested a sum of about sixty thousand pounds. But there was opposition to his proposal in Parliament—opposition that found a voice in the newly elected burgess, who so persuasively argued against the request that in the end the King had to settle for a total of thirty thousand pounds.[100] His Majesty was not amused to learn from one of the members of his Privy Chamber, Master Tyler, that "a beardless boy had disappointed all his purpose."[101] Obviously Thomas must have

---

[98] Ibid., 34.
[99] Ibid.
[100] Reynolds, *Field Is Won*, 51–52; Chambers, *More*, 87.
[101] Roper, *Lyfe*, 7.

appeared younger than his age, for he was already twenty-six at the time. In any event the King was determined to exact a price for this youthful indiscretion, and as the object of his wrath had little more in the way of personal wealth than the Carthusian monks with whom he associated, the monarch went after the father of this "beardless boy" instead, imprisoning the poor man in the Tower of London and charging him a fine of a hundred pounds.[102]

In the autumn of 1504,[103] at the end of his years spent with the Carthusians, More wrote to his friend John Colet. Expressing regret that Colet was away from London, he laments that he is thereby deprived of the wisdom of Colet's sermons and spiritual direction, the latter of which he seems to have felt in particular need of. He then complains of the way city life can stifle and choke the aspirations of the soul, as contrasted with the spiritually refreshing atmosphere of the countryside:

> In the city, what can incite a man to a good life, and does not rather, by a thousand devices call back him who is struggling to climb the hard tracks of virtue? One sees nothing but false affection and flattery on the one hand; hatred, quarrelling, and the wranglings of the law courts on the other. Wherever you look you see nothing but caterers, fishmongers, butchers, cooks, confectioners, poultrymen, all occupied in serving the body, the world and the devil! Even the houses block out a great part of the light, so that one cannot freely see the heavens; it is not the arc of the horizon that bounds the view, but the roofs of the houses.
>
> I cannot blame you if you are not tired of the country, where you see simple people, ignorant of the wiles of town, and wherever you turn your eyes, the beautiful face of the country refreshes you, the soft air exhilarates you, and the sight of the sky delights you.[104]

More's final decision to remain a layman in the world could not have been an easy one for him to make; we know this to have been the case from a comment he made to his daughter thirty years later, shortly before his death. While observing (on May 4, 1535) from the window of his prison in the Tower of London the first group of Carthusians sentenced to death by Henry VIII, More said to her:

---

[102] Ibid., 7–8.

[103] The editor of More's correspondence, Elizabeth Rogers, gives October 23, 1504, as the probable date of this letter (introduction to letter no. 3, in Rogers, *Correspondence,* 5).

[104] Latin original in ibid., 6–7; translation from E. M. G. Routh, *Sir Thomas More and His Friends, 1477–1535* (1934; reprint, New York: Russell and Russell, 1963), 25–26.

Lo, dost thou not see, Meg, that these blessed fathers be now as cheer-
fully going to their deaths as bridegrooms to their Marriage? Wherefore thereby mayest thou see, mine own good daughter, what a great
difference there is between such as have in effect spent all their days
in a straight, hard, penitential, and painful life religiously, and such as
have in the world, like worldly wretches, as thy poor father hath done,
consumed all their time in pleasure and ease licentiously.[105]

From a comment of Stapleton it appears that the above instance was
not the only occasion upon which More expressed such feelings of
regret in having chosen to remain in the world,[106] yet such comments,
coming as they do from the lips of a saint, should be seen in the same
light as the disquietude of the famous Curé d'Ars, Saint John Vianney, who, longing for a more perfect life of solitude and penance than
his own state as a parish priest, more than once attempted literally to
"run away" in order that he might devote himself to contemplation
in a cloistered monastery. But God willed otherwise, and invariably
John Vianney was forced to return to his station as a diocesan priest
of Ars, where so many thousands awaited his words of consolation
in the confessional. One need only look at the exemplary family life
of Thomas More's subsequent years, together with his high ideals of
lay spirituality and service to his Church, to understand why God
kept him in the world. While we cannot know the specific reasons
that entered into More's decision on a state of life, perhaps the best
explanation that has been offered is that provided by the author of
the so-called "Ro: Ba:" biography of the saint:

. . . [A]s God appointed that worthy man John Fisher, Bishop of Rochester, to be the Champion of the Clergy, so he reserved Thomas More in
the degree of the laity, to be the proto-Martyr of England that suffered
for the defence of the union of the Catholic Church.[107]

Stapleton's thoughts in this regard are equally valid:

. . . [P]erhaps it was that God, for his own greater glory, wished him to
remain a layman, to accept the honours and to meet the difficulties of
public life, and at the same time wished to keep his servant unspotted and
unharmed, and even to lead him to the highest perfection of sanctity.[108]

---

[105] Roper, *Lyfe,* 80–81.
[106] Stapleton, *Life,* chap. 2, pp. 8–9.
[107] Ro: Ba:, *Lyfe,* bk. 1, chap. 4, p. 26.
[108] Stapleton, *Life,* chap. 2, p. 9.

Finally there is the particularly eloquent observation of Cresacre More, who had good reason to be especially grateful for his great-grandfather's decision to embark upon family life:

> . . . God had allotted him for an other estate, not to live solitary, but that he might be a pattern to married men, how they should carefully bring up their children, how dearly they should love their wives, how they should employ their endeavour wholly for the good of their country, yet excellently perform the virtues of religious men, as, piety, charity, humility, obedience, and conjugal chastity.[109]

Toward the end of his life Thomas More himself was to reveal in the pages of one of his greatest apologetical works the beautiful ideals that he would have brought as a young man to the sacrament of matrimony; commenting on Saint Paul's words on the subject of marriage in his Letter to the Ephesians (Eph 5:25–27), he observed:

> Saint Paul here exhorteth men to love their wives, so tenderly that they should be of the mind, that to bring them to heaven they could find in their hearts to die for them, as Christ hath died for Christian people to bring them to heaven, and that men, to that intent that they may bring their wives to the glorious bliss of heaven, should here bring them well up in faith, in hope, and charity, and in good works, like as God hath washed his Church of all Christian people . . .[110]

As we have already seen above, Thomas More considered the English countryside a far more wholesome place than the city, and thus when he had decided upon his state in life, he was ultimately to ask for the hand of a young and simple country girl in marriage. She was the oldest of three daughters of John Colt, a citizen of Netherhall in Essex, whom More visited sometime in 1504 or at the beginning of 1505.[111] According to Cresacre More, all three of these young women were "very religiously inclined".[112] William Roper tells us that at first More found the second of the girls the most attractive and "best favoured", but when he considered that asking for her hand rather than for that of her older sister, Jane, would have deeply

---

[109] Cresacre More, *Life*, chap. 1, no. 5, pp. 29–30.

[110] *The Confutation of Tyndale's Answer*, ed. Louis Schuster et al., vol. 8 of *Complete Works of St. Thomas More* (New Haven: Yale Univ. Press, 1973), bk. 8, pp. 851–52. Hereafter cited as *CW* 8.

[111] Roper, *Lyfe*, 6; Chambers, *More*, 95; Reynolds, *Field Is Won*, 53.

[112] Cresacre More, *Life*, chap. 2, no. 1, pp. 46–47.

hurt the older girl, he, as Roper puts it, "of a certain pity framed his fancy" toward Jane and decided to marry her instead.[113] In a poem that More translated into Latin from the Greek only a few years after his marriage, we find a description of what a man should look for in choosing a wife; we have no reason to doubt that in these words there is at least some reflection of the young Jane Colt:

> And so, my friend, if you desire to marry, first observe what kind of parents the lady has. See to it that her mother is revered for the excellence of her character which is sucked in and expressed by her tender and impressionable little girl.
>
> Next see to this: what sort of personality she has: how agreeable she is. Let her maidenly countenance be calm and without severity. But let her modesty bring blushes to her cheeks . . . Let her glances be restrained; let her have no roving eye . . . Let her be either just finishing her education or ready to begin it immediately . . . Armed with this learning, she would not yield to pride in prosperity, nor to grief in distress—even though misfortune strike her down.[114]

The newly married couple first took up residence in a part of London known as Bucklersbury; here More was to reside for nearly twenty years, and it was here that all four of his children were born: Margaret (c. 1505–1544), Elizabeth (c. 1506–?), Cecily (c. 1507–?), and John (c. 1508/1509–1547).[115] Among those who knew More during the first years of his married life (1505 to 1511) was John Bouge, a parish priest who later entered the Carthusians. In a letter that he wrote shortly after the death of More, Father Bouge says that More was his parishioner while in London and that he had baptized two of More's children.[116] He was also More's spiritual director, probably from 1508 to 1510,[117] and thus was in a unique position to assess the state of the soul entrusted to him:

> This Mr. More was my ghostly child: in his confession to be so pure, so clean, with great study, deliberation, and devotion, I never heard many such: a gentleman of great learning, both in law, art, and divinity, having

---

[113] Roper, *Lyfe*, 6.

[114] "To Candidus: How to Choose a Wife", poem no. 143, in *CW* 3/2:185–87.

[115] Chambers, *More*, 98; Reynolds, *Field Is Won*, 53; Reynolds, *Saint Thomas More*, family tree chart.

[116] Chambers, *More*, 108–9.

[117] Daniel Sargent, *Thomas More* (New York: Sheed and Ward, 1933), 34.

no man like him now alive of a layman. Item, a gentleman of great soberness and gravity, one chief of the King's Council. Item, a gentleman of
little refection and marvellous diet.[118]

Our sources of information regarding this period of Thomas More's
life are few indeed, but we do have one major work of More's scholarship from these years: the translation into Latin of several of the
Greek works of Lucian. He and Erasmus collaborated on these translations, and the fruit of their labors, entitled *Luciani Opuscula . . . ab
Erasmo Roterodamo et Thoma Moro*, was published in Paris in November 1506.[119] The prefatory letter for More's portion of the book, addressed to King Henry VII's secretary, Thomas Ruthall, is of particular
interest, for in it More expresses his concern with the damage done
to the faith by unsubstantiated claims of miraculous occurrences and
private revelations that detract from, and can become confused with,
validated miracles and even Church doctrine and history. In this he
anticipated by well over a century the guiding principle of the Jesuit
scholars known as the Bollandists, who labored to produce scrupulously accurate accounts of the lives of the saints, devoid of question-
able legends, for their monumental work the *Acta Sanctorum*. More
begins by defending the value of reading the classical works of pagan
writers such as Lucian, for valid lessons may be derived from these
authors that can be applied within a Christian context. Thus Lucian's
dialogue *Philopseudes*, he notes, teaches us the pitfalls of mixing superstition with religion; similarly Christianity is done a grave disservice
by those who embellish the lives of the saints with unfounded and
fantastic tales:

> . . . [T]hey have not scrupled to stain with fiction that religion which
> was founded by [T]ruth [Himself] and ought to consist of naked truth.
> They have failed to see that such fables are so far from aiding religion
> that nothing can be more injurious to it. It is obvious, as St. Augustine
> himself has observed, that where there is any scent of a lie, the author-
> ity of truth is immediately weakened and destroyed. Hence a suspicion
> has more than once occurred to me that such stories have been largely
> invented by crafty knaves and heretics partly for the purpose of amusing
> themselves with the credulity of persons more simple than wise, and
> partly to diminish the true Christian histories by associating them with

---

[118] Quoted in Chambers, *More*, 109.
[119] Reynolds, *More and Erasmus*, 54–55.

fictitious fables, the feigned incidents being often so near to those contained in holy scripture that the allusion cannot be mistaken.[120]

More's words above should not be misunderstood as somehow con-
stituting a rejection on his part of all reported miracles other than
those contained in Sacred Scripture. We will later see from his own
writings elsewhere that he most certainly did believe in approved miracles involving the Eucharist, the Blessed Virgin Mary, and the saints.
Hence his criticism here is motivated, not by a naturalistic scepticism
toward the supernatural, but, quite to the contrary, by a genuine zeal
for the truths of his faith.

It was during this phase of his life that More appears to have first
met Antonio Bonvisi, arguably the closest of his friends. The son of a
prosperous, centuries-old family from the Italian city of Lucca, Bonvisi was born in December 1487, inheriting a career in banking and
the merchant trade from his ancestors. It is probable that More first
became acquainted with the young Italian merchant, some nine years
his junior, in 1505, when Antonio came on business to London, joining his uncle and two cousins to run a branch of the family's business
established in the English capital over thirty years earlier.[121] The Bon-
visis must have frequently hosted More at their house, judging from
the latter's comment in his last letter to Antonio some three decades
later that "for almost forty years now I have been, not a guest, but a
continual habitue of the Bonvisi household."[122] While More's use of
the term "almost forty years" may be merely an exaggerated estimate,
it may also indicate that he had been acquainted with the other members of the Bonvisi family in London prior to the arrival of Antonio in
1505. Although their fields of work differed vastly, More and Antonio
Bonvisi shared a common enthusiasm for the scholarship of Christian
humanism; moreover, judging from the anecdotes of their friendship
that have been preserved, Bonvisi's views regarding the Church seem
to have more closely approximated More's than did those of Erasmus.
Like Erasmus, Bonvisi expressed great admiration for More's intellectual prowess and poise, observing that the latter would during meals

---

[120] Quoted in ibid., 55–57; for original Latin text, see letter no. 5, 1506, in Rogers, *Correspondence,* 12–13.

[121] Elizabeth McCutcheon, " 'The Apple of My Eye': Thomas More to Antonio Bonvisi:
A Reading and a Translation", *Moreana* 18 (November 1981): 39.

[122] Letter no. 217, 1535, in Rogers, *Correspondence,* 560, 562, retranslated by McCutcheon,
"Apple", 55.

"wonderful deeply and clerkly [learnedly] talk with learned men, as well English as of other countries".[123] Bonvisi told of one particular occasion on which a foreign religious made the mistake of entering into debate with More, who in reply "set in a foot and coped with the said stranger", who "was much astonished and abashed to hear such profound reasons at a layman's hands".[124] More in turn clearly respected and admired the wisdom of his friend from Lucca, for it was through a conversation with Bonvisi that he came to a vastly deepened understanding of papal primacy, as we shall later see. On a more humorous note, More related in a letter to the humanist Martin Dorp (1515) how he once sat at table watching (undoubtedly with great fun) a learned Italian merchant—obviously Bonvisi—outwit a monk who was more intent on debate for its own sake than on the pursuit of truth. Bonvisi mischievously cited nonexistent chapters of various books of the Scriptures (for example, citing the twentieth chapter of a book that had only sixteen), to which the unsuspecting monk, not recognizing the trap, responded by attempting to explain these spurious passages, even going so far as to cite the commentaries of the famous medieval biblical exegete Nicholas of Lyra to support his interpretations.[125] We are left to conjecture how both More and Bonvisi managed to keep a straight face during this absurd exchange.

Did More and Bonvisi regularly exchange ideas on Christian spirituality? If so, one aspect in particular of Bonvisi's religious heritage would have struck a resonant chord with his English friend. In their travels across Europe as merchants and bankers, the descendants of the Bonvisi family had carried with them a pronounced devotion to the crucified Christ, manifested in their love for the most precious religious object of their native city, Lucca's *Volto Santo*, an ancient carved wood crucifix traditionally believed to be the handiwork of the disciple Nicodemus.[126] At England's Stonyhurst College there is preserved a fifteenth-century vestment embroidered with the image of Lucca's *Volto Santo* and with the inscription, "Pray for the soul of Luigi Bonvisi."[127] Might the Bonvisi family's love for the *Volto*

---

[123] Harpsfield, *Life,* 130.

[124] Ibid.

[125] Letter to Martin Dorp, October 21, 1515, in *CW* 15:51–55.

[126] C. Desmond Ford, S.J., "Good Master Bonvisi", *Clergy Review*, n.s., 27 (April 1947): 228.

[127] Ibid., 228 n.

Santo have been a contributing factor in the development of More's exceptional devotion to our Lord's Passion?

According to Roper, Thomas was during this period still living under the cloud of King Henry VII's wrath, who had evidently not forgotten the young man's action in Parliament. More even began planning to leave the country,[128] and perhaps with this in mind he visited the continental universities of Louvain and Paris in 1508.[129] But this tense situation ended with the death of the King in April 1509; the succession of his eighteen-year-old son, Henry VIII, to the throne must have brought a tremendous sense of relief to More and his family.

On September 3, 1510, More was appointed to the post of under-sheriff for London. In this capacity he, like the other under-sheriffs, served as legal advisor to the mayor and sheriffs of the city;[130] according to Erasmus, the job was not time-consuming, with More appearing in court to hear cases once a week (on Thursday afternoons).[131] Such a relatively light workload would have been to his advantage, for it would have left him more time to devote to his academic pursuits. But tragedy soon came upon the young lawyer. In 1511—sometime between late May and the end of the year—his wife, Jane, only twenty-three years old, fell ill and died.[132] Such a loss must have weighed very heavily upon her husband. Unfortunately, here again we are left only to speculate, for the sheer paucity of documentation regarding this phase of More's life prevents us from knowing anything further as to the nature of Jane's malady or the circumstances surrounding her death. Nonetheless, it is clear that More was immediately faced with the grave responsibility of providing for the proper nurturing of four very young children, the oldest no more than six and the youngest only two or three. Undoubtedly (as Erasmus testifies)[133] it was for this reason above all others that only a month after the passing of Jane, More married again. We learn of this second wedding from the letter of John Bouge mentioned earlier;[134] Father Bouge performed

---

[128] Roper, *Lyfe*, 8.

[129] Mentioned in letter of More to Martin Dorp, October 21, 1515, in *CW* 15:23.

[130] Chambers, *More*, 103.

[131] Erasmus, letter to Ulrich von Hutten, July 23, 1517, in Nichols, *Epistles*, 3:395–96.

[132] Chambers, *More*, 108.

[133] Letter to von Hutten, July 23, 1517, in Nichols, *Epistles*, 3:394.

[134] Chambers, *More*, 109.

the burial rites for Jane, and it was to Father Bouge that More came for his marriage to Alice Middleton, a widow about six to seven years older than he and the mother of several children, one of whom was still young enough to be brought into the More household.[135]

Perhaps Jane More had been willing meekly to accept her husband's unusual ways, but Dame Alice was most decidedly of quite a different stamp. Hence Father Bouge tells of her coming to him with the request that he would prevail upon her husband to set aside his hair shirt, a shirt that "tamed his flesh till the blood was seen in his clothes".[136] Alice was blunt and pragmatic, and her patience with More's scholarly friends appears to have worn thin at times; hence a wearied Erasmus commented at the end of one of his less pleasant stays on British soil, ". . . I am tired of the country, and feel myself becoming a stale guest to More's wife."[137] Years later, in the pages of his monumental apologetical work *The Confutation of Tyndale's Answer*, More humorously tells of a man attempting in vain to teach his wife—obviously Dame Alice—the wonders of earth science, using for the purpose a globe. The student, however, was rather uncooperative: "Now while he was telling her this tale, she nothing went about to consider his words, but as she was wont in all other things, studied all the while nothing else, but what she might say to the contrary."[138] Yet such comical qualities only endeared Dame Alice to her husband, who loved her as a conscientious housewife and a devoted stepmother to his children. More could not resist making many an affectionate jest at her expense; thus when she once berated him for a want of ambition, protesting that "I would not, I warrant you, be so foolish to be ruled where I might rule", More replied, "By my troth, wife, in this I dare say you say truth, for I never found you willing to be ruled yet."[139] On another occasion, when asked why both his first wife, Jane, and Dame Alice had been of petite stature, he responded that "if women were necessary evils, was it not wise to choose the smallest evil possible?"[140] Alice clearly enjoyed the teasing and knew how to respond good-naturedly in kind. Thus in reply to Erasmus'

---

[135] Reynolds, *Field Is Won*, 76, 78; Chambers, *More*, 109.

[136] Chambers, *More*, 109.

[137] Erasmus to Ammonius, August 1516, in Nichols, *Epistles*, 2:320.

[138] *CW* 8, bk. 6, p. 605.

[139] Harpsfield, *Life*, 106.

[140] Stapleton, *Life*, chap. 13, as paraphrased in Routh, *More and Friends*, 46.

tongue-in-cheek comment in one of his letters to More wishing the lady of the house a long life, Alice has her husband pen the following answer to his Dutch friend:

> My wife bids me give you a thousand greetings, and thank you for your very careful salutation, in which you wished her a long life, of which she says she is all the more desirous, that she may plague me the longer.[141]

Although More and his family spent nearly twenty years at their home in the Bucklersbury section of London, their subsequent residence, beginning in 1524, on the estate known as Chelsea was the one that would be immortalized in so many ways, especially in Hans Holbein's famous 1527 portrait of the Mores gathered together in one of Chelsea's spacious rooms. In Holbein's original sketch for his painting, one can easily spot many details that strongly suggest the depiction of a family about to begin prayers, perhaps the Divine Office. More himself is seated at the center of the picture, with his father seated on his right. Margaret Gigs, a girl More had adopted into his family when she was a child, leans over the shoulder of her adopted grandfather (John More), showing him the place in a book she is holding, which is probably a type of breviary known as a "book of hours"—no fewer than five of the figures in the portrait are holding such books. On Margaret Gigs' right, at the far left end of the picture, is More's second daughter, Elizabeth, aged twenty-one, who had married William Daunce two years earlier. Standing to the left of More is his only son and youngest child, John, aged nineteen, gazing down intently upon the book in his hands; John's wife, Anne, can be seen in the background, over More's right shoulder. To the left of John is Henry Pattison, the household jester More retained in his service to provide his family with plenty of innocent but hearty levity. It is Pattison who made the memorable pun some years later upon his master's resignation from high office, "Chancellor More is Chancellor no more."[142] Seated on the floor in front of John and Pattison are More's two other daughters, Cecily, aged twenty, and Margaret, twenty-two. Cecily had married Giles Heron on the same day that her sister Elizabeth had married William Daunce; Margaret had married

---

[141] More to Erasmus, December 15, 1516, in Nichols, *Epistles,* 2:448.

[142] John Farrow, *The Story of Thomas More* (New York: Image Books/Doubleday and Co., 1968), 147.

Hans Holbein the Younger. *The Family of Thomas More,* 1526.

William Roper in 1521.[143] Cecily appears to be fingering a rosary in her left hand, while Margaret, in the foreground, seems lost in deep thought. Lest there be any remaining doubt as to what the family is about to do, we find on the far right edge of the picture, immediately behind Cecily and Margaret, Dame Alice kneeling on a prie-dieu and glancing down at her book. But Holbein adds further details to his sketch, details that remind us that in his spirituality More sought, not to turn his back on the natural world, but rather to dedicate the good things of the world to the service of Almighty God. Hence we find at Dame Alice's side a little pet monkey, one of a host of animals that More had collected for the entertainment of his family. At the top of the picture, over the head of Margaret Gigs, Holbein has drawn a rough sketch of a stringed instrument, which is reflected in the subsequent depiction of several such instruments laid on a cabinet in later painted versions of this portrait. More enjoyed music and prevailed upon his wife to learn how to play the harp, the flute, the viol, and the spinet.[144] Hung at the top of the wall forming the background of the portrait is a small chime clock, a reminder of More's profound awareness of the inexorable passage of time—and the inexorable approach of death. This clock is the one and only object from the room in Holbein's sketch that has been preserved for posterity, a silent witness to the lives that unfolded before it over four and a half centuries ago.[145]

---

[143] The ages of More's children given here are those written onto Holbein's sketch (Chambers, *More*, 220). For the marriage dates of More's daughters, see Chambers, *More*, 182–83.

[144] Erasmus to Ulrich von Hutten, July 23, 1517, in Nichols, *Epistles*, 3:390, 394–95.

[145] Thomas Raworth, "St. Thomas More's Clock", *Month*, n.s., 7 (June 1952): 368–72.

CHAPTER II

Spirituality of the More Household

More had built for himself on the banks of the Thames not far from London a country house that is dignified and adequate without being so magnificent as to excite envy. Here he lives happily with his family, consisting of his wife, his son and daughter-in-law, three daughters with their husbands and already eleven grandchildren. It would be difficult to find a man more fond of children than he . . . You would say that Plato's Academy had come to life again. But I wrong More's home in comparing it to Plato's Academy, for in the latter the chief subjects of discussion were arithmetic, geometry and occasionally ethics, but the former rather deserved the name of a school for the knowledge and practice of the Christian faith.

— Erasmus, Letter to John Faber,
Bishop of Vienna, late 1532

More's decision to remain in the world by no means constituted an abandonment of the call to holiness that had motivated him to spend four years with the Carthusians. Indeed, if we are truly to understand More's public career as a statesman and scholar, as well as his private life as a husband and father, we must come to recognize him as fundamentally a man of God. Even his marvelous sense of humor stemmed from that peace of soul that only God can give. It is More's spirituality that binds together all the diverse threads of his thought and action. This immediately becomes evident in the daily horarium of the man, who rose at two o'clock in the morning, devoting the first five hours of his day to prayer and study.[1] He attended Mass

---

[1] R. W. Chambers, *Thomas More* (1935; reprint, Ann Arbor, Mich.: Ann Arbor Paperbacks, Univ. of Michigan, 1973), 178.

daily and often served the priest at the altar.[2] After the children had risen from bed, he would gather them together to recite the seven "Penitential Psalms" (Psalms 6, 32, 38, 51, 102, 130, 143) followed by the Litany of the Saints.[3] At meals More would have one of his children read aloud a passage from the Scriptures and, after it, an appropriate commentary or spiritual book (usually the Scripture commentaries of the popular medieval exegete Nicholas of Lyra), during which there was not a word of conversation. When the readings were done, a signal was given, according to monastic custom, with the words, "Tu autem, Domine, miserere nobis" (and do thou, O Lord, have mercy on us).[4] Conversation could now begin, first focusing upon the Scripture passage just heard but afterward turning to ordinary matters, with the household jester, Henry Pattison, injecting a goodly dose of honest humor.[5] In the evening, before retiring, he would assemble the entire household to recite Psalms 51 (the "*Miserere*"), 25, and 67, together with the Marian hymn *Salve Regina* and Psalm 130 (the "*De profundis*").[6] Also often included among More's own daily prayers were the fifteen "Gradual Psalms" (Psalms 120 to 134 inclusive) and Psalm 119 (the "*Beati immaculati*").[7]

More knew from his years at the Carthusians' Charterhouse the value of separating oneself in solitude from the noise of the world in order to hear the voice of God; indeed, the hustle and bustle of court life only seemed to convince him more deeply of the need to spend at least some time alone in prayer and meditation. Hence, to satisfy these aspirations he arranged for the construction of an oratory on the grounds of Chelsea, located at some distance from the family mansion house; this "New Building", as it was called, consisted of a chapel, a library, and a gallery.[8] It was to this place of quiet that

---

[2] Thomas Stapleton, *The Life and Illustrious Martyrdom of Sir Thomas More,* ed. E. E. Reynolds (Bronx, N.Y.: Fordham Univ. Press, 1966), chap. 6, pp. 62–64.

[3] Ro: Ba:, *The Lyfe of Syr Thomas More, Sometymes Lord Chancellor of England by Ro: Ba:,* ed. E. V. Hitchcock and Msgr. P. E. Hallett, Early English Text Society, original series, no. 222 (London: Early English Text Society, 1950), bk. 2, chap. 8, p. 126.

[4] Ibid., 127 (capitalization of Latin phrase modernized); Stapleton, *Life,* chap. 9, p. 89.

[5] Stapleton, *Life,* chap. 9, pp. 89–90.

[6] Ibid., 88–89.

[7] Ibid., chap. 6, p. 63.

[8] William Roper, *The Lyfe of Sir Thomas Moore, Knighte,* ed. Elsie V. Hitchcock, Early English Text Society, original series, no. 197 (London: Early English Text Society, 1935), 25–26.

More withdrew upon returning from Henry VIII's court functions in order to recollect himself.[9] And it was within the "New Building" that he sequestered himself every Friday so as to immerse himself from morning to night, and often all night, in prayer and spiritual exercises.[10] We learn of these ascetical practices from others, for at this time of his life he said nothing of them in his writings. But in his last years, and particularly during his imprisonment in the Tower of London, More did write quite a bit regarding the interior life, and it is in one of the works of this later period, his *Dialogue of Comfort against Tribulation*, that he speaks of the value of solitude; the passage seems unmistakably autobiographical:

> Let him also choose himself some secret solitary place in his own house as far from noise and company as he conveniently can. And thither let him some time secretly resort alone, imagining himself as one going out of the world even straight unto the giving up his reckoning unto God of his sinful living. Then let him there before an altar or some pitiful image of Christ's bitter passion, the beholding whereof may put him in remembrance of the thing and move him to devout compassion, kneel down or fall prostrate as at the feet of almighty God, verily believing him to be there invisibly present as without any doubt he is. There let him open his heart to God and confess his faults such as he can call to mind and pray God of forgiveness. Let him call to remembrance the benefits that God hath given him, either in general among other men, or privately to himself, and give him humble hearty thanks therefore. There let him declare unto God, the temptations of the devil, the suggestions of the flesh, the occasions of the world, and of his worldly friends much worse many times in drawing a man from God than are his most mortal enemies . . .[11]

In another of his late works, *De Tristitia Christi*, More once again reveals himself in speaking of the value of lifting the heart to God in the stillness of the night—as he must have found during his nocturnal watches in the "New Building":

> . . . [I]f we devote ourselves to meditation and prayer, the mind, collected and composed in that dark silence of the night, will find that it is

---

[9] Stapleton, *Life*, chap. 6, p. 63.

[10] Roper, *Lyfe*, 26; Ro: Ba:, *Lyfe*, bk. 2, chap. 1, p. 49.

[11] *A Dialogue of Comfort against Tribulation*, ed. Louis Martz and Frank Manley, vol. 12 of *Complete Works of St. Thomas More* (New Haven: Yale Univ. Press, 1976), bk. 2, chap. 16, pp. 164–65. Hereafter cited as *CW* 12.

much more receptive to divine consolation than it is during the daytime, when the noisy bustle of business on all sides distracts the eyes, the ears, and the mind, and dissipates our energy in manifold activities, no less pointless than they are diverse.[12]

Like a trusting child, More did not hesitate to present prayers of petition, as well as those of adoration, thanksgiving, and expiation, not only for himself but for others also. Thus, upon learning that any woman either of his own household or in the neighborhood was undergoing childbirth, he would immediately begin prayers for the mother and baby, not ceasing until he had learned that the delivery had gone safely.[13] When the life of his own daughter Margaret was hanging in the balance from a bout of the "sweating sickness" that had put her into a state of delirium, with the doctors unable to think of any way to save her, he resorted to the chapel of his "New Building" and there begged God to spare the life of his child. While thus in prayer, he remembered a remedy that the doctors had not; he went to them, and they promptly administered it to the girl in her sleep. For a while she seemed on the threshold of death, but thereafter a change for the better set in, and she fully recovered.[14]

More mandated that all the members of his household were to attend Mass on every Sunday and feast day; on the major feasts, including Christmas, Easter, Pentecost, and All Saints Day, all were expected to join him in attending the communal recitation of the nocturnal Office of Matins (the first hour of the Divine Office, celebrated around midnight), as well as the afternoon Office of Vespers.[15] On Good Friday as well as at other times, the family assembled in the "New Building" for a reading of one of the Gospel narratives of our Lord's Passion. At various points during the course of the reading, More would interject a few words of explanation, so as to elucidate the sacred texts.[16] This custom is yet another manifestation of his devotion to the mysteries of our Lord's suffering and death on the Cross. Eventually he was to begin setting down in writing his reflec-

---

[12] *De Tristitia Christi*, ed. and trans. Clarence H. Miller, vol. 14 of *Complete Works of St. Thomas More* (New Haven: Yale Univ. Press, 1976), 305–7. Hereafter cited as *CW* 14.

[13] Stapleton, *Life*, chap. 6, p. 67.

[14] Roper, *Lyfe*, 28–29; Stapleton, *Life*, chap. 6, pp. 65–66.

[15] Stapleton, *Life*, chap. 9, p. 89; Ro: Ba:, *Lyfe*, bk. 2, chap. 8, pp. 126–127.

[16] Stapleton, *Life*, chap. 9, p. 89; Ro: Ba:, *Lyfe*, bk. 2, chap. 8, p. 127.

tions upon the Gospel accounts of these events. Regrettably his *Treatise upon the Passion* was never finished, but in the portion that More did complete (of which we will have more to say in a later chapter) he has left us a prayer that reveals with what spirit he wished his family to participate in these readings in the "New Building":

> Good Lord, give us thy grace, not to read or hear this gospel of thy bitter passion with our eyes and our ears in manner of a pastime, but that it may with compassion so sink into our hearts, that it may stretch to the everlasting profit of our souls.[17]

More seems to have achieved for his family a remarkable balance in addressing the needs of the soul while not in any way neglecting the responsibilities and innocent joys of everyday life. While the "Ro: Ba:" biographer of More could truthfully say that each of those living under More's roof "had his time and task so set, either in reading spiritual books, prayers, and other virtuous exercises, that you would think it Mary and Martha's house, fit to give entertainment to their Creator",[18] such statements should not be misunderstood as implying that these spiritual exercises in any way stifled the normal features of family life. It is clear that More's intent in regulating his household was to avoid the all too common extreme of obsessive preoccupation with worldly affairs. As he was to say years later in one of his last apologetical writings, "so is it surely a very mad ordered life that hath but little time bestowed in any fruitful business, and all the substance idly spent in play."[19] It is however equally clear that More fostered in his family a healthy, ordered enjoyment of the natural world that God has given to mankind.

It is Erasmus who tells us what we have already observed—that his English friend delighted in observing and collecting different animals ranging from birds to weasels.[20] In one of his poems More expresses

---

[17] *Treatise upon the Passion,* in *Treatise on the Passion; Treatise on the Blessed Body; Instructions and Prayers,* ed. Garry E. Haupt, vol. 13 of *Complete Works of St. Thomas More* (New Haven: Yale Univ. Press, 1976), chap. 1, p. 52. This volume hereafter cited as *CW* 13.

[18] Ro: Ba:, *Lyfe,* bk. 2, chap. 8, p. 125.

[19] *The Answer to a Poisoned Book,* ed. Clarence Miller, vol. 11 of *Complete Works of St. Thomas More* (New Haven: Yale Univ. Press, 1985), bk. 1, chap. 8, p. 34.

[20] Letter of Erasmus to Ulrich von Hutten, July 23, 1517, in Francis M. Nichols, trans. and ed., *The Epistles of Erasmus: From His Earliest Letters to His Fifty-First Year* (1901–1918; reprint, New York: Russell and Russell, 1962), 3:392.

satisfaction in seeing a fly escape the snares of a spider.[21] As to his background in astronomy, William Roper tells of More on occasion accompanying Henry VIII to the roof of one of the King's palaces, where the two would observe and discuss the motions of the stars and planets.[22] More's adopted daughter, Margaret Gigs, and her husband, John Clement, were proficient students of medicine.[23] It has even been suggested that More took an interest in weather forecasting, judging from his vocal praise of Aristotle's *Meteorologica* (essentially a treatise on the earth sciences) in his October 1515 letter to Martin Dorp, wherein he says of this science:

> . . . I do not think . . . that any province of nature itself is more admirable than that which is closest to us and surrounds us, though about it we know so much less than about the position of the stars and the motions of heavenly bodies which are so far away from us.[24]

In addition to More's attendance of lectures concerning Aristotle's *Meteorologica* some years earlier,[25] further evidence of his specific interest in meteorology is provided by the following passage from his most famous work, *Utopia*: "They [the Utopians] forecast rains, winds, and all the other changes in weather by definite signs which they have ascertained by long practice."[26] It seems that More also enjoyed collecting curious objects for the entertainment of his family and friends, as Erasmus relates:

> . . . [I]f he meets with any strange object, imported from abroad or otherwise remarkable, he is most eager to buy it, and has his house so well supplied with these objects, that there is something in every room which catches your eye, as you enter it; and his own pleasure is renewed every time that he sees others interested.[27]

---

[21] See More's poem "The Hunting of a Spider", poem no. 42, in *Latin Poems,* ed. Clarence Miller et al., vol. 3, pt. 2 of *Complete Works of St. Thomas More* (New Haven: Yale Univ. Press, 1984), 125. Hereafter cited as *CW* 3/2.

[22] Roper, *Lyfe,* 11.

[23] Chambers, *More,* 184–85.

[24] Letter to Dorp, October 21, 1515, in *In Defense of Humanism: Letters to Dorp, Oxford, Lee, and a Monk,* ed. Daniel Kinney, vol. 15 of *Complete Works of St. Thomas More* (New Haven: Yale Univ. Press, 1986), 101–5 (quote on 101). Hereafter identified as *CW* 15.

[25] Ibid., 103.

[26] *Utopia,* ed. Edward Surtz, S.J., and J. H. Hexter, vol. 4 of *Complete Works of St. Thomas More* (New Haven: Yale Univ. Press, 1965), bk. 2, p. 161.

[27] Erasmus to Ulrich von Hutten, July 23, 1517, in Nichols, *Epistles,* 3:392.

Relentless in providing for the education of his children, More saw to it that his three daughters and one son all learned Latin and Greek, as well as the disciplines of theology, philosophy, logic, astronomy, and mathematics.[28] For practice he had the children, when he was away from home, write letters to him in Latin, to which he likewise responded in Latin.[29] On one such occasion (sometime between 1517 and 1520)[30] Margaret, Elizabeth, Cecily, and John received the following precious testament of their father's love:

> It is not so strange that I love you with my whole heart, for being a father is not a tie which can be ignored. Nature in her wisdom has attached the parent to the child and bound their minds together with a Herculean knot. Thence comes that tenderness of a loving heart that accustoms me to take you so often into my arms. That is why I regularly fed you cake and gave you ripe apples and fancy pears. That is why I used to dress you in silken garments and why I never could endure to hear you cry . . . Ah, brutal and unworthy to be called father is he who does not himself weep at the tears of his child . . . But now my love has grown so much that it seems to me I did not love you at all before.[31]

More's star pupil was his oldest daughter, Margaret, whose accomplishments utterly amazed her father's circle of scholarly friends, including the young Reginald Pole (who years later became the famous Cardinal Pole).[32] Sixteenth-century patristic scholars such as Jacobus Pamelius were indebted to her for discovering the solution to what was thought to be an irreversibly corrupted Latin transcription of a passage from the writings of Saint Cyprian. She was the first to recognize that the words "*nisi vos*" in the passage should actually be rendered *nervos*, a clarification that Pamelius dutifully attributed to Margaret in the notes to his 1568 edition of Saint Cyprian.[33] In a letter to Margaret, More tells of the astonishment evinced by Bishop John Vesey of Exeter upon seeing a sample of her Latin writing:

> I forbear to express the extreme pleasure your letter gave me, my sweet child. You will be able to judge better how much it pleased your father

---

[28] Chambers, *More,* 181.

[29] Ibid.

[30] Commentary, *CW* 3/2:413.

[31] Poem no. 264 (Latin with English translation), in *CW* 3/2:279–81.

[32] Stapleton, *Life,* chap. 5, p. 42.

[33] Ibid., chap. 11, p. 104, plus n.

when you learn what delight it caused to a stranger. I happened this evening to be in the company of his Lordship, John, Bishop of Exeter, a man of deep learning and of a wide reputation for holiness. Whilst we were talking I took out from my desk a paper that bore on our business and by accident your letter appeared. He took it into his hand with pleasure and examined it. When he saw from the signature that it was the letter of a lady, he was induced by the novelty of the thing to read it more eagerly. When he had finished he said he would never have believed it to have been your work unless I had assured him of the fact, and he began to praise it in the highest terms (why should I hide what he said?) for its pure Latinity, its correctness, its erudition, and its expressions of tender affection. Seeing how delighted he was, I showed him your declamation. He read it, as also your poems, with a pleasure so far beyond what he had hoped . . . He took out at once from his pocket a portague [a Portuguese gold coin] which you will find enclosed in this letter. I tried in every possible way to decline it, but was unable to refuse to take it to send to you as a pledge and token of his good-will towards you.[34]

More was deeply conscious of the richness and splendor of the Church's liturgy and of the different seasons of the Church calendar. Hence, as we have already noted, he was assiduous in attending daily Mass; his fluency in Latin would have enabled him to appreciate better the beauty of the liturgical texts. His esteem for the liturgy led him to participate more fully in whatever appropriate ways he could. In addition to serving the priest frequently as an acolyte, he would also sometimes carry the processional cross in parish processions.[35] He even joined his parish's choir, donning a surplice like an altar boy.[36] According to Erasmus, More could not sing,[37] and thus we are left to speculate as to just how appreciative the other choristers were of his voice. The saint's sense of profound reverence for holy places was such that when he was in church he would invariably refuse to talk or hear of any temporal matters.[38] So faithful was he to this habit that on one occasion, when during the Mass he was repeatedly summoned by the King, More replied that he would come, but only after he had finished paying homage "to a higher King". As Stapleton observes,

---

[34] Ibid., 106.

[35] Ibid., chap. 6, p. 64.

[36] Roper, *Lyfe*, 51; Ro: Ba:, *Lyfe*, bk. 2, chap. 1, pp. 51–52.

[37] Letter of Erasmus to Ulrich von Hutten, July 23, 1517, in Nichols, *Epistles*, 3:390.

[38] Stapleton, *Life*, chap. 6, p. 64.

Henry VIII did not resent this reply, for he was then still a "pious and God-fearing" monarch.[39]

In the sacraments More sought and found the strength and wisdom he needed to carry out his temporal duties. Hence whenever he was faced with any new matter of importance, he made a point of preparing himself by going to confession and receiving Holy Communion.[40] The sacramentals also had their place in his devotional life. He was known to go on pilgrimages to various shrines, making the entire journey (up to seven miles from his home) on foot.[41] During his tenure as Lord Chancellor, his friends would press him to ride on horseback (in virtue of his distinguished office) in the arduous processions held on the Rogation Days, but he absolutely refused. Alluding to the crucifix carried in the procession, he would reply: "I will not follow on horseback my Lord, who goes on foot."[42]

What do we know of Thomas More's spiritual reading? It is obvious that he made extensive use of the Bible; he even went so far as to assemble for himself a compilation of his favorite psalms, to which he resorted regularly.[43] As to what else he read, in the preface to one of his great apologetical works, *The Confutation of Tyndale's Answer*, he recommends English translations of three books that he feels will particularly "nourish and increase devotion": the *Meditationes Vitae Christi*, formerly attributed to Saint Bonaventure; the *Imitation of Christ* of Thomas à Kempis (which More identifies as "the Following of Christ" and attributes to the French ecclesiastical writer Jean Gerson); and the *Scale of Perfection* (or *Ladder of Perfection*) of Walter Hilton.[44] Significantly, two of the extant manuscript copies of the latter work are from the Carthusians' London Charterhouse and date from the era 1500–1510, coinciding with More's four years at this monastery.[45]

Kempis' classic, *The Imitation of Christ*, is so widely circulated and

---

[39] Ibid., 62–63; Ro: Ba:, *Lyfe*, bk. 2, chap. 1, p. 49.

[40] Roper, *Lyfe*, 72.

[41] Stapleton, *Life*, chap. 6, p. 64.

[42] Ibid.

[43] Ibid., 63.

[44] *The Confutation of Tyndale's Answer*, ed. Louis Schuster et al., vol. 8 of *Complete Works of St. Thomas More* (New Haven: Yale Univ. Press, 1973), preface, 37.

[45] Bernard Fisher, "English Spiritual Writers: 13: St. Thomas More", *Clergy Review*, n.s., 45 (January 1960): 3.

familiar to vast numbers of readers that a summary of its contents here would be superfluous. Suffice it to say that the *Imitation*'s prevalent theme of personally following and conforming oneself to Christ pervades More's spirituality, serving as one of the tenets of the Christian humanist movement of which he became a part. It should also be noted that the *Imitation*'s fourth book (absent from the first English translation but included in later editions from the early sixteenth century onward)[46] is devoted to one of the most dominant elements of More's spirituality: the Holy Eucharist. Thus we are not surprised to find that in More's own *Treatise to Receive the Blessed Body* his description of the soul as a house to be prepared for the coming of Christ in Holy Communion[47] is strikingly reminiscent of the following passage from the *Imitation*:

> I [Christ] am the Lover of all purity, and the generous Giver of all holiness. I seek a pure heart, and there is My resting place. Make ready for Me a great chamber, strewn with rushes—that is, your heart, and with My disciples I shall keep My Easter with you. If you desire that I should come to you and dwell with you, free yourself of the old filth of sin and cleanse also the habitation of your heart. Exclude the world and all the clamorous noise of sin, and sit solitary as a sparrow on the eaves of a house, and think upon your own offenses with great bitterness of heart, for a true lover will prepare for his beloved the best and the fairest place he can, for that is a sign of the love and affection of him who receives his friends.[48]

More's belief in a universal call to holiness, from which no state of life is either excluded or excused, is manifest in his recommendation to lay readers of Walter Hilton's *Scale of Perfection*, a work that the twentieth-century English monastic scholar Dom David Knowles has described as "in aim a *Summa* of the whole spiritual life".[49] Hilton, a fourteenth-century Augustinian canon, wrote the two books of the *Scale* several years apart, with the first addressing primarily the removal of the "image of sin" from the soul (the earlier stages of the spiritual life), and the second devoted to the restoration of the image of God in one's soul (the more advanced progression toward the con-

---

[46] Harold Gardiner, S.J., introduction, *The Imitation of Christ*, by Thomas à Kempis (Garden City, N.Y.: Image Books/Doubleday and Co., 1955), 12–13.

[47] *CW* 13:197–98.

[48] Thomas à Kempis, *Imitation*, bk. 4, no. 12, p. 226.

[49] Dom David Knowles, *The English Mystical Tradition* (New York: Harper, 1961), 104.

templative life). The *Scale* was by no means intended to offer an easy, watered-down spirituality; indeed, the immense success of this work among the Carthusians testifies to the high ideals and goals it sets for its readers. Yet the *Scale* attracted a surprisingly broad audience among the laity, who would have been pleased, as Thomas More undoubtedly was, with Hilton's assurance in the second book that the way of contemplation is potentially open to all who are willing to purify, humble, and mortify themselves for the love of God:

> There can be many different ways and diverse practices leading different souls to contemplation, for there are diverse exercises in working according to people's various dispositions and the different states they are in, such as seculars and those in religious orders. Nevertheless, there is only one gate.[50]

Hilton further observes that the call to such holiness is one to which not only all can respond but also one to which all should respond: ". . . [E]very rational soul should long with all its powers to draw near to Jesus and to become one with him through the feeling of his gracious invisible presence."[51]

An adequate synopsis of the *Scale*'s contents is beyond the scope of the present work, but among the more memorable images found in its pages is that of the soul as a pilgrim on its way to Jerusalem, intent on its destination regardless of the efforts of carnal desires, fears, and devils to dissuade it from its purpose:

> Keep up your desire, and say nothing else but that you want to have Jesus and to be in Jerusalem. And if they then perceive your will to be so strong that you will not spare yourself . . . but that your will is set ever onward, with one thing and one alone, turning a deaf ear to them as if you did not hear them, and keeping on stubbornly and unstintingly with your prayers and your other spiritual works, and with discretion according to the counsel of your superior or your spiritual father: then they begin to be angry and to draw a little nearer to you . . .
>
> But against all these annoyances, and all others that may befall, use this remedy: take Jesus in your mind, and do not be angry with them; do not linger with them, but think of your lesson—that you are nothing, you have nothing, you cannot lose any earthly goods, and you desire

---

[50] Walter Hilton, *The Scale of Perfection,* trans. John Clark and Rosemary Doward, Classics of Western Spirituality (New York: Paulist Press, 1991), bk. 2, no. 27, p. 245.

[51] Ibid., no. 41, p. 288.

nothing but the love of Jesus—and keep on your way to Jerusalem, with your occupation.[52]

Thoughts of a similar vein are to be found in More's English translation of the following words from the letters of Pico della Mirandola, wherein Pico admonishes his nephew not to be diverted from the pursuit of virtue by the revilements of worldly men:

> Let them therefore neigh, let them bawl, let them bark, go thou boldly forth [with] thy journey, as thou hast begun, and of the wickedness and misery consider how much thy self art beholden to God, which hath illumined thee sitting in the shadow of death . . . Dead be they, that live not to God . . .[53]

One of the hallmarks of the *Scale of Perfection* is Hilton's insistence on the soul's total assent to the teaching authority of the Church in the pursuit of perfection.[54] Thus for Hilton, the way of perfection is nothing other than the soul's interior progress in understanding and experiencing the Church's publicly taught doctrines, for it is precisely by fidelity to these beliefs that the soul is enabled to attain its full potential.[55] Hence, in Hilton's spirituality, submission to Christ and to His Mystical Body, the Church, are inseparable. Hilton likewise stresses the intrinsic value of the Church's recognized forms of vocal prayer, especially the Divine Office, in embarking on the way of perfection, for since the Office "is the prayer of holy church there is no vocal prayer so profitable for your ordinary use as that one".[56] Hilton's emphasis on the integral importance of the individual's relationship with the Church—that we can only truly live our Christianity in and with the Church—is one of the cornerstones of Thomas More's thought, as we will later see in the examination of his apologetical and devotional writings. And in the following description from the *Scale* of the sin of heresy, we find an anticipation of More's own perception of the motives underlying theological dissent:

---

[52] Ibid., no. 22, pp. 231–32.

[53] Letter of Pico to his nephew, July 2, 1492, appended to *Life of John Picus*, in *The Workes of Sir Thomas More Knight . . . in the English Tongue* (1557), as reproduced in *The English Works of Sir Thomas More*, ed. W. E. Campbell (London: Eyre and Spottiswoode; New York: Lincoln MacVeagh, Dial Press, 1931), 1:16.

[54] Hilton, *Scale*, bk. 1, no. 23, pp. 96–97.

[55] Ellen Ross, "Submission or Fidelity? The Unity of Church and Mysticism in Walter Hilton's *Scale of Perfection*", *Downside Review* 106 (April 1988): 140, 143–44.

[56] Hilton, *Scale*, bk. 1, no. 27, pp. 98–99.

A heretic sins mortally in pride, because he chooses his resting place and his delight in his own opinion and in what he says, and he supposes it to be true. That opinion and word is against God and holy church; and therefore he sins mortally in pride, for he loves himself and his own will and wit so much that he will not leave it even though it is plainly against the ordinance of holy church; but he wants to rest in it, as if in the truth, and thus he makes it his god. But he deceives himself, for God and holy church are so united and agreed together that whoever acts against the one is acting against both.[57]

In the earliest printed edition of the *Scale of Perfection*, dating from 1494, as well as in at least one early manuscript, another work of Hilton is included: his *Epistle on the Mixed Life*.[58] In view of the close relationship between this *Epistle* and the *Scale*, there is little reason to doubt that More would have been personally familiar with the former and that, in recommending the *Scale* to his readers, he may well have assumed that his advice would be applied to this shorter work of Hilton as well. When we actually examine the *Epistle on the Mixed Life*, there is all the more reason to believe that More made personal use of it in his own spiritual reading, for it is specifically written to advise those in the lay state or in positions of power and authority. One quotation, based upon the Gospel episode of the two sisters Martha and Mary (Lk 10:38–42), will suffice to demonstrate that the *Epistle* advocated the same synthesis of action and spirituality, the same sanctification of the temporal order with the service of God, that Thomas More lived:

> You should mix the works of the active life with spiritual works of the contemplative life, and then you do well. For you shall sometimes be busy with Martha to regulate and govern your household, your children, your servants, your neighbours, and your tenants: if they do well, encourage them and help them; if they do badly, teach them to better themselves, and chastise them. And you shall also check and wisely ensure that your possessions and worldly goods are rightly cared for by your servants, organized and properly spent, so that you can use them more plenteously to perform the acts of mercy to your fellow Christians. At other times you shall, with Mary, leave the bustle of the world and sit down at the feet of Our Lord in humility in prayers and holy thoughts and in contemplation of him, as he gives you grace. And so shall you

---

[57] Ibid., no. 58, pp. 128–29.
[58] Ibid., introduction, p. 33.

profitably go from the one to the other, deserving reward, and fulfil
both: and then you keep the order of charity well.[59]

The most popular English version of the pseudo-Bonaventuran
Meditationes Vitae Christi to which More refers in the preface to his
Confutation of Tyndale's Answer is that of the Carthusian Nicholas Love
(d. 1424), bearing the title *The Mirror of the Blessed Life of Jesus Christ*
and dating from about 1410, with the first printed edition appearing
in 1484.[60] Love's additions, deletions, and revisions to the Latin original are sufficiently frequent to justify categorizing him as something
more than merely a translator. Promulgated with the official authorization of the Church as an antidote to the heretical teachings of
John Wycliff (c. 1330–1384) and his followers, the *Mirror* is basically
a meditative synopsis of the life of Christ, presenting all the major
events from the Gospels in vivid language that more often than not
simply paraphrases or even directly quotes the Scriptures. In his introduction Love admits that some extrabiblical details or episodes are
included, but these, he explains, are added simply to aid the imagination of the reader in meditating upon each scene or mystery from
the Gospels. The *Mirror* went far in putting into the hands and hearts
of the laity the vernacular texts of many key Scripture verses, as can
especially be seen in the following passage regarding the Last Supper
discourse:

> First, he taught to them charity often, and most busily now when he
> said: "*Mandatum novum do vobis,* I give you a new commandment, and
> that is that ye love together, *ut diligatis invicem. In hoc cognoscent omnes,* and
> also in this one thing sovereignly all men shall know, *quia mei discipuli
> estis,* that ye be my disciples, *si dilectionem habueritis ad invicem,* if ye have
> love each to the other" [Jn 13:34–35]. And after that, how they should
> truly keep this charity by working in the love of him, he said to them
> thus: "*Si diligitis me, mandata mea servate,* if ye love me, keep my behests"
> [Jn 14:15]. And also after: "*Qui diligit me, sermonem meum servabit,* whoso

---

[59] Chap. 2, in R. N. Swanson, ed. and trans., *Catholic England: Faith, Religion and Observance
before the Reformation,* Manchester Medieval Sources Series (Manchester, England: Manchester
Univ. Press, 1993), 107.

[60] For mention of earliest printed edition of this work (that of Caxton), see A. W. Pollard and G. R. Redgrave, eds., *A Short Title Catalogue of Books Printed in England, Scotland,
and Ireland and of English Books Printed Abroad, 1475–1640,* 2d ed. (London: Bibliographical
Society, 1986), 1:140; see also introduction to Nicholas Love, *The Mirror of the Blessed Life
of Jesu Christ,* Orchard Books, vol. 10 (New York: Benziger Brothers, 1926), vi–vii, viii.

loveth me, he shall keep my word, *et Pater meus diliget eum,* and then shall my Father love him, *et ad eum veniemus et mansionem apud eum faciemus,* and we shall come to him and dwell with him" [Jn 14:23].[61]

In order to give readers a tangible framework to follow in their own prayer lives, the *Mirror* is divided according to the days of the week, assigning some of its meditations to Sunday, some to Monday, and so on, although Love acknowledges that he does not really expect most people to be able to complete all the reflections assigned to a given day. Those assigned to Friday, all concerning the Passion, are by far the most numerous, subdivided to coincide with the different hours of the Divine Office and to approximate the time of day when each successive event of the Passion transpired. As Love explains, he wants his readers to make an added effort in reflecting upon these mysteries that manifest with particular force Christ's love for us, the thought of which ought to "inflame and burn our hearts in his love":[62]

> . . . [T]o him that would search the Passion of our Lord with all his heart and all his inward affection, there should come many devout feelings and stirrings that he never supposed before. By the which he should feel a new compassion and a new love, and have new ghostly comforts, through the which he should perceive himself turned, as it were, into a new state of soul; in the which estate, those foresaid ghostly feelings should seem to him as a promise and part of the bliss and joy to come.[63]

There can be no doubt that Thomas More would have especially identified with the *Mirror*'s emphasis on what he would years later term "the spring (as it were) from which the stream of our salvation flowed forth, namely the death and passion of our Savior".[64] It is certainly plausible to suppose that in More's day-long spiritual exercises every Friday, of which we have already spoken, he followed essentially the horarium of Friday meditations provided by the *Mirror*. Indeed, in more than one passage the *Mirror* approaches the dramatic intensity and pathos that we will later find in More's final masterpiece on the Agony in the Garden, *De Tristitia Christi,* as when Love presents the striking image of Christ encountering a sea of angry and scornful faces as He goes to His death:

---

[61] Love, *Mirror,* pt. 4, chap. 39, p. 206.

[62] Ibid., pt. 5, chap. 40, pp. 212–13.

[63] Ibid., 213.

[64] *CW* 14:93.

They stand stiffly against him, all together; the princes and the Pharisees and the scribes with thousands of the people, crying all with one voice that he be crucified; and at the last the Justice, Pilate, gave the sentence that he be crucified; and anon that heavy cross was laid on his shoulders that were all rent and broken with wounds from his scourging. Now, furthermore, behold thy Lord Jesu so going forth with his cross on his back; and how then there ran out of the city at all its gates both citizens and strangers of all degrees, not only Gentiles, but also the foulest ribalds and wine-drinkers, not to have compassion on him, but to wonder upon him and scorn him. There is none that will know him by piteous affection, but rather with mud and other uncleanness they all despise and reprove him. And so, as the prophet saith, he is now *"a parable in all their mouths: and those that sit in the gates as judges speak against him; and those that drink wine in their lust make their songs about him"* [Ps 69:11–12].[65]

The *Mirror* could also be unflinchingly graphic in depicting the physical torments of the Redeemer:

Then ran out of his blessed body streams of that holiest blood abundantly on all sides from those great wounds; and he is so constrained and cramped that he cannot move anything except his head. And his body hanging only by those three nails, no doubt there is but that he suffered such bitter sorrows and pains that there is no heart that may think it or tongue tell.[66]

Descriptive passages such as this, intended to awaken the reader to the depth of what Christ suffered to save mankind, are echoed in the writings of More, and nowhere more than in the following lines from his *Dialogue of Comfort against Tribulation*:

. . . [I]f we could and would with due compassion, conceive in our minds a right Imagination and remembrance of Christ's bitter painful passion, of the many sore bloody strokes that the cruel tormentors with rods and whips gave him upon every part of his holy tender body, the scornful crown of sharp thorns beaten down upon his holy head, so straight and so deep, that on every part his blessed blood issued out and streamed down, his lovely limbs drawn and stretched out upon the cross to the intollerable pain of his forebeaten and sorebeaten veins and sinews, new feeling with the cruel stretching and straining pain far passing any cramp, in every part of his blessed body at once. Then the great long

---

[65] Love, *Mirror,* pt. 5, chap. 42, p. 230.

[66] Ibid., chap. 43, p. 233.

nails cruelly driven with hammers through his holy hands and feet, and in this horrible pain lifted up and let hang with the weight of all his body bearing down upon the painful wounded places so grievously pierced with nails, and in such torment without pity, but not without many despites, suffered to be pinned and pained the space of more than three long hours, till himself willingly gave up unto his Father his holy soul, after which yet to show the mightiness of their malice after his holy soul departed, pierced his holy heart with a sharp spear, at which issued out the holy blood and water, whereof his holy sacraments have inestimable secret strength, if we would, I say, remember these things in such wise, as would God we would, I verily suppose that the consideration of his incomparable kindness, could not fail in such wise to inflame our key cold hearts, and set them on fire in his love, that we should find ourselves not only content, but also glad and desirous to suffer death for his sake . . .[67]

From the scene of the Annunciation onward to Calvary and the Resurrection, the Mother of Christ is conspicuously prominent throughout the *Mirror,* yet another aspect of Love's work that would have appealed to More, as will later become evident from our exploration of his apologetical and devotional writings. The *Mirror* is particularly poignant in depicting the Blessed Virgin Mary's reaction to the Passion of her Divine Son:

. . . [F]or the first time his mother seeth how he is so taken and prepared for death; wherefore, sorrowful out of measure and having shame to see him so standing all naked—for they left him not so much as his small-clothes—she went in haste to her dear Son and clasped him and girt him about the loins with the kerchief of her head. Ah, Lord! in what sorrow is her soul now! Verily, I believe that she could not speak a word to him for sorrow, but she could do not more to him nor help him; for if she might, without doubt she would have done so. Then was her Son taken out of her hands in a rude manner and led to the foot of the cross.[68]

And again:

Seest thou now how ofttimes our Lady is this day dead; verily, as ofttimes as she saw done against her Son any new pain. Wherefore, now is fulfilled in her that which Simeon said to her, prophesying a long time

[67] Bk. 3, chap. 27, in *CW* 12:312–13.
[68] Love, *Mirror,* pt. 5, chap. 43, pp. 231–32.

before: "*Tuam ipsius animam pertransibit gladius*" (*His sword shall pierce
through thy heart* [Lk 2:35])—that is to say, the sword of his Passion and
sorrow, and that befell ofttimes on this day. But now truly the sword
of his spear hath pierced both the body of the Son and the soul of the
mother.[69]

While we cannot know for certain all the elements of the *Mirror
of the Blessed Life of Jesus Christ* that More assimilated into his own
inner life, his recommendation of this work, along with the *Imitation
of Christ* and Hilton's *Scale of Perfection*, gives us at least some insight
into his conception and understanding of what constitutes a fruitful
Christian spirituality.

More seems also to have esteemed a book on the subject of prayer
that, unlike the *Imitation of Christ*, which he mistakenly attributes to
Jean Gerson, was actually written by Gerson: *De oratione et ejus val-
ore*. He paraphrases an extended passage from it in his own *De Tristitia Christi* (see chapter 13).[70] It was Gerson's harmony of the Four
Gospels, entitled the *Monotessaron*, that More used as his guide in composing this latter work as well as for his *Treatise upon the Passion*.[71]

The writings of the Church Fathers clearly exerted a major influence upon Thomas More, most especially those of Saint Augustine.
Thus in his most monumental apologetical work, the *Confutation of
Tyndale's Answer*, he cites the authority of Saint Augustine twenty
times more than any other Church Father.[72] We have already seen
More as a young man lecturing upon Augustine's *City of God*, no
inconsiderable feat, for the latter is a work of enormous proportions,
as is the whole corpus of Augustine's writings. Any attempt to gauge
the influence of Saint Augustine upon the thought of Thomas More
would require a whole volume of its own. At this juncture two quotations from the *City of God* will suffice for our purposes. The first
that follows, concerning the fall of Satan and his angels, must have
been in More's mind as he wrote the introduction to his *Treatise upon
the Passion*, which begins with the same subject:

---

[69] Ibid., chap. 45, p. 240.

[70] *CW* 14:313–27.

[71] *CW* 14:621–23; *Treatise upon the Passion*, introduction, in *CW* 13:50–51.

[72] Fr. Louis L. Martz, S.J., *Thomas More: The Search for the Inner Man* (New Haven: Yale
Univ. Press, 1990), 37.

. . . [F]or us there are two societies of angels, one in the enjoyment of God, the other swelling with pride. The Psalmist refers to one in the verse: "Praise ye him, all his angels," and the Gospel records the speech of the prince of the other: "All these things will I give thee, if thou wilt fall down and worship me." One is aflame with the holy love of God; the other is reeking with the impure desire for its own exaltation. Since, as Scripture warns us, "God resists the proud, but gives grace to the humble," one group dwells in the highest courts of heaven; the other, hurled down, rages in the lowest regions of the air. One is tranquil with radiant holiness; the other is troubled with dark desires. One, by the will of God, aids us with kindness and avenges us with justice; the other, in arrogance, seethes with the desire of dominating and doing us damage. One group, as ministers of God's goodness, are free to do all the good they desire; the others are bridled by the power of God to keep them from doing all the harm they would. The good angels laugh at the others when these unwillingly do more good than harm by their persecutions; the latter envy the former when they bring their pilgrims home.[73]

The second quotation, in which Augustine stresses the goodness of all God's creation, brings to mind More's humanistic appreciation of the wonders of the universe, as well as his opposition to the Protestant reformers' conception of fallen man as being not only marred and damaged by original sin (as the Church professed and More believed) but *totally* depraved:

The explanation, then, of the goodness of creation is the goodness of God . . . It puts an end to all controversies concerning the origin of the world. Nevertheless, certain heretics remain unconvinced, on the ground that many things in creation are unsuitable and even harmful to that poor and fragile mortality of the flesh which, of course, is no more than the just penalty of sin. The heretics mention, for example, fire, cold, wild beasts, and things like that, without considering how wonderful such things are in themselves and in their proper place and how beautifully they fit into the total pattern of the universe making, as it were, their particular contributions to the commonweal of cosmic beauty. Nor have they observed how valuable they are even to us if only we use them well and wisely . . .

---

[73] Saint Augustine, *The City of God: Books VIII–XVI*, trans. Gerard G. Walsh, S.J., and Mother Grace Monahan, O.S.U., Fathers of the Church, vol. 14 (New York: Fathers of the Church, 1952), bk. 11, chap. 33, pp. 240–41.

Thus does Divine Providence teach us not to be foolish in finding fault with things but, rather, to be diligent in finding out their usefulness or, if our mind and will should fail us in the search, then to believe that there is some hidden use still to be discovered . . . This effort needed to discover hidden usefulness either helps our humility or hits our pride, since absolutely no natural reality is evil and the only meaning of the word "evil" is the privation of good.[74]

The two quotations given above should not be taken as sufficiently representative of the totality of More's intellectual debt to Saint Augustine. Yet, as we examine More's writings in the chapters to come, we will have the opportunity to see many additional examples of the Augustinian influence upon his heart and mind.

In view of the austere Carthusian roots of More's spirituality, it is not surprising that he chose to avail himself of two well-established monastic forms of bodily penance, the hair shirt and the discipline. Of the former we have already mentioned the testimony of Father John Bouge; elsewhere we learn that More even wore the hair shirt while sitting on the bench as Lord Chancellor but that he was most vigilant to conceal this particularly painful form of self-denial, making every effort to appear exteriorly no different from his peers.[75] He went so far as to hide it from his own family, confiding the secret only to his daughter Margaret, who did him the service of washing the hair shirt when necessary. But on one warm summer's day, when More was dressed in a collarless linen shirt, his daughter-in-law, Anne, evidently spotted the topmost edge of the secret "shirt of hair" and smiled; Margaret noticed her reaction and discreetly warned her father. Dismayed that his penance had been inadvertently revealed, he immediately corrected this oversight on his part without saying a word about it.[76] The actual hair shirt used by More has been preserved over a period of four and a half centuries and is now in the safekeeping of the Augustinian Canonesses of Newton Abbot, England,[77] a precious witness to the saint's firm belief in the need to "complete what is lacking in Christ's afflictions" (Col 1:24). His other instrument of

---

[74] Ibid., chap. 22, pp. 219–20.

[75] Ro: Ba:, *Lyfe,* bk. 2, chap. 1, p. 50.

[76] Roper, *Lyfe,* 48–49; Ro: Ba:, *Lyfe,* bk. 2, chap. 1, p. 50.

[77] R. W. Chambers, intro., *The Fame of Blessed Thomas More: Being Addresses Delivered in His Honour in Chelsea, July 1929* (London and New York: Sheed and Ward, 1933), 119; Stapleton, *Life,* chap. 6, p. 70 n.

penance, the discipline, consisted of thongs made from knotted cords with which he scourged himself on Fridays and on the eves of holy days, as well as during the "Ember days" (the special days of fasting and prayer that at that time were assigned to each of the four seasons of the year).[78] More was devoid of any vanity regarding his personal appearance, so much so that had it not been for the alertness of his personal attendant he would have forgotten even to change his clothes. He wore only the "simplest garments" unless the functions of his high office required otherwise. Once when he left the house in a pair of badly damaged boots, his secretary, John Harris, attempted to stop him, but he simply answered, "Ask my tutor to buy me a new pair."[79] With gentle teasing he knew how to reprove the excesses of vanity he observed in other members of the family. Hence, after being repeatedly begged by his daughter-in-law, Anne, for a pearl necklace, he finally presented her with a necklace of white peas.[80] In his *Dialogue of Comfort against Tribulation,* More tells of a man (undoubtedly himself) who more than once observed the pains his wife took to make herself more attractive by "straight binding up her hair to make her a fair large forehead" and by "straight bracing in her body to make her middle small". Her husband could not refrain from commenting on this senseless effort and told her, "Forsooth madame, if God give you not hell, he shall do you great wrong. For it must needs be your own of very right, for you buy it very dear, and take great pain therefore."[81]

More's love of God found expression not only in his prayer life but also in his fulfillment of Christ's command, ". . . [L]ove one another; even as I have loved you . . ." (Jn 13:34). The poor were regularly welcome guests at his table; he would also go to them himself, visiting the indigent families and bringing them financial support as needed. When in the office of Lord Chancellor he was precluded from going in person, he delegated others of the household to bring succor to these people on his behalf. The infirm and the elderly were particularly singled out for his favors; for these he provided a special home in his own parish of Chelsea where they could be lodged and cared for at his expense. To widows and orphans he provided his legal ser-

---

[78] Ro: Ba:, *Lyfe,* bk. 2, chap. 1, p. 50.

[79] Stapleton, *Life,* chap. 6, p. 69.

[80] Ro: Ba:, *Lyfe,* bk. 2, chap. 8, p. 129.

[81] Bk. 2, chap. 17, in *CW* 12:168−69.

vices gratis; a widow named Paula who had exhausted all her savings in the courts he took into his family and sustained as if she were his kinswoman.[82]

The filial love More bore toward his father was as genuine as his love for his children. Thomas' mother died when he was in his early twenties, but John More lived well into More's adult life, dying only five years before his illustrious son. In life and in death the younger More manifested his unchanging devotion. Thus while serving as Lord Chancellor it was his habit, on passing through Westminster Hall where John More sat as judge in the Court of the King's Bench, to pause and kneel down before his father to ask his blessing. This custom of his was all the more notable, for according to the anonymous author of the "Ro: Ba:" biography, at that time "men after their marriages thought themselves not bound to these duties of younger folks."[83] Thomas was most attentive to his father's spiritual and bodily needs in his last illness, and when the older More passed away, his son "with tears taking him about the neck, most lovingly kissed and embraced him, commending him into the merciful hands of almighty God"[84] and causing "many good prayers to be said for his soul's ease".[85]

More's lifelong recognition of the ephemeral nature of worldly success predisposed him to accept misfortune with extraordinary peace of mind. Hence when in the late summer of 1529 news reached him of a devastating fire that had destroyed part of his house, as well as all the barns filled with the newly harvested grain crop on his Chelsea estate, he was able to pen the following calming words to his wife on September 3 of that year:

> And whereas I am informed by my son Heron [Giles Heron, husband of More's daughter Cecily] of the loss of our barns and our neighbors' also with all the corn that was therein, albeit (saving God's pleasure) it were great pity of so much good corn lost, yet sith it hath liked him to send us such a chance, we must and are bounden, not only to be

---

[82] Stapleton, *Life,* chap. 6, p. 67.

[83] Ro: Ba:, *Lyfe,* bk. 2, chap. 3, pp. 59–60; Roper, *Lyfe,* 43; Nicholas Harpsfield, *The Life and Death of Sir Thomas More,* in *Lives of Saint Thomas More* (William Roper and Nicholas Harpsfield), ed. E. E. Reynolds, Everyman's Library, no. 19 (London: J. M. Dent and Sons, 1963), 84; Stapleton, *Life,* chap. 1, pp. 3–4.

[84] Roper, *Lyfe,* 44.

[85] Ro: Ba:, *Lyfe,* bk. 2, chap. 3, p. 60.

content, but also to be glad of his visitation. He sent us all that we have lost, and sith he hath by such a chance taken it away again, his pleasure be fulfilled; let us never grudge thereat but take [it] in good worth, and heartily thank him as well for adversity as for prosperity, and peradventure we have more cause to thank him for our loss than for our winning, for his wisdom better seeth what is good for us than we do ourselves. Therefore I pray you be of good cheer and take all the household with you to church, and there thank God both for that he hath given us and for that he hath taken from us, and for that he hath left us, which if it please him he can increase when he will, and if it please him to leave us yet less, at his pleasure be it.

I pray you to make some good ensearch what my poor neighbors have lost and bid them take no thought therefore, for and I should not leave myself a spoon, there shall no poor neighbor of mine bear no loss by any chance happened in my house. I pray you be with my children and your household merry in God . . .[86]

In the above letter there is an unmistakable echo of Job's words, ". . . [T]he Lord gave, and the Lord has taken away; blessed be the name of the Lord" (Job 1:21)—words that in the final and greatest crisis of his life five years later More was to write down for his own consolation. And it was in his final crisis—in the pages of his last work, *De Tristitia Christi*—that he was to pay his most eloquent tribute to God's loving providence:

He keeps hidden the times, the moments, the causes of all things, and when the time is right He brings forth all things from the secret treasure-chest of His wisdom, which penetrates all things irresistibly and disposes all things sweetly.[87]

Indeed, Divine Providence had great things in store for Thomas More.

---

[86] Letter no. 174, in Elizabeth Rogers, ed., *The Correspondence of Sir Thomas More* (Princeton, N.J.: Princeton Univ. Press, 1947), 422–23.

[87] *CW* 14:67–69.

CHAPTER III

Peace on the Eve of War: Christian Humanism in Pre-Reformation Europe

In the opening years of the sixteenth century, Thomas More was drawn into the intellectual movement that has come to be known as Christian humanism. More's translation of the life of the Italian humanist Giovanni Pico della Mirandola, of which we have already spoken, is one of the earliest indications of his interest in the movement, which had its roots in the larger phenomenon of the Renaissance inaugurated toward the end of the fourteenth century. As with the latter, Christian humanism promoted a renewed interest in the classic works of ancient Rome and Greece, but it more specifically sought to revitalize Christianity through a more intensive study of the original texts of the Scriptures and of the Fathers of the Church. The insights of theology were to be brought to bear in a more practical, immediate manner upon everyday life in order that souls might more closely imitate and follow Christ. Of course the individual whose name has become almost synonymous with Christian humanism is that of Erasmus of Rotterdam, in certain ways a somewhat enigmatic figure, who, as we have already mentioned, first met More in 1499. Over the years that followed, a growing circle of friends with shared interests and aspirations developed around Erasmus and More, including Bishop [Saint] John Fisher of Rochester (1469–1535), Dean John Colet of Saint Paul's Cathedral, London (1466–1519), Cuthbert Tunstall, who eventually became Archbishop of London (1474–1559), and from the continent Guillaume Budé (1468–1540), Johann Reuchlin (1455–1522), and later Juan Luis Vives (1492–1540). These men most certainly did not concur on all points, and indeed there were some

notable disagreements among them; but they were able to find sufficient common ground to cooperate in the pursuit of the same overall
goals.

The humanists' desire for accurate biblical texts crystallized in 1516
with the publication of Erasmus' edition of the New Testament, translated from Greek manuscripts into Latin and augmented with copious explanatory notes. Unfortunately, the new translation was marred
by errors and misprints, due at least in part to the impetuosity of
its progenitor, who had little patience with the chore of proofread-
ing.[1] Nonetheless, the work was truly a milestone in biblical scholarship and a remarkable achievement for its time, the value of which
was justly defended by such solidly orthodox figures as Bishop Fisher
and Thomas More. Bishop Fisher was himself engaged at this time
in putting together a harmony of the four Gospels (of which, regrettably, there is no surviving copy),[2] while in Spain, an ambitious new
edition of the entire Bible in three languages—Hebrew, Greek, and
Latin—was already in the making, under the auspices of the illustrious Cardinal Ximenes; this work, however, was not released until
1521.[3] As for Thomas More's interest in the new biblical scholarship,
we need look no farther than to his impassioned defense of Erasmus'
New Testament found in his October 1515 letter to Martin Dorp.[4]
His own use of the Bible was so extensive that the twentieth-century
French scholar Father Germain Marc'hadour was able to fill over a
thousand pages in publishing his survey of each and every citation of
Sacred Scripture that appears in More's works.[5]

The other textual *cause célèbre* of the Christian humanists was the
production of readily accessible printed editions of the Church Fathers. As in the field of biblical scholarship, here too Erasmus played
a leading role, beginning in 1516 with the publication of his impres-

---

[1] E. E. Reynolds, *Thomas More and Erasmus* (London: Burns and Oates, 1965), 98–100.

[2] Richard Rex, *The Theology of John Fisher* (Cambridge: Cambridge Univ. Press, 1991), 54.

[3] Basil Hall, "The Trilingual College of San Ildefonso and the Making of the Complutensian Polyglot Bible", in *The Church and Academic Learning*, ed. G. J. Cuming, Studies in
Church History, vol. 5 (Leiden, Netherlands: E. J. Brill, 1969), 123–34, 140–45.

[4] Letter of October 21, 1515, in *In Defense of Humanism: Letters to Dorp, Oxford, Lee, and
a Monk,* ed. Daniel Kinney, vol. 15 of *Complete Works of St. Thomas More* (New Haven: Yale
Univ. Press, 1986), 81–95. Hereafter identified as *CW* 15.

[5] Fr. Germain Marc'hadour, *The Bible in the Works of Thomas More,* two vols. in five parts
(Nieuwkoop, Netherlands: B. de Graf, 1969–1972). The first three "parts" (that is, books)
contain an inventory of More's scriptural citations.

sive edition, in nine folio volumes, of the works of Saint Jerome and culminating in 1530 with his *Opera Omnia* of Saint John Chrysostom. Over this period Erasmus also produced editions of Saint Cyprian (1520), Saint Hilary (1523), Saint Irenaeus (1526), and even a ten-volume edition of Saint Augustine (in 1529) (his editions of Origen and Saint Ambrose were published posthumously).[6] Although patristic publication did not get under way in earnest until after 1510,[7] the works of the Church Fathers had already begun to appear in print by the end of the fifteenth century (Erasmus was thinking about editing Saint Jerome as early as 1500).[8] In addition to Erasmus' contributions, there were in circulation a variety of other patristic volumes, including a 1467 edition of Saint Augustine's *City of God,* Georgius Trapezuntius' 1470 edition of Eusebius' *De evangelica praeparatione,* Leonardo Aretino's 1470–1471 edition of Saint Basil's *De legendis antiquorum libris,* and Ambrogio Traversari's 1498 edition of the works of Pseudo-Dionysius the Areopagite.[9]

In his frequent use of the Church Fathers in his writings, Thomas More was quite representative of his fellow humanists. Erasmus testifies to More's pronounced patristic interests in his famous description of the saint that appears in his letter of July 23, 1517, to Ulrich von Hutten: "He [More] also expended considerable labour in perusing the volumes of the orthodox Fathers . . ."[10] More's acclaimed lectures on Saint Augustine's *City of God,* given when he was only in his early twenties, demonstrate his mastery of this field at a young age, as well as the pride of place that he gave to the writings of the illustrious Bishop of Hippo. Perhaps it is no mere coincidence that the Spanish humanist Vives chose the pages of his own 1522 edition of Augustine's *City of God* to praise More's intelligence, learning, and integrity.[11]

---

[6] Cornelius Augustijn, *Erasmus: His Life, Works, and Influence* (Toronto: Univ. of Toronto Press, 1991), 100.

[7] Rex, *Theology,* 21.

[8] Augustijn, *Erasmus,* 100.

[9] Frederick Goff, ed., *Incunabula in American Libraries: A Third Census of Fifteenth-Century Books Recorded in North American Collections* (New York: Bibliographical Society of America, 1964), 66, 91, 214, 232.

[10] Francis M. Nichols, trans. and ed., *The Epistles of Erasmus: From His Earliest Letters to His Fifty-First Year* (1901–1918; reprint, New York: Russell and Russell, 1962), 3:393.

[11] R. W. Chambers, *Thomas More* (1935; reprint, Ann Arbor, Mich.: Ann Arbor Paperbacks, Univ. of Michigan, 1973), 177.

Among these scholars who were so geared to making full use of the relatively new medium of the printed word, it is no surprise that there should be found a shared enthusiasm for books. Such was particularly the case with Bishop John Fisher, who, though he was habitually austere in his personal possessions, nonetheless assembled a sizable library in his episcopal residence. According to an anonymous sixteenth-century biographer of the Bishop, Fisher's collection was "replenished with such and so many kind of books, as the like was scant to be found again in the possession of any one private man in Christendom".[12] In another passage the same author states: "He [Fisher] had the notablest library of books in all England, two long galleries full. The books were sorted in stalls, and a regestre of the names of every book hung at the end of every stall."[13] When following his arrest and imprisonment in 1534 the Bishop's belongings were confiscated, his books filled thirty-two "great pypes", that is, thirty-two casks, each of over a hundred gallons in capacity.[14] Erasmus was obviously well acquainted with Fisher's love for his library, as can be seen in a letter he wrote to the Bishop in September 1524: "I know how much time you spend in the library which is to you a very paradise."[15]

But Bishop Fisher was by no means alone in his enjoyment of books. It appears that on more than one occasion books sent to him by Erasmus were intercepted—at least temporarily—by Thomas More. The problem arose from Erasmus' practice of sometimes sending his letters and books for the Bishop via their mutual friend More. The letters evidently reached their destination in a timely fashion, but it appears More could not resist perusing the books before passing them on to their intended recipient. Hence in the summer of 1517 it was necessary for Fisher to write to Erasmus, complaining of a copy of Reuchlin's *De arte cabalistica* that had not yet arrived: "Your friend

---

[12] Fr. Francis van Ortroy, S.J., ed., "Vie du bienheureux martyr Jean Fisher: Cardinal, évêque de Rochester (+1535): Text anglais et traduction latine du XVI siècle", pt. 2, *Analecta Bollandiana* 12 (1893): 168.

[13] Ibid., pt. 1, *Analecta Bollandiana* 10 (1891): 166.

[14] Ibid., pt. 2, 168; E. E. Reynolds, *Saint John Fisher* (New York: P. J. Kenedy and Sons, 1955), 272.

[15] Reynolds, *Fisher*, 44; for original Latin text, see letter no. 1489, September 4, 1524, in *Opus Epistolarum Des. Erasmi Roterdami*, vol. 5, *1522–1524*, ed. P. S. Allen and H. M. Allen (Oxford: Clarendon Press, 1924), 537.

More has sent the letter, but still detains the book in his old way; as he did before with the *Oculare Speculum*."[16]

We find further evidence of More's fascination with books in a February 1516 letter to Erasmus describing his visit some months earlier with the scholar Jerome Busleyden of Mechlin; note what material possessions of Busleyden More values the most:

> He showed me his house so marvellously built and splendidly furnished
> and containing so many of those antiquities that, as you know, I find
> so fascinating. Above all there was his well-stocked library, and a mind
> even better stocked.[17]

When years later More erected on the grounds of his Chelsea estate a place apart for his private prayers and studies—his "New Building"—it featured a library that Stapleton describes as "large and valuable";[18] and we may safely assume from the ample scholarly citations in More's writings from this later period that the shelves were indeed well stocked.

Although the Christian humanists could sometimes be quite caustic in their criticisms of papal misconduct (as of Pope Alexander VI's worldliness or of Pope Julius II's warlike tendencies), a fairly recent study has found that, at least among German humanists, the majority of them did not see these personal failings of the men who occupied the See of Peter in their own day as a reason to cast any doubts upon the authority of the papal office. Thus in 1485 the humanist Rudolphus Agricola wrote to Pope Innocent VIII, ". . . [T]he power over all of our affairs has been transmitted to you by God",[19] while in 1506 Conrad Peutinger, a humanist from Augsburg, declared, "The Pontifex Maximus possesses a gift which has descended to him di-

---

[16] Bishop Fisher to Erasmus, June 1517, in Nichols, *Epistles*, 2:569; see also Fr. Edward Surtz, S.J., "More's Friendship with Fisher", *Essential Articles for the Study of Thomas More*, ed. R. S. Sylvester and G. P. Marc'hadour (Hamden, Conn.: Archon Books, 1977), 171.

[17] Letter of c. February 17, 1516, as translated in E. E. Reynolds, *The Field Is Won: The Life and Death of Saint Thomas More* (Milwaukee: Bruce Publishing Co., 1968), 100. For original Latin text, see letter no. 388 in *Opus Epistolarum Des. Erasmi Roterdami*, vol. 2, *1514–1517*, ed. P. S. Allen (Oxford: Clarendon Press, 1910), 197.

[18] Thomas Stapleton, *The Life and Illustrious Martyrdom of Sir Thomas More*, ed. E. E. Reynolds (Bronx, N.Y.: Fordham Univ. Press, 1966), chap. 4, p. 36; William Roper, *The Lyfe of Sir Thomas Moore, Knighte*, ed. Elsie V. Hitchcock, Early English Text Society, original series, no. 197 (London: Early English Text Society, 1935), 26.

[19] Noel Brann, "Pre-Reformation Humanism in Germany and the Papal Monarchy: A Study in Ambivalence", *Journal of Medieval and Renaissance Studies* 14 (fall 1984): 165.

rectly from God in Heaven . . ."[20] Even as strident a critic of papal behavior as Jacob Wimpheling was able to write in 1505 of the controversial Pope Julius II, "Let me humbly take refuge in the highest prince and sole head of the Church, the most merciful father of all the faithful, and the magnanimous and very constant defender of righteousness, Julius II, in whose power my salvation or damnation has been vested."[21]

While Thomas More does not frequently refer in his writings to the specific issue of papal primacy (he tends more often to speak in terms of the unquestionable teaching authority of the Church in general), he does quite explicitly assert this primacy in one of his most important apologetical works (the *Responsio ad Lutherum*).[22] There was obviously no doubt in the mind of More's principal polemical opponent, William Tyndale, that More was a "papist", judging from Tyndale's numerous comments to this effect in his *Answer unto Sir Thomas More's Dialogue*.[23] Moreover, it is highly significant that More never engages in the rather acerbic criticisms of papal misconduct so common among his fellow humanists, and so characteristic of his close friend Erasmus; this certainly suggests a deep reverence for the successor of Saint Peter, as does his reference to the Pope in a May 1519 letter (to the humanist Edward Lee) as the "best and greatest of primates, who ought to take precedence over all learned men's votes".[24] In another letter to a monk (1519–1520) he refers to Rome as the "citadel of our religion" and the Pontiff as "the supreme prince of Christendom" and "Vicar of Christ", who speaks "as if with the authority of a divine oracle".[25] As we will explore in a later chapter, More's understanding of just how crucial the issue of papal authority was within the larger context of the Church's teaching Magisterium

---

[20] Ibid., 166.

[21] Ibid., 169.

[22] *Responsio ad Lutherum*, ed. John M. Headley and trans. Sr. Scholastica Mandeville, vol. 5 of *Complete Works of St. Thomas More* (New Haven: Yale Univ. Press, 1969), bk. 1, chap. 10, pp. 139–41. For a full discussion of this and other passages in More's writings regarding the papacy, see chapter 6 of the present work.

[23] *An Answer unto Sir Thomas More's Dialogue,* in William Tyndale, *An Answer to Sir Thomas More's Dialogue, The Supper of the Lord and Wm. Tracy's Testament Expounded,* ed. Rev. Henry Walter, Parker Society, vol. 44 (1850; reprint, New York: Johnson Reprint Corp., 1968), 5–215 (passim).

[24] Letter of More to Edward Lee, May 1, 1519, in *CW* 15:167.

[25] Letter to a Monk, c. 1519–1520, in *CW* 15:271.

was to undergo a major transformation in the beginning of his career as an apologetical writer, a transformation that in the end would lead him to lay down his life without hesitation in defense of the Bishop of Rome's authority, not only over matters of faith and morals, but over the discipline of the Church as well.

There is reason to believe that the distinction between those who in the late fifteenth and early sixteenth centuries continued to adhere to the predominant theological movement of the Christian Middle Ages—scholasticism—and those who embraced the new Christian humanist approach to theology is not quite as clear-cut as has been assumed in some earlier studies of the period. The problem posed in drawing too sharp a division is particularly evident in the cases of Bishop Fisher and Thomas More. For all their devotion to the new methods of Christian humanism, neither hesitated to tap into scholasticism's findings whenever he saw fit, with Fisher resorting especially to Duns Scotus and More to Saint Thomas Aquinas. Both refer to Aquinas in their writings as the "flower of theology", a phrase they would have picked up from the writings of a man they both admired: Giovanni Pico della Mirandola.[26]

Stapleton relates a story in this regard from Thomas More's secretary, John Harris. While on one of his journeys by boat down the Thames, en route from Chelsea to London, More examined a newly published heretical pamphlet. After perusing its contents a bit, he brought to Harris' attention several passages and commented (as recorded by Stapleton):

> The arguments (said he) which this villain has set forth are the objections which St. Thomas puts to himself in such and such a question and article of the Secunda Secundae, but the rogue keeps back the good Doctor's solutions.[27]

This anecdote suggests, quite plausibly, that More was thoroughly familiar with the works of Saint Thomas Aquinas—how else could he have cited so spontaneously from memory the Angelic Doctor's words by "chapter and verse"? Hence it comes as no surprise that in the course of refuting the Protestant reformer William Tyndale's attacks against Thomas Aquinas, More pronounces the fol-

---

[26] Rex, *Theology*, 50, 62–64.
[27] Stapleton, *Life*, chap. 4, p. 35.

lowing tribute to the scholarship and sanctity of this great theologian:

> Now the wretch raileth by name upon that holy doctor Saint Thomas, a man of that learning that the great excellent wits and the most cunning men that the Church of Christ hath had since his days, have esteemed and called him the very flower of theology, and a man of that true perfect faith and Christian living thereto, that God hath himself testified his holiness by many a great miracle, and made him honoured here in his Church in earth, as he hath exalted him to great glory in heaven . . .[28]

Inspired by the Greco-Roman historians of the ancient world, the humanists inaugurated a revival in historical studies, of which Thomas More was to become a leading exponent in his own country. Although More found time to make only one contribution to this field—his unfinished work on the late-fifteenth-century reign of England's King Richard III—it was enough to shape the future of English historical writing for centuries to come. His familiarity with the work of other scholars in the historical field is evident from the biographer Stapleton's comment that "He studied with avidity all the historical works he could find."[29] Throughout his writings one can detect the influence of the classical Greek and Roman authors. And as to the historical research under way in his own age, it is known from a comment he makes in his 1533 apological work *The Debellation of Salem and Bizance* that More had read such contemporary works as Platina's *Vitae Pontificum* of 1479 and Hartmann Schedel's *Chronicon Chronicorum* of 1493. He was likewise acquainted with the scholarship of the humanists Robert Gaguin and Paulus Aemilius Veronensis.[30] In one of his last works, the *Treatise upon the Passion* (c. 1534), he evinces his familiarity with a famous Renaissance study of ancient coins, Guillaume Budé's *De Asse* (1515),[31] a book he had read thor-

---

[28] *The Confutation of Tyndale's Answer,* ed. Louis Schuster et al., vol. 8 of *Complete Works of St. Thomas More* (New Haven: Yale Univ. Press, 1973), bk. 7, p. 713.

[29] Stapleton, *Life,* chap. 2, p. 14.

[30] Richard Sylvester, ed., introduction to *The History of King Richard III,* vol. 2 of *Complete Works of St. Thomas More* (1963; reprint, New Haven: Yale Univ. Press, 1967), lxxiii, lxxxi–lxxxvii; *The Debellation of Salem and Bizance,* ed. John Guy et al., vol. 10 of *Complete Works of St. Thomas More* (New Haven: Yale Univ. Press, 1987), chap. 15, p. 114.

[31] *Treatise on the Passion; Treatise on the Blessed Body; Instructions and Prayers,* ed. Garry Haupt, vol. 13 of *Complete Works of St. Thomas More* (New Haven: Yale University Press, 1976), chap. 1, lecture 4, pp. 79–80, and notes, pp. 263–64. Hereafter cited as *CW* 13.

oughly according to a letter he wrote to the author some years earlier (in 1518).[32] More's early study of Saint Augustine's *City of God* (to which we have already referred) would have played a formative role in his conception of history, and indeed it is noteworthy that More's lectures on this work focused specifically upon its historical as well as its philosophical dimensions, as we are told by Stapleton.[33]

More's friendship with Bishop John Fisher is of particular interest in view of the common destiny of the two men as martyrs and canonized saints. There are numerous intellectual and spiritual parallels between the two: both were committed humanists, both deeply loved the Holy Eucharist,[34] and both fought with their writings the doctrinal revolt of the Reformation. There is a special poignancy in their shared devotion to the great penitential figure in the Gospels, Saint Mary Magdalen. Fisher went so far as to break with many of his fellow humanists in writing a treatise (in 1519) defending the traditional belief that the unnamed penitent woman who washed Christ's feet with her tears (Lk 7:36–50) and the sister of Martha and Lazarus called Mary (Jn 11:1–2; 12:1–8) were one and the same person as Mary Magdalen, out of whom Christ had cast seven devils (Mk 16:9).[35] More, who in his own writings evinces the same belief in this traditionally accepted identity of the Magdalen,[36] is unrestrained in his praise of Fisher's tract on the subject in a letter to the author: "Your lordship writes in a style that might well be that of Erasmus. As for the subject matter, ten Erasmuses could not be more convincing."[37] Elsewhere, in a letter to a monk (1519–1520) wherein he defends his friend Erasmus, More names among Erasmus' admirers Bishop Fisher, whom he describes in the most complimentary terms: "I will name, and most worshipfully I will name, the reverend father in Christ, John

---

[32] Letter no. 65, c. August 1518, in Elizabeth Rogers, ed., *The Correspondence of Sir Thomas More* (Princeton, N.J.: Princeton Univ. Press, 1947), 124.

[33] Stapleton, *Life,* chap. 2, pp. 7–8.

[34] Fr. Germain Marc'hadour, "Fisher and More: A Note", in *Humanism, Reform and the Reformation: The Career of Bishop John Fisher,* ed. Brendan Bradshaw and Eamon Duffy (Cambridge: Cambridge Univ. Press, 1989), 106–7.

[35] Ibid., 106; Rex, *Theology,* 65–77.

[36] *A Dialogue concerning Heresies,* ed. Thomas Lawler et al., vol. 6 of *Complete Works of St. Thomas More* (New Haven: Yale Univ. Press, 1981), bk. 1, chap. 2, p. 49; *Treatise upon the Passion,* chap. 1, lecture 4, in CW 13:76–77.

[37] Letter no. 74, to Bishop Fisher, 1519?, in Rogers, *Correspondence,* 136–37, quoted in English in Surtz, "More's Friendship with Fisher", 172.

the bishop of Rochester, a man as conspicuous for his virtue as he is for his learning and as eminent for both as any man living today."[38] More's admiration and respect for Fisher is likewise particularly evident in his May 1519 letter to the humanist Edward Lee regarding an intellectual dispute between the latter and Erasmus:

> . . . [Y]ou have submitted this entire quarrel to the judgment of the reverend father, the bishop of Rochester, to whom you have forwarded the volume of your annotations . . . you have chosen a peacemaker who is not only a particularly well-qualified judge because of his singular learning, which he now has the world to attest, but is also unlikely, because of his extraordinary piety, to let anything good in either book go to waste; a man who moreover loves both of you so much that he will devote all his energies to concord, and a man of such skill and resourcefulness that he will easily find a way to satisfy both of you.[39]

We come now to what is undoubtedly the most famous literary work of Thomas More: his *Utopia*, a brilliant tour de force of Christian humanism born in the relatively serene atmosphere of pre-Reformation Europe. Yet, to know only *Utopia* and not any of More's other writings is to know truly neither More nor *Utopia*. Hence, we must set this book in the context of what were More's professed beliefs both before and after he penned it, if we are not to misunderstand it. But before examining the contents of *Utopia*, we need to begin by reviewing the events in More's life from which it arose.

It was a diplomatic mission to the Netherlands inaugurated in May 1515 that ultimately provided More with just enough additional free time to devote himself to the writing of a new book. He was one of five delegates appointed by Henry VIII to represent England in negotiations with the Netherlands to be conducted in Bruges. By mid-July, however, the talks had reached an impasse that could only be resolved by high-level consultations on both sides. The negotiations went into recess, leaving More with plenty of leisure—time to think, time to converse with two Belgian humanist friends of Erasmus, Peter Giles and Jerome Busleyden, and time to write.[40] Gradually More set down on paper his vision of a hypothetical commonwealth situated in the

---

[38] Letter to a Monk, c. 1519–1520, in *CW* 15:269.

[39] Letter to Lee, May 1, 1519, in *CW* 15:179.

[40] Edward Surtz, S.J., ed., introduction to *Utopia*, vol. 4 of *Complete Works of St. Thomas More* (New Haven: Yale Univ. Press, 1965), xxviii–xxxi. Hereafter cited as *CW* 4.

New World, taking for his inspiration not only such ancient classics
of political theory as Plato's *Republic* and Aristotle's *Politics* but also the
amazing stories recorded in Amerigo Vespucci's account of his voyages to the newly discovered lands across the ocean (first published
in 1507).[41] In October More's diplomatic mission came to an end,
and he returned home with the manuscript of what was to become
book 2 of his new work. Enveloped once more in the hectic swirl of
daily duties, he found it far more challenging to bring to completion
book 1; even so, the offer during this time of an advisory post in the
service of the King provided him with further subject matter upon
which to write: the question of what good, if any, a scholar could do
in taking such a post.[42]

In the Belgian city of Louvain, the first edition of *Utopia* was published in Latin near the end of 1516.[43] In his letter to Peter Giles that
serves as a preface to the work, More apologizes that what his friend
thought would be ready to go to the printers in a month and a half
has taken a year to finish. He goes on to describe the difficulties he
has had in finding time to write his volume, most of which, as we
have seen, he encountered while working at home on what became
the first book of *Utopia* (after he had finished book 2). Every day he
must attend to questions of law; upon coming home from work, his
time is all but used up in conversing with his wife and children as well
as with his servants. More is quick to point out that these household
conversations are a necessary part of his responsibilities; nonetheless,
amid such things "the day, the month, the year slip away", with even
more time consumed by meals and sleep, the latter of which "takes
up almost half a man's life". Thus it was only by stealing some time
from eating and sleeping that he was able to complete his book.[44]

In certain respects *Utopia* can be likened to a short story, in that it
tells of a fictional meeting and conversation among three characters.
Two of the individuals are from real life: More and his friend the Belgian humanist Peter Giles. But it is the third character, the fictional
Raphael Hythlodaeus, who constitutes the key player in this narrative,

---

[41] J. B. Heffeman, "Vespucci, Amerigo", *New Catholic Encyclopedia* (1967), 14:631.

[42] Surtz, introduction to *Utopia*, *CW* 4:xxxi–xxxviii; Reynolds, *Field Is Won*, 101; P. A.
Duhamel, "Medievalism of More's *Utopia*", in Sylvester and Marc'hadour, *Essential Articles*
239, 243.

[43] Surtz, introduction to *Utopia*, *CW* 4:xxxviii; Reynolds, *Field Is Won*, 103–4.

[44] *Utopia*, prefatory letter to Peter Giles, *CW* 4:39–41 (quotes from 41).

the first book of which in large part follows the format of a Platonic dialogue (one of More's favorite literary devices). While on a diplomatic mission in Bruges, Belgium, More—having just attended Mass in the city's cathedral—is introduced by Giles to the sage Hythlodaeus, whom he learns has traveled on several voyages to the New World with the famous explorer Amerigo Vespucci. After the three sit down to converse in the garden of the house where More is lodged, Hythlodaeus begins to tell of his exploits in distant lands and of the laws and customs he found among different peoples.[45] Impressed by his learning and wisdom, Giles and More question him about why he has not entered into the service of one of Europe's crowned princes, who could benefit from his counsel (the very same prospect that More was at this time facing in real life). Hythlodaeus answers that such a post would deprive him of his freedom of action; moreover, kings would not be willing to follow the advice he would offer. Men are wont to think their own ideas best and quick to find fault with those of others.[46] Here with biting irony More has Hythlodaeus say, "Such proud, ridiculous, and obstinate prejudices I have encountered often in other places and once in England too."[47] Hythlodaeus goes on to relate a discussion he had concerning the punishment of criminals while a guest at the table of More's beloved boyhood mentor in real life, the late Cardinal Morton of Canterbury. Criticizing the use of capital punishment for thieves, Hythlodaeus argues that death is too cruel a penalty for petty theft, a crime to which men often resort not out of malice but rather out of desperation in their extreme poverty. Such poverty is frequently enough brought upon them by the greed of their wealthier countrymen. Even under the more severe Mosaic law, theft was not punishable by death; how then can it justly be so under the more merciful tenets of the New Testament? Furthermore, by inflicting the same sentence for theft as that assigned to murder, society in effect equates the taking of property with the taking of a human life—an inadmissible conclusion—and a thief is given little incentive to spare the life of the person most able to testify against him, his victim.[48] In this conversation Cardinal Morton proved himself a judicious listener, but the other guests did not. Hythlodaeus

---

[45] *CW* 4, bk. 1, pp. 47–55.
[46] Ibid., 55–59.
[47] Ibid., 59.
[48] Ibid., 59–75.

was dismayed by their duplicity, for they refused to admit any merit to his opinions until the Cardinal did so. It seems they were more concerned with flattering their host than with the honest examination of ideas. With men such as this in courtly circles, Hythlodaeus sees no reason to believe he would get a hearing were he to become a princely advisor.[49]

More remains unsatisfied with Hythlodaeus' reasons for refusing to counsel the high and mighty and presses the matter further. Hythlodaeus explains that his proposals would run counter to the greed and ambition of princes and hence would never be accepted by them.[50] Even so, More asks, is there not a value in accepting such an advisory post for the sake of at least influencing what "you cannot turn to good" so as to make it "as little bad as you can"?[51] Hythlodaeus responds by insisting that any accommodation or compromise on his part would only make him a participant in the very problem he would be trying to remedy.[52] The conversation now turns to the question of private versus communal ownership of goods, with Hythlodaeus advocating the latter practice, which he had the opportunity of seeing for himself in the island kingdom of Utopia.[53] Upon the request of Peter Giles, Hythlodaeus enters upon a lengthy account of the laws and customs of the Utopians, and it is this description that constitutes the second book of *Utopia*.

What sort of a society could be constructed using reason alone, unaided by the light of Divine Revelation? This is the fundamental question that More addresses in the second book of *Utopia*. It is only a theoretical question, but one that More felt needed to be raised in a society that had grown lax in the pursuit of its ideals. More's point was that even reasonable pagans could do better in many respects than sixteenth-century Christian Europe was doing in matters of government and social justice. That reason alone was not enough More makes sufficiently clear by incorporating into the values of his Utopians certain fallacious concepts, such as euthanasia and divorce,[54] practices that More most certainly did not condone, as is obvious from

---

[49] Ibid., 81–85.

[50] Ibid., 87–97.

[51] Ibid., 99–101 (quote on 101).

[52] Ibid., 101–3.

[53] Ibid., 103–7.

[54] Ibid., bk. 2, pp. 187, 189–91.

his other writings. Indeed, lest his readers misunderstand him, More is careful to end *Utopia* with the following disclaimer:

> . . . [M]any things came to my mind which seemed very absurdly established in the customs and laws of the people described—not only in their method of waging war, their ceremonies and religion, as well as their other institutions, but most of all in that feature which is the principal foundation of their whole structure. I mean their common life and subsistence—without any exchange of money.[55]

Those sufficiently familiar with More's life and writings will be able to recognize what concepts he did intend to advocate in *Utopia*. Note that the Utopians' laws and customs, such as their six-hour work day, which was considerably shorter than that of workmen in sixteenth-century Europe, all point to setting aside as much time as possible in every citizen's life for the pursuit of the arts and sciences; and those who excel in these studies are freed from all other work to devote themselves totally to higher learning.[56] It is obvious even from More's prefatory letter to Peter Giles, which we quoted earlier, that More knew from his own personal experience how difficult it was to "steal" time from the daily chore of earning a living in order to immerse oneself in the humanities. As to the Utopian policy on war, it would be a great mistake to equate it with the concept of pacifism in our own day. Yes, the Utopians were against war waged needlessly or for self-aggrandizement, as were More and his fellow humanists, who had seen too much of this kind of warfare in their own age. But Utopia did go to war when it was attacked by another nation or when an allied country needed the Utopians' assistance in defending itself or was suffering under the oppression of a tyrant.[57] In both books of *Utopia*, policies to redress social injustices and improve the status of the poor are advocated, revealing a genuine concern for the disadvantaged that is consonant with More's own record in public office, where he earned a reputation as the friend of the poor.

The Utopians' attitude of treating gold and silver as if they were next to worthless, suited only for the lowliest functions (such as for prisoners' chains),[58] is undoubtedly More's way of expressing a very

---

[55] Ibid., 245.
[56] Ibid., 127–29, 131, 159.
[57] Ibid., 199–201.
[58] Ibid., 151–157.

traditional disdain for the world's obsession with the pursuit of material rather than spiritual riches. Closely connected with this is More's use of elements of daily routine borrowed from that form of life that constituted the ultimate renunciation of material goods in the pursuit of spiritual ones: Catholic monastic life. Drawing upon his own firsthand knowledge of Carthusian practices, More has his Utopians observe a fixed horarium of daily activities, divided between work and recreation. During their meals, which are held in common, they listen to readings, as is done in monastic communities.[59] But by far the most conspicuous adaptation in Utopian society from monasticism is the concept of collective ownership in place of private property. As this idea was to be found not only in religious houses but was likewise advocated by Plato in his *Republic* and by several of the Church Fathers, its presence in More's *Utopia* should not be mistaken for some sort of nascent sixteenth-century precursor of Marxism. The Utopians pool their wealth, not in order to become mere tools of the state, as in a communist society, but rather for their own personal betterment, that each citizen may have sufficient leisure for pursuing the arts and sciences.[60] More does not himself see collective ownership as something a real society should implement, as he makes clear by his own closing comments at the end of Hythlodaeus' monologue in book 2,[61] as well as by his defense of private ownership in his *Dialogue of Comfort against Tribulation,* written years later.[62] There is likewise a warning against the forced redistribution of wealth in his 1529 work, *The Supplication of Souls.*[63] Utopia's collectivism serves rather as an indictment of the materialism that More had seen all too much of in Renaissance Europe.

The Utopians are not without religion; indeed, by unaided human reason they have arrived at a belief in a Supreme Being, though they differ among themselves as to who or what this Deity is and in other

---

[59] Ibid., 127, 141–45.

[60] Ibid., bk. 1, pp. 103–5; bk. 2, pp. 147, 159, 239–43.

[61] Ibid., bk. 2, p. 245.

[62] *Dialogue of Comfort against Tribulation,* ed. Louis L. Martz and Frank Manley, vol. 12 of *Complete Works of St. Thomas More* (New Haven: Yale Univ. Press, 1976), bk. 2, chap. 17, pp. 179–81.

[63] *Supplication of Souls,* bk. 1, in *Letter to Bugenhagen, Supplication of Souls, Letter against Frith,* ed. Frank Manley et al., vol. 7 of *Complete Works of St. Thomas More* (New Haven: Yale Univ. Press, 1990), 148–49.

details of their religious convictions. While in the absence of possessing the knowledge of Divine Revelation the Commonwealth does enjoin a tolerance of the multiplicity of religions among its people, it will not tolerate any denial of Divine Providence or of the immortality of the soul.[64] More tells us that in their worship the Utopians make much use of incense and candles,[65] interesting details for him to add in virtue of his vigorous defense of such things in his subsequent apologetical writings regarding Catholic liturgical and devotional practices. And in the starkness and darkness of Utopian churches[66] one can recognize yet another element borrowed from the austere ways of Carthusian spirituality.[67]

As to the public morality of the Utopians, they arrive at many of the same values as Christians despite their lack of guidance from Divine Revelation. Thus they firmly oppose and punish fornication, convinced that were such behavior to become common, the institution of marriage would be undermined.[68] In their regulations regarding population, there is no attempt to resort to birth control or abortion (practices certainly not unknown in other pagan societies). Although the Utopians have an odd policy (certainly not advocated by More) of redistributing grown children (aged fourteen or above) so that all families may be approximately the same size, it is explicitly stated that every family should consist of at *least* ten members and that there is *no rule* governing the number of children a family may have under the age of fourteen. When the population of a city exceeds its prescribed limit, the Utopians simply start a new city or colony elsewhere to handle the additional numbers.[69] In fact Utopia's population policies resemble more than anything else the statutes of certain religious orders such as the Carthusians, regulating the size of each monastery.[70] In Utopia the old and young are made to mingle with each other, so that youth may benefit from the wisdom of their elders;[71] moreover, traditional relationships between husband and wife,

---

[64] *CW* 4, bk. 2, pp. 217–23.

[65] Ibid., 235.

[66] Ibid., 231–33.

[67] Duhamel, "Medievalism of More's *Utopia*", 246.

[68] *CW* 4, bk. 2, p. 187.

[69] Ibid., 135–37.

[70] Duhamel, "Medievalism of More's *Utopia*", 246.

[71] CW 4, bk. 2, pp. 143, 235.

between parents and children, are by and large maintained.[72] Even the Utopians' non-Christian policy of allowing divorce is restricted to relatively few cases, for they believe that marriage is "seldom broken except by death".[73]

In reading *Utopia*, we must also be aware of More's unique sense of humor, which characteristically took the form of mock seriousness. Let us remember that he produced this work in large part as an entertainment for himself and for his friends. Who has not known the enjoyment of imagining a fictitious time and place? Would this not have been especially the case in the highly charged atmosphere of early sixteenth-century Europe, rife with stories of a fantastic New World an ocean away? More's intent to amuse is evident even in his prefatory letter to Peter Giles, wherein he asks his friend, who is cast as a participant in the imaginary conversation with Raphael Hythlodaeus, whether he remembers the length of a bridge in Utopia's capital city, and if he can recall the precise latitude and longitude of Utopia.[74] Understanding the joke, Peter Giles plays along by responding in kind in a letter to another humanist friend of theirs, Jerome Busleyden, wherein he is abashed to admit that at the precise moment when Hythlodaeus had told them the location of the island he was distracted by the cough of another person nearby.[75] As it was Giles who arranged for the publication of the first edition of *Utopia*, his letter along with More's prefatory letter were included at the beginning of the book;[76] wanting to add further to the fun, he also provided what he claimed was a poem in the Utopian tongue, and even added a presentation of the Utopian alphabet![77]

It is necessary, therefore, that we see *Utopia*, not as More's blueprint for the perfect society, but instead as a forum for the reevaluation of what values and goals a society should set for itself. More was, as it were, saying to a Europe that had the benefit of Christian revelation, "To thine own self be true";[78] if pagans can achieve as much as the Utopians do in constructing a more just society, cannot we as

---

[72] Ibid., 135, 137, 143, 147, 187–91, 233–35.

[73] Ibid., 189–91 (quote on 189).

[74] Ibid., prefatory letter of More to Peter Giles, 41–43.

[75] Ibid., prefatory letter of Peter Giles to Jerome Busleyden, 23.

[76] Surtz, introduction to *Utopia*, *CW* 4:lxxxiv–clxxxv.

[77] *CW* 4:19, and prefatory letter of Peter Giles to Jerome Busleyden, 23.

[78] Shakespeare, *Hamlet*, act 1, scene 3.

Christians do even more? Why then do we fare far worse? As More concludes:

> . . . I cannot agree with all that he [Hythlodaeus] said. But I readily admit that there are very many features in the Utopian commonwealth which it is easier for me to wish for in our countries than to have any hope of seeing realized.[79]

---

[79] *CW* 4, bk. 2, pp. 245-47.

CHAPTER IV

Excursus: The Church on the Eve of the Reformation

It is not possible to understand the course of events in sixteenth-century Europe that has come to be known as the Protestant Reformation without first gaining a grasp of the state of circumstances that preceded it and from which it arose. This is a point upon which most historians would agree, although just what those circumstances were and precisely how they precipitated the Reformation remain matters of intense debate. A discussion of these issues is essential in studying the life of Saint Thomas More, for in large part the "Reformation" that followed shaped the subsequent course of his life and ultimately brought about his untimely death.

It has come as a surprising discovery in a number of recent, in-depth studies of the pre-Reformation Church that in the early sixteenth century Catholicism was in many ways thriving—at least in England. The traditional image of a profoundly disillusioned laity, badly educated by an overwhelmingly corrupt and ignorant clergy and hungering for change, has not fared well amid the rigors of present-day research in this field. True, the Church had many grave internal problems to deal with, as we shall see shortly—it would be intolerably disingenuous to pretend otherwise—but the picture was not as bleak as it has often been portrayed.

Perhaps the most fascinating testaments to a far more vigorous pre-Reformation faith than previously assumed are the numerous catechetical and devotional works that came from the first printing presses of Catholic Europe in the fifteenth and early sixteenth centuries, years before Martin Luther published even a page of writing. There were little *Primers* to teach the laity the rudiments of their religion—especially the Ten Commandments and the sacraments—and devotional books to guide their participation in the Mass as well as to instruct them in prayer. In England alone the *Primer* went through no fewer than seventy-eight editions between 1501 and 1530.[1] A survey made by the French scholar Pierre Janelle found that roughly half of all books known to have been published in England between 1468 and 1530 (as listed in the British Museum's catalogue of early printed works) were on religious subjects (176 out of 349).[2] In the period from 1483 to 1532, the *Festival,* John Mirk's famous medieval English collection of model sermons for the use of preachers, was printed twenty-four times.[3] Hagiography proved quite popular, with six English-language printings of Jacobus de Voragine's *Golden Legend,* a widely disseminated thirteenth-century anthology of saints' lives, appearing between 1483 and the 1520s.[4] *The Arte or Crafte to Lyve Well,* a manual for the English laity first published in 1505 and translated from a French original, was particularly comprehensive in pedagogical content, covering the Ten Commandments, the precepts of the Church, the sacraments, the seven gifts of the Holy Spirit, the virtues, the seven deadly sins, and common prayers. Numerous illustrations printed from woodcuts accompany the text: thus with each sacrament there are two pictures, one of the sacrament itself, the other of its Old Testament prefiguration. In an illustration regarding the Our Father, Christ is depicted teaching this prayer to His apostles with the words (in English) appearing above their heads; similarly Moses and Aaron are shown in another woodcut featuring the Ten Commandments.[5] In one of several editions of the *Kalender of Shepherdes,* a popular volume containing an eclectic mixture of religious instruction and folklore that first appeared in 1503, there is a woodcut showing the pope and a coterie of bishops and ecclesiastics addressing the Blessed Virgin Mary, standing before them, with the words of the Hail Mary.[6]

Essential to the communication of the Christian faith is the apos-

---

[1] Christopher Haigh, *English Reformations: Religion, Politics, and Society under the Tudors* (Oxford: Clarendon Press, 1993), 26.

[2] Fr. Philip Hughes, "*The King's Proceedings*", vol. 1 of *The Reformation in England* (New York: Macmillan Co., 1951), 98–99.

[3] Haigh, *English Reformations,* 27.

[4] Hughes, "*King's Proceedings*", 99.

[5] Eamon Duffy, *The Stripping of the Altars: Traditional Religion in England, c. 1400—c. 1580* (New Haven: Yale Univ. Press, 1992), 81.

[6] Ibid., 82, plus plate 39.

tolate of preaching. Hence in evaluating the state of the Church at the close of the Middle Ages, it is necessary that we attempt to assess the quality and success of the sermons of this period in disseminating the message of the Gospel. While a cursory examination of the surviving texts may lend support to the widely held perception that late medieval preaching left very much to be desired, there is a recent (1992) in-depth study of French sermons from the fifteenth and sixteenth centuries that has to a large extent vindicated the preaching of this period in terms of both content and methods. Taking note of a wide consensus of evidence that late medieval sermons were attended by the laity in large numbers, the author of this new study, the Wellesley scholar Larissa Taylor, found that the preachers geared their words to capture the attention of the people and leave them with lessons they could easily remember and share with others. Drawing rather heavily on scriptural sources, these men presented the contents of the Bible in a colloquial manner, so as to make the Scriptures understandable to everyone. They had recourse to pedagogical methods, including visual means and dramatization, that are commonly recognized and accepted in the field of education. As to content, the message of the preachers was remarkably well balanced, presenting salvation as something attainable by all despite mankind's fall. Contrary to Protestant accusations, these men of the pulpit did not downplay the preeminence of faith and grace in the economy of salvation; nonetheless, they did teach that man was able "effectively [to] cooperate in his own salvation" and had to manifest not only faith but hope and love as well.[7] While they did present to the people the whole community of New Testament figures and the saints, the centerpiece of their sermons was the life of Christ, the events of which they depicted dramatically to their audiences in an effort "to capture the medieval imagination and inspire men and women to follow Christ".[8]

A commonly offered explanation for the Reformation is that it arose from, among other things, a pronounced feeling of "anticlericalism" —the laity's resentment of their clergy. In recent years the Oxford scholar Christopher Haigh has explored the issue in the case of England and found the evidence for widespread pre-Reformation anticler-

[7] Larissa Taylor, *Soldiers of Christ: Preaching in Late Medieval and Reformation France* (Oxford: Clarendon Press, 1992), 226–30 (quote on 229).

[8] Ibid., 230.

icalism to be weak or nonexistent.[9] Haigh notes that newer research has called into question the conventional assumption that the late medieval clergy were rife with ignorance and misconduct.[10] Moreover, rather than representing an elite and aloof class of citizens, most of the English clergy were sons of the poorer classes—pastors drawn from the very people they were called to serve.[11] In view of the financial hardships experienced by the majority of those entering the clerical state in early sixteenth-century England, it would be very difficult to explain the large number of vocations to the priesthood from among the laity during this period, together with the generous amount of voluntary financial support that the people were willing to give their priests, if anticlerical sentiments were common.[12] The known manifestations of hostility to clerics are relatively few in number and are often explainable by motives that are unique to the individual cases of hostility themselves—for instance, the resentment aimed at Cardinal Wolsey, which appears to have been directed more at the man himself than at priests in general.[13] Several of the most significant sixteenth-century works of anticlerical literature are the products, not of disinterested parties, but rather of early figures in the English Reformation, such as William Tyndale, Simon Fish, and Jerome Barlow.[14]

Surviving records of parish life from early sixteenth-century England are consistent in revealing a laity actively and devotedly engaged in the practice of their faith. Churchwardens' accounts from this period indicate a steady and generous stream of contributions toward the erection, adornment, and maintenance of churches and their furnishings. The commitment of the people to traditional forms of Catholic worship is manifest in the innumerable references to the acquisition of vestments, sacred vessels, and liturgical books for the celebration of Mass, as well as the addition or repainting of statues of the Blessed Virgin Mary and the saints.[15] England's church lay associations—the religious guilds and fraternities—were thriving institu-

---

[9] Christopher Haigh, "Anticlericalism and the English Reformation", *History* 68 (October 1983): 391–92, 402–3, 406.

[10] Ibid., 392–93.

[11] Ibid., 393.

[12] Ibid., 403–5.

[13] Ibid., 393–403.

[14] Ibid., 393–94.

[15] Haigh, *English Reformations,* 29–35.

tions in the early sixteenth century, as in London, where over eighty
such groups were in existence at this time; Lincolnshire had around
120 fraternities, Northamptonshire over a hundred.[16]

The Catholics of pre-Reformation England were intensely devoted
to the celebration of the Eucharist, evincing a strong liturgical sense
that drew them to attend Mass frequently and in large numbers. The
observations of a Venetian visitor to the country in 1500, while perhaps a bit exaggerated, are nonetheless particularly instructive in this
regard: ". . . [T]hey all attend Mass every day . . . they always hear
mass on Sunday in their parish church, and give liberal alms . . ."[17]

At first glance the records of how Mass was celebrated in the late
medieval Church would seem to suggest a liturgy that was kept somewhat at a distance from the people, with most of the service at least
partially concealed behind a rood screen, and even more so during
Lent, when a "Lenten veil" hung across the sanctuary; moreover,
the words of Mass were in Latin, a language most of the people did
not know, with the culminating words of consecration uttered in an
almost inaudible whisper. If this were all we knew of late medieval
practice, it might indeed seem difficult to understand, at least from
a purely human perspective, why the Mass was so extremely popular
with the laity. As a matter of fact, while the principal Mass of the
day would have been celebrated more or less along the lines we have
described, the innumerable Masses conducted at side altars were totally visible and fully audible to the laity.[18] Furthermore, despite the
language barrier, various means were employed to instruct the people
at least in the rudimentary meaning of what they were seeing and
hearing.

It is just such a basic understanding, coupled with a familiarity with
all the actions of the Mass as witnessed at the side altars (where the
people were able to stand and kneel at almost arm's length from the
priest),[19] that the laity would have brought with them in attending
the more solemn parish Mass conducted behind the rood screen. The
lessened "accessibility" of these more formal liturgies the laity would
have accepted as simply a visible expression of the sense of the sa-

---

[16] Ibid., 35–36.

[17] *A Relation, or Rather a True Account, of the Island of England,* trans. Charlotte Augusta
Sneyd (London: Camden Society, 1847), 23.

[18] Duffy, *Stripping of Altars,* 110–13.

[19] Ibid., 112–13.

cred that was an essential component in the celebration of this sacrament, for it was God Himself, they firmly believed, who became truly present on the altar.

But how was the Mass explained to the people? Over seven centuries earlier, in A.D. 747, the Second Council of Clovesho, England, mandated that the nation's priests were to instruct their flocks in the vernacular on the meaning of the Mass.[20] In the late twelfth or early thirteenth centuries there appeared a vernacular guide for the laity, *The Lay Folks' Mass Book,* a work that was still circulating in manuscript copies as late as the fifteenth century.[21] Describing the Mass as "the worthiest thing, of most goodness in all this world",[22] this work offered the reader a program for following attentively at least the major actions of the liturgy, while providing vernacular devotional prayers to be recited silently, echoing the themes of the particular portions of the service for which they were written. Thus the *Lay Folks' Mass Book* emphasizes the importance of the Gospel reading in these terms:

> If they are singing or saying mass, say your Our Father throughout, until the deacon or priest reads the gospel. Then stand up, and pay attention; for then the priest carries his book north, to the other corner of the altar, and makes a cross on the writing with his thumb . . . Then he next makes another on his face; for he has great need of grace, for then an earthly man shall speak the words of Jesus Christ, Son of the heavenly God. Both the readers and the hearers have great need, I think, of teachers how they should read and should hear the words of God, so beloved and dear.[23]

The private prayer that the *Mass Book* provides to be said following the priest's recital of the *Agnus Dei* (Lamb of God) begins with words that are almost a direct English translation of the Mass text: "Lamb of God, that may best take away the sins of the world, have mercy and pity on us, and grant us peace and charity . . ."[24]

---

[20] Second Council of Clovesho, canon 10, in J. D. Mansi, *Sacrorum Conciliorum Nova, et Amplissima Collectio* 12 (1766; reprint, Paris and Leipzig: Huberto Welter, 1901), col. 398.

[21] R. N. Swanson, trans. and ed., *Catholic England: Faith, Religion and Observance before the Reformation,* Manchester Medieval Sources Series (Manchester, England: Manchester Univ. Press, 1993), 78–79.

[22] Ibid., 83.

[23] Ibid., 85.

[24] Ibid., 90.

In addition to the *Lay Folks' Mass Book,* other lay guides to the Mass were composed up until the Reformation,[25] including a work of the fifteenth-century English poet John Lydgate, *The Virtues of the Mass,* which explained the *Kyrie* (Lord, have mercy) in these words:

> Kyrie and Christ, in number thrice three,
> Words of Greek, plainly to determine,
> Of mercy calling to the Trinity
> With ghostly grace his people to illumine,
> The number is token of the [angelic] orders nine,
> Our oraisons and prayers to present,
> To Christ Jesu most gracious and benign
> Goodly to accept the sign of our intent.[26]

It cannot be denied that the concept embodied in such books of pre-occupying the laity with private devotional prayers while the Sacrifice of the Mass is unfolding before them is unsatisfactory by modern standards. Nonetheless, it should be borne in mind that pre-Reformation catechesis did successfully instill in the people the supreme importance of the two most essential elements of the Mass that have come down to us from the Last Supper: the Consecration and Holy Communion. Unfortunately the people's highly developed sense of awe with regard to the latter—an intimate encounter with the living God—degenerated over the centuries into an excessive reticence to approach the Eucharistic Table. As a result, the majority of the late medieval laity received only once a year, at Easter. Even so, as parishioners flocked *en masse* to receive this one yearly Communion, they would have brought with them to the altar a heightened appreciation of the magnitude of what they were about to do—an appreciation engendered in part by the sheer infrequency with which they partook of this privilege.

It is when we shift our focus from England to pre-Reformation conditions on the Continent, especially in Germany, that we begin to grasp the darker aspects of the condition of the Church at this time—not that England was without its scandals—but things were worse across the Channel. Time and again throughout the fifteenth century,

---

[25] Duffy, *Stripping of Altars,* 118–19; Swanson, *Catholic England,* 78–79 n. 5.

[26] Text in *The Minor Poems of John Lydgate: Part I,* ed. Henry Noble MacCracken, Early English Text Society, extra series, no. 107 (London: Early English Text Society, 1911), 95.

the statutes of individual German bishops and of episcopal synods reveal the recurring necessity to condemn promiscuity among the ranks
of the clergy. Although there were regions of the country where the
conduct of the priests was generally above reproach, particularly in
the regions of Slesvig-Holstein to the northwest, the Rhineland in the
west, and in the southwestern corner of Bavaria known as the All-
gau, there were other large areas where clerical misconduct had taken
on serious proportions. These included Saxony (where Lutheranism
and the Protestant Reformation were subsequently born), Franconia
in Thuringia, and most of Bavaria.[27] And while many German parish
priests were financially hard pressed, as was the case in England, others, especially among the higher clergy, were living amid repulsively
opulent wealth.[28] Such behavior was all the more disillusioning when
it was found among those who had vowed themselves to a lifetime
of living the evangelical counsels of poverty, chastity, and obedience
—the members of religious orders. The institution known as the
benefice—an income allotted for the support of a priest in his parish
—was the object of numerous abuses, as avaricious clergymen accumulated for themselves the benefices of several parishes combined,
while neglecting to serve in all the posts they were receiving income
for. It is not difficult to intimate the source of such worldliness in
the sanctuary in view of the fact that when the Reformation began
the sons of princes held or controlled the episcopal seats of no fewer
than eighteen dioceses and archdioceses in Germany alone.[29]

It should be mentioned that a number of twentieth-century studies
of pre-Reformation Germany have succeeded in scraping away the
exaggerations of earlier historians to reveal that there were, side by
side with the real abuses, more than enough signs of vitality in the
life of the Church, including strong evidence of a deepening commitment to traditional forms of popular piety[30] comparable to what we
have seen in the case of England. In the nation that was the birth-
place of the printed word, at least fifty-nine published editions of
Thomas à Kempis' classic, *The Imitation of Christ,* had appeared by

---

[27] Hartmann Grisar, S.J., *Martin Luther: His Life and Work* (1930; reprint, Westminster, Md.: Newman Press, 1961), 126–27.

[28] Ibid., 127–28.

[29] Ibid., 129–30.

[30] Reinhold Kiermayr, "On the Education of the Pre-Reformation Clergy", *Church History* 53 (March 1984): 8.

the year 1500, and numerous other religious works, including sound collections of sermons to aid the clergy, were in demand.[31] Perhaps it is the early-twentieth-century Protestant historian Georg von Below who has most accurately characterized the mixed picture with which late medieval Germany confronts those who seek to understand it:

> We hear of grave defects . . . And again we hear of so many monasteries imbued with seriousness and character, of so many diligent efforts made for the improvement of the parochial clergy, of such eager solicitude for the faithful, of such fruitful fostering of studies within the Church, that we hesitate to assume that vice and loathsomeness ruled absolutely. We shall be compelled to establish the fact that gratifying and deplorable things are to be found side by side; that there are some phenomena which are depressing in the highest degree, but many others which are elevating; and that the relationship which they bore to one another was such as no one may venture to describe in numbers.[32]

Of course, crucial to the health of the entire Church was the state of affairs to be found in the See of Rome itself. As to the doctrinal integrity of the papacy, this remained totally secure as it always has (and as Christ promised it would)—no Renaissance pope ever tried to rewrite Catholic doctrine in order to excuse his own sins or ambitions. Having said this, we must nonetheless admit the deplorable failures of conduct in the lives of the Roman curia, especially the cardinalate, failures and shortcomings that in some instances appeared in the lives of the very men who became the successors of Saint Peter.

The scandals of greed, opulence, lust, and hunger for power in men consecrated to the service of the Church arose, not from some weakness or error in Catholic doctrine, which in fact has always condemned all these things; rather, such evils were the inevitable consequences of human weakness. The Church has never pretended to be a congregation of the sinless, nor could she be in view of Christ's words, ". . . I came not to call the righteous, but sinners" (Mt 9:13). But with regard to the hierarchy of medieval and Renaissance Europe, there were additional circumstances that all too frequently put especially weak men in particularly high ecclesiastical offices. Perhaps the single most important factor was the pressure and influence of earthly princes. From the beginning the Church has had to interact in one

---

[31] Grisar, *Martin Luther,* 133.
[32] Quoted in ibid., 130–31.

way or another with the "temporality", the powers of this world. In the early days of the Church, this interaction was a relatively simple matter, for the temporality refused any cooperation with Christianity and openly persecuted the Church. But with the fall first of Roman paganism and then of Roman political power, the Church, on the one hand, was faced with the opportunity to build a Christian civilization, a society permeated with Christian values, while, on the other, she found herself compelled to fill the chaotic political vacuum following the fall of the Roman Empire.

With the bloody invasions of Barbarian tribes from the north, wreaking social havoc, the Church was forced against her better judgment to enter deeply into the political arena—hence there arose the phenomenon of the papal states, lands governed by the popes. Many positive things came of the popes' direct involvement in government: for example, the papal states often served as a safe haven for the Jewish people fleeing violent anti-Semitic persecutions elsewhere.[33] But the papal states also imposed on the shoulders of the pontiffs many of the responsibilities of temporal rulers, consuming time and energy that could have been better spent in serving the pastoral needs of the Church. It also exposed the popes to the very real danger of becoming excessively worldly and preoccupied with the advancement of their own secular power and prestige or that of their families. By the early 1500s the Church found herself with a Vicar who eventually earned the dubious title of the "Warrior Pope": Julius II. Pope Julius' numerous forays into battle in defense of what he saw to be the interests of the papal states seem a far cry from Pope Saint Gregory the Great's vision of his office as that of a "servant of the servants of God". Even so, there is much to be said in Pope Julius' defense: he never compromised the teaching authority of the Church, and his patronage of the arts brought into being some of the greatest masterpieces ever produced, including Michelangelo's ceiling frescoes in the Sistine Chapel.

By the height of the Middle Ages most of Europe was being governed by Christian emperors and monarchs, who were in a powerful position to apply Christian principles to every sphere of life. Unfortunately, their behavior was often indistinguishable from that of pagan rulers, engaging in senseless territorial wars with their rivals. More-

---

[33] E. H. Flannery, "Anti-Semitism", *New Catholic Encyclopedia* (1967), 1:635–36.

over, keenly aware of the Church's influence over their own people, such kings and princes sought to manipulate the selection of local bishops, desirous of candidates who would in one way or another serve their own political agenda. A vacant bishopric came to be seen as a lucrative prize with which to reward the son of a rich noble and thereby forge and preserve valuable alliances. Obviously, the Church saw the office of a bishop as primarily that of a pastor in the service of his flock, not as a political reward to be handed out by kings; hence intense battles developed between the popes and the emperors over the episcopal selection process. On more than one occasion, when a pope took an especially heroic stand in opposing a secular ruler's attempts to violate the Church's prerogatives in this realm, the ruler retaliated by invading Rome itself, sometimes taking the pope prisoner or even setting up a rival puppet papacy.[34] Ultimately the Church succeeded in retaining her definitive authority over the election of new bishops, but with an eye to peace and reconciliation she found it necessary to forge an uneasy truce with the temporality and tolerated a considerable amount of input from the princes in the episcopal selection process. Sadly such influence from secular rulers led to the appointment and consecration of many an unsuitable or unworthy candidate. Once in office, men of this caliber served to perpetuate and worsen the problem, using their power or influence to bring about the appointment of further unsuitable candidates for important ecclesiastical positions, while opposing efforts at genuine reform. Needless to say, such bishops were scarcely immune from the temptation of exploiting for their own pleasure the Church's need to collect donations.

It is in this context, therefore, that we must see the problems facing the Church when Pope Julius II convened the Fifth Lateran Council on May 3, 1512. The opening speaker fully rose to the occasion. His name was Egidio Antonini, at the time Superior General of the Augustinian Order; he would later come to be known as Cardinal

---

[34] Thus in the years A.D. 1081 to 1084, the German Emperor Henry IV, angered by Pope Saint Gregory VII's valiant stand on the "investiture" issue, attacked Rome so as to depose the Pontiff and set in his place the antipope "Clement III"; nearly thirty years later the next to sit on the German throne, Henry V, usurping the authority of investiture, took Pope Paschal II prisoner (Rev. H. Mann, *The Lives of the Popes in the Middle Ages* [St. Louis: B. Herder; London: Kegan Paul, Trench, Trubner, and Co., 1910] 7:1910, 145–58; 8:51–68).

Egidio (or Giles) of Viterbo.[35] An ardent advocate of reform in religious life, Egidio saw the need for renewal throughout the Church as well, a renewal he wished to see initiated under the leadership of the pope.[36] For Egidio, the teaching authority of the papacy was beyond question, serving as the safeguard of the Church's precious unity; "What else is it to obey God than to follow Peter?", he once commented.[37] His unwavering obedience to the See of Rome, however, did not blind him to the real abuses that had appeared in the lives of recent popes as well as in the ranks of the Roman curia. Papal nepotism—preferment of relatives—he saw as a particular threat, violating the pontiff's charism of undivided fidelity to the one wife and family that his office had bound him to: the Church herself.[38] In view of the tremendous role cardinals have in the administration of the Church at the highest levels, as well as the fact that future popes are usually selected from their ranks, Egidio believed that the selection of candidates for the cardinalate should be free of all human biases and based instead on a candidate's virtues and intellectual gifts.[39] Clerical education was another of his reform priorities, for he considered sacred studies a key means of engendering a deep love for Christ.[40] It was thus with these convictions in his heart that Egidio was most eminently qualified to address with honesty what the Fifth Lateran Council needed most to accomplish:

> . . . [T]o root out vice, to arouse virtue, to catch the foxes who in this season swarm to destroy the holy vineyard, and finally to call fallen religion back to its old purity, its ancient brilliance, its original splendor, and its own sources.[41]

Egidio did not see the source of problems in any teaching of the Church: "Divine things certainly do not need correction", as he reminded the Council.[42] The Church needed a reform, not of her doc-

---

[35] John Olin, *The Catholic Reformation: Savonarola to Ignatius Loyola* (New York: Fordham Univ. Press, 1992), 40–41.

[36] John W. O'Malley, S.J., *Giles of Viterbo on Church and Reform: A Study in Renaissance Thought* (Leiden, Netherlands: E. J. Brill, 1968), 173.

[37] Ibid., 166–67.

[38] Ibid., 170–71.

[39] Ibid., 171.

[40] Ibid., 172.

[41] Olin, *Catholic Reformation,* 44.

[42] Ibid., 45.

trines, but rather of her members, most especially her hierarchy and clergy. It was in making this point that Egidio delivered the most famous line of his address: ". . . [M]en must be changed by religion, not religion by men . . ."[43] Well aware of the resistance from interested parties that would be encountered in attempting substantive reform, he urged the Council to action by painting the alternative of inaction in the darkest and most threatening terms:

> I see, yes, I see that, unless by this Council or by some other means we place a limit on our morals, unless we force our greedy desire for human things, the source of evils, to yield to the love of divine things, it is all over with Christendom, all over with religion, even all over with those very resources which our fathers acquired by their greater service of God, but which we are about to lose because of our neglect.[44]

In May 1514, two years after opening and under the authority of a new pope (Leo X), the Council finally approved a major reform measure that was subsequently issued as a papal bull with the title "Supernae dispositionis arbitrio". It stipulated reforms that were to extend even to the college of cardinals, who were to "abstain from luxury and pomp in their houses, table, furniture, and servants".[45] It likewise addressed in the clearest terms the deepest problem of all: the selection of unworthy candidates for ecclesiastical office:

> Since there is nothing more injurious to the Church of God than the promotion of unworthy prelates to the government of the churches, we ordain and decree that in the future vacant patriarchal, metropolitan, and cathedral churches as well as abbeys be filled in accordance with the requirements of the constitution of Alexander in the Lateran Council [the Third Lateran in 1179], that is, with persons of mature age, good moral character, and the necessary learning, and not at the instance of anyone . . .[46]

It is tragic that the provisions of this papal bull were not actually enforced—it might have made just enough difference to preserve the unity of the Church throughout Europe. Significantly, they were put

---

[43] Ibid.
[44] Ibid., 51.
[45] Ibid., 54, 59.
[46] Ibid., 56.

into force in Spain. There are undoubtedly a number of reasons (even geographical ones) why Spain was largely spared the turmoil of the Protestant Reformation, but one important factor must have been the country's primate in the crucial early years of the sixteenth century, Cardinal Francisco Ximenes de Cisneros (1436–1517), a model of Christian humanist dedication to the cause of ecclesiastical reform. Immediately upon his accession to the primatial see of Toledo in 1495, he communicated his reforming intentions to the canons of the cathedral: they were to abandon their sumptuous private residences and return to a traditional common life, for which he would provide them a suitable dwelling close enough to the cathedral for them to fulfill their liturgical duties there with regularity.[47] Having joined the Observantine Franciscans some eleven years earlier, the new Archbishop of Toledo was determined to continue living a life of personal austerity, setting an example for the clergy of his diocese.[48] In a 1497 diocesan synod, Ximenes laid out a plan of reform, calling for priests to reside in their own parishes and preach the Gospel to their flocks on all Sundays and Holy Days; each Sunday evening the young were to be called together by ringing the church bells, and after recital of the *Salve Regina,* they were to be instructed on the Creed, the Commandments, and the articles of the faith. The clergy were also to cease the iniquity of concubinage and frequently avail themselves of the sacrament of penance.[49] But in addition to such synodal decisions, Ximenes issued a number of his own reforming decrees. He was particularly vigilant in the selection of new candidates for important ecclesiastical offices, choosing only those of proven virtue and humility while rejecting any preferential treatment for those of high rank or birth. Any candidates who attempted avariciously to secure benefices for the sake of gain were summarily denied office.[50] So vigorous were his reforms of his own Franciscan order in Spain that approximately one thousand members of the Franciscan Conventuals, unwilling to

---

[47] Karl J. von Hefele, *The Life and Times of Cardinal Ximenez; or, The Church in Spain in the Time of Ferdinand and Isabella,* 2d ed. (London: Thomas Baker, 1885), 202.

[48] G. Cyprian Alston, "Ximenez de Cisneros, Francisco", *Catholic Encyclopedia* (1907), 15:729–30.

[49] Von Hefele, *Ximenez,* 209–10; John Olin, *Catholic Reform: From Cardinal Ximenes to the Council of Trent: 1495–1563* (New York: Fordham Univ. Press, 1990), 5.

[50] Von Hefele, *Ximenez,* 213.

give up their worldly amenities, left the country and settled in North Africa, where they entirely abandoned their Catholic faith and converted to Islam.[51]

In so many ways Cardinal Ximenes represented genuine Catholic reform at its best. Committed to the cause of Christian humanism, he founded a new university, the College of San Ildefonso at Alcala, which officially opened on July 26, 1508.[52] For his new institution, the Cardinal recruited scholars proficient not only in Latin but in Greek, Hebrew, and Aramaic as well. It was to these men that he entrusted the first great project of the new university—the preparation of a definitive published edition of the Bible that would provide, side by side, the texts of the Scriptures in three of these ancient languages (Latin, Greek, and Hebrew), as taken from surviving manuscripts (with Aramaic sources consulted as well).[53] Ximenes sets out the purpose of this ambitious endeavor in the prologue to what would come to be known as the Complutensian Polyglot Bible. Addressing Pope Leo X, he states:

> . . . [S]ince no version can translate faithfully all the force and naturalness of the original, especially when it treats of the language in which God Himself has spoken . . . we must go back, as St. Jerome and St. Augustine and other ecclesiastical authors warn us to do, to the fountains of holy Scripture to correct the books of the Old Testament according to the Hebrew text, and those of the New Testament according to the Greek text.[54]

Published in six volumes, the Complutensian Polyglot Bible proved to be a greater achievement than even Erasmus' 1516 New Testament; the volume of the Polyglot that contained the New Testament was actually printed two years before Erasmus' edition but was not released for distribution until 1521 (along with the other five volumes).[55]

In addition to his zeal for biblical studies, Cardinal Ximenes took a personal interest in preserving the liturgical heritage of his own nation, saving Spain's ancient Mozarabic Rite from total extinction

---

[51] Ibid., 215–17.

[52] Basil Hall, "The Trilingual College of San Ildefonso and the Making of the Complutensian Polyglot Bible", in *The Church and Academic Learning,* ed. G. J. Cuming, vol. 5 of *Studies in Church History* (Leiden, Netherlands: E. J. Brill, 1969), 121–22.

[53] Ibid., 122–34, 140–43.

[54] Ibid., 126.

[55] Ibid., 144–45.

by publishing a Mozarabic Missal in 1500.[56] Moreover, he concurred with Pope Leo X in recognizing the need to correct the inaccuracy of the Julian Calendar almost seven decades before Pope Gregory XIII officially inaugurated this much-needed scientific adjustment of the calculation of the solar year.[57] But perhaps one of the Cardinal's noblest traits was his adamant opposition to slavery in the New World. Taking action to stop this iniquitous practice, he even drew up a code in an effort to protect the rights of the native peoples.[58]

Unfortunately, early-sixteenth-century Europe did not have enough bishops with the vision and fortitude of Ximenes de Cisneros or Egidio of Viterbo. It was during the final days of the Fifth Lateran Council in March 1517 that Gianfrancesco Pico della Mirandola, the nephew of Thomas More's Pico (and author of the Pico biography More had dutifully translated) and a prominent layman in his own right,[59] made an almost prophetic statement of what the upcoming months would bring. While we cannot say for certain whether he delivered these words in person to the Council or sent them in a letter to Pope Leo, they undoubtedly served as one final warning of the catastrophe that lay in wait for Christianity:

> These diseases and these wounds must be healed by you, Holy Father; otherwise, if you fail to heal these wounds, I fear that God Himself, whose place on earth you take, will not apply a gentle cure, but with fire and sword will cut off those diseased members and destroy them; and I believe that He has already clearly given signs of his future remedy.[60]

---

[56] Known as the *Missale Mixtum*, the complete text of this missal is reprinted in vol. 85 of J.-P. Migne's *Patrologia Latina*.

[57] Von Hefele, *Ximenez*, 446.

[58] Alston, "Ximenez", 731.

[59] Paul Lejay, "Mirandola, Giovanni Francesco Pico della", *Catholic Encyclopedia* (1907), 10:351-52.

[60] Olin, *Catholic Reformation*, 55.

PART TWO

The Battle for the Soul of England

CHAPTER V

Dawn of the "New Men"

... [M]y increasing experience with those men frightens me with the thought of what the world will suffer at their hands.

— Thomas More, Letter to Erasmus, June 1533

The morning of October 31, 1517, found Thomas More miles from home and saddled with a task for which he had no relish. The King had dispatched him some weeks before on a diplomatic mission with Cardinal Wolsey to the northeastern French city of Calais. The intricacies of negotiation with the representatives of the French crown dragged on, and More longed to return to his family. Only six days earlier he had expressed his frustration in a letter to his friend Erasmus:

> Nothing could be more hateful to me than this mission. Here I am, banished to this little seaport, with its barren soil and wretched climate. If I hate legal business at home, where it pays me, you can imagine how it bores me here, where I am losing money over it.[1]

With unusual candor More here reveals his distaste for the legal profession, a distaste undoubtedly engendered by the way it kept him from devoting more of his time to higher pursuits. He knew he could not shun his responsibilities in the world, yet he could not help yearn-

---

[1] Letter of October 25, 1517, as quoted and translated in R. W. Chambers, *Thomas More* (1935; reprint, Ann Arbor, Mich.: Ann Arbor Paperbacks, Univ. of Michigan Press, 1973), 153; for original Latin text, see letter no. 688 in *Opus Epistolarum Des. Erasmi Roterdami,* vol. 3, *1517–1519,* ed. P. S. Allen and H. M. Allen (Oxford: Clarendon Press, 1913), 111.

ing for better things. He would have found some solace on that final morning of October at Mass in one of the churches or chapels of Calais—there is no reason to believe More did not remain faithful to his custom of daily Mass even while abroad. Most likely he would have attended a Mass celebrated by Cardinal Wolsey or by one of the priests in the Cardinal's retinue. The Gospel for the day (according to the English Missal of the time, the *Sarum Missal*) was taken from our Lord's Last Supper discourse, wherein Christ prays for the unity of His Church (Jn 17:11−26):[2]

> Holy Father, keep them in thy name, which thou hast given me, that they may be one, even as we are one. While I was with them, I kept them in thy name, which thou hast given me; I have guarded them, and none of them is lost but the son of perdition . . .

That same day around noon, in the German university town of Wittenberg, a thirty-four-year-old Augustinian monk made his way to the door of the city's castle chapel and posted upon it an invitation to debate a theological question, as was the long-established custom among the scholars of the Middle Ages and Renaissance.[3] On the notice the monk identified himself as "the reverend father Martin Lutther, Master of Arts and Sacred Theology".[4] His disputation consisted of ninety-five theses, among which was the following (no. 66): "The treasures of indulgences are nets with which one now fishes for the wealth of men."[5] The efforts to raise funds for the rebuilding of Saint Peter's Basilica in Rome had unfortunately become, in Germany and elsewhere, an occasion to abuse the consoling ecclesiastical dispensation known as the indulgence—the remission of at least a part of the temporal punishment due to sin granted to penitents by authority of the Church. The papal bull of Pope Julius II granting generous indulgences to those who donated to this massive project was seen by those among the clergy with avaricious ambitions as an

---

[2] Gospel for Vigil of All Saints in *The Sarum Missal in English* (1526 ed.), trans. Frederick Warren, Library of Liturgiology and Ecclesiology for English Readers, vol. 9 (pt. 2) (London: Alexander Moring, 1911), 552.

[3] Walther von Loewenich, *Martin Luther: The Man and His Work* (Minneapolis: Augsburg Publishing House, 1986), 109–10; H. G. Ganss, "Luther, Martin", *Catholic Encyclopedia* (1907), 9:442.

[4] *Career of the Reformer I,* ed. Harold Grimm, vol. 31 of *Luther's Works* (Philadelphia: Muhlenberg Press, 1957), 25.

[5] Ibid., 31.

opportunity to fill their own coffers at the expense of the Church and her people. Thus it was that Martin Luther's ninety-five theses on indulgences were proffered as a response to what was becoming an intolerable disgrace. But as the scholarship of recent decades has increasingly demonstrated, Luther's famed disputation of indulgences was but an outgrowth of a far wider-ranging theological agenda that he had begun to formulate over the preceding two years,[6] an agenda that sought not so much to correct abuses by reforming men, as Egidio of Viterbo had proposed at the Fifth Lateran Council, but rather to change the very doctrinal content of Christianity itself.

In the four years following the posting of his "Disputation" in Wittenberg, Luther wrote a plethora of tracts setting forth his ideas on a wide range of issues. Underlying all of his theology was his well-known proposition that a man is saved by faith alone—that good works are of no avail in that they cannot at all advance one's salvation or sanctification. It is on this basis that Luther rejected all acts of atonement or merit whatsoever: indulgenced prayers, fasting, pilgrimages, religious vows, and so on. He denied that there were seven sacraments as the Church had taught but affirmed rather that there were only two or three: baptism, the Eucharist, and perhaps penance (he was irresolute as to the latter).[7] Regarding the Eucharist, he declared that the Mass was not a sacrifice and hence Masses could not be *offered* to obtain the release of souls from Purgatory.[8] He denied the doctrine of transubstantiation, that is, the teaching that at the Consecration the substances of bread and wine are totally changed into the real Body and Blood of Christ, which retain the "accidents", that is, external forms (appearances), of bread and wine. Instead, he proposed that while the real Body and Blood of Christ did become present, the substances and not merely the "accidents" of bread and wine also remained after Consecration.[9] Furthermore, Luther denied that the eucharistic discourse of our Lord in the sixth chapter of the Gospel of Saint John was actually about the Eucharist.[10]

---

[6] Fr. Hartmann Grisar, S.J., *Martin Luther: His Life and Work* (1930; reprint, Westminster, Md.: Newman Press, 1961), 70–79, 89.

[7] *Babylonian Captivity of the Church,* in *Word and Sacrament II,* ed. Abdel R. Wentz, vol. 36 of *Luther's Works* (Philadelphia: Muhlenberg Press, 1959), 18, 124.

[8] Ibid., 35–36, 48, 54, 55.

[9] Ibid., 28–29.

[10] Ibid., 19.

With only two or three sacraments and no sacramentals, Luther needed a tangible unifying point of reference for his new creed. He soon found it in the concept of *sola scriptura*—the belief that the *Bible* is the *one and only* sure source of Christian doctrine, superseding any ecclesiastical authority. Luther appears to have first espoused the idea of *sola scriptura* during an inquest conducted by the Dominican cardinal Tommasso di Vio Gaetano (known as "Cardinal Cajetan")[11] in October 1518.[12] In his own published account of the meeting with the Cardinal, Luther declared that "the pope is not above, but under the word of God."[13]

If according to Luther the pope cannot pass definitive judgment on the interpretation of Scripture (as he bluntly asserts in his 1520 tract *To the Christian Nobility*),[14] with whom does such judgment reside? It belongs to all baptized Christians alike, he answers, even a "humble miller's maid, nay, . . . a child of nine if it has the faith", as stated in one of three sermons he preached in Erfurt, Germany, on October 21 and 22, 1522.[15] As Luther further declares in these Erfurt sermons, "You have been baptized and endowed with the true faith, therefore you are spiritual and able to judge of all things by the word of the Evangel . . . My faith is here a judge and may say: This doctrine is true, but that is false and evil. And the Pope and all his crew, nay, all men on earth, must submit to that decision . . ."[16] Earlier Luther had spelled out his exaltation of the private judgment of the baptized in his 1520 work *The Babylonian Captivity of the Church*:

> This glorious liberty of ours and this understanding of baptism have been taken captive in our day, and to whom can we give the blame except the Roman pontiff with his despotism? . . . he seeks only to oppress us with his decrees and laws, and to ensnare us as captives to his tyrannical power. By what right, I ask you, does the pope impose his laws upon us . . . ? Who gave him power to deprive us of this liberty

---

[11] O. Cameron, *The European Reformation* (Oxford: Clarendon Press, 1991), 101.

[12] Fr. Hartmann Grisar, S.J., *Luther*, vol. 4 (St. Louis, Mo.: B. Herder; London: Kegan Paul, Trench, Trubner, and Co., 1915), 388–89.

[13] "Proceedings at Augsburg, 1518", in *Career of the Reformer I*, 266–67.

[14] *The Christian in Society I*, ed. James Atkinson, vol. 44 of *Luther's Works* (Philadelphia: Fortress Press, 1966), 133–36.

[15] Grisar, *Luther*, 4:389.

[16] Ibid., vol. 2 (1913), 346.

of ours, granted to us in baptism? . . . [T]he church is smothered with
endless laws concerning works and ceremonies . . .

Therefore I say: Neither pope nor bishop nor any other man has the
right to impose a single syllable of law upon a Christian man without
his consent; if he does, it is done in the spirit of tyranny . . .

I lift my voice simply on behalf of liberty and conscience, and I con-
fidently cry: No law, whether of men or of angels, may rightfully be
imposed upon Christians without their consent, for we are free of all
laws.[17]

Luther's rejection of holy orders as a sacrament posed a problem
as to who constituted a valid minister for consecrating the Eucharist.
Luther offers his answer to this in his 1520 tract *To the Christian Nobility*, in which he announces that "whoever comes out of the water of
baptism can boast that he is already a consecrated priest, bishop, and
pope", although he does acknowledge that it would not be "seemly"
for an individual to exercise this priestly ministry without first being
called to do so by the community of believers.[18] He defines a priest
as "nothing else but an officeholder", devoid of any indelible or distinguishing sacramental mark other than that of baptism and who can
be appointed or deposed[19] at the will of the community:

. . . [W]hen a bishop consecrates [a priest] it is nothing else than that
in the place and stead of the whole community, all of whom have like
power, he takes a person and charges him to exercise this power on
behalf of the others . . . To put it still more clearly: suppose a group of
earnest Christian laymen were taken prisoner and set down in a desert
without an episcopally ordained priest among them. And suppose they
were to come to a common mind there and then in the desert and elect
one of their number, whether he were married or not, and charge him
to baptize, say mass, pronounce absolution, and preach the gospel. Such
a man would be as truly a priest as though he had been ordained by all
the bishops and popes in the world.[20]

Many had been scandalized by the infidelity of clergymen and religious who had broken their vows of celibacy—this was undoubtedly
one of the more odious forms of ecclesiastical misconduct sapping

---

[17] *Word and Sacrament II*, 70, 72.
[18] *Christian in Society I*, 129.
[19] Ibid.
[20] Ibid., 128.

the life of the Church in the early sixteenth century. Yet instead of seeking a return to the charism of chastity, Luther chose instead to sanction and codify its abrogation, declaring celibacy impossible to observe and calling for an end to the counsel of celibacy with his 1521 treatise *On Monastic Vows*.[21] He would later make the point further by taking a nun for his wife in 1525.[22]

Luther's concept of man as hopelessly depraved following Adam's fall in Eden, incapable of abstaining from sin and saved only by faith,[23] contained certain unavoidable implications regarding morality. For if a man's faith is the *sole* criterion by which he is to be judged by God, then logically he may *do* whatsoever he pleases. Indeed, such a libertine ethic might very well be inferred from the following passage appearing in one of Luther's early works:

> To sum up the whole argument, when it comes to the mitigation of laws and their right interpretation the only safe guide is love. Whatever is contrary to love can in no circumstances be imposed, nor can any law be interpreted to work against love, for no case of hardship or necessity works against love. To put it another way, whatever is not against love is a matter of free choice, permissible and sanctioned, especially in cases of necessity . . . nothing that is contrary to love, and nothing more than love, is or can be binding.[24]

Although Luther vigorously denied that his theology granted a license to sin, others saw such a license as an inevitable derivative of his teachings.[25] It is therefore not surprising that as Luther's ideas spread across the German countryside considerable social unrest quickly ensued. The reformer's propensity for tirades of ungovernable verbal abuse heaped upon his enemies also may have played a role in the increasingly explosive atmosphere. His calls for religious liberty among Christians stood in striking contrast with his intolerance of any who disagreed with him, whether it was the Church authorities whose teachings he rejected or the dissenters who, following in his footsteps, staked out theological positions even more radical than his own. Hence against the pope and his adherents, Luther pronounces

---

[21] Ganss, "Luther", 447–48.

[22] Ibid., 450.

[23] Ibid., 445.

[24] *The Judgement of Martin Luther on Monastic Vows* (1521), in *Christian in Society I*, 393.

[25] Grisar, *Martin Luther*, 266–68, 304.

an anathema in his *Babylonian Captivity* only a few lines after those on the freedom of the baptized Christian quoted earlier, declaring that:

> Unless they will abolish their laws and ordinances, and restore to Christ's churches their liberty and have it taught among them, they are guilty of all the souls that perish under this miserable captivity, and the papacy is truly the kingdom of Babylon and of the very Antichrist.[26]

Inflamed *partially* by Luther's teachings and rhetoric, but borne along also by legitimate grievances against the upper classes, the peasants of Germany rose up in an extraordinarily violent and anarchic revolt from 1524 to 1525 against their wealthy overlords, to which Luther responded by writing another tract—*Against the Murderous and Rapacious Hordes of the Peasants*—which called upon the German nobility to crush the rebellion.[27] The princes heeded his call, and in the enormous bloodshed that followed over one hundred thousand perished.[28]

Around Luther there gathered an inner circle of disciples who quickly became the cutting edge of the Reformation, advancing positions considerably more radical than those of their master yet consonant with the overriding ethos of dissent first unleashed by him. Most notable among these was Andreas Bodenstein von Karlstadt, dean of Wittenberg's university theological faculty,[29] who as early as May 1521 denounced the reservation of the Blessed Sacrament outside of Mass.[30] In July 1521 he resurrected the eighth-century Eastern heresy of iconoclasm by calling for the removal of all pictures and statues from the churches.[31] On October 9 of the same year, all but one of the forty monks of Wittenberg's Augustinian monastery (Luther's own monastery) announced their resolve to cease saying private Masses; included in this number was Gabriel Zwilling, who labeled the Mass a "devilish" institution.[32] In November twenty-eight

---

[26] *Word and Sacrament II*, 72.

[27] Grisar, *Martin Luther*, 278–85.

[28] Ganss, "Luther", 450.

[29] Clarence Miller, ed., introduction to *The Answer to a Poisoned Book*, vol. 11 of *Complete Works of St. Thomas More* (New Haven: Yale Univ. Press, 1985), xx–xxi. Hereafter cited as *CW* 11.

[30] Ganss, "Luther", 448.

[31] Ibid.

[32] Ibid.

of the Augustinians deserted their monastery;[33] Karlstadt, meanwhile, had stopped celebrating Mass.[34] By December Luther's men had excited the populace of Wittenberg to the boiling point; on December 3, several bands of students and townspeople stormed the parish church, where they chased the priests from the altar and took away the missals. The following day the rioters disrupted Mass at the Franciscan monastery, throwing stones through the cloister windows and demolishing the altar.[35] On Christmas morning Karlstadt finally reentered the sanctuary, but most definitely on his own terms. Celebrating what he termed an "evangelical Mass", and officiating without vestments, he told the people in his homily that they need no longer concern themselves with fasting before Communion or with being free of serious sin in order to receive the sacrament, for "faith alone makes us holy and righteous."[36] Continuing with the Mass, he altered the words of the liturgy so as to remove all references to the Eucharist as a sacrifice and refrained from elevating the Host at the Consecration. Communion followed, under both species (which was at that time not permitted), with each communicant taking the Host and chalice into his own hands. So nervous was one layman about participating in these prohibited practices that he dropped the Host and was too frightened to pick it up.[37] The next day Karlstadt flaunted his repudiation of clerical celibacy by celebrating his engagement to the daughter of a nobleman (the wedding took place three and a half weeks later).[38] Meanwhile more dissenters arrived in Wittenberg—the so-called "Zwickau Prophets"—who advocated among other things the elimination of infant baptism.[39] On January 11 (1522), the Augustinians, led by Gabriel Zwilling, demolished all but one of the altars in their monastery chapel and tore down all the religious images, burning them along with the sacramental holy oils.[40]

---

[33] Ibid.

[34] Ronald Sider, *Andreas Bodenstein von Karlstadt: The Development of His Thought, 1517–1525* (Leiden, Netherlands: E. J. Brill, 1974), 158.

[35] Ibid. 157.

[36] Ibid., 158, 159–60.

[37] Ibid., 160.

[38] Ibid., 160–61.

[39] Ibid., 161.

[40] Mark Edwards, Jr., *Luther and the False Brethren* (Stanford, Calif.: Stanford Univ. Press, 1975), 10; James Preus, *Carlstadt's Ordinaciones and Luther's Liberty: A Study of the Wittenberg*

By March 1522, Karlstadt had fallen into Luther's disfavor and eventually withdrew from Wittenberg,[41] but this did not deter him from pushing the edge of "reform" even farther. Perhaps in 1523, but certainly by late 1524, the renegade Lutheran disciple began advocating a completely symbolic understanding of the Eucharist, thus rejecting the doctrine of the Real Presence of the actual Body and Blood of Christ in the sacrament.[42] Luther vehemently opposed this radical concept, which as early as 1520 had been proposed to him in a letter from an elderly Dutch lawyer named Cornelius Hoen.[43] But by the early 1520s an entirely separate beachhead of dissent had begun developing in Switzerland around the figure of Ulrich Zwingli, a priest of Zurich who had read Hoen's letter to Luther and, unlike Luther, liked what he saw.[44] Although he had already begun arousing controversy with certain comments he had made about the papacy in his sermons, it was not until Lent of 1522 that Zwingli openly dissented from Church teaching by publishing a tract attacking the Church's laws of fasting and abstinence, thus siding with a group of Zurich citizens who had publicly defied the Church by eating meat on Ash Wednesday.[45] A familiar pattern of successive demands and defiances ensued. That same year Zwingli and ten other clerics petitioned the bishop of Constance (Switzerland) for an end to clerical celibacy, arguing that since he (Zwingli) and other clerics had already created scandal by their breaches of the vow of chastity, a dispensation to marry would supposedly remove their disgrace. Needless to say, the bishop did not comply with their request;[46] but they refused to accept No for an answer, and over the next two years illicit marriages of priests and nuns in Zurich became increasingly common (Zwingli himself married in 1524).[47]

By January 1523, Zwingli had adopted a eucharistic theology not

---

Movement, 1521–1522, Harvard Theological Studies, 26 (Cambridge, Mass.: Harvard Univ. Press; London: Oxford Univ. Press, 1974), 10; Ganss, "Luther", 448.

[41] Preus, *Wittenberg Movement*, 11.

[42] Introduction, *CW* 11:xxii (plus n).

[43] Ibid., xx.

[44] Ibid., xxiii.

[45] Fr. Philip Hughes, *A Popular History of the Reformation* (Garden City, N.Y.: Hanover House, 1957), 150; Wilhelm Meyer, "Zwingli, Ulrich", *Catholic Encyclopedia* (1907), 15:773.

[46] Meyer, "Zwingli", 773; George R. Potter, *Zwingli* (Cambridge: Cambridge Univ. Press, 1976), 79–81.

[47] Meyer, "Zwingli", 773; Hughes, *Popular History*, 151.

unlike Luther's in that he too rejected the sacrificial nature of the Mass and sought for a change in the wording of the eucharistic liturgy.[48] Soon thereafter (by June of the same year) he became opposed to reservation of the Blessed Sacrament outside of Mass.[49] Zwingli gradually shifted his views even farther from the eucharistic doctrines of the Church, so that by the end of 1524 he was openly espousing the purely symbolic conception of the sacrament already annunciated by Karlstadt but opposed by Luther.[50] In a move reminiscent of Karlstadt's reformed Christmas Mass, Zwingli chose Holy Thursday of 1525 as the day to debut his own free-lanced liturgy. Following the sermon, unleavened bread and wine were placed on a table in the nave of the church, after which a minister read one of the Scripture narratives of the institution of the Eucharist (that given in 1 Corinthians 11). Then, as all remained seated and while a minister read from the Last Supper discourse in the Gospel of Saint John (beginning with John 13), the bread was taken up and carried on wooden platters to each participant, who in turn would break off for himself a morsel and consume it. The wine was similarly administered.[51] Most certainly this ritual was not a Mass; there was no Consecration, and the entire Roman Canon was eliminated.

As in Wittenberg, so too in Switzerland did the specter of iconoclasm rear its head. In June 1520, a farmer of Toggenburg vandalized an image of the Crucifixion—an early indication of things to come.[52] Under the influence of sermons given by Zwingli and others that decried the veneration of religious images as idol worship, acts of violence and wanton destruction increased. Thus in September 1523, a panel depiction of the *Pieta* was defaced in a Zurich church, while at another in nearby Stadelhoffen three men vented their fury upon a large crucifix.[53] Less than a year later (June 1524), the government council of Zurich decided to divest the city of its so-called "idols"; under the personal supervision of Zwingli and two of his colleagues,

---

[48] Introduction, *CW* 11:xxiii; Potter, *Zwingli*, 149–50.

[49] Potter, *Zwingli*, 150–51 n, 158.

[50] Introduction, *CW* 11:xxiii; Potter, *Zwingli*, 156–58.

[51] Hughes, *Popular History*, 152–53; R. C. D. Jasper and G. J. Cuming, eds., *Prayers of the Eucharist: Early and Reformed* (London: Collins Publishers, 1975), 120–21.

[52] Carlos Eire, *War against the Idols: The Reformation of Worship from Erasmus to Calvin* (Cambridge: Cambridge Univ. Press, 1986), 79.

[53] Ibid., 79–81.

each church was stripped of all statues, paintings, altar decorations, and votive lamps. Even the walls were whitewashed, leaving the interiors stark and barren.[54] Chalices and monstrances were melted down for the minting of coins.[55]

We cannot say for certain precisely when Thomas More first heard of the burgeoning theological unrest in Germany, but it is known that in early March 1518, little more than four months after Luther posted his ninety-five theses in Wittenberg, Erasmus sent to More without comment a copy of the touted "Disputation".[56] By the end of the year some of Luther's other works had begun arriving on English soil, albeit in limited quantities.[57] It does not appear to have taken More terribly long to recognize the implications of the Lutheran agenda, for already in his "Letter to a Monk" dating from 1519 or 1520, he refers to the writings of Luther as "schismatic" and "heretical".[58] But in this same letter More likewise reveals his determination to fight those who would try to discredit the humanist movement by conflating its goals with those of Luther and his followers. He vigorously refutes the unnamed monk's criticisms of Erasmus' new Latin translation of the Greek text of the New Testament by pointing out that the Holy Father himself has given his approval to Erasmus' work in this regard.[59] Meanwhile sales of Luther's books in England grew apace. At Cambridge University the new ideas imported from Wittenberg were to draw together a circle of academics who in the early 1520s began meeting regularly for discussion at the "White Horse Inn".[60] Among those at Cambridge during this period was a young Scripture scholar named William Tyndale (1494?–1536),[61] the priest who was so soon to prove the most important theological figure in the

---

[54] Ibid., 82–83.

[55] Meyer, "Zwingli", 773.

[56] Mentioned in letter no. 785, from Erasmus to More, March 5, 1518, in Allen and Allen, *Opus Epistolarum*, 3:239.

[57] Carl S. Meyer, "Henry VIII Burns Luther's Books, 12 May 1521", *Journal of Ecclesiastical History* 9 (1958): 173.

[58] *In Defense of Humanism: Letters to Dorp, Oxford, Lee, and a Monk,* ed. Daniel Kinney, vol. 15 of *Complete Works of St. Thomas More* (New Haven: Yale Univ. Press, 1986), 263.

[59] Ibid., 201, 213–15, 227–59, 271.

[60] Fr. Philip Hughes, "*The King's Proceedings*", vol. 1 of *The Reformation in England* (New York: Macmillan Co., 1951), 133.

[61] James E. McGoldrick, *Luther's English Connection: The Reformation Thought of Robert Barnes and William Tyndale* (Milwaukee: Northwestern Publishing House, 1979), 36.

disintegration of England's one-thousand-year patrimony of Catholicism.

Near the end of January 1521, King Henry's ambassador to the German emperor Charles V, Archdeacon Cuthbert Tunstall, sent word across the Channel to Cardinal Wolsey that Luther—excommunicated that same month[62]—had published yet another controversial work, *The Babylonian Captivity of the Church.*[63] The arrival of the *Babylonian Captivity* in England subsequently elicited what is assuredly (and ironically) the single greatest piece of Catholic apologetical writing ever to issue from the pen of a reigning monarch: Henry VIII's *Defense of the Seven Sacraments (Assertio Septem Sacramentorum).* We know that already in April 1521 Henry had begun reading Luther's book. By July he had formulated and completed a comprehensive rebuttal of the *Babylonian Captivity,* a copy of which he sent to Pope Leo X.[64] Two months earlier (May 21) he explained in a letter to the Pontiff his reasons for writing *The Defense of the Seven Sacraments:*

> Whereas we believe that no duty is more incumbent on a Catholic sovereign than to preserve and increase the Christian faith and religion and the proofs thereof, and to transmit them preserved thus inviolate to posterity, by his example in preventing them from being destroyed by any assailant of the faith or in any wise impaired, so when we learned that the pest of Martin Luther's heresy had appeared in Germany and was raging everywhere, without let or hindrance, to such an extent that many, infected with its poison, were falling away, especially those whose furious hatred rather than their zeal for Christian truth had prepared them to believe all its subtleties and lies, we were so deeply grieved at this heinous crime . . . that we bent all our thoughts and energies on uprooting in every possible way, this cockle, this heresy from the Lord's flock . . . we determined to show by our own writings our attitude towards Luther and our opinion of his vile books; to manifest more openly to all the world that we shall ever defend and uphold, not only by force of arms but by the resources of our intelligence and our services as a Christian, the Holy Roman Church.[65]

---

[62] Scott Hendrix, *Luther and the Papacy: Stages in a Reformation Conflict* (Philadelphia: Fortress Press, 1981), 121, 123.

[63] Hughes, "*King's Proceedings*", 146–47.

[64] Ibid., 147.

[65] Letter of May 21, 1521, in *Assertio Septem Sacramentorum, or Defence of the Seven Sacraments,* ed. Fr. Louis O'Donovan, S.T.L. (New York: Benziger Brothers, 1908), 152–54.

Henry also states in the above letter that he had given the "learned and scholarly men" of his kingdom the task of examining Luther's works prior to condemning them. Their judgment was made manifest but a few days earlier (May 12), when in the presence of Cardinal Wolsey and a large assemblage of England's bishops, together with a considerable number of the laity, a pile of Lutheran books was consigned to the flames in the churchyard of London's Saint Paul Cathedral.[66] On this occasion, one of Thomas More's fellow humanists, the bishop of Rochester, John Fisher, gave a sermon that opened England's verbal challenge to the ever-widening encroachments of the continental reformers. Speaking with theological precision combined with metaphors borrowed from nature, Fisher addressed all the predominant motifs of Luther's new Christianity, refuting his theory of justification by faith alone as well as his attacks upon the authority of the papacy, the councils, the Church Fathers, and the Church's body of tradition. Yet rather than confining himself to a denial of Luther's doctrines, Fisher took a positive approach by explaining to the people the Church's teachings on these subjects.[67]

It was in the late spring of 1522, after returning to Wittenberg, that Luther first saw a copy of Henry's *Assertio Septem Sacramentorum*.[68] The English monarch's literary missive in defense of the Church was proving to be quite popular;[69] before the end of June 1522 a German translation of his work was in print.[70] On August 1, Luther's answer appeared—the *German Response to the Book of King Henry*[71]—which, in contrast to Henry's reasoned argumentation, was marred by copious vulgar *ad hominem* diatribes; one of the milder passages will suffice to illustrate this:

> . . . He condemns me as writing contradictory statements and as being in contradiction with myself. Here the miserable scribbler, lacking proper substance, has demonstrated with poisonous words how well he

[66] Meyer, "Henry VIII", 185–86.

[67] Fr. Edward Surtz, S.J., *The Works and Days of John Fisher* (Cambridge, Mass.: Harvard Univ. Press, 1967), 302–7.

[68] John M. Headley, ed., introduction, *Responsio ad Lutherum*, vol. 5 of *Complete Works of St. Thomas More,* trans. Sr. Scholastica Mandeville (New Haven: Yale Univ. Press, 1969), 722. Hereafter cited as *CW* 5.

[69] Hughes, "*King's Proceedings*", 147.

[70] Hendrix, *Luther and the Papacy,* 122.

[71] Ibid.

can manage to soil a lot of paper, a truly royal deed! . . . The boasting
king simply performs a trick of rhetorics: Luther is inconsistent—who,
therefore, can believe him? That is quite enough for the new defender
of the church, for this deity newly arrived in England.[72]

That such language and worse should be addressed to a head of state
constituted an affront to the entire English nation. There was a need
to respond firmly and decisively to this assault, yet with good reason
was it deemed inappropriate to dignify the *German Response* with a
direct answer from the King himself. Another would have to enter the
fray, and the man chosen for this unenviable task was Thomas More,
recently knighted and at the time a member of the King's Privy Council.[73] In one sense More's years of devotion to ecclesiastical studies
had finally come to fruition, for he was now given the opportunity
to use his humanist talents to defend the very beliefs that had so
absorbed his heart and mind. But in another sense this was a most
unfortunate way for him to have to begin his apostolate of Catholic
apologetical writing, for it seems that in addition to providing cogent
theological arguments More was also expected to redeem the King's
honor by responding somewhat in kind to Luther's low-minded mud-
slinging. Nevertheless, Thomas More's first major work of apologet-
ics, the *Responsio ad Lutherum* (*Response to Luther*)—published under
the pseudonym "William Ross" in 1523[74]—is replete with many a
brilliant passage truly worthy of the lofty soul who formulated them
and indicative of the even more extraordinary contributions he was
to make in years to come.

Shortly after issuing his vituperative answer to Henry's *Assertio
Septem Sacramentorum,* Luther brought to completion one of his most
significant projects, a German translation of the New Testament. Published in September 1522,[75] the Lutheran New Testament made su-

---

[72] Quoted in Erwin Doernberg, *Henry VIII and Luther: An Account of Their Personal Relations* (Stanford, Calif.: Stanford Univ. Press, 1961), 29.

[73] More became a member of the Privy Council in 1517; he was knighted in 1521 (E. E.
Reynolds, *The Field Is Won: The Life and Death of Saint Thomas More* [Milwaukee: Bruce
Publishing Co., 1968], 127, 145).

[74] The *Responsio* appeared in two editions during 1523, the first of which was printed under
a different pseudonym ("Ferdinand Barvellus"); it was withdrawn from circulation in order
to make way for an expanded and revised version—that with the pseudonym William Ross
(Headley, introduction, *CW* 5:832–34).

[75] Hendrix, *Luther and the Papacy,* 122.

perb use of the vernacular tongue and from a literary standpoint was a remarkable achievement.[76] The work was marred, however, by ideologically slanted translations of key passages.[77] Luther also provided prefaces that cast the Scriptures in the light of his own interpretations.[78] Several of the illustrations accompanying the text of the Book of Revelation conveyed a bluntly antipapal message, with the Beast and the Babylonian Whore both portrayed wearing the Roman tiara on their heads.[79] Hence, unlike the numerous pre-Reformation German translations of the Bible that had appeared in the fifteenth and early sixteenth centuries,[80] Luther's New Testament met with considerable opposition, for it was seen as little more than a pretext for disseminating the excommunicated monk's ideas. In England the German reformer's New Testament was eagerly read and pondered over by a young man named William Roper, whose enthusiasm for Luther knew no bounds. So smitten was he with the mystique of Lutheran doctrine (and so convinced was he of his own brilliance) that he longed to propagandize for the new ideas in every way he could.[81] In acting thus he greatly distressed his father-in-law—Thomas More —who attempted to change the mind of the headstrong lad, the husband of his beloved daughter Margaret, but to no avail. When debate proved fruitless, More had recourse to stronger measures, as he confided to Margaret:

> Meg, I have borne a long time with thy husband; I have reasoned and argued with him in those points of religion, and still given to him my poor fatherly counsel, but I perceive none of all this able to call him home, and therefore, Meg, I will no longer argue and dispute with him, but will clean give him over, and get me another while to God and pray for him.[82]

Under the gentle but irresistible influence of More's prayers, Roper soon abandoned the camp of the dissenters and became once again

---

[76] Ganss, "Luther", 447.

[77] Ibid.

[78] Von Loewenich, *Martin Luther*, 210–11.

[79] Andre Chastel, *The Sack of Rome, 1527*, Bollingen Series 35, no. 26 (Princeton, N.J.: Princeton Univ. Press, 1983), 72.

[80] Ganss, "Luther", 447.

[81] Nicholas Harpsfield, *The Life and Death of Sir Thomas More*, in *Lives of Saint Thomas More* (William Roper and Nicholas Harpsfield), ed. E. E. Reynolds, Everyman's Library, no. 19 (London: J. M. Dent and Sons, 1963), 100–102.

[82] Ibid., 102.

a faithful son of the Church,[83] in later years providing future generations with what is one of the most valuable and touching biographies of his illustrious father-in-law. This episode of Roper's dabbling in Lutheran ideology took place in the early 1520s,[84] shortly before or during the time More was called upon to write his *Responsio ad Lutherum;* thus the battle against heresy had become for him a personal battle as well. One can see this reflected in the sense of urgency and conviction with which More expresses himself in his apologetical writings; he had experienced firsthand the divisiveness engendered by theological dissenters and was determined to stand his ground against them.

In 1524 Luther was joined at Wittenberg by a new adherent from England—William Tyndale. As mentioned earlier, Tyndale had been among those at Cambridge University who had grown sympathetic to the Lutheran agenda. Desirous to produce a new English translation of the Bible, he had come to Germany with this purpose in mind after failing to obtain authorization for his project in his own country.[85] Although not yet a Lutheran when he first arrived in Wittenberg, the young English cleric was soon won over by the charismatic rebel monk and imbibed many of his ideas.[86] By July 1525, Tyndale had completed an English translation of the New Testament; he sought to have his texts published in Cologne, but the work was disrupted when the city's Catholic authorities had been apprised of what was going on. Thus the Cologne edition of Tyndale's New Testament contained only two of the four Gospels—those of Saint Matthew and Saint Mark. These, however, were plentifully annotated with English translations of Luther's biblical prologues and with ninety glosses that, like those of Luther, interpreted the Scriptures as the translator saw fit.[87] That Tyndale was intending even at this early juncture not simply to give the people the Bible in their own tongue but to change

---

[83] Ibid., 102–3.

[84] According to Harpsfield, this phase of Roper's life occurred around the time of his marriage to Margaret (ibid., 100); their marriage took place in July 1521 (Chambers, *More,* 182).

[85] Louis Schuster, "Thomas More's Polemical Career", in *The Confutation of Tyndale's Answer,* ed. Louis Schuster et al., vol. 8 of *Complete Works of St. Thomas More* (New Haven: Yale Univ. Press, 1973), 1158–59. Hereafter cited as *CW* 8.

[86] Ibid., 1159.

[87] Hughes, *"King's Proceedings",* 144–45.

Christian theology along Lutheran lines is quite evident in passages such as the following from the Cologne New Testament's opening prologue:

> The fall of Adam hath made us heirs of the vengeance and wrath of God, and heirs of eternal damnation; and hath brought us into captivity and bondage under the devil. And the devil is our lord, and our ruler, our head, our governor, our prince, yea, and our god. And our will is locked and knit faster unto the will of the devil, than could an hundred thousand chains bind a man unto a post. Unto the devil's will consent we with all our hearts, with all our minds, with all our might, power, strength, will and lusts . . .[88]

Having fled from Cologne with the incomplete copies of his work, Tyndale journeyed to Worms, where by March 1526 he had successfully published a complete edition of the New Testament, although this time without the glosses and prologues (it did, however, include an epilogue). Copies of the glossed Cologne edition reached England first, followed thereafter by six thousand copies of the Worms edition.[89] Like Luther's German Bible, Tyndale's New Testament was a notable literary achievement; in fact much of the text of the famous seventeenth-century King James Bible is identical to the sixteenth-century Tyndale translation.[90] Yet as with Luther, so too in the case of Tyndale, there were also some deliberate alterations of vocabulary that were intended to convey a meaning consonant with the English cleric's own quasi-Lutheran theology.[91] The Church in England recognized these elements in the Tyndale New Testament and sought to halt its dissemination in the country.[92] It is to be regretted that the bishops had not produced an authorized English translation of their own that would undoubtedly have undermined the reformer's allegations that in opposing his New Testament the hierarchy was re-

---

[88] Tyndale, *A Pathway into the Holy Scripture* (as collated with 1525 Cologne Prologue— quoted passage appears identically in the 1525 Prologue and the later *Pathway* version), in William Tyndale, *Doctrinal Treatises and Introductions to Different Portions of the Holy Scriptures,* ed. Rev. Henry Walter, Parker Society, vol. 42 (1848; reprint, New York: Johnson Reprint Corp., 1968), 17.

[89] Schuster, *CW* 8:1160; W. E. Campbell, *Erasmus, Tyndale and More* (Milwaukee: Bruce Publishing Co., 1950), 108–9; Hughes, *"King's Proceedings"*, 144–45.

[90] Hughes, *"King's Proceedings"*, 146.

[91] Ibid., 144.

[92] Ibid., 148.

ally trying to prevent the people from reading the Bible (as Tyndale charges in the preface to his 1530 translation of the Pentateuch).[93] There had been a number of English translations of the Scriptures during the Middle Ages, but the lack of a widely available, approved edition in the 1520s was exploited to the hilt by the Tyndale faction.

Despite the reformers' talk of a baptized Christian's ability to interpret the Bible without a hierarchy, Tyndale, like Luther, did not leave the people to judge Scripture for themselves but rather made every effort to propagate his own interpretations or those of his German mentor. Hence within months of the arrival in England of his New Testament, Tyndale published under separate cover *A Prologue upon the Epistle of St. Paul to the Romans* (1526), which, combining a direct translation of Luther's 1522 prologue to Romans with Tyndale's own observations, elaborates upon (among other things) the Lutheran doctrines of man's total depravity following the fall of Adam and predestination,[94] as in the following passage:

> In the ninth, tenth, and eleventh chapters he [Saint Paul] treateth of God's predestination; whence it springeth altogether; whether we shall believe or not believe; be loosed from sin, or not be loosed. By which predestination our justifying and salvation are clean taken out of our hands, and put in the hands of God only . . . thou hast of thyself no strength but to sin . . . thou canst never meddle with the sentence of predestination without thine own harm, and without secret wrath and grudging inwardly against God . . .[95]

While these events regarding Tyndale and his New Testament were transpiring, Thomas More was growing increasingly anxious over the spread of Luther's ideas across England as well as the Continent. In a letter dated December 18, 1526, More remonstrates with his old friend Erasmus for being slow in the completion of a book refuting Luther. He expresses concern that Erasmus must be ill (though obviously suspecting otherwise), for he cannot bring himself to believe that he would delay such a vital task for any other reason. But then More becomes more frank, suggesting that Erasmus' hesitation

---

[93] *William Tyndale's Five Books of Moses, called the Pentateuch, being a Verbatim Reprint of the Edition of M.CCCCC.XXX,* ed. Rev. J. I. Mombert (New York: Anson D. F. Randolph and Co., 1884), preface, 2–3.

[94] Schuster, *CW* 8:1166–68.

[95] Text of *A Prologue upon the Epistle of St. Paul to the Romans,* in G. E. Duffield, *The Work of William Tyndale* (Philadelphia: Fortress Press, 1965), 140–41.

is perhaps due to the fear of physical violence from the Lutheran partisans. Yet delay in answering the dissenters is costly and serves only to increase their numbers. Exhorting his friend to overcome any such fears, he summons him to action, whatever the risk:

> But if, according to some reports, the delay is due to the fact that you have been terrorized, and have lost all interest in the work, and have no courage to go on with it, then I am thoroughly bewildered and unable to restrain my grief. You have endured, dearest Erasmus, many, many struggles and perils and Herculean labors; you have spent all the best years of your life on exhausting work, through sleepless nights, for the profit of all the world; and God forbid that now you should so unhappily become enamored of your declining years as to be willing to abandon the cause of God rather than lose a decision.
>
> . . . [T]he whole world is waiting with expectation to receive from you, because you have given extraordinary proof of a heart that is valiant and trusting in God. It is impossible for me to doubt that you will continue bravely to exhibit such strength of spirit right up to your dying breath, even if there were a disastrous catastrophe.[96]

Earlier this same year More had completed his second apologetical piece, the *Letter to Bugenhagen*. As the title indicates, it was addressed to Johannes Bugenhagen, one of Luther's two closest aides (the other being Philipp Melanchthon). Ordained a priest in 1509, Bugenhagen joined the dissenters in Wittenberg in 1521 after having read Luther's *Babylonian Captivity* and his *Freedom of a Christian;* a year later he broke his vow of celibacy by marrying. Unlike Karlstadt, Bugenhagen contented himself with remaining in the shadow of his master, Luther, assisting and advising him in such projects as the translation of the Bible.[97] Nevertheless, he did make something of a name for himself by writing a number of polemical tracts, one of which was his *Letter to the English*. And it was to this short, pamphlet-sized work propounding the tenets of Lutheranism[98] that More responded.

The year 1527 saw the continued influx of heretical books from the

---

[96] Letter no. 38, from More to Erasmus, December 18, 1526, in Elizabeth Rogers, ed., *St. Thomas More: Selected Letters* (New Haven: Yale Univ. Press, 1961), 161–65 (quote on 162–63).

[97] Introduction, *Letter to Bugenhagen, Supplication of Souls, Letter against Frith,* ed. Frank Manley et al., vol. 7 of *Complete Works of St. Thomas More* (New Haven: Yale Univ. Press, 1990), xviii. Hereafter cited as *CW* 7.

[98] Ibid., xix.

Continent that were slowly but surely permeating England's academic institutions.[99] In the spring the first serious signs of trouble between King Henry and his Spanish consort, Catherine, surfaced,[100] but there were also events abroad that did not bode well for the future. As early as 1523, in his *Responsio ad Lutherum,* More had expressed the fear of what might ultimately come of Luther's doctrines of man as hopelessly sinful, incapable of bettering himself by good works and unbounded by obedience to authority or law:

> For just as very many of the princes look not without pleasure on a degenerating clergy, undoubtedly because they pant for the possessions of those who defect and hope to seize them on the grounds of abandonment, and just as those princes rejoice that obedience is withdrawn from the Roman pontiff with the hope that they will be able to dispose and divide and squander it all for themselves at home, so too there is no reason for them to doubt but that the people look to the time when they may shake off in turn the yoke of the princes and strip them of their possessions; once they have accomplished this, drunk with the blood of princes and revelling in the gore of nobles, enduring not even common rule, with the laws trampled underfoot according to Luther's doctrine, rulerless and lawless, without restraint, wanton beyond reason, they will finally turn their hands against themselves and like those earthborn brethren, will mutually run each other through. I pray Christ I may become a false prophet . . .[101]

As we have already seen, More's apocalyptic vision swiftly proved to be prophetic of events in Germany that reached their bloody climax in the Peasants' War of 1525. Even Luther, amid the chaos in his native land, soon recognized the dangers of the lawlessness he had unwittingly helped to engender, but this realization came too late;[102] he had already laid the theological foundations for anarchy. The year 1527 brought more ungovernable bloodshed and wanton destruction —this time in Christendom's capital. On May 6, 1527, the army of Emperor Charles V entered Rome. The troops, a mixture of Germans and Spaniards, unleashed upon the city a reign of terror in which thousands of innocent civilians were summarily massacred, women vi-

---

[99] Schuster, *CW* 8: 1168–69; Richard Rex, *Henry VIII and the English Reformation* (New York: St. Martin's Press, 1993), 115, 140–41.

[100] E. W. Ives, *Anne Boleyn* (Oxford: Basil Blackwell, 1986), 108.

[101] *CW* 5, peroration, 691–93.

[102] Grisar, *Martin Luther,* 282–83.

olated, churches and homes looted and burned.[103] Although the reasons for invading Rome were largely political, much (though not all) of the violence that ensued clearly stemmed from the contempt of the Lutheran German soldiers for all things Catholic. Having been taught by Luther to regard papal Rome as the "Babylonian Whore" and the "Seat of Antichrist", they treated her accordingly.[104] There were innumerable acts of sacrilege and barbarity that went far beyond the all too common cycle of looting and riotousness associated with wartime brutality. From a letter of one eyewitness to the carnage, Cardinal Giovanni Salviati, dated June 8, 1527, we learn some of the details of what transpired:

> The impiety and knavery which have been done [are] such [as] I am not able to write. Dead are all the innocent boys of Santo Spirito [Hospital], all the infirm are thrown in the Tiber, profaned and violated are all the monasteries . . . Burned is the great chapel of Saint Peter and of Sixtus . . . Stolen are the heads of the Apostles and the other relics . . . The Sacrament is trampled on and thrown in the mud . . .[105]

In another letter, dated June 15, 1527, Vincenzo da Treviso observed, "There is not a Christ in the churches that does not have one or two hundred lance wounds."[106] Word of the events that had transpired in Rome reached Thomas More and filled him with horror and disgust, as is evident from his own account of these happenings, which he wrote a year or so later in his *Dialogue concerning Heresies:* "Thus devised these cursed wretches so many diverse fashions of exquisite cruelties that I ween they have taught the devil new torments in hell that he never knew before . . ."[107]

It was in the spring of 1528 that Thomas More was brought into direct confrontation with the theological father of the English Reformation, William Tyndale. That year Tyndale published two new works, *The Parable of the Wicked Mammon* and *The Obedience of a Christian Man,* both of which constituted a defense of the reformers' doctrine

---

[103] Ludwig von Pastor, *History of the Popes from the Close of the Middle Ages,* vol. 9 (St. Louis, Mo.: B. Herder, 1910), 388–418.

[104] Chastel, *Sack of Rome,* 101–2.

[105] Author's own English trans. of letter to Baldassarre Castiglione, in Ludwig von Pastor, *Storia dei papi dalla fine del medio evo,* vol. 4, pt. 2 (Rome: Desclee and C. Editori, 1942), 725.

[106] Chastel, *Sack of Rome,* 107.

[107] *A Dialogue concerning Heresies,* ed. Thomas Lawler et al., vol. 6 of *Complete Works of St. Thomas More* (New Haven: Yale Univ. Press, 1981), bk. 4, chap. 7, 370–72 (quote on 372).

of *solafideism*—justification by faith alone,[108] although in the latter of these books the author seems more preoccupied than anything else with the demonization of the Church he had been born and raised in:

> Nevertheless this I say, that they [the hierarchy/clergy] have robbed all realms, not of God's word only, but also of all wealth and prosperity; and have driven peace out of all lands, and withdrawn themselves from all obedience to princes, and have separated themselves from the lay-men, counting them viler than dogs; and have set up that great idol, the whore of Babylon, antichrist of Rome, whom they call pope; and have conspired against all commonwealths, and have made them a several kingdom, wherein it is lawful, unpunished, to work all abomination. In every parish have they spies, and in every great man's house, and in every tavern and alehouse. And through confessions know they all secrets, so that no man may open his mouth to rebuke whatsoever they do, but that he shall be shortly made a heretic.[109]

Casting the clergy as oppressors who invent laws "violently [to] bind the lay-people, that never consented unto the making of them",[110] Tyndale calls upon the laity to question all ecclesiastical authority:

> . . . [A]ll their [the hierarchy's] study is to deceive us and to keep us in darkness, to sit as gods in our consciences, and handle us at their pleasure, and to lead us whither they lust; therefore, I read [i.e., advise] thee, get thee to God's word, and thereby try all doctrine, and against that receive nothing . . .[111]

Ironically it was in the pages of this very same work that as we shall later see Tyndale was to magnify to frightening proportions a king's power over his subjects. Yet throughout the *Obedience* Tyndale ex-udes a boundless self-confidence that he is right and the Church is "damnably" wrong, at one point not even hesitating to give himself a stature that strikes the reader as almost quasi-messianic:

> And as for mine authority, or who sent me, I report me unto my works, as Christ, John v. and x. If God's word bear record that I say truth, why should any man doubt, but that God, the Father of truth and of light, hath sent me; as the father of lies and of darkness hath sent you; and

---

[108] Carl R. Trueman, *Luther's Legacy: Salvation and English Reformers, 1525–1556* (Oxford: Clarendon Press, 1994), 83–84.
[109] *The Obedience of a Christian Man*, in *Doctrinal Treatises*, 191. Herafter cited as *Obedience*.
[110] Ibid., 147.
[111] Ibid., 324.

that the Spirit of truth and of light is with me, as the spirit of lies and of darkness is with you?[112]

More was nearing the zenith of his political career when he received a letter dated March 7, 1528, from a longtime friend, Cuthbert Tunstall—now Archbishop of London. It concerned the matter uppermost on both men's minds: the ever-increasing success of Luther's and Tyndale's propaganda on English soil. The Archbishop wished to enlist More in a new campaign against the dissenters— the "new men" as More called them[113]—a campaign to be waged on the reformers' own turf, the vernacular printed page. The situation was growing desperate and urgently required a forceful and articulate response:

> It is greatly to be feared . . . that Catholic faith may be greatly imperilled if good and learned men do not strenuously resist the wickedness of the aforesaid persons. That can in no way be better and more suitably done than if the catholic truth, which entirely confutes these mad teachings, is in like manner set out in its own language. The result will be that men unskilled in sacred literature, picking up these new heretical books, and together with them these same catholic books which refute them, will be able either to discern the truth for themselves, or else will be correctly advised and taught by others whose judgment is more acute.[114]

The strategy for challenging the dissenters was therefore clear and quite logical. But how was it to be carried out? Who would be capable of assuming the arduous responsibility of putting the case for the Church on paper and in proper English? The Archbishop continued:

> And since you, dearest brother, are distinguished as a second Demosthenes in our native language as well as in Latin, and you are in the habit of championing catholic truth most keenly in every discussion, you cannot better occupy your spare time (if you can steal any from your duties) than in publishing something in English which will reveal to simple and uneducated men the crafty wickedness of the heretics, and will better equip such folk against such impious supplanters of the Church.[115]

---

[112] Ibid., 282.

[113] *Confutation of Tyndale's Answer, CW* 8, bk. 7, p. 700.

[114] *English Historical Documents,* vol. 5, *1485–1558,* ed. C. H. Williams (New York: Oxford Univ. Press, 1967), 828.

[115] Ibid.

But if More was to succeed at this task, he would need to know his enemy; for this reason Tunstall now granted More authorization to read the heretical works he was to refute and advised him that he was sending him copies of a considerable number of them:

> . . . [I]t is a great step towards victory if you can spy out the enemy's plans, read his thoughts thoroughly and anticipate his aims. For if you set yourself to refute something which they will say they never meant, all your labour will be in vain.[116]

The Archbishop concludes with a rallying cry that is almost prophetic, summoning More to undertake this mission for the sake of the Church:

> Go forth boldly, then, to such holy work, by which you will both benefit the Church of God and lay up for yourself an immortal name, and eternal glory in heaven. We beseech you in God's name so to do, strengthening the Church of God with your support.[117]

More wasted no time setting to work on the first of two books directed against the teachings of William Tyndale—the *Dialogue concerning Heresies*.

In 1529, while More was writing his *Dialogue concerning Heresies*, an anonymous short work entitled *A Supplication for the Beggars* arrived in England. Although its actual author, Simon Fish, was only an obscure figure among the English reformers,[118] the *Supplication* nevertheless played a decisive role in forging an uneasy alliance between these dissenters and Henry VIII that ultimately severed the country from the Church. Addressed to "the king our sovereign lord", the booklet contained a furious assault upon the papacy and the clergy, alleging that the Church had stolen the supremacy that rightly belonged to the English crown; to make his case Fish even went so far as to recast the infamous King John (1199–1216) as a "righteous prince" victimized by power-hungry ecclesiastics:

> And what doth all this greedy sort of sturdy, idle, holy thieves, with these yearly exactions that they take of the people? Truly nothing, but exempt themselves from the obedience of your grace! Nothing, but translate all

---

[116] Ibid., 829.

[117] Ibid.

[118] Steven Haas, "Simon Fish, William Tyndale, and Sir Thomas More's 'Lutheran Conspiracy'", *Journal of Ecclesiastical History* 23 (April 1972): 125–26, 136.

rule, power, lordship, authority, obedience, and dignity, from your grace unto them! Nothing, but that all your subjects should fall into disobedience and rebellion against your grace, and be under them; as they did unto your noble predecessor king John . . .[119]

Fish goes on to endorse the concept of state absolutism first advocated by Luther several years earlier in something of a departure from the libertine views professed in the German reformer's earliest works.[120] Hence papal primacy was replaced with the primacy of a secular despot. Shortly before Fish's work appeared, Tyndale had vigorously asserted this same concept in his *Obedience of a Christian Man* (October 1528), proclaiming that:

> . . . God hath made the king in every realm judge over all, and over him is there no judge. He that judgeth the king judgeth God . . . and he that resisteth the king resisteth God, and damneth God's law and ordinance . . . Hereby seest thou that the king is, in this world, without law; and may at his lust do right or wrong, and shall give accounts but to God only.[121]

Tyndale's *Obedience* regrettably fell into the hands of King Henry, who afterward said of it, ". . . [T]his book is for me and all kings to read."[122] Similarly, Simon Fish's *Supplication* pleased the royal ego with its calls for the state to confiscate and make its own all Church properties.[123] The implementation of such ideas would not be long in coming. But Fish's book attacked the Church in other ways as well. By thoroughly defaming the clergy with indiscriminate and wildly exaggerated accusations aimed at weakening their credibility as teachers of the faith, Fish was undermining the Church's ability to communicate with her people. More recognized the threat and replied, evidently with great haste,[124] publishing that same year his *Supplication*

---

[119] *A Supplication for the Beggars,* in John Fox, *The Acts and Monuments of John Fox* (London: Seeley, Burnside, and Seeley, 1846), 4:660–61.

[120] Thomas Brady, "Luther and the State: The Reformer's Teaching in Its Social Setting", in *Luther and the Modern State in Germany,* ed. James Tracy, Sixteenth Century Essays and Studies, vol. 7 (Kirksville, Md.: Sixteenth Century Journal Publishers, 1986), 32–37.

[121] *Obedience,* 177, 178.

[122] John Strype, *Ecclesiastical Memorials relating Chiefly to Religion, and the Reformation of It and the Emergencies of the Church of England, under King Henry VIII, King Edward VI and Queen Mary I,* vol. 1, pt. 1 (Oxford: Clarendon Press, 1822), 172.

[123] *A Supplication for the Beggars,* in Fox, *Acts and Monuments,* 664.

[124] Introduction, in *CW* 7:lxv–lxvi.

of Souls. In addition to addressing the issue of clerical misconduct, a large part of More's work is taken up with a defense of the doctrine of Purgatory.

In 1530 Tyndale added more books to the print war. In January he published an English translation of the Old Testament's Pentateuch interlaced with interpretative glosses and prologues.[125] Some months later there appeared his *Practice of Prelates,* an unfortunate attempt to reconstruct Church history, in which, among other things, the papacy is depicted as a vinelike yew tree that had gradually choked the true Church:[126]

> And thus the pope, the father of all hypocrites, hath with falsehood and guile perverted the order of the world, and turned the roots of the trees upward, and hath put down the kingdom of Christ, and set up the kingdom of the devil, whose vicar he is . . .[127]

But Tyndale was also nettled by More's *Dialogue concerning Heresies* and decided to respond by setting to work on his *Answer unto Sir Thomas More's Dialogue,* which was published the following year,[128] written in very much the same vein as his *Obedience of a Christian Man* and *Practice of Prelates:*

> The pope first hath no scripture that he dare abide by, in the light; neither careth, but blasphemeth that his word is truer than the scripture. He hath miracles without God's word, as all false prophets had. He hath lies in all his legends, in all preachings, and in all books. They have no love unto the truth; which appeareth by their great sins that they have set up, above all the abomination of all the heathen that ever were, and by their long continuance therein, not of frailty, but of malice unto the truth, and of obstinate lust and self-will to sin.[129]

Meanwhile, continental Europe was to provide yet another demonstration of the cultural sensitivities of theological dissent in action, this

---

[125] Schuster, *CW* 8:1217–18.

[126] Ibid., 1218–21.

[127] *Practice of Prelates,* in Tyndale, *Expositions and Notes on Sundry Portions of the Holy Scriptures,* ed. Rev. Henry Walter, Parker Society, vol. 43 (Cambridge: Cambridge Univ. Press, 1849), 270.

[128] Schuster, *CW* 8:1142.

[129] Text in William Tyndale, *An Answer to Sir Thomas More's Dialogue, The Supper of the Lord and Wm. Tracy's Testament Expounded,* ed. Rev. Henry Walter, Parker Society, vol. 44 (1850; reprint, Johnson Reprint Corp., 1968), 104.

time in and around the city of Geneva. In October of 1530 troops from the Swiss city of Bern, a new stronghold of Ulrich Zwingli's doctrines, marched into Geneva; ironically they had been asked to come by the Genevans themselves, who were in need of assistance in a military confrontation with the kingdom of Savoy. Unfortunately for Catholic Geneva, the Bernese were obsessed with iconoclastic fever, having two years earlier eliminated all Catholic ceremonies in their own city. It seems the Bernese now took it upon themselves to impose their new values upon their allies. A nun of Geneva's Convent of Saint Claire, Jeanne de Jussie, tells of the path of wanton destruction forged by the soldiers as they passed through nearby villages on the way to the city. In Morge the troops quartered their horses in the cloister of the Franciscan monastery and desecrated the friars' chapel, starting a fire in the nave and throwing the consecrated Hosts into the flames, an action that our chronicler Jeanne likens to the tortures inflicted upon Christ by the soldiers of Caiaphas and Pilate. The Bernese completed their work by denuding the chapel, burning all its wooden statues and destroying the altar along with the stained-glass window behind it. Elsewhere in the suburbs of Geneva, the story was the same; everywhere they went, the soldiers vented their fury on all the religious images they found and even "poked out the eyes of the images with their pikes and swords, and spat on them, to deface and disfigure them".[130] These men of Zwinglian persuasion were also quite proficient in the destruction of Catholic books. Any priests who fell into their hands were beaten and stripped of their clerical robes. Especially perverse were their acts of sacrilege against the reserved Eucharist; tabernacles were broken and the Hosts thrown down to be trampled upon. In one case a consecrated Host was fed to a goat as the soldiers mockingly commented, "Now he can die if he wants, he has received the sacrament." The troops were, relatively speaking, somewhat more restrained upon entering Geneva itself, yet even here they did considerable damage to the city's religious houses.[131]

In 1532 there appeared in print the first part of Thomas More's single largest work, his *Confutation of Tyndale's Answer*, a comprehensive rebuttal of Tyndale's 1531 book *An Answer unto Sir Thomas More's*

---

[130] Jeanne de Jussie, *Le levain du Calvinisme,* cited in Eire, *War against the Idols,* 126.

[131] De Jussie, in ibid., 126–28.

Dialogue. Setting aside the Platonic dialogue format of his earlier work against Tyndale, More here chose instead to quote key passages from his opponent verbatim, after each of which he would give his own thorough reply. The comprehensiveness with which More refutes every conceivable argument of his opponent has been aptly described by Louis Schuster in the introduction to the Yale University edition of the *Confutation* (1973) as

> . . . labyrinthine . . . spun out of the legal mind night after sleepless night, alert to the nature of each bit of evidence as well as its reliability and strength under scrutiny, anticipating in lawyer-like fashion all the arguments of the opposition that might jeopardize one's case, leaving no escape clauses or loopholes untended, relentless in chopping away every supporting prop of the opponent's position until the very possibility of rebuttal seems confounded . . . One has the impression that every night during composition More fought the same battle on all fronts . . . [132]

In 1533 the second portion of the *Confutation* appeared, which in addition to continuing More's refutation of Tyndale also tackled the dissenters' concept of a church of the "sinless" raised by the reformer Robert Barnes (1495–1540) in his *Supplication . . . unto . . . King Henry the Eight.* (1531). [133] During this same period More devoted two apologetical treatises specifically to the defense of the Church's doctrines on the Holy Eucharist. The first of these, his *Letter against Frith,* served as a response to a treatise by the young dissenter John Frith that had advocated a Zwinglian, symbolic theology of the Eucharist. At first printed only for limited distribution in 1532, More's *Letter against Frith* was published for the public in December 1533, as was his *Answer to a Poisoned Book,* which brought his apologetical writings to a close. In the latter work More makes systematic use of patristic quotations in order to refute the anonymous treatise *The Supper of the Lord* (believed to have been written by either George Joye or William Tyndale), [134] which proffered a Zwinglian interpretation of Christ's eucharistic discourse in the sixth chapter of Saint John's Gospel. [135] Earlier in 1533 More had published two other apologetical

---

[132] Schuster, *CW* 8:1261.

[133] Rainer Pineas, *Thomas More and Tudor Polemics* (Bloomington, Ind.: Indiana Univ. Press, 1968), 120, 141.

[134] Appendix B, *CW* 11:343–50.

[135] Introduction, *CW* 11:lvi–lix; introduction, *CW* 7:cxxxii–cxli.

books, the *Apology* and the *Debellation of Salem and Bizance*—but as the contents of these have a particular bearing upon the conflict between King Henry VIII and the Church, we will reserve their discussion for a later chapter.

More was asked why he, a layman, lacking credentials as a Scripture scholar, should presume to "meddle" in theological disputation by writing, rather than leave such matters to clerics. In the preface to his *Confutation of Tyndale's Answer,* More counters that if the questions raised were subtle ones open to legitimate debate he would gladly yield the discussion to men more competent than he. But such is not the case with Tyndale, whose teachings assail clear and firmly established doctrines of the Church that a layman such as he can and should be sufficiently capable of defending. Moreover, he himself is an educated man, with a background in ecclesiastical studies comparable to that of his opponents; he has seen nothing in Tyndale's works that cannot be readily refuted.[136] In the heretical writings there is nothing of substance—only reckless statements and mockery of things sacred, expressed with tiresome verbosity (they "overwhelm the whole world with words").[137]

More's principal reason for writing is to give warning to gullible souls who, failing to recognize the pitfalls in heretical works, succumb in stages to their influence. Thus are they led to accept heterodox notions that at first may appear innocuous enough but which by degrees make even worse falsehoods palatable; thus the naïve are brought full circle to believing heresies that at the outset they never would have even countenanced.[138] As to the selection of the printed medium in defending the Church, More offers the following rationale in his first apologetical work, the *Responsio ad Lutherum:*

> . . . [T]here cannot be a more level plain for the struggle, or one less exposed to ambush, than a controversy carried on by means of published books, in which neither side can pretend, either that any point was falsely kept from the record by the secretaries, or later corrupted by forgers, or that anything had escaped him unforeseen in the heat of a hurried disputation. Rather, what he will have brought forward in the most ordered fashion—whatever he is able to bring forward at his leisure

---

[136] *Confutation of Tyndale's Answer, CW* 8, preface, 26–27.

[137] Ibid., 27.

[138] Ibid.

in accordance with the merits of the case—that will with honest fidelity appear in public.[139]

Although the work of apologetical writing is somewhat demanding, More notes, far more tedious is the task of reading the heretical works themselves (in order to refute them). More wishes that the dissenters' books and his would all just vanish into oblivion. But since the devil is making so many inroads and the heretical books are being spread about more and more, it is necessary that prudent and educated men should "set their pens to the book" in refutation of these false doctrines. Although such writings will not persuade the hard of heart, they will benefit those who have fallen into error through ignorance.[140]

Citing Luke 16:8, ". . . [T]he sons of this world are wiser in their own generation than the sons of light", More observes that the heretics of his day are more assiduous in propagating their doctrines than are the loyal, educated sons of the Church in defending the truths of the faith.[141] The situation, he explains, is comparable to that in the Garden of Gethsemane, for just as Judas busied himself in the night preparing to betray Christ while Christ's loyal disciples who remained in His company slumbered, so too in the current age (1500s) the dissenters lose no time in diligently setting about to write their attacks on Church teachings, while good men, articulate and possessed of more than enough erudition to refute such books, shrink from the task at hand and, in their sorrow over the deplorable state of affairs, neglect to "wake and pray and take the pen in hand".[142] Whatever other men may feel their obligation is, More will now fulfill what he sees as his duty, although he wishes it were not necessary for anyone to read a word of what he must now write.[143]

It was thus within a span of twelve years that Thomas More produced nine apologetical works, seven of which were written during the six-year period of 1528–1533, including the massive *Confutation of Tyndale's Answer,* which in its first edition filled over nine hundred

---

[139] *Responsio ad Lutherum, CW* 5, bk. 1, chap. 1, pp. 45–47.
[140] *Confutation of Tyndale's Answer, CW* 8, preface, 36.
[141] Ibid., 36.
[142] Ibid., 36–37.
[143] Ibid., 37.

folio pages.[144] Although every one of these works was born of particular circumstances, each of them does touch upon one or more of More's most common polemical themes: the nature of the Church, the authority of Scripture and oral tradition, the sacraments, and particularly the Eucharist. When taken as a unified whole, the apologetical works provide us with a mosaic of More's understanding of his faith. So rather than analyze each work separately, it is more to our purpose that we should present More's thoughts in a coherent synthesis in the pages to follow.

> This contest of Tyndale and More was the classic controversy of the English reformation. No other discussion was carried on between men of such preeminent ability and with such clear apprehension of the points at issue. To More's assertion of the paramount authority of the church Tyndale replied by appealing to scripture, with an ultimate resort to individual judgment. From such divergent premises no agreement was possible.[145]

---

[144] Hughes, "*King's Proceedings*", 149.

[145] E. Irving Carlyle, "Tyndale, William", in *Dictionary of National Biography,* vol. 57 (New York: Macmillan Co.; London: Smith, Elder, and Co., 1899), 427.

CHAPTER VI

"That They May All Be One": Thomas More's Defense of the Unity of the Catholic Church

> For every good man is bounden between truth and falsehood, the Catholic Church and heretics, between God and the devil, to be partial, and plainly to declare himself to be full and whole upon the one side and clear against the other.
>
> — Thomas More, *Apology*

It was at the Last Supper that Christ turned to His Heavenly Father and prayed that His disciples "may all be one . . . perfectly one" (Jn 17:21, 23), a prayer transcending time, offered for His beloved sons and daughters of every age. The unity of the Church, made manifest in the common profession of "one Lord, one faith, one baptism" (Eph 4:5), was a motif that pervaded Thomas More's ecclesiology. One might almost say that in a beautiful way this aspect of the faith "obsessed" him. While in conversation with his son-in-law William Roper, More confided to him that one of his three greatest wishes was that "where the Church of Christ is at this present sore afflicted with many errors and heresies, it were settled in a perfect uniformity of religion."[1] Elsewhere, in one of his apologetical works, More describes God as the "King of peace and unity" in contrast to Satan, whom he identifies as the "sower of dissension and king of rebel-

---

[1] William Roper, *The Lyfe of Sir Thomas Moore, Knighte,* ed. Elsie V. Hitchcock, Early English Text Society, original series, no. 197 (London: Early English Text Society, 1935), 24–25.

lion".[2] His preoccupation with the communal dimension of the faith is made manifest time and again in his letters, especially those of his last years, where we find him ending with the hope that "we may merrily meet in heaven".[3] But for More the unity of the Church was not some intangible, sentimental abstraction; rather, he believed in a concrete, visible unity of commonly professed beliefs, an unbroken continuity of faith that had already lasted fifteen hundred years.

More's thoughts on this subject were shaped in part by one of his favorite patristic expositions, Saint Cyprian's treatise *De unitate Ecclesiae* (*On the Unity of the Church*). Cyprian (d. A.D. 258) begins by setting the criterion for walking "in the footsteps of the conquering Christ":[4] if we are to escape eternal death and attain eternal life, we must keep His commandments. Thus how could any one claim faith in Christ, Cyprian asks, if he does not obey Christ? That there are those who profess to be Christian while rejecting Christ's commandments Cyprian sees as the work of Satan, who, frustrated by the conversion of so many to the faith, now resorts to deception by drawing souls from God under the guise of a false Christianity—heresies and schisms that stand in opposition to faith, truth, and unity.[5] Resorting to "plausible lies", the promoters of such theological dissension "offer night for day, death for salvation, despair under the offer of hope, perfidy under the pretext of faith, antichrist under the name of Christ".[6] Hence for Cyprian a unity of doctrine is essential to Christian unity, and it is in this context that he applies from Psalm 68 the words, "God who maketh men of one manner to dwell in a house" (Ps 68:6 [67:7], Douay trans.): "In the house of God, in the Church of Christ, those of one mind dwell . . ."[7] It is this expression of Cyprian's in particular that More cites repeatedly throughout his

---

[2] *The Confutation of Tyndale's Answer,* ed. Louis Schuster et al., vol. 8 of *Complete Works of St. Thomas More* (New Haven: Yale Univ. Press, 1973), bk. 7, p. 728. Hereafter cited as *CW* 8.

[3] Letter no. 218, from More to his daughter Margaret, July 5, 1535, in Elizabeth Rogers, ed., *The Correspondence of Sir Thomas More* (Princeton, N.J.: Princeton Univ. Press, 1947), 564.

[4] St. Cyprian, *The Unity of the Catholic Church,* in *Saint Cyprian: Treatises,* trans. and ed. Roy J. Deferrari, Fathers of the Church, vol. 36 (New York: Fathers of the Church, 1958), chap. 2, p. 96.

[5] Ibid., chaps. 2–3, pp. 96–97.

[6] Ibid., chap. 3, p. 98.

[7] Ibid., chap. 8, p. 103.

apologetical writings, writings inspired precisely by his determination
to do what he can to defend the unity of the Church.

But how does the Church achieve and preserve her unity in belief? It is in Christ's two promises that the Holy Spirit would lead
His Church into all truth (Jn 16:13) and that He would be with her
always, even unto the end of the world (Mt 28:20), that More sees
God's guarantee that His Church would faithfully transmit the living
tradition of the gospel down through the ages to all generations.[8] But
what precisely constitutes this living tradition? For More, the gospel
did not begin with the actual writing of the New Testament but rather
with the verbal teaching and living example of Christ Himself and
His apostles. Citing Saint John's words at the end of his Gospel that
"there are also many other things which Jesus did" that have been left
unwritten (Jn 21:25), More explains that when the inspired authors
of the New Testament set down in writing the words, actions, and
teachings of Christ, they did not record the totality of these things.[9]
Hence the sum total of the Christian creed consists both of what is
contained in the Scriptures and in what is preserved through the oral
tradition of the Church.

In defending oral tradition, More was in no way downplaying the
importance of Sacred Scripture. As a Christian humanist, he possessed a profound appreciation of the Scriptures, an appreciation amply demonstrated by the almost ceaseless biblical citations throughout
his written works. We have already seen More's enthusiastic support
of Erasmus' ground-breaking work in biblical scholarship. Nonetheless More's Christian humanist background also introduced him to
the invaluable contributions of the Church Fathers, whose writings
clearly manifested the existence of the Church's body of oral tradition
handed down from the apostles. More felt no uneasiness in professing
those Christian tenets that had been preserved only by the living oral
tradition, for the authority on which he accepted them—that of the
Catholic Church—was the same on whose authority he accepted the
Scriptures as the authentic Word of God. As More was frequently to
remind his readers, it is the Church that has established what is or is
not Sacred Scripture;[10] in this regard he was wont to cite the axiom

---

[8] See, for example, *CW* 8, bk. 1, p. 133.

[9] Ibid., bk. 3, pp. 311–13.

[10] See More's discussion of this in his *Supplication of Souls,* bk. 2, in *Letter to Bugenhagen,*

of Saint Augustine, ". . . I should not believe the gospel except as moved by the authority of the Catholic Church."[11]

Closely related to the transmission of the content of Divine Revelation through both the Scriptures and oral tradition is the belief that over the centuries the Church, continuously guided by the Holy Spirit, can attain a progressively deeper understanding of the deposit of faith, wherein a consensus arises regarding a hitherto undefined dogma—a "development of doctrine". In his *Confutation of Tyndale's Answer,* More brilliantly explains this process, distinguishing between those dogmas that God has imparted to His Church in such manner as to be fully and immediately recognized and those that have come to be recognized over the course of time. In his description of the latter we find a perfect synopsis of the development of such doctrines as those of the Immaculate Conception and the Assumption of the Blessed Virgin Mary:

> Sometimes he showeth it [the dogma] leisurely, suffering his flock to confer together and dispute thereupon, and in their treating of the matter, suffereth them with good mind and scripture and natural wisdom, with invocation of his spiritual help, to search and seek for the truth, and to vary for the while in their opinions, till that he reward their virtuous diligence with leading them secretly in to the consent and concord and belief of the truth by his Holy Spirit *qui facit unanimes in domo,* which maketh his flock of one mind in his house, that is to wit his Church. So that in the mean while the variance is without sin, and maketh nothing against the credence of the Church . . .[12]

But how, precisely, was the deposit of faith to be preserved from the encroachments of human error over the centuries? Were the Scriptures alone enough of an authority, as the Protestant reformers contended? No, More answers, the Bible alone was certainly not enough, for the written Word of God could in and of itself be interpreted by fallible men in any number of different ways. A supreme teaching authority

---

Supplication of Souls, Letter against Frith, ed. Frank Manley et al., vol. 7 of *Complete Works of St. Thomas More* (New Haven: Yale Univ. Press, 1990), 182–83. This volume hereafter cited as *CW* 7.

[11] *Contra Epistolam Manichaei,* chap. 5, no. 6, in *St. Augustin: The Writings against the Manichaeans and against the Donatists,* ed. Philip Schaff, vol. 4 of *A Select Library of the Nicene and Post-Nicene Fathers of the Christian Church* (1887, reprint, Grand Rapids, Mich.: William B. Eerdmanns Publishing Co., 1974), 131.

[12] *CW* 8, bk. 3, p. 248.

was needed, and More saw this need filled by a visible Magisterium, established within the Church by Christ Himself, who invested the apostles and their successors with this authority, and most especially Peter and his successors:

> Because of the steadfastness of Peter's faith, Christ made him the head and primate of His Church, as a rock standing in His own place, not as though Peter were immortal and so could hold office forever, but many would successively follow him into that office, and these not all of equal merit. Since this is so, even if the name "rock" does not fit them, is the power of the office for that reason not the same?[13]

As More intimates in the above passage, the unique teaching authority of the papacy is not dependent upon the personal virtues or lack thereof of the men who held the office. He notes that even with men in public office, citizens do not predicate their obedience upon the personal character of such leaders.[14] Elsewhere More defends the exercise of the Magisterium's teaching authority through the organ of the Church's general councils (what are known as ecumenical councils, official convocations of all or at least a representative number of the Church's bishops, convened by the supreme pontiff).[15] While it must be said that his understanding of the specific nature of papal infallibility and of the authority of popes relative to general councils seems to have lacked the full clarity[16] wrought so definitively centuries later by the First Vatican Council's pronouncements on these matters,[17] More does implicitly recognize, for all practical purposes, the papacy's charism of infallibility insofar as he repeatedly insists that Christ's promises to remain with His Church and to send the Holy Spirit effectively constitute a promise that He will never allow His Church to err in her teachings. As it is clear that he believed the

---

[13] *Responsio ad Lutherum,* ed. John M. Headley and trans. Sr. Scholastica Mandeville, vol. 5 of *Complete Works of St. Thomas More* (New Haven: Yale Univ. Press, 1969), bk. 1, chap. 10, p. 135. Hereafter cited as *CW* 5.

[14] Ibid., 141.

[15] Letter no. 199, from More to Thomas Cromwell, March 5, 1534, in Rogers, *Correspondence,* 499.

[16] See More's comments about the relationship between popes and general councils in ibid., 499.

[17] First Dogmatic Constitution on the Church of Christ, Vatican Council I, 4th session, July 18, 1870, especially chaps. 3 and 4, in John Clarkson, S.J., et al., *The Church Teaches: Documents of the Church in English Translation* (St. Louis, Mo.: B. Herder Book Co., 1955; reprint, Rockford, Ill.: Tan Books and Publishers, 1973), 94–102, especially 99, 102.

office of teaching in the Church to have been given to the pope and the bishops,[18] it follows that this inerrancy resides in the papacy itself. Indeed, More does not hesitate to endorse unequivocally the exposition of papal primacy presented in Bishop John Fisher's *Assertionis Lutheranae Confutatio,*[19] which contains about as clear an assertion of papal infallibility as any to be seen in his day; Fisher states: "To which judge shall we go, if not to the see of Peter? For that see will never lack divine assistance in handing down to us the certain truth about doubtful matters, especially matters concerning the faith."[20]

In a letter to Thomas Cromwell (March 5, 1534) More admits to having undergone a profound change in his perception of the issue of papal primacy[21]—a change that is surmised to have taken place sometime between the spring of 1521 and the summer of 1523,[22] when the Protestant Reformation was still in its earliest phase and More had yet to publish his first apologetical work (his *Responsio ad Lutherum* appeared in print shortly thereafter). More states that it was Henry VIII's vigorous assertion of papal primacy in his *Assertio Septem Sacramentorum* that caused him to start questioning his own previous assumptions that the unique primatial role of the papacy in the life of the Church was a human rather than a divine institution. He began studying the matter—it seems he had never really done so before—and if we are to judge from the testimony of two of More's contemporaries, Cardinal Reginald Pole[23] and the Spanish Dominican Pedro de Soto,[24] it did not take long for him to change his mind. Both Cardinal Pole, who as a fellow Englishman was an acquaintance of More's, and de Soto, who after More's death had the opportunity to

---

[18] *CW* 5, bk. 2, chap. 22, p. 627.

[19] More's reference to this work of Fisher appears in ibid., bk. 1, chap. 10, pp. 139–41.

[20] Richard Rex, *The Theology of John Fisher* (Cambridge: Cambridge Univ. Press, 1989), 106.

[21] Letter no. 199, in Rogers, *Correspondence,* 498.

[22] Introduction, *CW* 5:770.

[23] "Cardinal Pole's Speech to the Citizens of London, in Behalf of Religious Houses", in John Strype, *Ecclesiastical Memorials relating Chiefly to Religion, and the Reformation of It and the Emergencies of the Church of England, under King Henry VIII, King Edward VI and Queen Mary I,* vol. 3, pt. 2 (Oxford: Clarendon Press, 1822), no. 68, pp. 491–93 (spelling modernized in quotations that follow).

[24] De Soto's account appears as appendix B (and is mentioned briefly in the introduction) in *De Tristitia Christi,* ed. and trans. Clarence H. Miller, vol. 14 of *Complete Works of St. Thomas More* (New Haven: Yale Univ. Press, 1976), 1069–73 (appendix), plus 718 (introduction). *De Tristitia Christi* hereafter cited as *CW* 14.

meet and speak with a number of those who had known him personally, tell of More undergoing a definitive change of heart on this issue after a conversation with a close friend—Cardinal Pole says it was Antonio Bonvisi. According to Pole, while discussing the growing Protestant schism, More indicated that it was the dissenters' new tenets on the Holy Eucharist that troubled him the most, whereas their attacks on papal primacy seemed to him of lesser concern. No sooner had he said this than he began to have second thoughts, and confessing immediately to Bonvisi that he had spoken thus "without consideration", he asked him to come again to discuss this question. De Soto says that More told his friend "that he intended to read carefully and consider what one should hold on this matter, since he saw many men magnifying the authority of the Roman See but he himself did not clearly understand to what degree arguments from reason or authority established the authority of Rome". After a fairly short interval—Pole says it was only ten or twelve days, while de Soto says it was about a month—More and his friend met once again, and this time the former immediately began by reproaching himself, saying (according to Cardinal Pole), "Alas! Mr. Bonvisi, whither was I falling, when I made you that answer of the primacy of the Church?" More then shared with him the firm conclusion he had reached following his study, stating (as Father de Soto records it), "O my friend, how solid are the grounds on which the primacy of the Roman pontiff rests! In fact, it is not only most firmly established in the Christian religion but is itself the ground and foundation of all the rest." More proceeded to show his friend the texts he had found confirming papal primacy; neither Pole nor de Soto says what precisely these texts were, but we can arrive at some idea by returning to the testimony of More himself, who in his letter of March 5, 1534, to Cromwell states:

> But surely after that I had read his Grace's book therein [the *Assertio Septem Sacramentorum*], and so many other things as I have seen in that point by this continuance of these ten years since and more have found in effect the substance of all the holy doctors from Saint Ignatius, disciple to Saint John the Evangelist, unto our own days both Latins and Greeks so consonant and agreeing in that point, and the thing by such general councils so confirmed also, that in good faith I never neither read nor heard any thing of such effect on the other side, that ever could lead me to think that my conscience were well discharged, but rather in right

great peril if I should follow the other side and deny the primacy to be provided by God . . .[25]

More's comments regarding the papacy in his *Responsio ad Lutherum* give us a further insight into the sources that he had consulted in reaching his new understanding of papal primacy and provide us with the fullest exposition of his matured ideas on this matter. In fact, the textual revisions that More made to this, his first apologetical work, serve to demonstrate the change in his thinking, for while the first draft of the *Responsio,* probably composed at the beginning of 1523,[26] does to a certain extent offer a defense of the papacy, it is in the second draft, which became the final and published version toward the end of 1523,[27] that More definitively asserts papal primacy as a divine institution. As learned proponents of this doctrine, More lists Prierias (i.e., Silvestro Mazzolini), Ambrosius Catharinus, Johann Eck, Caspar Schatzgeyer, Johann Cochlaeus, Hieronymus Emser, Thomas Radinus of Piacenza, and Johann Fabri, observing that he had become familiar with the "sound and true reasoning" of their arguments partially through his own reading. But he reserves his most ardent praise for Bishop Fisher, who, More tells us, has totally clarified the issue of papal primacy by the proofs he has derived from the Gospels, the Acts of the Apostles, the Old Testament, and the consensus of the Latin and Greek Fathers.[28] So satisfied is More with the testimony of these men that he considers the question of papal authority a "closed issue".[29] Nonetheless, unashamed to identify himself as a "papist",[30] he takes the opportunity to add his voice to theirs:

> I am moved to obedient submission to this See by all those arguments which learned and holy men have assembled in support of this point; moreover, I am indeed moved not least by a fact which we have so often noticed; that not only has no one been hostile to the Christian faith without at the same time declaring war on that See, but also there has never been anyone who declared himself an enemy of that See with-

---

[25] Letter no. 199, Rogers, *Correspondence,* 498.
[26] Introduction, *CW* 5:832–34.
[27] Ibid.
[28] *CW* 5, bk. 1, chap. 10, pp. 139–41.
[29] Ibid., 141.
[30] Ibid., 183.

out shortly afterwards declaring himself also a notorious and foremost enemy and traitor both to Christ and to our religion.[31]

Although none of More's other apologetical works contains such a clear affirmation of papal primacy as we find in his *Responsio ad Lutherum,* it must be borne in mind that virtually all of these subsequent writings were composed and published in the politically explosive period from 1528 to 1533, during which the King was setting himself on a collision course with the Pope over the question of the validity of his marriage to Catherine of Aragon. It is obvious that under these delicate circumstances More would have judged it more discreet to speak of the absolute teaching authority of the Church in general, without specifically mentioning the pope, while there was still hope of reconciliation between Henry VIII and Rome. Such an explanation is borne out by More's March 5, 1534, letter to Cromwell, wherein he states that, in the composition of his *Confutation of Tyndale's Answer,* he had originally drafted an extended passage bringing together the various proofs in favor of papal primacy but that he later deliberately deleted this passage in view of the growing rift between the King and the Pope.[32] Despite this circumspection, More did retain in the published version of his *Confutation* the observation that from the days of the early Church onward good and learned Christian men have turned to the See of Rome for the resolution of any disputed questions regarding the faith, conforming themselves to the judgment of Rome, as did the Eastern Christians in the early general councils of the Church.[33] Moreover, it was during this very same period of his life that More chose to incur the King's wrath rather than compromise his by now firm belief in papal primacy; and it was at his trial, as we shall see later, that More was to make his climactic, uncompromising assertion of the supreme teaching and jurisdictional authority of the Bishop of Rome over the entire Church, a profession that he ratified with his own blood.

In addition to his beliefs in the primacy of the successor of Saint Peter and in the authority of the Church's ecumenical councils, More also believed in what has traditionally been called the *sensus fidei*— the shared assent of the entire Church to the tenets of the faith im-

---

[31] Ibid., 141.
[32] Letter no. 199, in Rogers, *Correspondence,* 500.
[33] *CW* 8, bk. 1, pp. 131–32.

planted in the hearts of individual Christians. Perhaps his most eloquent reference to this charism of the Church appears in his *Responsio ad Lutherum*:

> . . . [W]hereas He [God] wrote the old law first on stone, later on
> wood, yet always externally, He will write the new law inwardly by the
> finger of God on the book of the heart. Thus what lasted a very short
> time on harder material, He will cause to last forever on the most pliant
> material . . . The tablets made of rock were broken immediately; those
> of wood lasted a long time; but what He has written on the heart will
> last indelibly.
>
> On the heart, therefore, in the Church of Christ, there remains in-
> scribed the true gospel of Christ which was written there before the
> books of all the evangelists.[34]

While recognizing the *sensus fidei* of the faithful, More did not consider the Church a theological democracy, where revealed doctrine
could be determined by plebiscite. In response to Luther's protests
that "the authority of judging was snatched from the people" and
that the Church had fallen into error "through the stupid and superstitious obedience and patience of the people" to what he derisively
termed the "sacrilegious and abominable councils" of the bishops,[35]
More answered:

> . . . [D]o you think that while the matter is being examined the whole
> Christian people from the whole world should be called together at one
> time, as to an assembly of consuls to the Campus Martius, and their
> votes sought man by man? What sort of arrogation is it if the pastors
> before all others treat of the danger of the flock? To whom should the
> people rather wish that business delegated than to the bishops, to whom
> it especially belongs to be anxious about the safety of the people?[36]

If the Church has been instituted by God Himself with a visible
teaching authority and has been promised the continual and unerring
guidance of the Holy Spirit in transmitting to each generation the
deposit of faith, what is one to make of the phenomenon of theological dissent? Here we see the crux of More's disagreement with the
Protestant reformers. For More, the Catholic faith is a seamless gar-

---

[34] *CW* 5, bk. 1, chap. 8, p. 101.
[35] Luther, *Contra Henricum Regem Angliae*, quoted in *Responsio ad Lutherum*, *CW* 5, bk. 2, chap. 22, p. 627.
[36] *CW* 5, bk. 2, chap. 22, p. 627.

ment; assent to the Church's teachings means assent to *all* her teachings without exception: ". . . [H]e that forsaketh any truth of Christ's faith forsaketh Christ."[37] The introduction of new theological propositions that contradict doctrines already taught by the Church More sees, not as the work of the Holy Spirit, as the reformers claimed, but rather as instigated by the spirit of pride. Turning as he so often does to his favorite Church Father, he observes: ". . . [P]ride is as Saint Augustine sayeth the very mother of heretics."[38] It is a question, More believes, of having the humility to submit to the judgment of the Church; this is what the Church Fathers did and what they taught others to do as well.[39]

It was More's zeal for the unity of the Church that shaped his convictions in opposing theological dissent. Here again, Saint Cyprian's tract *De Unitate Ecclesiae* gives us an insight into More's thinking on this matter. Describing the seamless robe of our Lord as a symbol of the Church's unity, of which each baptized Christian who has "put on Christ" partakes, Cyprian warns that "He cannot possess the garment of Christ who tears and divides the Church of Christ."[40] Reflective likewise of More's perception of dissent is Saint Augustine's observation that "The body of Christ was left unbroken at the hands of His persecutors, but the body is not left unbroken at the hands of Christians."[41] For More, dissent constituted nothing less than a betrayal of Christ Himself. Thus in his last work, *De Tristitia Christi,* he compares dissenting clergymen to Judas: just as Judas greeted Christ in the garden with a traitor's kiss and salute, so too is the Lord saluted by those priests who, pretending to be His faithful followers, "consecrate the most holy body of Christ and then put to death Christ's members, Christian souls, by their false teaching and wicked example".[42] Dissenters, More observes, "make idols of their own false opinions"[43]

---

[37] *A Dialogue concerning Heresies,* ed. Thomas Lawler et al., vol. 6 of *Complete Works of St. Thomas More* (New Haven: Yale Univ. Press, 1981), bk. 4, chap. 16, pp. 420–21. Hereafter cited as *CW* 6.

[38] *CW* 8, bk. 6, p. 662.

[39] Ibid., bk. 7, p. 715.

[40] St. Cyprian, *Unity,* chap. 7, pp. 101–2.

[41] *Enarrationes in Ps. 33,* sermon 1, no. 7, as quoted in footnote of *Saint Augustine: Commentary on the Lord's Sermon on the Mount with Seventeen Related Sermons,* trans. Denis Kavanagh, O.S.A., Fathers of the Church, vol. 11 (New York: Fathers of the Church, 1951), 31.

[42] *CW* 14:389–91.

[43] *CW* 8, bk. 4, p. 485.

and would have the people "reject and refuse the faith" that "holy martyrs lived and died for".[44] That some reject the teachings of the Catholic Church and leave her because they refuse to accept her doctrines is, he points out, nothing new; many disciples left the company of our Lord upon hearing His teaching on the Real Presence of His Body and Blood in the Eucharist (Jn 6:66). But just as the Church survived in the disciples who did not desert Christ then, so shall she survive no matter how many may leave her for new heretical sects.[45]

In assessing their arguments, More observes that dissenters contradict themselves, denying all but what is clearly stated in Scripture while pronouncing the clearest biblical passages obscure, or even claiming to find support for their heterodox tenets in the very scriptural passages that contravene them. In their disputes they make the definition of the Church so ambiguous that in the end they conclude there is no Church on earth. Ultimately they set themselves so diametrically against the doctrines of the faith that there can be but two alternatives: either the dissenters are ungodly or else every Christian from "the time of Christ's passion" until now who has been reputed to be virtuous must be ungodly.[46] Furthermore, the dissenters teach as if they were the first to enunciate the true gospel. Was not the gospel preached by Christ, by the apostles, and by the Church Fathers the genuine gospel, More asks. To him the dissenters' assertiveness constitutes the height of presumption:

> Was no one saved from the time of Christ's passion until this present moment, when God finally chose you to save the world and preach the gospel of salvation to wretched mortals, corrupted and led astray until now by the apostles and evangelists?[47]

Even in the early days of the Reformation, the dissenters quickly splintered into a bewildering variety of sects, unable to agree among themselves; More compares their guidance to that of a crowd advising a man on how to find his way to a town, each pointing in a different direction.[48] The dissenters' exaltation of private judgment over the judgment of the Catholic Church ends in the doctrinal chaos of

---

[44] *Supplication of Souls*, bk. 1, in *CW* 7:167.

[45] *CW* 8, bk. 6, p. 671.

[46] *Letter to Bugenhagen*, in *CW* 7:95.

[47] Ibid., 29–31.

[48] *CW* 8, bk. 7, p. 772.

each man deciding for himself what is Scripture and how it is to be interpreted.[49]

If the dissenters would presume to claim the Christian Church has always professed what they now teach, or that she did sometime in the past, More challenges them to prove it.[50] Well aware of the reformers' efforts to drive an artificial wedge between the sixteenth-century Catholic Church and "the early Church", he observes that the only way to know what Christians believed a thousand years earlier is by reading their extant writings, and these only serve to confirm the teachings of the Catholic Church.[51] In condemning the Church of later ages by way of contrast to a supposedly more pristine early era, More catches Tyndale in something of a contradiction, for while according to the latter the dividing line between these two periods of Christian history is be found around the eighth century,[52] Tyndale nonetheless casts aspersion not only upon the later theologians of the Church but even upon Church Fathers and Doctors who lived and died in what he himself has defined as the early era of unadulterated Christianity.[53]

More is distressed to see how susceptible many a well-intentioned but gullible uneducated soul is to deception by the dissenters, whom they think are learned and upright men.[54] Even so, he sees no excuse for Christians to accept the testimony of any man, no matter how erudite or holy he may appear, if he asks them to believe himself rather than the Church—to accept his testimony rather than that professed in common for centuries by the Christian people and written in their hearts by the finger of God.[55] He perceived that the seeming success

---

[49] Ibid., p. 729.

[50] *Letter to Bugenhagen,* in *CW* 7:41.

[51] *CW 8,* bk. 7, p. 715.

[52] *An Answer unto Sir Thomas More's Dialogue,* in William Tyndale, *An Answer to Sir Thomas More's Dialogue, The Supper of the Lord and Wm. Tracy's Testament Expounded,* ed. Rev. Henry Walter, Parker Society, vol. 44 (1850; reprint, Johnson Reprint Corp., 1968), 8, 46, 145, 203. Hereafter cited as *Answer.*

[53] *CW 8,* bk. 6, p. 602; for Tyndale's view of the early Church, see *Answer,* 11; for his comments on the Church Fathers, see *Answer,* 48, and *The Obedience of a Christian Man,* in William Tyndale, *Doctrinal Treatises and Introductions to Different Portions of the Holy Scriptures,* ed. Rev. Henry Walter, Parker Society, vol. 42 (Cambridge: Cambridge Univ. Press, 1848; reprint, New York: Johnson Reprint Corp., 1968), 220, 329–30.

[54] *CW 6,* bk. 4, chap. 16, p. 418.

[55] Ibid., 419.

of heretical teachings often lay in their making Christianity a less demanding religion, a religion with "fewer rules", requiring less in the way of sacrifice or change in personal conduct:

> Luther claims it is a miracle that in such a short time so many Christians . . . went over to his heresies . . . As for people rushing headfirst into the life of freedom and sensual gratification he offers them—that seems about as much like a miracle as rocks falling downhill.[56]

More recognized that dissent did not make inroads overnight but rather achieved its ends by gradually desensitizing the faithful, as what is first considered utterly intolerable is with time given a hearing, gains a certain acceptability, and finally wins adherents:

> For the fact is that wherever this plague rages today most fiercely, everyone did not catch the disease in a single day. Rather the contagion spreads gradually and imperceptibly while those persons who despise it at first, afterwards can stand to hear it and respond to it with less than full scorn, then come to tolerate wicked discussions, and afterwards are carried away into error, until like a cancer (as the apostle says [2 Tim 2:17]) the creeping disease finally takes over the whole country.[57]

More already recognized that in some countries the adherents of the new beliefs were going to outnumber the "little flock" of Catholics who remained loyal to their Church.[58] Looking farther ahead, and building on what is implied in the Book of Revelation, More foresaw that a time would come following the spread of the gospel throughout the world when the faith would decline in Christian lands and the Church would be pressed so sorely by persecution that it would almost seem there were no Christian nations left; but this time would not last long.[59]

The image of the Church as a mother is an ancient one, expressed succinctly in Saint Cyprian's *De Unitate Ecclesiae:* "He cannot have God as a father who does not have the Church as a mother."[60] It is upon this image that More draws in stressing the contrast between

---

[56] *Letter to Bugenhagen,* in *CW* 7:31.

[57] *CW* 14:359.

[58] *CW* 8, bk. 7, p. 772.

[59] *Treatise upon the Passion,* chap. 4, lecture 2, in *Treatise on the Passion; Treatise on the Blessed Body; Instructions and Prayers,* ed. Garry Haupt, vol. 13 of *Complete Works of St. Thomas More* (New Haven: Yale Univ. Press, 1976), 173–74. Hereafter cited as *CW* 13.

[60] St. Cyprian, *Unity,* chap. 6, p. 100.

the Catholic Church and the newly founded sects of dissenters. As More explains, from the wholesome soil of the Scriptures both our true Mother the Church and those pretending to be our mother, the heretical sects, offer us fruit; that which the latter offer us is poisoned fruit, yet it is so cunningly proffered to us that it can be difficult to discern the difference until it is too late. Hence let us accept only the fruit our true Mother the Church offers us, no matter how un-appealing it may seem to our senses.[61] As to recognizing which is the true Church, how could we imagine that our loving Father in heaven would put us His children at risk of following the wrong sect and not make plainly known the identity of our real mother to those who are willing to learn the truth of the matter?[62] Turning to the image of the vine used by our Lord at the Last Supper (Jn 15:1-6), More sees this vine as representing the Church herself insomuch as she is the Mys-tical Body of Christ; the cut-off branches symbolize those who reject the Church's doctrines, so that no matter how green they may appear, they are doomed to wither, for they are severed from any nourish-ment.[63] Separated from Christ's Church, they are without Christ as their Head and lack the guidance of the Holy Spirit.[64] In addition to identifying her as the "Spouse of God",[65] More also describes the Church as Christ's "perpetual apostle", which she remains no matter how many nations may sever themselves from her and no matter how diminished in size she may become.[66] And in language replete with biblical allusions, More eloquently says of the Church that she is "set upon the high mountain of the stone that is Christ and therefore can never be hid".[67]

---

[61] *CW* 8, bk. 8, pp. 892-93.

[62] Ibid., 893.

[63] *CW* 6, bk. 2, chap. 5, pp. 206-7.

[64] *CW* 8, bk. 6, p. 669.

[65] Ibid., bk. 7, p. 725.

[66] Ibid., bk. 3, p. 252.

[67] Ibid.

CHAPTER VII

Scripture and the Church

The Bible and Tradition

The relationship of Sacred Scripture to the Church was in many ways the *cause célèbre* of the Reformation, as we have already seen in contrasting the reformers' insistence on the primacy of the Bible over all other authority—the idea of *sola scriptura*—with More's understanding of the Church as the living witness of the gospel, entrusted with both the written and the unwritten Word of God. As the issues of Scripture and oral tradition pervaded More's debates with his opponents, it will be necessary, at the risk of a certain degree of repetition, to explore these subjects in and of themselves, and at greater length.

Integral to More's deep love and veneration of Sacred Scripture was an unshakeable belief in its authenticity—that the Bible was a truthful and historically accurate account of God's dealings with mankind —that "the saying of our Saviour Christ is not a poet's fable, nor an harper's song, but the very holy word of almighty God himself."[1] Thus for More the veracity of the four Gospel narratives was beyond question:

> . . . [I]t is among Christian men more than shame to say it, that any of the four Evangelists should in the story write anything false, for then which of them might we trust, since we can be no more sure of the one than of the other.[2]

---

[1] *A Dialogue of Comfort against Tribulation,* ed. Louis Martz and Frank Manley, vol. 12 of *Complete Works of St. Thomas More* (New Haven: Yale Univ. Press, 1976), bk. 3, chap. 15, p. 240.

[2] *Treatise upon the Passion,* chap. 2, in *Treatise on the Passion; Treatise on the Blessed Body; Instructions and Prayers,* ed. Garry Haupt, vol. 13 of *Complete Works of St. Thomas More* (New Haven: Yale Univ. Press, 1976), 92. Hereafter cited as *CW* 13.

Directly challenging the *sola scriptura* premise, More asks the dissenters to show where in the Scriptures does it expressly say that Christ had made the apostles and evangelists write down every single word of His teachings that He willed to be taught to succeeding generations. Since the dissenters accept only what they can find stated in the Bible, they must therefore demonstrate the *sola scriptura* principle itself solely with the words of Scripture.[3] Hence More inquires of Luther's disciple Bugenhagen, ". . . [W]here did Christ with his own mouth teach you that we should believe only what he taught with his own mouth?"[4] Inasmuch as the Scriptures are but the inspired Word of God recorded in writing by His human instruments (the men who have written these inspired things down), any insistence on believing *only* the Scriptures would be tantamount, More warns, to believing more readily "the creature that wrote it, than God himself that inspired it".[5] When Tyndale attempts to defend the *sola scriptura* thesis by proposing that love of God and neighbor compelled the apostles to record all the necessary points of the faith as a safeguard against heretics, More asks how he can prove the apostles actually did this, for nowhere in the Scriptures does it say what Tyndale proposes.[6] It is simply fallacious to argue that God would not have left any of His Word unwritten lest any such unrecorded things be an occasion of doubts, dissension, and error; for the gospel was as much believed before it was written down as afterward, nor has the writing of the New Testament precluded doubts, dissension, and error as to the meaning of its content.[7]

If the dissenters rest their authority on Scripture, their authority to teach nonetheless remains in question, More points out, for the same Scriptures that they cite to support their positions are interpreted quite differently by the Church. How should the difference be explained? If Tyndale were to claim that the Scriptures are plainly and clearly

---

[3] *The Confutation of Tyndale's Answer*, ed. Louis Schuster et al., vol. 8 of *Complete Works of St. Thomas More* (New Haven: Yale Univ. Press, 1973), bk. 2, p. 158. Hereafter cited as *CW* 8.

[4] *Letter to Bugenhagen*, in *Letter to Bugenhagen, Supplication of Souls, Letter against Frith*, ed. Frank Manley et al., vol. 7 of *Complete Works of St. Thomas More* (New Haven: Yale Univ. Press, 1990), 57. This volume hereafter cited as *CW* 7.

[5] *CW* 8, bk. 3, p. 285.

[6] Ibid., 334–35.

[7] Ibid., bk. 2, p. 156.

understood to be in his favor, then why did not even one of the Church Fathers or Doctors, with all their learning and holiness, see and profess what was so evident and obvious to the dissenters? If, on the other hand, More adds, the Scriptures are obscure and difficult to interpret, then why should we think that the reformers have had any more success in divining the correct interpretation of the Bible than did all the Church Fathers, Doctors and saints since the time of Christ?[8]

More observes that the dissenters begin by refusing to accept anything they cannot find written in the Scriptures. Yet if they are shown that a particular practice is indeed found in the Bible, they reply by questioning whether it be fully found therein. By this course of argument they end in denying most of the sacraments, and the sacraments they retain are reduced (particularly by Tyndale) to nothing more than bare signs signifying only God's promises. But in such use of Scripture, not only do these dissenters set themselves against the interpretation of all the Church's Doctors and saints and the common faith of her people over fifteen centuries; they cannot even agree among themselves.[9]

More defended oral tradition with two principal arguments: (1) that the oral teaching of the gospel preceded the written Gospels, and (2) that the source for both the written teachings of our Lord, that is, the books of the New Testament, and the unwritten oral tradition passed down from apostolic times was one and the same—the Church —and hence it was illogical for the "reformers" to profess belief in the one (the Scriptures) while rejecting the other (oral tradition) as spurious. It is this latter line of reasoning that we find expressed in a key passage from Saint Augustine:

> Perhaps you will read the gospel to me, and will attempt to find there a testimony to Manichaeus. But should you meet with a person not yet believing the gospel, how would you reply to him were he to say, I do not believe? For my part, I should not believe the gospel except as moved by the authority of the Catholic Church. So when those on whose authority I have consented to believe in the gospel tell me not to believe in Manichaeus, how can I but consent? Take your choice . . . If you say, Do not believe the Catholics: you cannot fairly use the gospel

---

[8] Ibid., bk. 3, pp. 250-51.
[9] Ibid., bk. 2, pp. 156-57.

in bringing me to faith in Manichaeus; for it was at the command of the Catholics that I believed the gospel; —Again, if you say, You were right in believing the Catholics when they praised the gospel, but wrong in believing their vituperation of Manichaeus: do you think me such a fool as to believe or not to believe as you like or dislike, without any reason? . . . To convince me, then, you must put aside the gospel. If you keep to the gospel, I will keep to those who commanded me to believe the gospel; and, in obedience to them, I will not believe you at all.[10]

The above was a favorite passage of More's;[11] he uses it as a powerful proof text not only in his *Responsio ad Lutherum*[12] but also in his *Supplication of Souls* and, more extensively, in his *Confutation of Tyndale's Answer*.[13] In his *Apology,* while not explicitly citing these words of Augustine, he nonetheless presents the same argument, contending that both Luther and Tyndale only know what is or is not Sacred Scripture by accepting the centuries-old judgment of the Church in this regard; if therefore they trust the Church's decisions as to what the apostles and evangelists actually did or did not write, why should they not likewise accept the Church's judgment concerning the unwritten teachings of our Lord and His apostles?[14] But More enhances the latter argument by stressing that the Church was in existence and evangelizing peoples even before any of the New Testament books were written:

> . . . [I]f the Church were nothing bounden to believe, but only the things plainly written in scripture, . . . then had Christ's Church in the beginning been at liberty to leave a great part of Christ's own words unbelieved. For the Church was gathered and the faith believed, before any part of the New Testament was put in writing.[15]

---

[10] St. Augustine, *Contra epistolam Manichaei,* chap. 5, no. 6, in *St. Augustin: The Writings against the Manichaeans and against the Donatists,* ed. Philip Schaff, vol. 4 of *A Select Library of the Nicene and Post-Nicene Fathers of the Christian Church* (1887; reprint, Grand Rapids, Mich.: William B. Eerdmanns Publishing Co., 1974), 131.

[11] Notes, *CW* 8:1634.

[12] *Responsio ad Lutherum,* ed. John M. Headley and trans. Sr. Scholastica Mandeville, vol. 5 of *Complete Works of St. Thomas More* (New Haven: Yale Univ. Press, 1969), bk. 2, chap. 21, pp. 603–7.

[13] *Supplication of Souls,* bk. 2, in *CW* 7:182–83; *CW* 8, bk. 7, pp. 729–41.

[14] *The Apology,* ed. J. B. Trapp, vol. 9 of *Complete Works of St. Thomas More* (New Haven: Yale Univ. Press, 1979), chap. 5, p. 18.

[15] Ibid.

When Tyndale attempts to dismiss the question of how the dissenters can know what is or is not authentic Scripture by sanctimoniously answering, "Who taught the eagles to spy out their prey?",[16] More returns to Augustine's classic argument with delightfully comical mock-seriousness, reminding Tyndale that even his mentor Luther had conceded the role of the Church in determining what was Scripture:

> But now ye see well good readers by this reason, that Saint Augustine in respect of these noble eagles that spy this prey without the mean of the Church, was but a silly poor chicken. For he confesseth plainly against such high eagle heretics, that himself had not known nor believed the gospel but by the Catholic Church.
>   Howbeit it is no great marvel, since God is not so familiar with such simple chickens, as with his gay glorious eagles.
>   But one thing is there that I can not cease to marvel of, since God inspireth Tyndale and such other eagles, and thereby maketh them spy this prey themselves; how could it hap that the goodly golden old eagle Martin Luther himself, in whose goodly golden nest this young eagle bird was hatched, lacked that inspiration?[17]

As More observes in his *Confutation of Tyndale's Answer,* not even Tyndale could possibly believe that after the apostles had written their Gospels and Epistles they thenceforth no longer claimed to preach from their own authority as oral witnesses but instead based their authority on the new writings of either themselves or of their fellow apostles.[18]

More compares the distinction between Scripture and oral tradition with the laws of England: some of the country's laws have been written down, others have not, but would Tyndale accept only the written laws as binding?[19] And in virtue of Tyndale's presupposition that *all* of God's revelation has been written down,[20] it would follow analogously that since some of England's laws have been written down, *all* of her laws are in writing, and there are no unwritten laws. More

---

[16] *An Answer unto Sir Thomas More's Dialogue,* in William Tyndale, *An Answer to Sir Thomas More's Dialogue, The Supper of the Lord and Wm. Tracy's Testament Expounded,* ed. Rev. Henry Walter, Parker Society, vol. 44 (1850; reprint, Johnson Reprint Corp., 1968), 49. Hereafter cited as *Answer.*

[17] *CW* 8, bk. 7, p. 723.

[18] Ibid., bk. 2, p. 151.

[19] Ibid., bk. 3, p. 291.

[20] *Answer,* 26.

made this point because as a lawyer he was well aware that England did indeed have a whole corpus of unwritten law, just as the Church has her oral tradition.[21]

Rebuking Tyndale for suggesting that the Church has placed the merely human judgment of men above Holy Writ,[22] More stresses the equal force of Scripture and tradition, both of which are subject to the interpretation, not of men, but of "God and his Holy Spirit": ". . . [God] is as well to be believed without writing as with writing, and that himself and his Holy Spirit, understandeth his own writing better than all the creatures of the whole world."[23]

In accordance with Christ's promise at the Last Supper (Jn 16:13), More explains, the Holy Spirit has always instructed and will always instruct the Church in the truth as much through the unwritten word of oral tradition, written in the hearts of Christians, as through the Word of God inscribed on stone or in books of animal skin. These are the very same truths professed by the apostles, the martyrs, confessors, and Doctors, as well as by the majority of Christians throughout the centuries. Even the dissenters originally believed these truths, More adds; but having lost their powers of discernment they now condemn as evil those things that from the time of "Christ's death" to the present "all holy men, all good people, all true Christian nations" have believed to be good.[24]

Inveighing against the ceremonies of the Church's worship as neither serving the needs of one's neighbors nor rendering fitting honor to God, Tyndale contrasts Catholic practices with his own notion of an early Church devoid of ritual, in which nothing but the "pure word of God" was preached.[25] But what does Tyndale mean by the "pure word of God", More asks. If he is speaking of both the written and unwritten Word of God, then this is no different from what the Church preaches in their own day. If Tyndale were to raise the objection that contemporary preachers have added to the Word of God the ideas of the Church Doctors, More would answer that the writings of these Doctors who spent their lives studying, living, and proclaiming

---

[21] *CW* 8, bk. 3, p. 295.

[22] *Answer*, 9.

[23] *CW* 8, bk. 1, pp. 132–33.

[24] Ibid., 44–45.

[25] *Answer*, 11.

God's Word simply help us to understand and know God's Word.[26] If, on the other hand, Tyndale means by the "pure word of God" that only the written Word, Sacred Scripture, was preached in the early Church, then he cannot be referring to the very earliest days of the Church, when the evangelists had not yet set down the Gospels in writing:

> . . . Christ our Saviour himself preached more than his word written, and promised also without writing, and was believed then without writing, that he would send the Holy Ghost that should teach his Church all truth without writing, and Christ full truly fulfilled his promise without writing, and yet will not Tyndale now believe him without writing . . .[27]

More backs up his defense of the oral tradition of the Church with a battery of quotations from the Church Fathers, including passages from Origen (A.D. 184–254), Pseudo-Dionysius the Areopagite (fifth century or later), Saint Hilary of Poitiers (315–368), Saint Jerome (343–420), Saint Leo the Great (390–461), Saint John Chrysostom (347–407), Saint John Damascene (675–749), and Saint Augustine (354–430).[28] Thus the following passage from Origen's fifth homily on the Book of Numbers serves to counteract Tyndale's assertion[29] that the validity of a Christian ceremony is contingent upon its being understood or explained (what follows is More's own translation):

> In the observances of the Church, some things there are, which must of necessity be observed and kept, and yet the cause why appeareth not to every man. As (for example) that we kneel when we pray, and that of all parts of the heavens, we most specially turn us toward the east. I suppose that no man lightly knoweth the cause why. Moreover of the sacrament of the altar, either the manner in the receiving, or the guise and fashion of the consecration, or of the formal words and ceremonies used in baptism, and of the questions and answers used in the same: who may well open and declare the reason? And yet all these things though they be covered and hid, we bear upon our shoulders what time we in such wise accomplish and fulfill them, as we have received them of the great bishop Christ and his children, delivered and commended unto us.[30]

---

[26] *CW* 8, bk. 2, pp. 149–50.

[27] Ibid., 151.

[28] Ibid., bk. 3, pp. 368–75.

[29] *Answer,* 7, 30, 97.

[30] *CW* 8, bk. 3, pp. 368–69.

In assembling these texts from the Church Fathers, More turns to his favorite, Saint Augustine, no fewer than five times,[31] quoting among other passages the following unambiguous affirmation of oral tradition from Augustine's Epistle 54 to Januarius (the following is a modern translation):

> . . . [R]egarding those other observances which we keep and all the world keeps, and which do not derive from Scripture but from tradition, we are given to understand that they have been ordained or recommended to be kept by the Apostles themselves, or by plenary councils, whose authority is well founded in the Church. Such are the annual commemorations of the Lord's Passion, Resurrection and Ascension into heaven, the descent of the Holy Spirit from heaven, and other such observances as are kept by the universal Church wherever it is found.[32]

More defends his citation of John 21:25 as proof that not everything necessary to our faith is written in the Scriptures. Responding to Tyndale's claim that the passage refers only to Christ's miracles (insofar as it speaks of other things Christ *did* rather than other things He taught),[33] More argues that clearly our Lord's preaching must be included among the things that He *did* throughout His public ministry. John's Gospel is an account of both Christ's words and His miracles; hence the "other things" John refers to as remaining unwritten at the end of his Gospel would logically include words as well as miracles. Moreover, an examination of the contents of Saint John's Gospel reveals that the Evangelist did not record all of Christ's teachings, for there are teachings in the other three Gospels that are not included in his. And the same can be said of the other evangelists as well. Tyndale cannot escape this by claiming that God saw to it that the four Gospels when taken together encompass every necessary teaching, for he could never prove this to be so either by Scripture or by reason.[34]

More traps his opponent in a potential contradiction by noting that the Eucharist, one of the only two sacraments that Tyndale accepts, is not to be found anywhere in Saint John's Gospel if one accepts Tyn-

---

[31] Ibid., 371–74.

[32] Letter no. 54, c. A.D. 400, in *Saint Augustine: Letters,* vol. 1, *1–82,* trans. Sr. Wilfrid Parsons, S.N.D., Fathers of the Church, vol. 12 (New York: Fathers of the Church, 1951), 252–53.

[33] *Answer,* 96.

[34] *CW* 8, bk. 3, pp. 311–13.

dale's own interpretation of the Scriptures. For Saint John does not say anything about the institution of the Eucharist during his account of the Last Supper, and Tyndale refuses to accept that the eucharistic discourse of our Lord in John 6 pertains to the Eucharist. Hence how can Tyndale argue that John was referring only to miracles when at the end of his Gospel he says that there were other things he had not recorded?[35]

The Translation of Sacred Scripture

Thomas More was by no means opposed to the translation of the Bible into the vernacular. With his close friend Erasmus a prominent advocate of vernacular biblical texts, More believed that the good to be accomplished by placing the Scriptures into the hands of faithful Catholics more than outweighed whatever mischief dissenters might attempt to create by their abuse of the Word of God.[36] Thus we find him advocating methods of scriptural translation rather similar to those of our own day:

> . . . [I]t might be with diligence well and truly translated by some good Catholic and well learned man, or by diverse dividing the labour among them, and after conferring their several parts together each with [the] other. And after that might the work be allowed and approved by the ordinaries, and by their authorities so put unto print . . .[37]

In response to the charge that the clergy were trying to hide the Bible from the laity by banning Tyndale's English translation of the New Testament,[38] More answers that up to the fourteenth century there had been English translations of the Bible that were approved by

---

[35] Ibid., 313. For the passages in Tyndale relevant to this, see *Answer*, 29, 178–79, and *A Brief Declaration of the Sacraments* (c. 1533–1535), in William Tyndale, *Doctrinal Treatises and Introductions to Different Portions of the Holy Scriptures*, ed. Rev. Henry Walter, Parker Society, vol. 42 (1848; reprint, New York: Johnson Reprint Corp., 1968), 368–69.

[36] *A Dialogue concerning Heresies*, ed. Thomas Lawler et al., vol. 6 of *Complete Works of St. Thomas More* (New Haven: Yale Univ. Press, 1981), bk. 3, chap. 16, pp. 332, 340. Hereafter cited as *CW* 6.

[37] Ibid., p. 341.

[38] *The Obedience of a Christian Man*, in *Doctrinal Treatises*, 146–47, 160–61 (hereafter cited as *Obedience*); *William Tyndale's Five Books of Moses, called the Pentateuch, being a Verbatim Reprint of the Edition of M.CCCCC.XXX*, ed. Rev. J. I. Mombert (New York: Anson D. F. Randolph and Co., 1884), preface, 2–3.

the clergy and "by good and godly people with devotion and soberness well and reverently read".[39] Problems arose only when the heretic
John Wycliff (1329?–1384) endeavored to promote a new vernacular
edition of the Bible with the intent of using it to lend credence to his
own heterodox opinions. It was therefore in response to this abuse of
Scripture by Wycliff and his followers, More continues, that a council
of England's ecclesiastical authorities, convening at Oxford in the year
1408, ruled that from henceforth all translations of the Bible would
require approval at the diocesan level or from a provincial council before being allowed into circulation (More is here speaking of what is
known as the Arundel Constitution). In this context More notes that
the fourth-century Church Father and biblical scholar Saint Jerome
had warned that translation of the biblical texts was a dangerous task,
in view of the difficulties in accurately reproducing the meaning of
the original in a different tongue, with a different sentence structure.
The English law took what More saw as a reasonable approach to
the problem, neither prohibiting the reading of previous orthodox
translations of the Bible nor banning all new translations; the Wycliff
Bible was proscribed, not because it was new, but because it was badly
done. It was for this same reason that Tyndale's New Testament was
banned.[40] More admitted that there were clergymen who were afraid
to put the Bible into the hands of the laity for fear that there would be
abuses.[41] Nonetheless he could also testify from firsthand experience
as a layman, ". . . [I] myself have seen and can show you bibles fair
and old written in English, which have been known and seen by the
bishop of the diocese, and left in lay men's hands and women's too
such as he knew for good and Catholic folk that used it with devotion and soberness."[42] Moreover, More fully expected that the lack
of a widely accessible, authorized English edition would be rectified
in the near future:

> . . . [M]y mind giveth me that his Majesty is of his blessed zeal so minded
> to move this matter unto the prelates of the clergy, among whom I have
> perceived some of the greatest and of the best of their own minds well
> inclinable thereto already, that we lay people shall in this matter ere long

---

[39] *CW* 6, bk. 3, chap. 14, p. 314.
[40] Ibid., 314–16.
[41] Ibid., bk. 3, chap. 16, pp. 331–32.
[42] Ibid., chap. 15, p. 317.

time pass, except the fault be found in ourselves, be well and fully satisfied and content.[43]

More's comment about the King was not based merely on conjecture; in 1526 there had been published as a response to Martin Luther a letter of Henry VIII in which the King had stated:

> And if you do . . . not descant upon scripture, nor trust too much your own comments and interpretations, but in every doubt that shall insourge, learn the truth and incline to the same, by the advice of your pastoral fathers of the soul, it shall not only encourage well learned men to set forth and translate into our mother tongue many good things and virtuous, which for fear of wrong taking, they dare not yet do; but also that ye, by the good use thereof, shall take much good and great spiritual profit, which thing in you perceived, shall give occasion that such holy things, as evil disposed persons by false and erroneous translation corrupted . . . good men and well learned may be parcase in time coming the bolder, truly and faithfully translated, substantially viewed and corrected . . . to put in your hands, to your inward solace and ghostly comfort . . .[44]

More's hopes for a newly translated Catholic Bible in the English tongue during his lifetime were never realized, for only three years after his comments in this regard appeared in print, the English Church began to separate itself from communion with Rome. When in 1537 Henry VIII did grant approval for the publication of an English Bible, authorization was given to none other than Tyndale's version (as revised by Miles Coverdale).[45]

More is exasperated with Tyndale's use, in his Scripture translations, of novel vocabulary in the place of universally recognized and understood words, as if "all England should go to school with Tyndale to learn English."[46] He observes in Tyndale's texts of the Bible an uncanny consistency in changing the translation of certain key words; thus the word for "church" he renders as "congregation", that for "priest" he alters to "senior", and "grace" becomes "favor".[47] Tyn-

---

[43] Ibid., chap. 16, p. 344.

[44] "A Copy of the letters wherin Kyng Henry the eyght made answere unto a certayn letter of Martyn Luther", 1526, quoted in notes, *CW* 6:697–98 (spelling rendered closer to modern English).

[45] W. E. Campbell, *Erasmus, Tyndale and More* (Milwaukee: Bruce Publishing Co., 1950), 125.

[46] *CW* 8, bk. 2, p. 212.

[47] Ibid., 144.

dale himself, More adds, has admitted to having changed the translation of these words so as to reflect his own theology. And it was
precisely for this reason—Tyndale's heretical coloring of Sacred Scripture—that his translation of the New Testament was condemned.[48]
Hence More sees in the Tyndale texts a disingenuous manipulation
of the Word of God:

> For first he [Tyndale] would make the people believe that we should
> believe nothing but plain scripture . . . And then would he with his false
> translation make the people ween further that such articles of our faith
> as he laboreth to destroy, and which be well proved by holy scripture,
> were in holy scripture nothing spoken of, but that the preachers have
> all these fifteen hundred years misreported the gospel and englished the
> scripture wrong to lead the people purposely out of the right way.[49]

In his *Answer unto Sir Thomas More's Dialogue,* Tyndale admits that
he universally used the word "congregation" in place of "church"
when translating the Latin term *ecclesia* (in his English edition of the
New Testament), not because the word "church" was incorrect, but
because he believed the clergy had kept the people in ignorance of
the actual meaning of this latter expression by teaching that only they
—the clergy—were "the Church":

> Wherefore, inasmuch as the clergy . . . had appropriate[d] unto them-
> selves the term that of right is common unto all the whole congregation
> of them that believe in Christ; and with their false and subtle wiles had
> beguiled and mocked the people, and brought them into the ignorance
> of the word; making them understand by this word *church* nothing but
> the shaven flock of them that shore the whole world; therefore in the
> translation of the new Testament, where I found this word *ecclesia,* I
> interpreted it by this word *congregation.*[50]

Responding to this, More vehemently insists that he knows of no
Christian so ignorant as to think that the term "Church" means only
the clergy; rather, the clergy have always taught that the Church includes all the faithful. More acknowledges that there was a pious custom among Englishmen of referring to the clergy as the "church", but

---

[48] Ibid., 145.
[49] *CW* 6, bk. 3, chap. 8, p. 290.
[50] *Answer,* 13.

this was nothing more than a manner of speech and was understood as such.[51]

Tyndale proceeds to claim that even if "congregation" is not as specific a term as "church", the circumstances under which he uses it make its intended meaning clear.[52] More finds this explanation absurd —one might just as well replace the term "world" with the word "football" [i.e., a round ball], joining it with the context that people walk upon it and ships sail upon it, etc. Thus, he can give the word whatever meaning he wishes and justify the substitution. Moreover, the only "circumstances" that Tyndale has provided to elucidate his use of "congregation" are his heterodox tenets that there is no ordained priesthood distinguishable from the priesthood of all Christians[53] and that the Church consists, not of the common body of the Christian faithful, but rather of an invisible corps of unidentifiable chosen believers.[54] So far as More is concerned, Tyndale's motivation in replacing "church" with "congregation" is none other than to promote his own ecclesiology, in which the nature of the Church is radically redefined.[55]

Tyndale defends himself by arguing that since the word "church" can sometimes be used to refer to any body of individuals, it is thus as generalized a term as the word "congregation" and therefore interchangeable with the latter.[56] But More answers with a fundamental principle of linguistics: that the meaning of a word is determined by what it is commonly and normally used to mean in the particular language of which it is a part. Hence, as in common speech the word "congregation" is far broader a term than "church" and lacks the particular Christian significance of the latter word, any suggestion otherwise is inappropriate to the objective task of translation: "Thus may Tyndale abuse the holy name of church to any lewd thing that he list, but this is not the part of a translator."[57]

Answering Tyndale's contention that the Greek word at issue, *ecclesia*, was used first by the pagans and therefore did not specifically mean

---

[51] *CW* 8, bk. 2, pp. 164–66.

[52] *Answer*, 15.

[53] *Obedience*, 255.

[54] *Answer*, 30–33, 108–10, 113.

[55] *CW* 8, bk. 2, pp. 165–67.

[56] *Answer*, 15.

[57] *CW* 8, bk. 2, pp. 167–68 (quote on 168).

a body of Christians,[58] More explains that whereas in Greek there is no separate word for a Christian assembly, there is such a word in English—"church". Hence while the same word, *ecclesia*, must necessarily be used for both an assemblage of Christians and for non-Christian assemblies in Greek, these two distinct concepts can and should be differentiated in English. Thus while More readily agrees that *ecclesia* certainly should not always be translated as "church", he must likewise reject Tyndale's universal rendering of the word as "congregation". When in the New Testament the Greek term *ecclesia* specifically refers to a body of Christians, the specific English word for it—"church" —should be used instead.[59]

Addressing Tyndale's substitution of the word "image" for "idol" in his scriptural translations, More cites the following passage from Saint Paul's First Letter to the Corinthians (1 Cor 10:19–20):

> What do I imply then? That food offered to idols is anything, or that an idol is anything? No, I imply that what pagans sacrifice they offer to demons and not to God. I do not want you to be partners with demons.

In the above words, More stresses, it is clear that what is being condemned is not the use of images in and of themselves but rather the worship the pagans accorded to their false gods ("demons") that these images were made to represent. More reasons that if, on the one hand, the use of images in this case is reprehensible precisely because of who or what is being thereby worshipped (the false gods), it logically follows that the use of images in the worship of the true God and the veneration of His saints is a praiseworthy practice because of who is being worshipped (God) or honored (His saints). What More sees in Tyndale's translations is a deliberate attempt to equate all images used in worship with those particular images called idols that are dedicated to the worship of false gods. Hence Tyndale frequently translates the word for "idol" in the original text as "image" instead, a change that leads the unsuspecting reader to think that Holy Scripture forbids all religious imagery. Were Tyndale to justify the change with the defense that idols are a form of image and that therefore the terms are interchangeable, More would respond that by the same token one might just as illogically say that the word "devil" can be changed to

---

[58] *Answer*, 15.

[59] *CW* 8, bk. 2, pp. 168–72.

"angel" wherever it appears in the Scriptures, with the excuse that devils are, indeed, angels (albeit fallen ones).[60]

More's objections to Tyndale's English texts of the Scriptures concerned not only the question of faulty translation but also the interpretive commentaries with which Tyndale attempted to explain the Bible to his readers, as in the following gloss from the 1525 Cologne edition of his New Testament. It accompanies the passage from Saint Matthew's Gospel in which our Lord bestows primacy upon Saint Peter (". . . [Y]ou are Peter . . . whatever you bind on earth shall be bound in heaven . . ." [Mt 16:17–19]):

> Peter in the Greek signifieth a stone in English. This confession is the rock. Now is Simon Bar-Jona, or Simon Jona's son, called Peter, because of his confession. Whosoever then this wise confesseth of Christ, the same is called Peter. Now is this confession come to all that are true Christian. Then is every Christian man and woman Peter. Read Bede, Austin [Augustine] and Jerome, of the manner of loosing and binding and note how Jerome checketh the presumption of the Pharisees in his time, which yet had not so monstrous interpretations as our new gods have feigned.[61]

In the above gloss Tyndale is clearly attempting to recast one of the traditional proof texts of papal primacy in an entirely different light, giving it a new meaning consonant with his own theology, while at the same time adding a less than subtle slur against the popes ("our new gods"). It was commentaries of this nature that led More to say of the dissenters that they "ever ask for scripture as though they believed holy scripture, and yet when it maketh against them, they then with false and fond glosses of their own making do but mock and shift over in such a trifling manner that it may well appear they believe not scripture neither."[62]

More sees the dissenters as contradicting themselves by their very attempts to reinterpret Scripture; for if each person is, according to them, able to understand the bare Scriptures correctly, why do the proponents of personal interpretation continue to provide interpretations?

---

[60] Ibid., 172–76.

[61] Quoted in F. F. Bruce, *The English Bible: A History of Translations from the Earliest English Versions to the New English Bible* (New York: Oxford Univ. Press, 1970), 34–35 (spelling modernized).

[62] *Supplication of Souls*, bk. 2, in *CW* 7:176.

For all the scripture (they say) is open and plain enough. And therefore they put every man and woman unlearned in boldness and courage, to be in the scripture sufficiently their own masters themselves. But while they thus teach them, they forget that by their own teaching they should hold their peace themselves. And in deed so were it good they did, but if they taught better.[63]

More points out that the assent given to the Scriptures flows from the same faith by which assent is given to oral tradition. And just as it is possible through one's own insolence to yield to doubts regarding the latter, so is it possible to succumb to doubts about the former, even to the point of viewing Holy Writ as nothing but "fantasies". More wonders just how firm is the faith of those who say they believe nothing but the Bible, for despite their profession, they already deny a part of it—the two books of Maccabees, the contents of which contradict their denial of the existence of Purgatory. Just as conveniently, More adds, does Luther question the inspired character of the Epistle of Saint James, which clearly refutes his theology of faith without works.[64] Where might such selective acceptance of the canonically established Scriptures ultimately lead? More observes: ". . . [S]o might they by the same reason reject the remnant too, and so they will I ween at last . . ."[65] In his *Supplication of Souls*, he again addresses this issue, warning that the rejection of the Church's authority to determine what is or is not Scripture will in the end undermine the authority of all the Scriptures:

And surely if the Church might so be deceived in the choice of Holy Scripture that they might take and approve for Holy Scripture any book that were none, then stood all Christendom in doubt and unsurety whether Saint John's Gospel were Holy Scripture or not, and so forth of all the New Testament.[66]

---

[63] *The Answer to a Poisoned Book,* ed. Clarence Miller, vol. 11 of *Complete Works of St. Thomas More* (New Haven: Yale Univ. Press, 1985), bk. 3, chap. 4, p. 144.

[64] *CW* 8, bk. 2, p. 156; see also *Supplication of Souls,* bk. 2, in *CW* 7:180.

[65] *CW* 8, bk. 6, p. 639.

[66] *Supplication of Souls,* bk. 2, in *CW* 7:183.

CHAPTER VIII

Thomas More on the
Life of Grace in the Church

From the questions of how and in what form the content of Divine
Revelation has been entrusted to the Church and preserved by her
over the centuries, we pass on now to More's presentation of what
Divine Revelation specifically tells us about mankind's redemption.
At issue in the conflict between the Catholic Church and the vanguards of the Protestant Reformation were the nature of the fall of
man, the relationship between justification and faith, what role, if any,
an individual played in his own salvation, the exercise of free will,
and the channels of grace in the Church, most especially the seven
sacraments. Of course it is obvious from what we have already seen
of More's ecclesiology that he found the definitive answer to all these
questions in the unerring judgment of the Church, as promised by
Christ and effected by the guidance of the Holy Spirit. Nonetheless,
More was prepared to explain and defend the individual doctrines of
Christianity as need be; and in so doing, he reveals to us the sheer
breadth and depth of his own faith and convictions.

We may begin with the divisive issues surrounding mankind's fall
and his justification as effected by Christ. There is much to be said
for the historian Brendan Bradshaw's observation that More's Christian humanism played a key role in his response to Luther's excessively grim view of fallen human nature.[1] It is the Christian humanist
tradition that would have engendered in More a heightened sense of
the fundamental goodness of the human person, created in the image

---

[1] Brendan Bradshaw, "The Controversial Sir Thomas More", *Journal of Ecclesiastical History* 36 (October 1985): 545, 565–69.

of God, a reality enshrined only a few years earlier by Michelangelo on the ceiling of the Sistine Chapel. So much of what Christian humanism stood for stemmed from its vision of human nature, truly damaged by original sin, yet nonetheless capable of serving as the handmaid of grace, endowed with a free will that, in More's words, "doth . . . in such as have age and reason, work and walk on with God".[2] From this it becomes clear that Luther's doctrine of a hopelessly depraved human nature incapable of any good and deprived of a free will would have been repugnant to More. And it is this tenet of Luther that laid the foundation for the German reformer's *solafideism,* the concept that faith is the one and only thing required of a man in his salvation, to the exclusion of any operative role for whatever good actions he might perform. Here, too, Luther preaches a new dogma that would have been antithetical to the Christian humanists' emphasis upon the active pursuit of perfection in one's own life through the imitation of Christ. If as Luther claims good works are essentially of no avail, then what purpose is there in imitating Christ? Perhaps it is no mere coincidence that More in the preface to his *Confutation of Tyndale's Answer* tells his readers that he would rather see them reading Thomas à Kempis' classic *Imitation of Christ* than either his or Tyndale's polemical works.[3]

Like Luther, Tyndale in his earlier writings also insists that the actions by which one serves God—"good works" such as prayer, fasting, and almsgiving—are of no avail in the attainment of salvation and can even be idolatrous; for him, heaven is attainable only through faith in Christ's promises, joined of course to the merits of Christ's Passion, but nothing more.[4] Although Tyndale does admit that good works are an integral part of Christian life, he sees them as simply an outward manifestation and automatic outcome of faith, denying them

---

[2] *The Confutation of Tyndale's Answer,* ed. Louis Schuster et al., vol. 8 of *Complete Works of St. Thomas More* (New Haven: Yale Univ. Press, 1973), bk. 7, p. 799. Hereafter cited as *CW* 8. More mistakenly attributes the *Imitation* to the French ecclesiastical writer Jean Gerson.

[3] Ibid., preface, 37.

[4] *Parable of the Wicked Mammon,* in William Tyndale, *Doctrinal Treatises and Introductions to Different Portions of the Holy Scriptures,* ed. Rev. Henry Walter, Parker Society, vol. 42 (1848; reprint, New York: Johnson Reprint Corp., 1968), 46–47, 65, 103, 106, 122. Hereafter cited as *Mammon.*

any effective role in one's eternal destiny.[5] Thus in his *Obedience of a Christian Man* Tyndale states:

> . . . [W]hosoever goeth about to make satisfaction for his sins to God-ward, saying in his heart, This much have I sinned, this much will I do again; or this-wise will I live to make amends withal; or this will I do, to get heaven withal; the same is an infidel, faithless, and damned in his deed-doing, and hath lost his part in Christ's blood . . .[6]

Yet this view of Tyndale and other reformers, More demonstrates, is contradicted by Christ's own words in the Scriptures. If good works avail not, why does our Lord promise a reward to those who give so little as a cup of water to the thirsty (Mk 9:41; Mt 10:42)? Or why does Christ tell us that on the Day of Judgment heaven will be the reward of those who in life performed works of mercy for the poor and needy (and hell the punishment of those who have not done so [Mt 25:31–46]) if such acts are worthless? Even in the Old Testament, More shows, there is testimony to the value of good works performed with faith, hope, and charity in making satisfaction for sins, as in Sirach 3, which says that as water "extinguishes a blazing fire; so almsgiving atones for sin" (v. 30). This of course is not to say that good works alone are enough to save us—apart from the value given them by God and the merits of Christ's Passion, our works would avail nothing. Yet, More explains, "it hath pleased his high bounty to give so great a rich price for so poor and simple ware as are all men's works."[7]

Even faith itself Tyndale does not believe a man can do anything to attain—he sees it purely as an unmerited gift of God.[8] More replies that surely no one would ever deny that faith is a gift of God. Yet how is faith any less a gift if men by actively making an effort become the recipients of it? Is a gift, More asks, any less a gift simply because it is willingly taken by the recipient?[9]

---

[5] Ibid., 50, 45–56, 61.

[6] *The Obedience of a Christian Man,* in Tyndale, *Doctrinal Treatises,* 228. Hereafter cited as *Obedience.*

[7] *CW* 8, bk. 1, pp. 53–54 (quote on 54); bk. 4, pp. 402, 404.

[8] *Mammon,* 53, 56.

[9] *CW* 8, bk. 4, p. 504.

To Tyndale's claim that Catholics think they can keep God's law merely by relying on themselves,[10] More replies by denying that this has ever been the case; rather, it is the belief of the Church that man can indeed work toward his own salvation by keeping the law, but only with the help of God's grace. The Church continually warns the faithful against arrogantly thinking they can perform good works without relying totally upon the assistance of Almighty God. More sees Tyndale's accusation as stemming from his heretical denial that man has any freedom of will with which to keep the commandments of God.[11] Thus the question at issue is not salvation by works without faith but rather the reformers' proposition of salvation by faith without good works, wherein a man's actions are made to have no effectual bearing upon his redemption whatsoever, as if he could sin with impunity and need fear no consequences in the next life,[12] thereby "turning the nature of man into worse than a beast and the goodness of God into worse than the devil".[13] Tyndale's and Luther's attempts to soften the libertarian implications of their *solafideism* by proposing that faith like a tree necessarily yields a fruit of good works[14] makes no sense, for, as More explains, if good works are worthless, what good is the tree that produces such valueless fruit?[15]

For More, the reformers' doctrine of predestination—that regardless of anyone's conduct only a predetermined elect will be saved and that all others are predestined to damnation—is abominable; he cannot say enough in condemning this idea, branding it "detestable", "blasphemous", and the "very worst" of all heresies.[16] By "affirming that we do no sin of ourselves by any power of our own will but by the compulsion and handiwork of God",[17] it "maketh God

---

[10] *An Answer unto Sir Thomas More's Dialogue,* in William Tyndale, *An Answer to Sir Thomas More's Dialogue, The Supper of the Lord and Wm. Tracy's Testament Expounded,* ed. Rev. Henry Walter, Parker Society, vol. 44 (1850; reprint, Johnson Reprint Corp., 1968), 11. Hereafter cited as *Answer.*

[11] *CW* 8, bk. 2, p. 149; bk. 4, pp. 400–401.

[12] Ibid., bk. 4, pp. 402–3.

[13] *A Dialogue concerning Heresies,* ed. Thomas Lawler et al., vol. 6 of *Complete Works of St. Thomas More* (New Haven: Yale Univ. Press, 1981), bk. 4, chap. 17, p. 428. Hereafter cited as *CW* 6.

[14] *Mammon,* 50, 54–56, 61.

[15] *CW* 8, bk. 4, p. 401.

[16] *CW* 6, bk. 4, chap. 10, pp. 376–77; chap. 11, p. 400.

[17] Ibid., chap. 10, p. 377.

the cause of all evil, and such cruel appetite as never tyrant and tor-
menter had, ascribe they to the benign nature of almighty God".[18] In
rendering man's freedom of will null and void, More warns, predestination makes God indifferent to human conduct—indifferent to what
those predestined to salvation do, no matter how evil, and indifferent
to what those predestined to damnation do, no matter how good.[19]
By eliminating free will, it offers a false freedom that enslaves all and
a false virtue that engenders vice.[20]

Closely related to the issue of *solafideism* is the question of Christian
love—its role in our salvation and its proper motivations. Insistent
upon their notion of salvation by faith alone, More notes, the dissenters balk at the Church's teaching that salvation comes not only
through faith but through hope and love as well. They reject this despite the testimony of Scripture to the contrary (as in the First Letter
of Paul to the Corinthians [1 Cor 13:1–3, 13]).[21] More does believe
it is appropriate to consider the reasons for loving God—that He
ought to be loved, praised, and venerated by us for His goodness, as
well as for the gifts He has bestowed upon us.[22] But he cannot agree
with Luther's and Tyndale's insistence that the love and service of
God must not be prompted by what they brand as the "servile" and
"mercenary" motivations of either fear of punishment or the desire
of reward from God—that is, the desire for God's benefits.[23]

When Tyndale appears to concede that God's benefits are a valid
reason for loving God,[24] More makes the most of it by noting that
if, as Tyndale now admits, it is indeed appropriate to *love* God for
His benefits, then it would logically follow that it is proper to *serve*
God likewise for His benefits. And further, if it is right to love and
serve God for past benefits, may not He be loved and served as well
for benefits yet to come, for which we hope? If this is granted, then
one may rightly conclude that it is appropriate to love and serve God

---

[18] Ibid., chap. 12, pp. 402–3.

[19] Ibid., chap. 11, p. 400.

[20] *CW* 8, bk. 2, pp. 206–7.

[21] Ibid., bk. 1, p. 54; for an example of Tyndale's view in this regard, see *A Pathway into the Holy Scripture,* in Tyndale, *Doctrinal Treatises,* 15.

[22] *CW* 8, bk. 1, p. 51.

[23] Ibid., 51–52; for examples of Tyndale's view, see *A Pathway into the Holy Scripture,* 21, and *Mammon,* 62–66.

[24] *Answer,* 6.

for the very greatest of His benefits yet to come—heaven.[25] More-over, if "we may serve God with love", it follows that we may serve Him with the good works that flow from love—from a "faithful working charity".[26] Were Tyndale to counter (as he indeed does)[27] that such acts are worthless without faith, it would be a moot point, for surely nothing is worth anything apart from the goodness be-stowed upon it by God. What good is even faith itself if it is without charity?[28]

Tyndale, More observes, seems to think that the law of love enables those who believe as he does to judge all the laws of God (as well as those of man) and to decide how they are to be applied. Hence the dissenters presume that any interpretation they may make of the Scriptures is true, while that of the "holy men" of the Church they judge to be but false illusions.[29]

In answer to Tyndale's assertion that God's commandments are more properly kept if one seeks out the reason for the law and then judges the application of it according to the underlying reasons,[30] More warns that while it is true that there is a need for appropriate interpretation of God's commandments, this is not a task for the in-dividual to undertake on his own; for how can he presume that he is sufficiently competent to judge of the matter or that his judgment is not biased by the desires of his will? Let him turn rather to the recognized and venerable interpreters of Christian doctrine (that is, the Church Fathers and Doctors) and most especially to the solemn judgment of the Catholic Church herself—not an unknowable church composed exclusively of the elect as proposed by the reformers, but the Church to which all Christians except heretics belong, a Church that can never succumb to "damnable error".[31]

Indeed, More explains, the man who stubbornly insists on trusting his own conclusions rather than the judgment of the Church regard-ing the reason for a commandment of God is apt to end in breaking that very commandment. For it logically follows that if one such as

---

[25] *CW* 8, bk. 1, p. 52.

[26] Ibid., 55.

[27] *Answer*, 173.

[28] *CW* 8, bk. 4, p. 402.

[29] Ibid., bk. 1, p. 60, responding to Tyndale, *Answer*, 6–7.

[30] *Answer*, 6–7.

[31] *CW* 8, bk. 1, pp. 60–62.

Tyndale cannot determine the reason for a commandment, he would feel free to break it, having no reason to obey it:

> If our father Tyndale had been in paradise in the stead of our father Adam, he should never have needed any serpent or woman either to tempt him to eat the apple of the tree of knowledge. For when God had forbade him the eating thereof upon pain of death, as he forbiddeth us lechery upon pain of damnation; then would he have searched for the cause of the commandment. And when his wit would have found none because the flesh had there no need of taming; then would he have eaten on a good pace, and have thought that God almighty had but played the wanton with him, and would not be angry with him for an apple, and so would he by his own rule of searching have found out as much mischief as the woman and the serpent and the devil and all.[32]

Tyndale's insistence on finding a reason for God's commandments as the basis or even a precondition for obedience[33] More sees as opening the door to all sorts of troubling scenarios. Thus when Tyndale offers bodily self-control and sobriety as the only reasons for abstinence in food or drink,[34] does this mean that those who feel they have sufficiently mastered their appetites in this regard are free to indulge themselves on the Church's fast days? Mortification is indeed the reason for fasting, More continues, yet the Church, guided by the Holy Spirit, has seen fit to appoint specific days on which all Christians are to fast together, an action that cannot be made contingent upon the varying degrees of perfection or self-mastery to be found among her individual members. If men were left totally to themselves to decide when and if they needed to fast, they would end in fasting seldom if at all, as was now the case in Saxony under the influence of Luther.[35]

In Tyndale's theology of *solafideism,* the predestined, saved by faith alone, were free of all punishment for sin.[36] More asks how Tyndale could possibly deny that God allots to men certain temporal punishments in remission of their sins even after they have repented. How can he otherwise explain the punishment of the Israelites in the desert after they repented of the sin of idolatry, as related in the Book of Exodus, or the afflictions that the repentant David underwent in con-

---

[32] Ibid., 62.
[33] *Answer,* 6–7.
[34] Ibid., 6–7.
[35] *CW* 8, bk. 1, pp. 63–64.
[36] *Answer,* 22–23; *Obedience,* 228.

sequence of his sins of murder and adultery against Uriah the Hittite
(2 Sam 12:1–23)? While it is true that had God so willed, just "one
drop of Christ's precious blood" would have sufficed to atone for all
the punishments due in remission of these sins, God has actually ordained otherwise, More explains, in that He requires of men that they
undergo at least some consequences accruing from their evil actions,
lest they take the matter of sin too lightly and begin feeling free to
do evil as much as they want. Thus while the confession and absolution of a mortal sin (a "mortal offense") in the sacrament of penance
spares a repentant sinner "the perpetual banishment from the sight
of his [God's] face" and "the eternal torment of hell", God usually
leaves to the penitent a certain amount of temporal punishment to be
remitted either through good works and sufferings in this life or by
sufferings in the next life—in Purgatory, where others can also help
to relieve our debt in this regard. Although God normally requires
some form of satisfaction for sin, there can be exceptions, More admits, in view of God's "absolute merciful power, whereby he may do
when he will what he will".[37]

The Sacraments

Having upheld the Church's teachings on revelation and justification,
Thomas More was equally committed to defending the Church's principal means of dispensing the graces of the redemption—the seven
sacraments. Hence he considered the dissenters "most mad of all in
denying the sacraments which they find received and believed, used
and honored so clearly from the beginning".[38] While the dissenters
did not totally reject all the sacraments, they did deny four or five of
the seven recognized by the Church (confirmation, matrimony, holy
orders, anointing of the sick, and in most cases penance) and redefined the nature and workings of those remaining (baptism and the
Eucharist). Debate erupted over what constituted a sacrament, how
sacramental graces were conferred, and what was necessary for valid
reception. In the case of Tyndale, nothing was considered a sacrament
unless a "promise" made by Christ with regard to it could be found

---

[37] *CW* 8, bk. 2, pp. 210–11.
[38] Ibid., bk. 1, p. 120.

in the Scriptures.[39] Since he could find such "promises" only with baptism and the Eucharist, Tyndale believed that these were the only two sacraments instituted by Christ.[40] Among the sacraments he denied, his animosity seemed particularly directed against the sacrament of penance, which he characterizes as "a work of Satan . . . the falsest that ever was wrought, and that most hath devoured the faith",[41] and which he paints as a method of the clergy to oppress the laity: "Wherefore serveth confession, but to sit in thy conscience and to make thee fear and tremble at whatsoever they [the clergy] dream, and that thou worship them as gods?"[42] In fact Tyndale's obsessive opposition to this sacrament leads him more than once to make the absurd accusation that the clergy used confession as some sort of espionage system in an international conspiracy against the laity and temporal rulers:

> They [the hierarchy, the clergy] have feigned confession for the same purpose, to stablish their kingdom withal. All secrets know they thereby. The bishop knoweth the confession of whom he lusteth throughout all his diocese: yea, and his chancellor commandeth the ghostly father to deliver it written. The pope, his cardinals and bishops, know the confession of the emperor, kings, and of all lords: and by confession they know all their captives. If any believe in Christ, by confession they know him. Shrive thyself where thou wilt, whether at Sion, Charterhouse, or at the Observants, thy confession is known well enough. And thou, if thou believe in Christ, art waited upon. Wonderful are the things that thereby are wrought. The wife is feared, and compelled to utter not her own only, but also the secrets of her husband; and the servant the secrets of his master.[43]

To Tyndale's sacramental theology More counters that all seven sacraments are mentioned in the Scriptures: in addition to baptism and the Eucharist, which Tyndale admits, confirmation is mentioned in Acts 8:14–24, holy orders in 1 Timothy 4:11–16, matrimony in Ephesians 5:21–33, and extreme unction—the anointing of the sick —in James 5:14–15. Of the sacrament of penance More says that it is mentioned a number of times in the Scriptures (of course the most ex-

---

[39] *Obedience,* 252–55, 261, 273–74, 275–76; *Answer,* 172.

[40] *Answer,* 29.

[41] *Obedience,* 263.

[42] Ibid., 318.

[43] Ibid., 336–37; see also 281.

plicit reference to it is in John 20:21–23). If Tyndale will admit these references but denies they refer to sacraments on the grounds that no graces are explicitly promised with them, then how does he explain, More asks, Saint Paul's words to Timothy, for example, which indicate that graces were indeed conferred with the laying on of hands (in the sacrament of holy orders): "Do not neglect the gift you have, which was given you by prophetic utterance when the elders laid their hands upon you" (1 Tim 4:14).[44] In any event, More most certainly does not accept Tyndale's premise that the existence of each of the sacraments is dependent upon there being an explicit scriptural promise in each case. Criticizing Tyndale's erection of God's promises as the cause of His gifts, as well as his reduction of the sacraments to nothing more than bare signs of the promises, More observes that in reality both the promises and the sacraments betoken God's gift, which is ultimately wrought by God's goodness rather than by His promises. In the end our salvation is accomplished not by God's promises but rather by God Himself; the promises simply give us knowledge of the salvation accomplished by His goodness. Pressing this matter further, More points out that God "giveth not because he promiseth, but he promiseth because he will give". And indeed, it is the sacraments themselves rather than God's "promise" that can be said to be the proximate cause of God's gift.[45]

Tyndale likens the sacraments to a preacher in the pulpit: just as a preacher can announce the promises of Christ but cannot by his preaching bestow the fulfillment of those promises, so too, he asserts, the sacramental signs announce Christ's promises but are incapable of conferring any grace or effect therefrom.[46] Yet, as More warns, when this premise is combined with Tyndale's claim that a sacrament is invalid and void if the minister of the sacrament does not announce and explain the meaning of the sacramental signs to its recipients,[47] one is forced to conclude that if these things were true, then the sacramental signs are nothing but a waste of time. For if the minister performs what Tyndale defines as essential—the preaching of Christ's promises and the explaining of sacramental symbolism—

---

[44] *CW* 8, bk. 3, pp. 296–98.
[45] Ibid., bk. 1, pp. 106–7.
[46] *Answer*, 172; *Obedience*, 253, 256–57, 278.
[47] *Answer*, 30, 64–65, 76, 172; *Obedience*, 253, 276–77, 283.

what need is there for the signs themselves, such as the waters of baptism? More challenges Tyndale, who claims to believe nothing but what is plainly in the Scriptures, to show where in the Scriptures the sacraments are defined in this peculiar manner. The proof texts offered by Tyndale—Ephesians 5:26, 1 Peter 1:23, and James 1:18—which he cites on the grounds that they do not explicitly mention any role for the sacramental signs,[48] are not enough to confirm his proposition. The idea that omission necessarily excludes that which is omitted (in a text) is untenable.[49]

Tyndale's assertions notwithstanding, More finds in the Scriptures examples of sacramental signs being treated as necessary and effectual, as in Christ's nocturnal conversation with Nicodemus, during which our Lord states that "unless one is born of water and the Spirit, he cannot enter the kingdom of God" (Jn 3:5). Clearly the water mentioned here is something more than merely a "bare sign". More likens sacramental signs to a livery garment given to a poor man by a lord who tells him that if he wears it he will take him into his household as his servant, providing him with food and wages, but if he will not put on the garment he will not allow him into his home. Just as the livery garment is in and of itself unable to feed and pay its wearer but nonetheless facilitates the obtaining of sustenance for the poor man, in virtue of the nobleman's command (which renders the garment something more than a sign), so too are the sacramental signs, powerless in and of themselves, rendered more than merely ineffectual symbols by the promise of God.[50] But More goes farther, aligning himself with those Church Doctors and theologians (Saint Thomas Aquinas, Saint Bonaventure, and so on) who regard sacramental signs as not just facilitating the bestowal of graces, as in the livery garment analogy above, but as actual instruments of grace, endowed with power and influence by God to effect that which they symbolize[51] (subsequently the Council of Trent formally defined this as a teaching of the Church). Indeed, it seems only right that the signs accompanying the sacraments of the New Covenant should be of a higher order (and therefore effectual in some manner) than those of

---

[48] *Obedience,* 277–78, also 253.

[49] *CW* 8, bk. 1, pp. 95–98.

[50] Ibid., 99.

[51] Ibid., 99–102.

the Old Testament, which were only prefigurations of what was to come.[52]

More provides several different comparisons to elucidate his point. Thus he likens the external signs of the sacraments to medicine used in the restoration of a man's health. If God can cure an illness without resorting to any natural means, there is no reason why He cannot also heal a man in response to that man's faith in Him while allowing a natural instrument such as a medical treatment to play a role.[53] Of course in the case of sacramental signs such as water, holy oils, or the imposition of hands, More is not intending to suggest that these things have any natural properties capable of bringing about what is effected by God through them. Rather, his argument is that if God can perform a miracle directly, why can He not give to some element of His creation at a given moment a miraculous power it would not otherwise possess?[54] As an example, More cites our Lord healing one blind man by rubbing the sufferer's eyes with a mixture of clay and His own spittle (Jn 9:1–12). Obviously Christ could have restored the man's sight simply by willing it, as He had done on other occasions, yet here He chooses to wield His power over creation through this unusual means "to let them see that he not only could do it himself, but could also make the very dirt of the street able to do such cures as not all the plasters in all the surgeons' shops were able to attain unto".[55] As other scriptural examples, More mentions the woman healed of a hemorrhage by the touching of Christ's garment (Lk 8:42–48) and the healing of the Syrian army commander Naaman, whose leprosy disappeared when he washed in the waters of the Jordan as instructed by the prophet Elisha (2 Kings 5:1–14).[56] To the latter episode More makes only brief reference, simply noting that water was the agent here of God's miraculous intervention, yet we cannot but surmise that he is well aware of just how relevant this particular incident is to the debate he is engaged in. For when the prophet sent to Naaman the message that he should go and bathe seven times in the Jordan, the Syrian officer responded angrily, his reaction bearing some resemblance to the doubts of those who rejected the efficacy of

---

[52] Ibid., 99–100.
[53] Ibid., 98–99.
[54] Ibid., 103–4.
[55] Ibid., 104.
[56] Ibid., 103, 104.

sacramental signs: "Behold, I thought that he would surely come out to me, and stand, and call on the name of the Lord his God . . . Are not Abana and Pharpar, the rivers of Damascus, better than all the waters of Israel? Could I not wash in them, and be clean?" (2 Kings 5:11–12). But Naaman's servants remonstrated with him, asking why he should disbelieve that the miracle would occur just because the means (washing with water) seemed so ordinary (2 Kings 5:13); in the end they convinced their master and he was freed of his malady. Thus this miracle aptly demonstrates More's point that God can and does use lowly instruments, whenever He sees fit, to accomplish His designs.

The existence and validity of a given sacrament, More argues, is not as Tyndale claims contingent upon whether it can be shown by the Scriptures that God has fully revealed all its significations.[57] Of course More is by no means averse to providing reasons for sacramental signs when this can be done—such reasons regarding the meaning or significance of these signs, as well as their spiritual and even their bodily value, have, in more cases than not, been given.[58] Thus in the Old Testament God sometimes revealed the reason for his ceremonial instructions to the Israelites; but in very many instances he did not, as, for example, with the detailed prescriptions in the books of Exodus and Leviticus regarding the adornment of the Ark of the Covenant and the ceremonies associated with it (Ex 25–30, Lev 16). There is not even a reason provided for the important Jewish rite of circumcision.[59] Hence it is obvious that Tyndale cannot prove that the Israelites of the Old Testament were fully aware of what all their ceremonies symbolized; yet he could not possibly deny that it was both proper and meritorious for them to observe these ceremonies.[60]

In insisting that a Christian must know the reasons for a ceremony as a prerequisite to his accepting a rite, Tyndale caustically likens the use of the holy oils in the administration of the sacraments to being "smeared with unhallowed butter". In a similar vein he scoffs at the placing of salt on the tongue as a sacramental sign, as well as the use of vestments in the celebration of Mass.[61] More is scandalized by Tyn-

---

[57] Ibid., bk. 3, pp. 302–3, referring to *Answer*, 29.
[58] Ibid., bk. 1, p. 79.
[59] Ibid., 80.
[60] Ibid., bk. 3, pp. 302–3.
[61] *Answer*, 7.

dale's irreverence and sees in it evidence of a contempt for the very sacraments themselves.[62] Those, More explains, who having attained the use of reason receive the sacraments with devotion believe that in these sacraments they receive a gift of grace signified by the exterior signs and rites and that these exterior signs are themselves the very means established by God Himself by which the interior graces are conferred.[63] Dismayed by what he sees as the arrogance of Tyndale's demand of reasons for the external signs of God's sacraments, More asks whether Tyndale wishes to contend with God as to why, for example, He chose water rather than wine for baptism, since if we are to judge these matters by merely human reasoning, wine washes just as well as water does. Or, by human reckoning, would not butter suffice just as surely as oil for sacramental anointing? If Tyndale is given no reasons by God, will he then say we need no sacramental signs at all?[64] Alluding to Tyndale's seemingly self-serving interpretations of Scripture, More wryly comments:

> . . . [A]nd if God list not to make Tyndale an answer and tell him all this gear; then will he like a spiritual man set all such bodily ceremonies and sacraments at nought, and say God what he will, Tyndale will gloss his text as it please him, and then believe as he list who shall let him.[65]

Baptism

According to Tyndale, whoever does not understand the meanings of all the different external signs of the sacraments is no better receiving the sacraments than not receiving them.[66] Yet, as More notes, nowhere in the New Testament do either Christ or His disciples in speaking of baptism explain the reason why water should be used for this sacrament, as demanded by Tyndale. Hence, Tyndale is contradicting himself somewhat, for he claims that baptism is one of the two sacraments he does accept, yet by his definition one cannot receive a sacrament the external signs of which he does not know the reasons

---

[62] *CW* 8, bk. 1, pp. 76–77.

[63] Ibid., 77–78.

[64] Ibid., 79–80.

[65] Ibid., 80.

[66] *Obedience*, 276; *Answer*, 7, 30.

for.[67] Moreover, More warns, if we were to accept Tyndale's premise that without understanding or knowledge of God's promises the sacraments are to no avail, then one could logically conclude that all the children ever baptized might just as well have been left without the sacrament, since at their tender age they are incapable of learning the meaning of the sacramental sign of water.[68] As most English baptisms were of infants accompanied by their godparents, More asks whether Tyndale is referring to the knowledge of the candidates themselves or of their godparents. Unable to resist another jest at his opponent's expense, he wryly comments that if Tyndale means the lack of preaching these promises to the candidates themselves—infants—then "I deny not but that Tyndale sayeth right well and reasonable, and I shall speak to the parson of our parish that he shall preach to the child at the font, and tell him many good tales in his ear."[69] In the case of the godparents, More notes, there is no necessity to teach them on this occasion the promises of Christ in order to validate the sacrament, for they are already baptized Christians. Further, he reminds his readers that the Church has never taught that the validity of this sacrament depends on the understanding or even the faith of either the person performing the baptism or those acting as sponsors (thus even non-Christians could administer the sacrament if need be). Rather, they need only perform the rite prescribed by the Church and have the intention "to make the child Christian".[70] When Tyndale raises an objection to the use of Latin in the baptismal liturgy on the basis that it impedes the recipient unversed in this language from knowing and believing what Christ has promised regarding the sacrament, and thereby forestalls its valid reception,[71] More replies that since from the first days of Christianity in the country Latin has always been used in the baptismal rites of every English child, the acceptance of Tyndale's objection here would necessarily end in the absurd conclusion that there is not even one validly baptized Christian anywhere in England, with two possible exceptions—adult Jewish converts well versed in Latin (in sixteenth-century England Jews would have been virtually

---

[67] *CW* 8, bk. 1, pp. 81–82.
[68] Ibid., 83.
[69] Ibid., 94.
[70] Ibid.
[71] *Obedience,* 253, 276.

the only adult candidates for baptism) or, he adds with good-natured irony, "such English children as learned their [Latin] grammar in their mother's belly".[72]

The Sacrament of Penance

God established the sacrament of penance, More explains, in order to reconcile to Himself yet again those who have already been cleansed of their sins in baptism but who have subsequently succumbed to mortal sin; it is only through this sacrament that the fruits of baptism, lost through subsequent sins, can be recovered.[73] Utilizing a famous analogy from Saint Jerome to describe the role of the sacrament of penance in comparison with that of baptism, More likens baptism to a ship, as prefigured by the ark in which Noah and his family were safe but outside of which no one else survived amid the great Flood. When in the stormy seas of temptation a man succumbs and the "ship of his baptism" is broken, plunging him into the "deep sea of sin", God provides for him the sacrament of penance, a plank that the shipwrecked soul can take hold of and cling to while swimming (with God's help) to the safety of the shore.[74]

Citing a passage from the Letter to the Hebrews that speaks of how difficult it is for those who have fallen into serious sin after baptism to come again to full repentance (Heb 6:4–6), More points out that while the newly baptized are so totally cleansed in the sacrament that they are freed of all temporal punishment for their past sins, the same cannot be said for sins committed afterward; there must needs be satisfaction for these subsequent sins. Lest it be said that the merit of Christ's Passion cancels out all temporal punishment for these postbaptismal sins, More reminds his readers that even baptism, in applying Christ's sacrifice to us, does not remove the pain of undergoing bodily death (which is one of the consequences of original sin). Serious sin is not a matter so lightly to be dispensed with as to incur no significant consequences. Hence More finds the following words

---

[72] *CW* 8, bk. 1, p. 93.
[73] Ibid., bk. 2, p. 213.
[74] Ibid.

of the prophet Joel most instructive as to the manner in which one ought to repent:[75]

> "Yet even now," says the Lord, "return to me with all your heart, with fasting, with weeping, and with mourning; and rend your hearts and not your garments." Return to the Lord, your God, for he is gracious and merciful, slow to anger, and abounding in steadfast love, and repents of evil (Joel 2:12–13).

Appalled by Tyndale's assertion that the sacrament of penance is "a work of Satan",[76] More asks whether he would have us believe that all the Christians who have ever confessed their sins over the fifteen centuries since the time of Christ were all really serving Satan in doing so. Even Luther never uttered such blasphemous things against this sacrament as Tyndale; for all his other errors, Luther nonetheless acknowledged the value of confessing one's sins.[77]

Tyndale's contention that when a man sins he need do nothing more than simply repent within himself, and that anyone who attempts to offer God satisfaction (that is, penance) for his sins is "an infidel, faithless, and damned in his deed-doing",[78] is for More absurd. Without the need to make satisfaction for their transgressions, men would make light of sin and thus sin all the more freely:

> Neither purgatory need to be feared when we go hence, nor penance need to be done while we be here, but sin and be sorry and sit and make merry, and then sin again and then repent a little and run to the ale and wash away the sin, think once on God's promise and then do what we list.[79]

Extreme Unction (Anointing of the Sick) and Confirmation

Another sacrament denied by the reformers was that now named the "anointing of the sick" but which was known for many centuries as "extreme unction" in virtue of the fact that it was then administered only to those who were in imminent danger of death, that is, "*in ex-*

---

[75] Ibid., 213–215.

[76] *Obedience,* 263.

[77] *CW* 8, bk. 1, p. 89.

[78] *Obedience,* 228 (also 263–64, 284–85).

[79] *CW* 8, bk. 1, pp. 90–91.

tremis". More considers Tyndale's rejection of extreme unction to be built on two false premises: (1) that it cannot be a sacrament unless God's promises regarding it are plainly found in the written Word of God; (2) that in the case of extreme unction no such promise appears in the Scriptures.[80] As to the latter argument More immediately cites the fifth chapter of the Letter of James, which the Church has traditionally understood as clearly speaking of this sacrament:

> Is any among you sick? Let him call for the elders of the church, and let them pray over him, anointing him with oil in the name of the Lord; and the prayer of faith will save the sick man, and the Lord will raise him up; and if he has committed sins, he will be forgiven (James 5:14-15).

More points out that there most certainly is a promise expressed here —a promise of healing and forgiveness to the recipient of the sacrament. In response to Tyndale's claim that this healing spoken of in the above Scripture passage is attributed not to any sacrament but rather to "the prayer of faith",[81] More answers by asking why if this were true does Saint James make a point of mentioning the anointing with oil. Why should he do this if the oil is of absolutely no avail?[82] So confounded was Luther by this passage of Saint James, More notes, that he resorted to denying that this epistle was actually written by the apostle.[83]

In response to Tyndale's claim that the sacrament of confirmation is nowhere to be found in the Scriptures, and is therefore not a sacrament,[84] More counters by citing the following passage from the Acts of the Apostles that does indeed speak of a conferring of the Holy Spirit that is distinct from that which takes place in baptism:[85]

> Now when the apostles at Jerusalem heard that Samaria had received the word of God, they sent to them Peter and John, who came down and prayed for them that they might receive the Holy Spirit; for it had not yet fallen on any of them, but they had only been baptized in the name

---

[80] *Obedience*, 275.
[81] Ibid., 274-75.
[82] *CW* 8, bk. 1, pp. 87-88.
[83] Ibid., 88.
[84] *Obedience*, 273-74.
[85] *CW* 8, bk. 1, pp. 84-85.

of the Lord Jesus. Then they laid their hands on them and they received the Holy Spirit (Acts 8:14–17).

The Sacrament of Matrimony

As to matrimony, More explains that this "holy knot"[86] is indeed a sacrament, for it is a sign of God's union with the human soul and of Christ's union with His Church; and it is in the latter context that Saint Paul speaks of marriage as a sacrament in his Epistle to the Ephesians (chapter 5, especially verse 32).[87] More's coining of the expression "holy knot" for marriage brings to mind one of the ceremonies of the Church's nuptial rite found in his time in France and in at least some parts of Italy: the wrapping of the joined right hands of the bride and groom in the stole of the priest presiding at the wedding.[88] The union between husband and wife in matrimony, More points out, is also a sign of the grace conferred in God's drawing to Himself both the man and the woman receiving this sacrament, for "in that coupling of matrimony (if they couple in him) he coupleth himself also to their souls with grace."[89]

More contrasts Saint Paul's identification of marriage as a sacrament with Tyndale's assertion that matrimony is no more a sacrament than are the other images in Christ's parables, such as the mustard seed, the fisherman's net, or the leaven. Once again, the basis of Tyndale's position is that since he cannot find anywhere in the Scriptures a promise made by God that is signified by marriage, it cannot be a sacrament.[90] More counters by turning the principle of *sola scriptura* on its head: "Where read you then in scripture say we that God hath made you a promise that he never made promise nor never none would make, but he would first send you word by writing?"[91]

---

[86] Ibid., 87.

[87] Ibid., 86.

[88] Kenneth Stevenson, *Nuptial Blessing: A Study of Christian Marriage Rites,* Alcuin Club Collections, no. 64 (London: Alcuin Club/SPCK, 1982), 169–70, 237 (n. 43), 239 (n. 6).

[89] *CW* 8, bk. 1, p. 86.

[90] Ibid., 86–87, commenting on *Obedience,* 254.

[91] Ibid., 87.

To Thomas More the Holy Eucharist "is and ever hath in all Christendom been held of all sacraments the chief, and not only a sacrament but the very self thing also which other sacraments betoken, and whereof all other sacraments take their effect and strength".[92] We have already seen that in the earliest years of the Reformation it was the dissenters' attacks upon Catholic eucharistic doctrine that troubled More above all else. Although the Eucharist was one of the two sacraments that the reformers did accept, they were determined to redefine it to a greater or lesser extent. Dissent arose over two central tenets of eucharistic theology: the nature of the Mass and the specific nature of Christ's presence in this sacrament. As to the Mass, it was Luther who began the debate by denying that the celebration of the Eucharist was a real sacrifice, insisting moreover that the Mass cannot gain merits for anyone living or dead—hence it could not be "offered" for the souls in Purgatory. Of course the latter is really a corollary of Luther's theology of *solafideism,* in which only faith is necessary to salvation and good works of any kind are of absolutely no avail in making satisfaction for sins. Although his rejection of the Mass as a sacrifice was based in large part upon his insistence that the Letter to the Hebrews, in speaking of Christ as offering Himself once for all on Calvary (Heb 9:25–26; 10:10, 12, 14), precluded the existence of any other valid Christian sacrifice,[93] it nonetheless also stemmed from his *solafideism* in that he felt the Church, in speaking of the eucharistic celebration as a sacrifice, had turned it into a "good work", presuming to make men "all-powerful with God".[94] And Luther rejected the Roman Canon (the Eucharistic Prayer) of the Mass precisely because it referred to this sacrament as a sacrifice: "I have rejected the canon . . . because in utterly clear opposition to the gospel it calls sacrifices those things which are signs of God added to promises, offered to us to be received, not to be offered by us."[95]

---

[92] *Letter against Frith,* in *Letter to Bugenhagen, Supplication of Souls, Letter against Frith,* ed. Frank Manley et al., vol. 7 of *Complete Works of St. Thomas More* (New Haven: Yale Univ. Press, 1990), 234–35. This volume hereafter cited as *CW 7.*

[93] *The Abomination of the Secret Mass,* in *Word and Sarament II,* ed. Abdel R. Wentz, vol. 36 of *Luther's Works* (Philadelphia: Muhlenberg Press, 1959), 320.

[94] *Babylonian Captivity,* in *Word and Sacrament II,* 35, 47–48 (quote on 47).

[95] *German Response to the Book of King Henry,* quoted by More in *Responsio ad Lutherum,*

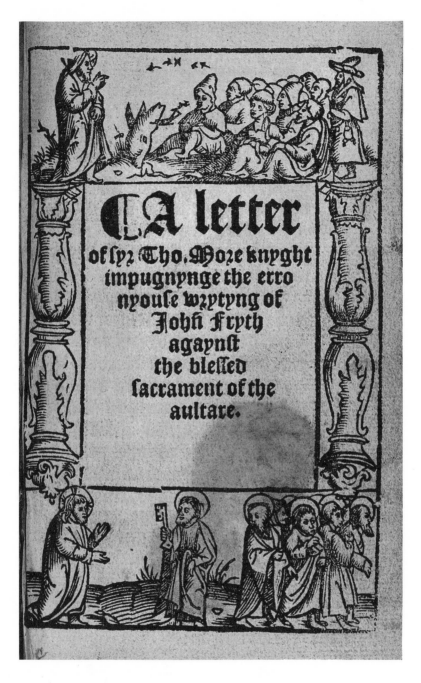

¶A letter

of fyr Tho. Moꝛe knyght
impugnynge the erro
nyoufe wꝛytyng of
John Fryth
agaynſt
the bleſſed
ſacrament of the
aultare.

Title page of Saint Thomas More's *Letter against Frith,* an apologetical tract on the Eucharist published in December 1533. Note at the bottom the depiction of Saint Peter standing before Christ in a re-creation of the scene of John 6:66–69, a vivid reminder of Petrine authority. More was imprisoned four months later.

The Real Presence of Christ in the Eucharist, defined by the Church as the substantial presence of the true Body and Blood, Soul and Divinity of Christ in this sacrament under the appearances (that is, "accidents") of bread and wine, was an even more fiercely contested issue of the Reformation. While it was again Luther who introduced the controversy by attacking the doctrine of transubstantiation, his was by far the least radical of the new definitions to be proffered by the dissenters in this regard. Luther accepted the real, substantial presence of Christ in the Eucharist but broke with the Church in insisting that following Consecration the substances as well as the appearances of bread and wine remained, subsisting together with the substances of Christ's Body and Blood. However, many of the other reformers totally rejected any substantial presence at all, interpreting this sacrament as only an outward symbol of Christ's spiritual presence, with the unchanged bread a symbol of his body and the unchanged wine a symbol of his blood. More's principal polemical opponent, William Tyndale, obviously shared this Zwinglian view of the Eucharist—the necessary outcome of his belief that the sacraments are nothing more than signs that "preach" God's promises. Tyndale's rejection of belief in the Real Presence, and, consequently, his rejection of any adoration of the reserved Eucharist, emerges in a number of passages from his writings, such as the following from his *Answer unto Sir Thomas More's Dialogue:*

> They [Christ and Saint Paul] say not, Pray to it [the Eucharist], neither put any faith therein. For I may not believe in the sacrament, but I must believe the sacrament, that it is a true sign, and it true that is signified thereby; which is the only worshipping of the sacrament: if ye give it other worship, ye plainly dishonour it.[96]

Earlier, in his *Parable of the Wicked Mammon,* Tyndale had spoken against thinking of God as dwelling in churches;[97] that this somewhat oblique reference constituted (among other things) a criticism of eucharistic worship is made clear years later in one of his last works, *A Brief Declaration of the Sacraments* (c. 1533–1535). Condemning eu-

---

ed. John M. Headley and trans. Sr. Scholastica Mandeville, vol. 5 of *Complete Works of St. Thomas More* (New Haven: Yale Univ. Press, 1969), bk. 2, chap. 16, p. 553. Hereafter cited as *CW* 5.

[96] *Answer,* 180.

[97] *Mammon,* 106.

charistic adoration as "the damnable idolatry which the papists have committed with the sacrament",[98] Tyndale goes on to declare:

> . . . [E]ven so deny I the body of Christ to be any more in the sacrament, than God was in the golden calves, which Jeroboam set up to be prayed to, the one in Bethel, and the other in Dan: for though God be present everywhere, yet if heaven of heavens cannot compass him to make him a dwelling-place (as the scripture testifieth), and much less the temple that was at Jerusalem, how should he have a dwelling-place in a little wafer or crumb of bread? God dwelleth not in the temple . . .[99]

Ironically, no matter how much Luther and the more radical dissenters differed in defining this sacrament, they were united in condemning the Church's reservation and adoration of the Eucharist outside of Mass.

More provides a succinct description of the Sacrament of the Altar, telling us that in the Mass,

> . . . [T]he very Body and Blood of our Lord is not only received by the priest himself and for himself, but is also for his own sins and other men's too, offered up to God as an holy host, oblation, and sacrifice representing the same sacrifice in which our Saviour both being the priest and the sacrifice, offered up himself for the sin of the world unto his Father in heaven, an acceptable sacrifice upon his painful cross . . .[100]

He observes that in denying the sacrificial nature of the Mass, Luther is breaking with all the Church Fathers and the Christians of every age, for from the earliest times the Eucharist has consistently been spoken of as a sacrifice or offering.[101] Addressing Luther's contention that a genuine sacrifice in the biblical sense cannot be both offered to God and consumed as the Eucharist is, More points out that the lamb of the Passover (Ex 12:3–10), which was undoubtedly a sacrifice in the biblical sense, was both totally immolated and totally consumed.[102] Responding to Luther's attempt to weaken the union of the Eucharist with the Sacrifice of Calvary, More reminds his opponent that Saint

---

[98] Text in Tyndale, *Doctrinal Treatises*, 381. This work originally bore the ungainly title, *A Fruitful and Godly Treatise Expressing the Right Institution and Usage of the Sacraments of Baptism, and the Sacrament of the Body and Blood of our Saviour Jesu Christ.*

[99] Ibid., 381–82.

[100] *CW* 8, bk. 1, p. 109.

[101] *CW* 5, bk. 2, chap. 16, pp. 551–53.

[102] Ibid., chap. 17, p. 567.

Paul explicitly links the Mass with the Cross when he says, "For as often as you eat this bread and drink the cup, you proclaim the Lord's death until he comes" (1 Cor 11:26).[103] As to Tyndale's accusation that those who attend Mass presume that they have done more than enough for God that day and need do no more,[104] More asks, "What man would be so foolish to think that he hath done enough for God?"[105] Elsewhere, in refuting the accusation that the teaching of the sacrificial nature of the Mass would require that Christ be crucified over again at each eucharistic celebration,[106] More presents the following words of Saint John Chrysostom to demonstrate that the uniqueness and nonrepeatability of Christ's immolation on Calvary was seen by the Church Fathers as fully compatible with the doctrine that each individual Mass is a sacrifice:[107]

> What is that then that we do? Do not we offer daily? Yes forsooth. But we do it in remembrance of his death. And this host is one host and not many. How is it one host and not many? For because that host was once offered, and was offered into the holiest tabernacle, and this sacrifice is a copy or example of that. We offer always the self same. Nor we offer not now one lamb, and tomorrow another, but still the same. This sacrifice therefore is one. For else because it is offered in many places at once, are there many Christs? Nay verily. For it is but one Christ everywhere, being both here whole, and there whole one body. For in like manner as he that is offered everywhere, is but one body and not many bodies; so it is also but one sacrifice.[108]

In defending the doctrine of the Real Presence of Christ in the Eucharist, More is at his very best. Appalled by those who denied this teaching, he observes that such dissenters "would destroy the leaven . . . which Christ hath himself put in our bread, such as for the more part would take his own blessed Body out of the Sacrament, and leave

---

[103] Ibid., chap. 16, p. 551.

[104] *Obedience*, 226–27.

[105] *CW* 8, bk. 1, p. 110.

[106] This charge is made in the anonymous *Supper of the Lord* (text in Tyndale, *An Answer to Sir Thomas More's Dialogue*, 227).

[107] *The Answer to a Poisoned Book*, ed. Clarence Miller, vol. 11 of *Complete Works of St. Thomas More* (New Haven: Yale Univ. Press, 1985), bk. 2, chap. 9, pp. 115–17. Hereafter cited as *CW* 11.

[108] St. John Crysostom, homily 17 on the Epistle to the Hebrews, as translated by More in ibid., 116.

there for our souls nothing but unsavory bread";[109] out of the Eucharist "take they the sweet kernel within, the blessed Body of Christ, and leave the people the shells".[110] Of the dissenters' attempts to reinterpret the Scriptures to justify their Zwinglian eucharistic theology, More comments: "Finally feign they not false glosses to corrupt the Gospel, and drive God out of Christendom, when they would expel Christ out of the Sacrament of the Altar?"[111]

In his exposition on our Lord's eucharistic discourse at Capernaum (Jn 6:25–71), presented in his most comprehensive treatise on the doctrine of the Real Presence, *The Answer to a Poisoned Book* (1533), More begins by noting that Christ often prepared His disciples for the deeds He was to perform by first instructing them with His words.[112] Such was particularly the case with the sacraments of baptism and the Holy Eucharist. Thus with baptism there was first our Lord's nocturnal discourse to Nicodemus (Jn 3:1–21). In the case of the "high Blessed Sacrament of the Altar",[113] Christ's words about the Eucharist in John 6 were themselves preceded by two miracles, the feeding of the five thousand (Jn 6:5–15) and the walk upon the waters (Jn 6:16–21), both intended to prepare the hearts of His listeners for the "marvelous high thing" He was about to teach them.[114] In the miracle of the loaves, More sees a foreshadowing of the "feeding of innumerable thousands with that one loaf that is his blessed Body in the form of bread".[115] He does not offer a specific reason for the miracle of our Lord walking upon the water, but we may reasonably assume that he would have interpreted it in the same way that he here explains the Savior's first words to the crowd that had followed Him to the other side of the lake after the multiplication of the loaves ("Truly, truly, I say to you, you seek me, not because you saw signs, but because you ate your fill of the loaves" [Jn 6:26]); by revealing their innermost thoughts, More points out, Christ manifests His divinity.[116] The power to walk on water was likewise a manifestation of His Godhead;

---

[109] *CW* 8, bk. 7, p. 709.
[110] Ibid., bk. 6, p. 639.
[111] Ibid. 640.
[112] *CW* 11, bk. 1, chap. 5, pp. 23–24.
[113] Ibid., 24.
[114] Ibid., 24–25.
[115] Ibid., 25.
[116] Ibid., bk. 1, chap. 6, p. 26.

one need only recall the following passage from the Old Testament Book of Habakkuk to see how such an action would have been perceived by those who witnessed it:

> Thou didst trample the sea with thy horses,
> the surging of mighty waters.
> I hear, and my body trembles,
> my lips quiver at the sound . . .
>
> (Hab 3:15–16)

After emphasizing the imperishable nature of that Food that is the Holy Eucharist as contrasted with the perishable nature of every carnal type of food,[117] More cites our Lord's speaking of the Eucharist as "the food . . . which the Son of man will give to you" (Jn 6:27) in order to stress the point that when we receive Holy Communion, it is Christ Himself who administers the sacrament to us:

> And therefore (as diverse holy doctors say) when the priest administers us this meat, let us not think that it is he that giveth it us, not the priest I say whom we see, but the Son of man Christ himself, whose own flesh not the priest there giveth us, but as Christ's minister delivereth us. But the very giver thereof is our blessed Savior himself . . .[118]

But God would not give mankind this inestimable gift of the Holy Eucharist without first asking something of us: "that you believe in him whom he has sent" (Jn 6:29). Commenting on this verse, More notes that faith is indeed a labor: "Ye verily, good readers, to believe well is no little work, and so great a work, that no man can do it of his own strength without the special help of God."[119] More points out a crucial turning point in the attitude of the crowd listening to our Lord's eucharistic discourse, for whereas in the euphoria that ensued from His multiplication of the loaves they were ready to crown Him king (Jn 6:15) and were at first captivated by His subsequent promise of "the true bread from heaven" (Jn 6:32), their attitude began to change as they came to realize that the Food of which He spoke was for the nourishment of the soul rather than to satisfy the cravings of the body. Hence they began to murmur and ask, "Is not this Jesus,

---

[117] Ibid., 27–29.
[118] Ibid., 29.
[119] Ibid., bk. 1, chap. 8, pp. 34–35.

the son of Joseph, whose father and mother we know? How does he now say, 'I have come down from heaven'?" (Jn 6:41–42).[120]

So as to demonstrate that our Lord intended His words, ". . . [T]he bread which I shall give for the life of the world is my flesh" (Jn 6:51), to be taken literally, More notes the reaction of the audience, who obviously thought this saying was not merely figurative, or they would not have "disputed among themselves" and asked, "How can this man give us his flesh to eat?" (Jn 6:52). Further, our Lord clearly intended them to understand the expression in a literal sense, for even upon hearing them murmur in this manner He nonetheless "more and more told them still the same, and also told them himself was God, and therefore able to do it."[121]

As always More turns to the Church Fathers to support his assertions. Throughout his *Answer to a Poisoned Book* he closely follows and explicitly cites the arguments of Saint John Chrysostom, directly translating into English, probably for the first time, several passages from Chrysostom's homilies on the Gospel of Saint John, including the following from his extraordinarily beautiful homily 46 on John 6 (here we provide a modern translation):

> . . . He [Christ] desired to prove the love which He has for us . . . And to show the love He has for us He has made it possible for those who desire, not merely to look upon Him, but even to touch Him and to consume Him . . . Let us, then, come back from that table like lions breathing out fire, thus becoming terrifying to the Devil . . .
>
> "Parents, it is true, often entrust their children to others to be fed, but I do not do so," He says; "I nourish Mine on My own flesh. I give Myself to you, since I desire all of you to be of noble birth . . ."
>
> The blood which we receive by way of food is not immediately a source of nourishment, but goes through some other stage first; this is not so with this Blood, for it at once refreshes the soul and instils a certain great power in it. This Blood, when worthily received, drives away demons and puts them at a distance from us, and even summons to us angels and the Lord of angels. Where they see the Blood of the Lord, demons flee, while angels gather . . .[122]

---

[120] Ibid., chap. 12, pp. 46–47.

[121] Ibid., bk. 4, chap. 3, pp. 154–56 (quote on 156).

[122] St. John Chrysostom, homily 46 on the Gospel of St. John, in *Saint John Chrysostom: Commentary on Saint John the Apostle and Evangelist,* trans. Sr. Thomas Aquinas Goggin, S.C.H., Fathers of the Church, vol. 33 (New York: Fathers of the Church, 1957), 468–69.

Refuting the claim that his favorite Church Father, Saint Augustine, talks of the Eucharist only as a sign,[123] More cites an epistle of Augustine (to "Eleusius, Glorius, and Felix") that speaks of Christ giving even Judas Iscariot the "price of our redemption" at the Last Supper. More asks what else the "price of our redemption" could be than Christ's own Body.[124]

Thus far we have focused our discussion on More's thoughts concerning the Eucharist within the context of the eucharistic celebration itself—the Mass. But what was his attitude toward the eucharistic devotions that had grown up around this sacrament, devotions that called upon the faithful to adore the Eucharist even outside the context of Mass? We know that by the fourteenth century public acts of eucharistic piety such as the carrying of the Blessed Sacrament in procession on the Feasts of Corpus Christi and Palm Sunday, as well as the reposition of the Eucharist in a splendidly adorned "Easter Sepulchre" from Good Friday to Easter Sunday, had become the norm across England.[125] More's belief in the validity of eucharistic worship outside the Mass is implicit in the displeasure he expresses with the dissenters' rejection or profanation of these customs, as, for example, in his *Letter to Bugenhagen:*

> Where do you think Luther was heading when he . . . refused to allow it [the Host] to be kept in the tabernacle and venerated in the church? He said that Christ did not institute the Eucharist for it to be venerated, but only for it to be received.[126]

In his *Dialogue concerning Heresies,* More includes among what he considers Luther's "abominable heresies" the German ex-monk's hatred for the Feast of Corpus Christi.[127] In book 4 of his *Confutation of Tyndale's Answer,* More describes the obstinacy of heretics who, among other things, out of disrespect for the Eucharist "cast the precious

---

[123] Such a claim is made in the anonymous *Supper of the Lord,* 259–60.

[124] *CW* 11, bk. 1, chap. 18, p. 74.

[125] A Palm Sunday eucharistic procession existed at Canterbury by the end of the eleventh century (*The Monastic Constitutions of Lanfranc,* ed. and trans. David Knowles [New York: Oxford Univ. Press, 1951], 22–26). As early as the thirteenth century the Eucharist was being placed in an Easter sepulchre on Good Friday at Salisbury (Pamela Sheingorn, *The Easter Sepulchre in England,* Early Drama, Art and Music Reference Series, no. 5 [Kalamazoo, Mich.: Medieval Institute Publications, 1987], 347–48).

[126] *Letter to Bugenhagen,* in *CW* 7:97.

[127] *CW* 6, bk. 4, chap. 2, p. 360.

Body of Christ out of the pyx".[128] In fact, More's criticism of Tyndale for his opposition to eucharistic worship emerges as a continuing refrain throughout the *Confutation,* appearing no less than twenty times. For More, eucharistic adoration is so integral a part of Christian belief that he considers Tyndale's attack upon this practice as sufficient in and of itself to destroy the reformer's theological credibility:

> . . . [H]e that considereth that Tyndale would have us so to believe in Christ . . . that we should believe . . . that once to kneel or pray thereto [to the Blessed Sacrament] were open and plain idolatry . . . shall soon feel that all his holy solemn tale of all his feeling faith is not worth a fly, but very faithless heresy.[129]

> It is also to be noted whereupon he groundeth this holy precept of his, that men should not pray to the Sacrament nor put any faith therein. He sayeth because that the Scripture doth not command it, therefore it is dishonour to the Sacrament to do it. Doth not these words alone teach us sufficiently, to know the mischief of that heresy by which they say that there is nothing to be believed without plain and evident Scripture, when we see now that Tyndale upon that doctrine of his, forbiddeth us to honour the holy Sacrament of the Altar?[130]

In contrast to Tyndale, More finds that, even aside from the oral tradition supporting the worship of this sacrament, there is more than sufficient justification for eucharistic adoration in the words of the Scriptures themselves:

> By these traditions . . . have we also the knowledge . . . to do divine honour unto the blessed Sacrament of the Altar, to which yet to say the truth never tradition needed. For since the Scripture is plain that it is Christ's own precious Body, which is not dead but quick, with that blessed soul and with them the Godhead inseparably joined; what frantic fool could doubt but it should be with divine honour worshipped, though neither God nor man beside that knowledge, had given us warning thereof?[131]

In reviewing the various promises of Christ that He would be with us until the end of the world (Mt 28:20), that His words would never pass away (Mt 24:35), that the Father and He would send the Holy

---

[128] *CW* 8, bk. 4, p. 424.
[129] Ibid., 395.
[130] Ibid., bk. 1, p. 118.
[131] Ibid., bk. 3, p. 367.

Spirit (Jn 14:26, 15:26), and that He the Son would come back to us (Jn 14:18), More reminds us that "Christ is also present among us bodily in the holy Sacrament. And is he there present with us for nothing?"[132] He explains further that in instituting the Eucharist and commanding its repeated celebration by His Church, our Lord "did in so commanding make a faithful promise, that himself would be for ever with his Church in that holy Sacrament . . . to abide perpetually with us, according to his own words spoken unto his Church, when he said, I am with you all days unto the end of the world . . ."[133] Drawing on the Old Testament, More observes that just as God supported the Israelites in their earthly pilgrimage by "walking with them in the cloud by day and in the pillar of fire by night", so much more does He now "assist and comfort us with the continual presence of his precious Body in the holy Sacrament".[134]

In his *Apology,* a defense of his apologetical efforts in the service of the Church, More likens the dissenters' verbal assaults against the teachings of the Church to a physical assault upon a Corpus Christi procession, wherein the assailants throw the vested participants and even the Blessed Sacrament itself into the mud—of course he was aware that in other parts of Europe verbal attacks had already escalated to outright physical desecration. Responding to the dissenters' demands that he should demonstrate impartiality in his refutations of them by also criticizing the clergy, More explains that this would be like expecting a man who had witnessed the disruption and desecration of the eucharistic procession either to ignore the violence done before his very eyes or, if he wishes to rebuke the assailants and rescue the Eucharist and the priests from their attackers, to show impartiality by heaping at least some abuse on the priests too. Of such "impartiality" More will have no part: "Surely for my part I am not so ambitious of such folks' praise, as to be called indifferent, nor will in writing against their heresies help them forth in their railing."[135]

---

[132] *CW* 6, bk. 1, chap. 20, pp. 114–15.
[133] *CW* 8, bk. 4, p. 467.
[134] *CW* 6, bk. 1, chap. 30, p. 182.
[135] *The Apology,* ed. J. B. Trapp, vol. 9 of *Complete Works of St. Thomas More* (New Haven: Yale Univ. Press, 1979), chap. 10, p. 51.

Tyndale was nearly as adamant in his attacks upon holy orders as he was in condemning the sacrament of penance, denying that there was any truly distinctive priestly ministry established by Christ other than the universal "priesthood" of the faithful spoken of in the First Letter of Peter (2:5, 9). Thus in his *Obedience of a Christian Man* he comments:

> Of that manner [as a Mediator between God and man] is Christ a priest for ever; and all we priests through him, and need no more of any such priest on earth, to be a mean for us unto God.[136]

Working from the above premise, Tyndale had to find a way to explain the nature of the ministry identified in the New Testament with the Greek word *presbyteros;* in doing so he reduced the Church's ministers to little more than elected sages, devoid of any really unique role in the celebration of the sacraments:

> By a priest then, in the new Testament, understand nothing but an elder to teach the younger, and to bring them unto the full knowledge and understanding of Christ, and to minister the sacraments which Christ ordained, which is also nothing but to preach Christ's promises . . .
> . . . Neither is there any other manner or ceremony at all required in making of our spiritual officers, than to choose an able person, and then to rehearse him his duty, and give him his charge, and so to put him in his room.[137]

Responding to Tyndale's claims that, with Christ a priest forever and all Christians priests through Him, there is no need for there to be ordained ministers to act as mediators between God and man, More observes that he finds all this to be nothing more than an effort by Tyndale to deny that the Mass is a sacrifice—that we do not need ordained priests to offer daily the same sacrifice that Christ offered once and for all on Calvary. It is this denial of the sacrificial nature of the Mass that explains Tyndale's and Luther's antagonism for the Canon (Eucharistic Prayer) of the eucharistic liturgy, which speaks of the sacrament as a sacrifice, a host, and an offering (in the Latin text of the Roman Canon, the sacrament is referred to three times

---

[136] *Obedience,* 255.
[137] Ibid., 256–57, 259.

as a sacrifice, four times as a host, and twice as an offering). More sees such an attitude as motivated by a contempt for the ordained priesthood:[138]

> This [the Canon] would they have us leave off for the only spite that they bear to priesthood, because they see that in this point that holy order of priesthood hath an excellent privilege, in which none angel hath the like authority.[139]

Availing himself of Tyndale's exhortation that one should read the two Epistles of Saint Paul to Timothy,[140] More uses two key verses from these same letters to demonstrate the validity of the Church's definition of the sacrament of holy orders. The passages he cites are: "Do not neglect the gift you have, which was given you by prophetic utterance when the elders laid their hands upon you" (1 Tim 4:14); and: "Hence I remind you to rekindle the gift of God that is within you through the laying on of my hands . . ." (2 Tim 1:6). In both these verses, More explains, it is clear that the sacrament is conferred by the sensible sign of laying hands upon the recipient and that the grace of the sacrament is bestowed precisely through this external action.[141] Tyndale is aware of these verses, but he belittles their sacramental significance by characterizing the laying of hands as nothing more than a gesture, as would be the patting of a boy's head by his elders.[142] Angered by this trivialization, More rebukes Tyndale for setting a double standard in claiming that the Scriptures have been misinterpreted while proposing new interpretations in order to explain away Scripture when it plainly contradicts his teachings.[143]

Tyndale then assails the anointing and tonsuring of those receiving the sacrament of holy orders; in an attempt to discredit such practices, he argues that neither Christ nor His apostles nor anyone else in the early Church was tonsured or anointed in this way, yet they preached and celebrated the sacraments all the same.[144] Tyndale's contention here provides More with another opportunity to introduce

---

[138] *CW* 8, bk. 1, pp. 112–15; Tyndale denies that the Mass is a sacrifice in *Answer*, 149.

[139] *CW* 8, bk. 1, p. 114.

[140] *Answer*, 18–19.

[141] *CW* 8, bk. 2, pp. 191–93.

[142] *Obedience*, 275.

[143] *CW* 8, bk. 2, p. 193.

[144] *Answer*, 18; *Obedience*, 258–59.

a touch of comic relief into his polemical debate with his opponent, while reminding readers of a significant flaw in the *sola scriptura* line of reasoning—that if a practice is not mentioned in the Scriptures it therefore did not exist in the early Church. More makes his point by humorously reminding his readers that nowhere does the New Testament specifically tell us that the apostles were themselves baptized:

> This is a worthy jest I promise you. If me listed here to trifle as Tyndale doeth I could ask him how he proveth that Saint Peter was never shaven [tonsured], since I suppose he never saw him, or if he would put me to prove that he was shaven, and therein when I could find no plain scripture for it, Tyndale would not believe me but if I brought forth his barber; I might tell Tyndale again that I were not bounden sith the scripture showeth it not, to believe him that Saint Peter was ever christened, till Tyndale bring forth his godfather.[145]

As to the role of anointing and tonsure in administering holy orders, More explains that he is certainly not claiming these two things constitute part of the matter (that is, essential elements) of the sacrament. In regard to the priesthood of Christ, it is irrelevant to ask whether He was ceremonially anointed or tonsured, for as *the* eternal High Priest, He obviously had no need of receiving the sacrament of holy orders at all. As for the apostles or any other priests of the early Church, they certainly could have received holy orders without anointing or tonsure, for the institution of such ceremonies was left to the judgment of the Holy Spirit, who taught these things to the Church as He saw fit over the course of time (More is again alluding to Christ's promise in John 16:13). But after the Holy Spirit had introduced these rites into the practice of the Church, it was only proper to insist on their observance thereafter as part of the rite of administering the sacrament of holy orders.[146]

When Tyndale asks what differentiates the oil used in the administration of confirmation from that used in administering holy orders or extreme unction,[147] More explains that while in all three instances the oil that is used has been blessed by a bishop, the oil serves as the very matter of the sacrament in the cases of confirmation and extreme unction, but serves in a lesser role—as part of the ceremony but not

---

[145] *CW* 8, bk. 2, pp. 193–94.
[146] Ibid., 193–95.
[147] *Answer*, 20.

as an essential element of the sacrament itself—in the case of holy orders. Similarly, holy water is in and of itself the same whether it is sprinkled on a man's forehead or is lying in a font, but when it is used in the act of administering baptism, it takes on the added role of being the matter of this sacrament, serving as "a means of purging the soul from sin and [of] infusion of God's grace, and of enabling the new regendred [i.e., re-created] creature to inheritance of heaven".[148] Again, More stresses that the sacrament of holy orders with its particular graces is conferred precisely through the action of the bishop laying his hands upon the recipient.[149]

Addressing Tyndale's premise that a priest who exercises his ministry unworthily is not really a priest at all,[150] More observes that if one were to accept such reasoning, then every Christian who acts unworthily would have to be considered unbaptized. Furthermore, since Tyndale sees priests as nothing more than officers in the Christian community, he should therefore conclude by his own reasoning that all men in public office, from the mayor to the sheriff, are necessarily devoid of their office or authority if they are unworthy men. Clearly such an anarchic scenario would be absurd.[151]

Refuting Simon Fish's demand in his *Supplication for the Beggars* that the clergy must be expected to perform manual labor,[152] More points out that such work was not required of the priests of the Mosaic law and that, while Saint Paul did indeed sometimes engage in physical labor (tent-making) in order to forestall criticism, the apostle nonetheless did not see himself under any obligation to do so (2 Th 3:7–9).[153] More reminds his readers that when Mary of Bethany chose to repose at the feet of Christ, our Lord defended her for having chosen the better part than her sister Martha, despite the fact that the latter was engaged in the noble labor of extending hospitality to "the best poor man and most gracious guest that ever was guested in this world".[154]

---

[148] *CW* 8, bk. 2, p. 195.

[149] Ibid., 198.

[150] *Answer*, 19–20.

[151] *CW* 8, bk. 2, p. 199.

[152] *A Supplication for the Beggars,* in John Fox, *The Acts and Monuments of John Fox* (London: Seeley, Burnside, and Seeley, 1846), 4:664.

[153] *The Supplication of Souls,* bk. 1, in *CW* 7:146.

[154] Ibid., 146–47 (quote on 147).

As we have seen, William Tyndale did not consider the priesthood a sacrament; for him all men and women are equally "priests".[155] From these premises he concluded that women are able to consecrate the Eucharist when necessary, an assertion he makes no less than three times in the course of his *Answer unto Sir Thomas More's Dialogue:*[156]

> If a woman, learned in Christ, were driven unto an isle where Christ was never preached, might she not there preach and teach to minister the sacraments, and make officers? The case is possible; shew then what should let, that she might not. "Love thy neighbour as thyself," doth compel. Nay, [you say] she may not consecrate. Why? If the pope loved us as well as Christ, he would find no fault therewith, though a woman at need ministered that sacrament . . .[157]

More finds Tyndale's suggestion of women priests ludicrous, as he is sure the faithful daughters of the Church down through the ages would:

> . . . [O]f as many good holy virtuous women as hath been in Christendom since Christ's death unto this day, was there never none yet but that her heart would have abhorred, if such an high presumptuous thought should once have fallen in her mind.[158]

More likewise notes that there is no historical precedent for such a practice in the Church:

> By what old story will he [Tyndale] show us, that Christian women be priests and were wont to sing Mass?[159]

Addressing Tyndale's novel assertion that from Christ's commandment in the Scriptures to love one's neighbor (Mt 22:39) it can be deduced that when needed women have the power to consecrate the Eucharist,[160] More expresses exasperation with the tenuousness of such an interpretation, complaining, "What is there that these folk may not prove by scripture, if they may deduce it thus and have their

---

[155] *Obedience,* 254–55.

[156] *Answer,* 18, 29–30, 176–77.

[157] Ibid., 176–77.

[158] *CW* 8, bk. 1, p. 92.

[159] Ibid., bk. 7, p. 807.

[160] *Answer,* 29–30, 176–77.

deduction allowed?"[161] With his characteristic humor he summarizes Tyndale's line of reasoning in these terms: If Mass is as necessary as the Church says it is, and if it is required that the Eucharist be celebrated in parishes at least on Sundays, it would follow that "if the priest be not at home, then some good wife may for a need step to the altar and say Mass in his stead because the scripture sayeth, love thy neighbor as thyself."[162] More proceeds to remind his readers of several examples from the Bible that demonstrate God's displeasure with those who attempt to arrogate to themselves a sacred office or privilege to which God has not called them. In the thirteenth chapter of the First Book of Chronicles (vv. 9–10) Uzzah is struck dead for having put out his hand to touch the Ark of the Covenant, something he was forbidden to do. In the Book of Numbers (chap. 16) Korah, Dathan, and Abiram were likewise smitten by God for demanding to perform the function of priests in defiance of the restriction of the priestly ministry to Aaron and his male descendants. And in the twenty-sixth chapter of the Second Book of Chronicles, King Uzziah falls from God's favor and is punished for entering the Temple to (in More's words) "play the priest and incense God himself".[163] Hence, for More, women cannot celebrate the Eucharist for the simple reason that God has not called them to this office; and no man or woman has the right to challenge the judgment of God:

> And Tyndale because a woman must love her neighbor as herself; will have her not touch the ark [of the Covenant] but the blessed Body of God, and boldly consecrate it herself, which neither the blessed mother of Christ, nor the highest angel in heaven, dared ever presume to think, because God had not appointed them to that office.[164]

Though More does not mention it explicitly, it is quite likely that he had in mind here one of the passages from the Letter to the Hebrews regarding the priesthood of Christ: "And one does not take the honor upon himself, but he is called by God, just as Aaron was" (Heb 5:4). But if women are not called to be priests, why is this so? Why are women able when necessary to administer the sacrament of baptism, yet not able to celebrate the sacrament of the Eucharist? Were Tyndale

---

[161] *CW* 8, bk. 3, pp. 259–60 (quote on 260).
[162] Ibid., 260.
[163] Ibid.
[164] Ibid.

to pose this question to him, More explains that he would answer that it is enough for us to know that God has so ordained—it is not necessary for us to know the specific reasons why:

> . . . I would give him none answer to that question, other than the ordinance of God's Spirit, which I see that God hath taught his Church, and else would he not suffer them to believe that it were well done, whereof no man is bounden to give a precise cause. But it were over much boldness to think that we could precisely tell the cause of every thing that it pleaseth God to devise . . .[165]

Furthermore, More stresses, God would not have allowed His Church to err in such a matter as this but rather would have taught her the contrary before then, had He so willed.[166]

More is amused by Tyndale's attempt to cast the question of whether women can celebrate Mass as a matter of equal rights—that women are somehow in "miserable servitude . . . because men will not suffer them to say Mass".[167] More is referring to the following passage from Tyndale's *Answer:*

> If a woman were driven into some island, where Christ was never preached, might she there not preach him, if she had the gift thereto? Might she not also baptize? And why might she not, by the same reason, minister the sacrament of the body and blood of Christ, and teach them how to choose officers and ministers? O poor women, how despise ye them![168]

"O the tender heart of piteous Tyndale", More groans. "He beginneth now by likelihood to look toward wedding he speaketh like a woer."[169] Elsewhere, responding to Tyndale's complaints that the Church suppresses dissent without a fair hearing of the dissenters' views,[170] More humorously alludes to his opponent's advocacy of women celebrating Mass, describing the future that would result were Tyndale to have his way:

> . . . [H]e [Tyndale] would have all things so far forth set at large, that he might bring first in doubt and question, and after in errors and heresies

---

[165] Ibid., 260–61 (quote on 261).

[166] Ibid., 261.

[167] Ibid., bk. 2, p. 191.

[168] *Answer*, 18.

[169] *CW* 8, bk. 2, p. 191.

[170] *Answer*, 42.

upon the question, every point of Christ's Catholic faith . . . then lo to make the Gospel truly taught, take away in any wise all the clergy clean, and let Tyndale send his women priests about the world to preach.[171]

It would hardly be fair to claim that More's opposition to Tyndale's proposal of women as celebrants of the Eucharist was motivated by "male chauvinism" or "sexism" on his part. More's daughters were among the most highly educated women of sixteenth-century Europe, a distinction they achieved precisely because their father believed firmly in training their young minds. There can scarcely be found a more eloquent Renaissance defense of the equal education of women than that given in More's letter to William Gonell, the tutor of his children (most probably written in May 1518):

> The harvest [of learning] will not be affected, whether it be a man or a woman who sows the seed. Both are reasonable beings, distinguished in this from the beasts; both therefore are suited equally for those studies by which reason is cultivated, and like a ploughed field, becomes fruitful when the seed of good precepts is sown.[172]

More understood the unique gifts that God has bestowed upon women, and among these, perhaps the most admirable, a woman's capacity to love—to love God and those He has entrusted to her. From the hour when the Blessed Virgin Mary, the Magdalen, and the other holy women gathered in the shadow of the Cross on the first Good Friday, the feminine gender has never been reticent in the worship and service of the Lord; seemingly in every age they have outnumbered men in filling the churches. Thus in seeking to show in his *Letter against Frith* the genuine spirit with which one should receive the Holy Eucharist, More illustrates his point by presenting the picture of a devout woman expressing her thanksgiving:

> . . . I trust every good Christian woman maketh a much better prayer at the time of her housel [Communion], by faithful affection and God's good inspiration suddenly. For she beside God's other goodness, thanketh him I think for his high singular benefit there presently given her, in that it liketh him to accept and receive her so simple and so far unworthy of

---

[171] *CW* 8, bk. 5, pp. 597–98.

[172] English translation as quoted in E. M. G. Routh, *Sir Thomas More and His Friends, 1477–1535* (1934; reprint, New York: Russell and Russell, 1963), 129; for Latin original, see letter no. 63, in Elizabeth Rogers, ed., *The Correspondence of Sir Thomas More* (Princeton, N.J.: Princeton Univ. Press, 1947), 122.

herself, to sit at his own blessed board, and there for a remembrance of his bitter passion suffered for her sins, to suffer her receive and eat not bread though it seem bread, but his own very precious Body in form of bread, both his very flesh, blood and bones, the self same with which he died and with which he rose again, and appeared again to his apostles, and ate among his disciples, and with which he ascended into heaven, and with which he shall descend again to judgment, and with which he shall reign in heaven with his Father and their Holy Spirit in eternal glory . . .

This lo in effect though not in words, can Christian women pray, and some of them peradventure express it much better too.[173]

Priestly Celibacy

More sees celibacy as a most appropriate state for priests in the service of Christ, who "was both born of a virgin and lived and died a virgin himself".[174] Citing our Lord's commendation of celibacy for those who are able to accept it (Mt 19:12), he asks what could be more suitable than "to take into Christ's temple to serve about the Sacrament only such as be of that sort that are content and minded to live after the cleanness of Christ's holy counsel" of chastity.[175] More notes that the advantages of continence in the realm of worship were not unknown even to the pagans; and among the Jews living under the Covenant of Abraham, the usage of temporary separation from one's own wife while in the priestly service of the Temple is evident from the conduct of Zechariah in the first chapter of the Gospel of Saint Luke (Lk 1:23–24).[176]

More observes that the Church forces celibacy upon no one; she simply chooses to admit to the priesthood only those who of their own free will promise to live a life of celibacy.[177] Although he admits that in the earlier centuries of the Church there were married men who were ordained, he stresses that even then celibacy was the preferred state for the clergy, as can be seen from the writings of the Church Fathers. Some who were married lived in continence after

---

[173] *Letter against Frith,* in *CW* 7:257–58.

[174] *CW* 6, bk. 3, chap. 13, p. 312.

[175] Ibid.

[176] Ibid.

[177] Ibid., 311, 312–13.

their ordination. With time, More explains, the observance of priestly celibacy became for all practical purposes the norm, eventually becoming accepted throughout Christendom (and finally codified in ecclesiastical law), recognized from experience as the best manner of life for the clergy. Even in the Greek Orthodox Church, he adds, which permits the ordination of married men, those who are unmarried before ordination are not allowed to marry afterward.[178]

As we have already seen from the early events of the Reformation, clerical celibacy was one of the first tenets of Catholic life to be rejected by Luther and the other reformers. While admitting that the unmarried state was sometimes appropriate when done for love of neighbor, Tyndale attacked the principal reason for celibacy—as a sacrifice for the love of God—with an iconoclastic fury:

> I may not vow for the chastity itself, as though it were sacrifice, to please God in itself; for that is the idolatry of heathen . . .
> . . . [T]o refer virginity unto the person of God, to please him therewith, is false sacrifice and heathenish idolatry.[179]

Tyndale even went so far as to interpret the following words in Saint Paul's First Letter to Timothy as an injunction mandating the marriage of clergymen:[180]

> Now a bishop must be above reproach, the husband of one wife, temperate, sensible, dignified, hospitable, an apt teacher, no drunkard, not violent but gentle, not quarrelsome, and no lover of money (1 Tim 3: 2–3).

As More is not slow to point out, this passage is clearly intended, not to prohibit celibacy, but rather to exclude from ordination those who have taken *more* than one wife.[181] Denying Tyndale's claim that celibacy is an "exceeding seldom gift", More points out that in reality many indeed have lived in celibacy; nor will he accept his opponent's argument that priests need to be married on the premise that celibacy makes a man too vulnerable to temptations of impurity.[182] If one were to accept such reasoning, More warns, one of two absurd

---

[178] Ibid., 310, 311.
[179] *Answer*, 160, 163.
[180] *Obedience*, 229–30.
[181] *CW* 6, bk. 3, chap. 13, pp. 303–8.
[182] Ibid., 308, commenting on *Obedience*, 230.

conclusions must necessarily follow from it: either that Christ erred in recommending celibacy, or that, since all priests must according to Tyndale be married, it is not permitted to ordain those living a state of life (celibacy) that God Himself has recommended.[183]

The Liturgy

Thomas More was obviously a man with a keen liturgical sense. Daily he attended Mass and recited at least a portion of the Divine Office; in his writings allusions to the liturgy are frequent enough to warrant our concluding that he was thoroughly versed in the Church's public forms of worship and that he participated in them attentively. Hence More was deeply concerned with addressing the reformers' assertion that the Church had strayed from the liturgical practices of the early Church—that the liturgy had become encrusted with needless embellishments over the centuries, while other aspects of early Christian celebration had been lost or suppressed. Repeatedly in the writings of the dissenters we find attacks on the gestures of the priest at Mass and upon the use of vestments, incense, gold and silver vessels, and even the texts of the prayers in the celebration of the sacraments. In addition the reformers demanded that the Church restore early customs no longer extant in the sixteenth century, such as Communion under both species for the laity. For More, neither liturgical change nor the lack thereof was, in and of itself, problematic. But how the Church celebrated the sacraments was to him a matter only for the Holy Spirit to determine. Building on his unshakeable belief in the divine origin of the Church, More reminds his readers that Christ promised to send the Holy Spirit upon the Church to "lead her into all truth" (cf. Jn 16:13) and that therefore the Church, in every universal decision, whether to make a change or to retain an old usage in her discipline, could not err, for such decisions were made by the Holy Spirit Himself acting through the Church. God may change a practice of Church discipline or retain it whenever He wills for whatever reason; He need not make the reason known to us:

> . . . [T]hrough the same Spirit, when He wishes, He changes certain things in His church as it pleases Him; and as God alone makes the

---

[183] Ibid., 309.

changes so God alone knows the reasons for changing. Only this does everyone know: whatever is changed throughout the whole church concerning the sacraments is changed with no one but God doing the changing, who, so that the whole church cannot err in matters of this sort, has promised that His Spirit will lead her into all truth and that He Himself will be with her even to the consummation of the world.[184]

More notes that we are even assured of the Holy Spirit's guidance of the Church in the name given the third Person of the Blessed Trinity by Christ Himself at the Last Supper—"Paraclete" (Jn 14:16–17, 26) —a name that means (among other things) "Comforter"; how could He be our Comforter, More asks, if He has left us "so comfortless" that we cannot be sure whether the Church is right or "in damnable error"?[185] Thus, just as God through His servant Moses had taught the Jewish people the rites and ceremonies with which they were to worship Him—ceremonies that would kindle their devotion—so has He taught His Church the proper forms of worship in celebrating the sacraments;[186] no one else has the authority to change these things:

> . . . I do not doubt that this practice which has already been followed throughout so many ages has been followed by the counsel of God . . . and unless it should please God that the practice be changed again, He would not otherwise allow the church to change it for the worse by human counsel, nor in the matter of the sacraments to be governed by a spirit other than His own Holy Spirit.[187]

Elsewhere, More cites a compelling illustration of the Church's authority to change a matter of discipline, noting how absurd it would be to argue that the decision reached by the apostles at the first Council in Jerusalem (Acts 15:6–29) barring the faithful from consuming animal blood or the meat of strangled animals is still in effect, as if the Church had not the power to revoke this decision in later times.[188]

But what of those who take it upon themselves to refashion the liturgy as they, rather than the Holy Spirit, see fit? In his last major work, *De Tristitia Christi,* More goes so far as to compare Judas' greeting and kiss in the Garden of Gethsemane with what he sees as the

---

[184] *CW* 5, bk. 2, chap. 6, p. 373.

[185] *CW* 8, bk. 3, p. 377.

[186] Ibid., bk. 2, p. 194.

[187] *CW* 5, bk. 2, chap. 5, p. 361.

[188] *CW* 8, bk. 3, p. 249.

pretended piety of laymen who, at the prompting of dissenting clergy, disobeyed what was then the Church's liturgical discipline by insisting upon receiving Communion under both species while condemning those who did not do likewise. More's criticism is here directed, not at the practice itself (the Council of Trent even gave some thought to allowing this form of Communion), but rather at the exercise of such a practice without the authorization of the Church. More adds that ironically many of those who insisted upon the laity receiving in this manner did not really believe in the Real Presence under either species; their attitude reminds him of Pilate's soldiers who did mock reverence to Christ, for such men, like the soldiers, genuflect before a reality they do not believe in.[189]

More's opponent, Tyndale, objected to the vestments and actions of the priest prescribed in the rubrics of the Mass precisely because such ceremonial actions increased what he viewed as the superstition and blind devotion of the people, a devotion lacking in the full understanding of the meaning of these things.[190] But were one to accept such reasoning, More responds, then by the same token one would have to accuse God of leading the Israelites into superstition by enjoining upon them His commandments regarding the sacrificial ceremonies of the Old Law, the ritual details of which the people did not understand.[191] When Tyndale asserts that the ceremonial actions in the liturgy serve only to give unbelievers material for mocking Christians,[192] More asks in reply whether we should be expected to surrender our venerable centuries-old liturgical traditions for fear that nonbelievers might scoff at us for practicing them. Does Tyndale really think that, were Christians to supply nonbelievers with reasons for their ceremonies, they would be satisfied? If one were to follow Tyndale's reasoning here to its logical conclusion, More continues, then we must disavow all the mysteries of our faith for fear the nonbelievers will scorn them.[193] Finally, to those who would argue in Tyndale's defense that his criticism is directed, not against the Mass itself, but only against certain ritual accretions that the priests fail to

---

[189] *De Tristitia Christi*, ed. Clarence H. Miller, vol. 14 of *Complete Works of St. Thomas More* (New Haven: Yale Univ. Press, 1976), 391–95.

[190] *Obedience*, 226–27; *Answer*, 11.

[191] *CW* 8, bk. 1, pp. 109–10.

[192] *Obedience*, 227.

[193] *CW* 8, bk. 1, pp. 110–11.

explain to their people, More answers that the man who is capable of mocking such time-honored devout practices is certainly capable of turning against the Eucharist itself.[194]

Addressing Tyndale's assertion that the ceremonies of the Church neither honor God nor help one's neighbor, nor avail in taming the passions,[195] More insists that the sacred rites do indeed accomplish all these things. For are not the hearts of the people lifted to God by their participation in such rites? How could ceremonies taught to the Church by the Holy Spirit fail to please and honor God? And as to one's neighbor, the faithful do indeed benefit each other in gathering to pray together, for otherwise there would be no distinction between prayer said alone and prayer said with others (More is obviously alluding here to our Lord's words in the eighteenth chapter of Saint Matthew: ". . . [W]here two or three are gathered in my name, there am I in the midst of them" [v. 20]). As channels of grace, the sacraments and rites of the Church also assist the faithful in overcoming temptation; the beauty of the ceremonies themselves brings peace to the soul, for "the more devoutly that they see such godly ceremonies observed, and the more solemnity that they see therein, the more devotion feel they themselves therewith in their own souls", with their passions quieted "at the voices of Christ's ministers in the choir, with organs and all together".[196]

The Observance of Sunday

More defends the Church's prohibition of "servile work" on Sundays and holy days from Tyndale's claim that Sundays are "servant to man" according to Christ's response to the Pharisees, "The sabbath was made for man, not man for the sabbath . . ." (Mk 2:27). More sees in Tyndale's interpretation an implicit license to do as one pleases on these days so long as one attends the days' Scripture services.[197] To Tyndale's assertion that we should not be too superstitious about this matter,[198] More answers that the people are already well aware

---

[194] Ibid., 111–12.
[195] *Answer*, 11.
[196] *CW* 8, bk. 2, pp. 159–61 (quotes on 161).
[197] Ibid., bk. 1, pp. 74–76, responding to *Answer*, 7, 66–67.
[198] *Answer*, 7.

that the Church permits them to do on Sundays whatever necessary work cannot be deferred to another day. He explains that our Lord, by saying, "The sabbath was made for man . . .", meant that this day of rest was instituted "for the spiritual benefit and profit of man", not that it was somehow the "servant unto man". According to the Scriptures, only God holds dominion over the Sabbath (". . . [T]he seventh day is a sabbath of solemn rest, holy to the Lord . . ." [Ex 31:15]); thus on this occasion Christ was not declaring every man "master and lord" over the Sabbath, but rather asserting His own divinity as "lord even of the sabbath" (Mk 2:28).[199] More pursues his case further by comparing the Sabbath to the function of a governor, whose office exists to serve the people, not so that the people may serve him, "yet is there no man among the people wont to call the governor his man, but himself rather the governor's man"; likewise Christ became man for us, yet no one would dare to speak of the Lord as his own servant.[200] But for More the issue at stake was something more important than how Tyndale used the word "servant"; it was rather the danger that Tyndale's ideas would lead the faithful to go beyond the acts of charity and truly necessary work permitted by the Church on Sundays and holy days, so that by stretching the definition of what was "necessary", the people would feel free to engage in labor that could honestly be performed on some other day instead. Such behavior would eventually eliminate the reverence of the faithful for holy days and render them virtually indistinguishable from work days.[201]

The Liturgy of Holy Week

Throughout Christian Europe up until the Reformation, the calendar of the Church and of her people reached its climax each year with the celebration of Holy Week.[202] In view of Thomas More's intense devotion to the mysteries of our Lord's Passion, it would be reasonable to assume that he participated with particular fervor in the sacred rites

---

[199] *CW* 8, bk. 1, pp. 74–75.

[200] Ibid., 75.

[201] Ibid., 75–76.

[202] For a comprehensive history of the rites of Holy Week, see my own work, *The Week of Salvation: History and Traditions of Holy Week* (Huntington, Ind.: Our Sunday Visitor, 1993).

of the Easter Triduum and that he would have found the reformers' virulent condemnations of the Church's Holy Week ceremonies especially disturbing. Fortunately we need not depend in this case upon mere suppositions; the references to Holy Week in the writings of More are conspicuously abundant and serve as further confirmation of his profound liturgical sense. Thus in book 1 of his *Dialogue concerning Heresies* (chap. 3) he mentions the "hallowing of the fire" and "of the font", a reference to two portions of the liturgy of the Easter Vigil, the blessing of the newly kindled Easter flame for the lighting of the Paschal candle and the blessing of the baptismal font later in the Vigil.[203] Again, in his *Confutation of Tyndale's Answer,* he lists among those things passed down to us by tradition "the hallowing of . . . [the] paschal taper" as well as the veneration of the Cross on Good Friday (what was known in England as the "creeping to the Cross").[204] Elsewhere, in his *Answer to a Poisoned Book,* More names the "creeping of Christ's cross" as one of the practices subjected to the irreverent mockery of dissenters.[205] It is also obvious that he attended the special communal celebrations of the Divine Office known as "Tenebrae", held during the last days of Holy Week. In addition to there being a note from More to his secretary, John Harris (regarding a correction to his *Treatise upon the Passion*), wherein he refers to the Wednesday before Easter as "Tenebrae Wednesday",[206] he provides in his *Dialogue concerning Heresies* the following beautiful interpretation of the most visually impressive rite associated with Tenebrae, the successive extinguishing of the candles on the hearse (Tenebrae candlestand):

> For yet stood still the light of faith in our Lady, of whom we read in the Gospel continual assistance to her sweetest Son without fleeing or flyttyng [deviating]. And in all other we find either fleeing from him one time or other, or else doubt of his resurrection after his death (his dear mother only excepted). For the signification and remembrance whereof the Church yearly in the Tenebrae lessons leaveth her candle burning

---

[203] *CW* 6, bk. 1, chap. 3, p. 56.

[204] *CW* 8, bk. 3, p. 367.

[205] *CW* 11, bk. 5, chap. 3, p. 223; also bk. 4, chap. 12, p. 186.

[206] Letter no. 48, from More to John Harris, January–April 1534, in Elizabeth F. Rogers, ed., *St. Thomas More: Selected Letters* (New Haven: Yale Univ. Press, 1961), 188.

still, when all the remnant that signifieth his apostles and disciples be one by one put out.[207]

The above passage has the added interest of providing further evidence of Carthusian influences upon More's spirituality, for his interpretation of the lone Tenebrae candle left burning was by no means a universal one (the candle was often seen as representing Christ Himself). While this Marian understanding of the candle can be found in the *Rationale Divinorum Officiorum* (Rationale of the Divine Offices) of the famous medieval liturgist William Durandus of Metz (1237–1296),[208] it is more likely that More originally assimilated the idea from the *Vita Christi,* a massive life of Christ written by the fourteenth-century Carthusian Ludolf of Saxony. Note the similarity to More's words in Ludolf's explanation:

> Then all the disciples sinned, and were extinguished in faith during those three days, except the Blessed Virgin, in whom alone the faith of the Church remained unshaken; in representation of which, in the matins of that triduum all the candles are extinguished except one alone, which remains lighted.[209]

The final years of Thomas More's life were to bring him into direct conflict with his sovereign, Henry VIII. Nonetheless, in one of his last works, the *Treatise upon the Passion,* More does not hesitate to speak movingly of his King's performance of the "Royal Maundy", the Holy Thursday ceremony of the washing of the feet:

> The example of Christ in washing the apostles' feet . . . much it hath been ever since, and yet in every country of Christendom in places of religion used it is, and noble princes and great estates use that godly ceremony very religiously. And none I suppose nowhere more godly than our sovereign lord the king's grace here of this realm, both in humble manner washing and wiping and kissing also many poor folks' feet after

---

[207] *CW* 6, bk. 1, chap. 18, p. 108.

[208] *Rationale Divinorum Officiorum* (Naples: Josephum Dura Bibliopolam, 1859), bk. 6, chap. 72, nos. 25–26, p. 515.

[209] *Vita Jesu Christi,* ed. A.-C. Bolard, L.-M. Rigollot, and J. Carnandet (Paris and Rome: Victor Palmé, 1865), pt. 2, chap. 59, no. 25, p. 615; English translation of passage from Rev. H. J. Coleridge, "Ludolf's Life of Christ", *Month* 17 (November–December 1872): 359.

the number of the years of his age, and with right liberal and princely alms therewith.[210]

On Liturgical Furnishings

Like so many other Christians down through the centuries, Thomas More saw no reason for conflict between zeal in the service of the poor and zeal for the proper adornment of the House of God. Of his solicitude for the needy, we have the testimony of Thomas Stapleton, who as we have already seen tells of More personally distributing alms to the poor and inviting them to his dinner table as well as maintaining a home for the indigent elderly and ill.[211] Yet he was likewise indefatigable in rendering the utmost honor and glory to the Almighty in his donations to the Church's worship. Thus in his own parish church of All Saints in Chelsea,[212] he provided for the construction of a new chapel and furnished it with all the appropriate accouterments and ornaments for the celebration of the sacred liturgy. The biographer "Ro: Ba:" specifies "Copes, chalices, Images" among the items that More donated to his parish;[213] in this regard, Stapleton mentions "much gold and silver plate".[214] To illustrate further More's eagerness for the adornment of the sanctuary, "Ro: Ba:" provides an amusing anecdote:

> So much he loved the beauty and glory of the house of God, that if he had seen a fair and comely man of personage, he would say, "It is pity yonder man is not a priest; he would become an Altar well." The like he would say of Jewels and precious stones . . .[215]

---

[210] *Treatise upon the Passion,* chap. 3, in *Treatise on the Passion; Treatise on the Blessed Body; Instructions and Prayers,* ed. Garry Haupt, vol. 13 of *Complete Works of St. Thomas More* (New Haven: Yale Univ. Press, 1976), 114.

[211] Thomas Stapleton, *The Life and Illustrious Martyrdom of Sir Thomas More,* ed. E. E. Reynolds (Bronx, N.Y.: Fordham Univ. Press, 1966), chap. 6, p. 67.

[212] This was its name in More's day (M. Barry O'Delany, "Memories of Chelsea", *Ave Maria,* n.s., 32 [August 9, 1930]: 178).

[213] Ro: Ba:, *The Lyfe of Syr Thomas More, Sometymes Lord Chancellor of England by Ro: Ba:,* ed. E. V. Hitchcock and Msgr. P. E. Hallett, Early English Text Society, original series, no. 222 (London: Early English Text Society, 1950), bk. 2, chap. 1, p. 50.

[214] Stapleton, *Life,* chap. 6, p. 63.

[215] Ro: Ba:, *Lyfe,* bk. 2, chap. 1, p. 51.

As a man, therefore, who knew how to be generous both to the poor and to God Himself, More was not going to let go unchallenged the claims of dissenters that the Church was filling her edifices with wanton opulence at the expense of the less fortunate in society. Indeed, he saw the poor themselves as eager to beautify the objects and places of worship, so as to preserve the sacred dignity with which the Church celebrated the Holy Eucharist:

> . . . [V]erily I can scant believe that any Christian people, although were they very poor, would at this day suffer the precious Blood of our Lord to be consecrate and received in wood, where it should cleave to the chalice and sink in and not be clean received out by the priest.[216]

The above passage is from More's *Dialogue concerning Heresies,* wherein he addresses a number of objections posed to the use of richly made, ornamented objects in the liturgy. For More there is no doubt as to the appropriateness of employing precious things in divine worship:

> . . . [I]t is very right and good reason that man serve him [God] again with the best, and not do as Cain did, keep all that ought is for himself, and serve his Master and his Maker with the worst.[217]

Responding to the claim in a book of the period, *The Image of Love,* that the saints and Doctors of the early Church would not have countenanced any such lavishness, More answers by citing the findings of the Renaissance scholar of papal history (and Vatican librarian) Bartolomeo Platina, who in his *Vitae Pontificum* (1479) describes gold and silver objects in the churches built by Constantine during the reign of Pope Sylvester I (A.D. 314–336).[218] Likewise he brings to the attention of his readers the even earlier Old Testament prescriptions of God Himself, stipulating the use of rich ornaments for the Ark of the Covenant and the Temple of Solomon.[219] Against the claim that in adorning the House of God, God's poor were thereby deprived, he counters by arguing that there are enough material goods to serve both the requirements of divine worship and the needs of the poor. Thus Luther's railings against the use of gold in the adornment of relics of the True Cross made no sense, More argues, when so much

---

[216] *CW* 6, bk. 1, chap. 2, p. 41.
[217] Ibid., 41.
[218] Ibid., 40–41, plus notes, 609.
[219] *CW* 6, bk. 1, chap. 2, pp. 41–42.

more gold went into the secular decoration of cups, knives, swords, spurs, painted clothes, posts, and even entire roofs; nor were these secular uses of gold exclusively confined to the uppermost strata of sixteenth-century society.[220] Moreover, the accusation that in giving costly things to the glory and honor of God one thereby deprives the poor is not a new charge. As More reminds his readers, it was posed by another long before—Judas Iscariot, who begrudged the precious nard with which Mary the sister of Lazarus anointed our Lord's head and feet, objecting, "Why was this ointment not sold for three hundred denarii and given to the poor?" (Jn 12:5), to which Christ answered, "Why do you trouble the woman? For she has done a beautiful thing to me. For you always have the poor with you, but you will not always have me . . . Truly, I say to you, wherever this gospel is preached in the whole world, what she has done will be told in memory of her" (Mt 26:10-11, 13).[221]

On the Responsibilities of Homilists

As one of the faithful who looked to his pastors for instruction, edification, and direction, Thomas More was well aware of the crucial role of preaching in the life of the Church. The biographer Stapleton relates that even as a young man More was quite diligent yet discriminating in attending sermons, going to hear preachers whose words were "truly pious and spiritual, and most moving to the heart", while avoiding those "whose only merits were pleasing oratory or subtle disquisition".[222] More passed this prudence on to his own children: of his daughters Erasmus notes both their remarkable ability to recall virtually everything they had just heard from the pulpit and their keen power of discernment:

> And if the priest has babbled something foolish, something impious, or something otherwise improper for a preacher—which we see happening frequently nowadays—they know whether to laugh or to ignore it or to express their indignation. Now that's the way to hear a sermon![223]

---

[220] Ibid., 50-51.
[221] Ibid., 49.
[222] Stapleton, *Life,* chap. 2, p. 9.
[223] Letter of Erasmus to William Budaeus, c. September 1521, quoted in Richard Marius,

More's most pointed words on the subject of preaching came in a letter written by him to the administrators of Oxford University in March 1518 or 1519. It appears from the testimony of Erasmus that his friend's comments were occasioned by the deliverance of a homily attacking the introduction of Greek studies into the Oxford curriculum.[224] Well aware that for many of his fellow laymen their knowledge of the faith came largely from what was taught in sermons, More would have been alarmed to see this invaluable means of catechesis squandered by a preacher who wasted his time in the pulpit giving his own subjective commentary on questions of learning, when there was such a pressing need to instruct the people about what mattered most —their salvation (note also More's passing reference to our Lord's continual presence in the reserved Blessed Sacrament):

> For could anyone with the least spark of Christian devotion in his heart not lament how the majesty of the sacrosanct office of preaching, which won the world over to Christ, is now being violated by the very men who are officially most responsible for upholding the authority of that function? Could anyone imagine a more blatant affront to the office of preaching than for a person who styles himself a preacher to step forth in the holiest season of the year and before a large audience of Christians, in the very temple of God, in the loftiest pulpit—in Christ's very throne, as it were—and in sight of Christ's venerable body, to turn his Lenten sermon into a bacchanalian travesty? How do you think those who stood listening received it when they saw their preacher, from whom they had come to hear lessons of spiritual wisdom, cavorting, guffawing, and monkeying around in the pulpit, and when those who had gathered there piously expecting to hear the words of life went away not recalling that they had heard anything but slurs against literature and impertinent preaching which had dishonored the office of preacher?[225]

Thomas More: A Biography (New York: Vintage Books, 1985), 224. For original Latin text, see letter no. 1233 in *Opus Epistolarum Des. Erasmi Roterdami,* vol. 4, *1519–1521,* ed. P. S. Allen and H. M. Allen (Oxford: Clarendon Press, 1922), 579.

[224] Daniel Kinney, ed., introduction to *In Defense of Humanism: Letters to Dorp, Oxford, Lee, and a Monk,* vol. 15 of *Complete Works of St. Thomas More* (New Haven: Yale Univ. Press, 1986), xxviii–xxxi.

[225] *Letter to Oxford,* in ibid., 135–37.

CHAPTER IX

The Sacramentals and Other Aspects of the Life of Grace

While the sacraments are undoubtedly the seven principal channels of grace in the life of Catholic Christians, the Church has always recognized a wide range of subordinate means by which grace is received through an action or the use of an object intended to direct the heart and mind to God. By the early sixteenth century, these "sacramentals" had become quite widespread and extremely popular, serving as a major means of engendering devotion among the people. But under the twofold pressure of *solafideism*'s rejection of "good works" for the sake of merit and *sola scriptura*'s denial of anything not explicitly mentioned in the Bible, sacramentals such as images, relics, blessings, and pilgrimages became the objects of the dissenters' most bitter condemnation and scorn. William Tyndale claimed that nothing of the material world could be dedicated to the worship of God:

> Fire, salt, water, bread, and oil be bodily things, given unto man for his necessity, and to help his brother with; and God that is a spirit cannot be served therewith . . .
> . . . Now God is a spirit, and will be worshipped in his word only, which is spiritual; and will have no bodily service.[1]

While conceding on the theoretical level that religious images could serve as helpful reminders of one's faith,[2] Tyndale nonetheless exco-

---

[1] *An Answer unto Sir Thomas More's Dialogue,* in William Tyndale, *An Answer to Sir Thomas More's Dialogue, The Supper of the Lord and Wm. Tracy's Testament Expounded,* ed. Rev. Henry Walter, Parker Society, vol. 44 (1850; reprint, Johnson Reprint Corp., 1968), 109, 125. Hereafter cited as *Answer.*

[2] Ibid., 59–60.

riated the veneration of images as it actually existed in the everyday life of the Church:

> And thus it appeareth that your ungodly and belly doctrine, wherwith ye so magnify the deeds of your ceremonies, and of your pilgrimages, and offering, for the deed itself, to please God, and to obtain the favour of dead saints . . . is but an exhorting to serve images; and so are ye image-servers, that is, idolaters.[3]

On the practical level Tyndale rejected all the sacramentals, from pilgrimages to holy water and blessed bread, claiming that such things restored health neither to the soul nor to the body.[4] He spoke with particular contempt of episcopal blessings, which he called "the wagging of the bishop's hand", charging that this action is "against Christ" and does "shame unto Christ's blood".[5]

Unlike his friend Erasmus and some of his humanist colleagues, Thomas More was not ashamed or embarrassed to defend the devotional practices of the Church, of which he himself made frequent use in his own spiritual life. And unlike Erasmus, More did not mock the simple piety of those ordinary faithful who "pour out their devotion to God in the churches"; defending such humble people from the dissenters' accusations of hypocrisy, More observed that King David did not consider it beneath his dignity to worship in song and dance with his people before the Ark of the Covenant.[6] Hence it was not unsympathetically that years earlier More translated the following words in his English text of the life of Pico della Mirandola: "The little affection of an old man or an old woman to Godward (were it never so small) he [Pico] set more by, than by all his own knowledge, as well of natural things as godly."[7] And in one of his last works, the *Treatise*

---

[3] Ibid., 62.

[4] *The Obedience of a Christian Man*, in William Tyndale, *Doctrinal Treatises and Introductions to Different Portions of the Holy Scriptures*, ed. Rev. Henry Walter, Parker Society, vol. 42 (1848; reprint, New York: Johnson Reprint Corp., 1968), 284 (hereafter cited as *Obedience*); *Answer*, 63–64.

[5] *Obedience*, 284.

[6] *Letter to Bugenhagen*, in *Letter to Bugenhagen, Supplication of Souls, Letter against Frith*, ed. Frank Manley et al., vol. 7 of *Complete Works of St. Thomas More* (New Haven: Yale Univ. Press, 1990), 93. Hereafter cited as *CW* 7.

[7] *Life of John Picus*, in *The Workes of Sir Thomas More Knight . . . in the English Tongue* (1557), as reproduced in *The English Works of Sir Thomas More*, ed. W. E. Campbell (London: Eyre and Spottiswoode; New York: Lincoln MacVeagh, Dial Press, 1931), 1:7.

upon the Passion, More commended the faith of those uneducated but devout souls who humbly reverence the Holy Eucharist, commenting that such simple believers are more pleasing to God than tepid clerics, no matter how learned they may be.[8]

Holy Images

Very much related to the subject of liturgical furnishings of which we have already spoken is the question of whether images—one of the most popular of the sacramentals—can legitimately be used in Christian worship. The basis for the dissenters' virulent rejection of all veneration of religious statues and paintings was their interpretation of biblical injunctions against the worship of pagan idols such as the following:

> You shall not make for yourself a graven image, or any likeness of anything that is in heaven above, or that is in the earth beneath, or that is in the water under the earth; you shall not bow down to them or serve them; for I the Lord your God am a jealous God . . . (Ex 20:4-5).

Many of the reformers took this passage, among others, to be a sweeping condemnation of the use of any images whatsoever in worship. But for More, such a broad interpretation could not be justified in view of God's instruction to Moses that molten angels be fashioned for the adornment of the Ark of the Covenant (Ex 25:18-20);[9] moreover, he points out, why had not such Fathers of the Church as Saint Augustine, Saint Jerome, Saint Basil, and Saint Gregory the Great found reason from the Scriptures for condemning the use of Christian images?[10] More explains that what was being forbidden in the Exodus passage above and elsewhere in the Old Testament was the adoration of false gods, wherein the molten or sculpted object was itself thought by the worshipper to be or to represent a deity other than the one true God.[11] This then was quite a different matter from

---

[8] *Treatise upon the Passion,* chap. 4, lecture 2, in *Treatise on the Passion; Treatise on the Blessed Body; Instructions and Prayers,* ed. Garry Haupt, vol. 13 of *Complete Works of St. Thomas More* (New Haven: Yale Univ. Press, 1976), 156. Hereafter cited as *CW* 13.

[9] *A Dialogue concerning Heresies,* ed. Thomas Lawler et al., vol. 6 of *Complete Works of St. Thomas More* (New Haven: Yale Univ. Press, 1981), bk. 1, chap. 2, pp. 38, 44-45. Hereafter cited as *CW* 6.

[10] Ibid., 38.

[11] Ibid., 45.

the veneration accorded by Christians to holy images, wherein adoration is directed to the triune God and not to the physical object
representing Him or to any other false deity. When the image is that
of a saint, the Christian renders the homage due only to God (that
is, *latria*) neither to the saint nor to his image; rather, the honor he
directs to the saint is like that given to the ambassador of a king, for
it redounds ultimately to God Himself.[12]

That one should express adoration to God or honor to a saint by
veneration of an image should not, More observes, seem so strange
to us: "When a man at the receipt of his prince's letter putteth off
his cap and kisseth it, doth he this reverence to the paper or to his
prince?"[13] Indeed, the use of images was rather a praiseworthy thing
that enhanced the devotion of the faithful; in this regard More, citing
a decree of Saint Gregory the Great, notes that "images be the books
of lay people wherein they read the life of Christ."[14] More then poses
the question of why, if it has always been considered acceptable to
venerate with a kiss a book containing the Gospels, the written record
of the life and Passion of Christ, it should not likewise be appropriate
to venerate a painting or sculpture depicting these same events.[15] Or
again, if it is acceptable to the reformers to honor the name of the
Lord, "Jesus", which is in and of itself nothing more than a word that
represents Christ to those who hear or read it, why is it not acceptable
to use "a figure of him carved or painted which representeth him and
his acts far more plain[ly] and more expressly"?[16] In addition, More
does not fail to remind his readers that it is a common and accepted
practice to take delight in the possession of images or other mementos
of those who are dear to us.[17]

Recognizing the need for quality artistry and craftsmanship in the
fashioning of religious images, More notes that a good image, like
a well-written book, is more effective in communicating its subject
matter than one poorly done, although he acknowledges there are exceptions to this principle in the case of images that "move a man for
some other special cause, as peradventure for some great antiquity or

---

[12] Ibid., 45⁻46.
[13] Ibid., 46.
[14] Ibid., bk. 4, chap. 2, p. 359.
[15] Ibid.
[16] Ibid., bk. 1, chap. 2, pp. 39⁻40 (quote on 40).
[17] Ibid., 47; chap. 3, p. 56.

the great virtue of the workman, or for that God showeth at the place some special assistance of his favor and grace."[18]

The Cross

In view of More's intense personal devotion to the mystery of our Lord's Passion, it should come as no surprise that he is especially adamant in his defense of the ultimate image of our faith, the cross, and particularly that most expressive form of the cross: the crucifix. He was convinced that, contrary to the claims of the reformers, God was pleased "to have the image of his blessed body hanging on his holy cross had in honour and reverent remembrance".[19] In making his case that if words can be used to remind us of God then so can images, More notes that the crucifix can elicit an even deeper devotion than sheer words alone: ". . . [T]hese two words Christus crucifixus do not so lively represent us the remembrance of his bitter passion as doth a blessed image of the crucifix, neither to lay man nor unto a learned."[20] Sceptical of those who might claim they have no need of a crucifix in their devotions, More does not see this image as merely a pedagogical device for the unlearned and spiritually uninitiated but rather as a most excellent means of stirring the hearts of all with a deeper love for the crucified Redeemer:

> And albeit that every good Christian man hath a remembering of Christ's passion in his mind, and conceiveth by devout meditation a form and fashion thereof in his heart, yet is there no man I ween so good nor so well learned, nor in meditation so well accustomed, but that he findeth himself more moved to pity and compassion upon the beholding of the holy crucifix than when he lacketh it.[21]

In dismissing as patently false an accusation by Tyndale that Catholics are taught only to pray in church, More responds to his opponent's further claim that while in church the faithful do nothing

---

[18] Ibid., bk. 1, chap. 2, p. 47.
[19] Ibid., 38.
[20] Ibid., 47.
[21] Ibid., bk. 1, chap. 3, p. 56.

but "say *Pater noster* unto a post"[22]—a caricature of the prayers said before crucifixes and before images of the Blessed Virgin Mary and the saints. While repeating his answer that these images are venerated not for themselves but for who and what they represent, More seems to sense that Tyndale's invective in this case is particularly aimed at the practice of reverencing images of Christ's Cross, which More here refers to as "the book of his bitter passion".[23] Defending the Good Friday ceremony of the veneration of the cross as it existed in sixteenth-century England, he explains that when (on this day) the faithful "do creep [on their knees] to the cross and kiss it and say a Pater noster at it; yet say we not the Pater noster to it but to God."[24] Elsewhere in his writings, appalled by Luther's virulent comments attacking the veneration of crosses and relics of the True Cross, More asks the Lutheran Bugenhagen, "Where did he [Christ] teach with his own mouth that his cross should be taken down and hidden away in the shadows somewhere lest gold be wasted in adorning it . . . ?"[25]

On the Giving of Blessings

Responding to Tyndale's caustic caricature of a bishop's blessing as the wagging of two fingers,[26] More observes that such an irreverent attitude toward the making of the sign of the cross comes as no surprise, considering the dissenters' disregard for crucifixes and even the True Cross itself. But Tyndale's scorn stands in contrast to the faith of Christians past and present who have always believed in the making of the sign of the cross—whether one crosses himself or another with God-given authority blesses him—for a blessing is "a kind of prayer and invocation of God's grace upon the party so blessed".[27] After relating an incident recorded by Saint Gregory Nazianzen wherein the pagan emperor Julian the Apostate, despite his hatred for the Cross, actually crossed himself in fear when confronted by diabolical visions,

---

[22] *The Confutation of Tyndale's Answer,* ed. Louis Schuster et al., vol. 8 of *Complete Works of St. Thomas More* (New Haven: Yale Univ. Press, 1973), bk. 2, p. 149. Hereafter cited as *CW* 8. For the cited passage in Tyndale, see *Answer,* 11.

[23] *CW* 8, bk. 2, pp. 149–50.

[24] Ibid., 150.

[25] *Letter to Bugenhagen,* in *CW* 7:57–59.

[26] *Answer,* 8; *Obedience,* 284.

[27] *CW* 8, bk. 1, pp. 128–29 (quote on 128).

More stresses how powerful the sign of the cross is in the face of temptation and expresses confidence that were Tyndale to happen upon the devil in the dark, "he would I warrant you cross and bless a pace."[28]

Relics

Humanist though he was, Thomas More did not consider it problematic to believe in relics and authenticated miracles. Indeed, he speaks unquestioningly of famous relics such as the mysterious "Holy Mandylion" of Edessa, a cloth bearing the image of Christ and venerated in the East up until the sack of Constantinople in 1204 (when it seems to have disappeared from the latter city)—what More identifies as an "image of his [Christ's] own face" sent (according to legend) by Christ Himself to the "king Abiagarus", that is, the first-century King Abgar V of Edessa. He likewise believed in the highly revered Veil of Veronica, another cloth bearing an image of Christ's "blessed visage", which for centuries attracted countless pilgrims to Rome.[29] He also accepts as genuine the account of the finding of the True Cross around A.D. 320 by Saint Helena, the mother of the Roman emperor Constantine.[30] More even expresses his belief in the legend that the Evangelist Saint Luke had painted on a table "the lovely visage of our blessed Lady his [Christ's] mother", a tradition that in More's time was associated with the famous ancient portrait of our Lady in the fourth-century Roman Basilica of Saint Mary Major.[31]

More finds precedents in the Old Testament for the Church's veneration of relics. Noting the instructions of the patriarchs Jacob and Joseph to their descendants that their remains were to be carried out of Egypt (Gen 49:29–32; 50:25), he sees as particularly significant an incident following the burial of the prophet Elisha, in which a dead man was raised to life when his corpse came into contact with the bones of the prophet (2 Kings 13:21). And as for the New Testament, More does not fail to remind his readers of the woman who was healed simply by touching Christ's garments (Mk 5:25–34).[32]

---

[28] Ibid., 129–30.
[29] *CW* 6, bk. 1, chap. 2, pp. 38–39.
[30] Ibid., bk. 2, chap. 9, p. 225.
[31] Ibid., bk. 1, chap. 2, p. 39.
[32] Ibid., bk. 2, chap. 9, pp. 224–25.

Responding to complaints that many relics must be fraudulent in view of the fact that in some cases two cities or shrines claim to possess the same relic of a particular saint, More explains how innocent human mistakes or misunderstandings can lead to seemingly contradictory claims with otherwise authentic relics. He cites as an example the case of the "head" of Saint John the Baptist preserved in the city of Amiens, France; though pilgrims speak of it as the whole head, the jaw from this relic is actually missing. There can be cases wherein two shrines, each reputed to possess the whole body of a saint, in reality possess only a part. In other instances a shrine remains revered even though most of the body of the saint once entombed there has long since been transferred elsewhere. Confusion can also arise from two different saints with the same name. Some relics may be mistakenly identified or lost due to past incursions by attacking nonbelievers, during which the relics would have been hurriedly stowed away.[33]

In a passage reminiscent of the eyewitness anecdotes provided by Saint Augustine in book 12 (chap. 8) of his *City of God,* More relates with childlike fascination the discovery of a number of hitherto hidden relics in the Benedictine Convent of Barking, an incident that occurred (by More's recollection) around the year 1500, when he was in his early twenties and perhaps had already begun contemplating a future with the Carthusians of the Charterhouse:

> As my self saw at the abbey of Barking besides London to my remembrance about thirty years past, in the setting an old image in a new tabernacle, the back of the image being all painted over and of long time before laid with beaten gold, happened to crack in one place, and out there fell a pretty little door, at which fell out also many relics that had lain unknown in that image God knows how long. And as long had been likely to lie again if God by that chance had not brought them to light. The bishop of London came then thither to see there were no deceit therein. And I among others was present there while he looked thereon and examined the matter. And in good faith it was to me a marvel to behold the manner of it . . . And diverse relics had old writings on them and some had none, but among others were there certain small kerchiefs which were named there our Lady's, and of her own working. Coarse were they not, nor were they large, but served as it seemed to cast in a plain and simple manner upon her head. But surely they were as clean seams to my seeming as ever I saw in my life, and were therewith as

---

[33] Ibid., 221–22.

white for all the long lying, as if they had been washed and laid up within one hour. And how long that image had rested in that old tabernacle that could no man tell, but there had in all the church none as they thought rested longer untouched. And they guessed that four or five hundred years ago that image was hidden when the abbey was burned by infidels, and those relics hidden therein.[34]

More observes that if through human error relics are mistakenly and unknowingly identified with the wrong saint or if an object that is no relic at all is innocently mistaken for a real relic and honored accordingly, there is no real harm done to the souls of those who reverenced these things—no more than if one unknowingly worshipped at Mass a host that through negligence or worse the priest had failed to consecrate.[35] In any event, the real issue that separated More from the dissenters was not so much whether a particular relic was valid but whether in principle any relic, no matter how authentic, should be the object of Christian veneration. For More, ultimately, the validity of this practice rests in the unfailing guidance of the Church by the Holy Spirit, who would never permit her to commend such a usage if it were reprehensible.[36]

Pilgrimages

As we have already seen, More personally took part in pilgrimages. In defending this practice, he does not claim to know the reason why God seems to favor being worshipped in certain places, places that are the destinations of pilgrimages. He can offer no other explanation than that "his [God's] pleasure in some place is to show more his assistance and to be more specially sought unto than in some other."[37] He gives as a scriptural example of this the pool of Beth-zatha mentioned in the Gospel of Saint John (Jn 5:2–9); the passage speaks of cures at this pool wrought by a miraculous stirring of the waters. No one can say why God chose to favor those who came to this particular place, yet obviously from the cures that happened there He did

---

[34] Ibid., 222.
[35] Ibid., 222–23.
[36] Ibid., 224.
[37] Ibid., bk. 1, chap. 4, p. 60.

indeed do so.[38] More considers it praiseworthy for a man or woman to journey with devotion to such places where God's assistance is made particularly manifest.[39]

Miracles

The attitude of Thomas More toward miracles and other preternatural occurrences provides a superb demonstration of his genuine Catholic humanism, a humanism that both knew how to engage in careful, rigorous scholarly inquiry that was willing to discard superfluities in the quest for truth yet could remain open to the reality that God can and does on occasion overrule the laws of nature to manifest His power, His wisdom, and His continuous involvement in the affairs of mankind. In his *Confutation of Tyndale's Answer,* More explains that it is the Holy Spirit who gives the Church the discernment to distinguish true miracles from those that are false; the Church therefore condemns false miracles, no matter how marvelous they may be.[40]

That More himself knew how to be circumspect in such matters is evident from his handling of the whole question of Elizabeth Barton, the so-called "Holy Maid of Kent", an English nun who was a contemporary of his (1506?–1534) and who claimed to have had mystical experiences and private revelations.[41] He first learned of this nun in 1525 or (more likely) 1526, when King Henry asked him to look over a document containing some of the purported mystic's own words that had been forwarded to the monarch by Archbishop William Warham of Canterbury. More found nothing particularly noteworthy or remarkable in this piece and told the King as much. About a year later (probably around Christmas of 1527), a Franciscan friar named Father Risby, who was lodged one night in More's house, raised the subject of Elizabeth Barton with him in a conversation following supper, but when the friar began to speak of a prophecy of Barton regarding the

---

[38] Ibid., 60–61.

[39] Ibid., 61.

[40] *CW* 8, bk. 3, p. 247.

[41] R. W. Chambers, *Thomas More* (1935; reprint, Ann Arbor, Mich.: Ann Arbor Paperbacks, Univ. of Michigan, 1973), 294–96. Except where noted otherwise, the account that follows is based upon More's letter to Thomas Cromwell, March(?) 1534, letter no. 197 in Elizabeth Rogers, ed., *The Correspondence of Sir Thomas More* (Princeton, N.J.: Princeton Univ. Press, 1947), 480–87.

matter of the King's marriage, his host would hear none of it. Not long thereafter another Franciscan, Father Hugh Rich, conversed with him about the "Holy Maid of Kent", but once again More refused to listen to any talk of revelations concerning the King, wisely noting that as Elizabeth Barton had seen the King herself, and therefore would have had the opportunity to relate to the monarch directly any such prophecies, there was no need for him to be informed of these things.

Father Rich spoke with him twice more on the experiences of Elizabeth Barton, but some of the tales he told regarding her seemed to More "very childish". He was particularly sceptical of a claim that she had somehow miraculously received Holy Communion at a Mass attended by the King at Calais; he deemed it "a tale too marvelous to be true".[42] Nonetheless, he was not ready to ascribe guilt to the supposed mystic herself, as he was thus far unsure whether these stories had actually originated with her or had been concocted by others. One day, while at the Brigittine Monastery of Syon in Isleworth, More was told by the priests there that they had met the woman and that some of them had "misliked" certain things regarding her. They sought his counsel, and he agreed to see the "Holy Maid" on the next occasion that she visited Syon. The interview initially left him with a favorable impression of the nun, for she seemed to evince a genuine Christian humility and prudence in her remarks. Their conversation throws light on More's own attitudes, for we see that he began their discussion by emphasizing to her that he had no interest as others had in hearing of her revelations but rather that he was motivated to speak with her by what he had heard of her great virtue and wished to be remembered in her prayers and devotions. Noteworthy is More's evident approval of her comment about what "great need folk have, that are visited with such visions, to take heed and prove well of what spirit they come of."[43]

Afterward More wrote a letter to the nun, phrased most deferentially, in which, after addressing her as "my right dearly beloved Sister in our Lord God" and comparing his position to that of Jethro advising Moses, who far surpassed him in dignity (Ex 18:12–27), he gently admonishes her to beware of telling her revelations regarding matters

---

[42] Letter no. 197, to Cromwell, in Rogers, *Correspondence*, 483.
[43] Ibid., 485.

of the Realm to those who have no need to hear them but only wish to satisfy their idle curiosity.[44] When later asked by the fathers of Syon Monastery to give his opinion of her, he told them of his favorable impressions but added the caveat that this was not a sufficient test of her genuineness, as this did not discount the possibility that she might be "very bad, if she seemed good, ere [before] I should think her other".[45] Subsequent events bore out the prudence of More's reserve, for Elizabeth Barton eventually declared her prophecies to be false and was executed under the charge of treason (nonetheless it does seem that she made her peace with God before dying). In this context we can readily recognize the wisdom of More's earlier advice to the Franciscan friar Father Rich, who had related to him the tales of this nun that he had found "too marvelous to be true":

> Father Rich, that she is a good virtuous woman, in good faith, I hear so many good folk so report her, that I verily think it true; and think it well likely that God worketh some good and great things by her. But yet are, you wot well, these strange tales no part of our creed; and therefore before you see them surely proved, you shall have my poor counsel not to wed yourself so far forth to the credence of them, as to report them very surely for true, lest that if it should hap that they were afterward proved false, it might diminish your estimation in your preaching, whereof might grow great loss.[46]

Having seen Thomas More's prudence in weighing the validity of claimed preternatural events, private revelations, and the like, we are better able to appreciate his genuine faith in occurrences of this nature that he found to be properly authenticated and approved by ecclesiastical authorities. It is obvious that More accepted eucharistic miracles as worthy of belief; indeed, in his defense of the Church's teaching on the Real Presence of Christ in the Eucharist as presented in his *Answer to a Poisoned Book,* he augments his already unassailable arguments by appealing to the additional testimony of "all the marvelous miracles that God hath showed for the blessed Sacrament yearly almost, and I ween daily too, what in one place and other".[47]

---

[44] Letter no. 192, to E. Barton, 1533(?), in Rogers, *Correspondence,* 465–66.

[45] Letter no. 197, to Cromwell, in Rogers, *Correspondence,* 486.

[46] Ibid., 487.

[47] *The Answer to a Poisoned Book,* ed. Clarence Miller, vol. 11 of *Complete Works of St. Thomas More* (New Haven: Yale Univ. Press, 1985), bk. 4, chap. 20, p. 203. Hereafter cited as *CW* 11.

Elsewhere, in his *Treatise upon the Passion,* More implies that he believes in authenticated miracles involving the "holy Blood of Christ out of the Sacrament" and in the phenomenon of "bleeding crucifixes" (what More calls a "crucifix striken").[48] In his *Supplication of Souls* he professes to believe in validated instances of apparitions and criticizes those who have an excessively sceptical attitude about the possibility of such occurrences.[49]

On occasion More himself pauses to relate a specific miracle, as with the following case—a preternatural phenomenon that was evidently observed by multitudes during the Good Friday ceremonies each year on the famous Crusaders' island of Rhodes and that only More has preserved for history:

> Ye might . . . upon Good Friday every year this two hundred years, till within this five years that the Turks have taken the town, have seen one of the thorns that was in Christ's crown bud and bring forth flowers in the service time, if ye would have gone to the Rhodes . . .[50]

It could be that More learned of this mysterious manifestation from one of his closest friends, the cleric William Lily, who in connection with a pilgrimage to Jerusalem had spent some time on the Mediterranean island acquiring a knowledge of Greek.[51]

More also gives as an example of a miracle verified by numerous and trustworthy witnesses the case of a twelve-year-old girl, the daughter of a respected knight, Sir Roger Wentworth. The girl was a victim of demonic possession, an affliction made manifest by "her mind alienated and raving with despising and blasphemy of God, and hatred of all hallowed things", as well as by her humanly inexplicable abilities to prophesy, to tell of events at other places as they happened, to discourse on scholarly subjects she had never studied, and to distinguish "the hallowed from the unhallowed" without any foreknowledge. When in her right mind, the girl was finally prompted to seek recourse at the shrine of Our Lady of Ipswich. Upon being laid before "the image of our blessed Lady", she at first reacted by going into horrifying contortions, but after this initial struggle she was suddenly and completely freed of the demon and restored to peace. Touched

---

[48] *Treatise upon the Passion,* chap. 4, lecture 2, in *CW* 13:147–48.
[49] *Supplication of Souls,* bk. 2, in *CW* 7:196–97.
[50] *CW* 6, bk. 1, chap. 13, pp. 84–85 (quote on 84).
[51] Chambers, *More,* 78; notes, *CW* 6:625.

deeply by this miracle that had liberated her from the bondage of Satan, the girl made up her mind to renounce the world and consecrate herself to Christ by entering the religious life, in which she persevered, living "well and graciously" thereafter.[52]

More notes that for those aspects of the faith most relentlessly attacked by dissenters, God performs miracles most abundantly—hence, all the miracles regarding the veneration of the saints and of holy images and relics, as well as those touching upon pilgrimages, the sacraments, and most especially the Holy Eucharist. Like the miracles in the days of the apostles, these latter-day manifestations testify to the Church's identity as Christ's "perpetual apostle".[53]

Honoring the Saints

From Luther's rejection of man's ability to do anything toward his own salvation in the way of merit, there stemmed his rejection of any special intercessory role for those who over the centuries had come to be recognized by the Church as saints; he likewise repudiated their function as examples of Christian virtue. Moreover, Luther essentially eliminated the commonly understood distinction of sainthood by emphasizing the identity of all the elect on earth or in heaven as "saints". Claiming that only the living could pray for each other, the dissenters insisted that Christ's role as man's sole Mediator with the Father precluded any intercessory role for those officially identified by the Church as "saints".[54]

While William Tyndale did acknowledge that there were distinctive saints whose lives were worthy of imitation,[55] he nonetheless essentially condemned the Church's veneration of saints, and especially prayer to the saints: "And then if our faith in God were greater than our fervent devotion to saints, we should pray to no saints at all, seeing we have promises of all things in our Saviour Jesus, and in the saints none at all."[56] Dead saints are not to be thought of as

---

[52] *CW* 6, bk. 1, chap. 16, pp. 93–94.

[53] *CW* 8, bk. 3, pp. 251–52.

[54] O. Cameron, *The European Reformation* (Oxford: Clarendon Press, 1991), 134–35.

[55] *Obedience*, 289.

[56] *Answer*, 95–96.

friends,[57] Tyndale declares; and like other dissenters, he levels against the Church the charge of idolatry in honoring the saints:

> They look on the miracles which God did by the saints . . . saying in their blind hearts, See what miracles God hath shewed for this saint; he must be verily great with God!—and at once turn themselves from God's word, and put their trust and confidence in the saint and his merits; and make an advocate, or rather a god of the saint . . .[58]

Accusing the Church of venerating as saints and martyrs men of avaricious and unworthy character,[59] Tyndale even resorts to casting England's most beloved martyr, Saint Thomas Becket, as a villainous figure who "for his mischief died a mischievous death".[60] In one of his final works, *William Tracy's Testament Expounded* (1534–1535), which he coauthored with John Frith, Tyndale (with Frith) proclaims that it is "damnable . . . to trust in the saints of heaven" and that the saints "abhor and defy" as "wicked idolaters" those who pray to them, reserving their prayers instead exclusively for a predestined elect, who, of course believing as Tyndale did, would never pray to a saint.[61]

As for the greatest of saints, Tyndale's attitude toward the Mother of God is cold at best, descending at times into carping attempts to diminish her unique stature in the Church. Thus he interprets Christ's words to His Mother at the marriage feast of Cana (Jn 2:1–11) as a rebuke: "And if there were no imperfectness in our lady's deeds, why did Christ rebuke her (John ii), when he ought rather to have honoured his mother?"[62] He thinks it conceivable that some other holy woman could equal Mary in holiness: "Wherefore if God gave his mercy, that another woman were in those two points [faith and love] equal with her, why were she not like great, and her prayers as much heard?"[63] Of the *Salve Regina* he remarks that "therein is much blasphemy unto our blessed lady; because Christ is our hope and life only, and not she."[64] He even makes the disdainful suggestion that the Blessed Virgin Mary if put to the test would have been capable

---

[57] *The Parable of the Wicked Mammon,* in Tyndale, *Doctrinal Treatises,* 66–67.
[58] *Obedience,* 184.
[59] Ibid., 291, 325.
[60] *Answer,* 131.
[61] Text in Tyndale, *An Answer to Sir Thomas More's Dialogue,* 278–79.
[62] *Answer,* 207.
[63] Ibid., 185.
[64] Ibid., 184.

of denying her Divine Son: "I would not swear on a book, that if our lady had been let slip as we other were, and as hard apposed, with as present death before her eyes, that she would not have denied some things that she knew true."[65] Equally bizarre is Tyndale's attempt to disprove Mary's sinlessness (in refutation of those who believed in her Assumption) by declaring with regard to the finding of the Christ Child in the Temple "how negligent she was to leave him behind her at Jerusalem unawares, and to go a day's journey ere she sought for him."[66]

More is both methodical and comprehensive in his defense of the Church's definition of the communion of saints. If we cannot honor the saints on the premise that such honor to mere creatures detracts from the honor of God Himself, More asks, then how can we explain God's commandments to honor such creatures here on earth as our parents or our rulers?[67] Catholics venerate the saints, he explains, not as alternate saviors but rather as those whom Christ particularly loves and with whose prayers and intercession on their behalf He will be particularly pleased. Indeed it is the Lord's will that the saints be honored, for the honor bestowed upon them is ultimately bestowed upon Him.[68] We venerate the saints as God's servants, as we would on earth welcome the servants of a great man we esteemed.[69] If the goodness we bestow upon our poor brethren is considered by Christ as bestowed upon Himself, as He tells us (Mt 25:40), and if those, as He says, who welcome His apostles and disciples welcome Him (Mt 10:40), assuredly those who honor the saints are likewise honoring Christ. Our Lord Himself showed that He would have His saints partake in His glory when He promised the apostles that they would be seated at His side on the final Day of Judgment (Mt 19:28). Moreover, He promised that Martha's sister Mary (whom More identifies as Mary Magdalen) would be honored throughout the world for her deed of anointing Him with ointment (Mt 26:13).[70] In the latter episode from the Gospels More also sees a refutation of those who

---

[65] Ibid., 207.
[66] *Obedience*, 316.
[67] *CW* 6, bk. 1, chap. 2, p. 48.
[68] *CW* 11, bk. 2, chap. 4, p. 105.
[69] *CW* 6, bk. 1, chap. 2, p. 48.
[70] Ibid., 48–49.

mock the lighting of candles and other devotional practices directed to the honor of God and His saints:

> But let them all by that example of that holy woman and by these words of our Saviour learn that God delighteth to see the fervent heat of the heart's devotion boil out by the body, and to do him service with all such goods of fortune as God hath given a man.[71]

> And yet was he [Christ] not ravished with the odor of her ointment, but with the delight of her devotion, in which he delighteth yet when any man doth the like.[72]

The dissenters seem to doubt whether the saints can either hear us or help us, More observes; yet how can we doubt whether they hear us? Their souls are not dead, and therefore as living souls the love and charity toward their fellowman that characterized them in this world cannot have diminished in the next. Indeed, More continues, the closer one draws to heaven, the greater is his solicitude toward his brethren here on earth, as was the case with the martyr Saint Stephen, who after seeing heaven opened prayed for his enemies who were stoning him (Acts 7:55–60). In view of this, is it conceivable that Saint Stephen would not pray for those who honor him on earth, now that he is in heaven?[73]

But even if the saints can hear us, can they help us? More notes that as the saints were certainly able to assist others while on earth where their human nature was as weak as ours, surely they can do so in heaven. But how can the saints respond simultaneously to so many prayers from so many places far and wide? More answers that if it is possible for us to see and hear in this world, it must certainly be possible for those in the next life to see or hear in some sense; it need not concern us how the saints are able to learn of affairs on earth.[74]

But why pray to the saints at all when we can pray directly to God Himself? More answers by noting that when we are ill we do not simply ask God to heal us, but we also seek treatment from a physician. Surely it is God who heals us when we recover, for He is behind everything the doctor does or uses, yet He wills to cure us

---

[71] Ibid., 49.
[72] *CW* 8, bk. 7, pp. 699–700 (quote on 700).
[73] *CW* 6, bk. 2, chap. 8, pp. 211–12.
[74] Ibid., 212–14.

by means of these natural instruments. In the same way He wills to help us through the intercession of His saints.[75]

That God will brook no rivals certainly does not mean that He forbids us to pray for one another. Even during our Lord's life on earth, More explains, He permitted people to come to His apostles rather than directly to Himself for help and allowed the Twelve to work miracles in His stead. On some occasions the apostles assumed the role of intercessors with Christ, presenting the petitions of others to their Master.[76] If this was the case when the apostles were with Christ on earth, it must surely be so now that they dwell with Him in heaven. God is pleased to have us honor and call upon His saints, "his especial beloved friends", for "it becometh us and well behoveth us to make friends of such as he hath in favour."[77] While it is true that we can ask the prayers of any dead person who to the best of our knowledge died at peace with God (since even souls in Purgatory can pray for us), we can only be absolutely certain of assistance from the canonized saints.[78] How, then, does the Church determine who is a saint? As in her doctrinal decisions, it is the Holy Spirit who guides the Church in unerringly recognizing true saints:

> . . . [W]hen the Church by diligent ensearch findeth the life of a man holy, and that thereto it is well witnessed that God by his miracles testifieth the man's blessedness and the favor in which he standeth with him in heaven, declaring by the boot and profit which he doth to many men for his sake that he will have him honored and had for hallowed in his Church here in earth, and this thing either by them that hath the cure of his Church after such diligence used, being by the canonization declared unto the people, or peradventure without canonization growing thereof (by the holiness well known and miracles many seen) so sure a common persuasion through the whole people of Christendom, that the person is accepted and reputed for an undoubted saint . . . we boldly may and well we ought in this case to trust that the grace and aid of God and his Holy Spirit assisting his Church hath governed the judgment of his ministers, and inclined the minds of his people to such consent.[79]

---

[75] Ibid., 214.
[76] Ibid., 214–15.
[77] Ibid., 215.
[78] Ibid., 216.
[79] Ibid., bk. 2, chap. 9, pp. 220–21.

More defends the practice of asking a particular saint to intercede with God for us in matters that, because of some aspect or detail of that saint's life, have traditionally become associated with him; thus of those who sought the intercession of Saint Apollonia, a third-century virgin martyr of Alexandria, Egypt, who lost her teeth during the tortures leading up to her death, More comments: "For as to pray to Saint Apollonia for the help of our teeth is no witchcraft, considering that she had her teeth pulled out for Christ's sake."[80] More explains that while it is true that we should seek first the Kingdom of God (Mt 6:33) and trust in God's promise that if we do so He shall see to our natural needs, nonetheless God does will that we should work for a living using our bodies, "having our hearts all the while in heaven". He expects us to ask Him for our material necessities— hence the petition for "our daily bread" in the prayer He Himself taught, the Our Father.[81] Such things are certainly not too trivial to petition heaven for: "But as for your teeth I ween if they ached well ye would yourself think it a thing worthy and not too simple to ask help of Saint Apollonia and of God too."[82]

More challenges the dissenters to a man-to-man comparison of their proponents with those of the Church, setting Saint Augustine against Luther, Saint Jerome against François Lambert, Saint Ambrose against Johann Oecolampadius, Saint Gregory the Great against Johannes Bugenhagen, Saint John Chrysostom against Tyndale, and Saint Basil against Simon Fish. Were the dissenters to add to the list on their side their own wives, More continues, he would not be able to match them directly, since these Church Fathers were not married, but he could set against them illustrious female saints: Saint Anastasia against Luther's wife, Saint Hildegard against Oecolampadius' wife, Saint Bridget of Sweden against Lambert's wife and Saint Catherine of Siena against Bugenhagen's wife.[83] As authorities affirming the doctrines of Purgatory and prayer for the dead, More additionally lists Saint Gregory Nazianzen, Saint Gregory of Nyssa, Saint Cyril of Jerusalem, Saint John Damascene, Saint Cyprian, Saint Hilary, Saint Bede, and Saint Thomas Aquinas.[84]

---

[80] Ibid., chap. 11, p. 232.
[81] Ibid., 233.
[82] Ibid.
[83] *Supplication of Souls*, bk. 2, in *CW* 7:209, plus notes, 373–75.
[84] Ibid., 210.

It is obvious from his writings that More firmly believed in the existence of angels. In one of his very last works, the *Treatise upon the Passion,* he offers a touching explanation of why God saw fit to create these beings:

> The glorious blessed Trinity . . . did when it pleased themselves, not of any necessity, nor for increase of any commodity, that their full and perfect, and not increasable bliss could receive thereby, but only of their mere liberal goodness, create of nothing, the noble high beautiful nature of angels, to make some creatures partners of the Creator's goodness.[85]

But not only did More believe in angels in general; he also accepted the Church's teaching that God has assigned to each of us an angel peculiarly our own to guide and assist us on our pilgrimage—a guardian angel. Thus in his *Dialogue of Comfort against Tribulation,* More recommends that the person battling temptation ask "his own good Angel" to intercede with God on his behalf.[86] In this same work he observes that God sometimes uses our guardian angels to plant within us good inspirations.[87] In his book on the subject of Purgatory, *The Supplication of Souls,* he has the souls in this place of purification express their gratitude to the guardian angels who came to their aid during life and who help them still:

> And among other right especially be we beholden to the blessed spirits our own proper good angels. Whom when we behold coming with comfort to us, albeit that we take great pleasure and greatly rejoice therein; yet is it not without much confusion and ashamedness to consider how little we regarded our good angels and how seldom we thought upon them while we lived. They carry up our prayers to God and good saints for us; and they bring down from them the comfort and consolation to us. With which when they come and comfort us; only God and we know what joy it is to our hearts and how heartily we pray for you.[88]

---

[85] *Treatise upon the Passion,* introduction, 1st point, in *CW* 13:3–4.

[86] *A Dialogue of Comfort against Tribulation,* ed. Louis Martz and Frank Manley, vol. 12 of *Complete Works of St. Thomas More* (New Haven: Yale Univ. Press, 1976), bk. 2, chap. 16, p. 155. Hereafter cited as *CW* 12.

[87] Ibid., bk. 1, chap. 3, p. 16.

[88] *Supplication of Souls,* bk. 2, in *CW* 7:227.

In one of the prayers with which he concludes each section of his *Treatise upon the Passion,* More asks the Trinity to make him receptive to the promptings of his angelic companion: "O glorious blessed Trinity . . . for thy tender mercy, plant in mine heart such meekness, that I so may by thy grace follow the motion [prompting] of my good angel . . ."[89] In yet another passage from this same work, More expresses his belief that the angels gather about the Blessed Sacrament to adore their God under the humble sacramental veils: "It seemeth also that by concomitance . . . there is everywhere evermore about this blessed Sacrament, a glorious heavenly company of blessed angels and saints, as divers holy doctors declare."[90]

The angels who remained faithful to God when Satan rebelled, More explains, were thereafter "so surely confirmed in grace" that from that time onward they have been incapable of sin or disobedience. We know this to be true, he continues, from God's teachings to His Church, while the angels know by means of God's promise communicated to them through the beatific vision, which they continually enjoy.[91] In his very last work, *De Tristitia Christi,* More testifies to the power of the angels by commenting that a whole army of mortals would shrink before so little as the "angry frown of a single angel".[92]

The Blessed Virgin Mary

One aspect of Thomas More's thought and spirituality that has invariably been overlooked is his devotion to the Mother of God, the Blessed Virgin Mary. As we have already seen, such devotion is implicit in More's recommendation of the pseudo-Bonaventuran *Meditationes Vitae Christi,* a work permeated with Marian themes. Yet his attitude toward the Blessed Mother is far more explicitly manifested in his zealous defense of every prerogative of hers, even those that had not yet been formally defined by the Church, as well as by the distress he exhibits over the dissenters' attempts to suppress prayers

---

[89] *Treatise upon the Passion,* introduction, 1st point, in *CW* 13:11.

[90] Ibid., chap. 4, lecture 2, in *CW* 13:148.

[91] *CW* 8, bk. 4, p. 437.

[92] *De Tristitia Christi,* ed. and trans. Clarence H. Miller, vol. 14 of *Complete Works of St. Thomas More* (New Haven: Yale Univ. Press, 1976), 499–501 (quote on 501). Hereafter cited as *CW* 14.

to her, and—most importantly of all—in the loving solicitude with which he speaks of her.

More believed in Mary's Immaculate Conception, in her perpetual virginity, and in the Assumption of her sinless body into heaven. Thus in his *Answer to a Poisoned Book,* decrying those who make irreverent "jest" of the Blessed Virgin Mary, he refers to her as "our blessed Lady the immaculate mother of Christ".[93] In his *Confutation of Tyndale's Answer,* he attests to the Church's belief that Mary was free of all personal sins.[94] More also believed that the Blessed Virgin experienced no travail in giving birth to her Divine Son.[95]

Among the truths of the faith preserved by oral tradition rather than the Scriptures, More names the perpetual virginity of the Blessed Mother and her Assumption into heaven, noting with regard to the latter that had Mary's body not been taken to heaven it would assuredly have been the object of at least as much veneration as the remains of the other saints. His point is that the absence of any cultus whatsoever as to Mary's remains lends confirmation to the belief that her body is not on earth but rather in heaven.[96] Belief in the Assumption has existed continuously over the centuries since the time of Mary's passing, More observes; hence it is by no means a new article of faith. Responding to Tyndale's flippant comment, "What help it me to believe that our lady's body is in heaven?",[97] he notes that it certainly is of use to us to believe all the truths that God has revealed to us—written or unwritten.[98]

More firmly believed that the Blessed Virgin Mary had vowed herself to a life of perpetual virginity even before the Annunciation. In his *Answer to a Poisoned Book,* he explains that Mary's question to the angel, "But how can this come about, since I am a virgin?" (Lk 1:34, Jerusalem Bible trans.)[99], does not allow for any other explanation, for the angel had just said to her that she "will conceive" (Lk 1:31) in the future. Hence as she was already betrothed to Joseph (Lk 1:27), and was certainly not beyond the age of childbearing as

---

[93] *CW* 11, bk. 5, chap. 3, p. 223.

[94] *CW* 8, bk. 4, p. 393.

[95] *Treatise upon the Passion,* introduction, in *CW* 13:27.

[96] *CW* 8, bk. 3, p. 366.

[97] *Answer,* 28 (spelling modernized).

[98] *CW* 8, bk. 3, p. 285.

[99] *The Jerusalem Bible, Readers' Edition* (Garden City, N.Y.: Doubleday, 1968).

was her kinswoman Elizabeth, there would have been no reason for her to ask, ". . . [H]ow can this come about . . . ?" Her virginity could have been an impediment to any future conception of a child in marriage only if she had previously made a vow to God to remain a virgin for the rest of her life. More also infers from this that Saint Joseph must have agreed beforehand to a life of celibacy with her, for it is most unlikely that she would have consented to a betrothal that she knew would threaten the keeping of her vow.[100]

The naturalness and spontaneity with which More introduces the Blessed Virgin into his discussions leads one to infer that she was habitually in his thoughts. Thus in his *Treatise upon the Passion,* while speaking of our Lord's special love for the Apostle Saint John, More does not fail to remind us that it was to John that Christ entrusted "his own dear heavy [sorrowful] mother".[101] Again referring to "the disciple whom Jesus loved" (Jn 21:20), this time in his *De Tristitia Christi,* and alluding to the tradition that this apostle remained celibate, More describes Saint John standing before the Cross by the side of "Christ's most beloved mother" as "two pure virgins standing together".[102] In this same work he expresses his opinion that since he could not see how the apostles could have been in a position to observe in the darkness every detail of our Lord's agony in Gethsemane as recorded in the Gospels, Christ Himself after His Resurrection must have described to both them and "His most loving mother" what He had suffered.[103] In yet another passage of *De Tristitia Christi* More names among the greatest of our Lord's mental sufferings in Gethsemane the thought of "the ineffable grief of His beloved mother".[104] Elsewhere, in his *Dialogue concerning Heresies,* More testifies to the steadfast faith of the Virgin Mary, whose fidelity to her Son in His Passion stood in sharp contrast with the failure of His apostles at that critical hour, her faith liturgically symbolized by the striking image of a lone candle left burning atop the hearse (Tenebrae candlestand) of Holy Week (see chapter 8 above). During an exposition on the perpetual virginity of the Blessed Mother in the same work, he waxes poetic as he describes the Incarnation as Mary's "celestial conception of her Maker, made

---

[100] *CW* 11, bk. 1, chap. 15, pp. 58–59; see also *CW* 6, bk. 1, chap. 25, pp. 150–51.

[101] *Treatise upon the Passion,* chap. 1, lecture 5, in *CW* 13:82.

[102] *CW* 14:571.

[103] Ibid., 189–93 (quote on 193).

[104] Ibid., 47–49 (quote on 49).

man in her blessed womb", and asks: ". . . [W]hat man could think it that ever God would suffer any earthly man after to be conceived in that holy closet taken up and consecrate so specially to God?"[105] Returning to the mystery of the Incarnation in the introduction to his *Treatise upon the Passion,* More reverently speaks of the second Person of the Blessed Trinity descending into the "blessed womb of the pure Virgin Mary" wherein He became man by the power of the Holy Spirit who overshadowed "the pure blood of her body".[106] In *The Supplication of Souls,* More has the souls in Purgatory testify that they receive comfort that "cometh at seasons from our Lady".[107] Finally, toward the end of his *Dialogue of Comfort against Tribulation,* he presents the consoling picture of Christ's "Immaculate mother" together with all the saints inviting us to the joys of heaven.[108]

There are other clues to More's filial love for the Mother of God scattered in his writings and in the recollections of those who knew him. From the biography of Thomas Stapleton we know that each night More and his family ended their day with, among other prayers, the well-known Marian hymn *Salve Regina*.[109] And in humorously listing the ever-deeper levels of poverty into which he anticipated his household would slide following his resignation from the office of Lord Chancellor, More ends by saying that if all else fails they could go begging "at every man's door to sing *Salve Regina,* and so still keep company and be merry together".[110] There is evidence that he frequented the Marian shrine of Willesden, for it was in one of Willesden's chapels that his two younger daughters were married in 1525, and it was from Willesden that he sent a letter to his secretary only a week prior to his imprisonment in April 1534.[111] Among the personal effects of More to have been preserved into the present century are two distinctly Marian objects of devotion: a rosary ring

---

[105] *CW* 6, bk. 1, chap. 25, p. 151.

[106] *Treatise upon the Passion,* introduction, 3d point, in *CW* 13:27.

[107] *Supplication of Souls,* bk. 2, in *CW* 7:227.

[108] *CW* 12, bk. 3, chap. 27, p. 315.

[109] Thomas Stapleton, *The Life and Illustrious Martyrdom of Sir Thomas More,* ed. E. E. Reynolds (Bronx, N.Y.: Fordham Univ. Press, 1966), chap. 9, pp. 88–89.

[110] William Roper, *The Lyfe of Sir Thomas Moore, Knighte,* ed. Elsie V. Hitchcock, Early English Text Society, original series, no. 197 (London: Early English Text Society, 1935), 52–54 (quotation on 54).

[111] Introduction, *CW* 6:486.

and a cameo depicting the head of the Blessed Virgin.[112] The prayer
More composed in the last few days before his execution begins with
the recitation of the *Pater noster* (the Our Father), the *Ave Maria* (the
Hail Mary) and the *Credo* (the Creed), while toward the end of the
prayer he inserts the well-known Marian versicle, "Pray for us, [O]
holy Mother of God, that we may be made worthy of the promises
of Christ."[113]

Among the facets of Luther's new theology that More took him
to task for was that he could "not abide the common anthem of our
Lady and the most devout *Salve Regina,* because we therein call that
blessed Virgin our advocate".[114] In his *Answer to a Poisoned Book,* More
complains of the dissenters' efforts to do away with the Rosary, describing them as casting rosary beads into the fire.[115] And in one of
his written exchanges with Tyndale, he thanks God that the devotion
of the people to the Blessed Mother was as yet still sufficiently strong
to dissuade his antagonist, who "forbiddeth folk to pray to her, and
specially misliketh her devout anthem of *Salve Regina*", from going
even farther than he already had in attacking the Church's beliefs and
practices regarding her.[116]

Devotion to the Heart of Christ

One particularly surprising find in the writings of Thomas More is
the significant number of references to the Heart of Christ, the "Sacred Heart" as it has since come to be called. These references, like
those touching upon the Blessed Virgin Mary, come so naturally that
they suggest a man who had long pondered the mysteries of the Heart
of Him who has loved us "with an everlasting love" (Jer 31:3). Undoubtedly related to this is More's emphasis on the mercy of God, a
theme we encounter throughout his works.

More's devotion to the Heart of Christ predates by nearly a hundred
and fifty years the famous apparitions regarding this devotion experi-

---

[112] R. W. Chambers, ed., *The Fame of Blessed Thomas More: Being Addresses Delivered in His
Honour in Chelsea, July 1929* (London and New York: Sheed and Ward, 1933), 119.

[113] "A Devout Prayer", in *CW* 13:228, 231.

[114] *CW* 6, bk. 4, chap. 2, p. 359.

[115] *CW* 11, bk. 4, chap. 12, p. 186.

[116] *CW* 8, bk. 3, p. 314.

enced by the French nun Saint Margaret Mary Alacoque (1647–1690) at Paray-le-Monial, yet we can find early forms of it going much farther back. At least one fairly explicit reference to the Heart of Christ can be found in the works of Saint Bernard (1090–1153),[117] as well as in the writings of his friend William of Saint Thierry (d. 1148), who speaks of entering "even into the Heart of Jesus, into the holy of holies, into the ark of the Testament, even into the golden urn, the soul of our humanity, containing in itself the manna of the divinity".[118] The thirteenth-century German nun Saint Gertrude (1256–1302) received private revelations regarding the Sacred Heart that certainly presage in some manner what later transpired at Paray-le-Monial. In his treatise *On Daily Work,* the influential fourteenth-century English mystic Richard Rolle calls upon the devout to reflect upon "the wide wound in His [Christ's] side through the which room is made for thee to find thy way to His heart".[119] We surmise, however, that the most likely source of More's devotion to the Heart of the Redeemer was none other than the religious order that in his youth, over a span of four years, had nurtured his highest aspirations—the Carthusians. Evidence of this devotion appears in Carthusian spirituality as early as the fourteenth century, most notably in the monumental *Vita Christi* of Ludolf of Saxony:

> The Heart has been wounded for us with a wound of love in order that we, by a return of love, might be able to gain access through the door of the side to his Heart, and there unite all our love to his divine love in such a manner as to make of them but one and the same love, as molten iron is blended with fire. For man should direct all his desires to God for the love of Christ, and in all things conform his will to the divine will, in return for that wound of love which he received for man on the cross, when the arrow of an unconquerable love pierced his most sweet Heart. Let us, then, remember what love exceeding great Christ has shown us in the opening of his side by opening to us therein full and free access to his Heart. Let us hasten to enter into the Heart of Christ . . .[120]

---

[117] St. Bernard, *In Cant.,* sermon 61, no. 4, quoted in Fr. J. V. Bainvel, S.J., *Devotion to the Sacred Heart: The Doctrine and Its History* (New York: Benziger Bros., 1924), 130.

[118] William of Saint Thierry, *De Contemplando Deo,* chap. 1, no. 3, quoted in Bainvel, *Devotion,* 130.

[119] Quoted in Fr. Herbert Thurston, S.J., "The Early Cultus of the Blessed Sacrament", *Month* 109 (April 1907): 389–90.

[120] *Vita Jesu Christi,* ed. A.-C. Bolard, L.-M. Rigollot, and J. Carnandet (Paris and Rome:

Devotion to the Heart of Christ appears even more frequently in the Carthusian writings of the fifteenth and sixteenth centuries, as in those of Dominic of Treves (1384?–1461), Denis the Carthusian (1394–1471), Henry Arnoldi (d. 1487), Pierre Dorland (1440–1507), and culminating in the works of More's contemporary, Lanspergius (d. 1539).[121] As for England, there is extant a pre-Reformation holy card distributed by the Carthusian Monastery of Sheen that depicts among the five wounds of Christ an easily recognizable and prominent image of the Sacred Heart.[122]

Significantly, the Heart of Christ is mentioned by More in his very first English book, his translation of the life of Pico della Mirandola, which he completed during or shortly after his "Carthusian years" (estimated to be 1501–1504). In one of the verses of an original poem by More included with the translation, he exhorts those assailed by temptation to turn their minds to the Passion of Christ and "Think on his precious heart carved in twain."[123] Elsewhere as here, such references quite appropriately appear when More is discussing the Passion of our Lord, as in his meditation on the Agony in the Garden, *De Tristitia Christi,* wherein he twice refers to the Sacred Heart as the "most gentle heart" of Christ,[124] and in another passage speaks of the Apostle Saint John holding "a special place in our Lord's heart".[125] In his *Dialogue of Comfort against Tribulation,* More, while enumerating everything that was done to the Savior in His Passion, mentions the piercing of "his holy heart" on the Cross,[126] an expression we find again in the fourth chapter of his *Treatise upon the Passion,* where he speaks of the blood and water that issued from the "holy heart of Christ", offering this incident as one of several possible explanations for the practice of adding water to the wine that is to be consecrated in the Holy Sacrifice of the Mass.[127] Likewise, in the course of de-

---

Victor Palme, 1865), pt. 2, chap. 64, nos. 14–15, p. 676; English translation from Bainvel, *Devotion,* 159–60.

[121] Bainvel, *Devotion,* 160–63, 178–80; *The Carthusians: Origin, Spirit, Family Life,* 2d ed. (Westminster, Md.: Newman Press, 1952), 41 n.

[122] Eamon Duffy, *The Stripping of the Altars: Traditional Religion in England c. 1400—c. 1580* (New Haven: Yale Univ. Press, 1992), figure 99.

[123] "The Twelve Weapons of Spiritual Battle", *Life of Picus,* 27.

[124] *CW* 14:49, 505.

[125] Ibid., 565.

[126] *CW* 12, bk. 3, chap. 27, p. 312.

[127] *Treatise upon the Passion,* chap. 4, lecture 2, in *CW* 13:151.

fending this same practice in his *Confutation of Tyndale's Answer,* More speaks of the blood and water welling out from Christ's "blessed heart upon the cross".[128] Returning to the *Treatise upon the Passion,* we find More observing that, even if all of Jerusalem had come to capture Christ, our Lord could have kept them all at bay with "one thought of his holy heart".[129] But perhaps the most moving of all of More's comments on the Heart of the Redeemer appears some pages later in the *Treatise,* as he discusses the Last Supper and reflects on our Lord's words, "I have earnestly desired to eat this passover with you before I suffer . . ." (Lk 22:15):

> And therefore, since he was now so near drawing to his passion which he had determined to suffer on the morrow, he like a most tender lover, longed with that last supper, to make them his farewell at his departing from them.
> Wherein as I before have said, appeared his wonderful loving heart . . .
> But he loved them so tenderly, that all the pain, sorrow, dread and fear that was toward him, could not so master and overwhelm his kind loving affection toward them, but that the desire and longing to make his last supper with them, so much increased greater, as he surely saw that his bitter passion drew nearer.[130]

Of Heaven, Hell, and Purgatory

Although More and his opponents were in agreement as to the existence of heaven, Tyndale among others proffered a bizarre theory that the souls of the just would not enter heaven until the end of the world,[131] an idea that More unhesitatingly rejects.[132] Elsewhere in his apologetical writings, More frequently mentions heaven in passing references as the final destiny and reward of the just. Years earlier he had translated the following words of Giovanni Pico della Mirandola regarding heaven from the collection of Pico's letters that he had cho-

---

[128] *CW* 8, bk. 3, p. 319.

[129] *Treatise upon the Passion,* chap. 2, in *CW* 13:93.

[130] Ibid., chap. 4, lecture 1, pp. 119–20.

[131] *Answer,* 118, 188–89; "Protestation made by William Tyndale, touching the resurrection of the bodies, and the state of the souls after this life" (extracted from preface to Tyndale's 1534 New Testament), quoted in Rev. Henry Walter, "Biographical Notice", Tyndale, *Doctrinal Treatises,* lxii–lxiii.

[132] *CW* 8, bk. 6, p. 625; bk. 7, p. 702.

sen to accompany his English edition of the Italian humanist's biography:

> Remember again how great things be promised and prepared for them, which despising these present things desire and long for that country whose king is the Godhead, whose law is charity, whose measure is eternity.[133]

More was eventually to speak most eloquently of heaven in one of his last spiritual works, *A Dialogue of Comfort against Tribulation,* which we will be exploring at length in a later chapter. Because of the reformers' questioning of whether there was really "fire" in hell, this place of eternal punishment for the damned does become a subject of discussion more than once in the polemical works of More. Thus in his *Supplication of Souls,* he describes hell in these terms:

> But whatsoever soul mishap to die in deadly sin and impenitent; since he is thereby fallen off forever from our Saviour Christ that was his foundation, and hath built up wretched works upon your ghostly enemy the devil, wherewith he hath so thoroughly poisoned himself, that he can never be purged; the fire shall therefore lie burning upon him forever, and his pain never lessened, nor his filthy spots never the more minished.[134]

In the midst of a discussion on the necessity of penance in his *Confutation of Tyndale's Answer,* More notes that when one repents of mortal sin and is absolved in the sacrament of confession, God in His mercy spares the penitent from undergoing the full sentence of "his high indignation, whereupon followeth the perpetual banishment from the sight of his face, and fruition of his glory into the eternal torment of hell".[135]

Purgatory, More explains, is "ordained for the punishment of such sins, as were either venial in the beginning, or from mortal turned to venial by the forgiveness of the mortality".[136] Of those in Purgatory, he observes:

> For though they be departed out of our company, yet them reckon we still for voyagers and pilgrims in the same pilgrimage that we be, toward

---

[133] Letter of Pico to his nephew, July 2, 1492, appended to *Life of Picus,* 17.
[134] *Supplication of Souls,* bk. 2, in *CW* 7:188.
[135] *CW* 8, bk. 2, p. 210.
[136] Ibid., bk. 3, p. 289.

the same place of rest and wealth that we walk, till they be passed once all the pain of their journey, and entered into the bliss of heaven.[137]

In the face of a wholesale denial of Purgatory by the reformers, More devoted much of his apologetical energies to the defense of this doctrine, most especially in the "Second Book" of his treatise, *The Supplication of Souls,* in which he responds to the dissenter Simon Fish's assertion in his *Supplication for the Beggars* that "many men of great literature and judgment" have concluded that "there is no purgatory; but that it is a thing invented by the covetousness of the spiritualty, only to translate all kingdoms from other princes unto them, and that there is not one word spoken of it in all holy Scripture."[138] As the title of More's work suggests, the arguments supporting the doctrine at stake are put by More into the mouths of the poor souls of Purgatory themselves, who tell the reader they are grieved by the dissenters' denial of Purgatory, not so much on their own account as out of fear for the salvation of their brothers and sisters on earth:

> Nor of all the heavy tidings that ever we heard here, was there never none so sore smote us to the heart as to hear the world wax so faint in the faith of Christ that any man should need now to prove purgatory to Christian men, or that any man could be found which would in so great a thing so fully and fastly believed for an undoubted article this fifteen hundred years begin now to stagger and stand in doubt . . .[139]

More explains that when we consider, on the one hand, God's justice in requiring the punishment of our sins and, on the other, His goodness in not punishing us forever once we have repented, one can only conclude that the punishment of contrite sinners must have a temporal limit. But since many die before there is time enough for them to undergo all the temporal punishment necessary to satisfy the justice of God, it must needs follow that this punishment be completed after death.[140] In answer to the objection that the merits of Christ's Passion totally cancel these debts, More points out that while God can and does in special cases forgive the entire debt of the sinner who repents with extraordinary fervor and love, His justice demands

---

[137] Ibid., bk. 5, p. 578.

[138] *A Supplication for the Beggars,* in John Fox, *The Acts and Monuments of John Fox* (London: Seeley, Burnside, and Seeley, 1846), 4:662.

[139] *Supplication of Souls,* bk. 2, in *CW* 7:170.

[140] Ibid., 173.

that under normal circumstances the sinner undergo at least some tangible consequences for his actions. If there were no punishment for vice, men would feel they could sin with impunity, no matter how numerous, how serious, or how prolonged their sins were, and that they need do no more after such deeds than "cry him [God] mercy as one woman would that treadeth on another's train".[141] How dangerous it is, More warns, to give people the impression that they can sin all they want in life and still go straight to the joys of heaven the moment they die, just so long as they manage to utter "three or four words" of remorse and nothing more before their final moment.[142] In this context the role of Purgatory as a deterrent to unbridled depravity becomes quite evident, for even should the sinner escape eternal damnation by the grace of a deathbed conversion (a grace he cannot presume beforehand will be given him), he must nonetheless first pay for the evil actions of his life by undergoing great suffering before crossing the threshold of heaven.[143] Thus the existence of Purgatory is a manifestation not only of divine justice but of God's mercy as well, for by dissuading men from sin it is instrumental in saving many from hell.[144] In response to his opponents' insistence that they will believe only what the Scriptures have to say, More presents a series of proofs for Purgatory from the Bible,[145] the most compelling of which is the testimony of the Second Book of Maccabees,[146] which speaks of Judas Maccabeus arranging for a sin offering on behalf of those dead in battle:

> . . . [A]nd they turned to prayer, beseeching that the sin which had been committed might be wholly blotted out . . . He [Judas Maccabeus] also took up a collection, man by man, to the amount of two thousand drachmas of silver, and sent it to Jerusalem to provide for a sin offering. In doing this he acted very well and honorably, taking account of the resurrection. For if he were not expecting that those who had fallen would rise again, it would have been superfluous and foolish to pray for the dead. But if he was looking to the splendid reward that is laid up for those who fall asleep in godliness, it was a holy and pious thought.

---

[141] Ibid., 173–74 (quote on 174).
[142] Ibid., 174.
[143] Ibid., 174–75.
[144] Ibid., 175.
[145] Ibid., 176–94.
[146] Ibid., 179–81.

Therefore he made atonement for the dead, that they might be delivered from their sin (2 Macc 12:42–45).

In answer to the dissenters' rejection of the two books of Maccabees as canonical parts of Scripture, More observes that Christ must have recognized their validity, for according to the Gospel of Saint John he participated in the Feast of the Dedication, a feast instituted by Judas Maccabeus as recorded in 2 Maccabees 10:5–8.[147] Among the other Bible texts he cites to support the doctrine of Purgatory (4 Kings [Vulgate] 20:1–7; 1 Sam 2:6; Zech 9:11; 1 Jn 5:16; Rev 5:13; Acts 2:24; Mt 12:32; Mt 12:36), More is able to make a particularly strong case with the following passage from the First Letter of Saint Paul to the Corinthians,[148] which indicates a purgation by fire after death as a prelude to salvation:

> Now if any one builds on the foundation with gold, silver, precious stones, wood, hay, stubble—each man's work will become manifest; for the Day will disclose it, because it will be revealed with fire, and the fire will test what sort of work each one has done. If the work which any man has built on the foundation survives, he will receive a reward. If any man's work is burned up, he will suffer loss, though he himself will be saved, but only as through fire (1 Cor 3:12–15).

At the end of his discussion of the scriptural evidence for Purgatory, More notes that even if no definitive proof texts could be found, this doctrine would be no less certain, for it has always been a professed belief of the Church—reason enough to accept it unreservedly.[149] Even Luther used to accept Purgatory, More adds, quoting the German monk's own earlier words defending the doctrine: "I am very sure that there is purgatory, and it little moveth me what heretics babble. Should I believe an heretic born of late scant fifty years ago, and say the faith were false that hath been holden so many hundred years?"[150] More ends the *Supplication of Souls* with an appeal to Christian charity, endeavoring to impress on his readers that the greatest alms we can bestow are the prayers and good works we perform to remit the sufferings of the needy, unseen souls in Purga-

---

[147] Ibid., 181.

[148] Ibid., 187–91.

[149] Ibid., 195.

[150] Luther, *Resolutiones disputationum de indulgentiarum virtute* (1518), quoted by More in ibid., bk. 2, p. 211.

tory;[151] so as to reinforce this point, More has the souls of Purgatory plead movingly on their own behalf:

> . . . [O]pen your hearts and have some pity upon us. If you believe not that we need your help, alas the lack of faith. If you believe our need and care not for us, alas the lack of pity. For who so pitieth not us, whom can he pity? If you pity the poor, there is none so poor as we, that have not a bratte [rag] to put on our backs. If you pity the blind, there is none so blind as we, which are here in the dark saving for sights unpleasant and loathsome till some comfort come. If you pity the lame, there is none so lame as we, that neither can creep one foot out of the fire, nor have one hand at liberty to defend our face from the flame. Finally if you pity any man in pain, never knew you pain comparable to ours; whose fire as far passeth in heat all the fires that ever burned upon earth, as the hottest of all those passeth a feigned fire painted on a wall . . .
>
> . . . Remember our thirst while you sit and drink; our hunger while you be feasting; our restless watch while you be sleeping; our sore and grievous pain while you be playing; our hot burning fire while you be in pleasure and sporting; so may God make your offspring after remember you; so God keep you hence or not long here; but bring you shortly to that bliss, to which for our Lord's love help you to bring us, and we shall set hand to help you thither to us.[152]

Mercy

The theme of God's mercy is a recurring one in the writings of Thomas More, one that we have already encountered in his translations from Pico della Mirandola. It appears time and again in his apologetical works, for More saw in the new doctrines of the reformers an implicit denial of God's mercy in the concept of predestination. It is a comment of Tyndale claiming that the Church has left the people ignorant of God's mercy[153] that elicits from More his most succinct declaration of the importance he gives to this subject:

---

[151] *Supplication of Souls,* bk. 2, in *CW* 7:205.

[152] Ibid., 225, 228.

[153] *Answer,* 11.

Now touching the mercy of our Lord, who can speak of Christ's passion and speak nothing of his mercy? This man is too mad to talk with. God's mercy is so great that no man can speak enough thereof.[154]

More finds in the mercy of God a patience and persistence with the unrepentant sinner, a refusal to give up or abandon a soul so long as there is still a chance of conversion. This loving persistence of God More sees expressed in the words of Christ from the Book of Revelation, "Behold, I stand at the door and knock . . ." (Rev 3:20):

Yet God, when man hath put him out of his dwelling, doth of his great goodness not always utterly leave him for his unkindness, but though if the man die ere God come in again, God shall of justice for his unkindness condemn him, yet he hovers still about the door of his heart, always knocking upon him to be by the free will of man let in with his grace into the house of man's heart again . . .[155]

The image of God incessantly knocking upon the door of a sinner's heart is one to which More resorts more than once, as in the following passage, wherein he speaks of God continuing to pursue, for as long as they live, those who have turned away from Him:

For as in the beginning God of his great mercy calleth upon all people both elects and reprobates to come to him, so doth he . . . call ordinarily upon them both of his like mercy still, as long as they live in this world here, and would . . . be as glad to find them again as ever he was to win them before, as the words of holy writ be plain in the Apocalypse, I stand at the door and knock.[156]

More also sees God's mercy manifested in the remission of even mortal sins, a remission that God offers to repentant sinners after suffering so relatively little on earth or in Purgatory—their sufferings drastically reduced by the application of the merits of Christ's Passion.[157] Elsewhere, in explaining that normally there must be temporal punishment for all sins, More allows for particular exceptions, as one cannot discount "the special privilege of God's absolute mercy" in certain cases. And it is by God's mercy that what is impossible to

---

[154] *CW* 8, bk. 2, p. 149.
[155] Ibid., bk. 4, p. 424.
[156] Ibid., 520–21.
[157] Ibid., 517.

man is accomplished, he adds, for such things are not impossible to God, as Christ tells us in Matthew 19:26.[158]

More's great confidence in the mercy of God was balanced by a realistic understanding of the justice of God; indeed, God's mercy and His justice are inexorably bound together. Thus More could not accept the idea that somehow a man could sin as much as he pleased and yet suffer no consequences so long as afterward he simply expressed a casual remorse to God for what he had done:[159]

> But we find it many times far contrary, that the over great regard of his mercy, turneth trust into presumption, and maketh men the more bold in sin so truly that neither love of God, nor desire of heaven, nor dread of hell, is able to pull them back.[160]

In the course of citing in his *Supplication of Souls* Christ's words regarding the uniquely unforgivable sin against the Holy Spirit (Mt 12:31–32), More seeks to assuage the fears of those who may be tempted to despair of God's mercy if they fall into the grievous sin of blasphemy by explaining that, while in the special case of which our Lord here speaks, the sinner, devoid of all grace, is "fixed and confirmed in an unchangeable malice", and never repents, at the same time there cannot be "any sin committed in the world so sore, so grievous, nor so abominable, but that if a man work with God's grace by contrition and heaviness of heart, with humble confession of mouth and good endeavor of penance, and satisfaction in deed against his thought, word and deed by which God was offended", he shall be forgiven. More felt it necessary to clarify this matter "lest some that read it might conceive a wrong opinion and a false fear drawing them toward despair, that if they mishappened (which our Lord forbid) to fall into blasphemy against the Holy Ghost, they could never after be forgiven how sore so ever they repented, or how heartily and how busily so ever they should pray therefore."[161]

---

[158] Ibid., bk. 2, p. 214.
[159] Ibid., bk. 1, pp. 90–91.
[160] Ibid., bk. 4, p. 513.
[161] *Supplication of Souls,* bk. 2, in *CW* 7:191–92.

With the reformers' rejection of any merit in the carrying out of good works came a repudiation, in whole or in part, of all acts of self-denial, such as fasting and abstinence. By contrast More, who himself wore a hair shirt every day, is vigorous to defend these practices. It is God's will, he explains, that remorse for sin should be expressed not only in the heart but in the body as well, through mortification. Humbling ourselves before God, we draw down God's mercy upon us by joining corporal penance to prayer for forgiveness, so as to manifest our grief in having offended Him.[162] In response to the dissenters' often repeated, virulent denunciations of corporal self-denial, More challenges them with two undeniable examples from the New Testament:

> You think all obedience of the body offered to God is hypocrisy. But it was not hypocrisy to Mary, who washed Christ's feet with her tears and dried them with the hair of her head. Coarse clothing is hypocrisy to you, but it was not hypocrisy to John the Baptist, who dressed in the skin of camels. Abstinence from food is hypocrisy to you, but it was not hypocrisy to John, who ate only locusts.[163]

Tyndale, who like his fellow dissenters denied any function for penance in reparation for sin, admitted only one reason for fasting: the mastery of the body.[164] Yet More finds Tyndale's position something of a contradiction, for despite his opponent's professed rejection of a role for philosophy in theological questions,[165] he has in this case offered nothing more than a philosopher's argument for the practice of fasting. Mastery of the body was also the reason why many a pagan philosopher in past ages both advocated and engaged in abstinence from certain foods. But among the Israelites of old and among Christian peoples, More continues, God has always enjoined fasting not only to control the desires of the flesh but also as a penance for one's sins, as well as to serve as a reminder that "we be now in the vale of tears."[166]

---

[162] *CW* 8, bk. 1, p. 65.
[163] *Letter to Bugenhagen,* in *CW* 7:93.
[164] *Answer,* 6–7.
[165] *Obedience,* 154–58.
[166] *CW* 8, bk. 1, pp. 64–65.

Scripture, More observes, clearly testifies that there are more reasons for corporal penance than simply the mastery of the flesh. Thus
when in the twenty-first chapter of the First Book of Kings (vv. 17–
29) Ahab the King of Samaria was threatened with the wrath of God
because of his great sins, he resorted to fasting and to clothing himself in sackcloth, not to tame his senses, but rather to humble himself
before God and punish himself for sinning, in the hope of winning
God's mercy, that he might be spared from the full force of divine
justice. And indeed his penance did find favor in the sight of God.[167]

Addressing the dissenters' rejection of the observance of fast days,
More comments on what they consider "the foolish fast of the Lent,
whereby there is taken away the evangelical liberty, that folk may not
eat flesh on Good Friday for compassion of Christ's passion":[168]

> And with this ordinance be they wondrous wroth, as though the Church
> ordained that folk should destroy themselves with forbearing their meat,
> and kill themselves with abstinence. And yet are the laws of the Church
> mitigated and made easy with exceptions and liberties almost more than
> enough, providing for sick men, children, old men, laborers, pilgrims,
> nurses, women with child, and poor folk, and well near as far as men
> might go but if these heretics be angry that the Church had not provided
> for gorbely gluttons too . . .[169]

Faith, Reason, and Philosophy

The reformers' contempt for medieval scholasticism, coupled with
their *solafideism* that excluded anything not conformable to their axiom of justification by faith alone, led them to a categorical rejection of a role for either the philosophical disciplines or the exercise
of reason in the realm of Christian theology. Such a stance was antithetical both to the tradition of the Church and to the Christian humanist perceptions of men such as More. Hence, responding to Tyndale's and Luther's complaints that the pope and the clergy are wrong
in mingling philosophy with theology,[170] More defends the place that

---

[167] Ibid., 66–67.

[168] Ibid., bk. 6, p. 631.

[169] Ibid.

[170] For Tyndale's position, see *Obedience*, 154–58.

philosophy holds in Christian life, arguing that in philosophy "all that we find true therein, is the wisdom given of God, and may well do service to his other gifts of higher wisdom."[171] As for reason, More sees it as the handmaid of faith, not competing with the latter but rather cooperating with it:

> . . . [R]eason must he needs have then that shall perceive what he should believe. And so must reason not resist faith but walk with her, and as her handmaid so wait upon her, that as contrary as ye take her, yet of a truth faith goeth never without her.[172]

But if reason is to serve its proper function, More goes on to explain, it must be exercised and trained by applying oneself to the study of the philosophical disciplines:

> Now as the hand is the more nimble by the use of some feats, and the legs and feet more swift and sure by custom of going and running, and the whole body the more agile and lusty by some kind of exercise, so is it no doubt but that reason is by study, labour and exercise of Logic, Philosophy and other liberal arts confirmed and quickened, and the judgment both in them and also in orators' laws and stories much ripened.[173]

In this context More is ready to defend the use of the thoughts and writings of pagan philosophers and poets, even in homiletics, when their ideas are found to be consonant with Christianity. Thus if Tyndale were to question the propriety of homiletic references to Aristotle or any other pagan philosophers or poets, More explains that he would counter that in so objecting Tyndale would be placing his apostolic judgment above that of Saint Paul, who mentions the philosophers in his Letter to the Romans (1:19–23) and even quotes the saying of a pagan Cretan poet in his Letter to Titus (1:12).[174] More also avails himself of Saint Jerome's analogy comparing the use of valid pagan philosophical wisdom with the spoils of pagan Egypt carried away by the Israelites when they were liberated under Moses:

> And as holy Saint Jerome sayeth, The Hebrews well despoil the Egyptians when Christ's learned men take out of the pagan writers the riches and learning and wisdom that God gave unto them, and employ the

---

[171] *CW* 8, bk. 1, p. 64.
[172] *CW* 6, bk. 1, chap. 23, p. 131.
[173] Ibid., 132.
[174] *CW* 8, bk. 2, p. 150.

same in the service of divinity about the profit of God's chosen children of Israel, the Church of Christ, which he hath of the hard stony pagans made the children of Abraham.[175]

Religious Life

One of the fundamental differences between Thomas More and his friend Erasmus rested in their widely divergent views of religious life. Erasmus, although an Augustinian monk himself, seems to have regretted his choice of this vocation and could find nothing good to say about it. More, on the other hand, who although a layman had spent four years of his early life seriously considering the cloistered state, had the deepest love and esteem for consecrated life, a love and esteem that remained with him to the very end. Although he could on occasion be quite critical of those religious whom he perceived as acting in ways unbecoming to the dignity of their vocation, he was determined to defend the faithful majority of men and women religious, who had chosen a state he envied, from the malicious words of dissenters such as Luther, who had condemned the very concept of monastic vows, and of Tyndale, who, as in the following passage, spoke of religious life with the utmost contempt:

> Neither is it lawful to forsake thy neighbour, and to withdraw thyself from serving him, and to get thee into a den, and live idly, profitable to no man, but robbing all men, first of faith, and then of goods and land, and of all he hath, with making him believe in the hypocrisy of thy superstitious prayers and pope-holy deeds.[176]

By stark contrast More, in a letter to a monk dating from around 1519–1520, speaks movingly of the service that those in religious life render to all mankind, especially by their prayers:

> I have no doubt at all that there is no good man anywhere who does not feel a great deal of heartfelt esteem for all religious orders, and certainly I myself have always regarded them not only with love but also with the utmost reverence, since it is my custom to honor the poorest man commended by virtue more than anyone distinguished for his riches or

---

[175] *CW* 6, bk. 1, chap. 23, p. 132.
[176] *Obedience,* 279.

admired for an illustrious birth . . . I am inclined to believe that the misery of this world is substantially alleviated by your pleading in its behalf (for if one just man's diligent prayer does a great deal of good, how much good must be done by the incessant prayer of so many thousands?) . . .[177]

It is in one of his earlier apologetical writings, his 1526 *Letter to Bugenhagen,* that More makes what is perhaps his single most eloquent statement on religious life:

Religious orders have produced a great many men of extraordinary sanctity. Although some monks have not always lived up to their order and some orders have degenerated to the behavior of the world around them, nevertheless the purest segment of the Christian people have always been found in religious orders. The members of these orders are far from following anyone other than Christ, for they are the ones primarily who sell what they have and give it to the poor and take up the cross and follow Christ. Dedicating their entire lives to vigils, fasts, and prayer, and following the Lamb in chastity, they crucify the vices and desires of the flesh.[178]

---

[177] *Letter to a Monk,* c. 1519–1520, in *In Defense of Humanism: Letters to Dorp, Oxford, Lee, and a Monk,* ed. Daniel Kinney, vol. 15 of *Complete Works of St. Thomas More* (New Haven: Yale Univ. Press, 1986), 275–77.

[178] *Letter to Bugenhagen,* in *CW* 7:53.

CHAPTER X

The Four Last Things

The Human Side of Apologetical Writing

In view of the sheer scope and depth of Thomas More's apologetical writings, we are left to wonder how he found the time to carry out such a monumental task during a period of his life when so much of his energy was allotted to the service of his King and his nation. We learn from his son-in-law William Roper that his writings were largely composed in the still of the night with time stolen from sleep,[1] as had also been the case some years earlier, when he formulated his *Utopia*. The bishops recognized that he had rendered them an enormous service in taking up his pen to defend the Church and decided to express their gratitude in a tangible way that they hoped would compensate him for all his labors. In convocation they decided to present him with an honorarium of four or five thousand pounds. But when a delegation of the bishops came to him with their gift, he politely refused it, explaining that he took great comfort in their satisfaction with his writings and that he looked only to God for any reward of his efforts, to whom all thanks in the matter truly belonged. Dumbfounded by his refusal, they attempted to prevail upon him to take it for his family's sake, but he remained resolute, telling them:

> Not so, my Lords, I had rather see it all cast into the Thames, than I, or any of mine, should have thereof the worth of one penny. For though your offer, my lords, be indeed very friendly and honorable, yet set I so much by my pleasure and so little by my profit, that I would not, in

---

[1] William Roper, *The Lyfe of Sir Thomas Moore, Knighte,* ed. Elsie V. Hitchcock, Early English Text Society, original series, no. 197 (London: Early English Text Society, 1935), 45–46, 48.

good faith, for so much, and much more too, have lost the rest of so many nights' sleep as was spent upon the same. And yet wish would I, for all that, upon condition that all heresies were suppressed, that all my books were burned and my labour utterly lost.[2]

The magnanimity of More's refusal is all the more poignant in light of the subsequent financial ruin into which he and his family were plunged so shortly thereafter during his imprisonment. More's comment that he would gladly sacrifice his writings to the flames in return for the eradication of all heresy serves to highlight what was his most pressing concern in his battle against theological dissent—the salvation of souls. Hence his apologetical works typically conclude with his hope and prayer that his opponents will be reconciled with the Church; at least one—Simon Fish, author of the *Supplication for the Beggars*—did make his peace with the Church before dying. At the end of his *Letter against Frith,* More prays that "God bless these poisoned errors out of his [Frith's] blind heart, and make him his faithful servant."[3] In the closing lines of his *Letter to Bugenhagen,* More directly invites his opponent to a change of heart:

> Abandon that ungodly sect . . . Return and rejoin the Catholic church. Then, in every way you can, correct what you corrupted for so many years with your preaching. Give up your illegitimate bishopric. Send away that unfortunate girl you whore with in the name of marriage. And spend the rest of your life in repentance for what you have done.
>
> If you do these things, Pomeranus [Bugenhagen]—and I pray to God you will—then will you truly joy in us, and instead of feeling sorrow that you are lost, we in turn will rejoice that you are found.[4]

What is perhaps More's most eloquent expression of how he viewed his opponents in the context of eternity appears in his 1533 work *The Apology:*

> As touching heretics, I hate that vice of theirs and not their persons, and very fain would I that the one were destroyed, and the other saved. And that I have toward no man any other mind than this (how loudly so ever these blessed new brethren the professors and preachers of verity

---

[2] Ibid., 46–48 (quotation on 48).

[3] *Letter against Frith,* in *Letter to Bugenhagen, Supplication of Souls, Letter against Frith,* ed. Frank Manley et al., vol. 7 of *Complete Works of St. Thomas More* (New Haven: Yale Univ. Press, 1990), 258.

[4] *Letter to Bugenhagen,* in ibid., 103–5.

belie me), if all the favour and pity that I have used among them to their amendment were known, it would I warrant you well and plain appear, whereof if it were requisite I could bring forth witnesses more than men would ween.

And sure this one thing will I be bold to say, that I never found any yet, but had he been never so bad, nor done never so much harm before; yet after that I found him once changed and in good mind to mend, I have been so glad thereof, that I have used him from thence forth not as an evil man or an abject, nor as a stranger neither, but as a good man and my very friend.[5]

Even in his exchanges with Tyndale, More could respond to menacing words with humor and charity. Thus when Tyndale sanctimoniously exhorts More to repent of his Catholicism lest his sinfulness rouse God and his blasphemies against "truth" and the Holy Spirit bring down upon himself the divine wrath,[6] More replies with mock seriousness:

These words when I read them, seemed me so pithy and so penetrating, set and couched in such an high spiritual fashion that they made me much to marvel what Tyndale had spied in me, and caused me to search my self . . . yet could I find in good faith neither in my breast nor in my book I thank God any such high blasphemies as Tyndale so highly cryeth out upon, except he call it an high blasphemy to call heresies heresies . . .

. . . I can no more I, but pray God amend him and make him a good man.[7]

Throughout More's apologetical writings we encounter time and again his irrepressible sense of humor, emerging spontaneously, as it does when, in commenting upon one of Tyndale's assertions (regarding the latter's denial of any ordained priesthood),[8] he dryly observes,

---

[5] *The Apology,* ed. J. B. Trapp, vol. 9 of *Complete Works of St. Thomas More* (New Haven: Yale Univ. Press, 1979), chap. 49, p. 167.

[6] *An Answer unto Sir Thomas More's Dialogue,* in William Tyndale, *An Answer to Sir Thomas More's Dialogue, The Supper of the Lord and Wm. Tracy's Testament Expounded,* ed. Rev. Henry Walter, Parker Society, vol. 44 (1850; reprint, Johnson Reprint Corp., 1968), 15.

[7] *The Confutation of Tyndale's Answer,* ed. Louis Schuster et al., vol. 8 of *Complete Works of St. Thomas More* (New Haven: Yale Univ. Press, 1973), bk. 2, pp. 180, 182. Hereafter cited as *CW* 8.

[8] *The Obedience of a Christian Man,* in William Tyndale, *Doctrinal Treatises and Introductions to Different Portions of the Holy Scriptures,* ed. Rev. Henry Walter, Parker Society, vol. 42 (1848; reprint, New York: Johnson Reprint Corp., 1968), 255–56. Hereafter cited as *Obedience.*

". . . [O]f such a scriptured man not very scripturely spoken."[9] And in a particularly amusing passage alluding to Tyndale's condemnation of the third-century Church Father Origen,[10] More whimsically describes how he had asked this Church Father to come and speak on his behalf, only to be turned down:

> And when I desired him [Origen] to take the pain to come and bear witness with me in this matter, he seemed at the first very well content. But when I told him that he should meet with Tyndale; he blessed himself and shrank back, and said he had rather go some other way many a mile than once meddle with him. For I shall tell you sir, quoth he, before this time a right honorable man very cunning and yet more virtuous, the good bishop of Rochester [John Fisher], in a great audience brought me in for a witness against Luther and Tyndale . . . But Tyndale as soon as he heard of my name . . . fell in a rage with me and wholly rated me, and called me stark heretic, and that the starkest that ever was. This tale Origen told me . . . Now in deed to say the truth it was not well done of Tyndale to leave reasoning and fall a scolding, chiding, and brawling . . . Fie for shame he should have favored and forborne him somewhat, and it had been but for his age. For Origen is now thirteen hundred years old or there about, and this was not much above seven years since.[11]

There is one episode related by More in his *Answer to a Poisoned Book* that deserves our attention insofar as it provides us with a passing glimpse of the personal and human side of More's toils, revealing him as something of a healthy perfectionist in his work.[12] One of his polemical adversaries, the anonymous author of *The Supper of the Lord* (1533), attempted to use a passage from his *Confutation of Tyndale's Answer* against him by claiming that More himself in the particular passage had acknowledged that the sixth chapter of Saint John's Gospel (the eucharistic discourse of our Lord at Capernaum) did not pertain to the Eucharist.[13] When More read this claim by his nameless opponent, supported, so it seemed, by the citation of a specific page in More's book, he thought at first that he must in-

[9] *CW* 8, bk. 1, pp. 113–14 (quote on 114).

[10] *Obedience*, 220.

[11] *CW* 8, bk. 2, p. 153.

[12] *The Answer to a Poisoned Book*, ed. Clarence Miller, vol. 11 of *Complete Works of St. Thomas More* (New Haven: Yale Univ. Press, 1985), bk. 5, chap. 2, pp. 216–19 (hereafter cited as *CW* 11); notes, *CW* 8:1569.

[13] *The Supper of the Lord*, in Tyndale, *An Answer unto Sir Thomas More's Dialogue*, 236–37.

deed have inadvertently failed to distinguish Tyndale's noneucharistic interpretation of John 6 from his own very different beliefs on the matter and had given readers the false impression that he shared Tyndale's views in this regard. More was ready to admit to having made an unintended misstatement in this case when he chanced to mention the matter in a conversation—probably with a group of his friends. After he had expressed his regret to them over having contradicted himself through an oversight, they attempted to reassure him that in such a long work a mistake or two was bound to slip by. But one woman asked him whether he had actually gone back to the passage and examined it to see if it actually said what his opponent claimed it did. More admitted that he had not, for it "irked" him even to look back at a mistake it was too late to correct; moreover, he could not imagine that his opponent would be so foolish as actually to cite the page number were he not sure his claim were indisputably true. Dismayed that More had not checked out his adversary's statement, the woman insisted that she would not believe the accusation until she had looked up the particular page in More's book herself:

> And therewithal she sent for the book, and turned to the very .249. side, and with that number marked also. And in good faith good readers, there found we no such manner [of] matter, neither on the one side of the leaf nor on the other.[14]

After looking further, they discovered that what was actually page 259 of the book had accidentally been labeled as page "ccxlix"—249—by the printers. On this latter page they did find More's discussion of the Eucharist with regard to the Gospel of Saint John, but it was obvious when they read the passage that More had certainly not misstated his position or contradicted himself. It was rather his opponent who through "either folly or falsehood"[15] had misread his words and had confused what More identifies as Tyndale's views with More's own beliefs.

As a postscript on the controversy over the proper translation of the Bible, there is at least one point of More's arguments that Tyndale seems eventually to have conceded, a point that has shaped the English rendering of one of the most famous lines from the Scriptures

---

[14] *CW* 11, bk. 5, chap. 2, p. 217.
[15] Ibid.

—the opening verse of the Gospel of Saint John. In his 1526 Worms translation of the New Testament, Tyndale rendered John 1:1 in these words: "In the beginning was that word, and that word was with God, and God was that word."[16] In his *Confutation of Tyndale's Answer* More recommended a change in the ordering of the last phrase, a change to "and the word was God".[17] Tyndale incorporated the latter wording into the 1534 edition of his New Testament,[18] and it is now the accepted rendering of the phrase in most English-language Bibles.

Interregnum:
The Four Last Things

As the theological battle of the Reformation gained momentum during the 1520s, Thomas More found himself gradually rising through the ranks of English government. Having been made a member of the King's Privy Council in 1517 as well as Master of the Court of Requests, he was knighted and appointed under-treasurer in 1521 and became Speaker of Parliament in 1523. Appointed Chancellor of the Duchy of Lancaster in 1525, he accompanied Cardinal Wolsey on another embassy to France that same year and again in 1527.[19] More's lot was one that many a man would have envied; so trusted a confidant of the King was he that His Majesty could scarcely bear to tolerate his absence from court and on more than one occasion personally visited his home, jovially strolling with More through the garden in convivial conversation. Even so, More entertained no illusions about his own seemingly lofty stature. It was after one such royal visit that he commented to his son-in-law William Roper:

> I thank our Lord, son, I find his Grace my very good lord indeed, and I believe he doth as singularly favour me as any subject within this realm. Howbeit, son Roper, I may tell thee I have no cause to be proud thereof,

---

[16] Text in *The Gospels: Gothic, Anglo-Saxon, Wycliffe and Tyndale Versions,* ed. Joseph Bosworth (London: Gibbings and Co., 1907), 441 (spelling modernized).

[17] *CW* 8, bk. 3, pp. 236–37.

[18] Text in *Tyndale's New Testament* (1534 ed.), ed. David Daniell (New Haven: Yale Univ. Press, 1995), 133.

[19] R. W. Chambers, *Thomas More* (1935; reprint, Ann Arbor, Mich.: Ann Arbor Paperbacks, Univ. of Michigan, 1973), 412 (index).

for if my head could win him a castle in France . . . it should not fail to go.[20]

As we have already observed, More was never a stranger to the bitter reality of death, having lost his mother when he was about twenty-one and his first wife, Jane, after only seven years of marriage. He had seen an outbreak of the "sweating sickness" in 1517 claim the lives of many, including a humanist friend.[21] Certainly there was enough in More's surroundings throughout his life to nurture his awareness of the proximity of death. It was in the chapel of the Mercers' Hall, the guild for which More transacted so much business over his earlier years, that in 1954 there was discovered buried beneath the floor a life-sized, painted stone effigy of Christ laid out in death on a bier.[22] It has been dated to More's time and may very well have been a familiar sight to him, consonant as it was with his own constant reflections upon death and upon the Passion of His Redeemer. We can be certain of the impact that the grim "dance of death" images of Saint Paul's Cathedral had upon More, for he himself speaks of them in the only ascetical work he wrote during his midcareer, *The Four Last Things:*

> For nothing is there that may more effectually withdraw the soul from the wretched affections of the body, than may the remembrance of death . . . if we not only hear this word death, but also let sink into our hearts, the very fantasies and deep imagination thereof, we shall perceive thereby, that we were never so greatly moved by the beholding of the dance of death pictured in [Saint] Paul's, as we shall feel ourselves stirred and altered, by the feeling of that imagination in our hearts.[23]

We cannot be sure just what was the specific impetus that led More to begin writing *The Four Last Things* around 1522, when he was in his forties, but the most likely reason is that he intended it as an instruction for his children—his daughter Margaret was also composing a treatise on the same subject matter at this time, undoubtedly with her father's warm encouragement. Although his original plan called

---

[20] Roper, *Lyfe*, 20–21 (quote on 21).

[21] Chambers, *More*, 152.

[22] Pamela Sheingorn, *The Easter Sepulchre in England,* Early Drama, Art and Music Reference Series, no. 5 (Kalamazoo, Mich.: Medieval Institute Publications, 1987), 239.

[23] *The Four Last Things,* in *The Workes of Sir Thomas More Knight . . . in the English Tongue* (1557), as reproduced in *The English Works of Sir Thomas More,* ed. W. E. Campbell (London: Eyre and Spottiswoode; New York: Lincoln MacVeagh, Dial Press, 1931), 1:77.

for a work that, as the title suggests, would discuss death, judgment, heaven, and hell, he completed only a small portion of the first section, devoted primarily to the subject of death and the seven principal vices.[24]

The centerpiece of *The Four Last Things* is the biblical text, ". . . [R]emember the end of your life, and then you will never sin" (Sir 7:36), which More sees as a more effective lesson in the pursuit of virtue and the avoidance of sin than the wise sayings of any ancient philosopher or secular sage. Turning to a favorite metaphor of Saint Augustine, that of God as the Divine Physician,[25] More explains that God gives us these words of Sirach as a prescription specifying four medicines for our souls. Neither costly nor unusual, these medicinal herbs can "be gathered all times of the year in the garden of thine own soul", for they are none other than the four last things—"death, doom [judgment], pain [hell], and joy [heaven]".[26] The prescription is a mild one, for it requires us only to *remember* these things, and the fourth, heaven, alleviates the unsavoriness of all the rest.[27] Indeed, the reception of these medicines of the soul brings a spiritual joy that exceeds any other happiness we can experience in this life—a joy that in the anticipation of heaven proved stronger in the lives of the martyrs than the pains of their tortures.[28] Yet if we are to experience spiritual joy, we must first detach ourselves from earthly pleasures:

> For like as the ground that is all foregrown with nettles, briars, and other evil weeds, can bring forth no corn till they be weeded out, so can our soul have no place for the good corn of spiritual pleasure, as long as it is overgrown with the barren weeds of carnal delectation. For the pulling out of which weeds by the root, there is not a more meet instrument, than the remembrance of the four last things . . .[29]

Seeing the remembrance of death as the most effective means of detaching the soul from earthly desires, More attempts to imprint the

[24] H. W. Donner, "St. Thomas More's Treatise on the Four Last Things and the Gothicism of the Trans-Alpine Renaissance", in *Essential Articles for the Study of Thomas More*, ed. R. S. Sylvester and G. P. Marc'hadour (Hamden, Conn.: Archon Books, 1977), 344–45.

[25] Rudolf Arbesmann, O.S.A., "The Concept of 'Christus Medicus' in St. Augustine", *Traditio* 10 (1954): 1–28.

[26] *The Four Last Things*, 72.

[27] Ibid., 72–73.

[28] Ibid., 73–74.

[29] Ibid., 74.

stark reality and inevitability of death upon his readers in a number
of vivid ways. Thus he presents a disturbing picture of one's own
deathbed, hemmed in on all sides by pains and troubles of soul and
body, nagged in one's final agony by worldly friends and family, "skip-
ping about thy bed and thy sick body, like ravens about thy corpse",
asking, "What shall I have . . . ?"[30] And in addition to all the sufferings that precede death, there is, More points out, the "intolerable
torment" of the soul's separation from the body at the moment of
death itself. Drawing as he so habitually does upon the example of
our Lord in His Passion, More notes that while Christ uttered no cry
of anguish "neither for the whips and rods beating his blessed body,
or the sharp thorns pricking his holy head, or the great long nails
piercing his precious hands and feet", He did cry out to His Father at
the moment when His "sacred soul" was to depart from His body.[31]
For us sinners there is also the threat of Satan, who, More warns, is
especially intent upon devouring us as we near death, knowing that it
is at the moment of death that "he either winneth a man for ever, or
for ever loseth him"—that no matter how firmly the devil may hold
sway over a man before death, the man may still escape from his grip
when death approaches, as did the good thief at the right side of our
Lord on the Cross.[32]

More observes that Satan can beguile those approaching death into
expending more efforts upon arranging the ceremonial details of their
own funerals than upon the preparation of their souls for eternity,
adding with irony that at least some of the mourners coming to such
a splendidly planned requiem may very well be "laughing under [their]
black hoods". He sees an absurd vanity in a man wasting his remaining time on such arrangements, "as though he thought that he should
stand in a window, and see how worshipfully he shall be brought to
church".[33]

Young and old alike, More warns, labor under the illusion that
death lies in their distant future, when in fact for the elderly it is
surely not long in coming, while for the young it may come all too
soon. Illness can serve as a reminder of death, a reminder that can

---

[30] Ibid., 78.
[31] Ibid., 77–78.
[32] Ibid., 78.
[33] Ibid., 79.

be expanded by thinking of our daily necessities of food and clothing as medicines in treating our incurable illness of a life that must inevitably end with death; moreover, even sleep is an image of death.[34] Just as a man traveling from one place to another is said to be on his way toward his destination whether he is only beginning his journey or is well advanced upon it, so too a man can be said to be dying throughout his life, from his mother's womb onward, for death is always walking with us.[35] In this context More compares our lot in this life to that of two condemned criminals en route to execution. If the cart that one criminal rides in to reach his place of execution must travel one mile, while the other must ride twenty or even a hundred miles, what difference does it make? Can the latter prisoner take much comfort in his life being prolonged by the longer route, if in the end he knows he must surely die?[36]

More goes on to show how the "medicine" of the remembrance of death can be utilized to turn us from the seven deadly sins, beginning with the "very head and root of all sins", pride. After speaking of pride in general, he singles out for particular consideration the vice of spiritual pride, the sin of hypocritical souls who fancy they "have the virtues that they lack" and think themselves "quick saints on earth".[37] Scorning the goodness of others, and envying praise that is not directed to themselves, such people grow furious when their fellowman fails to think as highly of them as they themselves do. This spiritual pride is particularly difficult to uproot, for whereas the gluttonous and the slothful have some recognition of their sins, those who have succumbed to spiritual pride think they have nothing to repent of. But even for stubborn souls such as these, More finds reason for hope in an image from the Book of Revelation that we have already seen him employ elsewhere (in his *Confutation of Tyndale's Answer*), and which he uses here for the very first time in his writings, that of "the knocking of our Lord, which always standeth at the door of man's heart and knocketh, whom I pray God we may give ear unto and let him in".[38] One of the ways Christ "knocks" is with the remembrance of death;

---

[34] Ibid., 79–81.
[35] Ibid., 81–82.
[36] Ibid., 82.
[37] Ibid., 82–83.
[38] Ibid., 83.

thus the sobering thought that, when death comes, spiritually proud men will face the danger of Satan attempting to drag them into hell with the sin of presumption can serve as "a right effectual ointment long before in their life to wear away the web that covereth the eyes of their souls".[39]

More moves on to other forms of pride, including vainglory, a delight in receiving praise—what is no more than a "blast of wind" from the mouths of men. Here again the remembrance of what lies ahead for the recipient of such praise and those praising him puts the matter in perspective: ". . . [W]ithin short time death shall stop their ears, and the clods cover all the mouths that praise them."[40] Then there is the achievement of worldly success, prosperity, and power, which shrivels to nothing upon the consideration of where it will all end:

> . . . [H]e that overlooketh every man . . . whom so many men dread and fear, so many wait upon, he shall within a few years, and only God knoweth within how few days, when death arresteth him, have his dainty body turned into stinking carrion, be borne out of his princely palace, laid in the ground and there left alone, where every lewd lad will be bold to tread on his head.[41]

More likens our lot in life both to a stage play and to a prison. As to the stage-play analogy, he compares a man's pride in his earthly prestige to the folly of a player taking pride in the rich costume he wears while on stage in the role of a lord. When the play is over, he will have to leave, not in the garments of a lord, but in his own clothes. We too, when the play of our life is done, must needs leave earth in just as much poverty as the player.[42] More's comparison of life to a prison is one of the most compelling analogies to appear in his writings, an image to which he will return years later (in his *Dialogue of Comfort against Tribulation*). As he explains the concept, earthly life is a prison that holds all men and women of whatever age or condition under sentence of death, from which there can be no escape. The prison is large, and the various prisoners spend their time laughing, crying, working, playing, or even building palaces for

---

[39] Ibid.
[40] Ibid.
[41] Ibid., 83–84 (quote on 84).
[42] Ibid., 84.

themselves, but inevitably one by one they will all be stripped and "shifted out in a sheet" for burial. In this light a man in authority can scarcely take pride in his position, for he is but one prisoner set above others until such time as the executioner's cart arrives to take him.[43]

More now proceeds to another of the deadly sins, envy, which he describes as the daughter of pride: envy so consumes a man that it can even reveal itself in his appearance, such that he "needeth none other image of death, than his own face in a glass". Envy is likewise confounded by the remembrance of death, for all the earthly goods or glory we might envy another for possessing will invariably be taken away when death comes, which will not tarry in arriving. Indeed, the more a man has, the more is he to be pitied, for his loss upon death will be all the greater.[44]

Wrath, "another daughter of pride", can be a lesser sin, More explains, when it results from a sudden, unexpected injustice done to us, "the rule of reason being letted for the while by the sudden brunt of the injury not forethought upon".[45] But it can also take a more grievous form in those for whom it has become habitual, rooted in pride, and revealing itself in an anger aroused by any gentle jokes about them or any opposition to or disagreement with their ideas. Such reactions serve to reveal that much of the cause for our wrath is an excessively high esteem of ourselves that takes offense whenever we are not treated as we deem fit. It is in this that the sin of wrath can be distinguished from righteous anger, for while the latter is roused by zeal for the honor of God, the former is inspired by a passion for our own honor. Indeed, we often grow angrier at an offense to ourselves than at an offense against God, as if we deemed ourselves more important than God.[46]

More sees the solution to wrath in the uprooting from the soul of its root pride. With pride removed there can grow a genuine love and reverence of God in the first place and a love and esteem of creatures, each in its proper order, for His sake.[47] Returning to his analogy of men on their way to execution, More applies the remembrance of

---

[43] Ibid., 84–85.

[44] Ibid., 85–86 (quote on 85).

[45] Ibid., 86.

[46] Ibid., 86–87.

[47] Ibid., 87–88.

death to the sin of wrath, observing that it is folly for us to grow angry with each other while we are all en route to our own deaths.[48]

More views covetousness as sheer folly, for it makes men continuously hoard and pile up riches for a future that never comes; in the end they die before they ever get to use all they have gathered, and their accumulated wealth falls into the possession of strangers. In their anxiety to save for the future, the covetous display a lack of trust in God, who has promised to provide all we need, as He does in Psalm 55, "Cast your burden on the Lord, and he will sustain you . . ." (v. 22), and in Matthew 6, ". . . [S]eek first his kingdom and his righteousness, and all these things shall be yours as well" (v. 33). There is nothing wrong in and of itself with working and providing for our future needs, More explains; rather, it is all worry over tomorrow's needs that our Lord expects us to set aside, "For the mind would Christ have clean discharged of all earthly care . . . that we should in heart, only care and long for heaven."[49] Indeed, there is no situation of material need so desperate as to justify our losing confidence in God; even if our plight were to end in death, we would be taken to the bosom of Christ as the poor man Lazarus was taken to the bosom of Abraham (Lk 16:19–22).[50]

". . . [I]t is not sin to have riches, but to love riches", explains More. If a man keeps himself from such inordinate love, he will see his possessions, not as his own, but rather as the "goods of God", entrusted to him by God, to whom he must render an account of their use. But the covetous man, proud in seeing himself as the owner of riches, sets his heart on his goods to the detriment of his love of God. Covetousness can lead to absurd behavior, as More observed with his own eyes in the case of a thief who on the day before his execution helped himself to a purse he was able to cut loose. When asked why he would commit such a useless petty theft on the eve of his hanging, he replied that "it did his heart good, to be lord of that purse, one night yet."[51]

Like the other vices, More observes, covetousness can be treated with the medicine of recalling death in that all a man may work to accumulate for himself will soon enough be lost by him when he dies.

---

[48] Ibid., 88.
[49] Ibid., 88–89/90.
[50] Ibid., 89/90–91/92.
[51] Ibid., 91/92–93/94.

Witness the parable of the rich man (Lk 12:16–21) who planned to expand his barns to hold all his possessions for years of enjoyment to come, only to have it said to him that he would die that very night: ". . . [A]nd the things you have prepared, whose will they be?" (Lk 12:20). To this More adds Saint Bernard's poignant question to the rich man, "Thou that hast gathered them, whose shalt thou be?"[52]

More ends his treatment of covetousness with two analogies. Thus the greedy hoarding of wealth is like a bright dream that vanishes when we die. And as death is like a robber who will certainly take everything from us, we should not stow away our possessions for the future, but rather put them to good use now while we still can by giving them to the poor, who can help us in turn with their prayers when we die.[53]

More traces gluttony back to Eve, in whom this vice was joined with pride in her act of taking and eating the forbidden fruit, upon which she had gazed in admiration: "And so entered death at the windows of our own eyes into the house of our heart, and there burned up all the goodly building, that God had wrought therein."[54] In this context More warns in no uncertain terms of the lust that can arise from the ungoverned use of the eyes:

> For when the eye immoderately delighteth in long looking of the beauteous face, with the white neck and round paps, and so forth as far as it findeth no let, the devil helpeth the heart to frame and form, in the fantasy by foul imaginations, all that ever the clothes cover . . . And therefore saith the holy prophet, Turn away thine eyes from the beholding of vanities [Ps 119:37].[55]

Harmful to both body and soul, gluttony so pampers the desires of the body that it impedes the soul's rule over it; with a touch of humor More remarks that in a gluttonous body "the soul can have no room to stir itself."[56] But even more deadly to the soul than gluttony are its two offspring, sloth and lust, which can lead to eternal damnation. From gluttonous feasts a whole range of debauchery ensues—

---

[52] Ibid., 93/94.
[53] Ibid., 93/94–95/96.
[54] Ibid., 95/96.
[55] Ibid.
[56] Ibid.

not only sloth and lust, but also evil conversation, foolhardiness, detraction, arguments, anger, and fighting.[57]

Interrupting his discussion of gluttony, More reiterates a major theme of his spiritual writings—that even in the present life virtue brings more joy than pain, whereas vice brings more pain than pleasure. More backs up his assertion with biblical texts: "In the way of thy testimonies I delight as much as in all riches" (Ps 119:14), and "The way of a sluggard is overgrown with thorns, but the path of the upright is a level highway" (Prov 15:19).[58]

More warns that gluttony is harmful to the health of the body, causing illnesses that require medicines or medical treatment. In this context he cites the advice of Plutarch, who likens those who live intemperately to the captain of a ship who, instead of plugging the leaks in his vessel, has his crew exert themselves pumping out the water that he could have kept out with so little effort.[59]

The remembrance of death here too serves as an antidote, More shows, for with the approach of death the glutton will barely be able to eat anything with the hands and mouth with which he was wont to gorge himself. This consideration, together with the thought that gluttonous living hastens the arrival of death, are reason enough for such a man to desist from intemperance.[60]

Scarcely four short paragraphs into his commentary on the sixth capital vice—sloth—More's *Four Last Things* is abruptly broken off in midsentence; evidently the opportunity never came for him to complete what he had so ably started. But before leaving this work, we will want to look at one more topic that More presents by way of excursus in an earlier section of *The Four Last Things:* his very sensible and practical advice on how to conduct oneself in conversation. He begins by explaining that it is not enough to control the tongue if the mind is not likewise governed in its thoughts. As the mind is never idle, it is incumbent upon us to occupy it with good thoughts, lest the devil fill it with evil ideas. As for speaking, More notes that, according to Scripture, there is both a time to open our mouths and a time to remain silent (Qo 3:7):

---

[57] Ibid., 95/96–97/98.
[58] Ibid., 97/98–99/100.
[59] Ibid., 99/100.
[60] Ibid., 101/102.

Whensoever the communication is nought and ungodly, it is better to hold thy tongue and think on some better thing the while, than to give ear thereto and underpin the tale. And yet better were it than holding of thy tongue, properly to speak, and with some good grace and pleasant fashion, to break into some better matter; by which thy speech and talking, thou shalt not only profit thy self as thou shouldest have done by thy well minded silence, but also amend the whole audience, which is a thing far better and of much more merit.[61]

But More not only provides advice on how to steer an idle or unwholesome conversation onto a more wholesome path; he also gives tips on how to make the best of a good conversation:

But if the communication be good, then is it better, not only to give ear thereto, but also first well and prudently to devise with thyself upon the same; and then moderately and in good manner if thou find aught to the purpose, speak thereto and say thy mind therein. So shall it appear to the presence [those present], that your mind was well occupied the while, and your thought not wandering forty miles thence while your body was there. As it often happeth, that the very face showeth the mind walking a pilgrimage . . . Which manner of wandering mind in company, may percase be the more excusable sometimes by some changeable business of the party; but surely it is never taken for wisdom nor good manner.[62]

---

[61] Ibid., 75–76 (quote on 76).
[62] Ibid., 76.

PART THREE

Love Strong as Death:
The Final Battle

CHAPTER XI

The "Great Matter"

His Majesty's Conscience

The marriage in 1509 of Henry VIII to Catherine of Aragon, daughter of Spain's most famous royal couple, Ferdinand and Isabella, certainly began happily enough. Eight years earlier the young Spanish princess had arrived in London to become the bride of Henry's brother Arthur, but within six months of their wedding Prince Arthur had died. In the wake of this tragic turn of events, the royal families of both nations still wished for a marital union that would bond their two countries together in peace. Thus it was that an appeal was made to the Holy See for a dispensation from the impediments of consanguinity that normally prohibited a widow from marrying her deceased husband's brother (according to the prevailing interpretation of canon law at the time). After weighing the issues involved, Pope Julius II granted the hoped-for dispensation in December 1503.[1] Yet by the time the actual papal bull granting the dispensation officially arrived in England (in 1505), plans for the solemnization of the marriage had been laid aside—the teenage Prince Henry and his father had had a change of mind. But with the death of Henry VII in April 1509, his son no longer hesitated about solemnizing his union with Catherine, and on June 11, the two were wedded in the Franciscans' church in Greenwich.[2] In their triumphal procession through London on the eve of their coronation thirteen days later, Catherine was dressed in white with her hair unbound ("hanging down to her back, of a very

---

[1] J. J. Scarisbrick, *Henry VIII* (Berkeley, Calif.: Univ. of California Press, 1968), 7–8, 192–93.
[2] Ibid., 8–13.

great length").[3] Both of these things served as public manifestations of the fact that Catherine's previous marriage to Arthur had never been consummated, and thus she was entering upon her married life with Henry as a maiden, an issue that was to weigh heavily in the tragic events to unfold some twenty years later.

After losing one son after another to death during pregnancy, birth, or infancy, Catherine bore in 1516 the couple's first daughter and their only surviving child, Mary. The years that followed, however, brought further woes, with Catherine's subsequent pregnancies ending in miscarriage or stillbirth.[4] Meanwhile the attention of the King was shifting from the woman to whom he had vowed himself to two women who satisfied his less noble inclinations: Elizabeth Blout, the sister of Lord Mountjoy, and Mary Carey, the married daughter of Thomas Boleyn. In 1519 Blout gave birth to the King's illegitimate son, Henry Fitzroy. The older Henry was growing increasingly apprehensive over the prospect of having no legitimate male heir to succeed him, and it was with this in mind that he began to groom his mistress' son for higher things.[5] But eventually Henry came to seek a solution to the succession problem elsewhere—in the bewitching eyes of yet another *femme fatale,* a woman who, unlike her sister Mary, aspired to far more than the role of royal courtesan. The King's enchantment with Anne Boleyn appears to have originated in the early part of the year 1526, although the matter did not take on conspicuous proportions until the spring of 1527.[6] By a not so strange coincidence, Henry's claims of an increasingly troubled conscience over the legitimacy of his marriage to Catherine developed apace with his desire for Anne. Yet it seems that the delicate conscience of the King did not deem it indelicate to write in the following terms to his latest fascination:

---

[3] Edward Hall, *The Lives of the Kings: Henry VIII* (1550 folio ed. entitled *The Triumphant Reigne of Kyng Henry the VIII;* reprint, London: T. C. and E. C. Jack, 1904), 1:5–7 (quote on 7).

[4] Retha Warnicke, *The Rise and Fall of Anne Boleyn: Family Politics at the Court of Henry VIII* (Cambridge: Cambridge Univ. Press, 1989), 48, 50; Scarisbrick, *Henry VIII,* 150; Garrett Mattingly, *Catherine of Aragon* (Boston: Little, Brown and Co., 1941), 174–75.

[5] Warnicke, *Anne Boleyn,* 44–46; Scarisbrick, *Henry VIII,* 147–48.

[6] E. W. Ives, *Anne Boleyn* (Oxford: Basil Blackwell, 1986), 108; E. W. Ives, "The Fall of Wolsey", in *Cardinal Wolsey: Church, State and Art,* ed. S. J. Gunn and P. G. Lindley (Cambridge: Cambridge Univ. Press, 1991), 291.

... [S]ince I parted from you, I have been told that the opinion in which I left you is now completely changed ... If this report is true I cannot enough marvel at it, seeing that I have since made certain I have never offended you. And it seems to me a very small return for the great love I have for you to be kept apart both from the presence and the person of the woman whom I most esteem in the world.[7]

Of course, in all fairness to Henry it should be said that he was in certain respects perhaps less predator than prey in this fatal tryst, for Anne was soon to demonstrate the aggressiveness of her own ambitions and desires, settling for nothing less than to become the next Queen of England.

The royal scruples over the wedding of 1509 were played out in a rather bizarre fashion on May 17, 1527, when the King was summoned—quite willingly—to a secret hearing on the validity of his marriage, conducted by Cardinal Wolsey and the Archbishop of Canterbury, William Warham, at what is now Westminster's Whitehall. Henry was to answer to the "charge" of having lived in sin for eighteen years with his brother's wife.[8] Two further sessions were held on the twentieth and the thirty-first (with a "proctor" standing in for the King), but events on the Continent were to put an end to this first stratagem for securing an annulment. The sacking of Rome that same month by the troops of Queen Catherine's nephew, Emperor Charles V, was soon followed by the capture and imprisonment of Pope Clement VII. Henry's inner circle anticipated that in the hands of Charles' army, Clement would not be anxious to risk the anger of the Emperor by making a decision that would deprive the Emperor's aunt of her dignity as Queen of England. In a rather farfetched scheme to remedy this potential impasse, Cardinal Wolsey was in July dispatched to France in order to seek appointment as a surrogate papal administrator who could carry out Pope Clement's duties for the duration of his incarceration.[9] Such an arrangement would give the English Cardinal the power to grant his king the annulment he desired without having to obtain Clement's consent. But the Pope had no intention of delegating the authority of his God-given office

---

[7] Undated letter of 1527 or 1528, in *English Historical Documents,* vol. 5, *1485–1558,* ed. C. H. Williams (New York: Oxford Univ. Press, 1967), 700 (letter no. 2).

[8] Scarisbrick, *Henry VIII,* 154–55.

[9] Christopher Haigh, *English Reformations: Religion, Politics, and Society under the Tudors* (Oxford: Clarendon Press, 1993), 90.

to anyone, nor were the French interested in advocating the English prelate's plan for a new Avignon quasi papacy.[10]

As Cardinal Wolsey's project was floundering on the Continent, an impatient King Henry was pursuing his own equally ill-advised course of action back at home. In September 1527 he sent to Rome his secretary, Dr. William Knight, with the draft of a proposed papal bull that would allow him to take Anne as a second wife while bypassing any decision about the status of Catherine with a preamble that matter-of-factly denied the validity of the 1509 marriage.[11] It is difficult to understand how a man as well versed in ecclesiastical studies as Henry could have thought that the Church would give her blessing to what amounted to bigamy, but then again, this would not be the last time that England's "Defender of the Faith" would prove himself unpredictable in the obsessive pursuit of his desires. Dismayed to learn of Knight's proposed mission as he passed through France on the way to Rome, Cardinal Wolsey immediately returned to England with the intention of advising his Sovereign. The idea of Anne Boleyn as Queen had come as a totally unexpected and most unpleasant surprise to the prelate, and he wanted to inform the King fully of all the ramifications. But it was too late. The Boleyns, old adversaries of the Cardinal, had played their hand well in his absence; on his return in late September, he was unable to obtain a private audience with Henry—in an arrogant display of her ascendancy, Anne refused to leave him alone with the King.[12] The decline and fall of Wolsey as Lord Chancellor and trusted royal advisor had begun.

Among the most innocent of victims to be caught up in the events unfolding at court was Queen Catherine. By all accounts she had been a faithful and pious wife to Henry for almost twenty years. It cannot be thought that the loss of one child after another weighed any less upon her shoulders than upon those of the King. If in her sorrows she withdrew more and more from the gaiety of court life to devote herself to prayer and penance, drawing upon the legacy of piety she had inherited from her mother, Isabella, she could scarcely be faulted for it. That she had no intention of abdicating the duties of her state in life was later made manifest when she adamantly refused

[10] Ibid.

[11] Paul Friedmann, *Anne Boleyn: A Chapter of English History, 1527–1536* (London: Macmillan and Co., 1884), 1:56–57.

[12] Ibid., 57–59.

the suggestion that she enter a convent to solve her husband's marital problems. She was kept in the dark as to Henry's plans to dispose of her until rumors began reaching her ears in May or June 1527.[13] Finally, on June 22 the King went to Catherine and told her himself of his doubts about their marriage.[14] She had already suffered through the deaths of all but one of her children, as well as the anguish of seeing her husband enter into two adulterous affairs with other women. Was she now to allow herself to be stripped of her God-given dignity as a married woman and to have her one surviving daughter stigmatized as the fruit of an unlawful union, all in order to make room on the throne for yet another of Henry's passing fancies? No, she would not consent to the annulment; and, as the King had feared, she wasted no time in sending word of her plight to Rome and to her nephew Charles.

Despite his humiliation at the hands of Anne Boleyn, Cardinal Wolsey managed to persuade Henry to change his instructions for Dr. Knight, and a message was dispatched to this emissary that reached him before he reached Rome. The proposed bull was to be scuttled, and in its place Wolsey's plan of acting as a papal surrogate authority was to be presented to the Pontiff. But in another foolhardy move made without Wolsey's knowledge, Henry also petitioned the Pope for a dispensation from the obstacle of consanguinity that ironically barred his proposed new marriage to Anne Boleyn—an obstacle he had incurred by having relations with Anne's sister Mary.[15] The same king whose conscience supposedly could not accept the validity of one dispensation of consanguinity was now seeking a second dispensation from the very same law. Pope Clement responded with a bull in December 1527 that stated there could be no such dispensation until the King's marriage to Catherine had been proven to be null and void. To settle the latter a commission was to be appointed, with both Cardinal Wolsey and a papal representative serving as the principal participants.[16] Wolsey knew he needed more than this to satisfy his increasingly impatient monarch, so he dispatched two more emissaries to Rome—Stephen Gardiner and Edward Foxe. This mission

---

[13] Warnicke, *Anne Boleyn*, 61.

[14] Friedmann, *Anne Boleyn*, 1:53.

[15] Ibid., 62–63.

[16] Scarisbrick, *Henry VIII*, 204; Peter Gwyn, *The King's Cardinal: The Rise and Fall of Thomas Wolsey* (London: PIMLICO, 1992), 502.

proved somewhat more successful, for the Pope made the concession of sending Cardinal Lorenzo Campeggio to England in October 1528 with a papal bull, the contents of which evidently gave both Campeggio and Wolsey the authorization to reach jointly a final and binding verdict on the marriage. But the Pontiff instructed the Italian Cardinal not to let the bull out of his hands and secretly told him to delay the case as long as possible in the hope that Henry would eventually change his mind on his own about the proposed annulment.[17]

Cardinal Campeggio appears to have been rather adept in employing delaying tactics, for the inquest into the King's "Great Matter" did not convene until May 31, 1529.[18] The proceedings were conducted at the Dominican house of Blackfriars, and for the second meeting of the commission on June 18, both Henry and Catherine were summoned to appear, although it was actually expected that on this occasion each would merely send a representative. Nonetheless, the Queen had resolved to take matters into her own hands and surprised the commission by appearing in person, pleading her case for herself.[19] But it was at the next meeting on June 21 that one of the truly defining moments of the whole crisis was destined to unfold. On this day both sovereigns were present. After a verbose explication by the King on, among other things, the sensitivities of his conscience, Catherine rose from her chair and, crossing the room to where Henry was seated, threw herself down on her knees before him, delivering with all the ardor of her Spanish temperament a plea for justice that Shakespeare was later to immortalize in his play *Henry VIII*:

> Sir, I beseech you for all the loves that hath been between us and for the love of God, let me have justice and right; take of me some pity and compassion, for I am a poor woman and a stranger, born out of your dominion. I have here no assured friends, and much less indifferent counsel. I flee to you as to the head of justice within this realm. Alas, sir, wherein have I offended you, or what occasion of displeasure have I deserved against your will or pleasure? . . . I take God and all the world to witness that I have been to you a true, humble, and obedient wife, ever comfirmable to your will and pleasure . . . being always well pleased and contented with all things wherein ye had any delight or dalliance;

---

[17] Ludwig von Pastor, *The History of the Popes from the Close of the Middle Ages,* vol. 10 (St. Louis, Mo.: B. Herder, 1914), 254–62.

[18] Ibid., 268.

[19] Scarisbrick, *Henry VIII,* 224.

whether it were in little or much . . . I loved all those whom ye loved only for your sake, whether I had cause or no, and whether they were my friends or my enemies. This twenty years I have been your true wife (or more), and by me ye have had divers children, although it hath pleased God to call them out of this world, which hath been no default in me.

And when ye had me at the first (I take God to be my judge) I was a true maid without touch of man; and whether it be true or no, I put it to your conscience.

After reminding Henry that both his father and hers were accounted wise monarchs, surrounding themselves with competent advisors who adjudged their marriage "good and lawful", the Queen pleaded for the opportunity to have recourse to counsel from her native land; and closing with the words, "to God I commit my case", she rose, curtsied to her husband, and withdrew.[20] Undoubtedly an awkward silence must have come over the entire assembly after such a speech as this, for the King found it necessary to respond in the most conciliatory of terms—at least for the moment—praising Catherine's virtues. But if the Queen's words had given Henry pause, it was not for very long. He resumed the justification of his cause by reminding the bishops present that they had all given their assent to the validity of his scruples—he had all their signatures and seals on a document to this effect. Archbishop Warham agreed that this was true. But there was one dissenting voice: "No, sir, not I, ye have not my consent thereto."[21] The voice was that of Bishop John Fisher. The tension was palpable.

As early as the spring of 1527, Cardinal Wolsey had requested and obtained the opinion of Bishop Fisher on the supposedly theoretical question of whether the pope has the authority to allow a man to marry his brother's widow. In Bishop Fisher's response, which was forwarded to the King on June 2 of that year, he admitted to the diversity of opinions among theologians on the marital question itself but found the reasoning that saw a man's wedding of his brother's childless widow as a breach of divine law rather weak. Nonetheless,

---

[20] George Cavendish, *The Life and Death of Cardinal Wolsey,* in Richard S. Sylvester and Davis P. Harding, eds., *Two Early Tudor Lives: The Life and Death of Cardinal Wolsey, by George Cavendish; The Life of Sir Thomas More, by William Roper* (New Haven and London: Yale Univ. Press, 1962), 83–85.

[21] Ibid., 85–87 (quote on 87).

he continued, even if the pros and cons of the case were of equal merit, he would give his assent to the judgment of the pope, for it is he that has the full authority to decide such a case and the power to grant a dispensation.[22] Thus when two years later, at the Blackfriars inquest, Bishop Fisher raised his voice to deny that he had concurred in the opinion of the other bishops as to the status of Henry and Catherine's marriage, it should not have come as a surprise to the King. Rather, it merely brought to the surface a growing tension that had already begun to develop between the monarch and the bishop. When the King heard Fisher's denial, a terse exchange ensued. "No hath," Henry answered, "look here upon this, is not this your hand and seal?" He showed the bishop the document, but when Fisher saw it he told him directly, "No, forsooth, sir, it is not my hand nor seal." The King then asked Archbishop Warham, who responded by affirming that the seal and signature were those of Fisher. But the bishop had no intention of backing down:

> That is not so, for indeed you were in hand with me to have both my hand and seal, as other of my lords hath already done, but then I said to you that I would never consent to no such act for it were much against my conscience, nor my hand and seal should never be seen at any such instrument (God willing) with much more matter touching the same communication between us.

Archbishop Warham was now embarrassed into making something of an admission, yet he nonetheless attempted to justify his actions: "You say truth, such words ye had unto me, but at the last ye were fully persuaded that I should for you subscribe your name and put to a seal myself, and ye would allow the same." Bishop Fisher replied: "All which words and matter, under your correction, my lord, and supportation of this noble audience, there is nothing more untrue." But the King's patience had run out, and, exasperated with what was happening to the proceedings, he put an end to the exchange by telling Fisher: "Well, well, it shall make no matter. We will not stand with you in argument herein, for you are but one man."[23] One man too many, it would seem. It is not improbable that from this day onward the fate of Bishop Fisher was sealed. As Englishmen under the Henri-

---

[22] E. E. Reynolds, *Saint John Fisher* (New York: P. J. Kenedy and Sons, 1955), 131–32.

[23] Cavendish, *Life of Wolsey,* 87–88.

cian rule were wont to remind themselves, "The wrath of the prince is death."[24]

But John Fisher was not the only man who was failing to give the King the answer he wanted to hear on the marriage question. Henry pressed his friend and counselor Thomas More to declare his opinion on the matter. After failing to persuade the King that he was not qualified to advise him on this issue, More reluctantly agreed to study the question. Subsequently he told Henry that as neither he nor the other counselors loyally bound to His Majesty's service were fit to function as objective advisors, the King could choose "such counselors . . . as neither for respect of their own worldly commodity, nor for fear of your princely authority, will be inclined to deceive you".[25] More now brought these honest brokers forward—the Church Fathers, including his beloved Saint Augustine. Their judgments were most certainly not to Henry's liking. Although he seemed to listen to More's presentation in good part, he refused to accept this as his counselor's final answer, for time and again he raised the issue with him.[26]

In the end the inquest at Blackfriars came to nothing so far as the King's purposes were concerned. The Queen refused to make any further appearances, nor would she recognize its authority to pass judgment. Instead, she appealed directly to the Holy See, and on July 13, 1529 (formally on the sixteenth), Pope Clement responded by ordering that deliberation over the marriage question be moved back to Rome.[27] On July 23, even before receiving word of the Pope's decision, Cardinal Campeggio adjourned the inquest for a summer vacation in keeping with Roman custom; the commission never met again.[28] The failure of these proceedings to accomplish Henry's plans spelled the end of Cardinal Wolsey's career as a statesman, and in the months that followed the King would show little in the way of mercy toward the man who had once been his trusted confidant. On October 9 a bill was passed by the King's Bench charging Wolsey with

---

[24] See the Duke of Norfolk's warning to Thomas More in William Roper, *The Lyfe of Sir Thomas Moore, Knighte,* ed. Elsie V. Hitchcock, Early English Text Society, original series, no. 197 (London: Early English Text Society, 1935), 71.

[25] Roper, *Lyfe,* 31–33 (quotation on 33).

[26] Ibid., 33, 49–50.

[27] Scarisbrick, *Henry VIII,* 225–26; Gwyn, *King's Cardinal,* 529.

[28] Gwyn, *King's Cardinal,* 527–29; Friedmann, *Anne Boleyn,* 1:93.

violation of the Praemunire Statute of 1391,[29] one of several English laws on the books since the fourteenth century that encroached upon papal authority over the country by forbidding appeals to Rome that in any way "touch our lord the king, against him, his crown and his royalty, or his realm".[30] On or about October 17 he was stripped of the office of Lord Chancellor that he had held for the past fourteen years.[31] After falling so precipitously into total disgrace, the Cardinal, exiled to his residence in Esher, where he was kept under house arrest, managed to stage a bit of a comeback during the following year, but this eventually brought down upon him a charge of treason, based on bogus allegations that he had tried to have the King excommunicated by the Pope and was attempting to build a political faction for himself in his Diocese of York.[32] On November 4, 1530, he was taken into custody for the journey back to London, where he was to be tried. But Wolsey never reached the city. Along the route the prelate fell ill and was unable to proceed farther than the Augustinian Abbey of Leicester, where he was allowed to take what proved to be his final rest. After two days at the Abbey, Wolsey predicted that he would not live beyond eight o'clock on the following morning. It was during that last night of his life that he pronounced judgment upon the moral compromises he had made in his service to the King: "If I had served God as diligently as I have done the king, he would not have given me over in my gray hairs."[33] The Cardinal faced death nobly, warning those about him both of the contagion of heresy from the Continent and of the danger that had destroyed him—the unbending will of Henry. Receiving the last rites, and finally at peace with God, he died at precisely the hour he had foreseen, eight o'clock on the morning of November 29, 1530.[34]

Upon Cardinal Wolsey's resignation from the chancellorship in mid-October of 1529, the King and his Council were faced with the necessity of filling the highest office in the kingdom with a suitable

---

[29] Ives, "Fall of Wolsey", 306–7.

[30] Reynolds, *Fisher,* 173.

[31] J. A. Guy, *The Public Career of Sir Thomas More* (New Haven: Yale Univ. Press, 1980), 31, 32.

[32] Gwyn, *King's Cardinal,* 599–601, 616.

[33] John Farrow, *The Story of Thomas More* (1954; reprint, New York: Image Books/Doubleday and Co., 1968), 127.

[34] Ibid., 127–28.

successor. The names of the Duke of Suffolk Charles Brandon and London's Archbishop Cuthbert Tunstall were both raised, but in the end a compromise candidate was selected—Thomas More. It was a choice that even Cardinal Wolsey, despite his disagreements with More, had advised, saying that he was "the aptest and fittest man in the Realm".[35] There was however one member of the King's Council disquieted by the selection—More himself. Thus it took a bit of angry persuasion on the part of His Majesty to compel his reluctant counselor to accept an office that represented the zenith of his public career. In the end More yielded, and at three o'clock in the afternoon of October 29, he stepped into the King's inner chamber and received from Henry's hands the supreme symbol of the authority with which he was now to be invested, the great seal of England. This simple ceremony made More officially the Lord Chancellor, but a public ceremony was carried out at ten o'clock on the following morning. Entering Westminster Hall, he was brought by the Dukes of Norfolk (Thomas Howard) and Suffolk to his seat presiding over the "court of Chancery". Norfolk announced to those present that he had been expressly charged by the King "to make declaration how much all England was beholden to Sir Thomas More for his good service, and how worthy he was to have the highest room in the realm, and how dearly his Grace loved and trusted him, for which . . . he had great cause to rejoice."[36] More replied by artfully deprecating his own abilities and added a telling remark: that in view of the downfall of his predecessor in this office, he had "thereof no cause to rejoice".[37] In reflecting upon his future as he stood in Westminster Hall, he may well have had in mind the sobering portrait of earthly success that he had envisioned some seven years earlier in his treatise *The Four Last Things:*

> If it so were that thou knewest a great Duke, keeping so great estate and princely port in his house . . . and at the sight of the pomp and honor showed him of all the country about resorting to him, while they kneel and crouch to him, and at every word barehead bigrace him, if thou

---

[35] Guy, *Public Career,* 31–32; comment of Cardinal Wolsey in Nicholas Harpsfield, *The Life and Death of Sir Thomas More,* in *Lives of Saint Thomas More* (William Roper and Nicholas Harpsfield), ed. E. E. Reynolds, Everyman's Library, no. 19 (London: J. M. Dent and Sons, 1963), 74.

[36] Roper, *Lyfe,* 39.

[37] Ibid., 39–40 (quotation on 40).

shouldest suddenly be surely advertised, that for secret treason lately detected to the king he should undoubtedly be taken the morrow, his court all broken up, his goods seized, his wife put out, his children disinherited, himself cast in prison, brought forth and arraigned, the matter out of question, and he should be condemned, his coat armor reversed, his gilt spurs hewn off his heels, himself hanged, drawn and quartered, how thinkest thou by thy faith amid thine envy, shouldest thou not suddenly change into pity?[38]

In the six years that lay ahead for More, these prophetic words were to become a bitter reality.

A Very Long Parliament

On November 3, 1529, shortly after the office of Lord Chancellor had passed from Cardinal Wolsey to Thomas More, Parliament was called to order in the presence of King Henry himself. In virtue of his new station it was the duty of More as the King's designated spokesman before this legislative body to open the new session with a speech enunciating the Sovereign's own agenda. On this and further occasions the task of delivering the King's message to Parliament was going to prove most distasteful to More. During the opening speech on November 3, he found himself in the awkward position of having publicly to disgrace his predecessor with a verbal barrage of criticism.[39] While More would undoubtedly have found fault with much of Cardinal Wolsey's actions, it is highly unlikely—in view of his veneration for the clergymen of the Church—that he would have willingly attacked a bishop in public had he not been constrained to do so by his office. Moreover, there is evidence to suggest that More's speech was actually an effort to protect the Cardinal from far worse attacks in Parliament that may have arisen from other quarters. As the Tudor scholar E. W. Ives recently commented (1991):

---

[38] *The Four Last Things,* in *The Workes of Sir Thomas More Knight . . . in the English Tongue* (1557), as reproduced in *The English Works of Sir Thomas More,* ed. W. E. Campbell (London: Eyre and Spottiswoode; New York: Lincoln MacVeagh, Dial Press, 1931), 1:86.

[39] R. W. Chambers, *Thomas More* (1935; reprint, Ann Arbor, Mich.: Ann Arbor Paperbacks, Univ. of Michigan, 1973), 240–41.

. . . More began with the required denunciation of Wolsey's offences, then announced that he had already been gently corrected, and ended by consigning the cardinal to insignificance as no more than a dire warning to others. Thomas More, one may suggest, was deliberately and on instructions, setting out to forestall an attack on the cardinal. Far from it being an example of political time-serving which stabbed in the back a man he had worked with for a decade, still less a contradiction of the king's secret wishes, the speech of the new chancellor was of a piece with the comfort and assistance which Henry was sending to the old [to Cardinal Wolsey].[40]

In addition to the matter of Cardinal Wolsey, More had also to present the King's call for a reformation of "divers new enormities . . . sprung amongst the people".[41] Fortunately More's conscience was spared in that he did not have to spell out precisely what reforms Henry might have had in mind. It would not take long to find out.

On the streets of London copies of Simon Fish's slanderous anticlerical tract *A Supplication for the Beggars* were circulating from the first day of the 1529–1530 session of Parliament.[42] Within Parliament itself the first signs of what would later evolve into a systematic campaign against the clergy emerged in the form of legislation that sought to redress legitimate grievances regarding probate, mortuaries, and pluralities[43] but which encroached upon ecclesiastical jurisdiction in its methods. Bishop Fisher was particularly alarmed at the implications of these measures. The anonymous sixteenth-century biographer of the Bishop provides his own reconstruction of a speech delivered by the prelate before Parliament at this time:

> My lords . . . consider what bills are here daily preferred from the Commons. What the same may sound in some of your ears I cannot tell; but in my ears they sound all to this effect, that our holy mother the Church, being left unto us by the great liberality and diligence of our forefathers in most perfect and peaceable freedom, shall now by us be brought into servile thralldom like a bondmaid . . . beware of yourselves and your country, nay, beware of the liberty of our mother the Church.[44]

---

[40] Ives, "Fall of Wolsey", 308.

[41] Hall, *Henry VIII*, 2:164.

[42] Steven Haas, "Simon Fish, William Tyndale, and Sir Thomas More's 'Lutheran Conspiracy'", *Journal of Ecclesiastical History* 23 (April 1972): 126.

[43] Reynolds, *Fisher*, 167.

[44] Fr. Francis van Ortroy, S.J., ed., "Vie du bienheureux martyr Jean Fisher: Cardinal,

Of course, interventions such as this by the good Bishop of Rochester were not adding to his prestige with His Majesty. Fisher could scarcely have had any illusions about the price he might soon have to pay for his courage in speaking out for his Church and his Queen. On July 11, 1530, the attorney general filed charges of praemunire in King's Bench against fourteen clerics; not surprisingly Bishop Fisher was among those named, as well as three other prominent episcopal supporters of Queen Catherine. It is supremely ironic and quite revealing of the real agenda behind this action in King's Bench that all fourteen were accused of having tacitly acquiesced in Cardinal Wolsey's exercise of legatine powers in violation of the praemunire statutes. Only one of these men could be considered a friend of the Cardinal, and a number of the rest had been among his opponents in various controversies over the years.[45] Later in the summer, praemunire charges were brought against two more individuals, one of whom was Anthony Husye, a layman. If the praemunire allegations of 1530 were intended as a shot across the bow for the clergy, then the naming of a layman among those accused may have served as an implied threat to the ecclesiastical court system that laymen such as Husye worked for as notary publics, advocates, scribes, and registrars.[46]

On July 13, 1530, the King sent a letter to Pope Clement VII, cosigned by his trusted noblemen as well as by several members of the English episcopate, which claimed that *many* universities had decided against the validity of Henry's marriage to Catherine and expressed growing impatience with the amount of time that Rome was taking to reach a judgment.[47] Henry was later to complain of having had to excuse his Lord Chancellor—Thomas More—from the duty of signing this challenge to the Holy See.[48] More as well as Bishop Fisher and Archbishop Tunstall could not bring themselves to put their signatures to such a document.[49] In September Pope Clement responded with firmness to the King's letter, reminding Henry that

---

évêque de Rochester (+1535): Text anglais et traduction latine du XVI siècle" (pt. 1), *Analecta Bollandiana* 10 (1891): 337–38 (spelling modernized).

[45] J. A. Guy, "Henry VIII and the Praemunire Manoeuvres of 1530–1531", *English Historical Review* 97 (July 1982): 481–86.

[46] Ibid., 486.

[47] Scarisbrick, *Henry VIII,* 259–60; Guy, *Public Career,* 129–30.

[48] Guy, *Public Career,* 140.

[49] Ibid., 130.

he himself was stalling the process by refusing to dispatch a delegate to Rome and that justice must be objectively served in pursuing the case regardless of the English monarch's past merits as a "Defender of the Faith".[50]

Over the summer and fall of 1530 Henry had been doing some reading—reading that would ultimately seal the fate of the Catholic Church in England. The scholars that the King had called upon to prepare a study of the marriage question were close enough to the completion of their task for him to begin perusing the manuscript of their magnum opus on the matter—the *Collectanea satis copiosa;* the original is marked in over forty places with the handwritten comments of Henry himself.[51] What Edward Foxe and Thomas Cranmer gave their sovereign was far more than another new strategy for achieving the sought-for annulment and remarriage; it was a historical and theological rationalization for a monarchal takeover of English Christianity—for the establishment of a theocratic English empire. Foxe and Cranmer's thesis was built on shaky grounds, such as the spurious correspondence between a fictitious second-century Christian English king, "Lucius I", and Pope Eleutherius, who is supposed to have declared Lucius the absolute vicar of God over England.[52] Yet in the end what mattered was that the *Collectanea satis copiosa* had flattered the royal ego, and this alone was enough to change history.

In the first weeks of 1531 the growing rift between King and clergy reached critical mass. On January 12 a convocation of the English bishops of the Canterbury province (encompassing all the dioceses in the southern half of the country) opened at Saint Paul's Cathedral in London to discuss a number of proposed reforms.[53] Henry and his men, however, soon provided the assembly with a far more immediate issue to settle. On January 16, the first day of the new session of Parliament at Westminster, a bill was introduced in the House of Lords offering pardon to the clergy for their alleged complicity in Cardinal Wolsey's violations of the praemunire statutes but requiring them to pay in compensation one hundred thousand pounds.[54] After

---

[50] Ibid.
[51] Guy, "Henry VIII", 495–96.
[52] Ibid., 496; Guy, *Public Career,* 132–33.
[53] Guy, "Henry VIII", 488; Haigh, *English Reformations,* 106.
[54] Ibid.

the bishops responded with an offer of forty thousand pounds,[55] they received an answer of sorts when on January 20 nine of those charged with praemunire in the summer of 1530 were once more summoned to appear before King's Bench. At the very least there was in the air an implied threat from the King that failure to pay the indemnity in full would leave every cleric of the Canterbury province in danger of facing similar praemunire charges.[56] The threat was well understood, and on January 24 the bishops conceded to pay the entire amount the King had asked for in installments spread over a five-year period.[57] But the King pressed them to agree to paying the entire amount at once in the event of war. In no mood for further concessions, the bishops went on the counteroffensive, refusing this proposal as well as the next—a slightly more conciliatory one—proffered by Henry. Drawing up their own list of conditions, the bishops stipulated that the King reaffirm the centuries-old rights of the Church guaranteed by the Magna Carta and that he delineate the precise limits of the prae-munire statutes.[58] Aroused by this challenge, Henry now resorted to iron-truncheon tactics. On February 7 Archbishop Warham read to the other bishops the King's blunt answer, couched in a series of five articles, the first of which proved to be the opening salvo of the most aggressive phase of the Henrician takeover of the Church in Eng-land. His Majesty had styled a new title for himself—"sole protector and supreme head of the English church and clergy"[59]—and he de-manded that the convocation recognize him as such. A heated debate began among the bishops about what they should do. Bishop Fisher led the fight against the proposed new title, but in the end it was he who would provide the convocation with a resourceful face-saving compromise. Upon his suggestion the bishops agreed on February 11 to recognize the king as "their singular protector, only and supreme Lord, and so far as the law of Christ allows, even Supreme Head".[60] It was the insertion of the phrase "so far as the law of Christ allows", proposed by Fisher after he heard it used by one of the King's spokes-men in the course of explaining the title, that made all the difference.

---

[55] Haigh, *English Reformations*, 106.

[56] Guy, "Henry VIII", 489.

[57] Ibid., 490–91; Haigh, *English Reformations*, 106.

[58] Haigh, *English Reformations*, 106; Guy, "Henry VIII", 491.

[59] Guy, "Henry VIII", 495.

[60] Chambers, *More*, 248.

In effect they were acknowledging Henry's supreme authority only insofar as it did not trespass upon or violate the "law of Christ", and of course for the bishops there was no distinction between the "law of Christ" and the law of the Church. Nonetheless, they well knew what interpretation the King was likely to give his newly won title, and thus it was that when Archbishop Warham read the revised text to the convocation for final approval there was a deafening silence. Finally the Archbishop said in a hesitant voice, ". . . [A]s silence signified consent, the new title should become fact."[61] The bishops had every reason to fear what might lie ahead. And Thomas More was as disconcerted as the bishops; in a letter dated only ten days after the February 11 "supremacy" decision in Convocation, Charles V's ambassador Eustace Chapuys reported that More was so troubled by recent events that he was anxious above all else to resign as Lord Chancellor.[62]

Satisfied that he had achieved as much as he could for the present, the King accepted the particulars of the bishops' last proposal as to how they would pay the one hundred thousand pounds for their pardon, and the relevant documentation regarding the grant was submitted to him in its final form in March. At the King's behest a new bill for pardoning the clergy was introduced in the House of Commons and passed that same month.[63]

During the rest of 1531, the opposing forces, locked in a battle over the future of the country, found themselves in an uneasy stalemate. On March 31 Parliament was adjourned until October; when October came the opening of Parliament was put off again, so that the body did not reconvene until January 1532. Not without reason Chapuys claimed these delays reflected indecision among Henry's advisors.[64] Evidence that Anne Boleyn's ambitions may have been outstripping even those of the King himself came in April 1531, when the monarch complained to the Duke of Norfolk that Anne was treating him worse than Catherine ever had.[65] But by the first weeks of 1532 Henry and his men were ready for a new concerted offensive against the Church. During January there was introduced in the House of

---

[61] Farrow, *More,* 142.

[62] Chambers, *More,* 279.

[63] Guy, "Henry VIII", 499–500.

[64] Haigh, *English Reformations,* 110.

[65] Ibid.

Lords a bill to deny the Pope "annates", the customary stipends he received upon the appointment of new bishops.[66] Although the proposal faced overwhelming opposition, the King was determined to force its passage and resorted to strong-arm tactics, intimidating the MPs into submission by personally appearing in the House of Lords three times during the deliberations. It passed—just barely—but ran aground again in the House of Commons. Finally, in what must have been a chilling scene, the King entered the Commons and ordered those voting for the bill to stand on one side of the hall, with those against it ordered to the other side. By March 26 Henry had succeeded in unnerving a sufficient portion of his opposition to achieve the ratification of the annates bill in both houses.[67] Even so, he did not implement the bill immediately, for he wished to hold its application in reserve as a bargaining chip with Rome.

While the King was busy muscling his legislation through Parliament, his "Master Secretary", Thomas Cromwell, was lending his hand to (if not actually masterminding) yet another ambitious new attack upon the clergy. On March 18, most likely at Cromwell's instigation, the Commons lodged before the King a complaint against the bishops, a "Supplication against the Ordinaries", asking for a reform of the ecclesiastical court system and of the canon law governing it. The first article of this petition was perhaps the most confrontational, attacking the Canterbury Convocation for enacting ecclesiastical legislation that lacked the consent of the laity and that trespassed upon the authority of the King and English law.[68] On April 27 the Canterbury Convocation presented its response, denying that there was any breakdown of relations between clergy and laity and defending the Church's exercise of jurisdiction over her court system. The bishops pointed out that whatever valid grievances did exist were the fault, not of the entire body of the clergy, but of certain individuals, nor did such failures discredit the ecclesiastical laws themselves.[69] Already incensed by an Easter Sunday homily of the Franciscan William Peto condemning the pursuit of a royal annulment (and delivered, no less, in His Majesty's presence), Henry reacted angrily to the bishops' response and now became resolute in the pursuit of the theocratic and

---

[66] Ibid.
[67] Ibid., 110–11.
[68] Ibid., 111–12.
[69] Ibid., 112–13.

imperialistic agenda of Cranmer and Foxe's *Collectanea satis copiosa*. On May 10 he sent to the Canterbury Convocation three unprecedented demands: (1) for the future the King would possess the power to veto any new ecclesiastical statute; (2) the current ecclesiastical legislation was to be evaluated by a panel composed jointly of laymen and clergy with the power to annul whatever Church laws they found fault with; (3) all ecclesiastical statutes left intact were thenceforth to derive their force from the authority of the King.[70] What Henry here proposed amounted to the surrender of the Church's spiritual autonomy into his hands—the reduction of the Church into little more than an agent and ward of the state. As Thomas More was later to remind his fellow countrymen, such demands constituted a flagrant breach of the 1225 finalized version of England's constitutional document, the Magna Carta (first signed in 1215 by King John), in which King Henry III, speaking for all his successors to the throne, had pledged "by this our present charter confirmed for us and our heirs for ever, that the English church shall be free and shall have all its rights undiminished and its liberties unimpaired".[71]

Henry VIII left little doubt as to whether he was going to let his namesake's submission to the Magna Carta limit his options in this regard when on May 11 he told thirteen members of the House of Commons:

> Well-beloved subjects, we thought that the clergy of our realm had been our subjects wholly, but now we have well perceived, that they be but half our subjects, yea, and scarce our subjects; for all the Prelates at their consecration, make an oath to the Pope, clean contrary to the oath that they make to us, so that they seem to be his subjects, and not ours . . .[72]

Shortly thereafter the King went farther still and demanded the power to convene all future councils of the Canterbury Convocation. On May 15, 1532, an aging and intimidated Archbishop Warham asked the Convocation to ratify Henry's proposals; six bishops yielded, which, together with the abbots who concurred, gave Warham enough votes to claim the Convocation's assent. He avoided the considerable opposition in the lower house of the Convocation by declaring the adjourn-

---

[70] Ibid., 114.

[71] *English Historical Documents*, vol. 3, *1189–1327*, ed. Harry Rothwell (New York: Oxford Univ. Press, 1975), 341.

[72] Hall, *Henry VIII*, 2:210 (spelling and punctuation rendered closer to modern English).

ment of the council before the latter body had a chance to vote on the matter. The next day—Thursday, May 16, 1532—the "Submission of the Clergy" was signed by Archbishop Warham, two other bishops, and four abbots at Westminster, with Thomas Cromwell looking on.[73] Within a few hours, Thomas More tendered his resignation from the office of Lord Chancellor: at three o'clock that afternoon he appeared in the garden of Westminster's York Place and put into the King's hands the symbol of More's erstwhile authority—the great seal of England—concealed in a white leather pouch.[74] All his human efforts to avert what he foresaw as nothing less than a disaster for his Church, his monarch, and his country were at an end.

More's resignation would result in drastic changes at Chelsea. No longer a high-ranking statesman, he had neither a reason nor the means to retain a large household staff. Even so, the ex-Lord Chancellor was assiduous in finding new positions for all the attendants he now had to send away.[75] Able to laugh at his own downfall, More availed himself of an opportunity to tease his wife about their change of status on the first holy day following his resignation. At the end of Mass in the parish church, during which the men and women would sit apart from one another, it was customary for an attendant of More's to come to his wife's pew and tell her, "Madam, my lord is gone"— a signal that her husband was ready to leave. On this morning, however, it was no servant but More himself who came to Dame Alice's pew, and, after bowing with great deference, he said to her, "Madam, my lord is gone."[76]

More must have felt a certain sense of relief in withdrawing from public office, for he was finally free to devote himself to the pursuits he loved the most. He says as much in a letter to Erasmus dated June 14, 1532, written less than a month after his resignation:

> It has been my constant wish almost since boyhood, dearest Desiderius [Erasmus], that some day I might enjoy the opportunity which, to my happiness, you have always had, namely, of being relieved of all public duties and eventually being able to devote some time to God alone and myself; at long last this wish has come true, Erasmus, thanks to the

---

[73] Guy, *Public Career,* 196–97.
[74] Ibid., 201.
[75] Roper, *Lyfe,* 52.
[76] Ibid., 55.

goodness of the Supreme and Almighty God and to the graciousness of a very understanding Sovereign. I have not, however, attained exactly what I had wished for. My prayer had been to reach the crowning point of my life healthy and vigorous, no matter how old, or at least without sickness and suffering, as far as one could expect at that age. Perhaps that was a little too bold; in any case, the answer to that prayer is at present in God's hands.[77]

The illness to which More refers consisted of chest pains of unknown origin.[78]

During the summer of 1532 a key player in the struggles between King and clergy left the stage—Archbishop Warham. The aging prelate died in August, not long after taking a firm stand against the idea of granting an annulment to Henry without the consent of Rome.[79] With the all-important See of Canterbury now vacant, the King had an opportunity to nominate for the office a candidate who could be expected to be more cooperative in the pursuit of his "Great Matter". In October he put forward the name of Thomas Cranmer, coauthor of the *Collectanea satis copiosa* that had shaped royal policy over the last year. At the time of Warham's death, Cranmer had been in Germany studying the theological tenets of Luther's "new men". It seems this English cleric was so anxious to apply what he had learned from his mentors that even before returning home he had decided to break his vow of celibacy and had made arrangements to marry a German woman. However, the King was not yet ready to cut the last thread of communion with Rome and hence wanted the Pope's recognition of his candidate for the See of Canterbury. A married archbishop simply would not do, and Cranmer had to return to England without his prospective consort.[80] Despite his circumspection in matters such as this, Henry was becoming increasingly audacious in other ways, going so far as to take Anne Boleyn with him on a state visit to France in October 1532.[81] By December Anne was pregnant.

---

[77] Letter no. 44, June 14, 1532, in Elizabeth Rogers, ed., *St. Thomas More: Selected Letters* (New Haven: Yale Univ. Press, 1961), 172–73.

[78] Ibid., 173.

[79] Reynolds, *Fisher*, 188–89.

[80] Friedmann, *Anne Boleyn*, 1:174–78; Albert Pollard, *Thomas Cranmer and the English Reformation: 1489–1556*, Heroes of the Reformation Series (New York: G. P. Putnam's Sons, 1904), 47–54.

[81] Haigh, *English Reformations*, 115.

If the child she was carrying was going to be framed as a successor to the English throne, it was expedient that the stigma of illegitimacy be neutralized with the marriage of the mother and father before the infant was born. Thus it was that on January 25, 1533, the King and his mistress were married in a secret ceremony without any authorization from the Pope.[82] When Parliament resumed that same month, Cromwell and the new Lord Chancellor, Thomas Audley, were already at work creating a legislative basis for the secret wedding. After a three-week battle in the Commons, both houses passed Cromwell and Audley's "Act in Restraint of Appeals",[83] which pompously announced that "this realm of England is an Empire" and forbade the making of any appeals to Rome regarding, among other things, matrimony and divorce cases.[84] Hence Queen Catherine's petitions to the Pope were rendered illegal.

On March 30, following the reception of a papal bull approving his election, Cranmer was consecrated archbishop, but not before privately pledging (four days earlier) in the presence of witnesses that he considered the vow of obedience he was about to make to the Pope as merely a form, declaring that he had no intention of honoring such a vow at the expense of his absolute obedience to the King alone.[85] The new archbishop was not slow to demonstrate his worth to his monarch; only two weeks after his consecration he wrote the first draft of a letter to the King, begging in the most obsequious manner for permission to commence the royal annulment proceedings. It seems the King himself chose to edit Cranmer's petition, correcting it in his own hand so as to render the text even more obsessively deferential toward his royal self. Thus, not satisfied with Cranmer's crouching phrase, "beseeching Your Highness most humbly upon my knees", he revised it to read, "prostrate at the feet of Your Majesty, beseeching".[86] Once the choreographed formalities of the archbishop seeking and obtaining permission were completed, Cranmer opened his annulment inquest on May 8. Both of England's episcopal conferences, the Canterbury and York Convocations,

---

[82] Warnicke, *Anne Boleyn*, 120–21.

[83] Haigh, *English Reformations*, 115–16.

[84] *English Historical Documents*, 5:738–41.

[85] Pollard, *Cranmer*, 56–57; Hilaire Belloc, *Cranmer: Archbishop of Canterbury, 1533–1556* (Philadelphia: J. B. Lippincott Co., 1931), 107–9.

[86] Mattingly, *Catherine*, 357.

were polled for their opinions of the case. Bishop Fisher courageously fought against the annulment, but in the end there were enough votes to give Archbishop Cranmer the results Henry wanted. On May 23, 1533, the Archbishop pronounced judgment against the validity of Catherine's marriage to the King. Five days later there came the inevitable sequel—Henry's marriage to Anne Boleyn was ruled to be licit.[87]

While Archbishop Cranmer busied himself with the task of changing Henry's wife on paper, the court was being tutored in the displacement of Catherine by Anne. On April 9—Wednesday of Holy Week—the Duke of Norfolk came at the head of a delegation to Catherine, requesting her to renounce her title as Queen of England, but even in the face of insulting threats she refused. A little later she received a message from the King informing her that it was his pleasure she should no longer term herself Queen or allow others to do so.[88] Three days later, at the Easter Vigil, Anne made her debut as the new queen in a cloth-of-gold gown, heralded by trumpets and accompanied by sixty maids of honor, with her train carried by the future Duchess of Richmond. An awkward scene followed the Mass, as Henry compelled his courtiers one by one to do her honor with the customary bow accorded to royalty.[89] On Easter Sunday, when the preacher at Saint Paul's Cross prayed in a loud voice for Anne instead of Catherine, almost the entire congregation rose in indignation and departed in the middle of the service.[90]

On May 29 Anne embarked from Greenwich for the Tower of London on a barge confiscated from Catherine of Aragon and two days later (on May 31) rode in state through the streets of London in a glittering spectacle as intimidating to spectators as it was dazzling.[91] The climax came on the morning of June 1 in Westminster Abbey, where, after being anointed with chrism from a gold, eagle-shaped ampulla, Anne was crowned Queen of England with Saint Edward's crown, a gold scepter being placed in her right hand and an ivory baton in her left. It was Anne's hour—her brief hour—less than three years later she would die under an executioner's axe on Tower Hill.

---

[87] Ibid.

[88] Friedmann, *Anne Boleyn*, 1:198–99.

[89] Ibid., 199; Ives, *Anne Boleyn*, 205.

[90] Friedmann, *Anne Boleyn*, 1:200.

[91] Warnicke, *Anne Boleyn*, 123–27.

But on this day of her triumph a great banquet was given in her honor at Westminster Hall, observed from a concealed vantage point by the King.[92] Was he taking note of who was present and who was not? If he was hoping to see the face of his former Lord Chancellor, his hopes were certainly disappointed. Thomas More was conspicuously absent from all the festivities, having declined the invitation of three old friends, the Bishops Cuthbert Tunstall, John Clerk, and Stephen Gardiner, who had asked him to accompany them to the coronation. They had even sent him twenty pounds to cover the cost of a new tunic for the occasion. Always gracious with his friends, More accepted the gift in order, he told them, that he might be the bolder in turning down their flattering request to join them for the ceremonies in London. In an effort to satisfy them as to why he would not come, he told them a story, drawn from the writings of the Roman historian Tacitus—that of a maiden charged with a crime in a land where the emperor prohibited capital punishment for virgins convicted of the offense in question. An advisor to the emperor proposed a diabolical solution—that the girl be "deflowered" so that she could then be "devoured". Applying the story to his own current situation and the proponents of the new order in England, More concluded, ". . . [I]t lieth not in my power but that they may devour me; but God being my good Lord, I will provide that they shall never deflower me."[93] In veiled terms he was telling his friends that while he could not escape the wrath of those against him at court, he would with God's help resist anything that violated his conscience. More knew that had he gone to the coronation his presence would have been taken as tacit approval of the divorce, the remarriage, and Henry's seizure of ecclesiastical authority; thus he could not in good conscience attend the proceedings, come what may.

Within six weeks of Anne's coronation, Pope Clement VII declared (on July 11) Henry's new marriage invalid, warning the King that if he did not separate from Boleyn by September he would be excommunicated. Responding with bullying tactics directed at the Pontiff, Henry activated the provisions of Parliament's 1532 annates bill and attempted to apply financial pressure to Clement by cutting off the an-

---

[92] Ibid., 126, 128–29.
[93] Roper, *Lyfe,* 57–59 (quotation on 59).

nate payments of the bishops to Rome—but to no avail.[94] In December 1533 the King's Council began a propaganda campaign, ordering sermons against the papacy. The Council also produced a pamphlet defending the annulment of the first marriage, asserting rather speciously that recent good weather, an interlude of peace, and the healthy birth of Henry and Anne's daughter Elizabeth manifested God's blessing upon the new marriage. Contending that the authority of the Pope was no different from and no greater than that of any other bishop outside his own diocese, the pamphlet pronounced any papal excommunication of the English King invalid.[95]

When in the early 1520s More first took up in earnest the task of defending the Catholic faith in writing, he could scarcely have imagined that this activity might eventually bring him into conflict with his Sovereign, who proudly bore the title "Defender of the Faith". Nonetheless, as Henry came to find in Protestant writings justifications for his course of actions regarding Anne Boleyn and the control of the Church, a confrontation was inevitable. It should be stated at the outset that there is no record of the King or his counselors directly challenging More over the contents of his actual writings. Nonetheless, there is reason to believe that with regard to at least two of More's later apologetical works—his *Apology* and his *Debellation of Salem and Bizance*—there must have been a growing undercurrent of royal consternation, for both books were composed to refute the anticlerical propaganda of one of the intellectual fathers of the new order in England, Christopher Saint German.[96] A common lawyer like More, Saint German had long since retired from active law practice when in 1528 he published the first part of his magnum opus on questions of English law, *Doctor and Student;* the second part soon followed in 1530. It was Saint German's revolutionary elevation of English common law to a par with natural law and canon law that was to make *Doctor and Student* a useful tool and Saint German a valuable ally to the Henrician regime in the growing Church-state conflicts of the 1530s. In 1531 Saint German himself applied his theories to these specific conflicts by issuing an appendix to *Doctor and Student,*

---

[94] Haigh, *English Reformations,* 117.

[95] Ibid.

[96] J. A. Guy, "Thomas More and Christopher St. German: The Battle of the Books", *Moreana* 21 (November 1984): 6, 23.

his *New Additions,* wherein he consistently decided in favor of the state.[97] Henry's men would have found in *New Additions* the solution they ultimately chose for the King's "Great Matter"—that the King acting through Parliament was "the high sovereign over the people, which hath not only charge on the bodies, but also on the souls of his subjects".[98] It was also in 1531 that Saint German involved himself in drafting parliamentary legislation that would implement the ideas of *Doctor and Student* and of *New Additions.*[99]

In late 1532 or early 1533, Saint German published a further work, *A Treatise concerning the Division between the Spirituality and Temporality,* which assumed a deep-seated enmity between the clergy and laity, setting forth both the reasons for this supposed enmity and a series of reforms to end the division along lines that were certainly not in the Church's favor.[100] It was this work that finally provoked More to respond in writing to his fellow lawyer's ideas with a book that appeared in print during Eastertide of 1533—the *Apology.*[101] Sharply refuting the *Treatise*'s stereotyping of the English clergy as corrupt, More saw Saint German as both exaggerating and fomenting discord between the spirituality and the temporality and rejected the *Treatise*'s erection of English common law over and above the Church's canon law. The *Apology* also provided the ex-Lord Chancellor with an opportunity to defend traditional ecclesiastical and governmental procedures for dealing with heretics as well as his own antiheresy actions while in office.[102] More was certainly taking his chances—he could not have been unaware that the publisher of the *Treatise concerning the Division,* Thomas Berthelet, regularly carried out publishing projects for the Henrician regime. It was also from Berthelet's presses that Saint German's *New Additions* had come in 1531. Thus in confronting Saint German, More was indirectly confronting the governmental propaganda campaign itself.[103]

The confrontation was extended when in September 1533, Saint

---

[97] Ibid., 8–11.

[98] Ibid., 9.

[99] Ibid.

[100] Ibid., 6, 12.

[101] Ibid., 6.

[102] Ibid., 6, 12–14; St. Thomas More, *The Apology,* ed. J. B. Trapp, vol. 9 of *Complete Works of St. Thomas More* (New Haven: Yale Univ. Press, 1979), passim.

[103] Guy, "Battle of the Books", 17–20.

German published a reply to More's *Apology*—a work entitled *Salem and Bizance*. Framed as a dialogue, *Salem and Bizance* focused on refuting More's defense of antiheresy procedures.[104] It elicited an amazingly swift response from the ex-Lord Chancellor—*The Debellation of Salem and Bizance,* which was printed in October of the same year.[105] By this time More's literary career had already become a matter for governmental surveillance, as can be seen in a report to Cromwell by his servant Stephen Vaughan, who was dispatched to Antwerp in early August to learn what he could about underground English publications:

> Master More hath sent often times, and lately, books unto Peto in Antwerp, as his book of the confutation of Tyndale, and Frith his opinion of the sacrament, with diverse other books. I can no further learn of More his practices, but if you consider this well, you may perchance espy his craft.[106]

Further evidence that More's writings were considered suspect by the Henrician regime is provided by the fact that some months later, in January 1534, More's publisher, William Rastell, was questioned by Cromwell on false allegations that the ex-Lord Chancellor had penned a rebuttal of the December 1533 royal propagandists' tract *Articles Devised by the Whole Consent of the King's Most Honourable Council.*[107]

In the autumn of 1533 the matter of Elizabeth Barton, the "Holy Maid of Kent", of whose prophecies against Henry and Anne we have already spoken (in chapter 9), came to a head with the arrest of the nun and several of her highly vocal supporters.[108] More's prudent circumspection in his brief contacts with this self-proclaimed mystic were not enough to prevent his name from being raised in the course of Cromwell's investigations of her adherents.[109] The ex-Lord Chancellor was essentially a marked man ever since his conspicuous absence during the coronation rites and celebrations for Anne Boleyn in June. By early February 1534 More found it necessary to clear his

---

[104] Ibid., 6–7, 14–16.

[105] Ibid., 6, 16–17; St. Thomas More, *The Debellation of Salem and Bizance,* ed. John Guy et al., vol. 10 of *Complete Works of St. Thomas More* (New Haven: Yale Univ. Press, 1987).

[106] Guy, "Battle of the Books", 21 (spelling modernized).

[107] Ibid.

[108] Alan Neame, *The Holy Maid of Kent: The Life of Elizabeth Barton, 1506–1534* (London: Hodder and Stoughton, 1971), 237–53.

[109] Ibid., 297, 199.

name in the Barton case with a lengthy letter to Cromwell, carefully documenting all his contacts with the "Holy Maid" and her supporters; he even included a copy of a letter he had written her, a letter that had been eagerly sought for by the investigators.[110] Afterward Cromwell led More to believe that he was fully satisfied with this account of his conduct regarding the nun.[111] Nonetheless, on February 21 there was introduced in the House of Lords a Bill of Attainder against Elizabeth Barton, her principal supporters, and certain of her associates that included the name of More among those charged with misprision of treason.[112]

More took up his pen again to assert his innocence in the matter, writing this time not only to Cromwell but to the King himself. To the former More proposed that he would be willing to defend himself before the lords in Parliament.[113] In lieu of this he was summoned in late February or early March before four members of the King's Council: Archbishop Cranmer of Canterbury, the Duke of Norfolk Thomas Howard, "Master Secretary" Cromwell, and More's successor to the office of Lord Chancellor, Thomas Audley.[114] The meeting proved to be a most decisive one, the real purpose of which was to confront the King's old friend, not on the Elizabeth Barton case, but rather on Henry's "Great Matter".

Upon arriving, More found himself being offered honor and wealth galore—if he would but concur with the judgment of Parliament and the universities by declaring his approval for the divorce and remarriage of His Majesty. The proposition bore an uncanny resemblance to one More knew from the Scriptures: "All these I will give you, if you will fall down and worship me" (Mt 4:9). When More refused it, his interrogators' conviviality swiftly evolved into threats. The King, they said, had charged them to tell him that "never was there servant to his sovereign so villainous, nor subject to his prince so traitorous

---

[110] Ibid., 297, 299–300; for the text of More's letter, see letter no. 197, in Elizabeth Rogers, ed., *The Correspondence of Sir Thomas More* (Princeton, N.J.: Princeton Univ. Press, 1947), 480–88 (Rogers appears to date this letter too late).

[111] Neame, *Barton*, 300.

[112] Chambers, *More*, 297.

[113] For letter to Cromwell, see letter no. 195, in Rogers, *Correspondence*, 469–70; for letter to Henry VIII, see letter no. 198 in ibid., 488–91.

[114] Chambers, *More*, 297–98; Roper, *Lyfe*, 64–68.

as he."[115] Then came a real surprise: His Majesty was having more royal regrets, not unlike those over his first marriage to Catherine. This time it concerned the work he had written against the teachings of Luther, the *Defense of the Seven Sacraments,* which in 1521 had won him the title "Defender of the Faith" from Pope Leo X. The Council now introduced the King's accusation that it was More who had instigated him to write so strongly in defense of papal authority. Disgusted with the intimidating words and with the absurd falsehood of this latest charge, More angrily answered: "My lords, these terrors be arguments for children, and not for me."[116] As to the King's book, More recounted that he had done nothing more than answer some questions that his Sovereign had posed to him while writing it; afterward he had also prepared the index. As for the book's treatment of papal authority, it was More who at that time—prior to the revision of his own thoughts on the papacy—had advised the King that this subject be "more slenderly touched" in view of the possible conflicts that might arise between Henry and the Pope—in his capacity as head of the papal states—over such temporal affairs as political disagreements with the other countries in Europe. It was the King who despite More's advice had insisted, "We are so much bounden unto the See of Rome that we cannot do too much honor unto it."[117]

Of course we know that Henry's defense of papal primacy in his book against Luther was one of the contributing factors in the subsequent transformation of More's own understanding of the subject in the early 1520s. Thus in recalling this earlier conversation with the King, More was certainly not disavowing his own support of papal primacy; he was simply reporting the conversation as it actually took place. Confident that the King would remember what had transpired, More ended by assuring the Council, ". . . [H]is highness will never speak of it more, but clear me thoroughly therein himself."[118] He proved to be right—this accusation regarding the book was never raised again. But this by no means meant that the ex-Lord Chancellor would be left in peace.

With the interrogation over, More headed home on the Thames,

---

[115] Roper, *Lyfe,* 65–67 (quotation on 66–67).
[116] Ibid., 67.
[117] Ibid., 67–68.
[118] Ibid., 68.

accompanied by William Roper. Anxious to learn whether his father-in-law had succeeded in having his name removed from the Bill of Attainder, Roper anticipated good news in virtue of More's cheerful demeanor following the interview. When the two were finally alone in the garden at Chelsea, the younger man remarked, "I trust, Sir, that all is well because you be so merry." "It is so indeed, son Roper, I thank God," More replied. "Are you then put out of the Parliament bill?", Roper asked. "By my troth, son Roper, I never remembered it." "Never remembered it, Sir? A case that toucheth yourself so near, and us all for your sake. I am sorry to hear it; for I verily trusted, when I saw you so merry, that all had been well." "Wilt thou know, son Roper, why I was so merry?" "That would I gladly, Sir." "In good faith, I rejoiced, son, that I had given the devil a foul fall, and that with those Lords I had gone so far, as without great shame I could never go back again."[119] More's reference to the devil taking a "foul fall" certainly suggests that he had indeed seen in the commissioners' offer of riches and honor a similarity to Satan's third temptation of Christ in the desert (Mt 4:8–11). Perhaps he was remembering Giovanni Pico della Mirandola's advice to his nephew based upon this Gospel episode, advice that More had translated as a young man in his twenties:

> Remember that all the time of our life is but a moment, and yet less than a moment. Remember how cursed our old enemy is; which offereth us the kingdoms of this world, that he might bereave us the kingdom of heaven, how false the fleshly pleasures; which therefore embrace us, that they might strangle us. How deceitful these worldly honors; which therefore lift us up, that they might throw us down. How deadly these riches, which the more they feed us, the more they poison us.[120]

The joy that More expresses at this juncture is the key to understanding all his subsequent actions; in suffering for his refusal to accept neither Henry's divorce and remarriage nor his assertion of supremacy over the Church, he saw himself as being "persecuted for righteousness' sake" (Mt 5:10). Like the apostles who rejoiced "that they were counted worthy to suffer dishonor for the name" (Acts 5:41), More

---

[119] Ibid., 68–69.

[120] Letter of Pico to his nephew, July 2, 1492, appended to *Life of John Picus*, in *The Workes of Sir Thomas More Knight*, 17.

rejoiced that he had taken a stance from which there was no honorable way of backing down, no means of escape. The relevance of the latter Scripture passage (Acts 5) to More's circumstances is underscored in that it is raised in the same context by Pico della Mirandola in his words to his nephew regarding persecution.[121] Hence unwilling to presume himself worthy of suffering for Christ, More had hitherto done what he could to avoid danger; but as God had now brought him to this extremity, he was confident that He would safely see him through it.

When the King learned the outcome of the interrogation, he was enraged, demanding that More's name remain in the Bill of Attainder. But when on March 6 the House of Lords asked Henry for permission to hear More for themselves, the royal counselors became alarmed at the prospects of an embarrassing defeat and pressed the King to yield. In turn Henry proposed that he would go to the House of Lords himself, believing that his royal presence would intimidate the lords into submission regardless of the impact of More's testimony. It was only after the personal pleading of Lord Chancellor Thomas Audley, along with a contingent of other Parliament members, that His Majesty reluctantly backed down and allowed the removal of More's name from the bill. There would be other ways to pursue More, his advisors assured him.[122] Learning from Cromwell of his father-in-law's reprieve, William Roper sent word to his wife, Margaret, at Chelsea.[123] When she conveyed to her father what she thought to be good news, he soberly replied, "In faith, Meg, *quod differtur non aufertur*" ("What is postponed is not abandoned").[124]

It was not long after this that Thomas Howard, Duke of Norfolk and one of the four Council members who had attempted to pressure More, personally warned the ex-Lord Chancellor as a former friend that it was "perilous striving with princes". "*Indignatio principis mors est*" (the wrath of the prince is death), he reminded him. Howard failed to appreciate that he was dealing with a man who had thoroughly reflected upon the utterly inescapable reality of death. "Is that all, my Lord?", More answered. "Then in good faith is there no more

---

[121] Ibid., 15.
[122] Chambers, *More*, 299–300.
[123] Ibid., 300.
[124] Roper, *Lyfe*, 71; Farrow, *More*, 157.

difference between your grace and me, but that I shall die today, and you tomorrow."[125]

On March 23, 1534, the Pope finally announced the decision that Henry had at first so impatiently awaited but which he was now prepared to ignore—Rome's judgment on the royal wedding of 1509. Catherine's marriage to Henry was declared totally valid, and the King was once again ordered to separate from Anne Boleyn or face excommunication (the September 1533 deadline for separation had been earlier extended by the Pope through the intervention of the King of France, Francis I).[126] In England Parliament was at this time nearing its Easter recess, but before it adjourned on March 30, yet another new act touching the King's "Great Matter" was passed—the "Act for the establishment of the King's succession".[127] This statute demanded, not only that all Englishmen recognize any children born from the union of Henry and Anne as the legitimate successors to the English throne, but also that they must profess the earlier 1509 marriage of the King to Catherine to be both null and against divine law and instead recognize as valid the Boleyn marriage. The statute even presumed to prescribe doctrine by stating that *no one* had the authority to grant a dispensation from the laws of consanguinity—an obvious denial of papal authority to do so. Anyone writing or acting in opposition to the King, the Boleyn marriage, or the children of this union would be charged with high treason, which was at that time punishable by one of the worst forms of death penalty imaginable —"drawing and quartering"—execution by disemboweling and dismemberment. Those who were found *only* to have *spoken* against the King, the marriage, or the children would be charged with misprision of treason and sentenced to life imprisonment, additionally suffering the confiscation of virtually all their property.[128] As a test of loyalty to the demands it contained, the "Succession Act" provided for an oath to be taken by all, the text of which was appended to the letters patent accompanying the ratified bill:

---

[125] Roper, *Lyfe*, 71–72.

[126] Haigh, *English Reformations*, 117, 118.

[127] Ibid., 118; Geoffrey de C. Parmiter, "Saint Thomas More and the Oath", *Downside Review* 78 (Winter 1959/1960): 5, 9 (quoted title of act on 5, spelling modernized).

[128] Parmiter, "More and the Oath", 5–9.

Ye shall swear to bear your Faith, Truth, and Obedience, alonely to the King's Majesty, and to the Heirs of his Body, according to the Limitation and Rehearsal within this Statute of Succession above specified, and not to any other within this Realm, nor foreign Authority, Prince, or Potentate; and in case any Oath be made, or hath been made, by you, to any other Person or Persons, that then you to repute the same as vain and annihilate; and that, to your Cunning, Wit, and uttermost of your Power, without Guile, Fraud, or other undue Means, ye shall observe, keep, maintain, and defend, this Act above specified, and all the whole Contents and Effects thereof, and all other Acts and Statutes made since the Beginning of this present Parliament . . . So help you God and all Saints.[129]

The act ordered that those who refused to take the oath were to be charged with misprision of treason and punished accordingly. On March 30—Monday of Holy Week—the new oath was immediately administered to every member of Parliament; not one of the MPs declined.[130]

On April 12, the Second Sunday of Easter, Thomas More and his son-in-law William Roper came into London to attend the sermon at Saint Paul's Cathedral. Afterward the two went to Bucklersbury, the old home More had originally shared with his first wife, Jane, and where his adopted daughter, Margaret Gigs, now lived with her husband, John Clement. It was in this place, full of bittersweet memories from the past, that More was confronted with the visitation he and his family had been dreading. The King's men had evidently learned of his whereabouts and now served him with a summons to appear the following day at Lambeth Palace to take the oath. More calmly returned home to Chelsea and spent his last night as a free man with his family, preparing them and himself for an uncertain future. When morning came More went to confession and then to Mass, receiving Holy Communion as he was wont to do when facing important events in his life. William Roper is very sparing in his description of what must have been a highly emotional scene for the whole family when his father-in-law departed Chelsea for the final time. He does tell us that in leaving More did not permit his wife and children to

---

[129] Ibid., 10.
[130] Haigh, *English Reformations*, 118.

follow him farther than the front gate, which he closed himself.[131] With a face darkened by sorrow he boarded the boat for Lambeth with Roper and four servants. It was in the moist morning air out on the Thames that More seems finally to have regained his inner peace in facing his future:

> Wherein sitting still sadly awhile, at the last he suddenly rounded me in the ear, and said, "Son Roper, I thank our Lord the field is won." What he meant thereby I then wist not, yet loath to seem ignorant, I answered: "Sir, I am thereof very glad."[132]

It is More himself who in a letter to his daughter Margaret gives us a detailed account of what transpired upon his arrival at Lambeth Palace.[133] According to More, it was he who was called to appear before the commissioners first, even though others had arrived before him; moreover he was the only layman summoned. The commissioners included Archbishop Cranmer of Canterbury; William Benson, Abbot of Westminster; Thomas Audley, More's successor to the office of Lord Chancellor; and Thomas Cromwell. Upon being asked to take the new oath to the succession, More requested to see the text of both the Succession Act and its associated oath. After reading the documents to himself, he explained to the commissioners that while he intended to impugn neither those who had composed this legislation nor those who had already sworn to it, he himself could not in good conscience do so. Lest they doubt his motives he even offered to take a separate oath affirming that it was purely for reasons of his own conscience that he would not take the succession oath. At this reply Audley expressed dismay, telling him that he was the first person to refuse to swear and warning him that such a refusal could only incur the King's distrust and displeasure. The commissioners then showed More the roll of names of those who had already taken the oath, but to no avail—he would not swear to it. Perhaps at a loss as to what to do next with their respected detainee, they ordered More out into the

---

[131] Roper, *Lyfe*, 72–73; Thomas Stapleton, *The Life and Illustrious Martyrdom of Sir Thomas More*, ed. E. E. Reynolds (Bronx, N.Y.: Fordham Univ. Press, 1966), chap. 15, p. 145; Ro: Ba:, *The Lyfe of Syr Thomas More, Sometymes Lord Chancellor of England by Ro: Ba:*, ed. E. V. Hitchcock and Msgr. P. E. Hallett, Early English Text Society, original series, no. 222 (London: Early English Text Society, 1950), bk. 3, chap. 9, pp. 189–90.

[132] Roper, *Lyfe*, 73.

[133] Letter no. 200, in Rogers, *Correspondence*, 501–7. This letter was written on or around April 17, 1535.

garden to await further instructions. It must have been an extraordinarily warm spring day, for More tells us that instead of going into the garden itself, he tarried in a room adjoining it so as to shelter himself from the heat. While there he caught glimpses of some of the others who had been summoned, including the clergy attached to the Archbishop of Canterbury, as well as the radical preacher and future Bishop of Worchester, Hugh Latimer, whose unseemly joviality under the circumstances surprised More. Only one was sent to join the ex-Lord Chancellor, a priest named Nicholas Wilson, who had likewise refused the oath; he was dispatched directly to the Tower.

Undoubtedly suspecting that there was a purpose in having him witness the spectacle of jolly Hugh Latimer and the other cooperative clergymen, More tells his daughter that when "they had played their pageant",[134] he was summoned before the commissioners for a second round of pressuring, being told that in the interval since his earlier interrogation many more had gladly taken the oath (in case he had not noticed). After repeating his refusal in the same terms as before, More explained that his unwillingness to disclose the reasons for his refusal stemmed, not from obstinacy as they believed, but rather from his concern that such a disclosure could only anger the King further. He would rather risk incurring his own harm than displease his monarch more than he was compelled to in refusing the oath. As the commissioners persisted in accusing him of stubbornness, More proposed to them that if the King commanded him, he would be willing to put his reasons in writing, on the condition that what he disclosed could not be used against him. He would even be ready to take an oath promising that if after revealing his objections a man was found that could adequately refute his concerns to the satisfaction of his conscience, he would consent to take the succession oath.

To this the commissioners answered that no assurance of immunity from prosecution for his written disclosures could be given, to which More replied that in the absence of such assurances his silence could not be construed as due to obstinacy. One of the participants, Archbishop Cranmer, now took hold of More's earlier statement that he condemned the conscience of no one who had sworn. Interpreting this remark as an admission of uncertainty about his own stance

---

[134] Ibid., 504.

against the oath, Cranmer asked why he did not choose to follow
his known duty to obey his King rather than persist in acting upon
his own uncertain opinion regarding the oath. In relating this exchange to his daughter, More professes being caught a little off guard
by the subtlety of Cranmer's argument, although when he goes on
to state that he was also given pause by it coming from "so noble
a prelate's mouth",[135] we have good reason to suspect in his words
a mock seriousness, the touchstone of all of More's humor. To the
Archbishop he answered that he believed this particular issue was one
that took precedence over his obligation to his prince. In an effort to
dispel the impression that he was somehow unsure of his own conscience, he also told Cranmer that he had reached his judgment after
lengthy consideration and study. Ending on a remarkably audacious
note, More added that if one were to take to its logical conclusion
Cranmer's proposition of royal will having precedence over all else, it
would follow that disputed moral questions could simply be resolved
by having the King pronounce upon them.

The Abbot of Westminster, William Benson, tried one final stratagem with their detainee by warning him he had good reason to doubt
his own judgment in view of the consensus to the contrary in Parliament. More acknowledged that Benson's argument would be valid if
he were truly standing alone in his opinions. But in fact he was sure
that in at least some points regarding the oath he was acting in union
with the whole "general council of Christendom"[136] as opposed to
the council of just one country. At this point, in a sudden outburst,
Cromwell swore that he would sooner lose his own son than see
More reject the succession oath, adding that this refusal threatened to
flame the King's suspicions of More's involvement in the Elizabeth
Barton case. More replied that be this as it may, there was nothing
he could do without endangering his soul.

In the evening, after his second session with the King's commissioners had come to an unfruitful end, More learned that Bishop Fisher
had likewise been questioned that same day regarding the oath.[137]
Four days later—on April 17—the ex-Lord Chancellor was transferred

---

[135] Ibid., 505.
[136] Ibid., 506.
[137] Ibid., 504.

from Lambeth Palace to the vast fortress complex of the Tower of London, where in a dimly lit cell of the so-called "Bell Tower"[138] he began the final chapter of his life.

---

[138] Since around the time of World War I, the Bell Tower has generally been recognized as the actual site of More's cell, although there has also been a tradition linking More to the Beauchamp Tower. For a discussion of the evidence, see E. E. Reynolds, "More's Cell in the Tower", *Moreana* 5 (November 1968): 27–28.

Saint Thomas More's cell in the Bell Tower, Tower of London.

CHAPTER XII

"To Bear the Cross with Christ": More's Inner Life in the Shadow of Death

With his imprisonment at the Tower of London on April 17, 1534, the life of Thomas More had finally come full circle. The world that over thirty years earlier he had contemplated leaving for the service of God he was now forced to leave for the service of God. In a strange way it was a return to familiar surroundings—to a solitary life within the confines of a cell, not unlike the life he shared as a young man with the Carthusians of the Charterhouse. And in the months to follow, this place was indeed to become a Carthusian house of sorts, with the arrest and imprisonment of six Carthusian monks, four of whom were from the Charterhouse itself. Such parallels did not escape More, for in one of his conversations with his daughter Margaret he confided to her that had it not been for his wife and children he would have enclosed himself long before in a cell just as narrow as that in which he now found himself.[1] Even over the many years in the world, More had prepared himself for this return to solitude; in particular there were the Fridays spent alone in prayer, study, and penance in the "New Building" at Chelsea. But he was now facing something beyond solitude: the very real prospect of a gruesome death. King and Parliament were inexorably expanding the definition of just what constituted treason, and that widening definition would eventually encompass More. In Tudor England

---

[1] William Roper, *The Lyfe of Sir Thomas Moore, Knighte,* ed. Elsie V. Hitchcock, Early English Text Society, original series, no. 197 (London: Early English Text Society, 1935), 76.

327

conviction on a charge of treason usually meant a sentence of death by disemboweling and dismemberment—"drawing and quartering", as it was euphemistically called. The strength of More's spiritual life would now be tested as never before. Yet it was primarily because of this culminating challenge to his faith that he was compelled to reveal in writing more of the secrets of his inner life than he had ever done.

As we have already noted, throughout More's life we find three predominant themes in his spirituality: mature reflection upon the reality of death, a profound devotion to the mysteries of the sacred Passion, and a deep love for the Holy Eucharist. Although these three elements were quite representative of the Catholics of his age, they are particularly characteristic of More himself, a manifestation of Christian humanism at its very best. These themes dominate the corpus of spiritual writings that More produced shortly before and during his prolonged imprisonment: *A Dialogue of Comfort against Tribulation,* the *Treatise upon the Passion, A Treatise to Receive the Blessed Body of Our Lord,* and *De Tristitia Christi.* While it is certain that the *Dialogue of Comfort* and *De Tristitia Christi* were written in the Tower, it appears likely that at least part of the *Treatise upon the Passion* was written before More's arrest. The *Treatise to Receive the Blessed Body* seems to have been written after the latter work, but we cannot be sure whether it was composed in the Tower. Nonetheless, it is clear that all these writings were produced at a time when More was at the very least anticipating his arrest, if it had not already taken place. There are also a number of minor compositions, especially prayers and annotations to the Psalms, as well as a collection of selected Scripture passages, much of which has survived in More's own handwriting and which can be safely dated to the period of his imprisonment. His extraordinary correspondence in the Tower with his daughter Margaret and with his friends we will reserve for the final chapter. Insofar as there is a successive treatment of ideas in the *Treatise upon the Passion,* the *Treatise to Receive the Blessed Body,* and *De Tristitia Christi* that in a certain sense makes the three works a unified whole,[2] we will not disrupt this continuity. Rather, we will set aside strict chronological

---

[2] Garry Haupt, introduction to *Treatise on the Passion; Treatise on the Blessed Body; Instructions and Prayers,* vol. 13 of *Complete Works of St. Thomas More* (New Haven: Yale Univ. Press, 1976), cxxxix. Hereafter cited as *CW* 13.

order and begin with the *Dialogue of Comfort,* one of the two works certainly written in the Tower.

A Dialogue of Comfort against Tribulation

Undoubtedly the most widely disseminated of More's Tower writings (aside from a few of his letters) is his *Dialogue of Comfort against Tribulation.* As the title suggests, in this work More once again resorts to one of his favorite literary forms, the dialogue, with the conversation passing back and forth between an elderly man named Anthony and his nephew, Vincent. The setting is contemporary Hungary, with the younger man seeking advice from his uncle on how to face the imminent threat of conquest of his Christian country by Moslem Turkish invaders. There can be no doubt that Anthony represents More himself, and the counsel he gives is intended especially for the members of his family, who are represented by the figure of Vincent. In this light the *Dialogue of Comfort* takes on somewhat daring connotations with respect to More's own situation at the hands of his enemies, who would necessarily be associated with the Turkish invaders. In our exploration of this work we will set aside the details of its external dialogue structure in order to concentrate on its inner message, for the *Dialogue of Comfort* is both a rich treasury of spiritual wisdom and an amazing testament of how a man faces persecution and martyrdom for Christ. All the ideas that follow are More's own. From time to time we will deviate slightly from the order in which he presents his thoughts so as to bring related subject matter together.

More begins with man's end. Reflecting upon death, he observes that if death can quickly befall a man in his youth, it most certainly will not be long in coming upon a man advanced in years.[3] Reminding his readers of Christ's reassurances to His followers that He will never abandon them, More asks how we could be disconsolate in any trial knowing that the Holy Trinity "be never one finger breadth of space, nor one minute of time from you".[4]

---

[3] *A Dialogue of Comfort against Tribulation,* ed. Louis Martz and Frank Manley, vol. 12 of *Complete Works of St. Thomas More* (New Haven: Yale Univ. Press, 1976), preface, 3–4. Hereafter cited as *CW* 12.

[4] Ibid., 5.

In a telling reference to what he was witnessing in his own time, More notes the disconcerting fact that there is no nonbeliever who persecutes Christians as maliciously as do apostates from the Christian faith.[5] But whatever torments the persecutors of our faith in this life may devise for us, such things pale by comparison with the everlasting horrors of hell.[6]

More now resorts to an image of our Lord encountered frequently in the writings of Saint Augustine: that of Christ the Physician. It is to Christ, the great Physician, that we must ultimately turn for comfort, More explains. The "medicines" of comfort offered by the ancient Greek philosophers are of some help, but these men knew nothing of the most consoling explanation of human suffering—that it is a means of earning favor in the sight of God. Nor did the pagan philosophers know of the grace by which God supports us in enduring tribulation for His sake. Christ the Divine Physician heals our wounds of sin with the medicine of His own precious blood.[7] Likewise, by the medicines with which Christ treats our tribulations we will have the strength to resist the temptation to complaint and discontent with which Satan would draw us from the temporal pains of this life into the eternal death of damnation in the next.[8]

In seeking spiritual consolation in the face of tribulation, one must begin with a firm foundation of faith, More continues. Just as a man devoid of human reason cannot be expected to derive profit from the tenets of human reason, neither can a man without faith derive comfort from the Word of God if he has no faith in it. But we need not only faith but a strong faith; we must make our own the words from the Gospel, "I believe; help my unbelief!" (Mk 9:24), and the disciples' petition, "Increase our faith!" (Lk 17:5). In the garden of our soul we must clear away the weeds of earthly distractions that dissipate our mind and plant the mustard seed of faith, so that it will grow into a vigorous tree, the branches of which will bear the fruit of the virtues through the work of the birds that will come to dwell there—the angels. With such faith we will be able to command the

---

[5] Ibid., 7.
[6] Ibid., 8–9.
[7] Ibid., bk. 1, chap. 1, pp. 9–12.
[8] Ibid., 11–12.

mountain of tribulation to remove itself from our heart, and it will do so (Mt 17:19).[9]

The desire of consolation from God is itself a consolation, for we know that He to whom we have turned in our troubles is able to help us in virtue of His omnipotence, and He will definitely help us in virtue of His infinite goodness and His promise to grant whatever we ask of Him.[10] Of course, in genuinely seeking consolation from God, one must be willing to leave to God the way He chooses to comfort us, whether it be in the form of the actual removal or mitigation of our sorrows or in the bestowing of strength and patience to endure our tribulations.[11]

God uses tribulations to bring a soul to conversion and amendment of life, as he did when he threw Saint Paul from his horse and blinded him on the road to Damascus (Acts 9:1–19); in the aftermath it was God the Physician who healed Paul's soul and body.[12] In a related passage several chapters later in the *Dialogue,* a passage that brings to mind those clergymen who told Henry VIII what he wanted to hear about his pursuit of annulment and remarriage, More speaks critically of certain clerics who deliberately refrain from warning a rich and powerful man of the peril his soul is in out of fear of angering him and on the false premise that admonitions will do him no good.[13] With irony More notes that good men often fear the most the loss of that which those who are in greatest danger fear the least—the loss of their souls through deadly sin.[14]

While we may pray with confidence unconditionally for such spiritual goods as an increase in faith, hope, and love, our prayers for relief from tribulation must be expressed as contingent upon God's holy will. He knows far better than we do what is best for us. Indeed, God may very well chastise us by granting our foolish wishes when, failing to resign ourselves in our prayers to His will, we importune Him for what He knows is bad for us.[15] Rather than stiffly dictating

---

[9] Ibid., chap. 2, pp. 12–13.
[10] Ibid., chap. 3, pp. 15–16.
[11] Ibid., 16.
[12] Ibid., chap. 4, p. 17.
[13] Ibid., chap. 14, pp. 44–46.
[14] Ibid., chap. 6, p. 20.
[15] Ibid., 21–22.

to God only one acceptable answer to our prayers, we should let the Holy Spirit frame the particulars of our petitions, for as Saint Paul says, ". . . [W]e do not know how to pray as we ought, but the Spirit himself intercedes for us with sighs too deep for words" (Rom 8:26). And if in our troubles the Holy Spirit is at work within us, what have we to fear? As Saint Paul reassures us, "If God is for us, who is against us?" (Rom 8:31).[16]

Tribulations that arise from one's own sins and failings can be turned to good account, for though at first they come upon a man against his will, he may thereafter willingly suffer them as a penance for his transgressions. Through repentance and patient acceptance, such tribulations are transformed into a medicine for the soul, as were the sufferings of the good thief crucified with our Lord on Calvary.[17] Moreover, not only do these tribulations endured in this life (and joined to Christ's Passion) make reparation for our sins; the patient and submissive endurance of them also merits us a greater reward in heaven. This is true both of the penances given to us by our confessor in the sacrament of reconciliation and of those we choose additionally to take upon ourselves.[18]

There are also tribulations that come upon us for no clear reason, that do not appear to be a punishment for some particular sin. These God sometimes sends as a way of deterring us from a sin we might otherwise be tempted to commit. They serve as a preventative medicine, to preserve a man from the sickness of sin. Thus to a good man who is wealthy God may send tribulation as an antidote to the world's blandishments, so as to "set a cross upon the ship of his heart and bear a low sail thereon, that the boisterous blast of pride blow him not under the water".[19]

But there are also certain tribulations sent neither to punish past sins nor to prevent future ones. Rather, they give a person with a more or less clear conscience the opportunity to win merit in the sight of God through patient endurance, as in the case of a man suffering under false accusations because he will not abandon the cause of justice or truth when confronted with a situation "where white is called black

---

[16] Ibid., 22–23.

[17] Ibid., chap. 8, pp. 24–27.

[18] Ibid., chap. 11, pp. 35–36.

[19] Ibid., chap. 9, pp. 27–30.

and right is called wrong".[20] Those undergoing such trials should not hesitate to take comfort in Christ's promises of mercy to the merciful and the Kingdom of Heaven to those persecuted for righteousness' sake (Mt 5:7, 10).[21] The application to More's own circumstances is fairly obvious.

In a brief excursus addressing the dissenters' objections to the Catholic doctrines of Purgatory and good works, More laments the detrimental effects of dissent upon the unity of the Church, leaving her vulnerable to her enemies from without:

> . . . [I]t is a right heavy thing to see such variance in our belief rise and grow among ourselves to the great encouraging of the common enemies of us all, whereby they have our faith in derision and catch hope to overwhelm us all . . .[22]

As we have here no lasting city (Heb 13:14), we should seek happiness, not in this world, but rather in the next. In the words of Ecclesiastes, there is a time to sow and a time to reap (Qo 3:2); in this life we must sow, watering the seed we plant here with our tears, that we may reap with joy in heaven, thus fulfilling the words of the Psalmist, "He that goes forth weeping, bearing the seed for sowing, shall come home with shouts of joy, bringing his sheaves with him" (Ps 126:6). Hence why should we envy those who seem to suffer so little in this world, when we remember that God chastises those He loves (Heb 12:6)? If our Lord and Master suffered, how can we His servants expect not to? Christ has told us that if any man would be His disciple, he must take up his cross and follow Him (Mt 16:24). How, then, can those without tribulations enter heaven? In this sense, therefore, the presence of trials in our lives is itself a consolation in that it is a sign of God's favor.[23]

But if tribulation is so beneficial, is it proper to pray that we or others be delivered from it? More explains that just as God teaches us the value of enduring tribulations, He likewise teaches that we should pray and labor for deliverance from such things. Indeed, God's very purpose in sending us a trial may be to prompt us to turn to

---

[20] Ibid., chap. 10, pp. 30-33.
[21] Ibid., 34-35.
[22] Ibid., chap. 12, pp. 37-38.
[23] Ibid., chap. 13, pp. 40-44.

Him for help. Moreover, God clearly commands us to assist others in need.[24]

While tribulation is ordered by God to a man's good, a person may nonetheless choose to respond to suffering in a detrimental way by turning to the flesh, the world, or even Satan for the consolation he refuses to seek from God. Even when faced with the approach of death, some such individuals try to escape the pangs of guilt and the thought of damnation in hell by turning to earthly diversions—card games, for example. But death finally comes, and "what game they came then to, that God knoweth and not I."[25] Some there are who after a life of refusing to turn from their sins are goaded by the devil to despair as death nears and the thought of their guilt overwhelms them. If at one time such a man considered the terrors of hell a mere fable, he no longer believes it to be so. But were he still to doubt the reality of hell, he will soon enough discover for himself that it is no fable.[26]

Although those who are suffering are more inclined to turn to God than those enjoying prosperity, nonetheless prayer may come more easily for a person free of tribulation than for a person racked with physical or spiritual torments. Even so, the prayer of a suffering person, be it nothing more than the lifting of his heart to God without a word, is far more pleasing to God than any prayer made in ease. Such was the case with the martyrs.[27] And More believes that the greatest prayers of our Lord were those He made during His Passion—both in His agony in Gethsemane, "when the heaviness of his heart with fear of death at hand so painful and so cruel as he well beheld it, made such a fervent commotion in his blessed body, that the bloody sweat of his holy flesh dropped down on the ground", and in His anguish on the Cross, amid "all the torment that he hanged in, of beating, nailing, and stretching out all his limbs, with the wresting of his sinews, and breaking of his tender veins, and the sharp crown of thorn so pricking him into the head that his blessed blood streamed down all his face".[28] While it is true that a man experiencing prosperity can certainly please God by his gratitude, there is, nonetheless, a greater

---

[24] Ibid., chap. 17, pp. 56–58.

[25] Ibid., chap. 18, pp. 59–62.

[26] Ibid., 61.

[27] Ibid., chap. 19, pp. 64–66.

[28] Ibid., 66–67 (quotes on 67).

value in tribulation patiently endured than in earthly comforts innocently enjoyed, for the former, unlike the latter, can lessen our time
in Purgatory and increase our reward in heaven.[29]

Remembering that in his tribulation God is all the closer to him,
the sick man should seek comfort in God alone, trusting in Him and
looking to Him for help that he may resign himself to His holy will.
He should pray in his heart and ask his friends and the priests to pray
for him. But let him begin by receiving the sacrament of penance,
which makes us "clean to God and ready to depart and . . . glad to
go to God".[30] Tribulation leads us to set our hearts less upon this
world, so that when our end comes and God calls us, we will not
greet His invitation with clenched teeth, loath to go to Him. Rather,
if we love Him so much that we long to go to Him, we will assuredly
be welcomed by Him.[31]

At the beginning of the second part of the *Dialogue of Comfort,*
More tells an amusing tale of a brother and sister—the sister entering
a cloistered convent and the brother going away to a university. When
some time later the brother returned as a doctor of divinity, he went
to the convent to visit his sister, whose piety he deeply esteemed. As
was customary in cloistered religious houses, they could speak only
through a grill set up for the purpose. After a touching greeting of
the one taking hold of the finger of the other between the bars of
the grating, the sister began to exhort her brother as to the vanity
of the world and the temptations of the flesh and the devil, advising
him on how to live temperately so as to save his soul. In her zeal,
however, she spoke too long without even realizing it, until finally
she interrupted her discourse to ask why her learned brother was not
sharing any of his wisdom with her. "By my troth good sister," he
answered, "I can not for you, for your tongue have never ceased, but
said enough for us both."[32]

More divides tribulations into three categories: those we freely take
upon ourselves; those we do not voluntarily take but willingly accept;
and those we cannot escape no matter what we do.[33] There is no need
of consolation for tribulation freely chosen—that is, the sufferings we

---

[29] Ibid., 67–69.
[30] Ibid., chap. 20, p. 76.
[31] Ibid., 75–77.
[32] Ibid., bk. 2, preface, pp. 79–80.
[33] Ibid., chap. 3, p. 86.

willingly impose upon ourselves as a penance for our sins and out of love for God; the benefits to be obtained for the soul through these mortifications are themselves a source of comfort.[34] For those undergoing the pains of penance and remorse for past sins, there is consolation in the thought of "the goodness of God's excellent mercy, that infinitely passeth the malice of all men's sins, by which he is ready to receive every man, and did spread his arms abroad upon the cross lovingly to embrace all them that will come".[35] Thus did God show His mercy to the good thief, who repented only when he was unable to steal anymore, yet who in his conversion was greeted by our Lord with greater jubilation in heaven than ninety-nine righteous men.[36]

God's great mercy to sinners even at the point of death, as in the case of the good thief, should not be misunderstood as a pretext for sinning with impunity until death approaches. For those who wait to the end to repent, the reward will not normally be commensurate to what it would have been had they lived a virtuous life. True, there are some who after a late conversion earn so much merit during the rest of their lives that their reward may equal or even excel that of others who have lived longer in virtue—such was the case with Saint Paul. Even so, the grace of repentance is a gift from God, and no one should be presumptuous enough to think that he will necessarily receive this grace after a life of sin and indulgence.[37]

In this world we find it necessary to wrestle with the fallen angels as we fight off temptations from the world and its pleasures, from the flesh, from pain, from our enemies, and even from our friends. But the more we are tempted (without yielding), the greater will be our merit; thus it is that Saint James tells us the experience of temptations should be a cause for joy (James 1:2).[38]

More now introduces an image of God's protective love for us— that of a hen sheltering her chicks under her wing—obviously inspired by Christ's own use of this analogy as recorded in Matthew 23:37. Should any of His children deliberately wander from Him into danger, God will "clucketh [them] home unto him"[39] like a mother

---

[34] Ibid., chap. 4, pp. 87–90.

[35] Ibid., 90.

[36] Ibid.

[37] Ibid., chap. 5, pp. 91–92.

[38] Ibid., chap. 9, pp. 100–101.

[39] Ibid., chap. 10, pp. 103–4.

hen saving her chicks from the predator. According to the Psalmist, God "will cover you with his pinions, and under his wings you will find refuge" (Ps 91:4); under His wings will we find safety when tempted, for "against our will can there no power pull us thence nor hurt our souls there."[40] And it is under His sheltering wings that we shall rejoice (Ps 63:7).[41]

More's citation of Psalm 91 above reflects the extensive use he makes of this psalm throughout much of the *Dialogue of Comfort;* thus in the words (according to the Vulgate edition of the Bible in use at that time), "His truth shall compass thee with a shield . . ." (Ps 91[90]:4[5], Douay-Rheims translation), he finds an assurance that God will shield with His truth those who trust in His assistance. This shield totally compasses those it protects, More observes, for the threat from Satan is fourfold.[42] It is through the interpretation of the following two verses from Psalm 91 that More will identify and explain these four forms of temptation:

> You will not fear the terror of the night,
> nor the arrow that flies by day,
> nor the pestilence that stalks in darkness,
> nor the destruction that wastes at noonday.
>
> (Ps 91:5–6)

Tribulation is called by the Psalmist the "terror of the night" because its origin is often obscure and unknown and thus dark as night; tribulation also inspires fear, as does the night. Even as young lions roaming in the night can only prey upon what God gives them leave to (Ps 104:20–21), so will a man be safe from predators in the night of suffering, for no matter what may happen to his body, his soul will be protected as long as he puts his trust in God. In the darkness of tribulation our fear may give us false alarms, but whatever may frighten us in this night, we will be secure if we put our hope in God.[43]

Pusillanimity in dealing with the fear of the night of tribulation can lead to the affliction of scrupulosity, an inordinate fear of falling

---

[40] Ibid.
[41] Ibid., 105.
[42] Ibid., chap. 11, pp. 105–6.
[43] Ibid., chap. 12, pp. 107–11.

into sin that can make a person morbidly afraid in everything he does. Such scruples nag the soul continuously, depriving one of peace so that good works are performed with weariness, bereft of spiritual comfort. The devil uses scrupulosity to try to make good men so preoccupied with God's justice that they forget God's mercy and lose heart:

> Thus fareth lo the scrupulous person, which frameth himself many times double the fear that he hath cause, and many times a great fear where there is no cause at all. And of that that is in deed no sin, maketh a venial, and that that is venial, imagineth to be deadly, and yet for all that falleth in them, being namely of their nature such as no man long liveth without. And then he feareth that he be never full confessed, nor never full contrite, and then that his sins be never full forgiven him, and then he confesseth and confesseth again, and cumbereth himself and his confessor both. And then every prayer that he saith, though he say it as well as the frail infirmity of the man will suffer, yet is he not satisfied, but if he say it again and yet after that again, and when he hath said one thing thrice, as little is he satisfied at the last as with the first, and then is his heart evermore in heaviness, unquiet and in fear, full of doubt and of dullness without comfort or spiritual consolation. [44]

While scruples are indeed troublesome for a virtuous man to undergo, an excessively tender conscience is certainly preferable to a conscience that is overly lax. Indeed, one of the pitfalls of scrupulosity is that a person may by the machinations of the devil be driven from the one extreme to the other, passing from inordinate rigor to permissiveness. Hence, rather than relying solely upon his own lights, a scrupulous person should seek out the guidance of a virtuous man, and especially that of a priest in the confessional, for "there is God specially present with his grace assisting his sacrament." [45]

In his discussion of scruples More certainly appears to be speaking as one who knew of this tribulation from his own experience. Significantly, among the notes that we find written by More in the *Book of Hours* he used during his imprisonment (which we will be examining at length later in this chapter), there is inscribed alongside Psalm 13 the comment that "He who has scruples in confession and is not satisfied in his own soul should pray this psalm." [46] When one

---

[44] Ibid., chap. 14, pp. 112–13.

[45] Ibid., 114, 119–21.

[46] *Thomas More's Prayer Book: A Facsimile Reproduction of the Annotated Pages*, trans. and ed. Louis Martz and Richard Sylvester (New Haven: Yale Univ. Press, 1969), 191.

reads this psalm it immediately becomes clear how truly consoling its words are to those who have suffered this inner affliction:

> How long, O Lord?
> Wilt thou forget me for ever?
> How long must I bear pain in my soul,
> and have sorrow in my heart all the day?
> How long shall my enemy be exalted over me?
>
> Consider and answer me, O Lord my God;
> lighten my eyes, lest I sleep the sleep of death;
> lest my enemy say, "I have prevailed over him";
> lest my foes rejoice because I am shaken.
>
> But I have trusted in thy steadfast love;
> my heart shall rejoice in thy salvation.
> I will sing to the Lord,
> because he has dealt bountifully with me.

(Ps 13)

Having over the years had to counsel several distraught souls contemplating suicide, More now treats of this delicate subject in the *Dialogue,* explaining that the temptation to kill oneself can repeatedly assail certain men and women, but with grace and sound direction they are able to resist it.[47] Of course there are some who seek suicide out of pride or anger, but for these something other than consolation is needed to dissuade them from their intended self-destruction.[48] The theoretical question of how to deal with a person who proudly claims he is inspired by God to commit suicide provides More with an opportunity to present guidelines on the discernment of spirits. He explains that the authenticity of a purported vision or private revelation can be determined by several means, including the disposition of the alleged seer, the character of the claimed revelation, and the conformity of the revelation to the law of God and to the teachings of the Church. If the seer exhibits pride following his experience, or if the revelation is merely sensational, rather than geared in some identifiable way to be spiritually profitable, or if the revelation contradicts God's law, it cannot be considered as of divine origin.[49]

---

[47] *CW* 12, bk. 2, chap. 15, pp. 122–23.
[48] Ibid., 123–24.
[49] Ibid., chap. 16, pp. 131–36.

As to those tempted to suicide out of despair, particularly despair over a grave sin, they should be counseled to have courage and trust in God's mercy, seeing the fall that occasioned their despondency as a timely warning of the danger they were in. As penitent sinners they will be lifted to their feet by God, and so strengthened with His grace that for this one fall they have suffered at Satan's hands they will give the devil a hundred falls in the future. Thus should they be reminded of the penitents Mary Magdalen, King David, and particularly Saint Peter, who fell through presumption but who did not afterward despair of God's mercy, so that by his tearful repentance he was fully restored to God's favor.[50]

In stressing that those suffering from the temptation to suicide should not fear to approach the sacrament of penance, More gives sound advice that is applicable in fighting all temptations, observing that no matter how grievous the tempting thought may be, it will not become a sin if it is resisted and rejected and if the person tempted calls to God for help. In this latter regard he recommends that one invoke the intercession of his guardian angel and of the saints "such as his devotion specially stand unto". The prayers of others here on earth should also be requested, especially the prayers of priests celebrating the Mass.[51] More's desire to reassure and calm fearful souls leads him to offer these consoling words:

> . . . [T]here is no devil so diligent to destroy him as God is to preserve him, nor no devil so near him to do him harm as God is to do him good, nor all the devils in hell so strong to invade and assault him as God is to defend him . . .[52]

As to the content and forms of prayer in fighting temptation, More recommends especially reflection upon Christ's Passion and the use of verses from the Psalms, such as, "Let God arise, let his enemies be scattered; let those who hate him flee before him!" (Ps 68:1). He also highly recommends the Litany of the Saints, noting its venerable history in the worship of the Church. More sees the words of our Lord, "Begone, Satan!" (Mt 4:10), as particularly effective against the

---

[50] Ibid., 145–46.
[51] Ibid., 152–55.
[52] Ibid., 153.

devil, along with the final words of the Our Father, "and lead us not into temptation, but deliver us from evil."[53]

Building upon the key scriptural text for his *Dialogue of Comfort,* Psalm 91, More identifies pride as "the arrow that flies by day" (Ps 91:5)—the arrow that appears during the short winter's day of our prosperity, raising us rapidly and then just as quickly plunging us back to earth. During that brief space when the arrow of pride bears us aloft, we haughtily look down upon our fellow men, yet the archer who shoots this arrow into our hearts is none other than Satan himself, whose intent is that when it inevitably falls back it will take us down into hell, just as it took him there.[54]

The temptation to pride amid prosperity is a real affliction for good men. Sometimes out of a pusillanimous fear of succumbing to pride, a good man in a high position may begin to neglect the duties of his state in life, mistakenly thinking that he must necessarily escape his prosperous circumstances in order to keep from offending God. True, for those who perceive they are unable to accomplish any good in a high position, which they find to be nothing more than a danger to their own souls, it is prudent for them to withdraw from their privileged station.[55] When, however, the latter is not the case, such a person should "temper his fear with good hope, and think that since God hath set him in that place (if he think that God have set him therein) God will assist him with his grace to the well using thereof."[56] Let him exercise mercy generously when called upon to administer justice and consider the poor his equals, for like them he entered the world poor and will leave it poor. Let him remember "the fearful pains of hell and the inestimable joys of heaven" and "use often to resort to confession", where he may lay open his heart to his confessor, who will remind him of all these things.[57] Moreover, let him sequester himself from time to time in prayer before an image of Christ in His Passion, where he may reflect upon his own sins as well as upon the blessings that God has bestowed upon him. Lamenting his weakness in the face of temptations from the flesh, the devil, the world, and

[53] Ibid., 155–56.
[54] Ibid., 157–60.
[55] Ibid., 160–61.
[56] Ibid., 161–62 (quote on 162).
[57] Ibid., 162–64 (quote on 164).

even from his friends, let him beg God in His mercy both to help
him resist and, should he fall, to rise and return to a state of grace.
He who does these things will undoubtedly be heard by God and
be preserved from spiritual harm in his high estate, where he will
perform his duties most beneficially.[58]

More now identifies "the pestilence that stalks in darkness" (Ps
91:6) as the devil who tempts us in two particular periods of spiritual
darkness—that of a soul on the verge of the dawn of grace and that of
a soul on the verge of falling from grace. This devil tempts souls with
insatiable carnal and worldly desires, drawing them into the darkness
where they cannot find their way (Jn 12:35). They wander, as it were,
in a maze, the center of which (should they come upon it) is hell itself.[59] Such was the case in our Lord's parable of the rich man who
stored up riches for himself, unaware that his life was about to end so
suddenly (Lk 12:16–21). Ironically, those meandering in this darkness
suffer many pains in the pursuit of their short-lived pleasures.[60]

As to the just who are blessed with earthly riches, they suffer the
tribulation of fear that they will succumb to the temptations of the
"pestilence that stalks in darkness". What is essential is not that they
dispossess themselves of all their property, but rather that they should
spiritually detach themselves from these material things and be willing to share at least some of their wealth with the poor. Yet how can
a rich man in good conscience keep *any* excess wealth for himself
in view of all the poor in the world? After pointing out that Christ
did not reproach the repentant tax collector Zacchaeus for pledging
the half rather than the whole of his riches to the needy (Lk 19:1–
10), More proceeds to argue against the concept of the collective
distribution of all wealth, noting that the existence of at least some
wealthier individuals in a society is actually necessary for the material
support of the poorer citizens, who often earn their livelihoods with
jobs that can be created only by men with the capital to undertake
such projects (as, for example, building construction).[61] Moreover,
our Lord's words, "Give to him who begs from you" (Mt 5:42),
should not be interpreted so literally that one ought to feel obliged to

---

[58] Ibid., 164–65; for a direct quotation from this passage, see chapter 2 of the present work.

[59] *CW* 12, bk. 2, chap. 17, pp. 166–68.

[60] Ibid., 168–69. For an amusing anecdote from this passage regarding Dame Alice, see chapter 2 of the present work.

[61] *CW* 12, bk. 2, chap. 17, 169–81.

give every single time he is asked, without any regard to how urgent the particular request is or whether the person asking is genuinely in need. Of course, we are always obliged to give when the need is urgent, whether the needy person is a friend or an enemy, but there are certain individuals to whom our obligations are greater—most especially, our own family.[62]

In the third part of the *Dialogue of Comfort,* More addresses what he considers the most dangerous of temptations for a just man: persecution for the faith—"the destruction that wastes at noonday" (Ps 91:6). Unlike other temptations, which come upon us stealthily in the night, this one Satan boldly launches against us openly amid the bright daylight of faith. Persecution is a particularly hazardous challenge, because it brings upon us at the same time both the allure of ease and comfort if we renounce our faith and the dread of torture and death if we remain steadfast in our religion. Unlike other sufferings that we cannot escape no matter how we respond to them, persecution tests us to a far greater degree in that we are offered a release from our pains if we deny our faith.[63]

More now begins to consider one by one the things that men fear the loss of in persecution (aside from life itself and one's freedom, which he will treat later): material possessions, fame, and authority. Material possessions in and of themselves add nothing to a man. And when one considers how readily whole kingdoms and empires fall or slip from the hands of one leader to another, how can anyone set much value on whatever accumulation of wealth he may happen to possess?[64] Why should we waste our love on possessions we can so easily lose and which only bring us anxiety over the possible loss thereof?[65] There are some who think of the land they own as a more permanent possession than other riches, as it is immovable and cannot be carried away. But they forget that while the land is immovable, they themselves are not, for they can be driven from their land, which they cannot take with them. To illustrate this point, More resorts to a clever personification of the land belonging to a prince, imagining what it might say about its owner's foolhardy ambitions:

---

[62] Ibid., 181–84.

[63] Ibid., bk. 3, chap. 2, pp. 200–201.

[64] Ibid., chap. 5, pp. 206–7.

[65] Ibid., chap. 6, pp. 208–9.

. . . [H]ow the ground on which a prince buildeth his palace, would loud laugh his lord to scorn, when he saw him proud of his possession, and heard him boast himself, that he and his blood are for ever the very lords and owners of that land, for then would the ground think the while in himself, ah thou silly poor soul, that weenest thou were half a god, and art amid thy glory but a man in a gay gown, I that am the ground here over whom thou art so proud, have had an hundred such owners of me as thou callest thyself, more than ever thou hast heard the names of. And some of them that proudly went over my head lie now low in my belly and my side lieth over them. And many one shall as thou doest now call himself mine owner after thee, that neither shall be akin to thy blood, nor any word hear of thy name. Who owned your castle Cousin three thousand years ago?[66]

There is great folly in desiring earthly possessions merely for the enjoyment of the present life. Such things actually bring us more pain than pleasure, what with "the labour in the getting, the fear in the keeping, and the pain in the parting from". Some wealthy men are slain for the riches they possess. Others never get to enjoy their riches, since they keep them out of sight under lock and key or buried in the ground, and thus "for fear lest thieves should steal it from them" they "be their own thieves and steal it from themselves."[67]

Another coveted possession is that of fame, the esteem and recognition of others. Yet such adulation constitutes nothing more than the "blast of another man's mouth"; to take pleasure in such accolades is to feed oneself with nothing but "wind". In his folly a person may imagine he is the subject of constant praise among others. But in reality, many of those he thinks go about talking of him never mention him at all. And even if there are those who speak well of him, they do not do so constantly or to every person they meet, as he would like to think. There are surely also those who speak ill of him or who praise him to his face while attacking him behind his back.[68] More relates the amusing story of a vainglorious prelate (suspiciously reminiscent of the late Cardinal Wolsey) who after delivering an oration asked those who came to dine with him that same day what they thought of his discourse, anxiously awaiting their flattery.[69] Nor

---

[66] Ibid., 207–8.

[67] Ibid., chap. 8, p. 210.

[68] Ibid., chap. 9, pp. 211–12.

[69] Ibid., chap. 10, pp. 213–16.

did they disappoint him, for each lavished his choicest praises upon his host's words. But by the time the last of them had his turn to speak—a learned ecclesiastic—there was no accolade left to bestow that had not already been used by the others. Yet he cleverly found a way to give his egotistical host precisely what he wanted without words:

> . . . [B]ut as he that were ravished unto heavenward, with the wonder of the wisdom and eloquence that my lord's grace had uttered in that oration, he brought forth a long sigh with an "Oh!" from the bottom of his breast, and held up both his hands, and lift up his head, and cast up his eyes into the welkyn [the heavens], and wept.[70]

While those seeking praise may ask others to be truthful with them, they cannot brook hearing the truth if it proves to be anything other than complimentary. Yet it is a truthful advisor that they should value over any flatterer. While criticizing the love of adulation, More also finds fault with those who through envy or coldness neglect to commend a man's genuinely good actions.[71]

In addition to property and fame, men also desire authority, but this too is a vain pursuit. The cares and obligations of being in a position of authority scarcely make such a lot in life worth pursuing. Those who attain great offices often lose their lofty status as quickly as they achieve it, and even when this is not the case, they invariably lose their coveted station soon enough through death.[72]

The anxious desire of earthly goods merely for one's own pleasure is reason enough to prefer the loss of such things to their attainment, for even though wealth, fame, and high office are innocuous in and of themselves, the worldly ambition to obtain them usually presages their misuse when ultimately attained. Thus, those anxious for authority are wont to abuse it when it is given to them; and those who long for material wealth are likely either to hoard whatever they do receive or to waste it on ostentatiousness and self-gratification.[73] Of course, those desirous of earthly goods only for their own pleasure will not admit this to be their intention but rather would have others think that they want these things in order to accomplish some higher

---

[70] Ibid., 215–16.
[71] Ibid., 217–19.
[72] Ibid., chap. 11, pp. 219–23.
[73] Ibid., chap. 12, pp. 223–25.

purpose. Nonetheless, persecution serves as a touchstone to reveal who is genuinely motivated by the desire to serve God in acquiring and using possessions and who is not. The former will be content to lose their goods rather than renounce their faith, whereas the latter will not.[74]

More now fields the question of whether it is permissible to escape persecution by compromising only some of our Christian beliefs.[75] His answer is a resounding No. Saint Paul asks how there can be any accommodation between darkness and light, between Christ and Belial (2 Cor 6:14–15), and our Lord Himself has stated in the Gospels that we cannot serve two masters (Mt 6:24). No, Christ will not countenance followers who make any exceptions whatsoever in their loyalty to Him:

> He will have you believe all that he telleth you and do all that he biddeth you, and forbear all that he forbiddeth you, without any manner exception. Break one of his commandments and break all; forsake one point of his faith, and forsake all, as for any thanks you get of him for the remnant.[76]

The blandishments of persecutors should not deceive us; if they seem to ask us to compromise relatively little now, they will ask for more later. Moreover, how can we be sure that any promise of security they make if we renounce our faith will be subsequently honored by them?[77] Even if a persecutor will honor his promise, how can our riches secured at the cost of displeasing God be safe from God's power to remove them if He so wills? Life is all too short; how long can we then expect to enjoy the riches we have salvaged by denying Christ? And when death invariably comes, not only will there be the sorrow of finally having to be parted from our possessions anyway, but far worse will be the grim and everlasting reality of our punishment in hell. Thus our Lord set at nought all consideration of renouncing Him for the sake of worldly goods when He asked what it would profit a man if he gained the whole world and lost his soul in the process (Mt 16:26).[78]

---

[74] Ibid., chap. 13, pp. 225–27.

[75] Ibid., chap. 14, pp. 229–31.

[76] Ibid., 230.

[77] Ibid., 231–33.

[78] Ibid., 233–37.

In the face of the impending loss of our possessions to the hands of persecutors, where should we hide them so that they may be safe? There is only one place where our goods will be totally secure, where the only thieves who can enter are those who have put all theft behind them to become righteous men. As our Lord Himself tells us, this place is heaven, in which our treasures will be free from corruption and where our hearts along with our treasures will be (Mt 6:19–21). For just as we would here on earth send our goods out of the land we were about to be driven from to the land where we expected to live the rest of our lives, much more so should we send them ahead to heaven, where we hope to spend all eternity. We can deposit our goods in heaven by putting them into the hands of the poor, for in doing so we put them into the hands of Christ Himself. There is also the consideration that as our worldly possessions grow up like weeds and brambles in the "ground of our hearts", strangling the Word of God sown there (Mt 13:22), our persecutors serve God's purpose in uprooting these weeds and brambles from our hearts by taking them away, so that the seed of God's Word is able to grow unhindered, warmed by the sunlight of grace.[79]

In dealing with the loss of possessions for Christ, we should also reflect that our Lord Himself suffered poverty for our sake. For throughout His life on earth He lived poorly without goods, lands, or high worldly office, so that we could be rich in heaven.[80]

But how does one overcome the fear of having to face possible torture or a painful death in a time of persecution? The answer is to be found in Christ's own sacred Passion—by contemplating "his great grievous agony".[81] If we are willing, our Lord will give us the grace to submit to His will as He did to His Father's will in Gethsemane, and we will be comforted by the Holy Spirit as He was comforted in the Garden by the angel. In this way will we be able to follow Christ and to "die for the truth with him".[82] If the thought of torture and death fills us with dread, this most certainly does not mean that we will fail when the time of trial comes; indeed, those who have experienced such fear beforehand have often stood their ground more firmly than those who seemed fearless at the outset. Moreover,

[79] Ibid., chap. 15, pp. 238–42.
[80] Ibid., chap. 16, p. 243.
[81] Ibid., chap. 17, p. 245.
[82] Ibid., 245–46.

God does not call all to martyrdom; hence, for some He provides that they will escape being put to the test lest they fail in the time of trial. Others He saves from the tortures of martyrdom by calling them from this life while they are still in prison awaiting their fate. There are still others whom He allows to undergo torture, but whose lives are subsequently spared, as (it is believed) was the case with Saint John the Evangelist. More takes comfort in Saint Paul's reassurance that God will not allow us to be tested beyond our strength (1 Cor 10:13).[83]

Persecutors may take us into captivity far from our native land, yet if our hearts are fixed upon God alone, this cannot really shake us, for God will be as close to us in a distant country as He is in our own. And how can separation from our own nation make us overwrought when we remember that on earth we are only pilgrims and that we have here no lasting city (Heb 13:14)? As to the loss of personal freedoms under the reign of a persecutor, are we not already enslaved somewhat by our sins? And was our time really employed so much more wisely when we were free than it is now that we are in bondage? Actually, the oppressive rule of persecutors is an opportunity provided by Divine Providence for us to gain merit with God and atone for our sins through our sufferings. For our sakes Christ was willing to humble Himself and take on the form of a slave. How, then, can we abandon Him who died to free us from the tyranny of Satan and refuse to endure a short period of bondage in return for the eternal freedom He has won for us?[84]

Returning to a concept found in two of his earlier writings, More now fully develops his analogy comparing the earth to a vast prison into which all enter under a sentence of physical death incurred through original sin. In this life the pains of sickness can restrict a man every bit as much as bindings on one's hands and feet in a narrow prison cell. With this in mind, we need not so greatly dread the possibility of imprisonment for our faith, for in a sense we are prisoners already. The fact that an actual prison allows us far less freedom of movement than does the "prison" of the world should not really trouble us; indeed, there are those who have willingly and con-

---

[83] Ibid., 246–48.
[84] Ibid., chap. 18, pp. 250–55.

tentedly embraced a life of close confinement by entering cloistered religious orders such as those of the Carthusians, the Brigittines, and the Poor Clares.[85] To make his point further, More tells of an amusing conversation that took place between a prisoner and a woman who came to visit him. There can be little doubt that what follows is nothing other than the substance of a real exchange between More and his wife, Dame Alice, that occurred while he was in the Tower, "in a chamber to say the truth meetly fair and at the least wise it was strong enough":

> . . . [A]mong many other displeasures that for his sake she was sorry for, one she lamented much in her mind, that he should have the chamber door upon him by night made fast by the gaoler that should shut him in. For by my troth quoth she, if the door should be shut upon me, I would ween it would stop up my breath. At that word of hers the prisoner laughed in his mind, but he durst not laugh aloud nor say nothing to her. For somewhat indeed he stood in awe of her, and had his finding there much part of her charity for alms, but he could not but laugh inwardly, while he knew well enough that she used on the inside to shut every night full surely her own chamber to her, both door and windows too, and used not to open them of all the long night. And what difference then as to the stopping of the breath, whether they were shut up within or without.[86]

Those afraid of imprisonment for their faith can take comfort in the fates of such biblical figures as Joseph, who, after lying in prison while his brothers walked free, subsequently became their support when they faced famine (Gen 37–45), and Daniel, who found freedom after surviving confinement in a den of lions (Dan 6:16–24).[87] But even if we cannot bring ourselves to think God will spare us in this manner, He will either surely spare us in some other way or grant us the greater privilege of dying for Him as did John the Baptist:

> Saint John the Baptist was (you wot well) in prison while Herod and Herodias sat full merry at the feast, and the daughter of Herodias delighted them with her dancing, till with her dancing she danced off Saint John's head, and now sitteth he with great feast in heaven at God's board,

---

[85] Ibid., chaps. 19–20, pp. 255–77.
[86] Ibid., chap. 20, p. 277.
[87] Ibid., 279.

while Herod and Herodias full heavily sit in hell burning both twain, and to make them sport withal, the devil with the damsel dance in the fire afore them.[88]

Finally we should remember that throughout His Passion our Lord was a prisoner for us; how can we refuse then to suffer imprisonment for Him? It is the ultimate folly to seek escape from a short imprisonment by denying Christ, only to suffer eternal imprisonment in hell.[89]

Addressing the fear of death itself, More notes that even in his own time there is a fairly large number of those who do not believe in an afterlife and hence dread death as the end of everything. Others fear death because after having lived sinfully they despair of any hope of salvation. Then there are those who, though they believe in life after death and want to be saved in the end, are nonetheless unwilling to detach themselves from the pleasures of this world, nor do they wish to relinquish these things until the very last moment.[90] As for those who are faithful to God, there are two fears associated with death to which even they are not immune—fear of pain and fear of shame. Yet whatever disgrace and degradation we undergo at the hands of a relative handful of persecutors cannot compare with the support accorded us by Christ and the host of His saints as they gaze upon us in our agony. Indeed, it is a glorious honor to die for Christ, as Scripture tells us: "Precious in the sight of the Lord is the death of his saints" (Ps 116:15).[91] Moreover, how can we be so proud as to refuse to undergo shame for the Lord our Master, who for us willingly underwent what was in His time accounted the most shameful and degrading form of death? Consider what shame and pain together Christ endured when He was crowned with such sharp thorns "that the blood ran down about his face", and after being given a reed as a scepter, He was subjected to the mock genuflections of His tormentors, who "beat then the reed upon the sharp thorns about his holy head".[92] A little later in the *Dialogue,* More will return to the thought of our Lord's Passion with even greater force, giving us an idea of

---

[88] Ibid.
[89] Ibid., 279–80.
[90] Ibid., chap. 22, pp. 283–87.
[91] Ibid., chaps. 22–23, pp. 287–91.
[92] Ibid., 291–92.

his own lifelong reflections upon this mystery by providing his most graphic depiction yet of Christ's agonizing torments on Good Friday (see the quotation of this passage in chapter 2).

Reason tells us that the enduring of a temporary pain is worthwhile if by it a greater good is gained thereof; such is the case with certain medical treatments (such as the surgical procedures in More's own day) that a reasonable man will willingly undergo. Should not, then, reason building on the foundation of faith enjoin us to accept a painful death in order to attain the eternal joys of heaven and escape the unending pains of hell?[93]

As to the terrible physical pains that can come with martyrdom, More now addresses the question of whether it is better to placate one's persecutors by exteriorly pretending to renounce the faith while interiorly continuing to adhere to it, and thereby escape the risk of faltering during torture and dying thereupon in apostasy. More finds such reasoning utterly unsound, comparing it to an unstable three-legged stool that collapses as soon as anyone attempts to sit upon it. In this analogy the three legs symbolize obsessive fear, false faith, and false hope. To begin with, it is absurd to think that the profession of one's faith in the face of persecution is a risky proposition, as if God would leave a person unaided and fail to grant him the grace to repent, abandoning him summarily to damnation, if he faltered while suffering for Him. Furthermore, those who deny their faith exteriorly have a false faith, no matter what they may claim to profess interiorly. Finally, it is nothing less than a presumptuous and false hope to assume that if we deny Christ for the present in order to satisfy our persecutors, we can count on the grace of reconciliation with God when the threat of persecution has passed. Nor can we count upon suffering an easier death thereafter, for natural death can be just as painful, if not more so, in its duration and intensity than violent death.[94]

The horrible end of those who renounce their faith to escape martyrdom becomes all the more evident when it is remembered that the pains of those who die in apostasy are but the prelude to the endless torments they will suffer in hell.[95] Yet few realize that hell is actually

---

[93] Ibid., chap. 24, pp. 292–94.

[94] Ibid., chap. 24, pp. 297–302.

[95] Ibid., chap. 25, pp. 302–4.

a manifestation of God's mercy to us—a means for directing our steps here on earth toward heaven:

> But surely God in that thing wherein he may seem most rigorous is very merciful to us, and that is (which many men would little ween) in that he provided hell. For I suppose very surely Cousin, that many a man and woman too, of whom there now sit some, and more shall hereafter sit full gloriously crowned in heaven, had they not first been afraid of hell, would toward heaven never have set foot forward.[96]

In view of our carnal fallen nature, which appreciates fleshly pleasures far more readily than spiritual joys, it is no surprise that we find the dread of the pains of hell a more compelling reason to remain faithful to God than the anticipation of the happiness of heaven. Yet we should strive to purify our affections so as to direct our hearts more toward the delights of the spirit than toward those of the flesh. If we succeed in doing so, the hope of "the sight of God's glorious majesty face to face" will give us greater solace and more incentive to suffer for Christ than any fears of hell can.[97]

Through prayer, spiritual reading, and meditation let us therefore kindle within ourselves a yearning for the surpassing joys of heaven. The man of the world thinks he cannot bring himself to desire anything other than the satiation of his carnal pleasures, yet it is obvious even from the experience of illness in this life how the cravings of the body can be turned to revulsion; how much more so in the next life will those fleshly gratifications that seemed so enjoyable here be viewed with loathing.[98] By contrast, so immense and beyond our imagining are the joys of heaven that even those of the most extraordinary sanctity in this life can know only the faintest taste of what awaits us, for no one while still on earth can experience the beatific vision. More directs our attention to the words of Isaiah (64:4) that Saint Paul reiterates in his First Letter to the Corinthians: ". . . [N]o eye has seen, nor ear heard, nor the heart of man conceived, what God has prepared for those who love him . . ." (1 Cor 2:9). But if these are to be the joys of every soul who enters heaven, even greater will be the reward of those who die for Christ, for as our Lord tells us, "To him who conquers I will grant to eat of the tree of life . . ."

---

[96] Ibid., chap. 26, p. 305.

[97] Ibid., 305–6.

[98] Ibid., 306–8.

(Rev 2:7). Despite all the tribulations he underwent, Saint Paul accounted his sufferings but little in comparison to the "eternal weight of glory" to come (2 Cor 4:17). Thus if we too are to attain this glory, we must be willing to follow Christ our Divine Head on the same path by which He walked into heaven—the path of suffering.[99]

If human lovers are so froward as to be willing even to die for their beloved without hope of any reward, so much more should we be willing to die for Christ, who will reward us for all eternity. If pagans have willingly endured terrible pain and death for the sake of their countries' defense or honor, merely to attain posthumous worldly renown, should not we be ready to do as much for Christ and thereby attain eternal honor and glory in heaven? And if even heretics have died for vainglory rather than recant, how shameful it would be if Catholics refused to lay down their lives for the true faith.[100]

In the closing pages of the *Dialogue of Comfort*, More sets before our eyes a vision of persecutors ranged before us—a formidable sight until he has us, on the one hand, consider the fiery depths of hell opening all about our feet, the only alternative left to us if we refuse to suffer for our faith (when called upon to do so), and, on the other hand, the ravishing beauty of "the Trinity in his high marvelous majesty, our Saviour in his glorious manhood sitting on his Throne, with his Immaculate mother and all that glorious company calling us there unto them"[101] if we remain constant. Upon beholding such a sight, what man would not gladly hazard a torturous death to reach heaven? As to our persecutors, let us remember that it is really not they but the devil himself with whom we are in battle, for it is he who seeks to devour us and can do so if we fall. What man, More asks, would distract himself over the bite of a pet dog when threatened by a lion? Even so, the devil can have no power whatsoever over us if we stand up to him, as Saint James tells us (James 4:7), for our strength in battling Satan comes, not from ourselves, but from Him who has already vanquished him—our Lord Jesus Christ. Hence how can we doubt God will sustain us in our weakness when we consider the vast number of martyrs, many of whom were no stronger than we

---

[99] Ibid., 308–11.
[100] Ibid., chap. 27, pp. 313–14.
[101] Ibid., 315.

are? Some of them were mere children. The strongest martyrs were nonetheless unable to endure their trials without the support of God, and the weakest among them found in God enough strength to stand up against the whole world.[102]

More's Scriptural Annotations and Prayers

In the sixteenth chapter of the second book of his *Dialogue of Comfort against Tribulation,* More offers a significant recommendation to those suffering from temptation: "Special verses may there be drawn out of the *psalter* against the devil's wicked temptations . . . which are in such horrible temptation to God pleasant, and to the devil very terrible."[103] In these words the reader senses an autobiographical revelation of the writer's own inner life, and with good reason. We are fortunate in that More's personal copy of the *Book of Hours* (an abbreviated version of the Breviary) has survived the ravages of time, revealing in a most remarkable and personal way the inner struggles of the saint during the fourteen and a half months of his imprisonment. For it is on the pages of this prayer book that we find written in the margins a series of annotations in More's own hand, some in the form of comments, others simply lines or cryptic, flag-shaped marks that draw attention to a particular verse or sequence of verses in the Psalms. From an examination of the passages delineated in this manner a picture emerges of a man seeking consolation and strength from God in the face of isolation, temptation, and dread.[104]

The notations apply various psalm verses to a multitude of personal vicissitudes: temptation, sickness, imprisonment, scruples, and slander. Even when a selected verse is highlighted with nothing more than a line, it is seldom difficult to understand the reason why More finds it particularly relevant to his own circumstances, as with the following from Psalm 27: "Though a host encamp against me, my heart shall not fear; though war arise against me, yet I will be confident" (Ps 27:3). Many verses are simply labeled as applicable to "tribulation". Not surprisingly, a preponderant number of the notations and markings touch upon the psalms traditionally associated with our Lord's

---

[102] Ibid., 315–18.

[103] Ibid., bk. 2, chap. 16, p. 156.

[104] *Thomas More's Prayer Book,* 189–203.

Passion, the subject of so much of More's thought; he could now understand as never before the sufferings the Psalmist describes. We see this especially with Psalm 38, so clearly a prophecy of the Passion that it has been used in the Divine Office of Good Friday for centuries. It is this psalm that elicits More's longest annotation (in the passages to follow, More's own words are given in italics):

> *A meek man ought to behave in this way during tribulation; he should neither speak proudly himself nor retort to what is spoken wickedly, but should bless those who speak evil of him and suffer willingly, either for justice' sake if he has deserved it or for God's sake if he has deserved nothing.*[105]

The psalm (22) that our Lord Himself quotes from while upon the Cross likewise receives considerable attention from More:

> *in [the time of] suffering with disgrace:* But I am a worm, and no man; scorned by men, and despised by the people (Ps 22:6).[106]

> *against demons:* Yea, dogs are round about me; a company of evildoers encircle me . . . (Ps 22:16).[107]

No word appears more frequently in More's annotations than "demons", identifying verses that he sees as invocations against their pernicious influence. As we have already seen in the *Dialogue of Comfort against Tribulation*, More attributed to the fallen angels a major role in tempting troubled souls, and there can be no doubt that while awaiting his fate in the Tower he considered himself truly under siege from "demons" in the literal and traditional sense of the word. Nonetheless, the sheer number of these annotations regarding devils in comparison to almost none mentioning evil men strongly suggests that More also intended to use the term as a discreet and oblique reference to the human enemies who were confronting him. This appears all the more the case when we examine the psalm verses along which such notes appear, for they usually speak more specifically of the machinations of wicked men than of demons. In the example of this that follows, the reader will also notice that More refers to one of his daily penitential practices (which he continued even in the Tower)—the wearing of a hair shirt:

---

[105] Ibid., 194.
[106] Ibid., 192.
[107] Ibid.

The demons taunt [us], but let us lie low; let us wear the hair shirt, let us fast and pray: But at my stumbling they gathered in glee, they gathered together against me . . . they impiously mocked more and more, gnashing at me with their teeth. How long, O Lord, wilt thou look on? Rescue me from their ravages, my life from the lions! (Ps 35:15–17).[108]

Entertaining no illusions about his own human frailty, More expresses on the pages of the *Book of Hours* a genuine humility. Hence his notes frequently ask for strength in temptation or for the grace of a particular virtue (hope, perseverance, and so on) or speak of repentance from sin:

trust: Even though I walk through the valley of the shadow of death, I fear no evil . . . (Ps 23:4).[109]

patience: For God alone my soul waits in silence, for my hope is from him. He only is my rock and my salvation, my fortress; I shall not be shaken (Ps 62:5–6).[110]

for one's sins: Remember not the sins of my youth, or my transgressions; according to thy steadfast love remember me, for thy goodness' sake, O Lord! (Ps 25:7).[111]

But More knew how to find Christian joy even amid the darkness of his cell. Hence we find delineated essentially the entire texts of Psalms 66 and 67, both of which speak of rejoicing in God, while other verses in Psalms 56 (v. 13), 73 (vv. 1–2), and 86 (vv. 7–13) are marked as expressions of thanksgiving, especially for deliverance from temptation. There are also notations that reveal More's ardor and longing for God:

[H]*appy the man who can say this from his soul:* As a hart longs for flowing streams, so longs my soul for thee, O God. My soul thirsts for God, for the living God. When shall I come and behold the face of God? (Ps 42:1–2).[112]

[T]*he prayer either of a man who is shut up in prison, or of one who lies sick in bed, yearning [to go] to church, or of any faithful man who yearns for*

---

[108] Ibid., 194.
[109] Ibid., 192.
[110] Ibid., 197.
[111] Ibid., 192.
[112] Ibid., 195.

heaven: How lovely is thy dwelling place, O Lord of hosts! My soul longs, yea, faints for the courts of the Lord . . . (Ps 84:1–2).[113]

Although More could not avoid being preoccupied to a certain extent with his own struggle, his profound sense of the communal dimension of the Church nonetheless remained with him throughout his imprisonment and found expression in a significant number of annotations that speak of praying for the needs of his fellow Christians, psalm verses marked as invocations "for the Christian people",[114] for the poor, for prisoners, and even for the King who was the cause of his misery:

a prayer for the people in [time of] plague, famine, war or other tribulation: O God, thou hast rejected us, broken our defences; thou hast been angry; oh, restore us . . . thou hast given us wine to drink that made us reel (Ps 60:1–3).[115]

for the king: Give the king thy justice, O God . . . May he judge thy people with righteousness, and thy poor with justice! (Ps 72:1–2).[116]

More's continued zeal for the "common corps of Christendom" is also reflected in his unique application of two verses from Psalm 106 as a warning to parents on their responsibilities in the raising and education of their children, matters to which More had demonstrated his own commitment years earlier with his own son and daughters:

[T]his they do who bring up [their children] badly: They sacrificed their sons and their daughters to the demons; they poured out innocent blood, the blood of their sons and daughters, whom they sacrificed to the idols of Canaan . . . (Ps 106:37–38).[117]

More takes note of the assurance given in Psalm 41 that those who assist the poor will be remembered by God in their hour of need. Though he was no longer in a position to help the needy by material means, he may well have found consolation in the thought that God would remember his past corporal works of mercy and come to His aid in his present distress:

---

[113] Ibid., 200.
[114] Ibid., 199.
[115] Ibid., 196.
[116] Ibid., 198.
[117] Ibid., 202.

alms for the poor man: Blessed is he who considers the poor! The Lord delivers him in the day of trouble . . . thou dost not give him up to the will of his enemies (Ps 41:1–2).[118]

On the first page of the hour of Prime for the Little Office of the Blessed Virgin in More's *Book of Hours,* above and below a woodcut of the Nativity, we find written in the saint's own hand something quite different from the terse psalm annotations we have encountered thus far:[119]

> Give me thy grace good Lord
> To set the world at nought

These are the opening words of a prayer that stretches over the next twenty pages of the *Book of Hours,* a verse or two per page. Clearly of More's own composition, it is, unlike the psalm annotations, totally in English. The prayer has a multifold structure that begins with the theme of detachment from the world:

> To be content to be solitary
> Not to long for worldly company
>
> Little and little utterly to cast off the world
> And rid my mind of all the business thereof

Having resolutely turned away from the vanities of the present life, More now raises his eyes to his Creator, to whom he looks for consolation and for whom he seeks to exert his heart:

> Gladly to be thinking of God
> piteously to call for his help
>
> To lean unto the comfort of God
> Busily to labor to love him

From the remembrance of God, More passes to the need for self-knowledge and compunction for one's sins:

> To know mine own vility and wretchedness
> To humble and meeken myself under the
> mighty hand of God

---

[118] Ibid., 194.
[119] "A Godly Meditation", in *CW* 13:226–27.

The thought of suffering willingly for Christ invariably brings to More's mind the Passion:

> To walk the narrow way that leadeth to life
> To bear the cross with Christ

Likewise the subject of death is one to which he must return:

> To have the last thing in remembrance . . .
> To make death no stranger to me

But the key to preparation for death is for More the same to which he always has recourse:

> To have continually in mind the passion that Christ
> suffered for me

Despite his difficult circumstances he does not cease to offer thanksgiving to his Creator:

> For his benefits incessantly to give him thanks

Here one of the dominant themes of More's *Life of John Picus*—the vanity of the world's passing pleasures—reemerges years later with all the more force:

> To buy the time again that I before have lost

> To abstain from vain confabulations
> To eschew light foolish mirth and gladness

> Recreations not necessary / to cut off
> of worldly substance, friends, liberty, life and all
> to set the loss at right nought for the
> winning of Christ

More ends by expressing Christian love for the authors of his misfortune:

> To think my most enemies my best friends
> For the brethren of Joseph could never have done
> him so much good with their love and favor as
> they did him with their malice and hatred.

> These minds are more to be desired of
> every man than all the treasure of
> all the princes and kings Christian and heathen
> were it gathered and laid together
> all upon one heap.

The rediscovery in 1963 of the original manuscript of *De Tristitia Christi* (of which we will speak in the next chapter) has also brought to light a hitherto unknown collection of More's favorite Scripture passages, written in his own hand on a series of pages at the back of the book.[120] Moving effortlessly back and forth from the Old Testament to the New, More informally arranges the passages by subject matter, providing a beautiful anthology that yet again manifests his deep knowledge of the Bible. Obviously intended for his own personal use, the Scripture passages are for the most part unaccompanied by any explanatory or interpretive notes—notes are not necessary, for the reasons behind the selection of the passages are self-evident. One series of verses reflects More's determination to overcome any temptations to bitterness toward his enemies:

> Do not rejoice when your enemy falls, and let not your heart be glad when he stumbles; lest the Lord see it, and be displeased . . . (Prov 24:17–18).

> Do not return evil for evil . . . (1 Pet 3:9).

> . . . [P]ray for those who persecute you . . . (Mt 5:44).

Another series of quotations is obviously selected so as to engender perseverance in facing the hardships of the present life through anticipation of eternal happiness in the next:

> What no eye has seen, nor ear heard, nor the heart of man conceived, what God has prepared for those who love him . . . (1 Cor 2:9).

Resignation to the will of God is yet another theme to be found in these passages:

> . . . [T]he Lord gave, and the Lord has taken away; blessed be the name of the Lord (Job 1:21).

---

[120] *De Tristitia Christi,* ed. and trans. Clarence H. Miller, vol. 14 of *Complete Works of St. Thomas More* (New Haven: Yale Univ. Press, 1976), 627–81.

The selections reach their greatest intensity in addressing the subjects of the Cross and death:

> . . . [T]he world has been crucified to me, and I to the world (Gal 6:14).

> My desire is to depart and be with Christ . . . (Phil 1:23).

> For to me to live is Christ, and to die is gain (Phil 1:21).

It is among the passages on death that More makes one of the only comments to be found on the pages of his scriptural anthology; reflecting upon a verse from the Second Book of Maccabees (2 Macc 6:19), he remarks:

> If a man saves his life by offending God, he will find the life he has saved in this way to be hateful . . . For you will remember that death still awaits you . . .[121]

Throughout his imprisonment More had wrestled with the issue of how a man finds the strength to face death for Christ, writing as we have already seen at great length on the subject in his *Dialogue of Comfort*. But amid the Scripture verses on the last pages of the "Valencia manuscript" he records an answer from the Song of Songs that is quite simple:

> . . . [L]ove is strong as death. . . (Song 8:6).

The hour was fast approaching for More to prove along with his Divine Master that love is indeed as strong as death.

---

[121] Ibid., 639.

CHAPTER XIII

The Drama of the Passion in Thomas More's Last Writings

. . . I had fully determined with my self, neither to study nor meddle with any matter of this world, but that my whole study should be, upon the passion of Christ and mine own passage out of this world.

— Thomas More, Letter to his
daughter Margaret, May 1535

Treatise upon the Passion

In William Rastell's 1557 edition of the complete English works of Thomas More, the text of the *Treatise upon the Passion* is prefaced with a long subtitle that delineates the intended scope of this work. Utilizing all four Gospel accounts, it was to be an exposition on all the events of our Lord's Passion, beginning with the convocation of the chief priests and scribes to decide upon His arrest and ending with the burial of Christ and the posting of the guards around His tomb.[1] It is not surprising that More would have begun with such an ambitious schema, for there can be no doubt from comments he makes throughout his writings that he was devoted to meditation upon the *entire* mystery of the Passion. We see this, for example, in the following observation he makes in his very last work, *De Tristitia Christi:*

---

[1] *Treatise upon the Passion*, title, in *Treatise on the Passion; Treatise on the Blessed Body; Instructions and Prayers*, ed. Garry Haupt, vol. 13 of *Complete Works of St. Thomas More* (New Haven: Yale Univ. Press, 1976), 3. This volume cited hereafter as *CW* 13.

. . . [N]othing can contribute more effectively to salvation, and to the implanting of every sort of virtue in the Christian breast, than pious and fervent meditation on the successive events of Christ's passion . . .[2]

Yet the *Treatise upon the Passion* as we actually have it is incomplete, covering only the Last Supper and the events leading up to it and ending with an extended discussion of the institution of the Eucharist. In all probability More began the *Treatise* sometime after his resignation as Lord Chancellor. In the course of writing it he would have become increasingly aware that his time as a free man was growing short, and thus he may well have begun curtailing his plans as to its scope. In any event, his subsequent arrest in April 1534 would have disrupted his work on the *Treatise*. With his imprisonment in the Tower, the continued composition of a work of this nature would have been difficult, as he no longer had access to the full range of scholarly sources from his own library. For the two works he is known to have written in the Tower—the *Dialogue of Comfort against Tribulation* and the *De Tristitia Christi*—he had to rely exclusively upon the relatively few books allowed him as a prisoner, together with his own memory of various sources. This is by no means to say that the latter two works are lacking in scholarship; indeed, *De Tristitia Christi* is arguably More's crowning literary achievement, as we shall later see. The lack of access to a library simply helped to make these works what the circumstances of their composition would have already essentially dictated—a more intimate and personal expression of More's genius. As for the *Treatise upon the Passion,* we encounter in its pages More the gifted teacher and man of faith who imparts to his readers a deepened understanding of the opening scenes of the Passion and of the theology of the Eucharist in a presentation imbued with the writer's love for his subject matter.

Not unlike the passion plays of the Middle Ages and the Renaissance, More's *Treatise upon the Passion* begins by setting the redemptive oblation of Christ in the widest possible context, as the event upon which all history—angelic and human—converges. He opens with the fall of Satan. More describes Lucifer as an angel who became filled with an arrogant self-love, presuming to deem himself God's equal; exalting himself, he was in punishment cast down from

---

[2] *De Tristitia Christi,* ed. and trans. Clarence H. Miller, vol. 14 of *Complete Works of St. Thomas More* (New Haven: Yale Univ. Press, 1976), 339–41. Cited hereafter as *CW* 14.

heaven with the other angels who took his part.[3] The fate of Satan, who reigns as "king over all the children of pride", should stand as a warning to all, whether of high or lowly estate. Those in lofty positions have reason to tremble at the thought of great angels being thrown down to hell for their pride.[4] Moreover, pride can make men foolish enough to exult in gifts they do not even possess, as in the case More gives of a girl who thinks herself beautiful, fancying that she is "well liked for her broad forehead, while the young man that beholdeth her, marketh more her crooked nose" (we suspect here an oblique reference to the broad forehead and memorable nose of Dame Alice).[5] But then there is a greater absurdity still, More continues: the folly of taking pride in one's material goods—in gold and silver, in jewels or fine clothing. As to the latter, he asks why a man should pride himself in wearing a garment of sheep's wool, considering that before it became his, "a poor sheep wore it on her back"— a poor sheep and nothing more.[6] Indeed, everything we have in this life is merely "borrowed ware" with which we must part upon death; as Saint Paul says, "What have you that you did not receive? If then you received it, why do you boast as if it were not a gift?" (1 Cor 4:7).[7]

From the fall of angels More passes to the great drama of mankind's creation and fall from grace. While God has endowed man with a soul possessed of understanding, memory, and will, in likeness to Himself, God's purpose, More believes, in giving the human person a lowly body formed from the "slime" of the earth was in order to protect it from succumbing to haughtiness as Satan did.[8] Upon the sight of Adam and Eve, clothed with innocence and immune from death amid the bliss of paradise, the devil was consumed with envy, the "daughter of pestilent pride", and resolved to destroy mankind, no matter what it cost him in further punishments, rather than allow these creatures with their lower natures to give honor to God and be raised to the fallen angels' once high place in heaven.[9] To accomplish his

---

[3] *Treatise upon the Passion*, introduction, 1st point, in *CW* 13:5–6.

[4] Ibid., 6–7 (quote on 6).

[5] Ibid., 7–8 (quote on 8).

[6] Ibid., 8.

[7] Ibid., 8–9.

[8] Ibid., introduction, 2d point, pp. 11–12.

[9] Ibid., 13–14.

end, More continues, Satan resorted to the vice that had succeeded in bringing about his own downfall—pride. Recognizing Adam's love for his wife, Lucifer sought to tempt Eve first by painting God as a liar who was envious of mankind achieving a knowledge of good and evil (Gen 3:4–5). Beguiled by his suggestions and desirous to become as a goddess, Eve ate the forbidden fruit and persuaded Adam to do likewise. No sooner had they done so than their flesh rebelled against their reason, and God pronounced His sentence of punishment upon the man, the woman, and their tempter.[10] Thus "poisoning them with his own pride",[11] Satan brought about the downfall of mankind:

> This is, lo, good readers the wretched change that our forefathers made, with falling into pride at the devil's false suggestion. In honor they were, and would not see it. Honor they sought, and thereby fell to shame. They would have waxed gods, and were turned into beasts . . .[12]

But God would not suffer Satan to glory in his victory, nor would He leave mankind eternally ruined by the devil's deception. Hence, as More figuratively expresses it, ". . . [T]he sharp justice of God and his tender mercy, entered into counsel together."[13] We find a similar "deliberation" between mercy and justice in the opening pages of Nicholas Love's *Mirror of the Blessed Life of Jesus Christ*.[14] As More explains, God ordained that mankind's redemption was to be achieved "by the cruel painful death of that innocent person, that should be both God and man", so that "recompense should be made unto God for man."[15] This work of redemption was to be an even greater work than that of creation itself. So as to demonstrate this point, More quotes from the *Exsultet*, the Church's hymn of praise and thanksgiving sung following the lighting of the Paschal candle during the Easter Vigil.[16] As translated in the current liturgy, the verse he cites asks:

---

[10] Ibid., 14–19.

[11] Ibid., 23.

[12] Ibid., 24.

[13] Ibid., introduction, 3d point, p. 25.

[14] Nicholas Love, *The Mirror of the Blessed Life of Jesu Christ*, Orchard Books, vol. 10 (New York: Benziger Brothers, 1926), pt. 1, chap. 1, pp. 10–15.

[15] *Treatise upon the Passion*, introduction, 3d point, in *CW* 13:27.

[16] Ibid., 26.

> What good would life have been to us,
> had Christ not come as our Redeemer?[17]

For some pages More temporarily digresses from his principal subject matter, embarking upon an excursus on two theological questions regarding the eternal fate of righteous non-Christians as well as the reasons why Christ's sacrifice has not totally canceled in mankind all the consequences of Adam's sin (such as death).[18]

Having set the stage, as it were, for the unfolding of the great drama of the redemption, More begins his exposition on the actual history of the Passion itself, using as his framework a Gospel harmony compiled by the French ecclesiastic Jean Gerson (1363–1429).[19] He adopts a format that provides the reader first with an English translation of the relevant passage from Gerson's Latin harmony, then with More's own commentary explaining the text, and concludes with an appropriate prayer (also composed by More). Opening with the Gospel verse, "Now the feast of Unleavened Bread drew near, which is called the Passover" (Lk 22:1), More turns to the typology of the Israelites' flight from Egypt under Moses and of the Passover meal that commemorated it. He explains to his readers that the events recorded in the Book of Exodus really did happen, but that these historical occurrences were also endowed by God with a prefigurative meaning, foreshadowing the greatest "Exodus" of all—that of all mankind, who ever since Adam's fall had been living under the slavery of Satan, just as the children of Israel had suffered bondage under Pharaoh. Just as Moses led the Israelites to freedom from their Egyptian taskmasters, so has Christ led us to freedom from ours—the devil and his cohort.[20] And just as the Israelites passed safely through the waters of the Red Sea while the forces of Pharaoh were in that same sea destroyed, so too our passage through the waters of baptism rescues us from danger, drowning the power of Satan over us. Recognizing the significance of the very name of the sea through which the children of Israel passed, More notes that the sacrament of baptism takes its force from "the

---

[17] *The Roman Missal: The Sacramentary* (New York: Catholic Book Publishing Co., 1974), 183.

[18] *Treatise upon the Passion*, introduction, 3d point, in *CW* 13:28–49.

[19] Ibid., introduction, "A Warning to the Reader", 50.

[20] Ibid., chap. 1, lecture 1, pp. 53–58.

red blood of Christ that he shed in his bitter passion".[21] Finally, the
Israelites' forty years of wandering in the desert serve as an image
of our own long, meandering sojourn in "the wild wilderness of this
wretched world"[22] that we must endure before reaching our final destination—heaven.[23]

Typology permeates the Passover meal as well, which our Lord
Himself celebrated with His apostles the night before He died. Thus,
More explains, the unblemished lamb prescribed by Moses (Ex 12:3–
10) is the figure of the unblemished Son of God, who was given the
title "Lamb of God" by His herald, Saint John the Baptist (Jn 1:29).
This immolated Lamb of the New Covenant becomes our food in the
Eucharist just as the immolated Paschal lamb served as food to the
Israelites.[24] The eating of only unleavened bread during the Passover
seder is seen by More to symbolize the love and truth with which we
should receive the Blessed Sacrament of the Altar.[25] But for More, the
marking of the Israelites' homes on the first Passover with the blood
of the Paschal lamb has particularly vivid typological significance:

> We must also with a bundle of the low growing herb of hyssop that
> signifieth humility, mark the posts and the hance [lintel] of the door of
> our house with the blood of the Lamb; that is to wit, have remembrance
> of his bitter passion, and his blessed blood shed therein. And likewise
> as with a bundle of hyssop, the bitter eysil [vinegar] and gall was given
> him to drink in the painful thirst of his passion, which he so humbly
> suffered, we should with a bundle of humility, as it were with a painter's
> pencil, dipped in the red blood of Christ, mark ourselves on every side,
> and in the hance of our forehead, with the letter of *Tau,* the sign of
> Christ's holy cross.[26]

In the striking down of Egypt's firstborn while the Israelites remained safe within their blood-marked dwellings, More finds further
symbolism: these firstborn of Egypt can be likened to the first motions of sin,[27] which cannot harm us so long as we do not venture

---

[21] Ibid., 58.
[22] Ibid.
[23] Ibid., 58–59.
[24] Ibid., 62.
[25] Ibid., 64.
[26] Ibid.
[27] Ibid., 63, 65.

abroad and expose ourselves to the occasions of sin, but rather remain sheltered by "that mark of Christ's bloody cross upon the posts of our house".[28] And just as the Israelites were instructed by Moses to eat their seder "in haste", with their belts about their waists, their sandals on their feet, and their staffs in hand (Ex 12:11), so too, neither are we to tarry as we flee from the slavery of Satan, but with our belts girt for unimpeded progress, our feet shod to protect our affections from defilement, and our staff in hand, "the remembrance of Christ's cross, to stay us with, and beat from us venomous worms", we are to be on our way.[29]

Having expounded the symbolism of the Passover setting for the Last Supper, More now turns his attention to the actions of the Savior as His Passion nears. Reflecting upon our Lord's completion of His instructions to His apostles in the final days before He was to suffer ("When Jesus had finished all these sayings . . ." [Mt 26:1]), More derives a lesson therefrom for us, in that just as Christ did not allow Himself to be delivered into the hands of His foes until He had finished His public ministry, likewise should we strive to complete the work God has given us in life before time runs out; indeed, we need to be most vigilant in this, for unlike Christ, we neither know nor can we determine the hour of our death:[30]

> For when death cometh, the dreadful mighty messenger of God, there can no king command him, there can none authority strain him, there can no riches hire him, to tarry past his appointed time one moment of an hour.[31]

Let us then not lose any time, More exhorts us, to the pursuit of empty passing vanities or, worse still, by succumbing to sin, but rather let us now say and do whatever our God-given duties require of us, lest we find ourselves lying unprepared upon our deathbed, "where we shall have so many things to do at once, and everything so un-ready, that every finger shall be a thumb, and we shall fumble it up in haste."[32]

---

[28] Ibid., 65.
[29] Ibid.
[30] Ibid., chap. 1, lecture 2, pp. 66–78.
[31] Ibid., 67.
[32] Ibid., 68.

In describing the various motivations of the Sanhedrin in deciding to apprehend Christ (Jn 11:47–53), More looks back at the events of Palm Sunday, reminding his readers that when some of the Pharisees called upon our Lord to silence the accolades of His disciples, He answered, "I tell you, if these were silent, the very stones would cry out" (Lk 19:40). More notes that these words were fulfilled on Good Friday, for when the cries of the crowd had changed from praise to denunciation, the rocks did indeed cry out in testimony to Christ: ". . . [A]nd the earth shook, and the rocks were split; the tombs also were opened . . ." (Mt 27:51–52).[33]

More sees in the convening of the Sanhedrin to decide upon action against Christ a demonstration that not every gathering of men is for good purposes. While Christ has promised to be present where two or three are gathered in His name (Mt 18:20), the same cannot be said of assemblies intent on doing evil, no matter how distinguished and respectable the participants may be: "For likewise as God is in the midst of the good council, so in the midst of an evil council, is there undoubtedly the devil."[34]

More remarks upon the niggardly price that Judas sold his Master for —thirty silver pieces. It demonstrates the folly of entering the service of the devil, who gives so little in return; whatever bit of pleasure he doles out to us entails pains that far outweigh it. Citing the testimony of Origen, More adds that Judas is the archetype of many who, claiming to be Christ's followers and disciples, (in More's words) "betray the truth, and cause to be spitefully killed, the faithful true doctrine of Christ".[35]

After discussing at some length the dating of the Last Supper, addressing the question of whether the evening of Holy Thursday constituted the beginning of Passover or fell on the day before it,[36] More examines the significance of our Lord's instructions to Peter and John regarding the arrangements for their Passover meal in the Upper Room. He sees Christ as wishing to celebrate the Passover in order both to comply with the law of Moses and to fulfill it with the institution of the Eucharist and the sacrifice of His own body on the "altar of the

---

[33] Ibid., chap. 1, lecture 3, pp. 71–72.
[34] Ibid., 73–74 (quote on 74).
[35] Ibid., chap. 1, lecture 4, pp. 79–82 (quote on 81–82).
[36] Ibid., chap. 2, pp. 86–92.

cross".[37] As to our Lord's mysterious manner of specifying how Peter and John were to find the place to arrange the supper (they were to look for an unnamed man carrying a water jug), More offers as one possible explanation the necessity of keeping the specific location of the meal from the ears of Judas lest he betray Christ into the hands of His enemies before He had celebrated the Last Supper (and instituted the Eucharist) with His disciples.[38] But More also views the incident as a manifestation of Christ's divinity, demonstrating His omniscience and His omnipotence; who other than God, More asks, could have by His Divine Providence arranged such a chance meeting between the disciples and the man with the water jug at the precise place He had foretold (the gate of the city)?[39]

Pondering the significance of Judas' continued presence among the apostles as they came to the Last Supper, More observes that just as this one disciple's treachery did not discredit the whole band of apostles, neither do the sins of malicious Christians take anything from the identity of the Catholic Church as Christ's holy Church. He also sees a lesson for us in Christ's observance of the Passover meal: just as our Lord was careful to keep the precepts of the Mosaic law while fulfilling them with the institution of the New Law, so should we be vigilant in keeping the precepts of the New Law. Moreover, the fact that, despite their lack of a home, Christ and His disciples were nonetheless provided with a lodging when they needed it for the Last Supper should serve as a reminder to us that we are pilgrims in this life, with no need for magnificent dwellings. While we have here "no lasting city" (Heb 13:14), in heaven we will be "for ever at home".[40]

Reflecting upon the words with which Saint John begins his account of the Last Supper in chapter 13 of his Gospel (". . . [H]aving loved his own who were in the world, he loved them to the end" [Jn 13:1]), More finds therein a summation and explanation of "all the whole piteous tragedy of his [Christ's] most bitter passion".[41] All that Christ did and suffered that night and the following day—from the washing of the disciples' feet to the Crucifixion—was but a manifesta-

---

[37] Ibid., 92.
[38] Ibid., 93–94.
[39] Ibid., 94–95.
[40] Ibid., 96–100 (quote on 99).
[41] Ibid., chap. 1, lecture 5, p. 82.

tion of His love. His was an unchanging love—"to the end"; because of this love He suffered "not only for his friends that were already his, but for his enemies, to make them friends of his".[42] More presents several different interpretations of this beautiful Gospel verse: some scholars, he explains, take John to mean that Christ loved His own to the utmost, "unto that extreme point of love, beyond which no man could go",[43] while others understand from these words that Christ's love was such that the nearer He drew to His death, the more tenderly did He show Himself to the apostles. Even Judas He would not drive away but rather "went about to mend him".[44] Still others say that "to the end" means that Christ's love was directed not merely to His disciples' fleeting earthly well-being but primarily toward their eternal happiness.[45] More endorses all three interpretations, noting that our Lord expressed His love "to the end" both in His words and in His actions at the Last Supper.[46] He also uses this verse of Saint John to remind us of the contrast between Christ's love and the fickle love of men. Can we be so sure of the support of friends in our hour of need, when we consider that our Lord Himself was deserted by His own upon His arrest? More exhorts his readers to learn to love God first and, then, all others for the love of God, warning against any love for creatures—even for one's own children—that diminishes the love we owe to God Himself.[47]

More reflects upon the wondrous humility of Christ in washing His apostles' feet, pointing out that He willed to do all this with His own hands—the laying aside of His outer garments, the filling of the basin with water, the washing itself, and the drying of their feet with a towel.[48] After discussing Saint Peter's reluctance to let his Master wash his feet, which stemmed from Peter's reverence for the "marvelous high majesty" of Christ,[49] More draws from this incident the lesson that we should never prefer any judgment or course of action

---

[42] Ibid., 82–83 (quote on 83).
[43] Ibid., chap. 3, p. 102.
[44] Ibid., 102–3 (quote on 103).
[45] Ibid., 103.
[46] Ibid., 103–4.
[47] Ibid., chap. 1, lecture 5, pp. 84–85.
[48] Ibid., chap. 3, pp. 105–6.
[49] Ibid., 106–7.

of our own, no matter how piously motivated it may seem, to whatever the will of God has ordained for us to do or not do; yes, even our consciences are accountable:

> Nor never shall God's precepts be obeyed, if every man may boldly frame himself a conscience, with a gloss [interpretation] of his own making, after his own fantasy put unto God's word.[50]

Our Lord washed His apostles' feet to give them an example, as His words afterward make clear (Jn 13:15); for, More explains, Christ did not teach His disciples to do anything He Himself did not first do. Would that all in positions of authority, from prelates to parents, always conformed their actions to their words as Christ did; those who fail in this More likens to a foolish weaver who with one hand unweaves what he has woven with the other.[51] Although, he adds, our Lord here was not instituting a new sacrament that would have required each of us to perform this very same physical action of washing others' feet, there is, nonetheless, a most praiseworthy tradition of reenacting Christ's gesture of humility among clergy, princes, and noblemen (he is referring to the Holy Thursday *Mandatum* rite); he cites, for example, the "Royal Maundy" that was performed each year by the King (as mentioned in chapter 8).[52]

In the fourth chapter of his *Treatise upon the Passion,* More addresses the institution of the Holy Eucharist. Considering those beautiful words of the Savior with which Saint Luke's account of the Last Supper opens, "I have earnestly desired to eat this passover with you before I suffer" (Lk 22:15), More offers two reasons why Christ was so particularly anxious to share this repast with His apostles: (1) that as He "loved them to the end" (Jn 13:1), He "like a most tender lover" would have therefore yearned to spend His final hours with them in this intimate manner, revealing thereby "his wonderful loving heart";[53] and (2) that He longed to bring to fruition the redemption of mankind with His own immolation on the Cross as well as to institute the sacrament that commemorated this same immolation (the Eucharist), but that before doing so, He would first "reverently finish

---

[50] Ibid., 112.
[51] Ibid., 113–14.
[52] Ibid., 114.
[53] Ibid., chap. 4, lecture 1, pp. 119–20.

the old Paschal'', that is, the Passover seder, which foreshadowed the oblation of the New Covenant.[54]

More sees the taking and drinking of the first "cup" mentioned in Saint Luke's account of the Last Supper (Lk 22:17–18) as marking the final action in Christ's celebration of the sacrificial meal of the Old Covenant. What followed was to be the first celebration of the new sacrifice of the New Covenant,[55] as explained by him in a brilliant two-sentence summation of the doctrine of the Holy Eucharist:

> After this done, our Savior Christ by and by in the stead of that old sacrifice of the Paschal Lamb so ended, did institute the new sacrifice, and the only sacrifice to be continued in his Church, the blessed Sacrament of the Altar. Which new sacrifice instead of that old sacrifice, and of all the old sacrifices which among the Jews fore-figured the very fruitful sacrifice of Christ's blessed Body upon the cross, should in his own Church of Jews and Gentiles together, continually with the selfsame Body and Blood offered in the Mass under the form of bread and wine, represent that sacrifice in which on Good Friday Christ once for ever, offered the selfsame Body and Blood in their proper form, to the Father upon the cross.[56]

More then points out the significance of various details of the institution of the Eucharist: from Saint Bede he borrows two ideas—that our Lord, in giving thanks before consecrating the bread, teaches us to begin "every good work" with thanksgiving to God; and that by giving with His own hand the Eucharist to the apostles, rather than allowing them to take it for themselves, He showed that He was offering Himself "of his own free will".[57] Undoubtedly thinking of those who had denied the dogma of the Real Presence in the Eucharist, More reasons that Christ would explain His selection of bread and wine as the species of His new sacrament as follows: that He would certainly not replace the lamb's flesh of the Old Testament sacrifice, which merely prefigured the New, with nothing more than the inferior inanimate substances of bread and wine when celebrating the new and superior oblation. Rather, He gives us a reality so much greater than either lamb's flesh or bread and wine, a reality (His true

---

[54] Ibid., 120.

[55] Ibid., 122–23.

[56] Ibid., 123.

[57] Ibid., 124.

Body and Blood) concealed, as it were, by the outward accidents of bread and wine.[58]

Regarding the actual words of institution, "This is my body . . ." (Lk 22:19–20; also Mt 26:26–28; Mk 14:22–24; 1 Cor 11:23–25), More observes that our Lord, in telling the apostles to "Do this in remembrance of me" (Lk 22:19), thereby indicated that He was establishing a new sacrament, a true sacrifice to be celebrated time and again down through the ages as the new sign of His Passion that has replaced the old sign, the Paschal lamb.[59] The words that both Saint Matthew and Saint Mark record as following the words of institution —"I tell you I shall not drink again of this fruit of the vine until that day when I drink it new with you in my Father's kingdom" (Mt 26:29; also Mk 14:25)—are, More believes, distinct from a very similar verse that in Saint Luke precedes the words of institution (Lk 22:18) and are spoken (in the case of Matthew and Mark) not merely of wine but of the Precious Blood of Christ in the Eucharist. For in all likelihood Christ did celebrate this sacrament again with His apostles, but only after the Resurrection.[60] More reassures his readers that the expression "fruit of the vine" in this passage poses no real problem, for its use here can be explained by the way the Scriptures on other occasions refer to a thing by the name of the former thing that has been converted into it—hence in Genesis God calls Adam dust: ". . . [Y]ou are dust, and to dust you shall return" (Gen 3:19). Moreover, did not Christ call Himself the "vine" (Jn 15:1), and thus could not the Precious Blood of Christ be appropriately described as the fruit of that vine that is His Body?[61]

In answer to a number of different arguments used to reject the dogma of the Real Presence, More here presents an exposition on the doctrine of transubstantiation. He begins by explaining that, following Consecration, the substances of bread and wine are totally converted into the true Body and Blood of Christ, but that the accidents of bread and wine ("whiteness, redness, hardness, softness, weight, savor and taste, and such other like")[62] remain, and since we know from experience that the accidents of an object cannot subsist sepa-

---

[58] Ibid., 124–25.
[59] Ibid., 126.
[60] Ibid., 129–32.
[61] Ibid., 131, 132.
[62] Ibid., chap. 4, lecture 2, p. 140.

rately from the substance of that object, we must accept this unique phenomenon in the Eucharist as nothing less than a miracle for which we should not expect God to provide us with a natural explanation.[63] After noting that with every sacrament there is both an outward sign and a sacred reality (a "holy thing") that the sign symbolizes, More notes that in the case of the Eucharist there are not one but two signs in addition to the reality contained by the sacrament that both signs point to: one sign is outward—the species of bread and wine—while the other is hidden and is both a sign of the Passion and a living reality—the Lord's actual Body and Blood.[64] Lest anyone question how something can be both a reality in itself and at the same time a sign representing that same reality, More cites two incidents from the Gospels that he believes show Christ at one and the same time truly present and a sign or symbol of Himself: His appearances to the two disciples on the road to Emmaus and to Mary Magdalen, both occurring after His Resurrection. In the first case, the risen Christ appears to the two disciples as a traveler, which More, working from Saint Augustine's interpretation,[65] sees as symbolic of our Lord's departure from this world to heaven in the Ascension; in the second, Mary Magdalen takes Him to be a gardener, a role that More, again drawing upon Augustine,[66] explains as symbolizing Christ's work of "planting the faith and other virtues in the garden of our souls".[67] Parenthetically we might add to More's line of reasoning here that Christ Himself is identified as a "sign" elsewhere in the Gospels: Simeon prophesied to the Blessed Virgin Mary that her Divine Son would be "a sign that is spoken against" (Lk 2:34).

More further distinguishes between two mysteries represented by the two signs of the Eucharist: the corporal Body of Christ and the Mystical Body of Christ. There is an important difference in that, while the Mystical Body of Christ—that is, the Church with all her

---

[63] Ibid., 140–41.

[64] Ibid., 141.

[65] Sermons 235 and 236, no. 2, in *Saint Augustine: Sermons on the Liturgical Seasons,* trans. Sr. Mary Sarah Muldowney, R.S.M., Fathers of the Church, vol. 38 (New York: Fathers of the Church, 1959), 228, 230, 232.

[66] *Tractate 121 on the Gospel of John,* no. 3, in *St. Augustine: Tractates on the Gospel of John 112–24: Tractates on the First Epistle of John,* trans. John W. Rettig, Fathers of the Church, vol. 92 (Washington, D.C.: Catholic Univ. of America Press, 1995), 58.

[67] *Treatise upon the Passion,* chap. 4, lecture 2, in *CW* 13:157.

members united under Christ the Head—is only symbolized in the Eucharist (it is "not contained therein"), the corporal Body of Christ —that is, His actual Body and Blood—is not just symbolized but is also truly present in this sacrament.[68] In addition, although they are neither sacramental signs nor are they represented by the signs of this sacrament, both the soul of Christ and His Godhead are present too in the Eucharist by "concomitance", for ever since the Incarnation, Christ's body has never been separated from the Godhead (even while the body lay in the sepulchre), while the soul of Christ, which albeit from its creation has always been joined to His Godhead yet did part from His body when He died on the Cross, has been rejoined with the body in the Resurrection and can never be separated from it again.[69] In virtue of the Godhead being present in this sacrament, not only is the second Person of the Holy Trinity found therein, but the Father and the Holy Spirit as well—by concomitance.[70]

More also reminds his readers that both the true Body and the true Blood of Christ are fully contained under each species, that is, under the visible form of bread or under the visible form of wine—hence the reason why the Church has not deemed it necessary for the faithful to receive Holy Communion under both species (even in our own day the practice is merely optional).[71] Conversely, the Church has always required both species for the celebration of the Mass and for the Communion of the celebrant, because both visible forms (the forms of bread and wine) are the signs of this sacrament, distinct from each other so as to commemorate the separation in death of Christ's Body from His Blood. Moreover, the Eucharist is also a sacrifice wherein is offered (as More describes it a bit later in his presentation) "the very flesh and blood of our Savior himself, immortal and impassible under the forms of bread and wine, representing the most acceptable sacrifice of the same flesh and blood offered up once for ever, mortal and passible upon the cross at his bitter passion".[72]

In regard to the relationship between the Holy Eucharist and the Mystical Body of Christ, More adds to what he has already said on this subject by pointing out that although the latter mystery is only symbol-

---

[68] Ibid., 142–43.
[69] Ibid., 146–47.
[70] Ibid., 148.
[71] Ibid., 147–50.
[72] Ibid., 147, 150, 155 (quote on 155).

ized in this sacrament, nonetheless this joining together of the faithful is actually brought about by reception of the real Body and Blood of the Lord their Divine Head in the Eucharist, for when Christ unites each of them with Himself sacramentally, they are thereby united with each other.[73]

More then explains the different titles for this sacrament. It is called the "Eucharist", the Greek word for "thanksgiving", because it is God's incomparable gift for which we should give great thanks. It is called "Communion", for in receiving it the faithful are united together in the Mystical Body of Christ. It is called the "Supper of the Lord" because it surpasses the Paschal meal that it fulfills and is one and the same supper as that instituted by Christ on Holy Thursday, in which the very same Body and Blood of Christ are made present and are received.[74]

As we near the abrupt end of the *Treatise upon the Passion* we find More completely preoccupied with defending the doctrine of the Real Presence of Christ in the Eucharist, as he had earlier done in his apologetical works. At one point he provides English translations of quotations supporting this dogma from no fewer than nineteen Church Fathers.[75] Passages such as this in More's last works demonstrate his continued commitment to the battle against theological dissent, despite his own increasingly constrained circumstances. The concluding words of the *Treatise,* which discuss the reception of the Eucharist, appear to contain in germinal and fragmentary form the ideas that are to be fully developed in the work to which we will turn next.

A Treatise to Receive the Blessed Body of Our Lord

Over the years, as we have seen, Thomas More devoted many a page of his writings to explaining and defending the Church's teachings regarding the Holy Eucharist. But it was in one of his very last works —*A Treatise to Receive the Blessed Body of Our Lord*—that he was to reveal the love that motivated all these efforts. It is evident that for at least the first months of his imprisonment More was permitted to

---

[73] Ibid., 154.

[74] Ibid., 154–56.

[75] Ibid., 160–70.

attend Mass at one of the chapels within the walls of the Tower complex,[76] most probably that of Saint Peter in Chains. Undoubtedly his sufferings within these walls would only have deepened his perception of both the immense consolation of Christ's Real Presence in this sacrament and of the inseparable bond that unites the Eucharist with the *mysterium Crucis,* the Passion of the Lord.

The subject of this treatise is the worthy and fruitful reception of Holy Communion, which More sees as achievable primarily through a proper preparation beforehand, together with a suitable period of thanksgiving afterward. While it is impossible for us ever to make ourselves sufficiently worthy to receive the body, blood, soul, and divinity of Christ, More explains, we can, with the help of God's grace, prepare ourselves in such a way that God in His infinite goodness and generosity will deem us ready for communion with Him in the sacrament.[77] Citing Proverbs 8:31, ". . . [M]y delights were to be with the children of men" (Douay-Rheims version), he notes that God not only condescends to be with us, but He actually "doth delight" in being with us, so long as we come to the sacrament with purified souls. Nor can we doubt that He delights to be with us, in view of the fact that in addition to becoming man in the Incarnation, He even underwent the Passion to redeem us.[78]

Such is God's patience, More continues, that He allows Himself to be bodily received even by those not in a state of grace; nonetheless, those who receive in this manner obtain no graces thereby but rather receive unto "their judgment, and their damnation". Moreover, they run the risk of falling into the power of the devil, as did Judas, who like them received Communion unworthily at the Last Supper.[79] In light of these considerations, there is good reason to be circumspect in preparing for this sacrament:

> And therefore have we great cause, with great dread and reverence, to consider well the state of our own soul, when we shall go to the board of God, and as near as we can (with help of his special grace, diligently

---

[76] See letter no. 209, from Margaret Roper to Thomas More, 1534, in Elizabeth Rogers, ed., *The Correspondence of Sir Thomas More* (Princeton, N.J.: Princeton Univ. Press, 1947), 539.

[77] *Treatise to Receive the Blessed Body,* in *CW* 13:191.

[78] Ibid., 191−92.

[79] Ibid., 192−93.

prayed for before) purge and cleanse our souls by confession, contrition, and penance, with full purpose of forsaking from thenceforth, the proud desires of the devil, the greedy covetousness of wretched worldly wealth, and the foul affection of the filthy flesh, and be in full mind to persevere and continue in the ways of God and holy cleanness of spirit . . .[80]

More warns that by unworthy reception we act like swine wallowing in filth, trampling underfoot "this pure pearl" that is the Eucharist with the dirty feet of our impure desires. Let us therefore take heed of Saint Paul's monition, "Whoever, therefore, eats the bread or drinks the cup of the Lord in an unworthy manner will be guilty of profaning the body and blood of the Lord" (1 Cor 11:27). In these words More sees unworthy reception equated with the crime of those who participated in putting Christ to death.[81]

From these considerations it becomes clear, More continues, that we should not hastily come to Holy Communion without first devoting sufficient time beforehand to examining our consciences. Of course no man can be absolutely certain of the state of his soul, yet nonetheless God is satisfied so long as we have examined ourselves to the best of our knowledge, making sure that there is no "poisoned spider or cobweb of deadly sin hanging in the roof" and that the "floor" of one's soul has been swept clean of any inappropriate thoughts.[82] We must also make sure that we come to the Lord's table fully believing that the sacrament we receive is not merely a symbol but is truly the very same Body that died on the Cross, the same Blood that was shed upon it; it is the same Body (and Blood) that rose from the dead, ascended to heaven, and sits at the right hand of the Father, and that is to come in judgment on the last day.[83]

It necessarily follows from belief in the Real Presence of Christ in the Eucharist that we must receive this sacrament with all possible humility and reverence. More compares what we are doing to the reception of an earthly prince into our own homes. What efforts we would make in such an event, he observes, to tidy our homes and set everything in order so as to show the prince our affection and esteem. If this be true for an earthly prince, how much more should

---

[80] Ibid., 193.
[81] Ibid., 193–94.
[82] Ibid., 194–95, 198 (quotes on 198).
[83] Ibid., 195–96.

we prepare for the "King of all kings", God Himself, who deigns to enter not merely our homes but our very bodies and souls? How can we ever do enough to ready ourselves to welcome such a King who, rather than putting us to any expense, instead imparts gifts to us, despite our many sins?[84]

If we are both to attain a true faith in the Eucharist and to make an appropriate preparation for its worthy reception, we must, More advises, ask God's assistance in prayer, without whose grace these things would not be possible to achieve.[85] Emphasizing the necessity of both deep humility and total trust in the mercy of God, he explains that in approaching the sacrament we should "of our own part, fear our unworthiness, and on his part trust boldly upon his goodness", an "inestimable goodness" that does not disdain "for all our unworthiness, to come unto us, and to be received of us".[86]

Turning to the Gospels in explaining what our attitude should be in receiving Holy Communion, More advises us to recognize the weakness of our faith and say with the man pleading for the healing of his possessed son, "I believe; help my unbelief!" (Mk 9:24), and join the apostles in asking, "Increase our faith!" (Lk 17:5). Furthermore, let us acknowledge our unworthiness and pray with the tax collector in the Temple, "God, be merciful to me a sinner!" (Lk 18:13), and with the centurion seeking the healing of his servant, "Lord, I am not worthy to have you come under my roof . . ." (Mt 8:8).[87]

Holy Communion, More reminds us, should be a time for humble reflection upon the Passion of our Redeemer, for the Eucharist is the memorial of His death; but it is also a time to rejoice in God's goodness to us. In a marvelous application of the Scriptures, More brings forward the example of Saint Elizabeth, mother of John the Baptist, who, when the Blessed Virgin had come to her, said in humility, "And why is this granted me, that the mother of my Lord should come to me?" (Lk 1:43), yet nonetheless rejoiced in exclaiming, ". . . [W]hen the voice of your greeting came to my ears, the babe in my womb leaped for joy" (Lk 1:44). If Elizabeth could rejoice that the Mother of God had come to her home despite her unworthiness, how much more should we not rejoice in this visitation of Christ into our very

---

[84] Ibid., 197–98.

[85] Ibid., 198.

[86] Ibid., 198, 199.

[87] Ibid., 199.

selves, despite our own unworthiness? Let us ask the Holy Spirit to help us imitate Elizabeth's example and respond to Christ's coming in this sacrament with both reverential fear and jubilation, so that we too can say that the child within us—our souls, which ought to be as much a child in innocence as was John the Baptist within his mother —leaps for joy.[88]

Having explained the importance of a suitable preparation for Holy Communion, More proceeds to lay great stress upon the importance of an extended period of thanksgiving following reception:

> Now when we have received our Lord and have him in our body, let us not then let him alone, and get us forth about other things, and look no more unto him . . . but let all our business be about him. Let us by devout prayer talk to him, by devout meditation talk with him. Let us say with the prophet: *Audiam quid loquatur in me dominus,* I will hear what our Lord will speak within me.
>
>   For surely if we set aside all other things, and attend unto him, he will not fail with good inspirations, to speak such things to us within us, as shall serve to the great spiritual comfort and profit of our soul.[89]

Drawing upon the episode of the two sisters Martha and Mary recorded in Saint Luke's Gospel (Lk 10:38–42), More observes that while we should imitate Martha in attending to whatever pertains to the outward honor of Christ and to the needs of His fellow guests, the poor, we should upon receiving Holy Communion also imitate Mary and "sit in devout meditation" to listen to what our Guest has to say to us. More urges his readers not to lose or squander this precious time in Christ's presence, for we cannot be sure if we will ever have this opportunity again in life (that is, each Communion could be our last). Rather should we press Him to remain with us and say with the two disciples on the way to Emmaus, "Stay with us . . ." (Lk 24:29). Nor will He depart from us, unless we by sin or worldly desires put Him away from us.[90] Let us not behave like those who on Palm Sunday welcomed Christ into Jerusalem with cries of "Blessed is he who comes in the name of the Lord!" (Mt 21:9) and "Hosanna in the highest!" (Mk 11:10), but who on Good Friday shouted, "Not this man, but Barab'bas!" (Jn 18:40), and "Away with him, away with

---

[88] Ibid., 199–201.
[89] Ibid., 201.
[90] Ibid., 201–2.

him, crucify him!" (Jn 19:15). Thus no matter how devoutly we may receive Him in Holy Communion on Easter Sunday, if we afterward return to a life of serious sin, we are no better than these Jerusalem crowds and, as it were, crucify Christ again (Heb 6:6).[91]

More ends his eucharistic reflection by setting before his readers one final example—that of the tax collector Zacchaeus. Just as Zacchaeus, when invited by the Lord to come down from the tree and take Him into his house, responded by quickly making amends for his past misdeeds, thus proving his sincerity (Lk 19:1-10), so too may we demonstrate that we have received Christ in the Eucharist with clean, resolute consciences and unwavering faith by performing good works. Thus will Christ be able to say of us as He said of Zacchaeus, "Today salvation has come to this house . . ." (Lk 19:9).[92]

De Tristitia Christi

It was in 1963 that the scholar Geoffrey Bullough made a most remarkable discovery in Valencia, Spain, at the Royal College and Seminary of Corpus Christi, established over three hundred fifty years earlier by Archbishop San Juan de Ribera. In the reliquary closet of Corpus Christi's Chapel of the Relics, secured within gilded doors, Bullough found a box made of tortoiseshell, resting next to a bound manuscript of Saint Vincent Ferrer's homilies. Inside the box was a small book bound with faded red and blue cloth; opening the cover he spotted the following inscription in Spanish, made by Archbishop Ribera himself:

> This book was sent to me by the Count of Oropesa, who told me that it belonged to Senor don Fernando de Toledo, to whom it had been given by the friar Father Pedro de Soto, Confessor to the Emperor, King, and Lord Charles V, *because it was by Thomas More and written with his own hand*.[93]

---

[91] Ibid., 202-3.

[92] Ibid., 203-4.

[93] Clarence Miller, "The Heart of the Final Struggle: More's Commentary on The Agony in The Garden", in *Quincentennial Essays on St. Thomas More: Selected Papers from the Thomas More College Conference,* ed. Michael Moore (Boone, N.C.: Albion [Appalachian State Univ.], 1978), 109 (emphasis added).

What Bullough had brought to light was by far the most precious manuscript of Thomas More to have been preserved for posterity: the original Latin draft of his very last literary work, *De Tristitia Christi* (The sadness of Christ), completed (intentionally or otherwise) less than a month before his execution. Although the text of this work was previously known through the preservation of a few secondary copies, most notably in an imperfect English translation by More's granddaughter Mary Basset, the discovery of the original draft, which had lain virtually unnoticed within Corpus Christi's walls for centuries, generated enormous interest in a work that had until then received inadequate attention. While the manuscript, with its numerous corrections and interpolations made by the author himself, is priceless enough in giving us an unparalleled opportunity to see More the writer formulating and revising his ideas on paper (revisions that reveal both the emotional intensity of his writing as he added words to amplify the most powerful passages and his zeal for honing the theological precision of his expressions),[94] it is the content of *De Tristitia Christi* that above all else makes the recovery from oblivion of this volume truly providential. In this, perhaps the most intimate of his works, More takes us into the Garden of Gethsemane with a serenity of spirit and controlled dramatic intensity that few authors have equaled, giving us a depiction of the suffering Son of God that is at once deeply human and truly majestic.

Thomas More begins with the conclusion of the Last Supper and from the outset draws lessons therefrom. He notes the nature of the conversation at the Last Supper table, contrasting it with the vacuous and sometimes even vicious talk that all too often occurs at meals. He also points out that the Last Supper ended with a hymn and, citing the belief of the medieval scholar Burgensis (c. 1353–1435) that this song (consisting of Psalms 113–18) was that known among the Jews as the "Hallel", compares this act of thanksgiving with the negligent thanks, muttered "through our yawns", offered by contemporary Christians for the bounty of the earth God has given them.[95] As More turns his attention to the principal subject of his work, that is, the Agony in the Garden, we now encounter what will become one of his major recurring themes—the idea of watching with the Lord in the night.

---

[94] Clarence Miller, introduction to *CW* 14:755, 756–58, 761–64, 766–67.

[95] *De Tristitia Christi, CW* 14:3–7.

He points out that our Lord did not take any rest following the Last Supper but went straight to the garden to enter into prayer. As to us, More adds, would that we were willing at least to think of Christ while we are at rest, in the spirit of Psalm 63 (v. 6: ". . . I think of thee upon my bed, and meditate on thee in the watches of the night . . ."). That this night prayer was a regular habit More justifiably concludes from Saint Luke's comment that our Lord went to the Mount of Olives "as was his custom" (Lk 22:39).[96]

In continuation of medieval traditions in this regard, More finds symbolic signification in every detail recorded by the four evangelists. Thus, for example, he saw in our Lord's ascending the Mount of Olives a call to raise our minds above the things of earth when preparing to pray. Similarly he finds hidden meanings in the place names "Mount Olivet", "Cedron", and "Gethsemane". Eloquently defending this form of biblical exegesis, More explains:

> . . . [S]ince not a single syllable can be thought inconsequential in a composition which was dictated by the Holy Spirit as the apostles wrote it, and since not a sparrow falls to the earth without God's direction, I cannot think either that the evangelists mentioned those names accidentally or that the Jews assigned them to the places (whatever they themselves intended when they named them) without a secret plan (though unknown to the Jews themselves) of the Holy Spirit . . .[97]

More notes that when our Lord went to Gethsemane, all of the apostles except Judas followed Him; thus the only apostle not to follow Him to prayer was treacherously hunting his Master instead, providing perhaps the starkest illustration of our Lord's words, "He who is not with me is against me . . ." (Mt 12:30). In this he sees a warning for us as well, that we may not leave Christ "after partaking of His favors and dining excellently with Him".[98]

Pointing out that Judas was obviously sure that he would find Christ at prayer in the garden, More returns to the subject of prayer in the night, criticizing those who attacked our Lord for eating and drinking with sinners as if He were lacking in prayer and self-denial. Yes, he explains, during the day, while the hypocritical Pharisee was busy making a pseudopious spectacle of himself on street corners, Christ

---

[96] Ibid., 7–9.
[97] Ibid., 9–25 (quote on 15).
[98] Ibid., 25–27 (quote on 27).

was lovingly ministering to the needy souls of sinners to bring them to conversion. But while the Pharisee was "snoring away in his soft bed", our Lord spent the night under the open sky praying to His Father. Again, More reminds us that when we wake in the night we should remember these "all-night vigils" of our Savior, and we should make some effort to "offer Him thanks" and pray for an "increase of grace" before falling asleep again; he adds that God will undoubtedly be most generous in rewarding even the smallest effort made in this regard.[99]

More now takes us deep into the Garden of Gethsemane to put before our eyes the unutterable scene about to unfold there. First there is Christ's command that eight of the apostles should remain where they were while He continued onward a bit, accompanied only by Peter, John, and John's brother James. Why were these three chosen to be more intimate witnesses of what was to follow? More cites Peter's faith, John's celibacy, and James' future destiny as the first apostle to undergo martyrdom. These were also the same three privileged to have seen Christ transfigured in glory on Mount Tabor, and thus were they the best prepared for this hour.[100] It was only after He was alone with Peter, James, and John that our Lord revealed His tormented state of mind, saying in their presence, "My soul is very sorrowful, even to death . . ." (Mt 26:38). Thus His agony began:

> For a huge mass of troubles took possession of the tender and gentle body of our most holy Savior. He knew that His ordeal was now imminent and just about to overtake Him: the treacherous betrayer, the bitter enemies, binding ropes, false accusations, slanders, blows, thorns, nails, the cross, and horrible tortures stretched out over many hours. Over and above these, He was tormented by the thought of his disciples' terror, the loss of the Jews, even the destruction of the very man who so disloyally betrayed Him, and finally the ineffable grief of His beloved mother. The gathered storm of all these evils rushed into His most gentle heart and flooded it like the ocean sweeping through broken dikes.[101]

So rich is the above passage that we must pause to draw out all its content. More considered the whole gamut of sufferings that weighed upon the heart of the Savior on that night. For not only did He suffer

---

[99] Ibid., 29–37.
[100] Ibid., 39–43.
[101] Ibid., 43–49 (quote on 47–49).

from the foreknowledge of every painful detail of His death agony on the Cross, with all the tortures that were to precede it; He was tormented at an even deeper level by the fates of His followers and His foes alike. For our Lord, whose very mission on earth was the salvation of all men, the loss of just one soul would have been an unfathomable tragedy; for is not Christ the Good Shepherd who leaves the ninety-nine sheep to go in pursuit of the one that has strayed (Mt 18:12)? In the eighteenth chapter of the Book of the prophet Ezekiel, it is written: "Have I any pleasure in the death of the wicked, says the Lord God . . . ?" (Ezek 18:23); one cannot begin to imagine what our Lord must have experienced as He contemplated the downfall of Judas. And then there was His agony at the thought of the indescribable anguish that was now to crush the heart of the most perfectly innocent of all His sheep—His own beloved Mother. She had known the cries of Rachel weeping for her children that rose from the streets of Bethlehem when Herod sent his henchmen to hunt down her Son; but it had not yet been His hour, and so He had been carried beyond their reach, cradled in her arms. But His hour had finally come—and His hour was to be her hour. There was now to be no escape—Saint Joseph was no longer there to lead the two to safety. Yes, the Passover lamb was to be eaten this night, but the blood that had sheltered the children of Israel in their homes when the firstborn of Egypt were struck down could not save her firstborn. No, her firstborn was the Paschal Lamb of the New Covenant, and His blood was to mark the lintels of all the new children of Israel, the children of the Church.

Following the passage upon which we have dwelt, More embarks on something of a digression of his own, but one most worthwhile and quite relevant to his own situation. He addresses the question of why our Savior allowed Himself to experience such dread and fear of His impending Passion and death. Were not such emotions unbecoming to the incarnate Son of God, who had exhorted His followers not to fear those who could kill only the body? Was not He, the King of Martyrs, to set an example of fearless fortitude in the face of such things? More responds that these objections stem from a misunderstanding of our Lord's words. In exhorting His disciples not to fear "those who kill the body but cannot kill the soul" (Mt 10:28), Christ was not condemning the quite natural and human fear one feels when death looms near; rather, He was addressing how we respond to that fear. It is only when out of fear a person denies his faith to escape suffering or death that he brings condemnation upon himself. Indeed, as More observes, there are times when one can and should flee persecution and death, so long as doing so in no way constitutes an implicit denial of Christ and does no "injury to His cause". Why else would our Lord have told His followers that "When they persecute you in one town, flee to the next . . ." (Mt 10:23)?[102] The apostles and many of the martyrs did just this, escaping from needless risks until the Lord saw fit to call them home by their giving witness with their blood. This does not mean that God has not sometimes prompted courageous souls to take the "initiative" by proclaiming their faith in potentially life-threatening situations even when not demanded of them. Nevertheless, God does not usually ask this of His faithful, and thus no one should be so presumptuous as deliberately to put himself in danger unless inspired to do so by God Himself.[103]

For most who face martyrdom, it is simply a question of whether they will suffer for Christ or deny Him. In this case, More explains, the Christian can rest assured that God has willed for him to undergo this trial, and therefore He will either provide him with a way to escape the danger without denying Him or provide him with all the grace and strength requisite to suffer and even to die for Him. He supports his point by citing a favorite passage of his from Saint Paul's First Letter to the Corinthians: "God is faithful, and he will not let you be tempted beyond your strength, but with the temptation will also provide the way of escape, that you may be able to endure it" (1 Cor 10:13). Thus More exhorts those finding themselves in "hand-to-hand combat with the prince of this world" and with "no way left to withdraw without disgracing the cause" to "cast away fear" and "be completely calm, confident, and hopeful".[104] More further reassures those under threat of death for their fidelity to Christ (and in this he is actually reassuring himself as well) that the great martyrs of ages past certainly suffered from fear; no less a figure than the Apostle to the Gentiles, Saint Paul, admitted to experiencing fear more than once (see 1 Cor 2:3 and 2 Cor 7:5).[105]

More now turns to the reasons why our Lord chose to experience dread to such a degree before His Passion. He begins by reminding

---

[102] Ibid., 49–63.
[103] Ibid., 63–67.
[104] Ibid., 69–71.
[105] Ibid., 73–81.

his readers of the heresies that have denied either the divine nature of Christ or His human nature. For More, our Lord's innumerable miracles refute the first heresy, while Gethsemane refutes the second. He sees Christ deliberately allowing Himself to undergo the emotions of sadness and fear so as to demonstrate that He was truly man.[106] But our Lord had other reasons as well for suffering as He did on Mount Olivet. More points out that the Savior has provided us with a supreme example to follow, so that in seeing His agony endured for our salvation we may not fail to accept trials for His sake or resent the just punishment of our sins.[107] And Gethsemane serves to give courage to those frightened by martyrdom:

> O faint of heart, take courage and do not despair . . . Trust me. I con-
> quered the world, and yet I suffered immeasurably more from fear, I
> was sadder, more afflicted with weariness, more horrified at the prospect
> of such cruel suffering drawing eagerly nearer and nearer . . . you, my
> timorous and feeble little sheep, be content to have me alone as your
> shepherd . . . See, I am walking ahead of you along this fearful road.
> Take hold of the border of my garment and you will feel going out
> from it a power which will stay your heart's blood from issuing in vain
> fears . . .[108]

After recapitulating his discussion of martyrdom, More invites his readers to reflect upon the scene in Gethsemane of our Lord pros-trating Himself on the ground in supplication to His eternal Father, providing us with the supreme model of humility:

> First of all Christ the commander teaches by His own example that His
> soldier should take humility as his starting point, since it is the founda-
> tion (as it were) of all the virtues from which one may safely mount to
> higher levels.[109]

The prayer of Christ in the garden serves as the point of departure for one of the most delightfully human passages in the *De Tristitia Christi*. For More launches upon an extended discussion of a prob-lem all Christians are all too familiar with—that of distractions in prayer:

---

[106] Ibid., 87–95.
[107] Ibid., 95–97.
[108] Ibid., 101–5.
[109] Ibid., 111–13 (quote on 113).

I wish that sometime we would make a special effort, right after finishing our prayers, to run over in our minds the whole sequence of time we spent praying. What follies will we see there? . . . Indeed we will be amazed that it was at all possible for our minds to dissipate themselves in such a short time among so many places at such great distance from each other, among so many different affairs, such various, such manifold, such idle pursuits.[110]

More continues by comparing the state of mind of those who pray distractedly with that of a person dreaming in his sleep. Often the distractions are reflected even in deplorable bodily deportment while at prayer; in this context he inveighs against a number of halfhearted ways of kneeling:

And even when we kneel down, we either place our weight on one knee, raising up the other and resting it on our foot, or we place a cushion under our knees, and sometimes (if we are especially spoiled) we even support our elbows on a cushion, looking for all the world like a propped up house that is threatening to tumble down.[111]

Such dissipation in mind or body we would not dare practice while conferring with any earthly prince, More argues; then how can we be so careless when speaking to Almighty God Himself?[112]

In a reflection on our Lord's interrupting His prayer to return to His disciples, only to find them asleep (Mt 26:40; Mk 14:37; Lk 22:45), More contrasts Christ's solicitude for the apostles with their negligence in sleeping while He suffered—how much more was His love for them than was theirs for Him.[113] And in a passage somewhat reminiscent of the *Improperia* (the "Reproaches") of the Good Friday liturgy, More draws out all that is implied in our Lord's gently reprimanding question to Peter in the garden, "Simon, are you asleep? Could you not watch one hour?" (Mk 14:37):

I always made much of you Simon, and yet Simon are you sleeping? I paid you many high honors, and yet Simon are you sleeping? A few moments ago you boasted that you would die with me, and now Simon are you sleeping? Now I am pursued to the death by the Jews and the

---

[110] Ibid., 113–19 (quote on 117–19).
[111] Ibid., 119–27 (quote on 125–27).
[112] Ibid., 129–35.
[113] Ibid., 157–59.

gentiles and by one worse than either of them, Judas, and Simon are you sleeping?[114]

In discussing our Lord's petition to His Father that if possible the cup of anguish might pass, More explains that when Christ spoke in this manner, He was speaking in virtue of His human nature. As true God and true man, He could act according to one nature or the other, depending on the circumstances. That the Scriptures record Christ's actions without distinguishing between what proceeded from one nature or the other should not confuse us, More argues, for in conversation we similarly speak of actions peculiar to either our body or our soul without differentiating between the two. As examples of this, he notes that we speak of the martyrs going immediately to heaven upon their deaths without specifying that only their souls have done so thus far (their bodies remain here on earth until the Day of Judgment), and that when we say a man is only dust and will "rot" in his grave, this naturally refers to his body but not his soul. Thus, it is one and the same Christ who said "I and the Father are one" (Jn 10:30) in virtue of His divinity and ". . . [T]he Father is greater than I" (Jn 14:28) in virtue of His humanity.[115]

In our Lord's repeated attempts to wake the slumbering apostles, More sees a lesson in how God prompts us to do what is right without forcing us:

> . . . [S]uch is God's kindness that even when we are negligent and slumbering on the pillow of our sins, He disturbs us from time to time, shakes us, strikes us, and does His best to wake us up by means of tribulations.[116]

We for our part are too foolish to recognize in tribulation the hand of God, "most loving even in His anger",[117] who is only allowing us to suffer in order to set us back on the road that leads to Him. More's observation in this regard brings to mind the verse from the Book of Proverbs, ". . . [T]he Lord reproves him whom he loves . . ." (Prov 3:12). Perhaps reflecting upon the thorny path that lay ahead for himself, More invites us to pray that God may lead us on toward our

---

[114] Ibid., 159–67 (quote on 165).
[115] Ibid., 181–85.
[116] Ibid., 197–203 (quote on 203).
[117] Ibid., 203.

final destiny: ". . . [W]e must intensely desire to run after you eagerly, O God, in the odor of your ointments, in the most sweet scent of your spirit."[118] When weariness or laziness is getting the better of us, he continues, then should we beseech God to "drag us along".[119] For when sloth sets in, the desire to pray is usually the first casualty. Thus, we should prepare ourselves in advance for such aridity of soul by asking God for the graces we will need to continue onward. We should even ask Him to send us those things that we may find most unpalatable but that He in His infinite wisdom knows are good for us and to deny us whatever would harm us, no matter how much we may later beg Him for such things in a moment of weakness.[120]

Reflecting upon the angel who came to our Lord in the garden (Lk 22:43), More brings his readers back to the bitter reality of Gethsemane by asking, "Do you realize how intense His mental anguish must have been, that an angel should come from heaven to strengthen Him?"[121] That Christ should have recourse to an angel was but further proof to More of the Church's teachings regarding the intercession of the saints and angels. If an angel could "console" Christ (albeit He needed no such assistance in virtue of His divinity), why cannot angels and saints assist us with their prayers?[122]

Saint Luke's reference to our Lord's bloody sweat (Lk 22:44) prompts More to express his agreement with the belief shared by most of the Church's scholars that the Savior in His bitter Passion suffered physical pains greater than that of any martyr ever, no matter how much more grievous and drawn out the tortures of some may appear by comparison with crucifixion. Noting the Church's interpretation of the prophet Jeremiah's words, "Look and see if there is any sorrow like my sorrow . . ." (Lam 1:12), as applicable to Christ Himself (an interpretation implicit in the way this text was used in the Divine Office of Good Friday, that is, at Tenebrae, for many centuries), More adds his own reason for believing that Christ's physical ordeal surpassed that of any other martyr. In view of the fact that "Christ, as the thought of His coming passion was borne in upon Him, was overwhelmed by mental anguish more bitter than any other mortal

---

[118] Ibid., 203–5 (quote on 205).
[119] Ibid., 205–7.
[120] Ibid., 209–11.
[121] Ibid., 221.
[122] Ibid., 223–27.

has ever experienced from the thought of coming torments", he adduces that the physical agony these mental torments anticipated must correspondingly have been the worst ever.[123]

Again More touches on the subject of martyrdom, explaining that there are two kinds of martyrs: those who although they greatly fear death accept martyrdom bravely when there is no valid means of escape; and those whom God inspires to expose themselves to danger and face death seemingly with little or no fear. As to which kind of martyr is more meritorious in the eyes of God, it is not for us to say: ". . . [J]ust who outranks whom in the glory assigned by God in heaven is not, I think, quite crystal-clear to us, groping as we are in the darkness of our mortality."[124]

At the end of this digression on martyrdom, More offers his readers some words of encouragement in undergoing trials for the Kingdom of God. In what is undoubtedly one of the most consoling passages of the *De Tristitia Christi,* he calls on us when we are in anguish to remember the agony of the Redeemer, so much worse than our own, and to pray in our agony that Christ may comfort us with "an insight into His".[125] And let us be mindful always to conclude any petition for deliverance as Christ did: ". . . [N]evertheless, not as I will, but as thou wilt" (Mt 26:39). If we make the effort to conduct ourselves in this manner, then just as the angel came to Christ in His torment, "so too each of our angels will bring us from His Spirit consolation that will give us the strength to persevere in those deeds that will lift us up to heaven."[126] Further, Christ offers us the reassurance that where He asks us to tread He has already passed before us:

> For after He had suffered this agony for a long time, His spirits were so restored that He arose, returned to His apostles, and freely went out to meet the traitor . . . Then, when He had suffered (as was necessary) He entered into His glory, preparing there a place also for those of us who follow in His footsteps.[127]

More now brings us to that climactic moment in the garden when Christ returns to His disciples a third and final time and, finding them

---

[123] Ibid., 227–37 (quote on 233–35).
[124] Ibid., 237–41 (quote on 239–41).
[125] Ibid., 253–55.
[126] Ibid., 255.
[127] Ibid., 255–57.

once again asleep, rebukes them in these words: "Are you still sleeping and taking your rest? Behold, the hour is at hand, and the Son
of man is betrayed into the hands of sinners. Rise, let us be going;
see, my betrayer is at hand" (Mt 26:45–46). Contrasting the slumber of the apostles who had followed our Lord to Gethsemane with
Judas' tireless determination to betray his Master, More sees a most
unfortunate similarity between the events of that night in Jerusalem
and what has happened down through the centuries up to his own
time. For does not this behavior of the eleven in the garden, he observes, resemble the "somnolence" of those bishops (their successors)
who have neglected the nurturing of their flock or who have failed
to give witness to the truth, while the enemies of Christ have been,
like Judas, relentlessly at work seeking to take Him and crucify Him
yet again?[128]

With the cowardly capitulation of nearly all of England's bishops to
the demands of a king bent on usurping the authority of the Church
still freshly engraved in his mind, More cannot refrain from lamenting
the damage done by the prelate who, whether through worldliness,
pusillanimity, or fear of putting himself at personal risk, abdicates his
duty of protecting his own flock. Of those bishops who do so out of
faintheartedness he observes:

> . . . [I]f sorrow so grips the mind that its strength is sapped and reason
> gives up the reins, if a bishop is so overcome by heavy-hearted sleep that
> he neglects to do what the duty of his office requires for the salvation of
> his flock—like a cowardly ship's captain who is so disheartened by the
> furious din of a storm that he deserts the helm, hides away cowering
> in some cranny, and abandons the ship to the waves—if a bishop does
> this, I would certainly not hesitate to juxtapose and compare his sadness
> with the sadness that leads . . . to hell . . .[129]

But for More "far worse" are those bishops who fail to carry out the
obligations of their sacred office out of fear for their own well-being.
Indeed, in giving witness when the faith is under attack, bishops are
called upon by Christ to do even more than others, for silence under
such circumstances would be tantamount to a denial of Christ:

> . . . He does not allow them to be concerned only about their own souls
> or merely to take refuge in silence until they are dragged out and forced

---

[128] Ibid., 257–61.
[129] Ibid., 261–65 (quote on 263–65).

to choose between open profession or lying dissimulation, but He also wished them to come forth if they see that the flock entrusted to them is in danger and to face the danger of their own accord for the good of their flock. "The good shepherd," says Christ, "lays down his life for his sheep."[130]

While More considers negligence in professing the faith comparable to the slumber of the apostles, and open denial of Christ out of fear comparable to Saint Peter's denial, he could only describe those who deliberately dissent in their teaching from the dogmas of the Church as the moral equivalent of Judas. Yet here he reminds his readers of the unfathomable mercy of God, who is willing to forgive even this sin; yes, Christ gave even Judas repeated chances, repeated gentle invitations, to repent:

> He deigned to stoop down at the feet of the betrayer and to wash with His innocent and most sacred hands Judas' dirty feet, a most fit symbol of his filthy mind. Moreover, with incomparable generosity, He gave him to eat, in the form of bread, that very body of His which the betrayer had already sold; and under the appearance of wine, He gave him that very blood to drink which, even while he was drinking it, the traitor was wickedly scheming to broach and set flowing.[131]

More finds Judas' signs of remorse in bringing back the silver pieces to the chief priests and in accusing himself of having betrayed innocent blood as evincing the powerful effects of Christ's overtures to this wayward soul:

> . . . I am inclined to believe that Christ prompted him thus far so that He might if possible—that is, if the traitor did not add despair to his treachery—save from ruin the very man who had so recently, so perfidiously betrayed Him to death.[132]

Thus in our Lord's dealings with Judas, More sees reason for hope that even the most hardened sinners can be brought to conversion. For if God in His infinite mercy was willing to pursue Judas so relentlessly that in the end it was only the betrayer's final sin of despair that thwarted his reclamation, will not He do the same for His other prodigal sons and daughters as well, if we but ask Him?

---

[130] Ibid., 265–71 (quote on 269–71).
[131] Ibid., 275–79 (quote on 277–79).
[132] Ibid., 279.

. . . [A]ccording to that holy advice of the apostle "Pray for each other that you may be saved," [James 5:16] if we see anyone wandering wildly from the right road . . . let us pray humbly and incessantly that God will hold out to him chances to come to his senses, and likewise that with God's help he will eagerly seize them . . .[133]

More pauses to consider the import of Christ's first words to the apostles when He finds them asleep a third and final time: "Sleep ye now and take your rest . . ." (Mt 26:45—Douay-Rheims translation). He believes there is a tone of irony, a grave though not flippant sarcasm in this expression, for it is clear from the words immediately following that it was no time to slumber, with Judas so near at hand. More is aware that some Catholic scholars do not see irony in this passage, among them his favorite Church Father, Saint Augustine. To those who would venture further to suggest that irony is inappropriate in the mouth of Christ, More responds by citing two other instances from the Sacred Scriptures where irony is employed, in one case by Saint Paul (2 Cor 12:13), in the other by the prophet Elijah (1 Kings 18:27 [3 Kings in Latin vulgate]).[134] Nonetheless, humbly referring to himself as "such a nobody as me",[135] More does not presume to know better in this matter than others.

Our Savior's words, "Rise and pray that you may not enter into temptation" (Lk 22:46), prompt More to speak yet again of the importance of prayer in the night. He begins by noting that Christ's command to rise teaches us that when waking from sleep to pray we cannot conquer our drowsiness "by a prolonged struggle, but rather we should break with one thrust the grip of the alluring arms with which it embraces us and pulls us down"; thus having shaken off "the very image of death", we may turn to God with our full vigor.[136] As a caveat to his earlier criticisms of distracted prayer, More offers his readers the reassuring advice of the ascetical writer Jean Gerson that involuntary distractions in no way detract from the merit of the original intention to pray, any more than the mental wanderings of a pilgrim on his way to a shrine could nullify his original decision to make the pilgrimage; indeed, our prayer, once begun with the right

---

[133] Ibid., 281–83 (quote on 281).
[134] Ibid., 287–301.
[135] Ibid., 301–3.
[136] Ibid., 303–7 (quotes on 305).

intention, continues throughout the day, so long as all our actions, of whatever nature, are ultimately directed toward the glory of God.[137]

Commenting on Christ's words that the hour of His betrayal had come and His betrayer was at hand (Mt 26:45–46), More sees this terrible moment in a sense repeated down through the ages, for whenever the Church is threatened by enemies from within or without, might we not say again that "the hour is at hand" when "the Son of man is betrayed into the hands of sinners"?[138]

After More embarks upon a digression concerning the sufferings of the Church in his own time (from which we have already quoted in an earlier chapter), he returns to the drama unfolding under the shadow of Gethsemane's olive trees and, in a powerful passage reminiscent of the poetic imagery of the Church Fathers, sets before our eyes the arrival of Christ's enemies as the ultimate confrontation between good and evil:

> They carry smoking torches and dim lanterns so that they might be able to discern through the darkness of sin the bright sun of justice, not that they might be enlightened by the light of Him who enlightens every man that comes into this world, but that they might put out that eternal light of His which can never be darkened.[139]

More pauses to consider the utter horror of what is about to take place. It is not a crowd of common criminals or ruffians that has come to do violence to the Christ; rather, this conspiracy is the work of respectable men of high office in Jewish society—men responsible for the upholding of God's law, but now bent on destroying His only begotten Son.[140] But more odious still is the fact that these are actually led by one of our Lord's own apostles, Judas.[141] And it is in Judas' kiss that More discerns the archetype for every act of pretended loyalty to Christ:

> In this same way Christ is approached, greeted, called "Rabbi," kissed, by those who pretend to be disciples of Christ, professing His teaching in name but striving in fact to undermine it by crafty tricks and stratagems. In just this way Christ is greeted as "Rabbi" by anyone who

---

[137] Ibid., 313–27.

[138] Ibid., 345–47.

[139] Ibid., 365.

[140] Ibid., 369–71.

[141] Ibid., 373.

calls Him master and scorns His precepts. In just this way is He kissed by those priests who consecrate the most holy body of Christ and then put to death Christ's members, Christian souls, by their false teaching and wicked example.[142]

At this juncture, More notes, our Lord is no longer tormented with dread, as He was but a short time ago while alone in prayer. For, having received Judas' duplicitous kiss, He now steps forward toward the crowd that has come to arrest Him and boldly asks, "Whom do you seek?" (Jn 18:4). In the same way, More explains, fearful souls should take courage in seeing that, just as they have shared in Christ's agony, so shall they receive the grace, when their hour of confrontation with the powers of evil has arrived, to rise to the occasion, provided they have been faithful in prayer and have resigned themselves to the holy will of their Creator: ". . . [B]y means of the wood of Christ's cross let down into the water of their sorrow, the thought of death, once so bitter, will grow sweet . . ."[143]

The mysterious crumbling to the ground of Christ's enemies in response to His first assertion of His identity ("When he said to them, 'I am he,' they drew back and fell to the ground" [Jn 18:6]) was, to More, an undeniable assertion of Christ's power over the entire situation; what they were about to do to Him would come about only because He had willed to allow them. Thus at the sound of His voice, which More likens to a bolt of lightning, the souls of His pursuers "melted" within their bodies. In this regard, More applies to Christ, the incarnate Word, one of the most famous verses from the Letter to the Hebrews, ". . . [T]he word of God is living and active, sharper than any two-edged sword . . ." (Heb 4:12).[144]

Following yet another digression on the interpretation of Sacred Scripture, and after stressing that the eleven apostles were protected from arrest or harm by our Lord Himself, More turns to Saint Peter's wielding of the sword against Malchus, slave of the high priest (Lk 22:50–51). In our Lord's rebuke of Peter's violent action ("Put your sword into its sheath . . ." [Jn 18:11]), he sees Christ admonishing His apostles to do battle, not with a sword of iron, but with "the sword of the word of God"; the sword of iron is properly the province

---

[142] Ibid., 389–91.

[143] Ibid., 411–17 (quote on 415–17).

[144] Ibid., 425–27, 431.

of the state and not of the clergy. Further, the sword can also be seen to symbolize the apostolic authority to excommunicate—a power the apostles and their successors may rightfully exercise as their own but which should be "kept hidden in the sheath of mercy" unless absolutely needed.[145]

Reflecting upon Christ's question to Peter, ". . . [S]hall I not drink the cup which the Father has given me?" (Jn 18:11), More observes that our Lord, who throughout His public ministry had taught us obedience to God, to parents, and to civil authorities, had now come to the culmination of His work, all done in obedience to His Heavenly Father. How could He refuse His Father, He asks Peter, at this supreme hour and "unravel in a single moment all of that most beautiful fabric I have spent such a long time weaving?"[146]

Christ's words, "But how then should the scriptures be fulfilled, that it must be so?" (Mt 26:54) are a reminder, More notes, to Peter, and to us as well, that the Passion of Christ was prophesied in innumerable passages of the Old Testament. How, then, could the redemption promised to mankind ever come about if the means ordained by God Himself for the accomplishment of that redemption were thwarted either by calling down angels from heaven (Mt 26:53) or by the sword of Peter?[147] In fact, More points out, by attempting to strike at those taking Christ to His Passion, Peter was inadvertently fighting against "the whole human race" by opposing the only way to our salvation.[148] Our Lord's action in the wake of Peter's rashness (Lk 22:51) evokes this beautiful comment from More:

> But now behold the most gentle heart of Christ, who did not think it enough to check Peter's strokes but also touched the severed ear of His persecutor and made it sound again, in order to give us an example of rendering good for evil.[149]

Christ, having reprimanded one of His own, now turned to confront the mob that had come to arrest Him: "Have you come out as against a robber, with swords and clubs? When I was with you day after day in the temple, you did not lay hands on me. But this is your

---

[145] Ibid., 471–81 (quotes on 477, 481 respectively).
[146] Ibid., 481–91 (quote on 491).
[147] Ibid., 501–5.
[148] Ibid., 503–5.
[149] Ibid., 505.

hour, and the power of darkness" (Lk 22:52–53). It is in his contemplation of these words that More reaches the zenith of his writing powers in the final pages of *De Tristitia Christi*. Christ is subtly warning the chief priests, Pharisees, and elders not to pride themselves on having trapped Him, More explains; for all their hostility they were unable to take Him even as He sat among them in the Temple, for He had not willed that they should have any power over Him until this hour:

> He lets them know that the foolish contrivances and maneuvers by which they labored to suppress the truth were powerless to accomplish anything against Him, but rather the profound wisdom of God had foreseen and set the time when the prince of this world would be justly tricked into losing his ill-gotten prey, the human race, even as he strove by unjust means to keep it.[150]

More then pauses over the words, "But this is your hour, and the power of darkness"; Christ was now about to pass from the company of His followers and into the hands of those who hated Him most, who would stop at nothing to destroy Him. Repeatedly our Lord had spoken of the coming of this hour; only a few days earlier He had said:

> Now is my soul troubled. And what shall I say? "Father, save me from this hour"? No, for this purpose I have come to this hour. Father, glorify thy name . . . Now is the judgment of this world, now shall the ruler of this world be cast out . . . (Jn 12:27–28, 31).

In this "hour" Christ willingly surrendered Himself into the hands of Satan that He might confound Lucifer's pride with the supreme act of humility; but for the moment, the enemies of Christ believed they had triumphed. So it is that More, finding our Lord's words in the garden regarding the "hour" richly imbued with dramatic force and meaning, puts into the mouth of the Savior a most poignant address to those who have raised their heel against Him:

> And so this is your hour and the power of darkness. This is the short hour allowed to you and the power granted to darkness, so that now in the dark you might do what you were not permitted to do in the daylight, flying in my face like winged creatures from the Stygian marsh . . . You

---

[150] Ibid., 523–25.

are in the dark when you ascribe my death to your strength. So too the governor Pilate will be in the dark when he takes pride in possessing the power to free me or to crucify me.[151]

In the lines that follow More reveals himself to be a man profoundly aware of the scope and magnitude of the battle within which he found himself immersed—a battle where good men were to strive against "principalities" and "powers" (Eph 6:12). The stakes were high—extremely high—the salvation or damnation of countless souls, the winning or losing of whole nations to the cause of Christ. He understood that the Christian martyr does not stand alone before his accusers. At his side are the martyrs of every time and place, all standing together "at a place called . . . Gabbatha" (Jn 19:13) before the judgment seat of Pilate, all standing with their Lord. Yes, the enemies of Christ are to have their hour, but their hour of illusory triumph is miserably brief:

> This is your short hour. This is that mad and ungovernable power which brings you armed to take an unarmed man, which brings the fierce against the gentle, criminals against an innocent man, a traitor against his lord, puny mortals against God.
>
> But this hour and this power of darkness are not only given to you now against me, but such an hour and such a brief power of darkness will also be given to other governors and other caesars against other disciples of mine. And this too will truly be the power of darkness. For whatever my disciples endure and whatever they say, they will not endure by their own strength or say of themselves, but conquering through my strength they will win their souls by their patience . . . So too those who persecute and kill them will neither do nor speak anything of themselves. Rather, the prince of darkness who is already coming and who has no power over me will instill his poison in the breasts of these tyrants and tormentors and will demonstrate and exercise his strength through them for the brief time allowed him. Hence my comrades-in-arms will be struggling not against flesh and blood but against princes and powers, against the rulers of the darkness of this world, against the spiritual forces of evil in high places.[152]

More now embarks upon a brilliant exposition built out of verses from Psalm 2, which significantly has been assigned for centuries to

---

[151] Ibid., 537–39.
[152] Ibid., 541–45.

the Divine Office for Good Friday and was thus part of Tenebrae, that is, the solemn public recitation of the Office for the last three days of Holy Week. In More's time Tenebrae for Good Friday was celebrated on the evening of Holy Thursday. As there is good reason to believe he was accustomed to attending Tenebrae (see chapter 8), we cannot help speculating that the juxtaposition of this psalm in his meditation on the events of the first Holy Thursday night may well have been inspired by this service:

> But although the nations have raged and the people devised vain things, although the kings of the earth have risen up and the princes gathered together against the Lord and against His Christ, striving to break their chains and to cast off that most sweet yoke which a loving God, through His pastors, places upon their stubborn necks, then He who dwells in the heavens will laugh at them and the Lord will deride them. He sits not on a curule throne like earthly princes, raised up a few feet above the earth, but rather He rises above the setting of the sun, He sits above the cherubim, the heavens are His throne, the earth is the footstool beneath His feet, His name is the Lord. He is the king of kings and the lord of lords, a terrible king who daunts the hearts of princes. This king will speak to them in His anger, and in His rage he will throw them into confusion. He will establish His Christ, the son whom He has today begotten, as king on His holy mountain of Sion, a mountain which will not be shaken. He will cast all His enemies down before Him like a footstool under His feet. Those who tried to break His chains and cast off His yoke, He will rule against their will with a rod of iron, and He will shatter them like a potter's vessel.[153]

More, seemingly borne along on a wave of inspiration, continues in this vein by borrowing a passage from Saint Paul's Letter to the Ephesians, which describes how the disciples of Christ are to arm themselves for battle, with truth as their belt, righteousness as their breastplate, faith as their shield, and the word of God as their sword (Eph 6:14–17). With such weapons as these, they will surely defeat Satan and his cohorts.[154] He then brings this address to an end by reiterating the theme with which he began—that time is short for those in rebellion against God:

---

[153] Ibid., 547–49.
[154] Ibid., 551–53.

. . . [T]he span of time allotted to your wanton arrogance is not endless but has been shortened to the span of a brief hour for the sake of the elect, that they might not be tried beyond their strength. And so this hour of yours and this power of darkness are not long-lasting and enduring but quite as brief as the present moment to which they are limited, an instant of time always caught between a past that is gone and a future that has not arrived. Therefore, lest you should lose any of this hour of yours which is so short, proceed immediately to use it for your own evil purposes. Since you seek to destroy me, be quick about it, arrest me without delay, but let these men go their way.[155]

Reflecting upon the rapid desertion of the apostles following Christ's reprimand of Peter, More observes how much more difficult it is to face death at the hands of an enemy with meekness and patience than to die striking out against him. This is illustrated by the apostles, who remained brave enough until Christ forbade them to fight those who had come to arrest Him. It is this incident that also finally settled for More a question that he tells us he had repeatedly pondered: whether Christ found *all* the apostles asleep in the garden when He came to them following His prayer to His Father or only those whom He had left nearby (Peter, James, and John). He concludes that all must have neglected Christ's admonition to watch and pray—this would explain why none had the patience to remain steadfast when they could no longer resort to fighting.[156]

Turning to the incident of the young man who fled naked after being seized by Christ's captors in the garden (Mk 14:51), More concludes that this individual was not one of the apostles but probably an attendant from the house where the Last Supper was held. Besides seeing this episode as proof that the crowd fully intended to arrest the apostles, More expresses his belief that the young man had come to Gethsemane and had lingered even after the flight of the disciples because he desired to follow Christ. He is confident that this man is in heaven now where someday hopefully we will all join him and learn from him the full story of what took place that night in the garden.[157]

---

[155] Ibid., 555-57.
[156] Ibid., 559-65.
[157] Ibid., 565-87.

More observes that in some situations we should flee from danger, while in others we should not. We ought to flee when there is no sin in doing so and we are in danger of falling into some other sin if we remain. But we must stand fast when God compels us to remain, for it is a serious sin to abandon the "battle station" that God has given us to guard.[158]

Finding significance in the fact that the young man was wearing only a linen cloth that broke loose easily when he was seized, More observes that just as a man in light and loose clothing can flee more easily than those in heavy or tight-fitting garments, so too a man encumbered by riches is far more vulnerable when danger comes than those who are detached from such things.[159] Moreover, there can be drawn from this episode an even more important analogy regarding the relationship between the body and the soul. As More explains, we must be willing to part with the garment that the soul puts on at the beginning of life and lays aside at its end—the body—rather than lose the soul through grave sin. Just as a snake breaks out of its old skin and emerges with its new by passing through thorns and thistles, so too should we be wise as serpents (Mt 10:16) and be willing to part with our bodies by passing through the thorns of suffering endured out of love for God, that we may be swiftly brought to heaven, there to emerge "shining and young".[160]

More now turns to the very moment when the crowd took custody of Christ, expressing the view that this did not take place until all the other events in the garden related by the four evangelists had transpired (Christ's words to His captors, the healing of the servant of Malchus, the flight of the apostles, and so on). It is here, with the words ". . . did they lay hands on Jesus", that More's exposition—and indeed his entire literary career—comes to an abrupt end.[161] It is believed that this sudden termination was dictated by the events of June 12, 1535, when the man who would betray More at his trial entered his cell and all of More's books and writing materials were confiscated. Whether determined purely by Divine Providence or by More's perfect timing and good literary sense, such an ending proved

---

[158] Ibid., 589–95.
[159] Ibid., 595–605.
[160] Ibid., 605–17 (quote on 617).
[161] Ibid., 619–25 (quote on 625).

most suitable, for his meditation had already covered every aspect of its declared subject matter—the Agony in the Garden. All that remained to him was to be led with his Master from Gethsemane to trial and death.

CHAPTER XIV

July 6, 1535

But if you live the time that no man will give you good counsel, nor no man will give you good example, when you shall see virtue punished and vice rewarded, if you will then stand fast and firmly stick to God, upon pain of my life, though you be but half good, God will allow you for whole good.

> — Thomas More,
> quoted in William Roper,
> *The Life of Sir Thomas More*

A More Intimate "Dialogue of Comfort": More's Correspondence in the Tower

The story of the last fourteen months of Thomas More's life is told largely through his correspondence with his family and friends—a precious testament to the love of God and the strength and beauty of human bonds forged under the shadow of the Cross. These letters afford us a window into More's soul as he deals with approaching death and the anguish of separation from his wife and children. Not surprisingly most of the extant correspondence from this period is to or from his daughter Margaret. There had always been a special affinity between the two, and in these last letters it reaches its fullest and most poignant expression. We have already had recourse to More's first letter to Margaret from the Tower, written on or shortly after his first day there (April 17, 1534), detailing the events of the previous Monday (April 13), when he answered the summons to appear before the King's commissioners at Lambeth.[1] His next letter, far shorter and more personal, was composed later that month or sometime in May; evidently he had at the time been deprived of writing instruments, for he himself states that he wrote it with a coal. It deserves to be quoted in full (including its postscript), for it sets the tone for all the correspondence that will follow:

> Mine own good Daughter,
>
>   Our Lord be thanked, I am in good health of body, and in good quiet of mind; and of worldly things I no more desire than I have. I beseech him make you all merry in the hope of heaven. And such things as I somewhat longed to talk with you all, concerning the world to come, our Lord put them in to your minds, as I trust he doth, and better too, by his Holy Spirit; who bless you and preserve you all. Written with a coal by your tender loving father, who in his poor prayers forgetteth none of you all, nor your babes, nor your nurses, nor your good husbands, nor your good husbands' shrewd wives, nor your father's shrewd wife neither, nor our other friends. And thus fare you heartily well for lack of paper.
>
> Thomas More, Knight.
>
>   Our Lord keep me continually true, faithful and plain, to the contrary whereof I beseech him heartily never to suffer me live. For as for long life (as I have often told thee Meg) I neither look for, nor long for, but am well content to go, if God call me hence tomorrow. And I thank our Lord I know no person living that I would had one philippe for my sake; of which mind I am more glad than of all the world beside.
>
>   Recommend me to your shrewd Will and mine other sons, and to John Harris my friend, and yourself knoweth to whom else, and to my shrewd wife above all, and God preserve you all, and make and keep you his servants all.[2]

In the third of More's Tower letters to Margaret, we find him deeply troubled by her last piece of correspondence, wherein she has attempted to persuade him, apparently halfheartedly, to take the oath. Reminding her that he has repeatedly explained to her already the impossibility of such a step, he confesses that the thought of his fam-

---

[1] See chapter 11, pp. 322–25, of the present volume.

[2] Letter no. 201, in Elizabeth Rogers, ed., *The Correspondence of Sir Thomas More* (Princeton, N.J.: Princeton Univ. Press, 1947), 507–8.

ily's grief and danger in consequence of his decision torments him even more than his own sufferings, yet "while it lieth not in my hand, I can no further but commit all unto God."[3] It is here that More quotes for the first time in his prison correspondence a verse from the Book of Proverbs to which he will turn regularly: "The king's heart is a stream of water in the hand of the Lord; he turns it wherever he will" (Prov 21:1). More uses it to stress one of the prevailing motifs of his last letters—the necessity of resigning oneself to the loving providence of God, which he often describes as the "hand" of God: ". . . I can no further go, but put all in the hands of him, for fear of whose displeasure . . . I suffer and endure this trouble." It is obvious from his Tower writings that to More the supreme example of such obedience to the divine will is that of Christ in Gethsemane, and hence this idea comes swiftly to the surface in his words to Margaret:

> . . . I beseech him [God] . . . give me grace and you both in all our agonies and troubles, devoutly to resort prostrate unto the remembrance of that bitter agony, which our Saviour suffered before his passion at the Mount. And if we diligently so do, I verily trust we shall find therein great comfort and consolation.[4]

To this letter that More undoubtedly found painful to write, Margaret responds with words of great love, telling him that in her grief over his absence she has found no small solace in reading over and over again his words, which she describes as "the faithful messenger of your very virtuous and ghostly mind".[5] Echoing his thoughts, as she will so often do in the correspondence to come, Margaret expresses her confidence that God "holdeth his holy hand over you", especially now that he has resigned himself completely to Him. The family has found much consolation, she continues, in remembering the edifying conversations he used to have with them. Unafraid to embarrass him with praise, she describes his heart as "a pleasant palace for the Holy Spirit of God to rest in", but ends on a very human note by expressing her envious desire of trading places with John à Wood, the servant assigned to attend to his needs in the Tower.[6]

---

[3] Letter no. 202, May (?) 1534, ibid., 509.
[4] Ibid.
[5] Letter no. 203, May (?) 1534, ibid., 510.
[6] Ibid., 510–11.

Whether from motives of genuine compassion or the hope of shaking More's resolve, permission was evidently granted by the King not long after this letter for Margaret to visit with her father from time to time. We find this mentioned by More in a brief note to all his friends, which concludes with what will become a regular refrain in his prison correspondence—a plea and pledge to exchange prayers: ". . . [P]ray for me, and I shall pray for you."[7] In August 1534, More's stepdaughter Alice Alington saw an opportunity to beg clemency for her stepfather from More's successor to the office of Lord Chancellor, Thomas Audley. Her attempt was unsuccessful, but it was this incident that formed the background for a most remarkable and poignant conversation between More and Margaret, as recorded in a letter purportedly written by the latter to Alice Alington. In his 1557 edition of More's writings, William Rastell expresses uncertainty about the authorship and even leaves open the possibility that More himself wrote it. Be this as it may, the letter is generally considered an authentic account of a real conversation between the two. As R. W. Chambers has put it, "The speeches of More are absolute More; and the speeches of Margaret are absolute Margaret. And we have to leave it at that."[8]

The incident begins with Margaret bringing to her father in prison a letter from Alice Alington relating Audley's negative response to her efforts on his behalf. As Audley had blamed More for obstinately holding out regarding the oath, it is Margaret's intent to show her father from the example of Audley's answer that persistence in his "scruple" will only succeed either in losing him the friends that can help him most or in making it impossible for them to do anything at all for him. Before sitting to converse, they recite together the seven penitential psalms and the Litany of the Saints. Although they at first engage in small talk, Margaret eventually broaches to him the matter of Alice's letter; yet More is not slow to gain the upper hand:

> With this my father smiled upon me and said: "What, mistress Eve . . . hath my daughter Alington played the serpent with you, and with a letter set you a work to come tempt your father again, and for the favor that

---

[7] Letter no. 204, 1534, ibid., 511.

[8] R. W. Chambers, "The Continuity of English Prose" (essay), quoted in introduction to letter no. 206, ibid., 514.

you bear him labour to make him swear against his conscience, and so send him to the devil?"[9]

More continues by reiterating that if it were possible for him to satisfy the King's wishes in this regard he most certainly would, but the fact remains that he cannot do so, as it would violate his conscience. He has given much thought to the matter over several years, and he is convinced that nothing can change his mind. Hence all he can do is accept from God whatever consequences may befall him as a penance for his sins. Acutely aware of his own human weakness, he most certainly has considered the worst that might happen to him, yet if he did not trust in God giving him the strength to endure whatever he must, he "would not have come here". Therefore, as it is only to God that he looks in this matter, he cares not whether men brand his refusal a "foolish scruple".[10]

To these words Margaret responds by giving him Alice's letter to read for himself, noting that Audley, an important and learned man, along with all the other nobles of England, believes otherwise. After reading over the letter twice, More begins by praising Alice for being such a good stepdaughter to him. As for Audley's comments, he replies that the two fables used by the new Lord Chancellor to make his point are not persuasive.[11] Deciding to refute the fables with a tale of his own, More tells Margaret of an unlearned man named "Company" who sat on a jury, the other members of which were all pressuring him to concur with them for fellowship's sake in finding the defendant guilty, even though he could not in good conscience bring himself to believe so. Finally, Company says to his companions:

> But now when we shall hence and come before God, and that he shall send you to heaven for doing according to your conscience, and me to the devil for doing against mine . . . if I shall then say to all you . . . play you the good fellows now again with me, as I went then for good company with you, so some of you go now for good company with me. Would ye go . . . ?[12]

---

[9] Letter no. 206, August 1534, ibid., 515.
[10] Ibid., 516.
[11] Ibid., 516–18.
[12] Ibid., 521–23 (quote on 523).

In light of this tale More asks his daughter whether he, who is accounted somewhat learned, can fail to do any less in following his conscience for the salvation of his own soul than did this unlearned juror. If he were to swear against his conscience simply to join company with those who have sworn supposedly in good conscience, shall they, when the time comes to "stand in judgment at the bar before the high Judge", join him for friendship's sake when he is sent to hell for doing what he believed was wrong?[13]

Margaret replies that it is not a question of taking the oath for fellowship's sake but rather a matter of conforming one's conscience to the judgment of so many upright and educated men, especially in view of the danger there is to one's soul in disobeying a law of Parliament. To this line of reasoning More answers by addressing first the point about Parliament, reminding his daughter that while there is an obligation to keep the laws of the land, no one is obligated to swear that every law is good, nor is he required to keep any temporal law that is unlawful in the sight of God. It is, he notes, not the law of any one country but rather the laws and decisions of a General Council of the Church that have authority to bind all universally and unquestioningly. More astutely observes that some of those who have now taken the Oath of Succession were formerly of his opinion in refusing it. Though many less than honorable reasons come to mind as to why a man might change his stance on this issue, he prefers to think these men incapable of acting from such motives and refuses to judge them.[14]

As to the number of those who differ with More on the oath, he expresses confidence that, whatever the case may be in England, throughout the whole of Christendom the majority of virtuous and learned men would concur with him at least in some of the reasons for his opposition; even more does he believe his view not to be a minority opinion among the citizens of heaven. In the writings of the saints and Doctors of the Church More likewise finds support for his views. Thus while he has made no attempt to persuade anyone to agree with him, he nonetheless likens the certainty of his own conscience in this matter to that of knowing God is in heaven—he hopes

---

[13] Ibid., 523–24.
[14] Ibid., 524–27.

that this assurance on his part will be of some comfort to Margaret.[15]
But he is able to see for himself that he has yet fully to convince her:

> When he saw me sit with this very sad . . . he smiled upon me and said:
> "How now daughter Marget? What how mother Eve? Where is your
> mind now? Sit not musing with some serpent in your breast, upon some
> new persuasion, to offer father Adam the apple yet once again?"[16]

Dejected, Margaret admits to having exhausted all arguments but
one—the argument that she herself has taken the oath (albeit, William
Rastell tells us, with an inserted clause stipulating consent only so far
as the law of God allows). His reaction to her pathetic confession
is classically Morean: "At this he laughed and said, 'That word was
like Eve too, for she offered Adam no worse fruit than she had eaten
herself.' "[17]

Once again More reassures his daughter that he has already given
due consideration to all the possible consequences of his stance, so
much so that many a night while still a free man he had lain awake,
"while my wife slept, and weened that I had slept too", contemplating his future. Even so, never did he waver in his decision as to
what he must do.[18] To this Margaret retorts that the contemplation
of what *may* befall is vastly different from facing the stark thought of
what *will* be; thus, were the time to come that the feared outcome
becomes an impending reality, her father may change his mind too
late to save himself from his fate. "Too late . . . ?", More answers,
"I beseech our Lord, that if ever I make such a change, it may be
too late indeed."[19] He has put his full trust in God's mercy and grace
to uphold him in whatever he may have to suffer for his decision.
When tempted by fear he will recall the Gospel episode of Saint Peter
sinking into the waves when his faith wavered (Mt 14:28–31) and
will do as Peter did then, calling to Christ for help, confident that the
Lord will take hold of him with His "holy hand" and save him from
drowning. Yet even were he to play the part of Peter further and fail
like Peter by swearing against his conscience, it is his hope that God

---

[15] Ibid., 527–29.
[16] Ibid., 529.
[17] Ibid.
[18] Ibid., 529–30.
[19] Ibid., 530.

will look upon him as He did upon Peter after his denials (Lk 22:61) and bring him like Peter to affirm once more the truth according to his conscience, ready to endure whatever pains or humiliation may ensue.[20] Thus More wishes his daughter to find peace of mind, as he has, in the loving providence of God:

> . . . [N]ever trouble thy mind for any thing that ever shall hap [to] me in this world. Nothing can come but that that God will. And I make me very sure that what so ever that be, seem it never so bad in sight, it shall in deed be the best.[21]

The father-daughter dialogue ends with More's prayer "that we may meet together once in heaven, where we shall make merry for ever".[22]

It is evident from a later letter of Margaret that Dame Alice had, like her stepdaughter, obtained leave to visit with her husband. In his biography of his father-in-law, William Roper has preserved for us one of these meetings, which, despite the grim setting and circumstances, provides that touch of comic relief we have come to expect whenever Dame Alice comes to the fore. We can do no better than let Roper relate the episode in his own words:

> "What the good year, Master More," quoth she, "I marvel that you, that have been always hitherto taken for so wise a man, will now so play the fool to lie here in this close, filthy prison, and be content thus to be shut up amongst mice and rats, when you might be abroad at your liberty, and with the favour and good will both of the King and his Council, if you would but do as all the Bishops and best learned of this realm have done. And seeing you have at Chelsea a right fair house, your library, your books, your gallery, your garden, your orchard, and all other necessaries so handsome about you, where you might in the company of me your wife, your children, and household be merry, I muse what a God's name you mean here still thus fondly to tarry."
>
> After he had a while quietly heard her, with a cheerful countenance he said unto her:
>
> "I pray thee, good Mistress Alice, tell me one thing."
>
> "What is that?" quoth she.
>
> "Is not this house," quoth he, "as nigh heaven as my own?"

---

[20] Ibid., 530–31.
[21] Ibid., 531–32.
[22] Ibid., 532.

To whom she, after her accustomed homely fashion, not liking such talk, answered, "Tilly vally, Tilly vally!"

"How say you, Mistress Alice," quoth he, "is it not so?"

"Bone deus, bone deus, man, will this gear never be left?" quoth she.

"Well then, Mistress Alice, if it be so," quoth he, "it is very well. For I see no great cause why I should much joy either of my gay house or of anything belonging thereunto; when, if I should but seven years lie buried under the ground, and then arise and come thither again, I should not fail to find some therein that would bid me get me out of doors, and tell me it were none of mine. What cause have I then to like such an house as would so soon forget his master?"[23]

On the day that More was first taken into custody (April 17) he had observed that another individual familiar to him had likewise been detained—the priest Nicholas Wilson, who had for a time been the King's confessor and chaplain. It was from this same Nicholas Wilson that he later received a letter asking his advice on what to do regarding the oath. As both men were now in prison for refusing the oath, and in growing danger of an even worse fate, More replied with the utmost caution and discretion, confining himself to reminding Wilson of all the patristic sources the two of them had consulted in reaching their opinions of the matter prior to their imprisonment: Saint Augustine, Saint Ambrose, Saint Basil, Saint Gregory, Saint Jerome, and Saint John Chrysostom. Beyond this More could tell him nothing as to what he should do now—each of them must simply follow what his own conscience dictated.[24] Eventually Wilson wrote again to his fellow prisoner, informing him of his decision to swear to the supremacy; More responded with a brief note in which he wishes him well but carefully refrains from expressing any judgment about Wilson's action. As always he ends by asking for an exchange of prayers with his correspondent.[25]

At some point between August 1534 and December of the same year, More was subjected to new punitive restrictions that cut off, at least for the time being, visits from his family. Moreover, he was denied permission to continue attending Mass, as he had been accus-

---

[23] William Roper, *The Lyfe of Sir Thomas Moore, Knighte,* ed. Elsie V. Hitchcock, Early English Text Society, original series, no. 197 (London: Early English Text Society, 1935), 82–84.

[24] Letter no. 208, in Rogers, *Correspondence,* 533–38.

[25] Letter no. 207, ibid., 532–33.

tomed to do in one of the two chapels of the Tower complex. We learn these details from a letter of Margaret to her father, wherein she indicates that the new measures did not come as a surprise to him, who had earlier forewarned his family of the probability of such a turn of events. While Margaret cannot contain her regret in no longer being free to engage in what she considers "the chief comfort" of her life—conversing with her father—she no longer speaks of dissuading him from his decision regarding the oath but, quite to the contrary, prays that he will stand firm in obeying God's will.[26]

More's answer to this letter begins with a salutation he will use more than once and which expresses one of the recurring themes of his prison correspondence: "The Holy Spirit of God be with you." In an effusive burst of emotion, he tells Margaret that were he to put down in writing what her "daughterly loving letters" meant to him, "a peck of coals would not suffice to make me the pens." Turning to the matter of the newly imposed restrictions he is experiencing, he warns her that the family may be subjected to sudden searches, as there seems to be some disbelief that he has really become a poor and destitute man. Nonetheless, such searches "can make but game to us that know the truth of my poverty".[27] More conjectures that the new restrictions may stem from suspicions or insinuations that he is guilty of something more than simply refusing the oath. Be this as it may, he is confident that so long as he does not fall in the judgment of God, he cannot suffer any real harm. He puts no stock in the judgment of the world, to which "wrong may seem right" and which pronounces his refusal of the oath a crime and his fear of God an obstinate opposition to the King.[28] How far such judgments are from the truth More believes should have been obvious to the members of the council that have questioned him on the oath, who could see for themselves how aggrieved he was in incurring the King's displeasure. It was to them that he said he would rather suffer whatever punishments he must than displease his King further by disclosing the reasons for his refusal. Even so, lest the King account his silence as obstinacy, he would willingly obey a direct order from his sovereign to make known to him personally these reasons, with the understanding that his disclo-

---

[26] Letter no. 209, ibid., 538–39.
[27] Letter no. 210, ibid., 540.
[28] Ibid., 540–41.

sure would not be used to convict him of breaking the supremacy statute. But Cromwell, More adds, told him quite frankly that even were the King to agree to such a plan, it would most certainly not be possible to guarantee immunity from prosecution under the statute if his response were found to violate it.[29]

More has heard talk that his continued refusal of the oath will ultimately compel the King to frame a new law against him. Although, he tells Margaret, he cannot bring himself to believe his prince and the men of Parliament would pass "such an unlawful law", he can do nothing to prevent this. And while he has had to struggle to overcome his fears, the spirit has since prevailed over the flesh, for he now resolutely sees it as "a case in which a man may lose his head and yet have none harm, but in stead of harm inestimable good at the hand of God".[30]

More confides to his daughter that with each passing day his fear of death is diminished by the thought that whatever years death may take from a man in this life are more than compensated for by his entrance all the sooner into heaven. As to the manner of one's death, there is little to be lost in dying while in good health, since there is scarcely any death by illness that comes without pain. Indeed, it is foolish to dread a death suffered for God, for if we manage to escape it, we will later find ourselves on the painful deathbed of our final illness wishing that God had taken us earlier instead. Moreover, "a man may hap with less thanks of God, and more adventure of his soul to die as violently, and as painfully by many other chances, as by enemies or thieves."[31] Thus, More reassures Margaret, he is at full peace with his decision come what may. Nonetheless, he cannot forget that Saint Peter, who was far less fearful of death than he, succumbed to fear and swore to deny Christ merely upon being confronted with the questioning of a "simple girl". He will therefore have recourse to his own prayers and those of his daughter in obtaining from God the grace to keep his resolve.[32] For More it is, as always, a matter of putting one's trust in God:

---

[29] Ibid., 541.
[30] Ibid., 542.
[31] Ibid., 542–43.
[32] Ibid., 543.

... I never have prayed God to bring me hence nor deliver me from death, but referring all things whole unto his only pleasure, as to him that seeth better what is best for me than my self do. Nor never longed I since I came hither to set my foot in mine own house, for any desire of or pleasure of my house, but gladly would I sometime somewhat talk with my friends, and specially my wife and you that pertain to my charge. But since that God otherwise disposeth, I commit all wholly to his goodness . . .[33]

Once more attempting to comfort Margaret with his optimism that the King will not pursue him further by unjust means (earlier in the letter he had reminded her what Proverbs 21:1 says about the hearts of kings being streams in the hand of God), More ends by exhorting her to "be merry in God".[34]

In More's next letter, written in reply to one from Margaret (the text of which has not been preserved), he rejoices in the spiritual wisdom she has expressed in writing of the vast difference between this passing world and the world that is to come "for them that die in God".[35] So pleased is he with her words that he quotes them, wherein she cites two verses from Saint Paul's Letter to the Philippians (1:21, 23) that we have already seen recorded by More, along with other favorite biblical passages, on the last pages of the "Valencia manuscript" of his *De Tristitia Christi*.[36] Margaret uses the verses in a prayer to "rest our love" in God so surely as to make Saint Paul's words of living and dying for Christ one's own,[37] and it is this prayer that More urges her to join him in saying daily:

And therefore good Marget, when you pray it, pray it for us both . . . that likewise as in this wretched world I have been very glad of your company and you of mine, and yet would if it might be (as natural charity bindeth the father and the child) so we may rejoice and enjoy each other's company, with our other kinsfolk, allies and friends everlastingly in the glorious bliss of heaven; and in the meantime, with good counsel and prayer each help other thitherward.[38]

---

[33] Ibid.

[34] Ibid., 542, 543‒44.

[35] Letter no. 211, ibid., 544.

[36] *De Tristitia Christi*, ed. and trans. Clarence H. Miller, vol. 14 of *Complete Works of St. Thomas More* (New Haven: Yale Univ. Press, 1976), 635.

[37] Letter no. 211, in Rogers, *Correspondence*, 544‒45.

[38] Ibid., 545.

Here we encounter, as we so often do in the prison correspondence, More's vision of the joy of being reunited with family and friends in heaven. Undoubtedly it stems from that same profound sense of the communion of saints and of the unity of the Church that we earlier discovered in his apologetical writings. Moreover, in view of this letter it is surely possible that More's selection of the two verses from Philippians 1 for his own scriptural anthology had directly resulted from Margaret's use of them here. In this context it is also noteworthy that More quotes from Margaret's letter the phrase, "to have an eye to mine end", words that bear a striking resemblance to one of the verses from More's own "Godly Meditation" that he wrote in the margins of his *Book of Hours:* "To have ever afore mine eye my death . . ."[39] Clearly father and daughter shared many ideas with each other over the years.

Margaret's confession of her own weakness pleases her father, for it demonstrates that both she and he do not trust themselves but rather look solely to God for support. More draws before her a lesson from Saint Paul, who in battling his own weakness begged God to deliver him from temptation. Yet God responded not by removing the temptation as Paul had asked but rather by willing him to suffer this trial so as to preserve him from pride, reassuring him with the words, "My grace is sufficient for you, for my power is made perfect in weakness" (2 Cor 12:9). Thus the weaker a man is, the more will God strengthen him, for as Saint Paul says elsewhere, "I can do all things in him who strengthens me" (Phil 4:13). Reiterating his trust that God will uphold him with His "holy hand", More likewise expresses his confidence that God in His mercy will not fail to uphold Margaret as well (in a matter of a few sentences More mentions God's mercy here no fewer than three times). Finally he draws his letter to a close with the excuse that it is late.[40] We are left wondering whether More did his writing by candlelight at night, or by the narrow shaft of sunlight that during the day would have streamed through the extremely small and solitary window of his cell.

In September 1534 Pope Clement VII died. His successor, Pope Paul III, began his pontificate with hopes that he could win Henry

---

[39] "A Godly Meditation", in *Treatise on the Passion; Treatise on the Blessed Body; Instructions and Prayers,* ed. Garry Haupt, vol. 13 of *Complete Works of St. Thomas More* (New Haven: Yale Univ. Press, 1976), 227. This volume hereafter cited as *CW* 13.

[40] Letter no. 211, in Rogers, *Correspondence,* 545–47.

back for the Church and avert a lasting English schism.[41] Moreover, Anne Boleyn's influence was waning, partly because of her failure to provide the King with a male heir and partly through the presence of a new rival for Henry's affections at court.[42] Nonetheless, when Parliament reconvened in November 1534, the King sought and obtained the most radical expression in law of his supremacy over the Church—the Supremacy Act. It had already passed in both houses by November 17:[43]

> . . . Be it enacted . . . that the King our sovereign lord, his heirs and successors kings of this realm, shall be taken, accepted, and reputed the only supreme head in earth of the Church of England called *Anglicana Ecclesia* . . . And that our said sovereign lord, his heirs and successors kings of this realm, shall have full power and authority from time to time to visit, repress, redress, reform . . . all such errors, heresies, abuses, offences, contempts, and enormities, whatsoever they be . . . any usage, custom, foreign laws, foreign authority, prescription or any other thing or things to the contrary hereof notwithstanding.[44]

The Supremacy Act formalized the de facto schism of England from the universal Church that had essentially existed ever since the fateful ratification of this title by the bishops of the Canterbury Convocation in May 1532. In the above passage from the Act, the words recognizing the King's authority to "visit, repress . . . reform" were to provide the legal basis in upcoming years for Henry's barbaric campaign to destroy England's monasteries. The line regarding foreign laws and authority was nothing less than an utter repudiation of all papal authority over the Church in England.[45]

By December 18, 1534, when Parliament recessed, both houses had passed a ruthless sequel to the Supremacy Act, the Treasons Act, which in effect menaced all Englishmen with the terror of death by drawing and quartering if they could be found in any way to have spoken against the King's title of supremacy over the Church. The bill met

---

[41] J. J. Scarisbrick, *Henry VIII* (Berkeley, Calif.: Univ. of California Press, 1968), 333.

[42] Paul Friedmann, *Anne Boleyn: A Chapter of English History, 1527–1536* (London: Macmillan and Co., 1884), 2:13, 34–37.

[43] Stanford E. Lehmberg, *The Reformation Parliament, 1529–1536* (Cambridge: Cambridge Univ. Press, 1970), 202.

[44] *English Historical Documents*, vol. 5, *1485–1558*, ed. C. H. Williams (New York: Oxford Univ. Press, 1967), 746.

[45] Lehmberg, *Reformation Parliament*, 202–3.

with considerable opposition, and in the end a symbolic concession had to be made in the wording before passage was finally secured: the insertion of the word "maliciously" in describing the intent of such speaking. Nonetheless, the addition of this term would prove to be a dead letter, for in the actual application of the law malicious intent was always assumed.[46] It was this bill that would eventually be used to destroy Thomas More and Bishop Fisher:

> Be it therefore enacted . . . that if any person or persons after the first day of February next coming, do maliciously wish, will or desire by words or writing, or by craft imagine, invent, practice or attempt, any bodily harm to be done or committed to the King's most royal person, the Queen's, or their heirs apparent, or to deprive them or any of them of the dignity, title or name of their royal estates . . . then every such person . . . shall be adjudged traitors; and that every such offence . . . shall be . . . adjudged high Treason . . .[47]

It was around Christmas of 1534 that Dame Alice wrote to the King in a desperate plea for mercy on behalf of her husband and her family. She describes More as continually ill over the eight months since his arrest—in Margaret's earlier purported letter to Alice Alington there was mention of him suffering from nocturnal leg cramps, kidney stones, and chest pains.[48] As for the family, Dame Alice tells the King that the latest acts of Parliament pertaining to her husband have taken from them much of what little property and income was left following earlier penalties. With the need to provide payments for the support of More as well as to supply the essential needs of the family, she is at a loss as to what to do. She stresses, however, that her greatest concern is for the well-being of her husband. As it is not out of malice but because of what she describes as a persistent "scruple" that More has refused the oath, Alice pleads with the King to release him so that he can quietly live out the rest of his life in the company of his family, supported only by such means as their sovereign deems appropriate.[49]

On December 22, More's fellow sufferer in the Bell Tower, John Fisher, wrote to Cromwell, explaining that he is extremely reluctant

---

[46] Ibid., 203–6, 213.

[47] Geoffrey de C. Parmiter, "The Indictment of Saint Thomas More", *Downside Review* 75 (April 1957): 153–54 (spelling and punctuation rendered closer to modern English).

[48] Letter no. 206, in Rogers, *Correspondence*, 514.

[49] Letter no. 212, c. Christmas 1534, in ibid., 547–49.

to write to the King—evidently Cromwell had made or conveyed
to him such a suggestion. Fisher believes that doing so would almost
certainly aggrieve his sovereign even more against him. In his inter-
rogations More had given the same reason for not addressing himself to the King directly. Nonetheless, out of deference to Cromwell's
wishes, the Bishop agrees to make an effort to write; whether he ever
actually did so is not known, for there is no record of any such correspondence. The second part of Fisher's letter to Cromwell addresses
the conditions of his imprisonment, which were even harsher than
those suffered by More in the cell below him, for unlike the latter,
he had never been a great favorite of Henry's. After begging for a
little decent clothing and food, he makes what he must know is a
futile plea for freedom and concludes with two simple requests for
the benefit of his soul:

> Other twain things I must also desire upon you: that one is that it may
> please you that I may take some priest with in the Tower by the assign-
> ment of master lieutenant to hear my confession against this holy time;
> the other is, that I may borrow some books to stir my devotion more
> effectually these holy days for the comfort of my soul. This I beseech
> you to grant me of your charity. And thus our Lord send you a merry
> Christmas and a comfortable to your heart's desire.[50]

On New Year's Day of 1535 More sent the beleaguered Bishop
Fisher a token of his friendship—an image of the Epiphany. On another occasion he was to send him an image of his patron, Saint John,
along with a supply of apples and oranges.[51] Fisher reciprocated with
such gifts as circumstances allowed—including half a custard.[52] It is in
January that we find More answering a letter from a priest ("Master
Leder") who, having evidently heard and believed a rumor that the
ex-Lord Chancellor had finally consented to take the Oath of Succession, wished to congratulate him for this very reason. Categorically
denying the story, More tells the priest of his trust that God will never
allow him to suffer such a fall, yet if ever he were to submit, it would

---

[50] E. E. Reynolds, *Saint John Fisher* (New York: P. J. Kenedy and Sons, 1955), 244–46 (quote on 246).

[51] Edward Surtz, S.J., "More's Friendship with Fisher", in *Essential Articles for the Study of Thomas More,* ed. R. S. Sylvester and G. P. Marc'hadour (Hamden, Conn.: Archon Books, 1977), 177.

[52] R. W. Chambers, *Thomas More* (1935; reprint, Ann Arbor, Mich.: Ann Arbor Paper-backs, Univ. of Michigan, 1973), 330.

not be from a change of conscience but rather from succumbing to torture and duress. Yet he cannot believe that the latter scenario will transpire; in view of Saint Paul's assurance that God will never allow us to be tempted beyond our strength (1 Cor 10:13), he is confident that with God's grace and the prayers of good people to uphold him, he will be able to remain firm. Addressing again the question of whether his refusal may be construed as obstinacy, More reiterates that he has refrained from writing to the King precisely because he fears angering him further in his regard. After citing once more the scriptural axiom that the heart of a king is in the hand of God (Prov 21:1), he ends on a strikingly ironic note by expressing the hope that those who have taken the oath may be as loyal to their sovereign as those who have refused it.[53]

During the winter and spring of 1535 the eventual fate of Thomas More—and of England—was being determined in large part by the shifting moods of the King and the complex web of power plays both within the English court and on the broader stage of continental Europe. Thus at a January 31 meeting with the French ambassador, Palamede Gontier, to discuss a proposed match of the one-year-old Princess Elizabeth with King Francis' son, Henry became enraged at Gontier's insinuation that there was still some question as to the legitimacy of Elizabeth's status. Two days later we find a haggard Anne Boleyn at a court ball confiding to Gontier her growing anxiety over her standing with the King.[54] Perhaps Anne's declining fortunes were the reason for the temporary improvement of conditions for More and Bishop Fisher during January and February. Even so, it was in the latter month that the Treasons Act went into effect, the law that would soon bring about the downfall of both prisoners. Meanwhile, the air was rife with mounting discontent directed against the King; in secret, plans were being formulated among some noblemen for the possibility of an overthrow of the Henrician regime.[55] By the end of February, however, Anne's rival for Henry's affections had fallen out of favor, with another taking her place—Margaret Shelton, a relative of Anne. This, paradoxically, together with Cromwell's support, seems to have helped reverse Anne's decline in status.[56] At the beginning of

---

[53] Letter no. 213, January 16, 1535, in Rogers, *Correspondence,* 549–50.
[54] Friedmann, *Anne Boleyn,* 2:50–52.
[55] Ibid., 48, 57–62.
[56] Ibid., 56–57.

March, the Boleyn faction's return to power encountered a setback when their ally Cromwell became sick. The illness eventually grew to life-threatening dimensions, with a full recovery not coming before the middle of April. During the interval Queen Catherine's allies attempted to win the King over, but whatever success they might have attained was soon thwarted by Cromwell, following his restoration to health, who resorted to threats and intimidation to silence support for Catherine.[57] A month earlier (in March) a preacher near Canterbury had boldly remarked, "Masters, take heed, we have nowadays many new laws. I know we shall have a new God shortly."[58]

On April 16, 1535, a signet letter engineered by Cromwell and bearing the King's stamp was issued,[59] proscribing anyone still loyal to the Pope:

> And where it is common to our knowledge, that sundry persons, as well Religious, as Secular Priests and Curates . . . do daily, as much as in them is, set forth and extol the jurisdiction and authority of the Bishop of Rome, otherwise called Pope; sowing their seditious, pestilent, and false doctrine; praying for him in the pulpit, and making him a God . . . more preferring the power, laws, and jurisdiction of the said Bishop of Rome, than the most holy laws and precepts of Almighty God; we . . . command you, that where and whensoever ye shall apperceive, know, or hear tell of any such seditious persons . . . that ye indelayedly do apprehend and take them, or cause them to be apprehended and taken, and so committed to ward . . . until upon your advertisement thereof unto us, or our Council, ye shall know our further pleasure . . .[60]

The diocesan clergy generally yielded to this pressure, but resistance did appear from some religious bodies, particularly the Carthusians, whose priors gathered at the London Charterhouse to confer on their opposition to the new measure. Their courage was rewarded accordingly by the Henrician regime. On or around April 20 the priors of the Charterhouse, of Axholme, and of Beauvale, together with the

---

[57] Ibid., 62–63.

[58] G. R. Elton, *Policy and Police: The Enforcement of the Reformation in the Age of Thomas Cromwell* (Cambridge: Cambridge Univ. Press, 1972), 15.

[59] Ibid., 231.

[60] John Strype, *Ecclesiastical Memorials relating Chiefly to Religion, and the Reformation of It and the Emergencies of the Church of England, under King Henry VIII, King Edward VI and Queen Mary I*, vol. 1, pt. 2 (Oxford: Clarendon Press, 1822), 208 (spelling and punctuation rendered closer to modern English).

prior of another religious community, the Brigittine Abbey of Syon, were imprisoned in the Tower.[61]

On April 26, 1535,[62] these four men—Richard Reynolds of Syon Abbey and the Carthusians John Houghton, Robert Lawrence, and Augustine Webster[63]—were brought to Westminster Hall for trial on the charge of high treason. Although they admitted to having denied the supremacy of the King over the Church, they pleaded that they had not done so maliciously. As the Treasons Act had appeared to stipulate malicious intent with the word "maliciously", the jurors could not concur on finding the four religious guilty. The judges insisted that any denial of the supremacy was by its very nature malicious; hence the inclusion of the word "maliciously" in the statute meant nothing in the way of a distinction. Yet even after this intervention the jury could not bring itself to agree on a conviction of the four. Such was not an acceptable outcome to the Crown. Taking immediate hold of the situation, Cromwell "in a rage went unto the Jury and threatened them" until they yielded and pronounced a guilty verdict. Afterward the jurors were "ashamed to show their faces".[64] The next day it was reported that Cromwell "hath had much ado with the judges and sergeants about certain of the Charterhouse".[65]

On the afternoon of April 30, only four days after the trial of Reynolds and the Carthusians, More was brought before the counselors for yet another round of questioning. More himself describes what transpired in a letter to Margaret written about three days later, which he begins by mentioning the sentencing to death of the four religious.[66] Although he professes not to know why they had been charged with treason, he undoubtedly must have sensed the reason and taken at least some comfort in thinking that several members of his beloved Carthusian Order had reached the same conclusion regarding their consciences as he had. He goes on to tell his daughter

---

[61] Friedmann, *Anne Boleyn*, 2:64; Chambers, *More*, 321–22.

[62] This date, rather than April 29, is given by Susan Brigden, *London and the Reformation* (Oxford: Clarendon Press, 1991), 228.

[63] Chambers, *More*, 320, 322.

[64] William Rastell, "Rastell Fragment", included in Fr. Francis van Ortroy, S.J., ed., "Vie du bienheureux martyr Jean Fisher: Cardinal, évêque de Rochester (+1535): Text anglais et traduction latine du XVI siècle" (pt. 2), *Analecta Bollandiana* 12 (1893): 254 (spelling modernized).

[65] Brigden, *London and the Reformation*, 228 n.

[66] Letter no. 214, May 2 or 3, 1535, in Rogers, *Correspondence*, 550–51.

that he is writing to her in order to quell any unwarranted fears or expectations she might be having as to his own fate—one source indicates that his concern to calm Margaret's anxieties was in this case particularly prompted by his belief that she was carrying a child.[67]

More then describes his latest interrogation, which was conducted in a chamber of the Tower complex by Cromwell together with the attorney general, Sir Christopher Hales, the solicitor general, Richard Rich, and two others, Thomas Bedyll and Sir John Tregonwell. Refusing an offer to sit with his questioners, he remained standing as Cromwell asked him whether he had seen the three latest pieces of parliamentary legislation touching his own case (the Supremacy Act, the Act of Treasons, and the Act of Attainder naming him and Bishop Fisher). More answered in the affirmative but noted that he had not expended much time upon the documents, not seeing a need to do so in his situation. Cromwell pressed on, inquiring specifically if he had read the first statute (the Supremacy Act) declaring the King supreme head on earth of the Church in England. When More admitted that he had, Cromwell told him that it was now the "King's pleasure" that he and the other counselors should demand an answer from him as to what he thought of this title. Seeing such a demand as a breach of trust, More replied that he had already expressed his mind to the King in this regard and was determined to refrain from involving himself further, choosing instead to remember the King and his counselors daily in his prayers. He wished simply to remove himself from all earthly preoccupations and to devote himself totally to thoughts of Christ's Passion and his own death.[68]

At this juncture More was sent out of the room and then called back a little later—obviously the counselors needed time to confer on a new strategy in dealing with their uncooperative detainee. Cromwell began anew by warning More that his imprisonment did not exempt him from loyal obedience to the Crown; in light of this, did he think the King had the authority to require compliance from him as he did of others? More answered that he would not contradict this assertion. Cromwell now made his threat more explicit, telling More that while those who complied would find favor with the King, those who obstinately did not would suffer the consequences under the law. But in

---

[67] Ibid., 551, plus introductory note on 550.

[68] Ibid., 551–52.

delivering this ultimatum, Cromwell revealed—whether wittingly or unwittingly—the real reason why it was so necessary to exact submission from the prisoner: his refusal of the oath was evidently leading other men to resist, to be "so stiff therein as they be".[69]

More responded by protesting that he had advised no one on this matter and that there was nothing further he could do, regardless of the consequences:

> I do nobody harm, I say none harm, I think none harm, but wish everybody good. And if this be not enough to keep a man alive in good faith I long not to live . . . And therefore my poor body is at the King's pleasure, would God my death might do him good.[70]

Cromwell seemed now to relent, assuring More that nothing he had said during the interrogation would be used against him; thereupon the prisoner was returned to his cell. More ends his account to his daughter by reminding her that whatever may come of this episode rests in the hand of God, for he trusts in the "goodness of God", so that "seem it never so evil to this world, it shall indeed in another world be for the best".[71]

As we related in an earlier chapter, More was with his daughter Margaret on May 4, 1535, when before their eyes Reynolds and the Carthusians were led away to their brutal execution at Tyburn, "bridegrooms" on their way to their marriage, as More described it. Dragged on hurdles through the streets of London, the four men maintained a dignified calm as one by one they were subjected to the barbaric torment of being hanged, disemboweled, and dismembered while the well-dressed courtiers of the King looked on. Even Henry himself was there, though in a disguise. Afterward the remains of the executed men were impaled on the city's gates.[72]

On May 7 More was questioned yet again, as was his fellow sufferer Bishop Fisher; in both cases the proceedings bore no results. Even so, May 7 proved to be the beginning of the end for both prisoners, as a man willing to lie and perjure himself entered the picture —Richard Rich—the new solicitor general. After the commissioners had finished with Fisher, Rich visited the Bishop in his cell, claiming

---

[69] Ibid., 553.

[70] Ibid.

[71] Ibid., 553–54.

[72] Brigden, *London and the Reformation,* 228; Chambers, *More,* 326.

to have been sent by Henry himself with a most confidential message. The King, he said, desired for the sake of his own conscience to learn from him his judgment of the supremacy issue. To this end, His Majesty had given his word as a prince that nothing Fisher would say in answer would be used against him, regardless of whether it contravened the laws pertaining to the supremacy. Rich even swore before him that he would disclose his reply to no one but the King. Fisher made the fatal mistake of taking Richard Rich at his word, and, desiring to comply with what he thought to be a personal appeal for spiritual direction from his sovereign, he divulged to the messenger the judgment he had so scrupulously refrained from revealing to any of his interrogators for over a year.[73]

That same month—in May 1535—Dame Alice wrote a short and desperate letter to Cromwell, begging for an audience with the King in order to plead on behalf of her husband and herself. So great was her financial hardship that she had been forced to sell some of her own clothing.[74] What response, if any, this pathetic appeal received is not known, but we can see from More's next letter to Margaret in early June that the King was in no mood for mercy. Once again More provides an account of still another interrogation that apparently took place on June 3, conducted by Archbishop Cranmer, Sir Thomas Audley, Thomas Boleyn (Anne Boleyn's father), Charles Brandon (Duke of Suffolk), and Cromwell. The latter communicated to More the King's displeasure with his answers at the last interrogation and conveyed to him the demand of His Majesty that once and for all he must either profess his recognition of Henry as supreme head of the Church in England or deny the title outright.[75]

Although deeply dismayed that the King thought ill of him, More could offer no other reply than that which he had already made; he could only hope that "the time shall come, when God shall declare my truth toward his Grace before him and all the world." Before such a time comes he may well have to suffer, yet since his conscience is at peace he does not see himself in any real danger, "for a man may in such case lose his head and have no harm." He is merely following the counsel that the King himself had given him upon entrance into

[73] Reynolds, *Fisher*, 259–61.
[74] Letter no. 215, May 1535, in Rogers, *Correspondence*, 554–55.
[75] Letter no. 216, June 3, 1535, in ibid., 555–56.

his sovereign's service—that he should look "first upon God and next upon the King . . . the most virtuous lesson that ever prince taught his servant".[76]

To these words Cromwell and Audley answer that the King may have recourse to the law to force a definitive reply from him. More responds that while he would not deny his sovereign's authority to pursue such a course, he cannot but think it harsh to demand that he who has neither acted against the Act of Supremacy nor spoken against it should be made either to affirm it at the peril of his soul or repudiate it at the peril of his body.[77]

Resorting to a more cunning line of reasoning, Cromwell reminds More of his past involvement as Lord Chancellor in the questioning of apprehended heretics. If it were permissible to demand that heretics answer whether they accepted the authority of the Pope, Cromwell asks, should it not likewise be permissible to demand that More now tell them definitely whether he accepts the supremacy of Henry over the Church as the law of the land declared? More answers that the two cases are not alike—the former was recognized without question throughout Christendom, whereas the latter is only the law of one country. A law of one country that contradicts that of the rest of Christendom in a matter of faith cannot oblige the conscience in the way that a universal law recognized throughout Christendom can.[78] There is lurking in this explanation of More an implicit affirmation of papal primacy (and his interrogators probably knew it), but he cautiously refrains from making it explicit.

In one final effort, Cromwell tries to persuade More to take an oath that would bind him to answering whatever questions would thereafter be put to him at the King's behest regarding the "King's own person", but not surprisingly More refuses. When his interrogators express wonder that he could so stubbornly cling to a view he seems unsure of, he replies that he is on the contrary quite certain as to his own decision; it is the decisions of other men that he refuses to judge. Obviously exasperated, the counselors pose yet another question to him: If he is as willing to leave this world as he claims, why doesn't he just speak his mind? More's answer is that which we encounter

---

[76] Ibid., 556–57.
[77] Ibid., 557.
[78] Ibid., 557–58.

time and again in the *Dialogue of Comfort against Tribulation* and *De Tristitia Christi:* It would be presumptuous for him to court death, and thus he does not seek it out, but if God Himself summons him to it he is confident that God in His mercy will give him the grace and strength he needs. Drawing to a close the fruitless interrogation, Cromwell tells More that he liked him much less this day than in their last meeting, so that he now believes he is acting out of ill intent. It is with this that More ends his account to Margaret of the meeting, adding that God knows he is acting in good will.[79]

Two weeks before the above interrogation—on May 20—Pope Paul III had named Bishop John Fisher a cardinal. Ironically the Pope thought this honor for the English prelate would please Henry.[80] News of the elevation reached England within the same month, eliciting an extremely violent reaction from the King. Upon learning that the traditional cardinal's hat had been sent from Rome and was ready to be sent across the English Channel from Calais, Henry immediately ordered Cromwell to find out from Bishop Fisher whether he would accept such an honor. The Bishop declared himself unworthy of this dignity but acknowledged that if asked by the Pope he would accept it on his knees for the good of serving Christ's Church. Upon learning of Fisher's answer, Henry angrily retorted, "Yea, is he yet so lusty? Well, let the pope send him a hat, when he will. But I will so provide that, whensoever it cometh, he shall wear it on his shoulders, for head shall he have none to see it on."[81] A letter of June 15 from the imperial ambassador Eustace Chapuys to his own sovereign (Charles V) adds that Henry threatened to "send the head [of Fisher] afterwards to Rome for the cardinal's hat".[82]

On June 11 three more Carthusians—Humphrey Middlemore, William Exmew, and Sebastian Newdigate—were tried in Westminster Hall for treason. Pleading not guilty, they contended with their judges, citing scriptural texts demonstrating papal primacy, but the proceedings ended predictably with a guilty verdict.[83]

On June 12, in a sign of things still worse to come, More suffered

---

[79] Ibid., 558–59.

[80] Reynolds, *Fisher,* 261–62.

[81] Ibid., 264.

[82] Quoted in ibid.

[83] Dom Lawrence Hendriks, *The London Charterhouse: Its Monks and Its Martyrs* (London: Kegan Paul, Trench and Co., 1889), 173–75.

the painful loss of his beloved companions in prison, his books. It was on or shortly before this day that he completed the final line of his last work on Christ's Agony in the Garden, *De Tristitia Christi*. As his books were being tied together for removal, More found himself engaged in conversation with the solicitor general, Richard Rich, the same man who had cunningly sealed the fate of John Fisher a month earlier by lying to the good bishop.[84] If Rich was now looking to trap more prey, More's legal mind seems to have evaded definitive capture in the course of their discussion. Even so, Rich found enough in the ex-Lord Chancellor's words to fabricate a case against More as lethal as the evidence he had against Fisher. If he could deceive a bishop of John Fisher's integrity, why could he not deceive a jury to bring down a Thomas More?

The following day—June 13, 1535—those coming to Sunday Mass throughout London heard both John Fisher and Thomas More condemned from the pulpit—on orders, of course, of the "supreme head" of the Church in England.[85] It seems the people had to be preconditioned for the imminent destruction of these two widely admired men. On Monday, June 14, both were interrogated again. This was the second time in three days for Fisher, as he had also been questioned on the same day that More's books were removed (June 12).[86] Three days later, on June 17, Bishop Fisher was taken to Westminster Hall to stand trial for high treason. His indictment charged that he "did on the 7th day of May . . . contrary to his allegiance, falsely, maliciously, and traitorously speak and utter these words in English to divers of his majesty's faithful subjects, viz., *the king our sovereign lord is not supreme head in earth of the Church of England.*"[87] Thus were the words that Richard Rich had deceived the Bishop into speaking used as the centerpiece of the prosecution's case. Hence it was that only one witness was called—Richard Rich. Following his testimony, Bishop Fisher addressed his accuser before the court:

> Sir, I will not deny that I so said unto you. But for all my so saying I committed no treason. For upon what occasion I so said and for what cause, yourself know right well.[88]

---

[84] Roper, *Lyfe*, 84–86.

[85] June 15, 1535, letter of Eustace Chapuys to Charles V, in Reynolds, *Fisher*, 265.

[86] Reynolds, *Fisher*, 267, 274–76.

[87] Ibid., 276.

[88] Rastell, "Rastell Fragment", 259–60 (quote on 260—spelling modernized).

Fisher then recounted Rich's message that the King had desired the Bishop's confidential counsel on the supremacy question, to be given under a guarantee of immunity; he also reminded Rich of his oath to divulge Fisher's answer to no one but the King himself. He continued:

> Now, my Lords . . . what a monstrous matter is this: to lay now to my charge as treason, the thing which I spake not until besides this man's oath. I had as full and as sure a promise from the king by this his trusty and sure messenger as the king could make me by word of mouth, that I should never be impeached nor hurt by mine answer, that I should send unto him by this his messenger, which I would never have spoken, had it not been in trust of my prince's promise and of my true and loving heart towards him, my natural liege lord, in satisfying him with declaration of mine opinion and conscience in this matter as he earnestly required me by this messenger to signify plainly unto him.[89]

But Bishop Fisher's arguments were in vain. Rich openly admitted that he had given him these assurances—but what did it matter? Fisher had spoken treasonable words, and that was enough, regardless of the circumstances under which they had been spoken. As William Rastell (publisher of the 1557 edition of More's English works) commented in his account of the trial, ". . . [P]ity, mercy, equity, nor justice had there no place."[90] The jury came back with the expected guilty verdict, though not without being subjected to threats lest they decide otherwise. Prior to the verdict, the Bishop spoke to the court in words that manifested both his holiness and his learning—words unrecorded for posterity, yet compelling enough to move several of the judges to tears.[91]

The Henrician regime rolled on in its relentless campaign to eliminate opposition. On Saturday, June 19, the three Carthusians tried and convicted of high treason eight days earlier were dragged to Tyburn and butchered to death.[92] At Sunday Mass the next day Fisher and More were denounced again from the pulpit.[93] Finally, on Tues-

---

[89] Ibid. (spelling modernized).

[90] Ibid., 260–61 (quote on 261, spelling modernized).

[91] Ibid., 261–62.

[92] Hendriks, *London Charterhouse,* 175.

[93] June 15, 1535, letter of Chapuys to Charles V, in Reynolds, *Fisher,* 265.

day, June 22, the imprisoned Bishop was awakened early with the message that he was to die that very morning. In reply Fisher calmly inquired of the lieutenant who had come to him what time it was and at what hour he was to go out. Upon learning that it was five in the morning and that he would be led to his execution at ten, he asked the officer to let him sleep another hour or two, as his illness had kept him up much of the night.[94] When Fisher later arose, he asked his servant, Richard Wilson, to lay out for him a clean white shirt and all his best clothing. Wilson was not a little amazed at this request, accustomed as he was to the Bishop's notable lack of solicitude in matters of dress. But Fisher told him, ". . . [D]ost thou not mark that this is our marriage day and that it behooveth us therefore to use more cleanliness for solemnity of the marriage?"[95] At about eleven the Bishop mounted the scaffold on Tower Hill—his sentence had been commuted from the usual traitor's death of drawing and quartering to execution by beheading, probably because of his poor health. After proclaiming to the onlookers that he had come "to die for the faith of Christ's Catholic Church", he laid his neck on the block and swiftly passed to the marriage feast of heaven.[96]

On June 25, Cromwell issued in the name of the King a circular letter to the justices of the peace, ordering a further crackdown on all opposition. All the clergy from the bishops to parish curates were under command to preach on "every Sunday and solemn feast" the new gospel of Henry's supremacy over the English Church and to excoriate the "great and innumerable enormities and abuses" of the papacy.[97] In a rage against all things Petrine, the Henrician regime sought to obliterate all ties to the See of Rome even on paper; hence bishops were additionally ordered:

> . . . [T]o cause all manner [of] prayers, orisons, rubrics, and canons in mass-books, and all other books used in churches, wherein the said Bishop [the pope] is named, utterly to be abolished, eradicated, and razed out, in such wise as the said Bishop of Rome, his name and memory,

---

[94] Rastell, "Rastell Fragment", 263.

[95] Ortroy, "Vie du bienheureux martyr Jean Fisher", 190–91.

[96] Rastell, "Rastell Fragment", 262, 264–65 (spelling modernized).

[97] Strype, *Ecclesiastical Memorials,* vol. 1, pt. 2, pp. 209–10 (spelling modernized); Elton, *Policy and Police,* 240–42.

for evermore (except to his contumely and reproach) may be extinct, suppressed, and obscured . . .[98]

Moreover, the smear campaign against the late John Fisher and against Thomas More was to be continued in no uncertain terms:

> We . . . will and desire . . . [that] ye do persuade, show, and declare unto the said people the very tenor, effect, and purpose of the premises in such wise . . . Showing also and declaring unto the people, at your said sessions, the treasons traitorously committed against us and our laws by the late Bishop of Rochester and Sir Thomas More, Knight who thereby, and by diverse secret practices of their malicious mind against us, intended to seminate, engender, and breed among our people and subjects a most mischievous and seditious opinion, not only to their own confusion, but also of diverse others, who lately have condignly suffered execution according to their demerits . . . And consequently, that all our faithful and true subjects may thereby detest and abhor, in their hearts and deeds, the most recreaunt and traitorous abuses and behaviors of the said malicious malefactors . . .[99]

On Sunday, June 27—only two days after this decree was issued— the preacher at Saint Paul's Cross (Simon Matthew) inveighed against Fisher and More in an effort to thwart the influence of their example:

> Of late ye have had experience of some whom neither friends nor kins- folk, neither the judgment of both Universities . . . nor the universal consent of all the clergy of this realm, nor the laws of Parliament, nor their most natural and loving prince, could by any gentle ways revoke from their disobedience, but would needs persist, giving pernicious oc- casion to the multitude to murmur and grudge at the King's laws: seeing that they were men of estimation and would be seen wiser than all the realm and of better conscience than other.[100]

There is extant the text of a letter from Thomas More to his Italian merchant friend, Antonio Bonvisi—the "apple of mine eye", as More was wont to call him—written shortly before his trial, although the specific date of it is unknown.[101] It is nothing less than an eloquent testament to the splendor of human friendship among those who love

---

[98] Strype, *Ecclesiastical Memorials*, 210 (spelling and punctuation rendered closer to modern English).

[99] Ibid., 210–12 (spelling and punctuation rendered closer to modern English).

[100] Elton, *Policy and Police*, 188.

[101] Letter no. 217, 1535, in Rogers, *Correspondence*, 559–63.

God. More begins by recalling that he himself had been warmly welcomed into the Bonvisi household for almost forty years; he marvels that Antonio has bestowed more favor upon him in his abject and disgraced state as a prisoner than have many others bestowed upon their prosperous friends. Such friendship, More observes, is undoubtedly "a high and a noble gift proceeding of a certain singular benignity of God".[102] He can only believe that God in His mercy had preordained to give him such a faithful friend to assist him in his hour of need. More prays that God will reward such loyalty and that He may take both of them from the turbulent world

> . . . into his rest, where shall need no letters, where no wall shall dissever us, where no porter shall keep us from talking together, but that we may have the fruition of the eternal joy with God the Father, and with his only begotten Son our Redeemer Jesus Christ, with the Holy Spirit of them both, the Holy Ghost proceeding from them both.[103]

"Long I to Go to God": Trial and Execution

London's Westminster Hall has changed relatively little in the nine hundred years since King William II first erected it about A.D. 1090; the only significant modifications, particularly in the roofing, were made by Richard II in the late 1300s. Thus it had already seen over four centuries of British history when Thomas More entered it on the morning of July 1, 1535. The sight of its familiar walls after over fourteen months of confinement must have evoked many bittersweet memories from his years as a barrister and judge; it was here that in passing to or from court he would pause to kneel for his father's blessing. Everything of his life and career had now come down to this one day—everything that had come before had been a preparation for it. In the preceding weeks his friends John Fisher, Richard Reynolds, and the Carthusians had all stood where now he stood. His time had finally come. It would be his final battle.

Upon coming into the presence of his judges, More heard for the first time the text of his indictment, which according to the practice of the time was in Latin. There were four counts containing a to-

---

[102] Ibid., 562.
[103] Ibid., 562–63 (quote on 563).

tal of eight charges.[104] The first count consisted of just one charge, accusing More of "maliciously" denying the King's title of supreme head of the Church of England by his refusal to answer questions put to him in this regard on May 7, 1535. Curiously the indictment goes on to repeat, in English, More's reply, as if it were reproachable: "I will not meddle with any such matters, for I am fully determined to serve God, and to think upon His Passion and my passage out of this world."[105] So it had come to this—even More's consuming devotion to the Passion was to be put on trial. The second count contained four charges: (1) that More had corresponded while in prison with a "traitor", the late Bishop Fisher; (2) that in his correspondence with Fisher he had encouraged him in his treasonous stance, informing him of his own refusal to answer the commissioners; (3) that he had used hostile language regarding the Act of Supremacy; and (4) that he had advised Fisher to answer on his own without having recourse to anything More had said, so as not to implicate him in a conspiracy between the two. The third count was comprised of two more charges: that in More's June 3 interrogation he had persisted in his incriminating silence and that, with the intent of engendering sedition, he had used the analogy of a two-edged sword to describe the Supremacy Act. With the fourth count containing the eighth and final charge, the dark figure of Richard Rich appears as it did at Fisher's trial; this count alleged that on June 12, More, in a conversation with Rich, had explicitly denied Parliament's authority to declare the King supreme head of the Church in England.[106] The indictment concluded:

> Thus the aforesaid jurors say that the aforesaid Thomas More falsely, traitorously and maliciously, by art imagined, invented, practiced and attempted entirely to deprive our lord the king aforesaid of his said dignity, title and name of his royal estate, namely, of his dignity, title and name of supreme head in earth of the Church of England, to the manifest contempt of the king himself and in derogation of his royal crown, against the form and effect of the aforesaid statutes and against the peace of our lord the king.[107]

---

[104] J. Duncan Derrett, "The Trial of Sir Thomas More", *English Historical Review* 79 (July 1964): 454.

[105] Parmiter, "Indictment", 159–60.

[106] Derrett, "Trial", 454.

[107] Parmiter, "Indictment", 161.

More knew his Latin and his law well enough to understand everything the indictment brought against him. Slowly, meticulously, and with only himself for his counsel, he proceeded to pick the charges apart so convincingly for the court that the state finally consented to drop the first three counts.[108] The prosecution could afford to do so, for the fourth count, after all, was built on far more secure ground —it was built on one man's willingness to perjure himself in order to get the job done of ridding the Crown of this meddlesome lawyer. The witness was called—Richard Rich.

Rich testified that on June 12 he spoke with More as the prisoner's books were being removed by two others, Sir Richard Southwell and a "Master Palmer". In the course of their conversation, Rich posed a theoretical question: If Parliament were to declare that he, Richard Rich, were King, would More accept him to be such? Answering that he would, More then countered with a theoretical question of his own: If Parliament were to declare that God was not God, would Rich assent to their decision? Rich replied that such a ruling certainly could not be accepted. But he had one more case for More to solve, an intermediate case: In view of the fact that the King had actually been made supreme head of the English Church, why did More not recognize him as such, in the same way that he would accept Parliament making Rich the king? According to Rich's testimony, More's answer was that while Parliament had the authority to name a king or depose him, it did not possess the same authority over the headship of the Church.[109]

We have seen time and again during his long imprisonment More's resolve not to speak ill of his enemies and persecutors or to fault the conscience of any man who differed with him. Yet even in the Tower More had not ceased to condemn in his writings those who distorted or denied truth; this was at the heart of his many years of fighting heresy, which he saw as the ultimate falsehood. Hence it was that in an unparalleled manifestation of righteous anger More denounced Rich and his testimony in the strongest terms:

> If I were a man, my lords, that did not regard an oath, I needed not, as it is well known, in this place, at this time, nor in this case, to stand here as an accused person. And if this oath of yours, Master Rich, be

[108] Derrett, "Trial", 456.
[109] Roper, *Lyfe*, 84–86, 87; Derrett, "Trial", 462–63.

true, then pray I that I never see God in the face; which I would not say, were it otherwise, to win the whole world.[110]

More now recounted for the court the conversation with Rich on June 12 as he remembered it. Unfortunately there is no extant record of More's version of the episode, but we know from William Roper that upon concluding his account he addressed his accuser directly:

> In good faith, Master Rich, I am sorrier for your perjury than for my own peril. And you shall understand that neither I, nor no man else to my knowledge, ever took you to be a man of such credit as in any matter of importance I, or any other, would at any time vouchsafe to communicate with you.[111]

More reminded Rich that he knew him quite well, as they had both been in the same parish for a number of years. Although he regretted having to say it, there could be no denying, explained More, that Rich had a bad reputation marked by dicing and an untrustworthy tongue. In the light of Rich's character, More asked the court whether it was plausible that after refusing to disclose his views to the King and his "honorable councillors" he would entrust his opinions in so grave a matter to a man of Rich's caliber: "Can this in your judgments, my lords, seem likely to be true?"[112]

More's compelling defense was threatening to upset the only count and charge that had survived from the original four-count, eight-charge indictment; something had to be done, and fast. The prosecution called two more witnesses: Sir Richard Southwell and Master Palmer, the men who had tied up More's books on June 12 while the prisoner and Richard Rich were having the disputed conversation. They, it was thought, would be able to corroborate Rich's testimony. But in court both men claimed to have been too busy with the books to have heard or taken notice of what was being said.[113]

With the presentation of testimony by the state completed, the defendant was given the opportunity to argue in his own defense one more time before the jury retired to reach a verdict. More gave five reasons why he believed his case should be dismissed: (1) that the in-

---

[110] Roper, *Lyfe*, 87.
[111] Ibid.
[112] Ibid., 87–89 (quote on 89).
[113] Ibid., 91; Derrett, "Trial", 465.

sertion of the term "maliciously" into the Treasons Act was intended to delineate situations such as his own, where there was no malice intended and none demonstrated in the evidence presented; (2) that the very way the Treasons Act uses the word "maliciously" precludes it being interpreted in anything but the narrow sense; (3) that the demonstration of malicious intent is as essential in applying this law as is the demonstration of the use of force in applying the law prohibiting forcible entry; (4) that the prosecution must demonstrate more than merely the *presumption* of malice, which is contradicted by the mutual trust that has consistently characterized More's relations with the King, manifest in among other things his ascent to the second highest office in the realm; and (5) that in the light of the latter there should be a presumption of innocence rather than guilt—although even if his refusal of the oath were interpreted as disloyalty, he was already serving a sentence for this act, and could not justly be sentenced for it further.[114]

Despite the strength of these arguments, the court overruled all of them and proceeded to send the jury out to reach a verdict. There was no repeat of the wild scene from the April trial of the Carthusians, when Cromwell menaced the jurors with threats upon their failure to return a guilty verdict. For the men charged with the task of deciding More's fate, the specter of seven clerics drawn and quartered and one beheaded in the last two months, set in the broader context of omnipresent Henrician and Cromwellian intimidation, scarcely lent itself to a reasoned weighing of the evidence, and thus it was that in only fifteen minutes[115] the jury came back with a predictable decision—guilty. Whether through nervousness or a deliberate effort to draw the proceedings to a hasty conclusion, the presiding judge, Lord Chancellor Thomas Audley, immediately began to declare the sentence for high treason. Even so, the lawyer who stood convicted before him knew his rights and did not hesitate to avail himself of them. Interrupting Audley, More declared: "My Lord, when I was toward the Law, the manner in such case was to ask the prisoner before judgment why judgment should not be given against him."[116]

---

[114] Derrett, "Trial", 465–67; Roper, *Lyfe,* 89–91.

[115] Thomas Stapleton, *The Life and Illustrious Martyrdom of Sir Thomas More,* ed. E. E. Reynolds (Bronx, N.Y.: Fordham Univ. Press, 1966), chap. 18, pp. 175–76.

[116] Roper, *Lyfe,* 92; Derrett, "Trial", 467–68.

Audley could not deny the point; suspending his pronouncement of the sentence, he commanded the defendant to speak his piece.

Feeling obliged not to presume his own fortitude in facing martyrdom, More had until now done all in his power to preserve his life. But with his fate finally sealed, he was at last free to reveal his convictions on the Henrician takeover of the Church in England. What More had said with his silence ever since his resignation from the office of Lord Chancellor in 1532 he would now declare openly for the entire nation to hear. If the imprisoned More had been misunderstood as passive and the victim of scrupulosity, all such illusions were about to be swiftly dispelled. The time had come for him to give the conscience of his country a living voice—a voice that would shake the rafters of Westminster Hall:

> Seeing that I see ye are determined to condemn me (God knoweth how) I will now in discharge of my conscience speak my mind plainly and freely touching my Indictment and your Statute, withal.
>
> And forasmuch as this Indictment is grounded upon an Act of Parliament directly repugnant to the laws of God and his Holy Church, the supreme Government of which, or of any part whereof, may no temporal Prince presume by any law to take upon him, as rightfully belonging to the See of Rome, a spiritual pre-eminence by the mouth of our Saviour himself, personally present upon earth, only to St. Peter and his successors, Bishops of the same See, by special prerogative granted; it is therefore in law, amongst Christian men, insufficient to charge any Christian man.[117]

More was speaking here with the same passionate language with which he had fought the Protestant reformers—and with good reason, for he saw the King's aggressive assertion of ecclesiastical supremacy as nothing less than a direct attack upon the unity and integrity of the Church. With his newfound freedom as a man about to die, he was finally able to avow in the most unambiguous terms the supreme authority of the See of Peter over the universal Church.

More proceeded to explain that as only one part of the Catholic Church, England had no more authority to make an ecclesiastical law of its own in opposition to that of universal Christendom than could

---

[117] Thomas More in Nicholas Harpsfield, *The Life and Death of Sir Thomas More,* in *Lives of Saint Thomas More* (William Roper and Nicholas Harpsfield), ed. E. E. Reynolds, Everyman's Library, no. 19 (London: J. M. Dent and Sons, 1963), 161.

one English city legislate against a decision of Parliament. Moreover, the Act of Treasons not only ran contrary to the law of God, but it also violated England's own corpus of legislation still in effect, including the Magna Carta, which promised "that the English church shall be free and shall have all its rights undiminished and its liberties unimpaired".[118] It even violated the King's own coronation oath, More added.[119] Henry seems to have agreed on this point, judging from a paraphrased English translation of the oath that bears modifications in the King's own handwriting. Before the modifications, the text as derived from the *Liber Regalis,* the liturgical book that governed English coronations for centuries, ran as follows:

> This is the oath that the king shall swear at the coronation, that he shall keep and maintain the right and the liberties of holy Church of old time granted by the righteous Christian King of England and that he shall keep all the lands, honours and dignities righteous and free of the crown of England in all manner whole without any manner of a minishment, and the rights of the Crown hurt, decayed or lost to his power shall call again into the ancient estate. And that he shall keep the peace of the holy Church and of the clergy and of the people with good accord. And that he shall do in his judgments equity and right and Justice with discretion and mercy. And that he shall grant to hold the laws and customs of the realm, and to his power keep them and affirm them which the folk and people have made and chosen. And the evil laws and customs wholly to put out and steadfast and stable peace to the people of his realm keep and cause to be kept to his power.[120]

Bear in mind that the above is essentially the oath that Henry, like his predecessors, had taken (in Latin) at his coronation in 1509. It clearly binds the monarch to guarantee the rights and liberties of the Church as More claimed. Here now is the same text with Henry's own subsequent deletions (the words crossed out) and insertions (the words in italics):

---

[118] *Magna Carta,* 1225 text, in *English Historical Documents,* vol. 3, *1189–1327,* ed. Harry Rothwell (New York: Oxford Univ. Press, 1975), 341.

[119] Roper, *Lyfe,* 93.

[120] Notes, *The Manner of the Coronation of King Charles the First of England at Westminster, 2 Feb., 1626,* ed. Rev. Christopher Wordsworth, Henry Bradshaw Society, vol. 2 (London: Henry Bradshaw Society, 1892), 19–20 (spelling and punctuation rendered closer to modern English).

~~This is the oath that~~ the king shall *then* swear ~~at the coronation~~, that he shall keep and maintain the *lawful* right and the liberties ~~of holy Church~~ of old time granted by the righteous Christian King of England *to the holy Church of England* ~~and that he~~ *not prejudicial to his Jurisdiction and dignity royal and that he* shall keep all the lands, honours and dignities righteous and ~~free~~ *freedoms* of the crown of England in all manner whole without any manner of a minishment, and the rights of the Crown hurt, decayed or lost to his power shall call again into the ancient estate. And that he shall ~~keep the peace of the holy Church and of the clergy and of the people with good accord~~ *endeavor himself to keep unity in his clergy and temporal subject[s]*. And that ~~he shall do~~ *he shall according to his conscience* in *all* his judgments *minister* equity ~~and~~ right and Justice ~~with discretion and mercy~~ *showing where is to be showed mercy*. And that he shall grant to hold the laws and *approved* customs of the realm, *lawful and not prejudicial to his crown or Imperial duty,* and to his power keep them and affirm them which the ~~folk~~ *nobles* and people have made and chosen *with his consent.* And the evil laws and customs wholly to put out and steadfast and stable peace to the people of his realm keep and cause to be kept to his power *in that which honour and equity do require.*[121]

Unfortunately the above handwritten alterations were not dated; we cannot, however, refrain from speculating that this redrafting of the coronation oath was done in the wake of More's comments in Westminster Hall, perhaps after Cromwell reported back to the King what had been said at the trial.

Returning to the issue of papal primacy, More observed that England had no more right to refuse obedience to the papacy than could a child refuse to obey his own father. He then reminded his listeners that England's communion with the See of Rome began with the arrival of Christianity itself in the country a thousand years earlier, which was brought by the missionary Saint Augustine of Canterbury at the instigation of Pope Saint Gregory the Great. More's words in this regard are paraphrased by Roper:

> For, as St. Paul said of the Corinthians: "I have regenerated you, my children in Christ," so might St. Gregory, Pope of Rome, of whom, by St. Augustine, his messenger, we first received the Christian faith, of us Englishmen truly say: "You are my children, because I have given to you everlasting salvation . . ."[122]

---

[121] Ibid.

[122] Roper, *Lyfe*, 93–94 (quote on 94).

Audley interrupted at this point to resurrect an argument More had heard before—that his obstinacy and "vehement" words against the Treasons Act were much to be marveled at, in virtue of the fact that he stood alone in his views against all of England's "Bishops, Universities and best learned men".[123] There was lurking in this statement a *non sequitur* that so many learned men could not possibly be wrong. Of course Audley also conveniently failed to mention that one bishop had differed from this apparent consensus—John Fisher—for which he was summarily executed. More countered by resorting to a consensus far broader than the university faculties of England:

If the number of Bishops and universities be so material as your lordship seemeth to take it, then see I little cause, my lord, why that thing in my conscience should make any change. For I nothing doubt but that, though not in this realm, yet in Christendom about, of these well learned Bishops and virtuous men that are yet alive, they be not the fewer part that be of my mind therein. But if I should speak of those which already be dead, of whom many be now holy saints in heaven, I am very sure it is the far greater part of them that, all the while they lived, thought in this case that way that I think now. And therefore am I not bound, my lord, to conform my conscience to the Council of one Realm against the general Council of Christendom. *For of the aforesaid holy Bishops I have for every Bishop of yours, above one hundred, and for one Council or Parliament of yours (God knoweth what manner of one), I have all the Councils made these thousand years. And for this one kingdom, I have all other Christian Realms.*[124]

All of More's speech must have stung the ears of his accusers and unsettled everyone in Westminster Hall, but there was nothing that could be done to stop him. Finally the Duke of Norfolk angrily shouted, "We now plainly perceive that ye are maliciously bent."[125] No, More answered, it was not malice but solely the obligation of his conscience that compelled him to declare his mind—God knew this to be true. Yet still free to speak the unspeakable, More had one final salvo for his persecutors, a reminder that in addition to suffering for his fidelity to the primacy of Peter he was also dying in defense of the indissolubility of Christian matrimony: "Howbeit, it is not for this supremacy

---

[123] Harpsfield, *Life*, 162.
[124] Roper, *Lyfe*, 94–95, plus Harpsfield, *Life*, 162, the latter in italics.
[125] Harpsfield, *Life*, 162.

so much that ye seek my blood, as for that I would not condescend to the marriage."[126]

More had spoken the truth and everyone knew it. Well aware of the hostility in so many quarters toward Anne Boleyn, Thomas Audley seemed caught off guard by the defendant's comments. Hesitant, he turned to the Lord Chief Justice of King's Bench, Sir John FitzJames, and asked whether the indictment was sufficient for conviction. He received an incredibly roundabout answer: ". . . I must needs confess that if the act of Parliament be not unlawful, then is not the indictment in my conscience insufficient".[127] Apparently FitzJames had been as unnerved by More's speech as had Audley. We do not know how long it took Audley to figure out the meaning of FitzJames' reply, but when he finally did, he began the sentencing of More:

> We command that Sir Thomas More, sometime knight, be carried back to the place from whence he came; and from thence to be drawn through the City to the public place of execution, there to be hanged till he be half dead, then to be cut down, his bowels presently to be taken out and burned, his head to be cut off, and his body to be quartered into four parts, and the body and head to be set up where the king shall appoint. So [the] Lord have mercy upon you![128]

The dreaded words having been uttered, More was given one final opportunity to speak—a chance to plead for mercy customarily given to convicts after sentencing. But More did not ask for mercy; instead he offered forgiveness:

> More have I not to say, my lords, but that like as the blessed Apostle St. Paul, as we read in the Acts of the Apostles, was present, and consented to the death of St. Stephen, and kept their clothes that stoned him to death, and yet be they now both twain holy Saints in heaven, and shall continue there friends forever, so I verily trust, and shall therefore right heartily pray, that though your lordships have now here in earth been judges to my condemnation, we may yet hereafter in heaven merrily all meet together, to our everlasting salvation.[129]

---

[126] Ibid., 162–63 (quote on 163).

[127] Roper, *Lyfe*, 95.

[128] Ro: Ba:, *The Lyfe of Syr Thomas More, Sometymes Lord Chancellor of England by Ro: Ba:*, ed. E. V. Hitchcock and Msgr. P. E. Hallett, Early English Text Society, original series, no. 222 (London: Early English Text Society, 1950), bk. 3, chap. 14, pp. 246–47.

[129] Roper, *Lyfe*, 96.

The trial was now over. Given over to the custody of Sir William Kingston, constable of the Tower, More was led from Westminster Hall out to the "Old Swan", a stairway close to the upstream, north-bank side of the old London Bridge.[130] It was here that Kingston, a good friend of More's, set aside his professional role as custodian of the prisoner and broke down in tears as he bade him farewell. Seeing his grief, More assured him that he would pray for him and his wife with the intention that they may all be reunited in heaven, there to be "merry for ever and ever". Kingston later told Roper that he was ashamed of his own weakness in contrast to More's fortitude, finding himself being consoled by the very one he should have been comforting instead.[131]

It is not clear whether More was taken back from the Old Swan to the Tower on foot or by boat on the Thames. There is on the river-front of the Tower complex a portal named the Traitor's Gate, built by King Henry III to facilitate the reception of convicts transported down the Thames in order to preclude the gathering of sympathetic crowds in the streets.[132] Henry VIII certainly had sufficient reason to fear such displays in the case of More. Whatever the case may be, it was at Tower Wharf that More caught sight of a most familiar face —that of his daughter Margaret. She and Margaret Clement (More's adopted daughter) had been waiting at this spot in the expectation that he would pass them. It is best left to Roper himself to tell what then transpired between his wife and her father:

> As soon as she saw him, after his blessing on her knees reverently received, she hastening towards him, and, without consideration or care of herself, pressing in among the midst of the throng and company of the guard that with halberds and bills went round about him, hastily ran to him, and there openly, in the sight of them all, embraced him, took him about the neck, and kissed him. Who, well liking her most natural and dear daughterly affection towards him, gave her his fatherly blessing and many godly words of comfort besides. From whom after she was departed, she, not satisfied with the former sight of him, and like one that had forgotten herself, being all ravished with the entire love of her

---

[130] E. E. Reynolds, *The Field Is Won: The Life and Death of Saint Thomas More* (Milwaukee: Bruce Publishing Co., 1968), 372.

[131] Roper, *Lyfe*, 97.

[132] Msgr. Laurance Goulder, "Thomas More's London", *Critic* 24 (December 1965/January 1966): 53.

dear father, having respect neither to herself, nor to the press of the people and multitude that were there about him, suddenly turned back again, ran to him as before, took him about the neck, and divers times together most lovingly kissed him; and at last, with a full heavy heart, was fain to depart from him; the beholding whereof was to many of them that were present thereat so lamentable that it made them for very sorrow thereof to mourn and weep.[133]

At some point during the return to the Tower, More's son, John, also came forward, kneeling to receive his father's blessing and kissing him; Margaret Clement likewise emerged from the bystanders to embrace and kiss him.[134]

After all the hours of deep emotional strain for More at Westminster Hall and Tower Wharf, it is not inconceivable that at the end of it he would have found a moment or two for a bit of comical relief at his own expense. Thus there is good reason to believe Edward Hall's story that when upon his return to the Tower More was asked to turn over his "upper garment"—a customary request for a convict's tunic—he took off his cap and handed it over, saying that it was the uppermost garment he had.[135] There is another incident recorded (albeit with certain differences) by two sources[136] that at some point Cromwell came to More in a last-ditch effort to make him change his mind on the oath, only to be told in response that he had indeed changed his mind—instead of shaving his beard before execution he would keep it so that it might share the fate of his head. When these words were reported back to the King, he is said to have dourly replied, "So does this man still mock us with his jests";[137] evidently Henry had lost his taste for More's humor, as had His Majesty's loyal chronicler, Edward Hall, who seemed to view the ex-Chancellor's jokes as insolent.[138]

For reasons unknown—perhaps a grudging gesture of mercy to a former friend, or more likely the desire to avoid politically embarrassing scenes in the streets—Henry commuted More's sentence from

---

[133] Roper, *Lyfe*, 98–99.

[134] Stapleton, *Life*, chap. 19, pp. 180–82.

[135] Edward Hall, *The Lives of the Kings: Henry VIII* (1550 folio ed. entitled *The Triumphant Reigne of Kyng Henry the VIII;* reprint, London: T. C. and E. C. Jack, 1904), 2:265.

[136] Stapleton, *Life*, chap. 16, pp. 161–63; Chambers, *More*, 343–44.

[137] Stapleton, *Life*, chap. 16, p. 163.

[138] Hall, *Lives of the Kings*, 2:265.

grisly execution by drawing and quartering at Tyburn to a somewhat more civilized and straightforward death by beheading at Tower Hill —the death penalty of the privileged classes. Undoubtedly More was grateful that his resolve would not have to be tested under the prolonged agony of the former manner of execution, but he could scarcely resist commenting on the irony of the King's so-called favor: "God forbid, the King should use any more such mercy unto any of my friends . . ."[139]

More knew that any day now could be his last. In the time that remained to him he continued his practices of penance. Stapleton tells of the prisoner scourging himself and, in a graphic effort to prepare his mind for the mystery of death, even wrapping himself in a linen sheet as if it were a shroud.[140] But finally More sensed the time had come to put aside his "spiritual weapons".[141] On Monday, July 5, he sent to his daughter Margaret his hair shirt and his discipline, along with a letter—his last—written with a piece of coal.[142] In addition to saying farewell to all his children, he expresses the hope that God will call him home on the morrow:

> I cumber you good Margaret much, but I would be sorry, if it should be any longer than tomorrow, for it is St. Thomas even, and the utas [octave] of Saint Peter and therefore tomorrow long I to go to God, it were a day very meet and convenient for me. I never liked your manner toward me better than when you kissed me last for I love when daughterly love and dear charity hath no leisure to look to worldly courtesy.
>
> Farewell my dear child and pray for me, and I shall for you and all your friends that we may merrily meet in heaven.[143]

More's linking of the next day—July 6—with Saint Peter and Saint Thomas Becket is rather revealing. July 6 was not itself the feast-day of Saint Peter but only the octave of that feast-day (June 29). Similarly, July 6 was only the *eve* of the feast commemorating the translation of the body of Saint Thomas Becket. More has therefore gone out

---

[139] Cresacre More, *The Life and Death of Sir Thomas Moore* (*1630*), facsimile of 1st ed., English Recusant Literature, 1558–1640, ed. D. M. Rogers, vol. 66 (Menston, Yorkshire, England: Scolar Press, 1971), chap. 10, no. 5, p. 335.

[140] Stapleton, *Life,* chap. 20, p. 187.

[141] Ro: Ba:, *Lyfe,* bk. 3, chap. 16, p. 257.

[142] Stapleton, *Life,* chap. 19, pp. 182, 185–86.

[143] Letter no. 218, July 5, 1535, in Rogers, *Correspondence,* 563–65 (quote on 564).

of his way to identify what he anticipates will be the day of his own death with these two saints in particular. The reasons are sufficiently obvious. For was he not dying to defend the primacy of the successors of Saint Peter? Moreover, was not his fate akin to that of Thomas Becket, who fell under the sword three and a half centuries earlier in upholding the rights of the Church against the encroachments of an English king also named Henry?

Curiously absent from this letter is any reference whatsoever to Dame Alice. Everything we know of More compels us to assume either that she was allowed to see him one final time or that he wrote another letter in his last days exclusively for her—a letter of which no record has survived.

More took time to compose a final prayer, marked as always by his love for the Eucharist and his devotion to the Passion. Addressing himself to the Holy Trinity, he prays that his lukewarmness may be transformed into warmth, that he may yearn for the sacraments, "and specially to rejoice in the presence of thy [Christ's] very blessed Body" in the Holy Eucharist, remembering in the context of the latter the Lord's sufferings. Asking that all may be made "lively members" of the Mystical Body of Christ, the Church, More ends by pleading on behalf of his enemies:

> Almighty God, have mercy on N. and N., etc. and on all that bear me evil will, and would me harm, and their faults and mine together, by such easy tender merciful means, as thine infinite wisdom best can devise, vouchsafe to amend and redress, and make us saved souls in heaven together, where we may ever live and love together with thee and thy blessed saints, O glorious Trinity, for the bitter passion of our sweet Saviour Christ. Amen.[144]

When morning came—July 6, 1535—it brought the news More had been expecting. At an early hour a personal friend, Thomas Pope, was sent to More's cell to notify him that he was to die before nine. Undoubtedly to the amazement of the sympathetic messenger, the prisoner welcomed the communication, expressing gratitude to the King both for putting him in this place where he could suitably prepare for his own end and for dispatching him so promptly from the

---

[144] "A Devout Prayer", in *CW* 13:230-31.

miseries of earthly life. Pope then notified More of Henry's wish that at his execution he should keep his comments to a minimum. More answered that it was good he told him this, for he had intended to speak at some length—though without saying anything with which his sovereign or anyone else could take offense. Nonetheless, he would totally comply with His Majesty's request. He did, however, have one thing to ask in return—might his daughter Margaret be permitted to be present at his burial? Pope assured him that Henry had already granted permission for his wife, children, and friends to attend his interment. When More replied with profuse thanks for the favor, Pope lost his composure and broke into weeping. More once again found himself offering solace to others as to his own fate, comforting his friend with the hope that eventually they would be merrily reunited for all eternity in heaven.[145]

More seems to have had the same idea as Bishop Fisher in viewing death suffered for Christ as an occasion for which he should dress festively. Thus he began changing into the silk camlet tunic he had received from Antonio Bonvisi, much to the consternation of the lieutenant of the Tower, for a convict's garment was customarily forfeit to the executioner. Citing the example of Saint Cyprian, who gave thirty gold pieces to his executioner, More was only too glad to allow such a fine piece of clothing to become the property of the man who, as far as he was concerned, was about to do him a great service in sending him out of this world; but the lieutenant would hear none of it. In the end More reluctantly yielded, donning instead a rough gray tunic belonging to his servant John à Wood.[146] Into his hands he took a small red cross[147] and emerged from the darkness of his cell into the daylight of a summer morning.

It was a journey of roughly six hundred feet from the Bell Tower to the place of execution, Tower Hill. Judging from the number of incidents reported to have occurred as More made his way to the scaffold, there must have been something of a crowd gathered along the route. One woman came up to him to offer him a cup of wine, but he refused it with the words, "My Master had vinegar and gall,

---

[145] Roper, *Lyfe,* 100–102.

[146] Ibid., 102; Stapleton, *Life,* chap. 20, pp. 187–88.

[147] Stapleton, *Life,* chap. 20, p. 187.

and not wine, given him to drink."[148] The Henrician chronicler Edward Hall tells of another woman present who called upon More to make a statement regarding a legal case of hers that he had handled while in office; to this impertinent request he replied, not without humor, "Good woman, have patience a little while, for the King is good unto me that even within this half hour he will discharge me of all businesses, and help thee himself."[149] When yet another woman loudly taunted him with the accusation that he had given a "wrong judgment" against her, More replied, "Woman, I am now going to my death. I remember well the whole matter; if now I were to give sentence again, I assure thee I would not alter it. Thou hast no injury, so content thee, and trouble me not."[150]

As his end neared More found himself offering solace to others one final time. There was a man in the crowd from Winchester who some years earlier had been deeply troubled by temptations to despair; when all else failed, a friend brought him for counseling to Thomas More, who was then Lord Chancellor. As we have seen with his *Dialogue of Comfort against Tribulation,* More evidently had a reputation for helping those prone to thoughts of suicide. He did what he could to advise the man, yet at first it seemed in vain. More then resorted to prayer, "earnestly beseeching Almighty God to rid the poor man of his trouble of mind".[151] More's prayers were answered—the man recovered his peace and thereafter regularly came to see his benefactor. But when upon More's imprisonment he was no longer able to speak with him, his old temptations to despair returned. Learning of More's condemnation, he journeyed from Winchester to London in the hope of seeing him again. It was in this desperate state that he came to Tower Hill on the morning of July 6. Waiting along the route to the scaffold, he pushed through the crowd and cried out to the prisoner as he passed, "Master More, do you know me? I pray you, for our Lord's sake, help me. I am as ill troubled as ever I was." "I remember thee full well," More answered; "Go thy ways in peace, and pray for me, and I will not fail to pray for thee." From that day

---

[148] Ro: Ba:, *Lyfe,* bk. 3, chap. 17, p. 259.

[149] Hall, *Lives of the Kings,* 2:265 (spelling modernized).

[150] Ro: Ba:, *Lyfe,* bk. 3, chap. 17, pp. 259–60.

[151] Ibid., 260 (originally in Stapleton, *Life,* chap. 6, p. 66).

onward, peace returned to his soul and he was never again disturbed by this affliction.[152]

When the ex-Lord Chancellor reached the scaffold an officer lent him a hand as he mounted the stairs, More jesting, "When I come down again, let me shift for myself as well as I can."[153] He then addressed the bystanders, albeit briefly in compliance with the King's wishes. If Henry had hoped to stunt More's eloquence with his stipulation of brevity on the scaffold, he certainly did not succeed. Asking those present to pray for him, while promising to "pray for them elsewhere",[154] More called upon the crowd to bear witness "that he should now there suffer death in and for the faith of the holy Catholic Church".[155] After pleading for prayers that the King might receive "good counsel", he declared "that he died the King's good servant but God's first".[156] Kneeling down on the scaffold platform, he recited Psalm 51—the "*Miserere*":

> Have mercy on me, O God,
> according to thy steadfast love;
> according to thy abundant mercy
> blot out my transgressions . . .

> (Ps 51:1)

After several other prayers, he turned to his executioner, who was evidently downcast, and said, "What, man, pull up thy spirits, and be not afraid to do thy office."[157] When the latter knelt to make the customary request for forgiveness from the man he was charged to execute, More kissed him and joked about the shortness of his own neck. Blindfolding himself, he laid his head down on the chopping block but pulled his beard aside, telling the hangman, "I pray you let me lay my beard over the block lest ye should cut it."[158] Then, with

---

[152] Ibid., 260–61 (also Stapleton, *Life*, chap. 6, pp. 66–67).

[153] Hall, *Lives of the Kings*, 2:265 (spelling modernized).

[154] *Paris Newsletter*, in Chambers, *More*, 349.

[155] Roper, *Lyfe*, 103.

[156] *Paris Newsletter*, in Chambers, *More*, 349.

[157] Ro: Ba:, *Lyfe*, bk. 3, chap. 17, pp. 261–62 (quote on 262).

[158] Hall, *Lives of the Kings*, 2:265–66 (quote on 266; spelling modernized); Stapleton, *Life*, chap. 20, p. 189.

one swift stroke, he passed to that unseen country that all his life he
had so longed to see.

> . . . [F]orget I not that I have a long reckoning and a great to give account of,
> but I put my trust in God and in the merits of his bitter passion, and I beseech
> him give me and keep me the mind to long to be out of this world and to be
> with him. For I can never but trust that whosoever longs to be with him shall be
> welcome to him . . .[159]

Even in death the King would not allow More to return to his own
family. His body was buried, albeit in their presence, in the chapel
where he probably attended his last Mass as a prisoner, Saint Peter in
Chains. Years later Margaret Roper's maid, Dorothy Colley, was able
to recall for the biographer Thomas Stapleton a remarkable incident
concerning the interment. She had accompanied Margaret that day
as she journeyed across the city to the Tower, stopping at churches
along the way and bestowing alms upon the poor. As they neared their
destination, Margaret realized she had brought no linen with which
to wrap her father's body; they would have to stop and buy some,
but her purse by now had nothing left. Her maid Dorothy proposed
that she should simply go into a shop nearby for the linen and buy
it on credit. Margaret replied that as an unknown in the neighborhood she would not be trusted to pay in this manner; nonetheless
she asked Dorothy to try. So the maid went into a shop, with the
intent that when the merchant asked for payment she would look into
her purse and, upon finding nothing, promise him that she would get
the money from her mistress and return to pay him. Yet when she
opened the purse in the presence of the merchant, she found within
it precisely the amount of money needed to pay for the linen. It can
scarcely be imagined what a consolation this little miracle must have
been to More's grief-stricken daughter.[160]

Although More's body was allowed something of a decent burial,
the Henrician regime intended a far different fate for the head of the
martyr. As was customary with beheaded traitors, More's head was
parboiled and impaled on Tower Bridge as an intimidation and threat

---

[159] Letter no. 208, Thomas More to Dr. Nicholas Wilson, 1534, in Rogers, *Correspondence*,
537.
[160] Stapleton, *Life*, chap. 20, pp. 191–92.

to the King's subjects. It would have eventually been hurled into the river had not Margaret bribed the executioner to let her take it.[161] She kept it with her the rest of her life, and when she died, only nine years later, she was buried "with her father's head in her arms as she had desired".[162]

---

[161] Reynolds, *Field Is Won*, 381.

[162] Rev. John Lewis, preface to his 1729 edition of the Roper biography of More, quoted in Hugh Albin, "Opening of the Roper Vault", *Moreana/Thomas More Gazette* 16 (1979): 34. The head relic is now in the Roper vault of Saint Dunstan's, Canterbury.

Epilogue: The Aftermath

Of how many of my most faithful friends have I not been robbed in these stormy days! Long since by the death of William Warham, Archbishop of Canterbury; recently by that of William Mountjoy, of the Bishop of Rochester and of Thomas More, who was the chief magistrate of his country, whose heart was whiter than snow, a genius such as England never had before, nor ever will have again . . .

— Erasmus, *Ecclesiastes,* Preface,
August 1535

In his death Thomas More was spared the agony of witnessing what would follow. From a purely human standpoint it would seem that all his years of work and prayer to preserve the unity of the Church, culminating in his supreme sacrifice on Tower Hill, had been in vain. A few followed his example, but not many. By the summer of 1536 Henry VIII and his "Master Secretary" Cromwell had inaugurated the wholesale plundering and destruction of England's monasteries, one of many manifestations of a politically driven religious fanaticism that was to express itself time and again in the obliteration of a thousand years of English Christian art and literature. Over the centuries that followed, More's worst fears about where doctrinal disunity would ultimately lead were realized, with the divinity of Christ and the very existence of God coming under question in large segments of European society.

But does all this really mean that Thomas More's life and death were in vain? The answer can be found in the words of the Prophet Isaiah: ". . . I said, 'I have labored in vain, I have spent my strength for nothing . . . yet surely my right is with the Lord, and my recompense with my God' " (Is 49:4). Like the flame of the Tenebrae candle that More had seen as symbolizing the unquenchable faith of the Blessed Virgin amid the darkness of Good Friday, so too the flame of Catholicism in England went into hiding yet never died. Driven out

453

of the splendid surroundings of medieval cathedrals, it had to flee into the dark recesses of attics, where Masses were celebrated in secret. It was guarded by men and women who over the course of the late sixteenth and seventeenth centuries were willing to die that the flame might be kept alive for their children and their children's children. In the nineteenth century this undying flame gradually reemerged into the open, where it was rediscovered by such men as John Henry Newman, who found it to be a most "kindly light" to lead them to God. By the late twentieth century, Catholicism had grown to become yet again the single largest communion of practicing Christians in all of England.[1]

Indeed, More's recompense was with his God. On May 19, 1935, Thomas More and his friend Bishop John Fisher received the highest honors of the Church they loved. During the canonization ceremony in Saint Peter's Basilica, Pope Pius XI said of the former:

> The other star of sanctity that traced a luminous path across that dark period of history was Thomas More, Lord Chancellor of the King of England. Endowed with the keenest of minds and supreme versatility in every kind of knowledge, he enjoyed such esteem and favour among his fellow-citizens that he was soon able to reach the highest grades of public office. But he was no less distinguished for his desire of Christian perfection and his zeal for the salvation of souls. Of this we have testimony in the ardour of his prayer, in the fervour with which he recited, whenever he could, even the Canonical Hours, in the practice of those penances by which he kept his body in subjection, and finally in the numerous and renowned accomplishments of both the spoken and the written word which he achieved for the defence of the Catholic faith and for the safeguarding of Christian morality. A strong and courageous spirit, like John Fisher, when he saw that the doctrines of the Church were gravely endangered, he knew how to despise resolutely the flattery of human respect, how to resist, in accordance with his duty, the supreme head of the State when there was question of things commanded by God and the Church, and how to renounce with dignity the high office with which he was invested. It was for these motives that he too was imprisoned, nor could the tears of his wife and children make him swerve from the path of truth and virtue. In that terrible hour of trial

---

[1] John Beaumont and John Walsh, "Is There a Catholic Revival in England?", *Fidelity* 13 (June 1994): 25.

he raised his eyes to heaven, and proved himself a bright example of Christian fortitude. Thus it was that he who not many years before had written a work emphasizing the duty of Catholics to defend their faith even at the cost of their lives, was seen to walk cheerful and confident from his prison to death, and thence to take his flight to the joys of eternal beatitude.[2]

Pope Pius ended his homily with a stirring invitation to his separated brothers and sisters of England:

Let those who are still separated from Us consider attentively the ancient glories of their Church which were at once a reflection and an increment of the glories of the Church of Rome. Let them consider, moreover, and remember that this Apostolic See has been waiting for them so long and so anxiously, not as coming to a strange dwelling place, but as finally returning to their paternal home. In conclusion, let us repeat the divine prayer of Our Lord Jesus Christ: "Holy Father, keep them in Thy name whom Thou hast given me; that they may be one as we also are." Amen.[3]

Forty-seven years later, in a May 1982 visit to England, Pope John Paul II took the occasion of a homily in London's Westminster Cathedral to speak of both More and Fisher:

London is particularly proud of two outstanding saints, great men also by the world's standards, contributors to your national heritage, John Fisher and Thomas More.

John Fisher, the Cambridge scholar of Renaissance learning, became Bishop of Rochester. He is an example to all Bishops in his loyalty to the faith and in his devoted attention to the people of his diocese, especially the poor and the sick. Thomas More was a model layman living the Gospel to the full. He was a fine scholar and an ornament to his profession, a loving husband and father, humble in prosperity, courageous in adversity, humorous and godly. Together they served God and their country—Bishop and layman. Together they died, victims of an unhappy age. Today we have the grace, all of us, to proclaim their greatness and to thank God for giving such men to England.[4]

---

[2] "The Two New Saints" (homily at canonization), *Tablet,* June 1, 1935, 694.

[3] Ibid., 695.

[4] "Vengo al Servizio dell'Unita nell'Amore", homily at Westminster Cathedral, May 28, 1982, *Insegnamenti di Giovanni Paolo II 5:2, 1982 (Maggio-Giugno)* (Vatican City: Libreria Editrice Vaticana, 1982), 1899.

As to the relevance of Thomas More's life and writings in the modern world, the answer to this can best be expressed in the words of our Lord: "He who has ears, let him hear" (Mt 13:9). The battles that Thomas More fought are not over—in a certain sense they are more acute than ever, as is intimated in the comment of G. K. Chesterton on the importance of Thomas More with which we began this book. Father Germain Marc'hadour, one of the greatest and most widely respected More scholars of the present age, perhaps put it best in a prophetic article he published in 1961:

> It may be that the near future will face all of us with the problem of harmonizing, or simply reconciling, our loyalty to Caesar with our loyalty to God . . . Caesar, moreover, is no longer a monarch; he is a cabinet, or a party . . . he is public opinion, which shapes—and is shaped by—the newspapers, the broadcasts, the schools . . .
>
> If we may bring a few examples, there are today fields of conduct, such as divorce, sexual behavior and education, the use of artificial contraceptives, abortion, mercy-killing, nationalization, film censorship, and a few more, in which a Catholic, especially if he is a lawyer, a doctor, a nurse, or a teacher, will find himself alone against practically everyone else in his profession . . .
>
> As in penal days, the Catholic will sometimes be alone of his species in the whole street . . . He will even find fellow Catholics ready to taunt him . . . In extreme cases fidelity to the doctrine of Mother Church will mean worse than corporal death: it will alienate from a man the trust and esteem of the people he likes, or even loves, best . . . The prospect of this social disqualification, of this civic annihilation so to speak, is as strong and effective a pressure as the old forms of physical duress . . . thousands will apostatize simply because they see no rational justification for the Church's position on a number of points, and they have not enough faith, on the other hand, to cling to her through sheer obedience . . .
>
> . . . If ever we lack wisdom to decide where the golden measure of Christian obedience lies, or grace and energy to carry out its implications when we are bleakly isolated in a hostile environment, let us turn to him [More]. The obedience of one man redeems the sins of many. The fervent intercession of one saint can remedy the sickly reluctance of many tepid Christians. He is a dangerous patron and a dangerous friend, "a nuisance of a saint," who never believed in being carried to heaven on a featherbed. He will not teach us an easy way, but he will show us

where we can find the comfort we need to suffer our freely accepted discomforts.[5]

In the words of his *Dialogue of Comfort against Tribulation,* Thomas More invites us to go forth with Christ in His Passion and "die for the truth with him".[6] Are we, then, willing to live and die for Christ? It is the heartfelt wish of this author that all of us, like Thomas More, may say Yes to our Lord knocking upon the doors of our hearts, that "we may meet in heaven together, where we shall be merry for ever and ever."[7]

---

[5] Fr. Germain Marc'hadour, "Obedient unto Death: A Key to St. Thomas More", *Spiritual Life,* n.s., 7 (fall 1961): 216–18, 221.

[6] *A Dialogue of Comfort against Tribulation,* ed. Louis Martz and Frank Manley, in vol. 12 of *Complete Works of St. Thomas More* (New Haven: Yale Univ. Press, 1976), bk. 3, chap. 17, p. 246.

[7] Thomas More to Sir William Kingston, in William Roper, *The Lyfe of Sir Thomas Moore, Knighte,* ed. Elsie V. Hitchcock, Early English Text Society, original series, no. 197 (London: Early English Text Society, 1935), 97.

Bibliography

Albin, Hugh. "Opening of the Roper Vault in St. Dunstan's Canterbury and Thoughts on the Burial of William and Margaret Roper". *Moreana/Thomas More Gazette* 16 (1979): 29‒35.

Alston, G. Cyprian. "Ximenes de Cisneros, Francisco". In *Catholic Encyclopedia*. 15:729‒31. 1907.

Augustijn, Cornelius. *Erasmus: His Life, Works, and Influence*. Toronto: Univ. of Toronto Press, 1991.

Augustine, Saint. *Saint Augustine: The City of God: Books VIII‒XVI*. Trans. by Gerard G. Walsh, S.J., and Mother Grace Monahan, O.S.U. Fathers of the Church, vol. 7. New York: Fathers of the Church, 1952.

————. *Saint Augustine: Commentary on the Lord's Sermon on the Mount with Seventeen Related Sermons*. Trans. by Denis Kavanagh, O.S.A. Fathers of the Church, vol. 11. New York: Fathers of the Church, 1951.

————. *Saint Augustine: Letters*. Vol. 1, *1‒82*. Trans. by Sr. Wilfrid Parsons, S.N.D. Fathers of the Church, vol. 12. New York: Fathers of the Church, 1951.

————. *Saint Augustine: Sermons on the Liturgical Seasons*. Trans. by Sr. Mary Sarah Muldowney, R.S.M. Fathers of the Church, vol. 38. New York: Fathers of the Church, 1959.

————. *St. Augustine: Tractates on the Gospel of John 112‒24: Tractates on the First Epistle of John*. Trans. by John W. Rettig, Fathers of the Church, vol. 92. Washington, D.C.: Catholic Univ. of America Press, 1995.

————. *St. Augustin: The Writings against the Manichaeans and against the Donatists*. Vol. 4 of *A Select Library of the Nicene and Post-Nicene Fathers of the Christian Church*. Ed. by Philip Schaff. 1887.

Reprint, Grand Rapids, Mich.: William B. Eerdmanns Publishing Co., 1974.

Bainvel, Fr. J. V., S.J. *Devotion to the Sacred Heart: The Doctrine and Its History.* New York: Benziger Bros., 1924.

Baker, Howard. "Thomas More at Oxford". *Moreana* 11 (November 1974): 6–11.

Beaumont, John, and John Walsh. "Is There a Catholic Revival in England?" *Fidelity* 13 (June 1994): 22–36.

Belloc, Hilaire. *Cranmer: Archbishop of Canterbury, 1533–1556.* Philadelphia: J. B. Lippincott Co., 1931.

Bosworth, Joseph. *The Gospels: Gothic, Anglo-Saxon, Wycliffe and Tyndale Versions.* London: Gibbings and Co., 1907.

Bradshaw, Brendan. "The Controversal Sir Thomas More". *Journal of Ecclesiastical History* 36 (October 1985): 535–69.

Brady, Thomas. "Luther and the State: The Reformer's Teaching in Its Social Setting". In *Luther and the Modern State in Germany.* Sixteenth Century Essays and Studies, vol. 7, ed. by James Tracy, 31–44. Kirksville, Md.: Sixteenth Century Journal Publishers, 1986.

Brann, Noel. "Pre-Reformation Humanism in Germany and the Papal Monarchy: A Study in Ambivalence". *Journal of Medieval and Renaissance Studies* 14 (fall 1984): 159–85.

Brigden, Susan. *London and the Reformation.* Oxford: Clarendon Press, 1991.

Bruce, F. F. *The English Bible: A History of the Translations from the Earliest English Versions to the New English Bible.* New York: Oxford Univ. Press, 1970.

Cameron, O. *The European Reformation.* Oxford: Clarendon Press, 1991.

Campbell, W. E. *Erasmus, Tyndale and More.* Milwaukee: Bruce Publishing Co., 1950.

Carlyle, E. Irving. "Tyndale, William". In *Dictionary of National Biography.* 57:424–31. New York: Macmillan Co.; London: Smith, Elder, and Co., 1899.

The Carthusians: Origin, Spirit, Family Life. 2d ed. Westminster, Md.: Newman Press, 1952.

Cavendish, George, and William Roper. *Two Early Tudor Lives: The Life and Death of Cardinal Wolsey, by George Cavendish; The Life of Sir Thomas More, by William Roper.* Ed. by Richard S. Sylvester and Davis P. Harding. New Haven and London: Yale Univ. Press, 1962.

Chambers, R. W., ed. *The Fame of Sir Thomas More: Being Addresses Delivered in His Honour in Chelsea, July 1929.* London and New York: Sheed and Ward, 1933.

————. *Thomas More.* 1935. Reprint, Ann Arbor, Mich.: Ann Arbor Paperbacks, Univ. of Michigan Press, 1973.

Chastel, Andre. *The Sack of Rome, 1527.* Bollingen Series 35, no. 26. Princeton, N.J.: Princeton Univ. Press, 1983.

Coleridge, Rev. H. J. "Ludolf's Life of Christ". *Month* 17 (November–December 1872): 337–70.

Cyprian, Saint. *Saint Cyprian: Treatises.* Trans. and ed. by Roy J. Deferrari. Fathers of the Church, vol. 36. New York: Fathers of the Church, 1958.

Derrett, J. Duncan. "The Trial of Sir Thomas More". *English Historical Review* 79 (July 1964): 449–77.

Doernberg, Erwin. *Henry VIII and Luther: An Account of Their Personal Relations.* Stanford, Calif.: Stanford Univ. Press, 1961.

Donner, H. W. "St. Thomas More's Treatise on the Four Last Things and the Gothicism of the Trans-Alpine Renaissance". In *Essential Articles for the Study of Thomas More,* ed. by R. S. Sylvester and G. P. Marc'hadour, 343–55. Hamden, Conn.: Archon Books, 1977.

Doyle-Davidson, W. "The Earlier Works of Sir Thomas More". In *Essential Articles for the Study of Thomas More,* ed. by R. S. Sylvester and G. P. Marc'hadour, 356–74. Hamden, Conn.: Archon Books, 1977.

Duffy, Eamon. *The Stripping of the Altars: Traditional Religion in England, c. 1400–c. 1580.* New Haven: Yale Univ. Press, 1992.

Dulhamel, P. A. "Medievalism of More's *Utopia*". In *Essential Articles for the Study of Thomas More,* ed. by R. S. Sylvester and G. P. Marc'hadour, 234–50. Hamden, Conn.: Archon Books, 1977.

Durandus of Metz. *Rationale Divinorum Officiorum.* Naples: Josephum Dura Bibliopolam, 1859.

Edwards, Mark, Jr. *Luther and the False Brethren.* Stanford, Calif.: Stanford Univ. Press, 1975.

Eire, Carlos. *War against the Idols: The Reformation of Worship from Erasmus to Calvin.* Cambridge: Cambridge Univ. Press, 1986.

Elton, G. R. *Policy and Police: The Enforcement of the Reformation in the Age of Thomas Cromwell.* Cambridge: Cambridge Univ. Press, 1972.

Erasmus, Desiderius, of Rotterdam. *Desiderii Erasmi Roterodami: Opera Omnia.* Vol. 5. Lyons: Peter Vander, 1704.

———. *The Epistles of Erasmus: From His Earliest Letters to His Fifty-First Year.* Trans. and ed. by Francis M. Nichols. 3 vols. 1901–1918. Reprint, New York: Russell and Russell, 1962.

———. *Opus Epistolarum Des. Erasmi Roterdami.* Ed. by P. S. Allen, H. M. Allen, and H. W. Garrod. 12 vols. Oxford: Clarendon Press, 1906–1947.

Farrow, John. *The Story of Thomas More.* New York: Image Books/ Doubleday and Co., 1968.

Fisher, Bernard. "English Spiritual Writers: 13: St. Thomas More". *Clergy Review,* n.s., 45 (January 1960): 1–10.

Flannery, E. H. "Anti-Semitism". In *New Catholic Encyclopedia.* 1:633–40. 1967.

Ford, C. Desmond, S.J. "Good Master Bonvisi". *Clergy Review,* n.s., 27 (April 1947): 228–35.

Fox, John. *The Acts and Monuments of John Fox.* Vol. 4. London: Seeley, Burnside, and Seeley, 1846.

Friedmann, Paul. *Anne Boleyn: A Chapter of English History, 1527–1536.* 2 vols. London: Macmillan and Co., 1884.

Ganss, H. G. "Luther, Martin". In *Catholic Encyclopedia*. 9:438–58. 1907.

Gleason, John B. *John Colet*. Berkeley, Calif.: Univ. of California Press, 1989.

Goff, Frederick, ed. *Incunabula in American Libraries: A Third Census of Fifteenth-Century Books Recorded in North American Collections*. New York: Bibliographical Society of America, 1964.

Goulder, Msgr. Laurance. "Thomas More's London". Photographs by Daniel Frasnay. *The Critic* 24 (December 1965–January 1966): 42–55.

Grisar, Fr. Hartmann, S.J. *Luther*. 6 vols. St. Louis, Mo.: B. Herder; London: Kegan Paul, Trench, Trubner, and Co., 1913–1917.

———. *Martin Luther: His Life and Work*. 1930. Reprint, Westminster, Md.: Newman Press, 1961.

Guy, John A. "Henry VIII and the Praemunire Manoeuvres of 1530–1531". *English Historical Review* 97 (July 1982): 481–503.

———. *The Public Career of Sir Thomas More*. New Haven: Yale Univ. Press, 1980.

———. "Thomas More and Christopher St. German: The Battle of the Books". *Moreana* 21 (November 1984): 5–25.

Gwyn, Peter. *The King's Cardinal: The Rise and Fall of Thomas Wolsey*. London: PIMLICO, 1992.

Haas, Steven. "Simon Fish, William Tyndale, and Sir Thomas More's 'Lutheran Conspiracy' ". *Journal of Ecclesiastical History* 23 (April 1972): 125–36.

Haigh, Christopher. "Anticlericalism and the English Reformation". *History* 68 (October 1983): 391–407.

———. *English Reformations: Religion, Politics, and Society under the Tudors*. Oxford: Clarendon Press, 1993.

Hall, Basil. "The Trilingual College of San Ildefonso and the Making of the Complutensian Polyglot Bible". In *The Church and Academic Learning*. Vol. 5 of *Studies in Church History,* ed. by G. J. Cuming, 114–46. Leiden, Netherlands: E. J. Brill, 1969.

Hall, Edward. *The Lives of the Kings: Henry VIII.* 1550 folio edition entitled *The Triumphant Reigne of Kyng Henry the VIII.* Reprint, 2 vols. London: T. C. and E. C. Jack, 1904.

Harpsfield, Nicholas, and William Roper. *Lives of Saint Thomas More* (Roper biography and Harpsfield biography). Ed. E. E. Reynolds. Everyman's Library, no. 19. London: J. M. Dent and Sons, 1963.

Hefele, Karl J. von. *The Life and Times of Cardinal Ximenez; or, The Church in Spain in the Time of Ferdinand and Isabella.* 2d ed. London: Thomas Baker, 1885.

Hendriks, Dom Lawrence. *The London Charterhouse: Its Monks and Its Martyrs.* London: Kegan Paul, Trench and Co., 1889.

Hendrix, Scott. *Luther and the Papacy: Stages in a Reformation Conflict.* Philadelphia: Fortress Press, 1981.

Henry VIII, King. *Assertio Septem Sacramentorum, or Defence of the Seven Sacraments.* Ed. by Fr. Louis O'Donovan, S.T.L. New York: Benziger Brothers, 1908.

Hilton, Walter. *The Scale of Perfection,* Trans. by John Clark and Rosemary Doward. The Classics of Western Spirituality. New York: Paulist Press, 1991.

Hughes, Fr. Philip. "*The King's Proceedings*". Vol. 1 of *The Reformation in England.* New York: Macmillan Co., 1951.

—————. *A Popular History of the Reformation.* Garden City, N.Y.: Hanover House, 1957.

Ives, E. W. *Anne Boleyn.* Oxford: Basil Blackwell, 1986.

—————. "The Fall of Wolsey". In *Cardinal Wolsey: Church, State and Art.* Ed. by S. J. Gunn and P. G. Lindley, 286–315. Cambridge: Cambridge Univ. Press, 1991.

John Chrysostom, Saint. *Saint John Chrysostom: Commentary on Saint John the Apostle and Evangelist: Homilies 1–47.* Trans. by Sr. Thomas Aquinas Goggin, S.C.H. Fathers of the Church, vol. 33. New York: Fathers of the Church, 1957.

John Paul II, Pope. *Insegnamenti di Giovanni Paolo II. 5:2, 1982 (Maggio-Giugno).* Vatican City: Libreria Editrice Vaticana, 1982.

Kempis, Thomas à. *The Imitation of Christ*. Ed. by Harold Gardiner, S.J. Garden City, N.Y.: Image Books/Doubleday and Co., 1955.

Kiermayr, Reinhold. "On the Education of the Pre-Reformation Clergy". *Church History* 53 (March 1984): 7–16.

Knowles, Dom David. *The English Mystical Tradition*. New York: Harper, 1961.

Lehmberg, Stanford E. *The Reformation Parliament, 1529–1536*. Cambridge: Cambridge Univ. Press, 1970.

Loewenich, Walther von. *Martin Luther: The Man and His Work*. Minneapolis: Augsburg Publishing House, 1986.

Love, Nicholas. *The Mirror of the Blessed Life of Jesu Christ*. Orchard Books, vol. 10. New York: Benziger Brothers, 1926.

Ludolf of Saxony. *Vita Jesu Christi*. A.-C. Bolard, L.-M. Rigollot, and J. Carnandet. Paris and Rome: Victor Palme, 1865.

Lupton, J. H. *A Life of John Colet, D.D.* London: George Bell and Sons, 1909.

Luther, Martin. *Career of the Reformer I*. Ed. by Harold Grimm. Vol. 31 of *Luther's Works*. Philadelphia: Muhlenberg Press, 1957.

————. *The Christian in Society I*. Ed. by James Atkinson. Vol. 44 of *Luther's Works*. Philadelphia: Fortress Press, 1966.

————. *Word and Sacrament II*. Ed. by Abdel R. Wentz. Vol. 36 of *Luther's Works*. Philadelphia: Muhlenberg Press, 1959.

Lydgate, John. *The Minor Poems of John Lydgate: Part I*. Ed. by Henry Noble MacCracken. Early English Text Society, extra series, no. 107. London: Early English Text Society, 1911.

Mann, Rev. Horace. *The Lives of the Popes in the Middle Ages*. Vol. 7. St. Louis: B. Herder; London: Kegan Paul, Trench, Trubner, and Co., 1910.

————. *The Lives of the Popes in the Middle Ages*. Vol. 8. St. Louis: B. Herder; London: Kegan Paul, Trench, Trubner, and Co., 1910.

Mansi, J. D., ed. *Sacrorum Conciliorum Nova et Amplissima Collectio*. Vol. 12. 1766. Reprint, Paris and Leipzig: Huberto Welter, 1901.

Marc'hadour, Fr. Germain. "Obedient unto Death: A Key to St. Thomas More". *Spiritual Life*, n.s., 7 (fall 1961): 205–21.

———. "The Death-Year of Thomas More's Mother". *Moreana/ Thomas More Gazette* 16 (1979): 13–16.

———. "Fisher and More: A Note". In *Humanism, Reform and the Reformation: The Career of Bishop John Fisher,* ed. by Brendan Bradshaw and Eamon Duffy, 103–8. Cambridge: Cambridge Univ. Press, 1989.

———. "Thomas More's Spirituality". In *St. Thomas More: Action and Contemplation: Proceedings of the Symposium Held at St. John's University, October 9–10, 1970.* Ed. by Richard Sylvester, 123–59. New Haven: Yale Univ. Press, 1972.

Marius, Richard. *Thomas More: A Biography.* New York: Vintage Books, 1985.

Martz, Louis L., S.J. *Thomas More: The Search for the Inner Man.* New Haven: Yale Univ. Press, 1990.

Mattingly, Garrett. *Catherine of Aragon.* Boston: Little, Brown and Co., 1941.

McCutcheon, Elizabeth. " 'The Apple of My Eye': Thomas More to Antonio Bonvisi: A Reading and a Translation". *Moreana* 18 (November 1981): 37–56.

McGoldrick, James E. *Luther's English Connection: The Reformation Thought of Robert Barnes and William Tyndale.* Milwaukee: Northwestern Publishing House, 1979.

Meyer, Carl S. "Henry VIII Burns Luther's Books, 12 May 1521". *Journal of Ecclesiastical History* 9 (1958): 173–87.

Meyer, Wilhelm. "Zwingli, Ulrich". In *Catholic Encyclopedia.* 15:772–75. 1907.

Miller, Clarence. "The Heart of the Final Struggle: More's Commentary on the Agony in the Garden". In *Quincentennial Essays on St. Thomas More: Selected Papers from the Thomas More College Conference,* ed. by Michael Moore. Boone, N.C.: Albion (Appalachian State Univ.), 1978.

More, Cresacre. *The Life and Death of Sir Thomas Moore (1630)*. Facsimile of 1st ed. English Recusant Literature, 1558–1640, ed. by D. M. Rogers, vol. 66. Menston, Yorkshire, England: Scolar Press, 1971.

More, Saint Thomas. *The Complete Works of St. Thomas More*. New Haven: Yale Univ. Press, 1963–.

> Vol. 2. *The History of King Richard III*. Ed. by Richard Sylvester. 1967.
> Vol. 3, pt. 2. *Latin Poems*. Ed. by Clarence Miller et al. 1984.
> Vol. 4. *Utopia*. Ed. by Edward Surtz, S.J., and J. H. Hexter. 1965.
> Vol. 5. *Responsio ad Lutherum*. Ed. by John Headley; trans. by Sr. Scholastica Mandeville. In 2 parts. 1969.
> Vol. 6. *A Dialogue concerning Heresies*. Ed. by Thomas Lawler et al. In 2 parts. 1981.
> Vol. 7. *Letter to Bugenhagen, Supplication of Souls, Letter against Frith*. Ed. by Frank Manley et al. 1990.
> Vol. 8. *The Confutation of Tyndale's Answer*. Ed. by Louis Schuster et al. In 3 parts. 1973.
> Vol. 9. *The Apology*. Ed. by J. B. Trapp. 1979.
> Vol. 10. *The Debellation of Salem and Bizance*. Ed. by John Guy et al. 1987.
> Vol. 11. *The Answer to a Poisoned Book*. Ed. by Clarence Miller. 1985.
> Vol. 12. *A Dialogue of Comfort against Tribulation*. Ed. by Louis Martz and Frank Manley. 1976.
> Vol. 13. *Treatise on the Passion; Treatise on the Blessed Body; Instructions and Prayers*. Ed. by Garry Haupt. 1976.
> Vol. 14. *De Tristitia Christi*. Ed. and trans. by Clarence H. Miller. In 2 parts. 1976.
> Vol. 15. *In Defense of Humanism: Letters to Dorp, Oxford, Lee, and a Monk*. Ed. by Daniel Kinney. 1986.

————. *The Correspondence of Sir Thomas More*. Ed. by Elizabeth F. Rogers. Princeton, N.J.: Princeton Univ. Press, 1947.

————. *The English Works of Sir Thomas More*. Ed. by W. E. Campbell. Vol. 1. London: Eyre and Spottiswoode; New York: Lincoln MacVeagh, The Dial Press, 1931.

————. *St. Thomas More: Selected Letters*. Ed. by Elizabeth F. Rogers. New Haven: Yale Univ. Press, 1961.

————. *Thomas More's Prayer Book: A Facsimile Reproduction of the Annotated Pages*. Trans. and ed. by Louis Martz and Richard Sylvester. New Haven: Yale Univ. Press, 1969.

Monti, James. *The Week of Salvation: History and Traditions of Holy Week*. Huntington, Ind.: Our Sunday Visitor, 1993.

Neame, Alan. *The Holy Maid of Kent: The Life of Elizabeth Barton, 1506–1534*. London: Hodder and Stoughton, 1971.

O'Delany, M. Barry. "Memories of Chelsea". *Ave Maria*, n.s., 32 (August 9, 1930): 176–79.

Olin, John. *Catholic Reform: From Cardinal Ximenes to the Council of Trent: 1495–1563*. New York: Fordham Univ. Press, 1990.

————. *The Catholic Reformation: Savonarola to Ignatius Loyola*. New York: Fordham Univ. Press, 1992.

O'Malley, John W., S.J. *Giles of Viterbo on Church and Reform: A Study in Renaissance Thought*. Leiden, Netherlands: E. J. Brill, 1968.

Ortroy, Fr. Francis van, S.J. "Vie du bienheureux martyr Jean Fisher: Cardinal, évêque de Rochester (+ 1535): Text anglais et traduction latine du XVI siècle". *Analecta Bollandiana* 10 (1891): 121–365; 12 (1893): 97–287.

Parmiter, Geoffrey de C. "The Indictment of Saint Thomas More". *Downside Review* 75 (April 1957): 149–66.

————. "Saint Thomas More and the Oath". *Downside Review* 78 (winter 1959/60): 1–13.

Pastor, Ludwig von. *History of the Popes from the Close of the Middle Ages*. Vol. 9. St. Louis, Mo.: B. Herder, 1910.

————. *The History of the Popes from the Close of the Middle Ages*. Vol. 10. St. Louis, Mo.: B. Herder, 1914.

————. *Storia dei Papi dalla Fine del Medio Evo*. Vol. 4, pt. 2. Versione Italiana di Mons. Pio Cenci. Rome: Desclee and C. Editori, 1942.

Pineas, Rainer. *Thomas More and Tudor Polemics.* Bloomington, Ind.: Indiana Univ. Press, 1968.

Pius XI, Pope. "The Two New Saints" (Homily at Canonization of Saints Thomas More and John Fisher, May 19, 1935). *Tablet,* June 1, 1935, 694–95.

Pollard, Albert. *Thomas Cranmer and the English Reformation: 1489–1556.* Heroes of the Reformation Series. New York: G. P. Putnam's Sons, 1904.

Potter, G. R. *Zwingli.* Cambridge: Cambridge Univ. Press, 1976.

Preus, James. *Carlstadt's Ordinaciones and Luther's Liberty: A Study of the Wittenberg Movement, 1521–1522.* Harvard Theological Studies, vol. 26. Cambridge, Mass.: Harvard Univ. Press; London: Oxford Univ. Press, 1974.

Rashdall, Hastings. *English Universities—Student Life.* Vol. 3 of *The Universities of Europe in the Middle Ages,* rev. ed., ed. by F. M. Powicke and A. B. Emdem. Oxford: Oxford Univ. Press, 1936.

Raworth, Thomas. "St. Thomas More's Clock". *Month,* n.s., 7 (June 1952): 368–72.

Rex, Richard. *Henry VIII and the English Reformation.* New York: St. Martin's Press, 1993.

———. "A Note on St. John Fisher and Erasmus". *Journal of Ecclesiastical History* 40 (October 1989): 582–85.

———. *The Theology of John Fisher.* Cambridge: Cambridge Univ. Press, 1991.

Reynolds, E. E. *The Field Is Won: The Life and Death of Saint Thomas More.* Milwaukee: Bruce Publishing Co., 1968.

———. *Margaret Roper: Eldest Daughter of St. Thomas More.* New York: P. J. Kenedy and Sons, 1960.

———. "More's Cell in the Tower". *Moreana* 5 (November 1968): 27–28.

———. *Saint John Fisher.* New York: P. J. Kenedy and Sons, 1955.

———. *Saint Thomas More.* New York: P. J. Kenedy and Sons, 1953.

————. *Thomas More and Erasmus*. London: Burns and Oates, 1965.

Ro: Ba:. *The Lyfe of Syr Thomas More, Sometymes Lord Chancellor of England by Ro: Ba:*. Ed. by E. V. Hitchcock and Msgr. P. E. Hallett. Early English Text Society, original series, no. 222. London: Early English Text Society, 1950.

Roper, William. *The Lyfe of Sir Thomas Moore, Knighte*. Ed. by Elsie Vaughan Hitchcock. Early English Text Society, original series, no. 197. London: Early English Text Society, 1935.

Ross, Ellen. "Submission or Fidelity? The Unity of Church and Mysticism in Walter Hilton's *Scale of Perfection*". *Downside Review* 106 (April 1988): 134–44.

Rothwell, Harry, ed. *English Historical Documents*. Vol. 3, *1189–1327*. New York: Oxford Univ. Press, 1975.

Routh, E. M. G. *Sir Thomas More and His Friends, 1477–1535*. 1934. Reprint, New York: Russell and Russell, 1963.

Sargent, Daniel. *Thomas More*. New York: Sheed and Ward, 1933.

Scarisbrick, J. J. *Henry VIII*. Berkeley, Calif.: Univ. of California Press, 1968.

Schuster, Louis. "Thomas More's Polemical Career". In *The Confutation of Tyndale's Answer*, ed. by Louis Schuster et al. *Complete Works of St. Thomas More*, 8:1137–268. New Haven: Yale Univ. Press, 1973.

Sheingorn, Pamela. *The Easter Sepulchre in England*. Early Drama, Art and Music Reference Series, no. 5. Kalamazoo, Mich.: Medieval Institute Publications, 1987.

Sider, Ronald. *Andreas Bodenstein von Karlstadt: The Development of His Thought, 1517–1525*. Leiden, Netherlands: E. J. Brill, 1974.

Sneyd, Charlotte Augusta, trans. *A Relation, or Rather a True Account, of the Island of England*. London: Camden Society, 1847.

Stapleton, Thomas. *The Life and Illustrious Martyrdom of Sir Thomas More*. Ed. E. E. Reynolds. Bronx, N.Y.: Fordham Univ. Press, 1966.

Stevenson, Kenneth. *Nuptial Blessing: A Study of Christian Marriage Rites*. Alcuin Club Collections, no. 64. London: Alcuin Club/SPCK, 1982.

Strype, John. *Ecclesiastical Memorials Relating Chiefly to Religion, and the Reformation of It and the Emergencies of the Church of England, under King Henry VIII, King Edward VI and Queen Mary I*. Vol. 1. Oxford: Clarendon Press, 1822.

Surtz, Edward, S.J. "More's Friendship with Fisher". In *Essential Articles for the Study of Thomas More*, ed. by R. S. Sylvester and G. P. Marc'hadour, 169–79. Hamden, Conn.: Archon Books, 1977.

———. *The Works and Days of John Fisher*. Cambridge, Mass.: Harvard Univ. Press, 1967.

Swanson, R. N. *Catholic England: Faith, Religion and Observance before the Reformation*. Manchester Medieval Sources Series. Manchester, England: Manchester Univ. Press, 1993.

Taylor, Larissa. *Soldiers of Christ: Preaching in Late Medieval and Reformation France*. Oxford: Clarendon Press, 1992.

Thurston, Fr. Herbert, S.J. "The Early Cultus of the Blessed Sacrament". *Month* 109 (April 1907): 377–90.

———, trans. and ed. *The Life of Saint Hugh of Lincoln*. London: Burns and Oates, 1898.

Tyndale, William. *An Answer to Sir Thomas More's Dialogue, The Supper of the Lord and Wm. Tracy's Testament Expounded*. Ed. by Rev. Henry Walter. Parker Society, vol. 44. 1850. Reprint, New York: Johnson Reprint Corp., 1968.

———. *Doctrinal Treatises and Introductions to Different Portions of the Holy Scriptures*. Ed. by Rev. Henry Walter. Parker Society, vol. 42. 1848. Reprint, New York: Johnson Reprint Corp., 1968.

———. *Expositions and Notes on Sundry Portions of the Holy Scriptures*. Ed. by Rev. Henry Walter. Parker Society, vol. 43. Cambridge: Cambridge Univ. Press, 1849.

———. *The Work of William Tyndale*. Ed. by G. E. Duffield. Philadelphia: Fortress Press, 1965.

————, trans. *Tyndale's New Testament* (1534 edition). Ed. by David Daniell. New Haven: Yale Univ. Press, 1995.

————, trans. *William Tyndale's Five Books of Moses, called the Pentateuch, being a Verbatim Reprint of the Edition of M.CCCCC.XXX.* Ed. by Rev. J. I. Mombert. New York: Anson D. F. Randolf and Co., 1884.

Warnicke, Retha. *The Rise and Fall of Anne Boleyn: Family Politics at the Court of Henry VIII.* Cambridge: Cambridge Univ. Press, 1989.

Warren, Frederick, trans. *The Sarum Missal in English* (trans. of 1526 ed.). 2 vols. The Library of Liturgiology and Ecclesiology for English Readers, vols. 8 (pt. 1) and 9 (pt. 2). London: Alexander Moring, 1911.

Williams, C. H., ed. *English Historical Documents.* Vol. 5, *1485–1558.* New York: Oxford Univ. Press, 1967.

Wordsworth, Rev. Christopher, ed. *The Manner of the Coronation of King Charles the First of England at Westminster, 2 Feb., 1626.* Henry Bradshaw Society, vol. 2. London: Henry Bradshaw Society, 1892.

Art Credits

Page 2: Page from More's *Book of Hours* with the first words of his "Godly Meditation." Used with permission of Yale University Press. Source: *Thomas More's Prayer Book*, edited by Louis L. Martz and Richard Sylvester, Yale University Press, 1969, page 3.

Page 55: Hans Holbein the Younger. *The Family of Thomas More, 1526.* Kunstmuseum, Basel, Switzerland. SCALA/Art Resource, New York.

Page 199: Title page of More's *Letter Against Frith*, used with permission of the Folger Shakespeare Library.

Page 326: Daniel Frasnay (photographer), photograph of the bell tower where St. Thomas More was kept while imprisoned in the Tower of London, seen in Msgr. Laurance Goulder's article "Thomas More's London", *Critic 24*, December 1965–January 1966, page 50. Used with permission of the Thomas More Association, Chicago, Illinois.

Excerpt Credits

The author and publisher wish to express their appreciation to the following for permission to reprint materials:

Analecta Bollandiana, "Vie du bienheureux martyr Jean Fisher: Cardinal, évêque de Rochester (+ 1535): text anglais et traduction latine du XVI siècle", vol. 10 and 12.

Augsburg Fortress, *Luther's Works*, vol. 36: *Word and Sacrament II*, © 1959. *Luther's Works*, vol. 31: *Career of the Reformer: I*, © 1957. *Luther's Works*, vol. 44: *The Christian in Society I*, © 1966.

Benziger Bros., *Devotion to the Sacred Heart: The Doctrine and Its History*, © 1924. *Assertio Septem Sacramentorum*, or *Defence of the Seven Sacraments*, © 1908. *The Mirror of the Blessed Life of Jesu Christ*, © 1926.

Bruce Publishing Company, *The Field Is Won: The Life and Death of Saint Thomas More*, © 1968.

Burns and Oates Ltd., *Thomas More and Erasmus*, © 1965.

Cambridge University Press, *War against the Idols: The Reformation of Worship from Erasmus to Calvin*, © 1986. *Policy and Police: The Enforcement of the Reformation in the Age of Thomas Cromwell*, © 1972. "The Fall of Wolsey", in *Cardinal Wolsey: Church, State and Art*, © 1991. *The Theology of John Fisher*, © 1991. *An Answer to Sir Thomas More's Dialogue, The Supper of the Lord and Wm. Tracy's Testament Expounded*, © 1968. *Doctrinal Treatises and Introductions to Different Portions of the Holy Scriptures*, © 1968. *Expositions and Notes on Sundry Portions of the Holy Scriptures*, © 1849.

Catholic University of America Press, *Saint Augustine: The City of God*, books VIII–XVI, © 1952. *Saint Augustine: Commentary on the Lord's Sermon on the Mount with Seventeen Related Sermons*, © 1951. *Saint Augustine: Letters*, vol. 1 (1–82), © 1951. *Saint Cyprian: Trea-*

Princeton University Press, *The Correspondence of Sir Thomas More*, © 1947.

Russell and Russell, Inc., *The Epistles of Erasmus: From His Earliest Letters to His Fifty-First Year*, © 1962.

Sheed and Ward, *The Fame of Sir Thomas More: Being Addresses Delivered in His Honour in Chelsea, July 1929*, © 1933. *Spiritual Life*, "Obedient unto Death: A Key to St. Thomas More", Fall, 1961.

The Tablet, "The Two New Saints", (Homily at Canonization of Saints Thomas More and John Fisher, May 19, 1935, English Translation), June 1, 1935.

University of Michigan Press, *Thomas More*, © 1973.

William B. Eerdmanns Publishing Co., *A Select Library of the Nicene and Post-Nicene Fathers of the Christian Church*: vol. 4: *St. Augustin: The Writings against the Manichaeans and against the Donatists*, © 1974.

Yale University Press, *St. Thomas More: Action and Contemplation: Proceedings of the Symposium Held at St. John's University, October 9–10, 1970*, © 1972. *A Dialogue Concerning Heresies*, © 1981. *A Dialogue of Comfort Against Tribulation*, © 1976. *De Tristitia Christi*, © 1976. *In Defense of Humanism: Letters to Dorp, Oxford, Lee and a Monk*, © 1986. *Latin Poems*, © 1984. *Letter to Bugenhagen, Supplication of Souls, Letter Against Frith*, © 1990. *Responsio ad Lutherum*, © 1969. *St. Thomas More: Selected Letters*, © 1961. *The Answer to a Poisoned Book*, © 1985. *The Apology*, © 1979. *The Confutation of Tyndale's Answer*, © 1973. *Thomas More's Prayer Book: A Facsimile Reproduction of the Annotated Pages*, © 1969. *Treatise on the Passion; Treatise on the Blessed Body; Instructions and Prayers*, © 1976. *Utopia*, © 1965. *Two Early Tudor Lives: The Life and Death of Cardinal Wolsey, by George Cavendish; The Life of Sir Thomas More, by William Roper*, © 1962.

Index